Progressive Politics in
the Democratic Party

Progressive Politics in the Democratic Party

Samuel Untermyer and the Jewish Anti-Nazi Boycott Campaign

Richard A. Hawkins

BLOOMSBURY ACADEMIC
LONDON • NEW YORK • OXFORD • NEW DELHI • SYDNEY

BLOOMSBURY ACADEMIC
Bloomsbury Publishing Plc
50 Bedford Square, London, WC1B 3DP, UK
1385 Broadway, New York, NY 10018, USA
29 Earlsfort Terrace, Dublin 2, Ireland

BLOOMSBURY, BLOOMSBURY ACADEMIC and the Diana logo
are trademarks of Bloomsbury Publishing Plc

First published in Great Britain 2022
This paperback edition published by Bloomsbury Academic in 2023

Copyright © Richard A. Hawkins, 2022

Richard A. Hawkins has asserted his right under the Copyright,
Designs and Patents Act, 1988, to be identified as the author of this work.

Series design by Adriana Brioso
Cover image: Portrait of lawyer Samuel Untermeyer. (© Underwood And Underwood/
The LIFE Images Collection/Getty Images)

All rights reserved. No part of this publication may be reproduced or
transmitted in any form or by any means, electronic or mechanical,
including photocopying, recording, or any information storage or retrieval
system, without prior permission in writing from the publishers.

Bloomsbury Publishing Plc does not have any control over, or responsibility for,
any third-party websites referred to or in this book. All internet addresses given
in this book were correct at the time of going to press. The author and publisher
regret any inconvenience caused if addresses have changed or sites have
ceased to exist, but can accept no responsibility for any such changes.

A catalogue record for this book is available from the British Library.

Library of Congress Cataloging-in-Publication Data
Names: Hawkins, Richard A., Dr. author.
Title: Progressive politics in the Democratic Party: Samuel Untermyer and the
Jewish anti-Nazi boycott campaign / Richard A. Hawkins.
Description: London, UK; New York, NY: I.B. Tauris, 2022. |
Includes bibliographical references and index.
Identifiers: LCCN 2021025994 (print) | LCCN 2021025995 (ebook) |
ISBN 9781788317405 (hardback) | ISBN 9781786726353 (epub) |
ISBN 9781786736413 (pdf) | ISBN 9780755606290 (ebook other)
Subjects: LCSH: Untermyer, Samuel, 1858-1940. | Jewish lawyers–United States–Biography. |
Human rights workers–United States–Biography. |
Zionists–United States–Biography. | Anti-Nazi movement–United States–History. |
Democratic Party (U.S.)–History.
Classification: LCC KF373.U58 H39 2022 (print) | LCC KF373.U58 (ebook) |
DDC 340.092 [B]–dc23
LC record available at https://lccn.loc.gov /2021025994
LC ebook record available at https://lccn.loc.gov /2021025995

ISBN: HB: 978-1-7883-1740-5
PB: 978-1-3502-7857-8
ePDF: 978-1-7867-3641-3
eBook: 978-1-7867-2635-3

Typeset by Deanta Global Publishing Services, Chennai, India

To find out more about our authors and books visit
www.bloomsbury.com and sign up for our newsletters.

Contents

Preface	vi
List of abbreviations	viii
List of Illustrations	xi
Introduction	1
1 The making of an American Jewish leader: Untermyer's education and career as a Wall Street lawyer, 1858–1940	15
2 Mr Untermyer goes to Washington: The Wall Street poacher turned Bryanite gamekeeper, 1897–1914	47
3 Untermyer's quest for national public recognition, 1914–40	87
4 Untermyer as a Zionist leader in the 1920s: To be or not to be?	119
5 Untermyer's finest hour: The boycott of Nazi Germany in the 1930s	147
Conclusion	181
Epilogue	185
Notes	187
Bibliography	271
Index	296

Preface

This book began with an essay on Samuel Untermyer commissioned by the *American National Biography* in 1996.[1] After the essay had been edited Oxford University Press shared it with Untermyer's grandson, the nuclear engineer Samuel Untermyer II. He was frustrated that his brother, Frank, had not completed a biography of their grandfather, on which he had been working for many years. Samuel II asked a trusted family friend, James (Jim) Welsh, to contact me to enquire whether I would be interested in writing a biography of his grandfather. I agreed and the initial research was generously funded by Samuel II. Jim has been a constant advocate and supporter of the project. After some initial displeasure with his brother's decisive action, Frank selflessly shared his research and Untermyer family lore with me. Samuel Untermyer's great-nephew, the lawyer and diplomat Peter Rosenblatt, has also shared information with me. Peter's brother, the late Richard Rosenblatt, shared with me the Untermyer family photographs which had been inherited from their grandmother, Samuel Untermyer's sister Addie. In addition, Rabbi Peter Schweitzer, a descendant of Untermyer's great-aunt Adelheid, has also shared family papers with me.

Samuel Untermyer discouraged prospective biographers during his lifetime. However, he did agree to numerous biographical dictionary entries and newspaper and magazine biographical profiles. After Untermyer's death his children also discouraged biographers[2] with the exception of youth worker Charlotte Himber, the author of a biographical essay.[3] Apart from Frank and I only one other person has attempted to write a biography of Untermyer, the wife of a post-war Guggenheimer & Untermyer lawyer,[4] the late Manhattan Family Court Judge, Nanette Dembitz.[5] Her grandfather, Louis Dembitz, as a Czech Jewish immigrant lawyer in Louisville, Kentucky, became a leading member of the Republican Party and in 1860 was one of the three nominators of Abraham Lincoln at the Chicago National Convention. Dembitz's great-aunt Fredericka was the mother of US Supreme Court justice Louis D. Brandeis.[6] However, although Dembitz was an accomplished lawyer, the Untermyer biography defeated her. She only completed four draft chapters during the mid-1960s and later abandoned the project after failing to find a publisher.[7] One of the principal challenges was an apparent lack of source material. Only a small fraction of Untermyer's private papers had survived. They had been donated to the American Jewish Archives (AJA). Furthermore, at that time the Guggenheimer & Untermyer law firm archive was bound by client confidentiality. Subsequently after the dissolution of the law firm in 1986[8] the firm's archive was destroyed. Frank Untermyer succeeded in saving a small part of this archive which he stored for many years at his family's Brant Lake estate in upstate New York. Some of those papers which survived the attention of the local mice were bequeathed by Frank to the AJA.

Numerous librarians, archivists, local historians and genealogists have assisted me during the last two decades. Among them are Kevin Profitt, senior AJA archivist (now retired), Camille Servizzi, AJA archivist (also now retired); Elisa Ho, the current AJA senior archivist and her colleagues Joe Weber, Julianna Witt and Aliza Spicehandler; historian Dr Moshe Mossek, a former director of the Israel State Archive; and Günter Steiner, Archivöberinspektor Staatsarchiv Augsburg, Bavaria, Germany. I acknowledge Dr Tracy Conrad, MD, proprietor of the *Willows Inn*, Untermyer's former Palm Springs' winter villa, for generously funding a research trip in 2001 to the Californian desert resort and hosting me during my stay. I would also like to acknowledge a British Academy Small Grant in 2006 which funded a visit to Columbia University's Rare Book and Manuscript Library to research the records of the Non-Sectarian Anti-Nazi League to Champion Human Rights. In addition, the Thyssen Foundation funded me to present a paper at the 'Boycott and Embargo – The Political Uses of Economic Power in the Twentieth Century' conference held at the Ruhr-Universität Bochum, Germany, 10–11 October 2008. Lastly, I would like to thank the German Historical Institute Washington for including my entry on Samuel Untermyer in their online resource *Immigrant Entrepreneurship: German-American Business Biographies, 1720 to the Present*.[9] An earlier version of Chapter 4 was published as an article in the *Australian Journal of Jewish Studies*. Chapter 5 includes revised content from articles published in *American Jewish History* and *Management & Organizational History*. I thank the editors of these journals for their permission to reuse content.

Abbreviations

ACLU	American Civil Liberties Union
AE	Albert Einstein
AEP	Albert Einstein Papers
AFL	American Federation of Labor
AH	American Hebrew
AHS	Abba Hillel Silver
AHSP	Abba Hillel Silver Papers
AJA	American Jewish Archives
AJC	American Jewish Committee
AJCong	American Jewish Congress
ASO	Adolph S. Ochs
ASOP	Adolph S. Ochs Papers
BC	Bainbridge Colby
BCP	Bainbridge Colby Papers
BDE	Brooklyn Daily Eagle
BU	Brandeis University
BVC	Bertha V. Corets
BVCC	Bertha V. Corets Collection
CG	Carter Glass
CGP	Carter Glass Papers
CUL	Columbia University Libraries
CW	Chaim Weizmann
EMH	Edward Mandell House
EMHD	Edward Mandell House Diary
EMHP	Edward Mandell House Papers
FMD	Florence Marshall Diaries
FUPP	Private Papers of the late Prof. Frank Untermyer
G&U	Guggenheimer & Untermyer
GU&M	Guggenheimer, Untermyer & Marshall
JDB	Jewish Daily Bulletin

JDC	American Jewish Joint Distribution Committee
JHS	Jacob Henry Schiff
JHSC	Jacob Henry Schiff Collection
JMB	James M. Beck
JMBP	James M. Beck Papers
JML	Jones Memorial Library
JWV	Jewish War Veterans
JNUL	The Jewish National University and Library
KKK	Ku Klux Klan
LAC	Library and Archives Canada
LAS	Laurence A. Steinhardt
LASP	Laurence A. Steinhardt Papers
LCC	Lynchburg Circuit Court
LCMD	Library of Congress Manuscripts Division
LDB	Louis Dembitz Brandeis
LDBC	Louis Dembitz Brandeis Collection
LM	Louis Marshall
LMC	Louis Marshall Collection
LV	Lynchburg Virginian/Lynchburg Daily Virginian/Daily Lynchburg Virginian
MA	Manuscripts and Archives
MID	Military Intelligence Division
NA	United States National Archives and Records Administration
NSANLCHRR	Non-Sectarian Anti-Nazi League to Champion Human Rights Records
NYDT	New York Daily Tribune/New York Tribune
NYEP	New York Evening Post
NYH	New York Herald
NYHT	New York Herald Tribune
NYMA	New York Municipal Archive
NYPL	New York Public Library
NYT	New York Times
NYS	New York Sun
NYTCR	New York Times Company Records
PAAA	Politisches Archiv des Auswärtigen Amts

PI	Philadelphia Inquirer
PU	Princeton University
RBML	Rare Book and Manuscript Library
RDFUASC	Robert D. Farber University Archives & Special Collections Department
RL	Robert Lansing
RLP	Robert Lansing Papers
RPHSFA	Rabbi Peter H. Schweitzer's Family Archive
SSC	Small Special Collections
SSW	Stephen Samuel Wise
SSWC	Stephen S. Wise Collection
SD	Samuel Dickstein
SDC	Samuel Dickstein Collection
SGMML	Seeley G. Mudd Manuscript Library
SU	Samuel Untermyer
SUC	Samuel Untermyer Collection
TNA	United Kingdom National Archives
UA	University Archives
UL	University of Louisville
UVL	University of Virginia Library
WA	The Weizmann Archive
WES	Washington Evening Star
WGM	William Gibbs McAdoo
WGMP	William Gibbs McAdoo Papers
WJB	William Jennings Bryan
WJBP	William Jennings Bryan Papers
WRH	William Randolph Hearst
WRHP	William Randolph Hearst Papers
WRHS	Western Reserve Historical Society
WSJ	Wall Street Journal
WW	Woodrow Wilson
WWP	Woodrow Wilson Papers
WZO	World Zionist Organization
ZOA	Zionist Organization of America
YUL	Yale University Library

Illustrations

Illustration 1
Miniature of Therese Landauer Guggenheimer Untermyer, c. 1850s   16
Courtesy Peter Rosenblatt

Illustration 2
Photograph of Isidor Untermyer, c. 1860s   17
Courtesy Richard Rosenblatt

Illustration 3
Photograph of Untermyer Family on Vacation in Lapland, c. 1880s   22
Courtesy Frank Untermyer

Illustration 4
Thomas Powers's 'A Hit! – "Crushed to Earth" Pleases All' Cartoon, 1905   36
New York Evening World, 14 April 1905, 3.
Courtesy Library of Congress

Illustration 5
Udo J. Keppler's '"Watcher Got?": A Quiet Game of Freezeout in
    Life Insurance Gulch' Cartoon, 1906   53
Puck, 3 October 1906, 1.
Courtesy Al Holden

Illustration 6
Boardman Robinson's 'Gulliver Before the Lili-Pujoans' Cartoon, 1912   68
New York Daily Tribune, 20 December 1912, 1.
Courtesy Library of Congress

Illustration 7
Oscar Cesare's 'Who Said Panic?' Cartoon, 1912   69
New York Sun, 20 December 1912, 9.
Courtesy Library of Congress

Illustration 8
Oscar Cesare's 'The People Demand Stock Exchange Legislation' Cartoon, 1913   73
New York Sun, 5 April 1913, 7.
Courtesy Library of Congress

Illustration 9
Photograph of Samuel Untermyer and Albert Einstein,
    Palm Springs, 7 February 1933   126
Courtesy of Samuel Untermyer II

Illustration 10
Photograph: The Fearless Champion of Jewish Rights, New York Harbour,
    6 August 1933   155
Courtesy American Jewish Archives

Introduction

Kenneth D. Wald in his recent book on the foundations of American Jewish liberalism has observed that scholars 'have given relatively short shrift to the explicitly political dimensions of Jewish life in the United States'. This, he argues, 'has also left unsolved the key puzzle in modern American Jewish political behavior. Jews today [2019] rank among the most pro-Democratic and politically liberal constituencies in the United States'. In fact, political science theory would suggest that 'As a relatively wealthy, highly educated, and upper-status community, Jews should be more Republican and politically conservative than other Americans.'[1] In Wald's exploration of the historical roots of American Jewish liberalism he overlooks Samuel Untermyer, the Progressive Jewish Democrat.

Untermyer did not begin life as a liberal or, in the parlance of his era, as a Progressive. At the beginning of his career, he was a conservative Democrat. James M. Beck, a conservative Democratic, and later Republican, lawyer and politician, was one of Untermyer's close friends.[2] Untermyer is unusual because while it is common for people to gradually shift from liberalism to conservatism as they age, the alternative is not. This transition began in the 1890s and it seems likely liberal Republican Louis Marshall was invited by Untermyer to join his law firm in 1890[3] not just because he was a specialist in equity cases and appellate court work[4] but also because his civil rights advocacy offered Untermyer's firm an early form of corporate social responsibility. Initially Untermyer's liberalism was restricted to his support for his new partner's endeavours. However, at the beginning of the 1900s he became an advocate for economic and financial reform as part of the Progressive faction of the Democratic Party. This will be explored in Chapters 2 and 3.

Untermyer's liberalism was not restricted to economic and financial reform. He was a staunch supporter of female suffrage. Untermyer told William Gibbs McAdoo in 1916 he was and had been 'upwards of 25 years an ardent champion of suffrage . . . To me a democracy in which the suffrage is denied to one-half the population is a misnomer.'[5] Untermyer was to serve as a member of the Advisory Committee of the Men's League for Woman Suffrage.[6] Brooke Kroeger has described him in a recent book as a 'suffragent'.[7] As early as 1910 Untermyer had lobbied the New York State Legislature in support of a Female Suffrage Bill.[8] The same year Untermyer's Yonkers' country estate Greystone was host to the first of four lectures given by suffragist Ida Husted Harper.[9] Untermyer observed in a letter to Max Eastman in 1913:

> Those who belittle the public importance of the movement toward woman suffrage do not realize the injustice of woman's status before the law in [New York] and other states with respect to property and domestic rights under man-made laws

... The marriage relation should be one of partnership and community of interest. Instead of this we have the barbarous situation whereby the husband has the right under the law absolutely to disinherit the wife. All the personal property acquired by him is his own. She has no claims upon it, even when there are no children.[10]

Untermyer's wife Minnie was also a supporter of women's suffrage, although before 1909 she had been 'too timid to express' her 'views publicly'.[11] However, in October of that year she resigned from the anti-suffrage League for the Civic Education of Women which she had served as vice-president and announced her intention to join both of New York's leading suffrage societies: the Equality League of Self-Supporting Women and the New York State Suffrage Association. Minnie subsequently became a member of both organizations.[12] By 1915 she had also been elected an officer of the German American Committee of the Woman Suffrage Party. Minnie and her husband organized a mass rally of German Americans on behalf of the committee at New York's Terrace Garden in October of that year. They brought the keynote speaker, their friend, the former secretary of state William Jennings Bryan over from New Jersey in their motor car.[13]

Untermyer strongly supported the 1915 New York state female suffrage amendment which was on the ballot in the November election. In early October, his Yonkers estate was the venue for a big suffrage party in honour of Olive Whitman, the wife of the governor of New York.[14] In a speech delivered at the end of October on the centenary of the birthday of suffragist Elizabeth Cady Stanton, he observed that the state of the law with regard to women's rights was a shame to civilization, and that there was no democracy without suffrage. He referred specifically to the divorce laws of New York State, which did not allow a divorce on the grounds of desertion or cruel and inhuman treatment.[15] Untermyer also supported birth control.[16] In the November state election the amendment was decisively rejected.[17] Undeterred, in 1917 he became a member of the Men's Advisory Committee of Carrie Chapman Catt's Woman Suffrage Party's campaign in support of another Woman Suffrage Amendment on the ballot in the November state election.[18] At the beginning of October he spoke at the campaign's first big mass meeting,[19] and at the end of the month he proudly marched with the women in the suffrage parade in New York City.[20] This time the voters passed the amendment which gave women full suffrage. New York was the first East Coast state to do so. It was a major victory for the suffrage movement.[21] Untermyer then worked with the Woman Suffrage Party to prepare the necessary laws which he had agreed to draft.[22]

Untermyer also helped Alice Paul's more militant Congressional Union for National Suffrage and National Women's Party who campaigned for a national women's suffrage amendment to the US Constitution which Untermyer had supported since at least 1914.[23] His wife was a member of the party's national advisory council.[24] In May 1916 Untermyer asked McAdoo to try to arrange a half-hour meeting with Abby Scott Baker, the party's press officer, to make the case for the administration giving its support to the amendment.[25] The following year the party picketed the White House to try to secure Woodrow Wilson's support for the amendment. When Wilson pardoned sixteen of the pickets who had been sentenced to sixty days in Virginia's Occoquan workhouse, Untermyer advised Baker, their spokeswoman, that they could not be compelled to accept the pardon. Baker blamed McAdoo for the incarceration of the pickets.[26]

In his early career Untermyer was against organized labour. Samuel Gompers later recalled he had observed to him in 1888 that 'labor unions were the curse of the country'.[27] However, Untermyer became a supporter of labour unions in later life, several of which he represented pro bono in disputes.[28] The International Ladies' Garment Workers' Union were so grateful for his determining contribution to their victory in the ten-week 1921–2 cloak makers' strike that they presented him with a solid gold loving cup.[29] Untermyer explained why he had become a supporter of labour unions in 1915,[30] observing

> Capitalism is more powerful, more rampant, more despotic, and less controlled by law or public sentiment with us than in any other country. It lacks the most elemental sense of justice and fights every inch of the way regardless of the merits of the controversy. Of all its blunders its blindness to and disregard of the welfare of the industrial workers who are Its chief asset is the most flagrant, short-sighted, and unpardonable.[31]

Anticipating the 1930s New Deal he also favoured maternity benefits and insurance against sickness, invalidity, and unemployment, all contributed to by the employer, by the state, by the community, such as they had in other countries.[32] Untermyer also supported a minimum wage.[33]

Later, in 1921 that he testified before the US Senate that although if an open shop were possible, he would be in favour of it because it was more consistent with the American concept of personal liberty, in practice there was no such thing. He observed that

> I think it must generally be agreed that the peace and happiness and comfort and welfare of the community would require that organized labor should be recognized and encouraged, rather than the nonunion shop, where that labor does not have a fair chance in any way against organized capital, as it is at the mercy of concentrated capital.[34]

Untermyer also testified that he opposed companies refusing to employ union members. He noted that this was the practice of the Bethlehem Steel Co. in which he was a large holder of stock. Untermyer said that he had opposed this company policy for many years.[35] He also testified that he supported collective bargaining.[36] His testimony regarding Bethlehem Steel was not hypocrisy. For example, in 1919 Untermyer had represented the Actors' Equity Association free of charge in a dispute with New York City theatre managers, even though he had investments in theatre properties.[37]

Untermyer's support for labour unions included those organized by African Americans. In 1934, Major General Ralph H. Van Deman, a retired former Military Intelligence Division (MID) officer who ran a private espionage network to assist the then-under-resourced MID, commissioned a lengthy report on Untermyer from the American Vigilant Intelligence Federation of Chicago.[38] It accused Untermyer of engaging in activities in support of 'Communist programs' in part because of his sympathy for the African American sleeping car porters.[39] In late November 1926 Untermyer had attended the first interracial labour dinner ever given by the earliest successful African American labour union, the Brotherhood of Sleeping Car Porters. He told them, 'The two biggest fakes in America are the open shop and the company union.' He applauded their fight against these 'two fakes' in the Pullman system[40] and promised that he would assist them in presenting their case to the US Railway Mediation Board[41] in an appeal for improved conditions. Untermyer cited figures which he said showed the Pullman Company could afford to pay the porters higher wages.[42] The *Topeka Plaindealer* observed that Untermyer's 'strong, biting words belied the shadow of sickness that darkened his face. His message took on the solemnity and dignity of prophecy as he gave wise counsel and encouragement for the struggle'.[43] He was to be one of several prominent legal advisers to the union.[44] An investigation was begun into the Brotherhood's demands in May 1927 by former governor Edwin P. Morrow of Kentucky, a member of the United States Board of Mediation, and William F. Mitchell, the board's statistician.[45] The *Pittsburgh Courier* observed on 2 July 1927:

> Like Darrow, Mencken, John Haynes Holmes and other prominent white men, Mr. Untermyer does not lose his voice when the wronged party is a Negro. He speaks out strongly and hits from the shoulder irrespective of race, color or creed. Not satisfied with having made a monetary contribution to help along with the organization work of the Brotherhood of Sleeping Car Porters, he has written a powerful letter to the president of the Pullman Company demanding that the vicious policy of discharging active members of the union be discontinued. Says he in criticism of this policy:
>
> 'It will injure the quality of the service your Company offers the travelling public. The avenue to high morale and better service is in cooperation with legitimate desires such as the formation of a union of their own and not frustrated by fear.'
>
> With such a powerful ally as Mr. Untermyer, these Negro workers should have less difficulty in winning their fight. When white men who have no immediate personal interest in the matter come willing to the assistance of black workers, there seems to be little excuse for these workers themselves not to do their utmost.[46]

However, later in July Morrow concluded that without the cooperation of the Pullman Company he had no power to arbitrate under the Railway Labor Act. Pullman did not cooperate.[47]

Untermyer also later demonstrated his support for the African American community by bequeathing 1,691 books from his Law Library, including a hundred or more volumes of his most famous cases to Howard University Law School. His collection joined those from Louis Marshall's library which Jacob Billikopf had persuaded his cousin James to donate after his father's death in 1929.[48]

Jason Shulman observes that the history of the United States since the First World War is packed with 'Jewish characters—as litigants, lawyers, judges, journalists, and professors. That American Jews have been disproportionately drawn to the speech protection of the First Amendment is at once obvious and yet surprisingly absent from American or legal history'. Shulman singles out Untermyer as an early advocate who played a key role.[49]

Untermyer was a strong supporter of press freedom as illustrated by the Panama Libel Case. In October 1908, the New York *World* published an article alleging various people associated with President Theodore Roosevelt's administration had profited from the purchase by the federal government of the Panama Canal Company. The story was also taken up by the *Indianapolis News*.[50] Roosevelt responded by instructing the federal government to sue the *World* and the *Indianapolis News* for criminal libel. On 17 February 1909 the Grand Jury of the District of Columbia handed down indictments against Joseph Pulitzer, owner of the *World*, and Delevan Smith and Charles E. Williams, owners of the *Indianapolis News*, together with the Press Publishing Company, the corporation which published the *World* and Caleb M. Van Hamm and Robert H. Lyman of the managing staff of that newspaper.[51] The *World* decided to fight the extradition of Pulitzer, Van Hamm and Lyman to Washington, DC.[52] They retained Untermyer's friend De Lancey Nicoll to represent them against the federal government. The indictments proved to be ineffective because the three men were unlikely to voluntarily go to the capital to be arrested.[53]

However, Roosevelt then got a Federal Grand Jury in New York to issue indictments in early March against the Press Publishing Company and Van Hamm, managing editor of the *World*, on the ground that twenty-nine copies of the offending issues had been circulated at the military reservation at West Point. No indictments were issued against Pulitzer or Lyman. At this point Untermyer became involved in the case, as attorney for Vann Hamm. Nicoll continued as counsel for the Press Publishing Company.[54] On 15 March Untermyer entered a plea of not guilty for Van Hamm.[55] The case collapsed at the end of January the following year in what was seen as a victory for the freedom of the press.[56]

Untermyer also believed that the press should be objective. Anticipating Walter Lippmann and Charles Merz's seminal *New Republic* article 'A Test of the News'[57] by almost a year, he observed to Upton Sinclair in 1919,

> The newspapers no longer confine their editorial views and policies to the editorial page where they legitimately belong. Almost every news item of importance is treated editorially from the point of view of the policy of the paper and the news is garbled and distorted in order to establish the points sought to be printed.[58]

Untermyer was opposed to Socialism because he believed it was a 'beautiful, iridescent dream'.[59] Nonetheless when agents of the New York State Legislature's Lusk Committee, which was investigating 'Red' subversion, raided the Rand School, a left-wing institute owned by the American Socialist Society in New York in July 1919, he was quick to come to its defence. He told the *New York Times*:

> I am a pronounced anti-Socialist, but a pronounced believer in free speech. I understand that the Rand School is controlled by intellectuals among the Socialists who believe in promulgating their doctrines through lawful methods and who are opposed to the radical left wing.
>
> The Lusk committee is doing incalculable harm by its unlawful methods and is driving law-abiding citizens into the arms of the radical wing of the party. I never have known anything as lawless as the Lusk committee, as when the Rand School people appealed to me . . . The open contempt of the Lusk Committee for law and order is a flagrant example of lawlessness.[60]

Untermyer sent a letter to Senator Clayton R. Lusk in defence of the Rand School.[61] Untermyer represented pro bono the American Socialist Society before the New York Supreme Court in opposing an injunction by State Attorney General Charles D. Newton to restrain it from continuing instruction and sale of radical literature through the Rand School of Social Science and the Rand School Bookstore. The state also made motion for a receiver. Both were preliminary to a trial to annul the charter of the American Socialist Society and to close the Rand School and Bookstore.[62] Thomas Wirth suggests that 'Untermyer was driven, at least partly, by political motivations in taking on the Rand School case. As a Democrat and supporter of progressive reform, smashing the Republican-led Lusk Committee had more than minor political significance for his party at the state level.'[63] On 28 July in a telegram Untermyer accused Newton of issuing every day for weeks falsehoods concerning the Rand School and conducting a 'libelous' newspaper campaign against it. In the same telegram to Newton, Untermyer also summarized the issues involved in the case:

> Never since the famous Dred-Scott [sic] fugitive slave case was there a cause in the courts in which such momentous issues were involved. We are about to learn whether an educational institution, teaching among other things economic and social science, and recognized as an auxiliary to the Socialist Party of America, operating within the law, and which appeals only to legal and orderly methods of agitation and consistently deprecates violence and revolution, is, in times of peace, to be denied the personal liberty and freedom of speech and of the press granted it by our Constitution, and whether the hateful process of force and seizure of its books and papers, to prevent which the founders of our Republic provided with such scrupulous care, may with impunity be abused and set aside by public officials elected by the people and charged with the enforcement of the law.[64]

On 30 July the New York Supreme Court dismissed the attorney general's action.[65] One of the members of the Rand School, Max Eastman, reported that

> Samuel Untermyer went in and scared the Attorney General to death. He tried to get a postponement, Untermyer insisted on immediate trial, he said he wasn't prepared, and the judge dismissed the case! It was the 'motion to revoke the

charter' of the Rand School. I think that will cramp his style a little when it comes to indicting us. I hope so. I don't want to be tried again for a while.[66]

The attorney general tried unsuccessfully to reopen the case in October, an action which Untermyer said was persecution.[67] However, Todd J. Pfannestiel observes, 'since the State lacked any new, substantial evidence, and was also unable to meet Untermyer's demand for an immediate trial, Justice Gavegan once again dismissed the charges.'[68] So the Lusk Committee instead drew up new laws, including a licensing statute, to suppress the school. These were enacted in 1920 but vetoed by Governor Alfred E. Smith. After his defeat by Nathan L. Miller in the November 1920 gubernatorial election, the Lusk Laws, including the licensing statute, were re-enacted in 1921. The school declined to apply for a license. The state attorney general then applied for injunction to stop its teaching. The school challenged the injunction in the state courts. While an appeal against an adverse decision in the appellate court was pending, Miller was defeated by Smith in the gubernatorial election of November 1922. Smith's return to office was followed by the repeal of the Lusk legislation, and thus the proceedings against the school stopped.[69] Zechariah Chafee, Jr. observes that 'The cause of liberal education was won, not in the courts but at the polls.'[70]

Untermyer support for civil liberties continued in the 1920s. In April 1920 he assisted the five Socialist Assemblymen who were ousted from the New York State Assembly at the behest of Speaker Thaddeus C. Sweet and Senator Lusk after an investigation by the Assembly Judiciary Committee.[71] In the September special election Untermyer gave his support to the five men as a protest against their expulsion, although he opposed their beliefs.[72] All of the five Socialists were re-elected[73] and re-seated in the Assembly.[74] Sweet then contrived to oust the five again. This time the Republicans supported two of their Socialist colleagues, and thus only three of the five were ousted. The other two Socialists then resigned.[75] Once again Untermyer condemned the ouster. He observed, 'It is another attack on our democratic institutions. The voters who elected these men, however greatly we may differ from their views, are entitled to be represented.'[76]

The Socialists were not the only victims of wartime hysteria and its post-war aftermath. In 1921 Untermyer represented his friend German-born Sir Edgar Speyer, a former member of the British branch of the private banking firm of Speyer & Co. of Frankfurt and New York.[77] He had resigned as a Privy Councillor in 1915 after having been subjected to a campaign of political persecution in Britain.[78] In the spring of 1919 Speyer, who had moved to the United States, was informed by the British home secretary that the revocation of his naturalization certificate was under consideration. Untermyer succeeded in persuading the British government to appoint a commission to take evidence in the United States, at which he and his son, Irwin, represented Speyer. Every witness with a knowledge of the facts testified before Judge Morgan J. O'Brien from April to June 1921. O'Brien's subsequent report dismissed all the American charges against Speyer. Speyer assumed that the proceedings against him would be dismissed. However, at the revocation hearing in October the British government presented different charges against him.[79] In December 1921, the British home secretary revoked Speyer's British naturalization and removed him from the

Privy Council. Untermyer described the British government's action 'as cruel political persecution'.[80]

During the 1920s Untermyer supported the work of the American Civil Liberties Union (ACLU). He supported its purpose

> to protect our civil liberties and to cry out against the ever growing invasion of the most sacred rights of citizenship guaranteed by the Constitution of a land that dares not call itself the home of liberty – the denial of peaceful, lawful assembly and freedom of speech...
>
> In these days of complex social and economic conditions our obvious weapon would of course be the press, which should be our first and last bulwark against all forms of oppression. We should be able to turn to it as our natural ally, for freedom of speech and lawful public assemblage are no less dear to us than is freedom of the press. They go hand in hand. If one can be suppressed, why not the other? All of them taken together constitute our last ditch fortifications against despotism.[81]

In 1924 Untermyer represented the ACLU in a case in which three lawyers, four members of the United Mine Workers of America and several newspaper men were assaulted and falsely arrested by agents of the Vinton Colliery Company, during a bitter strike against the Appalachian coal mine owners.[82] The following year he supported the ACLU's protest against the conviction of one of its directors, Roger N. Baldwin, and seven others for unlawful assemblage in Paterson, New Jersey, during the 1924 silk strike. Untermyer also agreed to assist the ACLU with the Paterson Seven's appeal against their conviction before the New Jersey Supreme Court in January 1926.[83] When the court upheld the conviction in November 1927, he promised to take the case to the US Supreme Court if necessary, observing that

> There was no law or ordinance of the City of Paterson requiring any sort of license or permit to hold a meeting in the square, nor did the police suggest that it should not be held. It would be difficult to conceive anything more important to a free and liberty loving people than the eventual outcome of this test case.[84]

Earlier in 1925 the Communist Shapurji Saklatvala, a British Member of Parliament, had been denied entry to the United States by the State Department to attend the Inter-Parliamentary Union Congress in Washington, DC. Untermyer observed as member of the ACLU's Saklatvala protest committee that America's

> recent attitude toward freedom of speech is contrary to all our traditions and to the spirit of our institutions. We can well afford to tolerate the expression of every point of view of government, however dangerous or absurd we believe it to be. In point of fact, there is less liberty of speech and action and more intolerance in this vaunted land of liberty than in any European country outside of Russia and Southeastern Europe. The reversal of our traditional policy that was made necessary by the war and supposed to be a purely war policy continues

to be more and more pronounced, until our Government has reached a state of permanent hysteria.[85]

In October 1925 the Passaic, New Jersey, textile mill owners cut their workers' wages by 10 per cent. The workers responded by forming a union and in early 1926 began a strike[86] for improved wages and working conditions together with union recognition. The New Jersey police responded on behalf of the mill owners with exceptional violence. Untermyer was one of several lawyers and other public figures who supported the strikers.[87] In April he appeared before the US Senate Committee on Manufactures in support of a proposed investigation into the strike and presented an affidavit on behalf of the ACLU. Untermyer pledged if an investigation were granted, he would act as counsel for the strikers.[88] The committee decided not to act.[89] Untermyer believed that the New Jersey police and committing magistrates were the lawbreakers, not the strikers. He noted all the violence had been committed by the police.

> Such wanton despotism and lawlessness have rarely been witnessed. If the published reports are true, the officials have literally inaugurated and are pursuing against the strikers a veritable reign of terror in which human rights and our vaunted liberties and freedom of speech are being grossly outraged.
>
> The unnecessary brutal manner in which the attempted parade of the children of the strikers is reported to have been charged into and suppressed is difficult to understand, except on the theory that there is no such thing as the right of protest by the men who are on strike and their families.[90]

Toward the end of April, the governor of New Jersey, A. Harry Moore, offered the services of a mediation committee he had appointed to arbitrate in the strike.[91] However, Untermyer observed that in his opinion the strikers 'no longer need[ed] outside mediation'[92] and, as Jacob A. Zumoff notes, advised them not to have anything to do with Moore and his committee.[93] Although the strikers ignored Untermyer's advice, Moore was not willing to negotiate with their Communist leader, Albert Weisbord.[94] So the strike continued until the end of the year. Four of the mills granted a substantial part of the workers' demands while the other five conceded better conditions without union recognition.[95] Zumoff argues that the Passaic strikers pioneered many of the labour protest techniques that were to become important in the 1930s.[96]

Untermyer's new-found support for labour unions was not unconditional. One of the bills resulting from the New York State Legislature's Lockwood Housing Investigation Committee for which he acted as counsel was a labour union regulation bill. In January 1923 Untermyer took part in a debate with his friend[97] Morris Hillquit, the Socialist lawyer, on the proposed bill. The chairman, Oswald Garrison Villard, introduced Untermyer with a joke.

> I am tempted to introduce the next speaker as a reformed lawyer, (laughter) for I am told there was a time when Mr. Samuel Untermyer devoted himself exclusively to his profession and to the amassing of wealth. It must have been a long time

ago for I can't seem to recall it. I can only recall that for a long time past he has been giving us extraordinary examples of enlightened and patriotic citizenship. (Applause.)[98]

Untermyer argued for the bill which was aimed at addressing the building industry labour unions' racketeering that the Lockwood Inquiry had revealed. Hillquit argued against the bill. The bill was not enacted.[99]

Untermyer had a keen interest in criminal justice. He was a member of the Prison Association of New York which had made a major contribution to the reformation of the state's sixty or so county jails.[100] Untermyer was an opponent of capital punishment. For some years he was a member of the committee of which Lewis Edward Lawes was chairman.[101] Lawes was the progressive warden of Sing Sing State Prison, a New York State Prison located at Ossining.[102] Untermyer was also a long-standing member of the League for the Abolition of Capital Punishment. In January 1926 he accepted a place on its National Executive Committee.[103] Two years later he took part in a debate with state senator William Lathrop Love on whether capital punishment should be abolished.[104] Untermyer suggested that the real motive of the State of New York in inflicting capital punishment was not to protect society but to cater to a vicious subconscious instinct.

> The attitude of the State proves that behind all our virtuous protestations and pretended revulsion there lies the subconscious, brutal instinct of the Colonial Puritan who within the space of less than two centuries danced about the stake at which women and children were burned alive for petty offences.[105]

Untermyer believed that the irrevocability of the punishment was one of the strongest arguments against the death penalty.

> To say that our system is as yet the best that we can or should devise is to fly in the face of all experience. We know that innocent men have been and are occasionally convicted and executed. For every such instance that happens to reach the light of day, how many have gone undisclosed we do not know, but those of us who have had experience in the courts can well conjecture and we stand aghast at what is happening in our midst, especially to poor and friendless.
>
> The thought that the law has put these cases beyond the reach of correction is abhorrent to our sense of justice and humanity.
>
> So long as the convicted man is with us the agitation for the correction of injustice is kept alive, but when he is gone that stimulus disappears.[106]

Untermyer also cited the pernicious influence of public opinion.

> The War taught us that in times of passion and public excitement all things are possible, with inflamed public sentiment and the spirit of revenge in the air. I attribute much that is evil and savage and little that is worth while in us to

'war psychology'; but it at least taught us how cruel can be man to man when influenced by passion.

Is not the percentage of probable error too high to warrant an irrevocable penalty? . . .

Many of us doubtless recall the case of Leo Frank in 1915 in Georgia, convicted of outraging and murdering a young girl. He was sentenced to death. Impartial investigators concluded that he was innocent and that the guilt lay with a negro named Conly, connected with the establishment of which Frank was at the head. Governor Slaton, in the face of a wide public demand for Frank's execution, aroused by the yellow press, bravely commuted the sentence, became satisfied of Frank's innocence, of which there was no doubt. The mob broke into the jail and lynched Frank.[107]

Samuel Untermyer's liberalism was made possible by the wealth generated by his law practice. By the turn of the twentieth century, he had achieved his goal of accumulating $5 million.[108] Later in 1920 he was estimated to be worth $40 million[109] which placed him among the wealthiest Americans.[110] Untermyer's wealth took the form of real estate and securities.[111] He was not afraid of conspicuous consumption. As well the enjoyment gained from it, it also signalled he was successful and helped him attract additional high fee-paying clients. In the early 1890s he purchased a townhouse on fashionable 5th Avenue.[112] This was followed by the acquisition in 1899 of Greystone, the former country estate of Samuel J. Tilden, at an auction for $171,500. He also purchased a tract of land adjacent to the estate for $50,000. The house itself, a massive three-storey structure with a tower, contained thirty-one rooms. The previous owner had let Greystone become dilapidated. Untermyer hired the architect Joseph Henry Freedlander to alter the building, the approaches and the grounds. It was estimated Untermyer's total outlay for Greystone, including his improvements, was $550,000.[113] Untermyer also purchased a large selection of fine art for the house.[114] He had become a collector at the beginning of the 1890s.[115] Untermyer is remembered for his courageous purchase of James McNeill Whistler's celebrated 'Nocturne in Black and Gold' in 1892.[116] The artist Edward Burne-Jones had testified in a British libel suit against John Ruskin in 1878 that the 'Nocturne in Gold and Black', which the American Impressionist completed in two days, was neither a work of art nor worth 200 guineas. Untermyer paid 800 guineas for the painting.[117] By 1904 the interior of the house was the last word in luxury.[118] His second cousin, Beatrice Lowenstein Magnes, who was a friend of his daughter Irene, later recalled Greystone 'was more like a museum than a home'.[119] Among Untermyer's prized possessions was Benjamin Disraeli's buhl desk. The journalist James Creelman noted Greystone resembled 'the domain of some prince, rather than the home of a plain citizen . . ., a home that requires five miles of fences and the care of a hundred and fifty men'.[120] The art critic Guy Pène DuBois subsequently suggested Untermyer's Greystone was inspired by Versailles,[121] although it is more likely the Germanophile lawyer was partly inspired by Sans Souci.

However, Untermyer's greatest joy came from what he regarded as living works of art, flowers. Untermyer's passion for flowers came from his mother. His childhood home in Lynchburg had always been filled with flourishing plants. He later recalled, 'From the time I could understand anything, I have regarded flowers as an inseparable part of daily life.'[122] The gardens at Yonkers became his pride and joy.[123] He once observed to a journalist, 'I am told my profession is the law. But my real affection is my greenhouse.'[124] Sir Edgar Speyer believed his gardens ranked among the finest anywhere.[125] Untermyer began to appear in court with a fresh flower, such as a carnation, in his lapel.[126] Soon he decided that only a fresh orchid grown at the Greystone greenhouses was appropriate for his image, and henceforth never left home in the morning without one in his lapel.[127]

At the turn of the twentieth century many of America's wealthiest men owned yachts. In 1903 Untermyer acquired the *Scud*, an 83-foot-long steam yacht.[128] It had been built in 1901 specifically for its speed.[129] Untermyer soon became involved in a rivalry with another yacht owner on the Hudson River and was pleased to establish the *Scud* was faster.[130] When he was in residence in Greystone Untermyer also used his yacht to travel to and from work in Manhattan when the weather was hot.[131] By 1913 the yacht became outmoded and Untermyer sold it to John Francis Strauss, a fellow attorney.[132] During the First World War when he was unable to partake in his annual European vacation, he first chartered the houseboat (an early twentieth-century superyacht) *Osiris* from his client Julianna Farquhar Ferguson for the winter season 1915–16.[133] In December 1916 he acquired his own houseboat, the twin-screw power 125-foot *Nirodha*, one of the most expensive and luxurious crafts of her type in the world. It was later valued at $125,000.[134] The yacht was used both for vacations and to entertain clients and friends such as William Jennings Bryan.[135] Untermyer owned the *Nirodha* for over a decade.[136]

Like many millionaires of his era Untermyer also used his wealth to financially support a mistress, Irish immigrant Margaret Roche Rice.[137] She was the daughter of a gentlemen farmer[138] and the niece of a surgeon general in the Indian Army.[139] In 1906 Untermyer arranged Margaret's marriage to a gay Hungarian independent scholar,[140] Imre Jösicka-Herczeg,[141] the adopted son of a nobleman, in order to be able to accompany her in society.[142] Marguerite, as she subsequently styled herself, had two wards, John and Molly Tackaberry, who were her nephew and niece.[143] Molly was to marry William 'Billy' Gibbs McAdoo, Jr., the son of one of Untermyer's friends, in 1922.[144] Untermyer established a trust to provide for Marguerite and Imre.[145] They often accompanied him and his wife Minnie to social events.[146] They also vacationed together as two couples.[147]

In 1930 Untermyer leased an apartment at 927 5th Avenue.[148] His 5th Avenue townhouse had been razed in 1926 two years after the death of his wife and replaced by an office building.[149] Untermyer also acquired a winter villa, the Willows, in the southern Californian desert resort Palm Springs, in October 1930.[150] Untermyer later described what attracted him to Palm Springs.

> It is right in the heart of the desert, surrounded by snow-capped mountains. It is the deadest place on earth. All that we have is climate! When it doesn't rain the sun is hot and beautiful. The air is perhaps the dryest in the world. 'Sun-baths' are the principal diversion.[151]

Untermyer had the residence renovated as a beautiful concrete Mediterranean-style house[152] and surrounded by fine landscaping. Molly McAdoo was his interior decorator. Untermyer's first winter season at his villa was 1930–1.[153] The villa had no dining room. In January 1931 Untermyer converted the patio into a dining room. He observed to his friend William Gibbs McAdoo, 'When we get through with the place I am sure it will be thoroughly comfortable, thanks to Molly's indefatigable industry and good taste.'[154] Molly and her aunt Marguerite were to be frequent guests at the Willows.[155]

Untermyer was a very difficult man to work for. His butlers seldom stayed in his employment for long. The exception was the last butler, Louis Blair, who had immigrated to the United States in 1913. Originally known as Karel Bleha, he had been born in the small Bohemian town of Červené Pečky in 1898.[156] After he entered Untermyer's employment he became a naturalized American citizen with the new name of 'Louis Blair' in July 1928.[157] He was to accompany Untermyer on all his trips in the United States and abroad. By 1934 Blair was sometimes described as his 'secretary'.[158] He was one of Untermyer's most trusted employees and according to Untermyer family tradition was able to read his employer's mind. This was a remarkable advancement from his early life in Bohemia as a farm labourer. Blair was gay. Unlike many of his contemporaries Untermyer did not have a problem with this.[159] In 1933 Laurence A. Steinhardt helped his uncle attempt to get Jack Warner to find a job for Blair's twenty-one-year-old boyfriend Kenneth Gordinier at the Warner Bros. studio in Brooklyn or New York.[160] Untermyer's two sons did not approve of Blair. During the last months of Untermyer's life Alvin and Irwin found Blair drunk one night with two teenage boys in the kitchen of his father's 5th Avenue apartment. They took the opportunity to dismiss Blair while their father was too ill to object.[161]

Untermyer cannot be fully understood without the context of his childhood, education and highly successful career as a Wall Street lawyer. This will be explored in the first chapter. The second and third chapters will explore his role as a Progressive Democratic politician, in particular, the Pujo Investigation and his support for the Wilson administration. The fourth chapter will explore Untermyer's role as a Jewish steward during the 1920s, specifically looking at his involvement in the lawsuits against the anti-Semite Henry Ford and his support for the Zionist Project in Palestine. The fifth and final chapter will explore Untermyer's leadership of the anti-Nazi boycott in the United States and elsewhere in the world during the 1930s.

1

The making of an American Jewish leader

Untermyer's education and career as a Wall Street lawyer, 1858–1940

Samuel Untermyer was born in pre-Civil War Lynchburg, Virginia, the son of Bavarian immigrants from Swabian *Judendörfer*.[1] His mother, Therese Landauer, preceded his father in immigrating to the United States. Born in Hürben on 10 April 1827,[2] her father, Raphael Israel Landauer, was an ironmonger and wine merchant.[3] Her mother, Johanna Jonas Landauer, was the daughter of Abraham Jonas (also known as Abraham ben Jona Schwab). He was the last Court Jew and factor to the House of Öttingen-Spielberg, a small south German principality.[4] The Princes of Öttingen always installed one of their Court Jews as leader of the Jewish community 'because of the many services they rendered to the State'.[5] The principality ceased to exist in 1806 because Napoleon incorporated it into the Kingdom of Bavaria.[6]

In 1847 a marriage was arranged to Salomon Guggenheimer, who had immigrated to the United States in in the early 1840s and established a dry goods store in Lynchburg, Virginia, with his brother Nathaniel.[7] The two brothers were sons of Abraham Guggenheimer, a wealthy Rötgerber (red tanner)[8] and leather merchant.[9] Salomon returned to Hürben for the marriage on 28 July. Therese's dowry was 2,100 Bavarian *gulden* which was the equivalent of about $860.[10] Her marriage was short-lived. Salomon died on 17 October 1848,[11] a few months after the birth of his son, Randolph, on 20 July.[12] In his will Salomon noted Therese possessed 11,000 *gulden* (the equivalent of about $4,500), which he wanted to remain her property, and $400 invested in the dry goods store which he also wanted her to have.[13] R.G. Dun & Co. estimated that Therese's total property amounted to $6,000.[14] Therese was soon remarried. On 24 February 1850 she was married to Isidor Untermyer by the Rev. Maximillian Josef Michelbacher of the Congregation Beth Ahabah in Richmond.[15] Therese and Isidor had seven children: Iva,[16] Ellen (Helen),[17] Isaac,[18] Samuel, Morris (Maurice),[19] an unnamed child who died in infancy,[20] and Addie.[21] Samuel, who was born on 6 June 1858, was their fourth child. He outlived all his siblings.

Isidor Untermyer was a tailor who had immigrated from Kriegshaber in 1844 probably with his sister Adelheid. He may have first lived in Richmond. After three years he moved to Lynchburg.[22] He had been born on 8 May 1811[23] in the village of Kriegshaber in the vicinity of Augsburg. Isidor was the younger son of Isaak

Illustration 1 Miniature of Therese Landauer Guggenheimer Untermyer, *c*. 1850s.

Untermayer, who was a master butcher, and Jette Guggenheimer, a paternal aunt of Salomon Guggenheimer.[24] The earliest record of the Untermayer family in Kriegshaber is a 1789 document referring to the Jewish meat broker Untermayr. Isidor's father is first recorded in a document from 1794 referring to Isac unter Mayr.[25] Yehuda Shenef suggests that Isaak had also been known as Isaak ben Mayer. He apparently adopted the name Untermayer to avoid confusion with another man with the same name. He suggests that Isaak Untermayer was the son of Meir ben Simon (1730–1800). Meir was the son of Shimon ben Meir (1698–1775), who in turn was the son of Meir ben Sanwil Ulmo (1655–1735). Many of the influential Ulmo family were famous rabbis and scholars. They were descendants of Jews expelled from the Free Imperial City of Ulm in 1499. If Shenef is correct it is possible Samuel Untermyer was named after Meir ben Sanwil Ulmo.[26] After the death of Meir ben Simon, his widow became head of the family. When she died, the family home was divided between Isaak and his older brother Zacharias in November 1821. Zacharias occupied two-thirds of the building and his brother, Isaak, the remainder.[27] Isaak Untermayer died in 1838 and Jette the following year. Under the Bavarian Matrikel-Gesetz (registration law) a commercial business was inherited by the eldest son. Younger sons were not normally permitted to establish their own business

Illustration 2 Photograph of Isidor Untermyer, c. 1860s.

or to marry.[28] Accordingly, Isidor's elder brother, Max, inherited the family business in November 1839.[29] So there had been no future for Isidor, the younger son, in Bavaria.

In April 1850 Isidor established a short-lived partnership with Therese's former brother-in-law, Nathaniel, a dry goods store, Guggenheimer & Untermyer,[30] anticipating by many years the eponymous law firm of the same name. The partnership was dissolved after the store was destroyed in a fire. Fortunately, it was insured.[31] Untermyer's father then established his own dry goods store which was to specialize in clothing.[32] In 1859 he also established an apparel manufactory,[33] the output of which included African American slave clothing.[34] The following year Isidor was one of the directors of the newly incorporated Lynchburg Savings Bank.[35] There was no rabbi in Lynchburg which is why he had been married in Richmond. Although there were sufficient Jews residing in Lynchburg to form a congregation by the outbreak of the Civil War,[36] the city's first synagogue was not opened until 1897.[37] So Isidor served as religious leader on high holidays.[38] He was also a member of the Congregation Beth Ahabah in Richmond.[39]

Untermyer was aged three when the American Civil War began. It is not known how he was educated when he reached school age during the war. His half-brother

Randolph had been sent by their mother to board with Untermyer's paternal aunt, Adelheid Mendelson, in New York City where he was educated at one of the public schools and after her death at a boarding school.[40] There were no public schools in Lynchburg at this time.[41]

After the outbreak of the war Untermyer's father expanded into military supplies.[42] He also formed an equal partnership with Samuel W. Shelton to manufacture tobacco in a speculative venture.[43] During the war Untermyer's mother invested in real estate in Lynchburg and in neighbouring Jonesborough, Tennessee. She was assisted by her nephew, Max Siesfeld, who had joined the Untermyer household in 1861. He acquired on her behalf a boarding house on Lynchburg's Main Street.[44] Later in 1863 Siesfeld acquired on her behalf a commercial property on Jonesborough's Main Street for $30,000. It was subsequently transferred to Untermyer's father with the proviso it was for the 'sole separate and exclusive use and benefit' of his wife Therese 'and not to be liable for [his] contract debts or liabilities'.[45] Herman Cone, who was married to her first husband's niece Ellen,[46] owned an adjacent property.

After the defeat of the Confederacy in 1865 Isidor Untermyer was bankrupt. He died the following year on 24 March. A committee of Freemasons escorted his body to Richmond, where he was buried in the Hebrew Cemetery.[47] At the time of his death his businesses were heavily in debt. The total estate was valued at $543 (including $6,000 in Confederate money valued at $10). Debts against the estate amounted to $22,274.25.[48] The debts related to the clothing store rather than the tobacco factory.[49] Unfortunately debts due to Isidor incurred before the end of the Civil War were impossible to collect because of the Stay Laws passed by the Virginian General Assembly. They suspended temporarily the collection of debts incurred during the Civil War, the last one until 1 January 1868.[50]

Fortunately, Untermyer's mother's business interests were separate from those of his father, so his family was able to survive the depressed business conditions in post–Civil War Lynchburg.[51] Her boarding house at 167 Main Street became her main source of income. Untermyer's half-brother Randolph had returned from New York City after the war. He established Randolph Guggenheimer's Dry Goods Emporium on the ground floor of the boarding house.[52] He initially did good business. However, his success was short-lived. R.G. Dun & Co. reported in February 1868 he had used his status as a minor to evade payment of debts.[53] In May his mother took over the business. R.G. Dun & Co. reported she was selling the goods out of which her son had cheated his creditors.[54]

In the summer of 1868 Untermyer's mother decided Lynchburg 'did not offer her opportunities for education which her boys and girls needed'.[55] Her sole purpose in life was to secure her children's welfare through a 'thorough education'.[56] She had already sent Untermyer's older brother Isaac to New York City, where he had enrolled at Public School No. 35 at the beginning of the previous year. Since Adelheid Mendelson had died in 1864[57] Isaac probably boarded with his mother's nephew Adolph (Abraham) Levinger.[58] Levinger had immigrated to New York City in 1854 with his brother Mathias.[59] By the following year Levinger had established himself as a lawyer[60] and was admitted to the bar in 1859.[61] Untermyer's mother, he and his siblings moved to New York City where his brother Randolph was to enrol at the beginning of October on a two-year law course at the University of the City of New York (later renamed New York University).[62] Therese subsequently sold her real estate in Lynchburg with the assistance of Levinger.[63] She also sold her real estate in Jonesborough.[64]

Untermyer's mother established a 'first class Jewish boarding house' at 2 and later also 3 Livingston Place opposite Stuyvesant Square just to the north of Little Germany.[65] Among her first boarders were her sister-in-law Adelheid's daughter Sophia and her husband Benedict Lowenstein. They had married the previous year.[66] From 1878 the boarding house was relocated successively to three different premises in the Lenox Hill district just opposite the lower south-eastern side of Central Park.[67] Lenox Hill was 'Society's outer periphery until the 1890s'. Only a handful of the wealthy 'braved such proximity to the tenement world'.[68] The Untermyers' neighbours included Mayer and Babette Lehman. Mayer Lehman had come to the United States from Bavaria in 1847 to join his brothers Emanuel and Henry in Montgomery, Alabama. They became prominent cotton merchants. After the Civil War they moved to New York City, where Emanuel had established a branch of their business shortly before the Civil War. The firm of Lehman Brothers was to be transformed into an investment bank. Untermyer and his brother Isaac became lifelong friends of Mayer's son, Herbert, who was born in 1878.[69] Untermyer later represented Lehman Brothers as a lawyer.[70]

As well as keeping a boarding house Untermyer's mother was a caterer for weddings and other social events on New York's East Side,[71] and also became a real estate investor again from 1873 with the assistance of her nephew Adolph.[72] In 1882 she retired and purchased with a $8,000 mortgage a three-storey house at 106 East 92nd Street in the Goat Hill neighbourhood immediately north of Lenox Hill.[73] Two years later in gratitude for their mother's selflessness Untermyer and his brother Isaac took over the mortgage and had a $32,000 'first class' four-storey-high stoop brownstone house designed by architects Hugo Kafka & Co. built for her and their families at 9 East 92nd Street between Madison and 5th Avenues. This was before they purchased houses for themselves.[74] Prague-born Kafka designed many prominent buildings both in New York City and elsewhere in the state.[75] In retirement Untermyer's mother made two visits to her relatives in Bavaria: the first in 1883, the second in 1887. She subsequently became an invalid and died in 1895.[76]

Untermyer was educated at the Boy's Public School No. 35 on 13th Street near 6th Avenue. Dr Thomas Hunter, the progressive principal, was a Protestant political refugee from Ireland. He believed in equal opportunities for Jews and opposed corporal punishment. Untermyer later became a member of the Thomas Hunter Association which held annual dinners in their teacher's honour after his retirement.[77] Up to his bar mitzvah in 1871 he was destined to become a rabbi and had acquired a good knowledge of Hebrew so that he could fluently read much of the Talmud. Although he later claimed economic necessity required to abandon this career path,[78] it is much more probable he rebelled against his orthodox mother. The following year Untermyer passed the examination required to enrol in the College of the City of New York's one-year Introductory Collegiate Course.[79] The class was the equivalent of high school and prepared young men to enter college.[80] He ranked 132 out of a class of 169 and achieved results of 2030 out of a possible score of 3700.[81] His older brother Isaac was a much better student. He had ranked 23 out of an Introductory Class of 205 three years earlier.[82] After Untermyer completed the class he worked as a clerk for three years at the law office of his cousin Adolph and half-brother Randolph.[83]

In later years, the Guggenheimer and Untermyer families would claim that their family law firm was founded by Randolph Guggenheimer instead of Adolph Levinger. Levinger's clientele included German American brewers, bankers and manufacturers. In addition to practicing law, he founded a brewery with his brother Mathias. This was later relocated from Manhattan to College Point, Long Island (now part of the New York City Borough of Queens). After Guggenheimer graduated from New York University Law School in 1870 he formed a partnership with Levinger, which became an uptown branch of his cousin's original downtown firm. While Untermyer was an apprentice, a bank in which Levinger had an interest failed. It was then claimed that Levinger was responsible for some monies which were unaccounted for. He was arrested, charged with embezzlement and bailed. Untermyer's mother was one of his guarantors. Levinger absconded after dissolving his partnership with Guggenheimer, whose business was hereafter conducted at the former uptown branch. Untermyer's mother and her fellow guarantors hired a former New York City detective, Charles Heidelberg, to track him down. Levinger succeeded in alluding Heidelberg and subsequently died of yellow fever in Havana, Cuba.[84] It is not clear whether Levinger was guilty of embezzlement. However, the College Point brewery had become insolvent at about the same time as the alleged embezzlement.[85]

At the beginning of October 1876 Untermyer followed in his brother Isaac's footsteps and enrolled at Columbia College of Law (later to become Columbia Law School). To enrol he had to meet a new admission requirement introduced by the college's trustees which applied to all applicants from 1876 apart from graduates of literary colleges. All other candidates for admission had to be at least eighteen and have received a good academic education, including the level of Latin required for admission to the Freshman Class of the College.[86] According to one of the trustees, white-shoe lawyer George Templeton Strong, the requirement was introduced to 'keep out the little scrubs (German Jew boys mostly) whom the School now promotes from the grocery counters in Avenue B to be "gentlemen of the bar"'.[87] The Warden of the Law School, Professor Theodore W. Dwight, had successfully opposed the extension of the period of study from two to three years.[88] Law classes were held in the afternoon in the first year and in the morning in the second year.[89] Untermyer was taught by Dwight and later recalled

> As a teacher, Professor Dwight was a genius. As an educator, his like will probably never be reproduced. His force, character, and learning left an ineffaceable impress on his students that lasted throughout their lives and was a never-ceasing source of guidance and inspiration ... He taught the science and fundamental principles of the law in an enduring, illuminating, and fascinating way and as they have never since been inculcated.[90]

While he was at Columbia, he met Louis Marshall, who became his lifelong and closest friend. Marshall completed the law course in one year. He lacked the funds to pay for the minimum two years of fees required to graduate. Both Untermyer and Marshall were members of Columbia Law Club and took part in mock trials.[91] While he was a student Untermyer also continued working at his half-brother Randolph's law firm.

He later claimed as 'the little fellow with the Cantor's beard' he had been representing clients in court since the age of sixteen including eight times in the Court of Appeals before he was admitted to the Bar.[92] When he graduated in May 1878,[93] he was over a year below the minimum age required to take the New York State bar examination.[94] To help overcome this obstacle he changed the date of his birth to 2 March 1858. In a probably typical early case, Untermyer represented a woman in 1881 before the New York Supreme Court claiming surplus monies in a property transaction.[95]

After the tragic demise of Levinger in 1876, Guggenheimer appears to have retained his cousin's German American clientele, including, for example, the brewer Henry Clausen, Jr.[96] He had also joined Tammany Hall before his cousin's death. He was an active supporter of Boss Tweed from as early as 1871.[97] Guggenheimer ingratiated himself with Tammany, and this enabled him to develop a lucrative real estate development business alongside his law practice.[98] In 1885 Guggenheimer made his brothers Isaac and Samuel name partners.[99] The latter was to be the catalyst that transformed Guggenheimer & Untermyer into a Wall Street law firm that successfully challenged the hegemony of the white-shoe WASP firms. John Oller has characterized Untermyer as 'the anti-white shoe corporate lawyer'.[100] Later after his half-brother Randolph's untimely death in 1907[101] Untermyer became senior partner.[102] His brother Isaac had left the partnership in 1905 to found a separate firm, Untermyer, Stein & Stiefel; otherwise, he probably would have become senior partner.[103] After this firm was dissolved in 1909 Isaac returned to the family firm.[104] During Untermyer's time as senior partner the only non-Jewish partner during his lifetime, Arthur Manley Wickwire, joined the firm in 1911 as a specialist in railroad cases.[105] These were an important part of the firm's business from the end of the nineteenth century.

Untermyer's girlfriend during the early 1880s was a German American Protestant dressmaker, Minnie Carl. Their first two children, Edwin and Leonard Alvin (known as Alvin), were born out of wedlock on 12 November 1881 and 1 December 1882, respectively.[106] Edwin died at the age of four months. Untermyer's mother's strong opposition to a marriage outside their faith probably explains why it did not take place until 6 October 1883. Untermyer and Minnie were married by Rabbi Adolph Huebsch of the Congregation Ahawath Chesed, a conservative Reform rabbi. Minnie remained an observant Protestant for the rest of her life.[107] There were two further children born in wedlock: Irene, born on 17 August 1884,[108] and Irwin, born on 2 February 1886.[109]

Minnie was the daughter of German immigrants from Zeulenroda in the Thuringian Vogtland. Her paternal grandfather, Johann Erdmann Traugott Carl, was one of the last surviving German veterans of the Napoleonic Wars. Returning to Zeulenroda at the end of the wars he learned weaving skills and founded a cotton and half-woollen fabric manufactory.[110] Later when the Battle of Nations Monument in Leipzig was consecrated by Kaiser Wilhelm II on 18 October 1913, Johann was one of six veterans honoured in the official commemorative booklet.[111] Perhaps her grandfather's story explains why Minnie was a staunch German nationalist. Her father, Manilius, was a veteran of the American Civil War who had fought on the Union side.[112] The Untermyer and Carl families later claimed that he had been part of the 1848 German Revolution and immigrated to St. Louis with Carl Schurz.[113] In fact, Minnie's father had immigrated with her mother Pauline and older brother Alvin in 1854.[114] During the Civil War

Illustration 3 Photograph of Untermyer Family on Vacation in Lapland, c. 1880s. Samuel Untermyer, Minnie Untermyer, Alvin Untermyer, Irwin Untermyer, Irene Untermyer, Governess, and three Laplanders.

Carl he fell in love with Louisa, the wife of a comrade-in-arms, Lieutenant Colonel Francis Ehrler. Louisa had already had at least two previous extramarital affairs. Minnie's father subsequently deserted her mother and eloped with Louisa to New York City leaving his cuckolded comrade, who had been cashiered for being drunk on duty, to die in hospital from erysipelas on 8 March 1865.[115] Minnie's deserted mother became a boarding housekeeper In St. Louis. She subsequently moved to New York City too. Minnie's mother forced Manilius to support her and her children, although he remained with Louisa for the rest of his life.[116]

In his early years as a lawyer, Untermyer's firm offered a full service to its clients, including representation in divorce cases. He represented clients in many high-profile cases. Untermyer was extremely successful in exposing the transgressions of their wives perhaps with Louisa Ehrler who had wronged his mother-in-law in mind. For example, in 1900 Daniel Guggenheim discovered his brother, William, had recently married Grace Brown Herbert, a Californian divorcee with a colourful past. Guggenheim told his brother if he did not divorce his non-Jewish wife, he would be disowned. The following year to avoid a scandal the divorce took place in Chicago.

Grace got a one-off payment of $150,000. She squandered her settlement and tried to blackmail the Guggenheims for $250,000 in return for her silence. They refused. Grace's lawyer tried to get the divorce overturned in 1912 by claiming she had never been a resident of Illinois. The last witness in the lawsuit was Untermyer, who testified that he had not told Grace to come to Chicago to get a divorce.[117] The court refused to annul the divorce but found Untermyer had committed fraud.[118] The State Attorney of Illinois began disbarment proceedings against Untermyer.[119] However, the case was subsequently dropped.[120]

Gregory J. Kupsky argues that 'German-ness was no small part of Untermyer's self-identification.'[121] Being a Germanophile and able to converse in the German language certainly helped Untermyer retain and attract new German American business clients for the firm. In an 1883 case, *Betz v. Baur*, where he represented John F. Betz, a German American brewer from Philadelphia, he defeated a white-shoe law firm with some of the best legal talent in New York.[122] In an action arising from this case, Betz also sued Henry Daily, Jr., a prominent white-shoe New York lawyer, for conspiring with the New York partners of Betz to issue notes in the firm's name, for which Mr Betz would be liable. Untermyer and Richard S. Newcombe[123] represented Betz. Daily was defended by leaders of the bar who had appeared on either side in the Beecher-Tilton trial in 1875, including William A. Beach and William Fullerton. After a trial before the New York State Supreme Court, a verdict of $49,000 was obtained for Mr Betz.[124] Daily's appeal was dismissed with costs in June 1885.[125] Untermyer was to represent numerous brewers, in particular German Americans, up until the beginning of prohibition. Betz's nephew, the brewer David G. Yuengling, Jr., was an especially lucrative client. After Yuengling's bankruptcy in 1897 his upstate New York estate at Brant Lake was acquired by Untermyer's brother, Maurice. After his death, the property was passed on to Untermyer[126] and subsequently his son Irwin.[127]

In 1888 Untermyer's brother, Isaac, identified an opportunity to make money as a company promoter in London. The low rate of return on British government bonds created an opportunity to float American free-standing companies on the London Stock Exchange. These companies could offer British investors a better rate of return.[128] Untermyer also claimed the credit for this idea. He later recalled he had been earning only $100,000 a year in 1886. The company promotions set him on his path to achieve his goal of accumulating a fortune of $5 million.[129] During the next three years Untermyer and his brother Isaac successfully promoted the floatation on the London Stock Exchange of six brewery companies: New York Breweries (1888), John F. Betz and Son's Brewery (1888), Frank Jones Brewing Company (1889), United States Brewing Company (1889), The City of Baltimore United Breweries (1889), New England Breweries (1890); two mid-western companies: Chicago and North-West Granaries (1889), Pillsbury-Washburn Flour Mills (1889); the Blake & Knowles Steam Pump Works (1890) and the Harney Peak Consolidated Tin Company (1890).[130] Samuel Untermyer was also almost certainly the promoter of the Cincinnati Breweries Company[131] and the Otis Steel Company[132] in 1889. The former acquired two breweries in Ohio the following year, including the Jung Brewing Company of Cincinnati.[133] Some of the breweries involved in the flotations were pre-existing clients such as John F. Betz of Philadelphia. In the case of some of the companies they were acting on behalf of other American law firms, in the case of the two mid-western companies: Levy Mayer[134] of Kraus, Mayer & Stein of Chicago.[135] Untermyer and his brother placed over $45 million of British capital in the United States in the three years up to 1892.[136] They earned more than $1 million in commissions and fees.[137]

The company promotions brought Samuel Untermyer to national and international prominence. It introduced him to a network of important men and institutions in the world of late-nineteenth-century international finance and politics. He and his brother worked closely with a City of London financier of German Jewish heritage, Leopold Salomons.[138] Untermyer made many influential lifelong friends in the City of London including Henry Isaacs,[139] whose son Rufus was to become a prominent early-twentieth-century British politician. Frank Crisp, a prominent City of London solicitor,[140] was another lifelong friend from this period. Crisp introduced Untermyer to the pleasures of gardening. In 1889 Crisp acquired Friar Park, a large estate at Henley-on-Thames,[141] where over the next ten years he developed a large garden.[142] Together with the gardens at Hampton Court Palace[143] it may have helped inspire the garden Untermyer later developed at his Yonkers estate in the early twentieth century. After Crisp's retirement Untermyer worked with another London firm, Burn & Berridge.[144] Sir Thomas H. D. Berridge, a partner in the firm, also became a good friend.[145]

The British free-standing companies organized by the Untermyer brothers were to provide the firm with legal work for many years even where other law firms had originally represented the American companies involved such as Pillsbury.[146] The British companies managed their American investments through American boards of management. This also generated work for Samuel Untermyer. For example, he was on the board of management of the New England Breweries Company for many years assisted by his brother-in-law, Alvin Carl.[147] He also continued to work with the group of investment trusts founded by Salomons. For example, Untermyer represented the Industrial & General Trust in a New York case in the early 1900s.[148]

In 1889 Untermyer was recognized by the New York City Bar when he was one of several members selected as special guests to meet President Benjamin Harrison as part of the city's celebration of the centennial of George Washington's inauguration.[149] Four years later the first biographical essay on Untermyer was published. The essay in the new *National Cyclopædia of American Biography*[150] was the first of many to be published during his lifetime. It marked his emergence as a man of national stature. He first appeared in *Who's Who in America* in the fourth edition published in 1906.[151] Later he was to have more space allocated to him in *Who's Who* than any other American.[152]

The 1893 essay marked the first time a myth about Untermyer's father appeared in print. He claimed his 'father was a wealthy planter in Virginia, who served as lieutenant in the Confederate army'.[153] Untermyer's half-brother Randolph subsequently also invented a story about his father in an unpublished biographical essay. Not only was his father a tobacco planter but the Guggenheimer family had been settled in Virginia for many years.[154] Untermyer's brother Maurice named a short-lived son Robert Edward Lee in 1892 in honour of the Confederate general.[155] Untermyer's story was to be further embellished over the years. For example, by 1906 the myth had morphed into

Untermyer, the father, was a tobacco planter. Like the Guggenheimers, who served in the Confederate army, he was devoted to the Confederate cause, and had showed his faith in it by investing heavily in Confederate bonds. He was on the street in Lynchburg when the news of Lee's surrender was told to him; he had a weak heart and the shock killed him then and there. Mrs. Untermyer and her boys were left almost penniless.[156]

By 1930 his father had also become the owner of 1,200 slaves which, if true, would have made him the owner of the largest number of slaves in the history of the American South.[157] In fact he had owned only four female slaves in 1860.[158] Untermyer's embrace of 'Lost Cause' mythology was part of a reinvention of himself. However, it is unlikely he really had much sympathy for the 'Lost Cause'. He seldom visited his home city, Lynchburg, not least because it was also the birthplace and a fiefdom of his archenemy, the segregationist Democratic Party politician Carter Glass.[159]

The 1893 biographical essay notes that Untermyer was one of the chief promoters and president of the Harney Peak Tin Mining, Milling and Manufacturing Co. of New York, which owned tin-mining claims in South Dakota, the first tin ever discovered in the United States. Furthermore, by appearing before the House Ways and Means Committee in February 1890, he had succeeded in having a tariff of four cents a pound on imported tin included in the Wilson Tariff Act of 1890.[160] This was to be the first of many appearances at congressional hearings. The company had been founded in 1884. Untermyer had become its counsel in 1885, and president in 1888. It was floated in the City of London as free-standing company in 1890. No tin was ever commercially produced at Harney Peak.[161] Although there had been allegations that Harney Peak was a fraudulent promotion as early as 1887, it seems unlikely that Untermyer would have included Harney Peak among his achievements if he had knowingly been involved in fraud.[162] Indeed in 1894 when the British investors accused of fraud began lengthy litigation against Untermyer and his fellow promoters in the United States he told Marshall:

> From what I am told of the complaint it is a mass of lies and misrepresentations but the trouble is that it will probably prove sufficiently sensational for the newspapers and I figure most prominently in dealings. I feel somewhat uncomfortable about that kind of publicity. It promises to be a bitter trial.[163]

Untermyer also asserted in a newspaper interview that he had no knowledge of mining and never claimed to have. He had been influenced in his judgement by the reports of the English experts.[164] The Harney Peak fiasco was not resolved until the summer of 1908, when Untermyer reached an agreement with the British investors in London.[165] The affair helped teach him 'the importance of preventing the "hawking" of an enterprise'.[166]

In February 1894 Louis Marshall joined Untermyer's firm[167] as a name partner unlike Moses Weinman, who had been the first non-family member to become a partner in 1890.[168] Marshall was the only non-family member to be made a name partner in the history of the firm which is an indication of his importance. Untermyer had invited

Marshall to join his firm in 1890. It took four years of persuasion before he agreed. Negotiations were successfully completed in mid-January 1894.[169] Harry Hoffman, Untermyer's private secretary from 1908 to 1916, and after his death a partner in the firm,[170] later recalled:

> Mr. U ... brought down from Syracuse N.Y. Louis Marshall who had made a great name up-state and offered him a partnership guaranteeing him a large annual income, which always exceeded paid guarantee. Mr. Marshall was a brilliant lawyer and a Republican, but Mr. U. was a Democrat. So that it was convenient if influence was needed with either administration. I recall some cases where Mr. U. would have Mr. Marshall sit in on some of his trials so that Mr. Untermyer's great skill as a trial lawyer and Mr. Marshall's attendance would make a splendid record for possible appeal, and made an unbeatable combination.[171]

Following Marshall's death in 1929 Guggenheimer, Untermyer & Marshall reverted to its original name after his son, James, left the firm at the beginning of 1931.[172] He subsequently founded his own law firm in 1934.[173]

Following the City of London company promotions Untermyer organized a variety of trusts in the United States that also generated additional income for him and his firm. The journalist James Creelman later noted Untermyer was one of the first lawyers in the early 1890s to realize the economic advantages of corporate combinations[174] and was the legal leader 'in the centralizing movement' which 'engulfed the industries of the whole country'.[175] They included the wallpaper, lithographic printing, enamelware, umbrella and steam pump industries.[176] Untermyer's friend Herbert H. Lehman also later recalled Untermyer 'was instrumental in forming a good many of the so-called trusts, and made a great deal of money out of it'.[177] The enamelware trust included a company founded by Adolph Steinhardt,[178] who had married Untermyer's sister Addie in 1889.[179]

In the case of the lithographic printing trust, the leading party, Joseph Palmer Knapp, was a long-standing client. Some indication of Knapp's importance was the severe dressing-down Untermyer gave Marshall after Knapp was inconvenienced by a bout of absent-mindedness by his partner.

> To-day Knapp rang me up over the telephone... I told him I did not know anything about the present status of the matter of the child's school as you left no memo. behind you... Knapp wanted to know what answer there was to the application...
>
> Knapp's naturally a little out of humor at matters so near to him left hanging in the air...
>
> Mr. [Edward] Neary [the chief stenographer] just reports that... he found [in your desk] the signed application of Mr. Knapp. I do not know quite what we are to say to Mr. Knapp about it. I suggest that you make the explanation yourself. I am tired of it.[180]

Untermyer had helped Knapp arrange loans to buy control of his father's engraving business in 1891.[181] The following year Untermyer arranged the sale of stock in the Knapp Company to the lithographers F. Heppenheimer's Sons of New Jersey.[182] In 1896 he helped

Knapp merge his company with a dozen of his competitors, including Heppenheimer's, to create the American Lithographic Company.[183] As American Lithographic's capacity expanded, Knapp sought new printing business. For example, in 1903 Untermyer negotiated an Associated Sunday Magazines franchise with Adolph S. Ochs on behalf of Knapp for the *New York Times* and *Philadelphia Public Ledger*.[184] In 1906 Knapp bought control of James Crowell's publishing house and his two magazines, *Farm and Fireside* and the *Woman's Home Companion*, for $750,000. This business was incorporated as the Crowell Publishing Co.[185] Untermyer and Thomas W. Lamont of the Bankers Trust Co. helped Knapp by becoming minority shareholders in the company.[186] Untermyer became a long-term investor in Knapp's business.[187] Later in 1919 following the death of Robert J. Collier, the Crowell Publishing Co. purchased his publishing house, P.F. Collier and Son, which included *Collier's Weekly* and a large subscription book business.[188]

One of the trusts, the Columbia Straw Paper Co., resulted in an embarrassing scandal. It was alleged that Untermyer and his partners had engaged in stock watering at the expense of the straw paper mill owners. Untermyer later denied there had been any stock watering. He noted that the promoters had misrepresented their venture because it did not include all the straw paper mills. Furthermore, shortly afterwards straw paper was superseded by manila paper made from wood pulp. Untermyer lost $150,000 of his own money in the venture.[189] There was lengthy litigation which reached the US Supreme Court, where Louis Marshall, Charles A. Dupee and Monroe L. Willard were unsuccessful in their defence of Untermyer and his partners.[190] Although the Supreme Court concluded on 22 January 1900 that the paper mill owners had been defrauded, it was unable to offer them any redress. It upheld the judgement of the lower court in favour of Untermyer's syndicate. He must have felt relieved that his firm was not identified as party to the fraud in newspaper reports on the Supreme Court's decision.[191]

However, the Columbia Straw Paper affair was not over. In August 1896 William E. G. See had started legal action against the Columbia Straw Paper Co. in the state Court of Chancery in New Jersey, where the company was registered, at the request of various banks, including the First National Bank of Chicago.[192] The case was litigated for several years. Untermyer and his co-defendants settled out of court in June 1905 agreeing to the payment of $170,000 to the receiver.[193] Hence he was not amused when Vice-Chancellor Henry C. Pitney published in August 1906 what purported to be an April 1905 decision in favour of See.[194]

The last major trust that Untermyer helped organize in the 1890s was the United Fruit Company of Boston. The company was incorporated in New Jersey on 30 March 1899.[195] It brought together fruit importing companies in Baltimore, Philadelphia, New York and Boston.[196] The new company owned banana plantations in the Caribbean and Central and South America. It also owned and chartered a fleet of ships (later known as the Great White Fleet).[197] In the summer of 1902 Untermyer helped organize the extension of the trust to Great Britain. This gave United Fruit a monopoly of the Jamaica fruit trade and control of the British as well as the American banana markets.[198] United Fruit soon acquired or destroyed most of its competitors.[199] Untermyer and his firm acted on behalf of United Fruit for over forty years.[200] He was a director of the company from October 1901 to July 1908.[201]

During the 1890s Untermyer also began to take an interest in the newspaper publishing business. In early 1896 he befriended a fellow Southern Jew, Adolph S. Ochs, who had come to New York from Chattanooga, Tennessee, in 1896 and purchased the *New York Times* for $75,000. Untermyer represented a rival and unsuccessful purchaser.[202] He was so impressed by Ochs that two years later he lent him $15,000.[203] Untermyer also purchased shares in the *New York Times*.[204] This was one of several investments in newspaper and magazine publishing companies during his lifetime which included The Brewers' Journal, Inc.[205] Untermyer's financial support for the *New York Times* was further strengthened during the financial panic of 1907. Ochs had a note with the Bank of America that matured at the end of 1907 and had been informed it was unlikely to be renewed. Untermyer took up the note in exchange for a cheque from Ochs for $5,700, a note for $20,000 payable by Ochs in two months and a note for $25,000 payable by Ochs in four months.[206] Three years later Untermyer offered to purchase $100,000 or more of new *New York Times* bonds. However, the issue was a success and Ochs did not need to take up Untermyer's offer.[207] Untermyer became a lifelong friend of Ochs, and also of Louis Wiley, who was one the publisher's leading executives from 1896, serving as the business manager of the *New York Times* from 1906 until his death in 1935. Wiley's brother-in-law, Abraham Benedict, was a Guggenheimer, Untermyer & Marshall partner from 1900 to 1917.[208]

Untermyer's firm also continued to represent the brewing industry during the 1890s, including a trade association representing about one-sixth of the total production of beer in the United States, the Brewers Exchange of New York.[209] In March 1896 Untermyer was retained by the New York State Brewers' and Maltsters' Association to challenge the enactment by New York State of the Raines Liquor Tax Law of 1896.[210] He paid the eminent white-shoe lawyer Joseph H. Choate a fee of $100,000 to join his legal team, which also included Louis Marshall and Ashbel P. Fitch, to challenge the constitutionality of the bill in the New York Supreme Court and subsequently the Court of Appeals on behalf of the brewers. Choate's powerful address to the Court of Appeals failed to persuade it of the merits of the brewers' case.[211] The Raines Act was part of an increasingly hostile attitude on the part of state legislators that began to have adverse effects on the business of Guggenheimer, Untermyer & Marshall's brewer clients.[212] It was just as well the firm began to diversify its client base during the 1890s.

Among Untermyer's new clients were textile and apparel companies including B.B. & R. Knight of Providence, Rhode Island, which produced a well-known brand of cotton goods, 'Fruit of the Loom'.[213] In common with many other companies he represented, his fee was partly paid with stock in this company.[214] Later in 1910 Untermyer helped his friend Sol Warfield Davies organize the International Cotton Mills Corporation which he represented for several years.[215] He also represented his relative, Moses H. Cone, who founded the Cone Export & Commission Company in 1890, with its principal office in New York City. Moses was the son of Herman Cone. Moses's company handled the output of the cotton mills of North Carolina. Three years later Cone established in Greensboro, the Southern Finishing Mills – the first of its kind in the South equipped to finish cotton goods of the finer grade in a first-class manner. In 1895 Cone and his brother Ceasar decided to expand their business further. They constructed and put into operation the following year the large mill known as the Proximity. Within ten years another mill was constructed, White Oak, which was the largest denim mill in the world.[216] Untermyer was to act as a lawyer for Moses.[217] Moses's son Bernard also started his career as a lawyer at Guggenheimer, Untermyer & Marshall in 1897, including representing clients in court alongside Untermyer. He left the firm in 1904 to return to Greensboro to join his family's business.[218]

In 1896 Untermyer became involved with the mining industry again with Samuel Newhouse,[219] a mine promoter. Newhouse joined with Thomas Weir to acquire the Highland Boy Gold Mining Company and other properties in Bingham Canyon in Utah. He secured capital from Untermyer on his own account and as a representative of European investors for the venture which the lawyer organized on the London Stock Exchange as the Utah Consolidated Gold Mines Ltd. The properties were purchased to extract gold, but high-grade copper was discovered. Newhouse pushed for the construction of a copper smelter, which began operation in May 1899.[220] Untermyer also helped Newhouse and Weir organize another company in London, the Boston Consolidated Copper and Gold Mining Company, Ltd., in May 1898.[221] Five years later Untermyer organized Newhouse Mines & Smelters in New York to reopen and develop the Cactus Mine in Copper Gulch, Utah. The company built a model town for its workers called Newhouse.[222] In 1909 the company found itself with some $200,000 of debt, partly past due. Untermyer served as counsel with Isidore H. Kramer for the committee which reorganized the company as South Utah Mines & Smelters. It resumed operations in September 1910.[223] The mine was exhausted in mid-1914 and ceased production.[224]

Untermyer's firm represented a number of other copper mining companies, including Leonard and Adolph Lewisohn's eponymous Lewisohn Brothers[225] and the Boston and Montana Consolidated Copper & Silver Mining Co. in which Leonard was the principal investor until its acquisition by William A. Rockefeller, Jr. and Henry H. Rogers in 1900.[226] A few years after the death of Leonard Lewisohn in 1902,[227] his brother Adolph invited Untermyer in January 1906 to become a director and an investor in his new company, the General Development Company, which was organized to examine, develop and finance mining properties in the United States, Canada and Mexico, which, when they attained self-supporting production, were turned over to operating subsidiary companies.[228] Untermyer was one of the largest stockholders. Its earliest investments were in mines in Montana, Colorado, Arizona and Guanajuato, Mexico.[229] Probably the most successful early project was the Miami Cooper Company which was organized in 1907 to develop a copper deposit near Globe, Arizona.[230] Another later project which was also a great success was the South American Gold and Platinum Company organized in 1916 to develop properties in Columbia.[231] The *Duluth Evening Herald* observed in 1907 that the Lewisohns had 'had phenomenal success in their various mining ventures in every quarter of the globe.'[232] With the General Development Company Adolph Lewisohn more than upheld the family tradition with this speculative venture's periodically high dividends, the highest of which was the amazing 60 per cent paid out in June 1909. By the early 1920s the company had expanded into Canada and New Zealand.[233]

Although Untermyer was involved in most of the turn-of-the-twentieth-century copper deals[234] he was not directly involved in the creation of the Amalgamated Copper

Co. in April 1899, contrary to speculation at the time.[235] However, in 1905, Thomas W. Lawson, a stockbroker, claimed that in 1898 he had double-crossed Untermyer, 'the Machiavelli of the New York Bar', on behalf of Standard Oil as part of the negotiations that led to the creation of the Amalgamated Copper Co., causing his clients to allegedly lose several million dollars.[236] Untermyer refuted Lawson's account.

> As a work of the imagination pure and simple it deserves to rank with the realistic romances of Jules Verne and the Baron Munchausen. Of course, nobody outside of a lunatic asylum nowadays confuses Lawson's yellow tales of fiction with facts.[237]

Henry H. Rogers and William A. Rockefeller, Jr. of Standard Oil employed Untermyer as counsel to sue Lawson for libel.[238]

The Guggenheim brothers were perhaps the most important of Untermyer's new mining clients. Untermyer was to become Daniel Guggenheim's 'most trusted legal adviser'.[239] In turn he regarded Guggenheim as a 'friend'.[240] In 1899 Untermyer helped the Guggenheims establish the Guggenheim Exploration Company in New Jersey with a capital of $6 million.[241] His share of his firm's fee appears to have been in the form of shares which by 1911 were reported to worth around $500,000 in present market value. His partners, his brother Isaac and Moses Weinman, were also shareholders.[242] The company was modelled on Guggenheimer, Untermyer & Marshall's client, the Rothschilds' Exploration Company.[243] A year and half later in 1901 Untermyer helped Daniel Guggenheim bring about a consolidation with the 'Smelting Trust' that left the Guggenheim Brothers in control of the reorganized American Smelting and Refining Company. This required a compromise with Standard Oil that reinstated the United Metals Selling Company as American Smelting's sole selling agency abroad with a 1 per cent commission on all metals handled.[244] However, the rivalry between the Guggenheims and Standard Oil was not completely over. In 1905 the financier Bernard M. Baruch acquired for the Guggenheims two large smelting companies on the US Pacific Coast, Tacoma Smelting and Selby Smelting & Lead, to prevent Standard Oil from becoming serious competitors to the Guggenheims on both the Pacific Coast and in Alaska. Baruch recalled that this transaction led to his first business meeting with Untermyer, 'one of the shrewdest lawyers of that day'. Untermyer tried to bargain down Baruch's fee of $1 million. When Baruch protested, he asked him if he intended to 'hold up' the American Smelting & Refining Company. Daniel Guggenheim resolved the dispute by agreeing to pay the full fee.[245]

Untermyer's firm assisted the Guggenheims in the development of their Latin American empire.[246] An investment in Mexico proved unsuccessful.[247] The Guggenheims' investments in Chile proved to be much more successful. In 1909 Untermyer oversaw the Guggenheims' initial investment, $4 million in the Braden Copper Mines Co. The company owned a copper mine, mills, smelters and a railway line in Chile.[248] Four years later the Guggenheims established a second company, the Chile Copper Co., to develop a new mining property acquired the previous year by their newly formed Chile Exploration Co. at Chuquicamata, a mountain made up of hundreds of millions of tons of low-grade copper ore.[249] By July 1915 the Guggenheims had spent about $30 million on the development of Chuquicamata. Untermyer observed to William Gibbs

McAdoo that it had 'already been demonstrated to be by far the richest and greatest copper property in the world. It is said to be [worth] intrinsically over $300,000,000'.[250] Chuquicamata was connected to the port of Antofagasta by a branch of the British-owned Antofagasta (Chili) and Bolivia Railway Co.[251] Untermyer was American counsel to this railway and its Delaware registered subsidiary, the Bolivia Railway Co.[252]

The Guggenheims also continued to invest in American copper mining. In 1905 they gained control of the Utah Copper Company.[253] Untermyer invested in the company because he was 'impressed with the character and ability of the [Guggenheims] and by the prospects of the properties'.[254] In 1909 he began negotiating a consolidation of the copper industry on behalf of the Guggenheims.[255] On 5 January 1910, a special meeting of the shareholders of the Boston Consolidated in London agreed to a merger with Utah Copper.[256] Untermyer is reputed to have received a fee of $775,000 to bring about the merger. Paul D. Cravath was quoted as saying he had never received as big a fee.[257] Untermyer's fee was the highest one ever received apart from the possible exception of one of between $750,000 and $1 million reputedly earned by his white-shoe rival William Guthrie in 1902 as counsel to the widow of a railroad magnate.[258] It is not surprising the London *Economist* had observed in 1908 that Untermyer was 'probably the best-known corporation lawyer in the United States'.[259]

The Guggenheims also invested in Alaska. However, they lacked the resources to invest on the scale they wanted. So they initially formed an alliance with J.P. Morgan & Co. and other financiers. They invested in the Copper River and Northwestern Railway Co. to construct a 400-mile railway into the interior from Valdez.[260] In July 1906 the Guggenheims formed the Alaska Syndicate with J.P. Morgan & Co. to make further investments.[261] The syndicate acquired a 40 per cent share of the Kennecott Mines Co. in November. The company's Bonanza Mine was reputedly one of the greatest copper deposits ever found. It was the reason the Guggenheims had backed the construction of the new railway. The syndicate acquired the remaining 60 per cent of Kennecott in April 1909.[262] Untermyer provided professional advice to Daniel Guggenheim on Alaska as he did regarding the brothers' other ventures.[263]

After the copper merger of 1910 Samuel Newhouse withdrew from the mining industry and focussed on real estate. He built the first skyscraper in Salt Lake City, followed by two more. He was already well known for his acquisition with his brother Mott of part of Manhattan's famous Flatiron site in 1899, a deal in which he was represented by Untermyer.[264] Unfortunately Samuel Newhouse did not prove to be as talented a real estate developer as a mining promoter. He overextended himself and began borrowing money from Untermyer.[265] By 1917 he was involved in costly litigation with Untermyer, his son Irwin, and Harry Hoffman.[266] In June 1918 Untermyer and Newhouse reconciled their differences. Newhouse observed that 'Untermyer made a very fair and generous settlement with me, and our difficulties have been adjusted amicably'.[267] The following year Newhouse's half interest in the Newhouse Realty Co. was acquired by the Bonneville Hotel Co. Untermyer retained his half interest in the business.[268]

The Guggenheims also became involved in the Nipissing Mines Company, a silver mine being promoted by William Boyce Thompson in Canada's Yukon Territory. Thompson was one of Untermyer's Yonkers neighbours.[269] In November 1906 Thompson solicited the interest of the Guggenheims, who sent the mining engineer John Hays Hammond to report on the mine. Hammond's report was favourable. The Guggenheim Exploration Company acquired a block of shares in the company, whose president was Samuel Newhouse. David Guggenheim became worried about the validity of title to Thompson's mine. Untermyer arranged a meeting between Thompson and Guggenheim on 1 December. The meeting was not a success and the mine's stock crashed.[270] The public reacted badly and, although the Guggenheims were not at fault, in order to restore confidence, they reimbursed the 150 clients who had invested in Nipissing through the Guggenheim Exploration Company.[271] It was subsequently established that the doubt regarding the validity of the title to the property was without foundation.[272]

Untermyer also represented an estranged Guggenheim brother, Benjamin. In 1899 Untermyer organized a pump works trust for him, the International Steam Pump Company of New York. This involved the consolidation of five competing plants transacting 90 per cent of the steam pump business of the United States.[273] In April 1903 Untermyer incorporated an English combination, the Worthington Pump Company, to control steam pump, engine and water works on a similar basis as the International Steam Pump Company in the United States. The new combination acquired, along with other interests, all of the European and part of the remaining foreign business of the Worthington Pumping Engine Co., Henry P. Worthington and the George F. Blake Manufacturing Co. which had previously been controlled by the International Steam Pump Co. He also acquired James Simpson & Co. of England for the new company. The company also established two new factories: one in Germany and one in Russia. Benjamin Guggenheim was the president of the new company, and the majority of the stock and the bonds of the new company were held by the International Steam Pump Co. or its subsidiary companies.[274] Herbert H. Lehman later recalled that the Worthington Pump Company was Lehman Brothers' first big underwriting job. He inferred Benjamin Guggenheim was not a good manager.[275] Guggenheim went down with the *Titanic* in 1912. After his death, the International Steam Pump Co. went into receivership.[276] Untermyer had sold his stock, relinquished his directorship and resigned as counsel of the company in the summer of 1904.[277]

In early 1915 together with Bernard M. Baruch, Charles Hayden and Dwight Morrow, Untermyer advised the Guggenheims on the reorganization of their business interests. They decided that all the Guggenheim copper investments should be consolidated, and that the Guggenheim Exploration Co. should be dissolved.[278] In May a new corporation, the Kennecott Copper Corporation, was formed. It acquired the Kennecott Mines Co. the following month. In December, the new corporation acquired the Exploration Co.'s investments in Utah Copper and Braden Copper and the Alaska Syndicate's interest in the Copper River and Northwestern Railway and the Alaska Steamship Co.[279] This allowed the Guggenheims to sell most of their interest in the new company at a time of high copper prices. However, Untermyer retained a large number of shares in the company.[280]

After the victory of Untermyer's half-brother Randolph as Tammany's candidate for president of the Council in the municipal election of 1897, their firm was immediately rewarded with new business. Earlier in 1897, the United States Fidelity and Guaranty

Company of Baltimore had come to New York to establish a branch office. Tammany Hall boss Richard Croker agreed to support the establishment of the branch in return for which Andrew Freedman,[281] 'the one intimate whom [he] trusted with his financial matters',[282] was elected third vice-president of the company and resident director in New York.[283] Untermyer's firm was appointed counsel for the company's New York office.[284] This was the beginning of a lucrative professional relationship and personal friendship between Untermyer and Freedman.[285] Untermyer later recalled that

> Andrew Freedman was my old and intimate friend . . . He was an aggressive fighter but he had a heart of gold and a capacity for friendship rarely equalled. There was no sacrifice he was not willing to make for a friend. He had a philosophy on that subject to which I subscribe but to which all men will not agree.[286]

Freedman came from a similar background to Untermyer. He was the son of a Bavarian Jewish immigrant dry goods importer.[287] Freedman had initially followed his father into the dry goods trade, but had branched out into the real estate business, in which he was very successful. In the early 1890s he further branched out into the sports business when he was appointed receiver for the Manhattan Athletic Club in 1893. He attracted all the major eastern colleges for their football and other contests. In 1895 he acquired a controlling interest in the New York Giants baseball club.[288] It proved to be a very profitable investment. Untermyer's firm became legal counsel for the club from 1897. Freedman sold the club after the 1902 season.[289]

Fitzpatrick and Buse observe that 'Freedman had contacts with influential bankers and industrialists, and before long he was executing bonds [on behalf of United States Fidelity and Guaranty] for public officials, financial institutions, and such corporations as the Manhattan Railway Company, Metropolitan Street Railway Company, Erie Railroad, the New Haven, Central Railroad of New Jersey and New York and Queens County Railways.'[290] As legal counsel for the United States Fidelity and Guaranty New York office, Guggenheimer, Untermyer & Marshall further benefitted from the opportunity to offer its services as legal counsel to these corporations.

Freedman was one of the men responsible for initiating the first subway (underground railway) line in New York City, which is probably the most important accomplishment of the mayoralty of Robert A. Van Wyck. Although an underground railway had first been discussed in 1868, it had been repeatedly opposed by the existing street railway companies who made it profitable for Tammany Hall to support them. However, by the late 1890s Tammany Hall decided it could no longer resist progress. Bids were invited for the construction of the first subway line. On 16 January 1900, the Rapid Transit Board announced that John B. McDonald, an experienced contractor, a frontman for Freedman, had been successful with a $35 million bid.[291] However, McDonald lacked the capital to build the line as did Untermyer and Freedman. Freedman introduced the financier August Belmont to McDonald. Belmont decided to back McDonald[292] on the advice of his friend Cornelius Vanderbilt III.[293] It proved challenging to underwrite the project. However, with Belmont's backing for the project Freedman was able to convince United States Fidelity and Guaranty to arrange a $5 million bond in February 1900 for McDonald to cover the first section of subway. One million dollars of suretyship was written, the company retaining $250,000, and three other surety companies each agreeing to underwrite a similar amount. McDonald provided a $4 million personal bond which was to be funded by investors in the Rapid Transit Subway Construction Company which was to be established to construct the line. This company was subsequently acquired by the Interborough Rapid Transit Company (IRT) in 1902.[294] Untermyer was to be actively involved with the IRT for the rest of his life. However, during the company's first two decades he denied this on more than one occasion. He observed that it had its own in-house attorneys[295] and also suggested that his only investment had been in some bonds on which he had made a loss.[296] However, an investigation by a New York State Joint Legislative Committee in 1916 found evidence which suggested that Untermyer and his firm had been actively involved with the IRT in its early years.[297]

Furthermore, Untermyer was involved in the attempt by Freedman and his associates to consolidate rapid transit in New York City. On 24 January 1906 they formed the Interborough-Metropolitan Company. Under an agreement with August Belmont two days later this company acquired a large majority of the capital stocks of the IRT, the Metropolitan Street Railway Company and the Metropolitan Securities Company. In September 1907 to further the consolidation the holding company succeeded in placing the Metropolitan Street Railway and an affiliated company, the New York City Street Railway, in federal receivership.[298] Opponents of the consolidation petitioned for state receivership instead. After temporarily taking over from Paul D. Cravath at short notice, Untermyer unsuccessfully opposed state receivership in the state Supreme Court on behalf of the two companies.[299] The case was appealed all the way to the US Supreme Court which found in favour of the federal receiverships.[300]

Untermyer and Freedman also attempted to break the Theatrical Syndicate's domination of Broadway. Their friend Samuel S. Shubert, a West Prussian Jewish immigrant, was a fellow member of Tammany Hall.[301] Beginning in 1897 Shubert and his brothers Lee[302] and Jacob J. had built a theatre chain upstate and then from March 1900 in New York City.[303] Although the Shuberts had an in-house lawyer from the beginning of 1900, William Klein,[304] they also employed Untermyer as outside legal counsel.[305] Untermyer helped represent the brothers in a dispute over a theatre lease in May 1902.[306] Two years later Untermyer helped Klein incorporate the various components of the Shuberts' business.[307]

The Theatrical Syndicate had been formed in August 1896 by producers Samuel F. Nirdlinger (known as Nixon) and J. Frederick Zimmerman of Philadelphia and Charles Frohman, Al (Albert) Hayman, Marc Klaw and Abraham Lincoln Erlanger of New York.[308] The syndicate sought to secure exclusive booking control of all of the important theatres in the United States. The number of theatres under syndicate control grew from thirty-three in 1896 to as many as eighty-three in 1896. The syndicate also indirectly controlled many other theatres through booking contracts. Alfred L. Bernheim suggests at its highpoint the syndicate probably booked at least 700 theatres, including all those of any significance. The syndicate argued that the elimination of cut-throat competition benefitted everyone in the theatre business. In return, it derived income from the profits of its pooled theatres and the commissions or fees from booking.[309]

Untermyer had become involved in an attempt to break the syndicate's control in April 1905 when he agreed to represent David Belasco against the Theatrical Syndicate. Belasco was a Californian-born Jewish playwright and producer who had become involved in a dispute in 1902 with syndicate members Klaw & Erlanger, who refused to allow him to perform the play 'Du Barry' in New York City. In response, he had leased Oscar Hammerstein's Republic Theatre on 44th Street, near Broadway, which he had refurbished and renamed the Belasco Theatre. A further dispute with Klaw & Erlanger the following year led Belasco to break completely with the syndicate and manage his own bookings independently of them in a fight that was said to have cost him almost $1 million.[310]

A Joseph Brooks had brought a suit for the dissolution of a partnership which he alleged had existed between him and Belasco. Belasco responded by claiming that Brooks was a dummy partner for Klaw & Erlanger and sued them. Justice James Fitzgerald of the New York Supreme Court decided that the cases would be tried together.[311] In the trial Belasco testified that Abraham Erlanger had threatened to crush him.[312] During Untermyer's cross-examination of Erlanger he engaged in an ill-tempered exchange with Brooks's attorney, Abraham Gruber, which was immortalized by the *New York Evening World*'s cartoonist Thomas Powers.[313]

'Your Honor,' said Mr. Gruber, addressing Justice Fitzgerald, 'I want this to go on the records, I never saw so smart a lawyer as Mr. Untermyer.'

'And I want it to go on the records', retorted Mr. Untermyer. 'I never saw such a pestiferous lawyer as Mr. Gruber.'

'You are the most oleaginous man I know,' said Mr. Gruber. 'I am attempting to try this as a lawyer.'

'What kind of a lawyer?' sneered Mr. Untermyer[314]

The high point of the trial was the testimony of Leslie Carter, a well-known actress, who was called by Untermyer in rebuttal to tell of a conversation between Belasco and Samuel F. Nixon. She confirmed that Belasco had told Nixon that Klaw & Erlanger were his secret partners in starring the actor David Warfield in *The Auctioneer*.[315] The testimony in the trial was completed on 26 April.[316]

At the beginning of the trial Belasco had negotiated an agreement with a fellow enemy of the Syndicate, Samuel S. Shubert. They agreed that his shows would be presented only in theatres owned by the Shubert brothers. He also agreed to purchase theatres together with them.[317] By 1905 the Syndicate had decided the brothers represented a threat and begun a campaign of repression against them. While Judge Fitzgerald was deliberating Sam Shubert was killed in mid-May in a train accident at Harrisburg, Pennsylvania. After they had recovered from the tragedy, the surviving brothers regrouped. In July 1905 with the support of Belasco they formally broke off relations with the Syndicate and extended their alliance to include Harrison Grey Fiske, the editor of the *New York Dramatic Mirror*. The various theatrical interests of the Shuberts, including some thirty theatres, were brought together as 'Sam S. and Lee Shubert, Incorporated' at the beginning of September.[318] In October Joseph Rhinock of Covington, Kentucky, and Max Anderson and George B. Cox of Cincinnati agreed

Illustration 4 Thomas Powers's 'A Hit! – "Crushed to Earth" Pleases All' Cartoon, 1905.

to finance the construction of eighteen new theatres in the West and Canada for the Shuberts by investing between $300,000 and $400,000.[319]

On 19 December 1905 Judge Fitzgerald ruled against Belasco. Following Fitzgerald's decision 'John Doe' proceedings were begun before Justice William E. Wyatt in the Court of Special Sessions in what was reported as a serious attempt to destroy the so-called Theatrical Syndicate. The action was prosecuted by Assistant District Attorney Isidor J. Kresel on behalf of New York County District Attorney William Travers Jerome, assisted by Untermyer, representing Belasco, Fiske, James S. Metcalf, the drama critic of *Life* magazine, and others who had formed an organization to fight the syndicate.[320] However, Justice Francis M. Scott of the New York Supreme Court stopped the investigation with a writ of prohibition on 22 December.[321] Belasco did not give up; he re-engaged Untermyer to bring an anti-trust prosecution under the State of New York's Donnelly Act. Untermyer collected a great amount of testimony, including from Lee Shubert, which he took to District Attorney Jerome. He agreed to take on the case and convened a grand jury which held hearings in late January. The grand jury then brought in a true bill of conspiracy against the syndicate. Abraham Erlanger engaged Levy Mayer of Chicago and another New York law firm on behalf of the syndicate. Mayer and his associates moved to dismiss the indictment. The case was heard by Justice Otto A. Rosalsky, who in June 1907 dismissed the case, ruling that theatrical amusements were not objects of trade or commerce.[322] Belasco subsequently decided to return to the syndicate in April 1909 because they offered him more favourable terms than the Shubert brothers.[323]

Nonetheless by 1912 John Tenney argues that the Shubert brothers had 'in a sense' won the war with the syndicate by proving it wrong in its belief that it would not have to share the theatrical field.³²⁴ The previous year the Shuberts reorganized their corporation. In late 1911 Untermyer and Freedman acquired a third of the $1 million corporation. Cox, Rhinock and the Shuberts jointly held the other two-thirds.³²⁵ Untermyer and Freedman hoped that they could bring about an understanding between the Shubert brothers and the syndicate. During 1912 they tried to purchase the Klaw & Erlanger interests on behalf of the Shubert brothers. Untermyer and Freedman were unsuccessful notwithstanding rumours of further negotiations in early 1913. At some point Untermyer transferred his stock to his son, Alvin. Alvin and Freedman transferred their stock to Cox in 1913 for $582,000.³²⁶ However, this was not the end of Untermyer and Freedman's association with the Shuberts. During that year they financed three new theatres for the Shuberts: the Shubert (in memory of their brother Sam), the Booth and the 44th Street Theatres.³²⁷ The first two theatres were designed by architect Henry B. Herts,³²⁸ and Foster Hirsch notes that they 'have been ever since the geographical center of the Broadway theater district'³²⁹ Untermyer retained a one-half interest in the Booth and Shubert theatres, and a one-third interest in the 44th Street theatre after the latter's death in 1915.³³⁰

Freedman died in December 1915. At his funeral Untermyer led the pallbearers who included key figures associated with the IRT such as De Lancey Nicoll, Cornelius Vanderbilt III and August Belmont, and others such as his friends Louis Wiley of the *New York Times* and Richard Croker, Jr.³³¹ The greater part of Freedman's estate of $7 million was left in his will for the creation of a foundation to establish an Andrew Freedman Home, a non-sectarian home for financially distressed gentlefolk. His brother received $50,000 and several other comparatively small bequests. His mother and sister, Belle Freedman, were left a life interest in one half of the residuary estate. The other half and the remainder after the deaths of his sister and mother reverted to the foundation.³³² Daniel B. Freedman explained that his brother had

> felt always a deep sympathy for men and women, especially husbands and wives, who had been of good circumstances but had been unfortunate in their declining years. He believed that there was no institution now existing which provided for this class. It was his idea that those who were helped by [the Andrew Freedman Home] should not consider themselves in any way as objects of charity, but as enjoying all that a real home afforded.³³³

Untermyer was entrusted with the fulfilment of Freedman's bequest. Freedman named twenty-four persons to act as trustees of the home for at least a year. The names of those still alive at the reading of the will included some of the most powerful men in New York City such as Untermyer, August Belmont, Jacob H. Schiff and Nathan Straus.³³⁴ Schiff assisted Untermyer during the first couple of years of planning the fulfilment of Freedman's vision for the home.³³⁵ This is contrary to the popular belief that the Jewish Wall Street bankers ostracized Untermyer after the Pujo Investigation. Although Untermyer was criticized for spending too much money on the construction and furnishing of the building for the home, he argued that Freedman had intended that there would 'be little of the institutional about it'.³³⁶ The home was opened on 25 May 1924 by Untermyer, who was to serve as the first president of the board of trustees of the Andrew Freedman Home.[337] He observed that it was an 'eloquent and convincing answer to attacks upon our capitalistic system . . . It demonstrates once more that the honest accumulation of wealth goes hand in hand with public service'.[338]

As well as re-entering the mining industry at the turn of the twentieth century Untermyer and his firm also became involved in the railroad industry for the first time.[339] Swain estimates that during the last quarter of the nineteenth century companies accounting for as much as one third of America's railroad mileage had been in receivership at least once.[340] Legal fees could be substantial because of a labyrinth of legal proceedings. Untermyer became active in the industry when a relatively small percentage of America's railroad mileage was in receivership.[341] Leslie Hannah notes that J.P. Morgan & Co. had made their largest profits from railroad organizations during the 1890s. Untermyer's firm entered this lucrative business just as the bank's interests were shifting elsewhere.[342] In 1930 Untermyer recalled that during the late 1890s he had intervened in the reorganization of the insolvent Union Pacific Railroad by interesting British investors. He claimed that President McKinley had called on him to scare American bankers into paying the federal government a better price for the railroad.[343] This is a reference to a last-minute bid for the railroad in late October 1897 by an English syndicate headed by the London stockbroking firm Coates, Son & Co.[344] Although the Coates Syndicate's bid was rejected[345] it forced the syndicate headed by Jacob H. Schiff of Kuhn, Loeb & Co. to pay the federal government an extra $8 million for the railroad.[346] Untermyer's name is not mentioned in either the press coverage or in McKinley's correspondence. Untermyer's uncharacteristic failure to take the credit for the organization of the Coates Syndicate during Schiff's lifetime is probably explained by the fact he was one of the banker's friends. It is possible Untermyer, a Democrat, intervened on behalf of his half-brother, Randolph, who was a McKinley Democrat.[347] At the time, the McKinley administration was being attacked for being in collusion with the Schiff syndicate to sell the Union Pacific for less than it was worth. Untermyer's successful intervention assisted the Republican Party in the upcoming elections at the beginning of November, in particular the Ohio gubernatorial and state legislature elections.[348]

The first railroad receivership Untermyer was involved with was the reorganization of the Birmingham, Sheffield and Tennessee River Railway Co. in 1899 when he represented the London investment trust Industrial & General Trust against the railroad's receivers.[349] This was followed by the Detroit Southern Railroad Co. receivership in 1904. It was appointed on the petition of bondholders in the railroad.[350] Untermyer was counsel to a committee representing preferred and common shareholders in the railroad.[351] The following year he represented a syndicate headed by tobacco, insurance and transportation tycoon Thomas Fortune Ryan[352] which successfully wrested control of the Seaboard Air Line in a 'sensational fight' from its president, John Skelton Williams.[353] The syndicate's members[354] also included bankers James A. Blair[355] and Sol Davies Warfield.[356] In 1908 the Seaboard Air Line went into receivership and Warfield was appointed one of the receivers. Untermyer was appointed counsel at his suggestion and played a leading role in the railroad's reorganization.[357] Sol Davies Warfield became a good friend. Warfield's niece, Wallis, later achieved fame as a friend of a member of Britain's royal family.[358]

Untermyer was also involved with the Kansas City Southern Railway Company. In 1905 he was employed by Herman Sielcken, of the New York coffee brokerage firm Crossman & Sielcken, to help him wrest control of the railway from Edward H. Harriman and his associates.[359] The Harriman syndicate had seized control of the company's predecessor, the Kansas City, Pittsburg and Gulf Railroad in 1899[360] from its founder, financier Arthur Edward Stilwell. In May Sielcken succeeded in ousting the Harriman syndicate. Untermyer was elected one of the new directors of the railroad[361] and was its general counsel for many years.[362] For example, he represented the railroad in a case before the US Supreme Court in 1913.[363] Untermyer also had an amendment to the laws relating to the judiciary enacted in 1915 by the US Congress to allow appeals from the federal circuit court and the federal circuit court of appeals to the US Supreme Court where a federal question is involved but not set out and stated on the bill.[364] It enabled Untermyer as counsel for the railroad to appeal another case to the US Supreme Court in 1915.[365]

From 1910 Untermyer also represented a committee of first mortgage bondholders of the Wabash Pittsburgh Terminal Railway Company against the interests of George J. Gould, the son of railroad magnate Jay Gould. The railroad had entered receivership in 1908.[366] Untermyer was a champion of the rights of minority stockholders, advocating that the civil remedies of federal anti-trust law be extended to them.[367] He represented committees of minority stockholders of the Rutland Railroad from 1910 and opposed the transfer of its stock and control by the parent railroad, the New York Central and Hudson River Railroad, to New York, New Haven & Hartford Railroad,[368] whose president, Charles S. Mellen, was working on behalf of J.P. Morgan, Sr.[369] The New York Central sold one half of its Rutland stock to the New Haven in 1911. But Untermyer succeeded in preventing the New Haven from acquiring the other half.[370] Untermyer also represented the minority stockholders of the St. Joseph & Grand Island Railway from 1911 to protect their interests against the parent company, the Union Pacific Railroad. In 1914, the United States District Court of Nebraska ruled that the Union Pacific must give control of St. Joseph & Grand within sixty days to the minority shareholders, otherwise a receiver would be appointed by the court.[371]

In 1914 mining financier Nathan L. Amster[372] a Chicago, Rock Island & Pacific Railroad bondholder, began a campaign of newspaper advertising alleging malfeasance against the Reid-Moore syndicate which controlled it.[373] To make sure the legal end of his fight received proper attention Amster engaged the services of Untermyer.[374] The lawyer subsequently became counsel to a protective committee formed by Amster representing minority bondholders.[375] Untermyer's friend Sol M. Stroock later became co-counsel.[376] On the opposing side was a committee under the chairmanship of James N. Wallace, president of the Central Trust Company of New York, affiliated to the Reid-Moore syndicate.[377] In November Untermyer won a victory for Amster in the circuit court of appeals. Judge Henry G. Ward postponed the foreclosure of the company by the syndicate and condemned the prevailing practice of trust company presidents serving as chairmen of protective committees for the bonds of which their trust company was mortgage trustee.[378]

In addition to Amster's legal action, the Interstate Commerce Commission's chief counsel, Joseph W. Folk, carried out an inquiry into the Rock Island railroad. In October

1914 a letter in the *Railway Age Gazette* questioned Folk's impartiality, suggesting he was too close to Amster's attorney, Untermyer.[379] Folk held hearings in June 1915 where Untermyer represented the Amster Committee.[380] Folk subsequently published a report on the Rock Island railroad which was very critical of the syndicate which controlled it.[381]

Meanwhile the railroad had entered receivership at the behest of the Reid-Moore syndicate.[382] After further lengthy litigation[383] in October 1916 the two sides agreed to join together to produce a reorganization plan. Untermyer was one of the new committee's counsels.[384] In January 1917, a reorganization plan was agreed.[385] The terms of the compromise settlement included the purchase by the syndicate leaders, Daniel G. Reid and William H. Moore, of $5,000,000 of 6 per cent preferred stock of the railway company, the payment by them of $500,000 and all the costs of the litigation.[386] Untermyer retained an interest in the railroad industry for the rest of his life. During the Great Depression of the 1930s he advocated government ownership of America's railroads as an alternative to bankruptcy.[387]

In 1911 Untermyer took on the Waters-Pierce Oil Company as a new client. The following year the company accused the Standard Oil Company of conspiring to get control of their company. They alleged in the 1912 annual election of directors that representatives of the Rockefellers, John D. Archbold, Henry M. Flagler, and other Standard Oil magnates tried to vote by proxies a majority of Waters-Pierce stock with a view to putting Standard Oil representatives in charge of the Waters-Pierce Oil Company.[388] Untermyer represented the faction led by the president of Waters-Pierce, Henry Clay Pierce, in New York and Samuel W. Fordyce, Jr. in Chicago, the litigation taking place in both cities.[389] Untermyer believed that the dissolution of the oil trust was a farce. He undertook to show by the witnesses he examined that the old crowd was still in control of the former subsidiaries and was trying to bring the Waters-Pierce Company into subjection.[390]

The most memorable part of the case came at the end of May when Untermyer cross-examined John D. Rockefeller. Untermyer, the master of the art of cross-examination,[391] met his match in Rockefeller. Rockefeller, cool, smiling and ingenuous, withstood two hours of questioning giving very few direct and positive answers. Finally, an exasperated Untermyer conceded defeat.

> Mr. UNTERMYER. I think that is all, Mr. Rockefeller.
> Mr. ROCKEFELLER. I hope you won't spare me. I will be glad to stay as long as you want me, and sincere desire is -.
> Mr. UNTERMYER. I object.
> Mr. ROCKEFELLER. You object to the sincere desire?
> Mr. UNTERMYER. I have been so filled up with professions to-day that I would like to get some facts.

With that Rockefeller was excused. As he left the stand the *New York Times* reported he put his arm on Untermyer's shoulder and said, 'I'm afraid I was a little stupid to-day and didn't understand all of your questions thoroughly.'[392] The case was concluded in November when the Standard Oil interests agreed to sell to Henry Clay Pierce all their holdings in the Waters-Pierce Oil Co.[393]

Another important new client in 1911 was the publisher William Randolph Hearst[394] who also became a political ally. Untermyer had fallen out with his friend Adolph S. Ochs, so he needed a new newspaper publisher ally. He invested in the ten-year bonds issued by Hearst the following year secured by the earnings of his International Magazine Co.[395] Untermyer urged Hearst to become the Democratic Party candidate for New York City mayor in the winter of 1917 and the following winter while they were on vacation in Palm Beach to enter the gubernatorial contest. There was also speculation that Untermyer was supporting a run by Hearst in the 1920 presidential election.[396] He represented Hearst in his attempt to break the monopoly of Associated Press. As Untermyer observed to his friend Upton Sinclair

> The Associated Press today controls a practical monopoly of the news of the World. We have gotten so closely in touch with the rest of the World and the cost of foreign news has grown to be so great that no newspaper of importance can exist today without an Associated Press franchise. If you will study the Articles of Association of the Associated Press, you will find that such a franchise is unobtainable on any terms without the consent of the competitors in the particular locality for which it is to be used which means that no competing newspaper can start up in any locality without buying out an existing paper that has a franchise.[397]

Hearst was disciplined by Associated for refusing to obey its order to change the title of the Oakland edition of the *San Francisco Examiner*.[398] Untermyer sought an injunction in the New York Supreme Court which was granted in October 1915.[399]

Hearst had created the International News Service in 1909 to compete with Associated Press.[400] In January 1917, the Associated Press sought an injunction against the International News Service. Untermyer represented Hearst again. The Associated Press accused the International News Service of publishing news gathered by the former organization for the exclusive use of its members. Untermyer argued in court that pilfering from bulletin boards and early editions had been common practice for years. He declared that 'The Associated Press has always taken the attitude that its members are the aristocrats of the newspaper world and that we are the upstarts.'[401] Judge Augustus Noble Hand of the United States District Court for the Southern District of New York ruled in favour of Associated Press.[402] The case eventually ended up before the US Supreme Court, where Untermyer appeared on Hearst's behalf in May 1918 alongside Senator Hiram W. Johnson of California, Henry A. Wise and William A. De Ford.[403] Untermyer summarized the questions involved as follows:

> Is there a right of property in news or knowledge of the news or in the quality of 'firstness' in the news that will survive its publication by the gatherer in any of the newspapers to which it has been delivered for the express purpose of publication and sale until the gatherer of the news and all of its customers have secured their reward; or does this news become public property as soon as it has been published by any of the papers to which it has been surrendered without restriction for that specific purpose? In other words, is there a sanctity

of property right reserved to the news gatherer against the effects of publication as to matter that is admittedly uncopyrightable greater than that given by the statute to copyright matter?[404]

The Supreme Court ruled against Hearst on 23 December 1918 by 5 to 3. Justices Oliver Wendell Holmes, Joseph McKenna and Louis D. Brandeis dissented.[405] Untermyer believed he had lost the case because it was the height of the war. Hearst's 'newspapers were not sufficiently subservient to the British and French propaganda with which the country was being flooded'. Untermyer believed the dissenting opinions 'undoubtedly voice the Law as it should be'.[406] Despite losing the case Untermyer and Hearst remained good friends.[407]

In January 1912 Untermyer announced his retirement from Guggenheimer, Untermyer & Marshall. His brother Isaac and Moses Weinman also retired at the same time. Untermyer ceased to be a partner but, unlike the other two, continued to be listed with the firm's partners as 'counsel'. The remaining partners continued to practice under the same firm name. Louis Marshall succeeded Untermyer as senior partner, a position he held until his death in 1929.[408]

Marshall's ambition had not been to succeed Samuel Untermyer as effective head of the firm. Instead, he had set his heart on being elevated to the US Supreme Court. In 1909 Untermyer and the other partners had unsuccessfully lobbied the Taft administration to promote Marshall's candidacy for a vacant seat following the death of Justice Rufus W. Peckham.[409] Unfortunately it would appear that President Taft had very early on decided to nominate Judge Horace Harmon Lurton of Tennessee.[410] The following year Marshall asked his friends Jacob H. Schiff and Judge Mayer Sulzberger to recommend him to Taft for another vacancy created by the death of Justice David Josiah Brewer. They secured an audience with Taft in early April.[411] Afterwards Sulzberger reported back to Marshall that Taft had created the impression that he might possibly be on the list of candidates for a future vacancy.[412] In 1949 Rabbi Stephen S. Wise recalled a story allegedly told to him by Taft in 1911 about the meeting. Taft told Wise he had asked Schiff twice, 'if you were President, would you name Sam Untermyer's partner to the Supreme Court?' In fact, according to Wise, he had already decided to nominate Charles Evans Hughes.[413] Sulzberger's letter to Marshall suggests that Wise's account is incorrect. Matt Silver has also questioned the veracity of Wise's recollection, noting that the evidence suggests that Taft had not yet decided Hughes was to be his nominee. Furthermore, he points to Marshall's own belief that Taft had been prejudiced against him by an editorial by Arthur Brisbane in the *New York Evening Journal* falsely claiming that Marshall was opposed to the Preventorium Nathan Straus was seeking to establish at Lakewood, New Jersey. According to Marshall Brisbane had subsequently proceeded to Washington to oppose Marshall's nomination on this false charge.[414] In fact Untermyer had represented the co-owner of the Preventorium, Max Nathan. Nathan, in response to concerns from neighbouring property owners about 'diseased' children in the Preventorium, proposed moving the institution. He was willing to donate his half of the property to fund the move. The other co-owner, Nathan Straus, vociferously resisted.[415] Silver notes that the firm's 'legal handling of the case was beyond reproach',[416] but in his opinion 'Untermyer's public presentation of the affair was clumsily impolitic and self-defeating' and that this 'contributed to the drubbing endured by his firm as a whole.'[417]

The *Bench and Bar* were correct in expressing scepticism regarding Untermyer's 'retirement' predicting instead 'greater activity'.[418] Indeed while he pursued other time-consuming projects which will be the subjects of Chapters 2–5, he also remained highly active in legal practice until the early 1930s. One of the justifications for the retirements in 1912 was to pass on the firm to the next generation of the family, Untermyer's two sons, nephews, and Louis Marshall's son James. However, none of them were able to meet Untermyer's exacting standards, except possibly his nephew Laurence A. Steinhardt. As counsel Untermyer chose clients and cases that interested him. Two of the four chapters of Nanette Dembitz's unfinished biography concern Helen Elwood Stokes of Denver divorce case[419] and, after her ex-husband's death, her fight for her dower rights.[420] Untermyer responded to criticism that he was wasting his talent by involving himself in the second case by observing

> I would not have been willing at my time of life to have dedicated months of my energies to a bitter, unpleasant and exhausting law suit for the mere protection of private rights, not even for the vindication of the honor of that brave little lady and her children, important though that be. This task could have been left to younger men. To me there was something far bigger and of an urgent and commanding public character involved in the task. It was the safeguarding of the administration of justice against the pollution of perjury on a scale never before dared, that primarily appealed to me. The proportions of the conspiracy to rob this lady of her fair name and to disgrace her children, and its reckless challenge to our ineffective judicial system are staggering beyond belief.[421]

Untermyer also continued to take an active interest in corporate law. He continued to represent his friend Sol Davies Warfield and the Seaboard Air Line railroad. The Seaboard Air Line played a prominent role in the Florida land boom of the 1920s. Untermyer also helped reorganize the railroad after Warfield's death in 1927.[422] He also took on new clients. For example, during the 1920s he represented an Anglo-American syndicate who were financing eighteen of the heirs of the late Ottoman sultan Abdul Hamid II, who claimed ownership of oil fields in Mesopotamia (modern-day Iraq). In 1904, the sultan had transferred ownership from the Ottoman state to the royal estate vast tracts of potentially oil bearing land after a survey by Carlouste Sarkis Gulbenkian.[423] Clarence W. Barron told William Boyce Thompson, Untermyer's Yonkers' neighbour, that the syndicate hoped to capture a $50 million commission.[424] Untermyer and his associates claimed that the oil fields were purchased by the sultan with funds from his personal estate and he was the personal owner with a title as good as any person could have for real property. The fact that the Young Turks had deposed the sultan in 1908 did not impair his title to the property or the right of his heirs to inherit it.[425] Untermyer met with Secretary of State Charles Evans Hughes at the beginning of December 1922 to secure the support of the State Department for the submission of all claims to the oil fields in Mesopotamia to an impartial tribunal or to The Hague Tribunal.[426] After further meetings with Untermyer, Hughes instructed America's

Acting High Commissioner in Constantinople (Istanbul) in mid-January 1923 that while the Department would accord proper diplomatic support to American citizens and interests, it did not engage in favouritism, and could grant no special privileges to any one American company it would deny to another.[427] The American negotiators did indeed ensure that the Lausanne Treaty of 1923 provided for arbitration.[428] However, the Anglo-Turkish Mixed Arbitral Tribunal reached an adverse decision in December 1930 when it declared that it was not competent to deal with claim of the heirs of the sultan.[429] In the meantime the American government had reached an agreement in 1928 with Britain on behalf of an American consortium made up of Standard Oil of New Jersey, Standard Oil of New York and three other companies giving it a share of 23.75 per cent in the output of Iraq's oil.[430]

Untermyer also represented Hollywood movie moguls after he retired. Harry Warner and William Fox were also friends. He believed that there was a new art form, 'the film', and used to go the movie theatre in Yonkers regularly. Untermyer liked historical films. His favourite movies included Fred Niblo's *Ben Hur* (1925) and Alfred E. Green's *Disraeli* (1929) starring George Arliss. The gardens of his Greystone estate were used as locations for two silent movies during the summer of 1923. The first, *Zaza*, produced by Paramount's Long Island studio, starred Gloria Swanson in a screen adaptation of the play that had made Leslie Carter famous on the Broadway stage under the management of Untermyer's client David Belasco. The second *Twenty-One*, which starred heartthrob Richard Barthelmess, was released by First National in early 1924.[431]

In 1929 Untermyer was an arbiter in a dispute between Warner Brothers and American Telephone and Telegraph Company (AT&T) over a licence for the use of equipment manufactured by the latter for making sound pictures.[432] The following year Untermyer was also retained by William Fox. Fox had been his client before. In 1911 and 1912 he had helped represent Fox against the Motion Picture Patents Company. At that time Fox had owned a chain of cinemas in New York City that had had its licence to rent films from the Motion Picture Patents Company revoked. Untermyer had accused this company of being a monopoly and defended Fox's right to run a film exchange without paying part of his profits to the big producers. Judge Learned Hand granted Fox an injunction on the grounds that the Motion Picture Patents Company was an unlawful combination.[433]

Fox subsequently became a film producer as well as an exhibitor. By the late 1920s he controlled Fox Film Corporation and its affiliated Fox Theatres Corporation through Class B stock with voting control. Early in 1929, Fox Theatres acquired control of Loew's Inc., which, besides its large theatre interests, controlled Metro-Goldwyn-Mayer, a leading producer. Fox also purchased the British Gaumont Company, motion picture distributors and owners of some 300 cinemas in Great Britain. However, by October it was clear that Fox had overextended himself. He had acquired the Loew shares on margin. Two of his creditors, Harry L. Stuart, of the investment bank Halsey, Stuart & Co. of Chicago and New York, and John E. Otterson, president of Electrical Research Products, Inc. (ERPI), a subsidiary of AT&T, agreed to bail Fox out in exchange for control over the voting stock in Fox Film and Fox Theatres. In early December Fox agreed to vest control of the two companies in a voting trust made up of himself, Stuart and Otterson. However, Fox soon discovered that Stuart and Otterson had effectively seized control of his companies. Meanwhile all over the country, suits were begun against Fox companies.[434]

Fox believed that Halsey, Stuart & Co. were seeking a receivership so that the bank could exercise a fifteen-year preferential financing contract and the ERPI could enforce a fifteen-year talking picture apparatus licence.[435] Fox knew that Untermyer was counsel for Warner Brothers in an ongoing case against AT&T,[436] and met with him to discuss the case one morning early in January 1930 in Atlantic City, where he occupied a penthouse on top of the President Hotel in an effort to help his asthma.[437] Fox told him the bankers were forcing him to the wall and the lawyers he had spoken to had sided with Stuart and Otterson. Untermyer explained that both Stuart and Otterson had close ties with J.P. Morgan & Co. None of the bankers and lawyers who did business with J.P. Morgan & Co. would want to associate themselves with Fox. Untermyer said that Fox was correct in his appraisal of the dangers of his position. It would take a tremendous effort to save Fox, but he was willing to make the attempt. His firm would need a $100,000 retainer. If Untermyer could salvage something for him, so that Fox was not completely wiped out, he would expect a total fee of $1 million. Fox agreed to pay the retainer.[438]

Untermyer put together a syndicate made up of the Bancamerica-Blair Corporation, Lehman Brothers and Dillon, Read & Co. to refinance Fox's two companies.[439] However, the syndicate subsequently concluded that the amount of money required to rehabilitate the Fox companies was much greater than originally anticipated.[440] The re-financing plan unravelled. Fox's friend Albert M. Greenfield, the Philadelphia financier, found a potential buyer for his stock in the Fox corporations, the Chicago utilities magnate, Harley L. Clarke.[441] Midday on Monday 7 April Clarke signed an agreement to pay $20 million for Fox's voting shares. Stuart lent Clarke some of $20 million and arranged bank loans for the rest.[442] Untermyer endeavoured to ensure that the press reported the agreement in a way that saved Fox's face. Clarke paid Untermyer the remaining $900,000 of his fee. Besides the $1 million from the Fox companies, Fox sent Untermyer a personal check for $250,000. Untermyer returned it saying that he wanted no more than a fair fee, which he had fixed in the $1 million bill to the companies.[443]

Untermyer's last major endeavour as a corporate lawyer involved the aftermath of the suicide in March 1932 of the Swedish 'match king' Ivar Kreuger. In late April Untermyer became counsel together with former secretary of state Bainbridge Colby for a committee of holders of debentures of the Kreuger & Toll Company. It and its sister company, the International Match Company, were bankrupt.[444] Untermyer regarded it as the 'world's greatest swindle'.[445] He visited Sweden in July 1933 in an effort to obtain for his clients a share of the $2½ million that was said to have been salvaged from the affairs of the corporation.[446] It was fortuitous that Untermyer's nephew, Laurence A. Steinhardt, was appointed American ambassador to Sweden by Roosevelt in 1933. He was able to do work associated with the Kreuger business on behalf of Untermyer in Stockholm.[447] In early November Untermyer and Steinhardt held a conference at Greystone with twenty-four American and foreign businessmen and economists, including Jacob Wallenberg,[448] the managing director of Stockholms Enskilda Bank. The meeting was an informal one to discuss plans that were being made to salvage properties of some of the Krueger companies.[449] Wallenberg played a leading role in the negotiations with Untermyer's committee on behalf of the Swedish banks, and later also the Swedish Match Co.[450] The *Svenska Dagbladet* reported at the end of November that 'America's foremost' lawyer's negotiations with Wallenberg and the stakeholders had made 'a good start'.[451] The negotiations were successfully concluded during 1935[452] allowing a distribution of funds to the debenture holders the following year.[453] The legal work associated with the committee continued for several more years. Untermyer's nephew, Eugene, did most of the day-to-day work.[454]

The Kreuger and Toll committee marked the end of Untermyer's long career as a corporate lawyer. The anti-Nazi boycott, which is the subject of Chapter 5, was to take up most of his time during the next few years. However, he still found time to occasionally represent high-profile clients, a good example being Pierre Dreyfus, the son of Captain Alfred Dreyfus, who had been the victim of institutional anti-Semitism in the French Army at the end of the nineteenth century. Untermyer was acquainted with Dreyfus because he was president of the Comité de Défense des Juifs Persécutes, one of France's most active anti-Nazi boycott organizations. Dreyfus had attended a world boycott conference Untermyer organized in Amsterdam in 1933.[455] In 1936 Dreyfus learnt that Warner Brothers were making a film called *The Life of Emile Zola*, the writer who interceded on behalf of his father. In November he wrote a letter to Untermyer asking whether he could obtain a copy of the screenplay for him. In response to Untermyer's intervention Warner Brothers provided Dreyfus with a copy of the final script. He suggested certain changes, which were accepted.[456]

2

Mr Untermyer goes to Washington

The Wall Street poacher-turned Bryanite gamekeeper, 1897–1914

Tuesday 2 November 1897 was election day in New York City. Untermyer's half-brother, Randolph Guggenheimer, was on the Tammany Hall ticket as a candidate for election as President of the City Council. Boss Richard Croker had rewarded Guggenheimer for his long service to Tammany Hall with his first nomination for an elected political office.[1] Florence and Louis Marshall spent the evening at Untermyer's home where the latter had a ticker (a telegraphic machine that printed out data on a strip of paper) installed for the election results.[2] Guggenheimer was elected by the largest vote on his ticket.[3]

Guggenheimer had been a late addition to Tammany's ticket. The original candidate for president of the City Council had been Jacob Ruppert, Jr., a thirty-year-old German American brewer. However, Tammany Boss Croker had ordered his name taken off the ticket in early October because the brewers would not respond with a campaign fund of $50,000, which it had been agreed that Ruppert should raise for Tammany. Guggenheimer had been chosen by Croker because he could furnish a 'bar'l' well filled for the Tammany campaign. The *New York Press* noted that Guggenheimer had many wealthy friends.[4] A McKinley Democrat, he had voted for the successful Republican candidate in the previous year's presidential election.[5] So Guggenheimer also had the potential to widen the appeal of the Tammany ticket. Untermyer actively supported his half-brother's campaign. He helped secure the support of the New York brewers for the entire Tammany ticket.[6]

During the period Untermyer became politically active he had two role models from his extended family: a cousin, Herman Myers, and his half-brother, Randolph Guggenheimer. The former was mayor of Savannah, Georgia, from 1895 to 1897 and 1899 to 1907.[7] Lauren Beth Aker describes Myers as a Progressive Democrat.[8] Myers often visited New York.[9] Untermyer had represented Myers and his brothers, Sigo and Fred S.,[10] in a law suit against two New York City banks in 1891.[11]

Guggenheimer, as noted earlier, served as president of New York City Council, and periodically as acting mayor, between 1897 and 1901. He was responsible for several progressive initiatives, including a proposal for municipal workers to collect leftover food from the well-off, restaurants, hotels and boarding houses to feed the destitute of the city.[12] He also supported a proposal for a free public library.[13] In 1900 Guggenheimer drew attention to the underpayment of young girls in factories, stores and shops. He advocated a new state law fixing a minimum wage rate for girls and children. Guggenheimer also declared himself a supporter of equal rights for women. For example, he believed that 'College women are in no respect, except perhaps in physical strength and endurance, the inferiors of men.'[14] The *Brooklyn Daily Eagle* suggested Guggenheimer advocated equal pay for women.[15] Another Brooklyn newspaper reported in August 1900 that Guggenheimer hoped to win the Democratic nomination to be the candidate to succeed Robert A. Van Wyck as mayor the following year.[16] However, it appears to have been misinformed. Guggenheimer announced in early September he would not be seeking the nomination and would be returning to his law practice at the end of the following year.[17]

Untermyer and his family had not supported Bryan as the Democratic candidate in the 1896 presidential election. In the 1900 presidential election his half-brother Randolph and brother Maurice had initially tried to prevent Tammany Hall from supporting Bryan's candidacy for the Democratic nomination.[18] However, in June Untermyer publicly endorsed Bryan saying he was 'enthusiastically in favor' of him.[19] He became a 'personal and political friend' of Bryan, who regarded him as the 'biggest lawyer' he was acquainted with.[20] Untermyer had for many years been known as a sound money man. However, he put this belief aside because he supported Bryan's opposition to imperialism. He agreed with Bryan that America did not need to own a country or a people to trade with them. Untermyer observed, 'As a patriotic citizen I would rather have free-silver than the approval of the present foreign policy if put to the alternative, which we are not.'[21] He supported Bryan again in the 1908 presidential election, observing during the campaign that the Democratic Party candidate was 'a bigger man and better beloved than at any other time in his career. He has lived to see his Ideas of corporate control, for which he was denounced and derided and his good faith attacked, appropriated by his opponents'.[22] Untermyer also made two donations of $1,000 and $1,500 to Bryan's campaign fund.[23]

As already noted in his earlier career Untermyer had been a conservative. Gregory Weinstein later recalled that during the 1880s Untermyer had participated in the debates on current events held by the Young Men's Union of the Ethical Society on Sundays at the Workingmen's School. '[T]he two Samuels – Untermyer and Gompers – would discuss labor conditions from opposite viewpoints to the keen enjoyment of the audience.'[24] At the time of these debates Untermyer was well known for his conservative position on labour unions. For example, he became well known in his role as 'counsel for the boss brewers', the United States Brewers Association, during a boycott of 'pool beer' by labour union members in 1888.[25] Gompers, who was one of the union officials representing the workers during the boycott,[26] later became one of Untermyer's political friends. However, at the time Untermyer's friends were from a very different political circle which included James M. Beck, a conservative lawyer. Beck remained a close friend even after Untermyer's transformation into a Progressive Democrat.[27]

Untermyer's decision to become actively involved in Progressive Democratic politics was possibly with the view to becoming a US senator after his retirement from his law firm or securing a high-profile government position when a Democratic candidate was next successful in winning the presidency. He served as one of New York's delegates to the Democratic National Conventions of 1904, 1908, 1912, 1916, 1932 and 1936. He was also a delegate at large from New York at the 1920 convention.[28] As part of this quest Untermyer also became a campaigner for economic and social reform. In a letter to Adolph S. Ochs in August 1902 he observed

> There never was a time when we were confronted with graver problems or when a purer higher patriotism was required of our public men & of the organs & moulders [sic] of public opinion. To my mind the prompt & stringent regulation of the Trusts & the control of all public utilities is the most pressing & important of all such questions. There [sic] continued operation under present conditions is a serious menace to our future & a fraud upon the people. As a Democrat & a believer in States rights I have been reluctantly forced to the conclusion that they shall be placed under national control by a comprehensive Constitutional Amendment providing for national corporation laws & quickly too before they grow stronger than the people themselves . . .
> I have seen something of the internal workings of these 'innocuous' octopuses: I <u>know</u> that their tendency is irredeemably bad.[29]

It is probable Untermyer was also motivated by rivalry with J.P. Morgan, Sr. As a Wall Street lawyer Untermyer was professionally acquainted with Morgan and visited him at his home to work on contracts, on one occasion in 1908 saving a valuable rug from a spark from an open wood fire.[30] The first case in which Untermyer was on the opposing side to Morgan was in 1903 and 1904 when he represented a Bondholders' Protective Committee in litigation following the failure of the United States Shipbuilding Co. It had been organized by J.P. Morgan & Co. in 1902 as a consolidation of the larger shipbuilding companies and had included the Bethlehem Steel Co., which was controlled by a J.P. Morgan & Co. syndicate.[31] Although Untermyer claimed that he intended no attack on J.P. Morgan & Co. and referred to Morgan in interviews about the case in a respectful manner,[32] the banker was reputedly very angry that the United States Steel Corporation and the Bethlehem Steel Co. were dragged into the resulting shipbuilding scandal.[33] In February 1904 Untermyer succeeded in persuading the receiver to accept a reorganization plan largely the same as the one he had originally proposed the previous year.[34] The reorganization was completed by the end of 1904. The company was renamed the Bethlehem Steel Co. and Untermyer became the largest shareholder apart from the company's president, Charles M. Schwab.[35] His fee was 15,000 shares with a nominal value of $8 each. By 1915 they had risen in value to around $300 each, making it worth $4½ million.[36]

Susie J. Pak notes that the first time Untermyer gave a speech on the American economy was on 3 November 1904.[37] He delivered it to a noon meeting of the Commercial Travelers League in New York City on the eve of the presidential election that year. He began by observing that

> We In New York and the East . . . are living in a fool's paradise—in an atmosphere of unconscious corporate influence. The men in control of the destinies of these

corporate interests are of course men of brains, industry, and Ingenuity. The love of wealth and of the power that comes from wealth dominates these giants of industry, and accounts largely for their success. Our admiration for their intellectual strength and resourcefulness has blinded us to the game they are playing at the expense of the public welfare. The wholesome object lesson of a few of them serving jail sentences is the only effective way to remind the others that lawbreaking is not business.

Later in the speech he delivered a critique of Republican candidate President Theodore Roosevelt's policy on the trusts.

Our President has often been quoted as telling us that there are 'good' trusts and 'bad' trusts. The only 'good' trust is one that's dead or bankrupt because it has failed to become a trust . . . Presumably the President thinks they are all 'good' since there has been no effort to punish any of them. If the definition of a 'good' trust is one that contributes to the Republican campaign fund and a 'bad' trust is one that helps the Democrats, I imagine they have all been good up to this time.

After a discussion of Roosevelt's record, he ended his speech with a reflection on the current state of the debate about the regulation of the trusts.

I charge the Republican Party with insincerity and false pretense on this great question. It Is trying to deceive the public as to Its attitude by pretending to prosecute the trusts while shielding them from the laws to which they are amenable. It has set up an academic controversy that has harmed no one, under cover of which the real lawbreakers are being granted Immunity from prosecution. It is in partnership with the most vicious of these violators of the law. In return for protection the party is furnished with the sinews with which to wage war upon the integrity of the ballot and to corrupt and subvert our political institutions.

I am neither a radical nor an alarmist. The radicals are the small body of reckless and foolhardy rich and powerful men who are victimizing the people and imperiling the industrial future of our country . . . The conservatives are those who are sounding the note of warning and pleading for the enforcement of the law while there is yet time. Let us have a President and an Attorney General who will give an object lesson in the difference between a financier and a buccaneer that will teach respect and fear for the law![38]

The *New York Times* in an editorial on Untermyer's speech fully endorsed his analysis asking whether Roosevelt could be trusted to take the action required against the trusts.[39]

The Republican lawyer Henry Wollman, a friend of Untermyer's law firm partner Louis Marshall,[40] responded to the speech with a light-hearted commentary.

This week my distinguished associate in the Shipbuilding case, my esteemed friend Samuel Untermyer, who is now of counsel for Henry H. Rogers, the active head and front of Standard Oil, advocated [the Democratic Party's presidential candidate] Judge [Alton B.] Parker's[41] election because the trusts favored Roosevelt. If anything were needed to show the accuracy of Judge Parker's statement made In Connecticut on Thursday that 'every trust in this country, Including the Standard Oil trust, is doing what it can to elect that ticket' (meaning the Roosevelt ticket), Mr. Untermyer's speech would confirm that pronouncement. Mr. Untermyer is counsel for the great Pump Trust or combination and other Important combinations; in fact, although a comparatively young man, he might be said to be one of the fathers of combinations in this country, and that's why he favors Parker, the slayer of trusts. Francis Lynde Stetson, the general counsel of the Steel Trust, of the Erie, the Northern Pacific, the Southern and many other railroads, and general counsel for J. P. Morgan & Co., ardently supports Parker.

Wollman went on to name several other prominent corporate lawyers who represented trusts together with one of the most important financiers in the affairs of the Tobacco Trust who were supporting Parker in the election. He observed it 'certainly must make the trusts of this country shudder when they think how faithless their high officers and counsel are in favoring Parker, who is going to destroy them'.[42]

In his speech Untermyer had referred to a secret investigation of the trusts being carried out by the Department of Commerce and Labor. A few weeks after the election the first report of James R. Garfield, Commissioner of Corporations, which was made public by the Secretary of Commerce and Labor. Garfield proposed the federal control of the trusts. Corporations should be required to have a federal franchise or license to engage interstate commerce.[43] Untermyer responded by observing:

> I do not agree with Mr. Garfield that his remedy of a license or franchise from the federal government is a practical or effective means of restraint. It will be overcome by organizing sub-companies in the states in which the corporation does business.
>
> *The only effective remedy is one which absolutely takes away from the States the right to grant charters to corporations that are engaged in interstate commerce and places this power in the hands of the federal government.*[44]

It is notable that Untermyer had made no reference to J.P. Morgan in his Commercial Travelers League speech contrary to some of the speeches he was to give about trusts a few years later. It is possible Untermyer's subsequent enmity toward the banker arose after he became 'Morgan's deadly rival' in the field of fine Scotch collies.[45] In 1903 Untermyer had adopted one of Morgan's hobbies, dog breeding. One of his first dogs was acquired from the banker.[46] Morgan had bred collies since the early 1890s.[47] Untermyer was to spend large sums of money on dogs to compete with him in dog shows.[48] He built the Greystone Kennels at his Yonkers country estate to house them, which were described by the *New York Tribune* as being 'conducted upon an almost military basis'.[49] Unlike Morgan, who was a dog lover, Untermyer appears to have adopted this hobby to rile the banker.[50]

From the mid-1900s Untermyer publicly advocated economic and financial reform. He first called for economic reform in a feature interview in 1905 with the

New York Times. He called for the principle of state supremacy to be surrendered to give the federal government control of corporations and more authority to counter corporate fraud. Untermyer did not think there was any danger in investing the federal government with more power over the national economy. This was the only way the domination of the economy by the trusts could be defeated.[51] During the next few years Untermyer gave further thought to the ills of the American economy and the potential remedies.

Untermyer challenged the American economic and financial system in his legal practice beginning with insurance. He was already familiar with the industry. His client James Hazen Hyde had controlled the majority of the Equitable Life Assurance Society's stock. The society's executives sought to remove Hyde from the control of the society in 1905 and mutualize the Equitable by giving the policyholders the right to elect the directors. In response, Hyde sold his stock to Thomas Fortune Ryan. The scandal led to New York State establishing the Armstrong Committee to investigate the insurance industry, whose counsel was Charles Evans Hughes.[52] From this point onwards Untermyer was to cross paths with Hughes frequently in both the legal and political worlds.[53] The following year, Untermyer lobbied for state bills in New York and Ohio to strengthen the position of policyholders versus insurance company managers by making it easier for them to elect trustees who were truly representative.[54] He also created the International Committee of Policy Holders of the New York and Mutual Life Insurance Companies to replace their managements.[55] The committee's members included Progressive Democratic and Republican politicians such as ex-governor Henry Roberts of Connecticut, Governor John A. Johnson of Minnesota, Governor Frank Hanly of Indiana, Congressman William Alden Smith of Michigan and Governor Napoleon B. Broward of Florida.[56] In an address to the Insurance Committee of the Ohio Legislature in March, Untermyer denounced the insurance industry as 'a bottomless sink of corruption'.[57] He also condemned 'the defiant and unrepentant attitude' of the two companies towards their policy holders.[58] Untermyer declined to be nominated as a member of the International Policy Holders slate. His justification was that

> If in the final analysis it will appear that I have in any way contributed to the success of a movement which will rescue these vast assets from the grasp of the speculative Wall Street financiers, where they have been used for doubtful schemes of high finance and to corrupt Legislatures and political parties, and to place them in honest, conservative hands selected by the owners of the properties, I shall be more than content with having had the high privilege of taking part in the performance of so great a public duty.[59]

Both the Mutual and New York Life employed dirty tricks against the committee.[60] The latter company was unsuccessfully challenged by Untermyer in the New York Supreme Court.[61] A cartoon by Udo J. Keppler on the front page of an October issue of the satirical magazine *Puck* depicted Charles A. Peabody, president of Mutual Life, and Alexander E. Orr, president of New York Life, playing poker with Samuel Untermyer in a Wild West saloon, each of them holding a handful of 'Proxies' in one hand and a pistol in the other.[62] The victory of the official slate in the trustees' elections held in mid-December[63] was not confirmed by the Inspectors of election until the following June.[64] Roscoe Carlyle Buley, an insurance industry corporate historian, suggests Untermyer's methods antagonized many policyholders and that he was suspected of aspiring to control as dictatorial as the existing regime.[65] In January Untermyer had met with Governor Charles Evans Hughes in Albany to urge that he recommend fair insurance election legislation.[66] However, the legislature failed to act and so at the end of September Untermyer conceded defeat on behalf of the committee.[67]

Later in 1910 the New York State Department of Insurance published a report on an examination of the Mutual. Untermyer considered it a vindication of the claims he had made on behalf of the international policyholders.[68] Charles A. Peabody responded by alleging that Untermyer had secretly sought to betray the policyholders in the election of 1907. Untermyer sued him for libel.[69] Peabody responded with an insult.

Illustration 5 Udo J. Keppler's '"Watcher Got?": A Quiet Game of Freezeout in Life Insurance Gulch' Cartoon, 1906.

> I do not think it worth while to spend any time considering Mr. Untermyer's libel suit. I have not much money, but I have enough to pay any damage which Mr. Untermyer's reputation could suffer.[70]

Untermyer was incensed that Peabody's statement and comment on his reply and libel suit had been published by the *New York Times*. He considered it to be a personal betrayal of him by Adolph S. Ochs. He wrote a lengthy letter to him, of which the following extract captures the spirit of the whole.

> Only a man whom you trusted as your friend could have done me the hurt and injury that you did me. I shall never cease to feel the pain of it and yet if it were possible that there is an explanation I should be glad to know it for my friendship for you has not been of the superficial kind and I should hate to feel that you were incapable of friendship. Perhaps I am judging you by too high a standard. I only know how sacred friendships are to me & what I would have done under like circumstances.[71]

There was a break in their friendship. However, they subsequently mended fences in 1918 and became good friends once more.[72]

Untermyer also challenged the banks after he was appointed counsel for the receiver of the Munroe & Munroe 'laundry' brokerage firm in December 1904.[73] He exposed the role of the National City Bank of New York in the Montreal and Boston Copper Co. stock washing scandal.[74] He compelled the implicated vice-president of the bank, Archibald G. Loomis, to resign in January 1905.[75] Subsequently a syndicate including Samuel Newhouse and Untermyer organized the acquisition of Montreal and Boston Copper by the Dominion Copper Co. of Toronto.[76]

During this period Untermyer and his firm also represented a number of Wall Street banks, including Lehman Brothers,[77] Lazard Frères[78] and the Banker's Trust Co. For example, Untermyer represented a syndicate including Benjamin Strong, Jr., vice-president of the Banker's Trust Co., in the reorganization of the Southern Iron & Steel Co. from 1911 to 1913.[79] He was assisted in the legal work by his law firm partners Arthur Manley Wickwire and Alvin, his eldest son. The assets of the company were sold at auction on 31 January 1913. The sole qualifying bid was from a syndicate represented by Wickwire.[80] The Banker's Trust Co. also acted as depository for a committee of the bankrupt Western Maryland R.R. Co.'s bondholders and stockholders which Untermyer represented in 1908.[81]

The Panic of 1907, which took place in October, exposed the perils of a country without a central bank. J.P. Morgan Sr. had to intervene to prevent a collapse of the financial system. The panic had been caused by a failed attempt by two speculators to corner the stock in a copper company. This led to a run on a trust company, the Knickerbocker Trust.[82] Untermyer was involved in the aftermath of the panic as counsel to a committee of depositors in the Knickerbocker Trust who hoped to rehabilitate the company.[83] His client Andrew Freedman had $200,000 invested in the company.[84] By late November Untermyer had drawn up a plan for the reorganization of the company.[85] He was opposed by a rival depositors' committee whose counsel Herbert L. Satterlee was the son-in-law of J.P. Morgan.⁸⁶ Satterlee's committee blocked both Untermyer's plan and subsequent attempts at a compromise. Untermyer blamed Morgan.

> From the beginning, we offered again and again, orally and in writing, to leave every disputed question to Mr. J.P. Morgan and to Mr. Francis Lynde Stetson, his counsel. There was no spirit of compromise present at any stage . . .
> So far from our committee having blocked any plan for rehabilitation, as certain interested persons would like to have it understood so as to shift the responsibility in case of failure, we have . . . abandoned plan after plan which we considered more favorable to depositors in order to meet the general view.⁸⁷

A financial journal which supported Satterlee's plan accused Untermyer of unnecessarily delaying and obstructing it.⁸⁸ Despite Untermyer's best efforts the depositors backed a rival reorganization plan supported by Morgan.⁸⁹

Susie J. Pak has observed, 'Morgan's role in the Panic of 1907 added to his legendary status, but it also fueled the political movement for financial reform.'⁹⁰ Untermyer was one of the leading reform advocates. Pak suggests that

> Though he was . . . a strong critic of Theodore Roosevelt's distinction between 'good' and 'bad' trusts, Untermyer's ideas on state responsibility were more in line with that of Roosevelt's New Nationalism than Wilson's New Freedom. He believed in the power of an activist government . . .⁹¹

From 1909 he returned to the fray to give speeches and publish articles in journals and newspapers over the next few years advocating federal legislation to reform the American economic and financial system. He focussed on three different areas: trusts, stock exchanges and the banking system. Untermyer believed existing federal law on trusts needed to be greatly strengthened. In a statement in June 1909 to the *New York Times* with reference to a recent lawsuit by his client Adolph Segal, a Pennsylvania sugar refiner, against the Sugar Trust (the American Sugar Refining Co.),⁹² he argued that the trusts were 'enthroned'.⁹³ The following year he produced a four-point plan to deal with the trusts.⁹⁴ In a speech to the National Civic Federation in January 1911 Untermyer argued that the big trusts were too powerful to be successfully prosecuted by the government. He also referred to two major anti-trust cases currently before the US Supreme Court. He assumed the Court would uphold the judgments of the Circuit Court of Appeals dissolving the trusts. But he questioned if they were enforceable in practical operation.⁹⁵ The same month he also advocated the absolute abolition of what he described as 'the financial device known as the 'holding company', describing it as a 'recent financial abomination.'⁹⁶ In July, after the US Supreme Court had ruled on the anti-trust cases, *The North American Review* published an article by him entitled 'The Remedy'.⁹⁷ He noted that the impact of the rulings had been lessened because the Attorney General had decreed 'that no criminal prosecutions would be considered until after the expiration of the time fixed for compliance with the decrees of the Court'.⁹⁸ His remedy included the enforced organization under federal law of every corporation engaged in interstate or international trade, the prohibition of the holding company, the protection of the rights of minority shareholders, the prohibition of the ownership by corporation of stocks of other corporations and the creation of a regulatory court or commission similar to the Interstate Commerce Commission.[99] Untermyer subsequently produced a refined federal corporate regulation plan for the National Civic Federation.[100] In November he testified before the Senate Committee on Interstate and Foreign Commerce. He outlined his views on corporation control and proposed legislation based on his National Civic Federation plan.[101] Untermyer followed up his testimony with an article in the magazine *World To-Day*[102] and further speeches, including one at a New York Economic Club dinner.[103] The following April Untermyer took part in a debate with his friend Morris Hillquit on the resolution 'That Socialism was the Only Solution to the Trust Problem' at Carnegie Hall organized by the Intercollegiate Socialist Society. Untermyer argued for government regulation rather than government ownership. The *New York Press* noted that 'The striking fact of the debate was, however, that Hillquit was not as emphatic in his denunciation of trusts as was Untermyer'.[104]

Untermyer also advocated the regulation of America's stock exchanges. In February 1911, in a letter to New York City mayor, William J. Gaynor, Untermyer observed

> The Stock Exchange should not be regarded as a private Club, but as one of the most powerful National and International financial agencies in the world. Its powers at present are the most despotic and uncontrolled of any known Public Institution and they ought to be subject to review. If you are disposed to take up the subject in the form of proposed legislation it would afford me great pleasure to contribute as a public service such of my time and attention as would be needed.[105]

Later at the end of the year Untermyer called for legislation to regulate the New York Stock Exchange.[106] The following year he invited the stockbroker Bernard M. Baruch to visit him at Greystone to discuss possible legislation affecting stock manipulation and rehypothecation. He warned that 'Unless the dominating spirits in charge of the [New York] Stock Exchange are sufficiently far-sighted and statesmanlike to realize the drift of public sentiment' extremists might take advantage to 'imperil the usefulness of the Stock Exchange which if conducted under proper legal safeguards [he regarded] as one of our most useful and necessary institutions'. Baruch declined the invitation and instead suggested Untermyer meet with the law committee of the exchange and its counsel.[107]

In the early-twentieth-century stocks were traded by brokers in every state and territory. Stock exchanges could be found in most states and territories.[108] Unlike in Britain, there was not one dominant stock exchange equivalent to the London Stock Exchange. The New York Stock Exchange could only claim to be first among equals. Furthermore the New York Stock Exchange was not the only stock market in the city. The Consolidated Stock Exchange of New York and the outdoor New York Curb Market provided alternative stock markets.[109] However, the New York Stock Exchange was the most prestigious of the three markets. Its membership was dominated by the white Anglo-Saxon Protestant elite and together they formed one of the most powerful financial institutions in the United States. Many of the New York Stock Exchange's members were to come to regard Untermyer as a bête noire.[110] He was to discover that the New York Stock Exchange was an even more powerful adversary than J.P. Morgan & Co.

Untermyer also advocated the reform of the national banking system. In September 1911 he gave an interview in Paris before his departure for the United States, in which he pointed to the 'Money Trust' as the greatest peril facing the United States. He also observed action against the concentration of money power must come quickly if it were to afford relief.[111] At the end of December he gave a seminal address on 'Is There a Money Trust?' to the Finance Forum of New York City's West Side YMCA. He began by observing that were Congress to investigate it would find that there was no such thing and certainly none that was in violation of the law.[112] However, he further observed

> If, however, we mean by this loose elastic term 'Trust' as applied to the concentration of 'Money Power' that there is a close and well-defined 'community of interest' and understanding among the men who dominate the financial destinies of our country and who wield fabulous power over the fortunes of others through their control of corporate funds belonging to other people, then our investigators will find a situation far more serious than is popularly supposed to exist.[113]

He believed it would be difficult to find an adequate remedy, although improved banking and currency laws would help mitigate the 'constantly increasing danger'. Untermyer's proposed remedies included an independent 'scientific money system' with a 'Reserve National Bank'.[114] He warned inaction was 'likely to lead to a moneyed oligarchy more despotic and more dangerous to industrial freedom than anything civilization has ever known'.[115] Untermyer recommended several other legislative reforms.[116]

One of Untermyer's objectives may have been a seat in the US Senate, although he often denied this. In March 1911, his name was suggested as a compromise candidate at the 'famous breakfast conference', held at the Executive Mansion in Albany during a deadlock over the choice of candidate. This was before senators were elected by the popular vote. Governor John Alden Dix, Tammany Hall Boss Charles F. Murphy, who arrived at Albany a few hours after the conference, and state senator Franklin D. Roosevelt accepted Mayor Gaynor's suggestion of Untermyer as a way out of a difficulty. Later Untermyer was informed that certain interests were decidedly opposed to him. Then he learned that Roosevelt had switched entirely and was openly opposing him. Anxious to find out the identity of the opposing interests, Untermyer went to Francis Lynde Stetson, who informed him that he, Morgan, and all the allied Wall Street and steel interests were decidedly opposed to him for various reasons. Among them were Untermyer's role in breaking up the Shipbuilding Trust in 1904, his championship of the policyholders of the Mutual Life Insurance Company and his general opposition to Morgan interests.[117] Stetson subsequently denied that Morgan had opposed Untermyer as a senator.[118] Boss Murphy subsequently proposed James A. O'Gorman, who won the support of the Democratic Party caucus. O'Gorman was the last senator elected by the New York State Legislature.[119]

Untermyer's main objective was the enactment of federal legislation to strengthen the regulation of banking, the stock exchange and trusts. He sought out like-minded congressmen and senators. In July 1911, Charles A. Lindbergh, an Insurgent Republican member of the House from Minnesota,[120] introduced a resolution proposing the appointment of a committee to find out whether there was a 'Money Trust'. The resolution was adopted in committee and favourably reported. It was rumoured that Untermyer was the real force behind Lindbergh's resolution.[121] Lindbergh had been trying to stymie Senator Nelson Aldrich's proposed central bank which was favoured by Wall Street banks such as National City Bank. As he later observed

> Lest the purpose of my starting the original Money Trust probe be misconstrued, I here state that it was not for the purpose of discovering the Money Trust. Long before that time it was known by those who had carefully studied the problem that there was a money power combination that operated and controlled the country's finances and carried on its operations in a shameful manner. The purpose and actual effect of my original resolution was a flank move, to defeat the special interests in their attempt to fasten on the people of this country the so-called Aldrich Banking and Currency Plan for 50 years. This plan was an attempt on their part to make the greatest steal from the people that has ever been made.[122]

Hearings were held on Lindbergh's resolution in mid-December.[123] Afterwards Lindbergh received a letter from Untermyer urging him not to abandon his resolution calling for an inquiry into the operations of the so-called Money Trust.[124]

On 5 January 1912, the *New York Times* reported that there was a general expectation in the New York City financial district that Untermyer would be chosen as counsel to the committee that was to investigate the so-called Money Trust. It was noted that he had retired a few days before from active participation in the routine work of his law firm.[125] On the same day William Jennings Bryan's *The Commoner* signalled his support by reprinting Untermyer's interview on the Money Trust published in the New York *World* the previous September.[126] In mid-January Untermyer went to Washington to consult with the House Committee on Rules, which was considering the advisability of investigating the so-called Money Trust. Untermyer attended a conference with Congressman Robert Lee Henry[127] together with Secretary of Commerce and Labor Charles Nagel and Attorney General George W. Wickersham.[128] By late January the congressional Democratic leaders were either openly opposing an investigation or at least not supporting it. Henry, who did support an investigation, summoned Untermyer to appear before the House Committee on Rules in the hearing on the proposal to order an investigation.[129] Untermyer was the first to testify. In his testimony he sought to curb the enthusiasm of some more ardent members of the committee.[130] Untermyer suggested that

> Individual instances of abuses would be gone into by the committee, I imagine, only for the purpose of illustrating the defect in the system, not for the purpose of injuring any individual or institution; because, I take it, that this is not intended to be a promiscuous fishing expedition into the private affairs of the people, but is intended as an important and serious undertaking that will take a long time, that is going to be very extensive, and that should be very profitable.[131]

In his statement Untermyer also proposed including the operations of the New York Stock Exchange within the scope of the inquiry. After further debate in the House of Representatives, agreement was reached to carry out the investigation.[132]

On 7 February, a Democratic Party caucus was held to discuss the Money Trust investigation where his appointment was opposed by Carter Glass, a Virginian congressman. Glass favoured the Philadelphia lawyer William Glasgow, Jr. as an alternative. However, he declined the invitation.[133] Glass later recalled that he then yielded to the argument that 'it takes a thief to catch a thief'. According to his account

> the committee finally agreed to designate Untermyer purely upon the theory that having personally participated in the illicit transactions which it was designed to expose, he would be better able to reveal the irregularities of his former associates.[134]

One of Untermyer's allies informed him that Glass had defamed him at the Democratic caucus. He wrote to Glass asking for an explanation. Glass replied that although he was aware of the Harney Peak and Columbia Straw Paper scandals, he had not referred to them in the caucus. However, he had read an extract from a letter Untermyer had written to Henry in which he had made an 'offensive allusion to the banking and currency committee of the House, of which I am a member, practically charging that the committee could not be trusted to investigate the so-called money trust'.[135]

Untermyer in reply to Glass observed that he had assumed that his letter to Henry would be regarded as confidential and did not expect it to be released to the press. He said that he had had reports from members present at the caucus about what Glass had said regarding the Columbia Straw Paper case. He also cited the following report from the *Richmond Virginian* of 8 February,

> Carter Glass of Virginia, a member of the Committee on Banking and Currency, denounced Samuel Untermyer of New York who has been advocating an investigation and whom Mr. Henry quoted. Mr. Glass said that Mr. Untermyer's corporation record was bad.

Untermyer demanded to know exactly what documents Glass had in his possession.[136] Glass replied that the court records were none of Untermyer's business because he had not made use of them. He accepted that Untermyer's letter to Henry had been confidential but reiterated that the assertions in it were untrue.[137]

As well as confronting Glass directly Untermyer also wrote to his cousin, Charley Guggenheimer, in Lynchburg enquiring about him.[138] He replied

> Regarding Congressman Carter Glass, he is a personal friend of mine. Of course, I cannot say anything regarding any assault that he may have made upon you.
>
> I was raised with him and know him personally very very well. I differ with him on many things in Politics, but must state that he is always on the level, square, courageous in everything that he does, but bitter as the devil. He can hate stronger than any man I ever knew. With it all, I am his friend and have always found him true.[139]

Meanwhile Henry had temporarily been outmanoeuvred by his opponents in the Democratic caucus. Arsene Pujo of Louisiana, the Chairman of the House Banking and Currency Committee, had introduced a resolution proposing an investigation of the Money Trust by standing committees. Lindbergh and Henry argued for a stronger resolution with more powers, but the House voted in favour of the Pujo Resolution.[140] However, fifty or more Bryanite Democrats threatened to form an alliance with the Republicans in the House for a 'real' Money Trust investigation. Majority leader Oscar Underwood was forced to allow an amendment to the resolution directing the Banking and Currency Committee to investigate the matters referred to in Henry's House Resolution 405.[141] Untermyer, disturbed by a hostile report in the *New York Evening Sun* on 29 February[142] that Henry had suggested his name as counsel to the Money Trust investigation, sent a telegram to him that night saying he would not accept the position. He observed that

> Never having taken active part in politics it is, however, rather amusing to learn that I have political entanglements. I am curious to know what they are, as I have been for ten years consistently fighting corrupt high finance from the time of the United States Shipbuilding and life insurance cases to the present cases. I am deeply interested to know the nature of the financial affiliations referred to.[143]

Charles Shields observes Untermyer did not want to be seen to be volunteering but instead wanted to be invited.[144] Several weeks later in mid-April, Henry and several Democratic members of the House Banking and Currency Committee spent several days in conference with Untermyer at Greystone. Untermyer tried to convince them that to be more effective the subcommittee needed additional power. He said that he would consent to work as counsel only if he could have full control of the inquiry.[145] Shields, citing a confidential source, says Untermyer

> saw Pujo as amiable, but not overly accomplished and used him accordingly, often in a condescending manner. Pujo was originally disgruntled by some of the things which were being done in the direction of influencing the trend of the Investigation but eventually acquiesced.[146]

Pujo agreed to accept Untermyer's terms. On 21 April Untermyer was engaged as counsel and Major Edward Howard Farrar of New Orleans, a close friend of Pujo, as associate counsel to the committee. Untermyer accepted with the understanding that the resolution under which the committee would act would be restored to its original form, substantially as introduced by Henry, so as to give scope to the inquiry.[147] Pujo succeeded in getting the House to pass a revised resolution while its opponents were out of town.[148] J.P. Morgan, Jr. reported the disturbing news to his father that their belief that there would be a less intrusive investigation had been upset by the appointment of Untermyer as counsel 'who refused to take that position unless more drastic resolution than that already suggested was passed'.[149]

The Pujo Committee began its investigation in May. Pujo held a meeting with Untermyer at Greystone to discuss the progress of the inquiry in early June. Untermyer expressed his concern that the agitation and the opposition of the big financial interests were beginning to have their effects. However, Pujo said that the investigation would not be stopped by the refusal of some banks to respond to the committee's request for information, or because of the failure of the Senate to pass the Pujo amendment to the national banking law to give the committee broader powers, or because of the lack of funds with which to conduct the investigation.[150]

On 6 June, the Pujo Committee held its first hearing in New York City. The first witness was William Sherer, manager of the New York Clearing House. Untermyer said that Sherer's testimony showed that the Clearing House was an illegal combination wielding autocratic power and exercising monstrous regulation over the nation's banking industry and enabling its members to levy an annual tax of $50 million from the rest of the United States.[151] Frank A. Vanderlip, chairman of the committee of the Clearing House Association, responded by accusing the committee, and in particular Untermyer, of making inaccurate and defamatory statements about the business of his association.[152] Untermyer in turn challenged the members of the Clearing House Association who had criticized the inquiry to testify before the Pujo Committee.[153]

The inquiry was adjourned at the end of June until the autumn. Although it was not the custom for legislators to work during the summer heat, Robert T. Swaine claims that Untermyer persuaded the committee to adjourn because the Roosevelt–Taft fight was getting all the newspaper headlines.[154] In fact the future of the inquiry was under threat because the Senate Finance Committee was holding up an amendment to the banking law which had been passed by the House of Representatives in May. Untermyer claimed Senators Boise Penrose and Joseph W. Bailey were blocking a report on the amendment on behalf of Wall Street bankers Morgan and Stillman. Untermyer cabled his friend Bryan asking him to use his influence through publicity and otherwise to force consideration of the amendment in the Senate before it adjourned for the summer.[155] The bill was reported just before the close of the session, and there was an adverse vote of seven to six, with Bailey voting with the Republicans against the bill. In late November Untermyer informed Bryan the bill was now on the Senate calendar and observed he was sure it could be passed with his assistance if it could be forced to a vote.[156] Bryan replied that he would be 'pleased to render you any possible assistance'.[157] The bill was forced to a vote and passed by the Senate allowing the inquiry to resume.

In late June, the Democratic Convention had been held in Baltimore. Woodrow Wilson, the governor of New Jersey, won the Democratic Party nomination. Untermyer later claimed after Wilson' death that he was 'a close personal friend'[158] who shared an interest in detective novels.[159] Although Wilson regarded him as a friend,[160] Untermyer exaggerated the strength of their bond. Furthermore, Wilson was to prove an unreliable friend and after he won the presidency did little to publicly recognize Untermyer.[161] After Wilson had assumed office Untermyer mostly relied upon intermediaries such as his friend Bryan, the president's first secretary of state. He also cultivated new friendships. He became a very good friend of both Wilson's private adviser, Colonel Edward M. House,[162] and Wilson's son-in-law and first treasury secretary, William Gibbs McAdoo. Later, after they were no longer part of the Wilson administration, his friend Joseph W. Folk, a former Progressive Democratic governor of Missouri, acted as his intermediary.[163] Untermyer's significant presence in national politics throughout Wilson's administration is not fully reflected in the multivolume history of his presidency by Arthur S. Link, the leading specialist on Wilson. He includes Untermyer only in the first two of the five volumes (out of eight originally planned).[164]

Untermyer's support for Wilson caused great concern in the New York banking community. Vanderlip wrote to James Stillman, chairman of the board of directors of the National City Bank,[165] alleging that Untermyer's

> whole ambition is to, in some way, get a whitewash for his character. He has offered a hundred thousand dollars (all of this is quite confidential of course) if he can be assured of a foreign mission. Indeed, he would give any amount for an important one, and has even the audacity to think that he might possibly be appointed to England. Wilson will make no promises whatever and they have accepted only $10,000 as yet and probably will accept no more. He would also like to be Attorney General. Morgenthau says that, of course is quite impossible, although he could imagine that he might be sent to some post of about the grade of Italy.[166]

Wilson won the nomination with the assistance of Bryan. As soon as he learnt of Wilson's nomination Untermyer sent him the following Marconigram on 3 July.[167]

> I congratulate our country on its great opportunity to destroy Wall Street government and accomplish lasting economic reform. Consider me unreservedly enlisted provided all Wall Street assistance is refused.[168]

Untermyer, who had been a delegate at the convention, also sent Wilson a letter on the same day in which he further observed

> The result is a splendid triumph in popular government over what seemed at one time to be almost insurmountable obstacles on the part of the great financial interests that have steadfastly and bitterly opposed your nomination.[169]

From that time onwards Untermyer kept Wilson informed on the progress of the Money Trust investigation.[170] Ironically, according to McAdoo, Untermyer had not been present during the vote and his alternate had been directed by Tammany Hall Boss Murphy to vote for Governor Champ Clark, although Untermyer was, according to Wilson's campaign manager, William F. McCombs, a 'loyal Wilson man' and a large contributor to his campaign fund.[171] Untermyer had contributed $7,000 to the Wilson campaign in early 1912 and, after Wilson was nominated as the Democratic Party's presidential candidate, contributed another $10,000.[172]

On his return to New York from his European summer vacation at the end of August Untermyer renewed his attack on J.P. Morgan. He said in an interview with the *New York Times* it must have been a troublesome question for Morgan to decide between choking off the pending Pujo bill through President Taft's allies in the Senate and obtaining immunity for the Steel and Harvester Trusts. For almost six months the progress of that bill had been blocked in the Senate after having been passed almost unanimously by the House. Untermyer also observed

> It was very considerate of Mr. Morgan not to announce that he was supporting Gov. Wilson, but I can well understand his grievance against the Baltimore Convention for rejecting Gov. Harmon, whom he and his associates did their best to ram down our throats
>
> I wonder whether these gentlemen in Wall Street will ever realize that the country is heartily sick and tired of their blighting and corrupting influence in our political life, and that their support is justly the heaviest handicap a candidate can have, notwithstanding the funds which they may secretly feed to his campaign?[173]

Untermyer's thinking reflected that of Bryan, who had advised Wilson's friend House the previous December:

> I am glad Governor Wilson recognizes that he has the opposition of Morgan and the rest of Wall Street. If he is nominated it must be by the Progressive Democrats, and the more progressive he is the better.[174]

Untermyer went on in the interview to predict the dawn of a new era.

> we are on the horizon of a new era. The change comes none too soon, for the patience of the people is well-nigh exhausted, and justly so. Old-age pensions, insurance against accident, participating insurance against sickness and unemployment to which the employer, the employe, and the State contribute, prohibition of child labor, conservation of the health of mothers and children, are no longer experiments. They are now an essential part of the established policy of civilized government. We are already in the rear van of the line of progress on all these questions. We should add to these reforms that of the State industrial life insurance and thus release the most thrifty and deserving classes of our toilers from the grip of the private industrial life insurance companies that are extorting almost double the legitimate cost of insurance and accumulating a rapidly increasing surplus that is being used in ways that are dangerous to the community...
>
> There is no merit in the argument that by recognizing these just claims of labor we shall so increase our costs of production as to impair our ability to compete in the world's markets. Germany finds itself able to inaugurate these and many other social reforms that have so largely improved the condition of its people that emigration has ceased and its workmen are enjoying a degree of prosperity unknown to-day in any other part of the world, our own country not excepted, and yet she is able to drive us out of any of the world's markets in which we come into competition.[175]

In mid-September Vanderlip had a meeting with Henry Morgenthau, Jr., who was chairman of Wilson's finance committee.

> My conversation with Morgenthau left me more pessimistic about the political outlook than I have been at all... I think Wilson is really pretty well imbued with the 'Money Trust' idea, and I fear that he lacks the sincerity that I believed at one time he had... Morgenthau tells me that Untermyer is preparing for a thorough going campaign to begin after the election – I believe the date is November 20th – and has got a lot of men working on it now... There has been a lot of talk this week of subpoena service being out after pretty much everybody, but I do not think there is anything in it, although the chances are that we will be in for all the sensation that Untermyer can make, later on. I think the special point of attack will be the Clearing House. Happily, my term as chairman expires next month.[176]

Untermyer was delighted by Wilson's victory in the November general election. He wrote to McAdoo to thank him for his part in the result.

> Permit me to add to the chorus of congratulation and express my recognition of the great ability and untiring industry with which you have conducted your end of the campaign. It was well worth doing and I can imagine your satisfaction at the splendid outcome.[177]

Wilson appointed McAdoo Secretary of the Treasury, a decision which was welcomed by Untermyer[178] and his fellow Progressive Louis D. Brandeis.[179] However, Untermyer was undoubtedly disappointed not to be recognized by Wilson. Indeed, back in June, *Twentieth Century Magazine* had included him as Treasury Secretary in a fantasy non-partisan progressive administration.[180] After Wilson's victory the *Mexican Herald* noted that Untermyer's name was also mentioned as a possible attorney general. But his appointment 'was considered rather improbable, because it would be too much like "waving a red flag at Wall Street"'.[181]

In early November Untermyer held a meeting with Dr H. Parker Willis, the expert employed by the subcommittee of Banking and Currency, of which Glass was chairman. Willis reported to Glass

> it is clear to my mind that Mr. Untermyer contemplates a general campaign from the opening of Congress onward aimed at the idea of gathering to himself all the functions entrusted to the Banking and Currency Committee as a whole. He intends to retire from business [and] the legislative sub-committee, and to put himself forward as a banking and currency legislator on behalf of the money trust subcommittee.[182]

Glass was alarmed by this turn of events and thought Untermyer's action 'as nothing short of treasonable'.[183] He wrote to a fellow member of his subcommittee, Congressman Robert J. Bulkley, that

> As far as I am concerned I do not intend for a moment to tolerate such impertinence and, if my committee agrees with me, I shall bring the matter to the attention of the Banking and Currency Committee and insist upon the dismissal of Untermyer who never should have been employed.[184]

He also sent a letter to Pujo, who had decided not to seek re-election in the general election,[185] seeking his assurance that Untermyer was acting without his authority.

> I feel sure that you do not share with Mr. Untermyer this extraordinary view of the functions of our respective sub-committees. The division of our particular duties was, as you know, clearly indicated by the full committee on Banking and Currency; and I regard this action of Mr. Untermyer's as characteristic impertinence on his part. I am writing to you all frankness with the confident expectation that you will put a stop to Mr. Untermyer's activities in the direction indicated, and thus save me the trouble of bringing the matter to the attention of our Banking and Currency Committee with a view to ascertaining whether Mr. Untermyer's surreptitious interference with the distinct work of my sub-committee is to be tolerated.[186]

Pujo replied that the allegations regarding his subcommittee were unfounded and that to the contrary he had refused to consider such proposed action.[187] During the second half of November the *New York Times* reported a possible split between Pujo and Glass and that the former was furious with Untermyer. However, Pujo was not concerned by the issue raised by Glass. He suspected Untermyer was leaking self-serving reports on his committee's investigations to the press. Untermyer denied the charge against him and remained counsel to the committee. However, associate counsel Farrar resigned for personal reasons.[188]

Glass spoke with Untermyer during the second half of November to voice his concern that the counsel was scheming against him. In response to this meeting Untermyer wrote Glass a conciliatory letter on 22 November denying the allegation observing that his 'statement as to what had been said to you came to me like a thunderbolt out of a clear sky'. He expressed the hope that when Pujo and Glass met the following week they would find a way to combine the work of their two subcommittees.[189] Glass's subcommittee met on 2 December and unanimously declined Untermyer's invitation to coalesce.[190]

The same day Lindbergh criticized the Pujo Committee for its slow progress. He also condemned the Taft administration for its refusal to help the committee.[191] Perhaps in response to Lindbergh's criticism, a few days later Untermyer sent letters to J.P. Morgan & Co., Speyer & Co. and Kuhn, Loeb & Co. He asked a great many questions concerning the business done by those firms, their interest in various banks and trust companies, their security holdings, syndicate participation and profits therefrom, and their control over railroads and industrial corporations through interlocking directors.[192] This request posed a difficult problem. New York attorney Paul D. Cravath, counsel for Kuhn, Loeb & Co., observed that

> I think the present attitude of most of [the bankers] is to give somewhat fully information which concerns their own affairs but to be strict in refusing to give information regarding the affairs of customers. Kuhn, Loeb & Co. see no objection to stating the aggregate amounts of the purchases of securities which they have made jointly with other bankers. As they now feel, they are disinclined to give any information regarding participations which they have received from or awarded

to other bankers except aggregates. They are indisposed to give any information regarding what may be termed private loans.[193]

Untermyer also held a meeting in late October at the Lotos Club with several leading bankers to obtain data regarding the operation of the Clearing House.[194]

In mid-December, the Pujo Committee began to hear the testimony of most of the prominent bankers of the United States. Walter E. Frew, a director of the Bankers Trust Company, revealed to Untermyer its phenomenal rise through a 'voting trust' of three men closely identified with J.P. Morgan & Co. to the control of $168 million in deposits. Frew was also president of the Corn Exchange Bank of New York and chairman of the Clearing House Committee of the New York Clearing House. He was a reluctant witness and had to be pushed by Untermyer. Frew also revealed how the Guaranty Trust Company through another 'voting trust' of three men identified with J.P. Morgan & Co. controlled $200 million in deposits.[195]

Frew's testimony was followed by that of Frank K. Sturgis, chairman of the Law Committee of the New York Stock Exchange. Untermyer got Sturgis to reveal that the stock exchange did not take notice of the alleged manipulation of stocks by pools or syndicates, the test of legitimacy of the transactions being in his opinion the payment of commissions. Moral questions and stock exchange questions were 'very different things'.[196]

By early December 1912 Pujo had decided there was sufficient evidence to consider proposing legislation for the regulation of the stock exchanges. Robert S. Winsmore, the Wall Street correspondent of the *Philadelphia Inquirer* and former stockbroker,[197] saw this proposed 'destructive legislation' as 'disturbing'. He noted a seat on the New York Stock Exchange had just sold at the lowest price recorded since the panic days of 1907 and 1908. This reflected how worried Wall Street was.[198] It became clear by mid-December that Untermyer's secondary focus on the stock exchanges was having an impact on public opinion. Winsmore reflected:

> The Pujo Investigating Committee which should be called the Untermeyer [sic] committee, has given Wall Street much to think about during the week, and it may well be that the thinking has not brought peace of mind to the financial community. Beyond doubt Mr. Untermeyer [sic] has scored heavily off the Stock Exchange, although many Stock Exchange members profess not to think so. It is true – and unfortunately so – that the Exchange cannot and will not recognize the great change that has taken place in public opinion during the past few years.[199]

Mary O'Sullivan, in her recent history of the US securities markets between 1866 and 1922, argues that the stock exchange witnesses 'fared much worse' than the bankers and that the exchange 'emerged from this experience with a seriously tarnished reputation'.[200] She also quotes a leading investment banker's observation that the stock exchange did not have 'an altogether sound case'.[201]

On 18 December Untermyer cross-examined J.P. Morgan. Morgan's personal assistant Belle da Costa Greene had observed earlier in the autumn that he had been severely affected by Untermyer's Money Trust investigation. She referred to the lawyer as 'underbred, disgusting and scoundrelly' and that he was 'like a nasty little Italian flea attacking a mountain lion'.²⁰² Morgan was forced to sit and wait while Untermyer examined other witnesses. The elderly banker was furious at this deliberate insult, and, when he was finally called to testify, he was beside himself with rage. However, Morgan did not evade Untermyer's questions and gave revealing answers. At 3 p.m. the subcommittee adjourned. The hearing resumed at 10.30 a.m. the next day.²⁰³ The most well-known exchange between Untermyer and Morgan concerned a man's character.

> Mr. UNTERMYER. Is not commercial credit based primarily upon money or property?
> Mr. MORGAN. No, sir; the first thing is character.
> Mr. UNTERMYER. Before money or property?
> Mr. MORGAN. Before money or anything else. Money can not buy it.
> Mr. UNTERMYER. So that a man with character, without anything at all behind it, can get all the credit he wants, and a man with the property can not get it?...
> Mr. MORGAN. Because a man I do not trust could not get money from me on all the bonds in Christendom.²⁰⁴

Earlier in his testimony Untermyer had tried to get Morgan to agree that there was a Money Trust. He suggested to Morgan that he wanted to control everything.

> Mr. MORGAN. What I say is this, that control is a thing, particularly in money, and you are talking about a money control – now, there is nothing in the world that you can make a trust on money.
> Mr. UNTERMYER. What you mean is that there is no way one man can get it all?
> Mr. MORGAN. Or any of it, except ---
> Mr. UNTERMYER. Or control of it?
> Mr. MORGAN. Or control of it?
> Mr. UNTERMYER. There is no way one man can get a monopoly of money?
> Mr. MORGAN. Or control of it.
> Mr. UNTERMYER. He can make a try at it?
> Mr. MORGAN. No sir; he can not. He may have all the money in Christendom, but he can not do it.²⁰⁵

Two of New York's newspapers published a cartoon of Untermyer the day after Morgan completed his testimony. Boardman Robinson's satirical 'Gulliver before the Lili-Pujoans' on the front page of the *New York Tribune* reimagined Morgan as Jonathan Swift's Gulliver and Untermyer as a Lilliputian.²⁰⁶ Oscar Cesare's sinister 'Who Said Panic?' in the New York *Sun* depicted Untermyer and Bryan, both dour looking, with a gibbet in the background surrounded by dead bodies from which hung a placard saying, 'For Those Who Would Cause Panic – Wilson'. This was a reference to the president-elect's 'Haman' speech of 17 December in which he threatened to hang from a metaphorical gibbet any man or group of men who sought to threaten the business interests of America by precipitating a financial panic. Although Untermyer was no Jacobin, the

Illustration 6 Boardman Robinson's 'Gulliver Before the Lili-Pujoans' Cartoon, 1912.

Sun, whose proprietor was a political enemy, probably wanted to undermine the Pujo Investigation.²⁰⁷

Morgan died a few weeks later on 31 March. Untermyer made a generous tribute to him when he learnt of his death.

> With the death of Mr. Morgan, . . . the world loses one of its most conspicuous figures, and our country sustains the irretrievable loss of a generous, patriotic citizen of rare breadth and public usefulness. The art world, and especially our Metropolitan Museum, will never be able to replace him.
>
> Whatever may be one's views of the perils to our financial and economic system of the concentration of the control of credit, the fact remains and is generally recognized that Mr. Morgan was animated by high purpose and that he never knowingly abused his almost incredible power.²⁰⁸

Illustration 7 Oscar Cesare's 'Who Said Panic?' Cartoon, 1912.

However, Untermyer had told Colonel House the day before

> if anyone was to have the power J.P. Morgan had had during the past twenty-five years, he thought he was as good a man for it as anyone he knew.[209]

His son, J.P. Morgan, Jr. blamed Untermyer for his father's death. However, in public J.P. Morgan & Co. tried to stop the two episodes being linked together by the general public.[210] In private, J.P. Morgan, Jr. was unhappy that his father's physician had issued a statement that referred

> to Pujo as one of the causes of father's illness. We have all here maintained the note which he struck so well in Washington that he was much too big to be annoyed by miserable little things like that . . . There is no use in letting that little rascal Untermyer smile a happy smile and say 'I brought it off after all'.[211]

John Douglas Forbes argues that the banker's antipathy towards Jews dates from this time.[212]

Meanwhile the committee broke for Christmas and did not reconvene again until January. George F. Baker of the First National Bank of New York was the first to testify when the committee reconvened in January. Untermyer got him to admit that overconcentration of banking control was a danger to the United States and that financial concentration had reached its acceptable limit.[213] J.P. Morgan, Jr. reported to his father that he thought 'The beast was both rude and insulting to him.'[214] Untermyer then cross-examined several insurance industry leaders in an attempt to show a close working alliance between the big life insurance concerns and certain leading financiers in New York.

Untermyer also cross-examined George W. Perkins, a former J.P. Morgan & Co. partner. He must have been gratified that Perkins conceded that investors should be protected by the incorporation of the stock exchange. Untermyer also got Perkins to concede that he found financial concentration disturbing and that it was the result of inadequate currency and banking laws.[215]

The day after Perkins's testimony Untermyer's friend Jacob H. Schiff of Kuhn, Loeb and Co. testified. Unlike in the case of Morgan, Untermyer did not try to intimidate Schiff. The banker testified that he did

> not believe in concentration through holding companies . . . I believe in concentration through individuals . . . I think individuals should have every possible freedom: I do not believe in anything that will limit individual freedom . . . I would not limit the individual by law to buy anything he pleases . . . I would let nature take its course.

Although Schiff was against many of the abuses Untermyer was trying to outlaw, he reiterated several times his belief that they could all be resolved by unregulated market forces.[216] Several other bankers testified before the subcommittee recessed for a month on the afternoon on 24 January.[217]

During the recess Untermyer and Pujo were authorized to visit Jekyll Island in Georgia on 7 February to take testimony from retired industrialist William A. Rockefeller, Jr., who was not well enough to travel to Washington. However, although Untermyer claimed he had heard Rockefeller was well enough to play golf, the retired tycoon said he had never played a game of golf in his life. Untermyer started to question him, but his physician intervened to observe it was obvious that Rockefeller was unfit to testify. Untermyer and Pujo agreed not to proceed any further.[218] Untermyer then travelled down to Palm Beach, where he spent two weeks writing the first draft of the committee's report.[219] The subcommittee resumed its inquiry on 25 February and completed its work the following day.[220]

On the eve of the completion of the Pujo Committee's report at the end of February 1913 J.P. Morgan & Co. delivered a letter to Pujo which contained a general denial of the existence or possibility of a Money Trust.[221] The final version of the Pujo Committee's report was published at the end of February. The majority report confirmed the existence of a Money Trust while the minority report denied its existence but conceded a perilous concentration of power. The report recommended legislation regarding the clearing house, the stock exchange and control of money and credit, which it incorporated in two bills.²²² The *New York Times* editorial said of the majority report:

> The committee deals with fancied troubles, and with imaginary remedies. It is out of its depth, and while wishing to do good would take great risks of doing harm. The gentleman whose name the report bears will not be a member of the next Congress, and the submission of the report is likely to be the climax of his career. It is well that we know the worst of the money trust on the very highest authority. We now can sleep more calmly o' nights, sharing the repose which may be anticipated for the report.²²³

Some of Wall Street's bankers believed that Untermyer had failed to prove his case against J.P. Morgan & Co.²²⁴ However, J.P. Morgan & Co. recognized that the Pujo Report had caught the public mood as J.P. Morgan, Jr. observed to Stillman

> The Untermyer enquiry [sic] and the press generally have indicated a feeling on the part of the public that J.P. Morgan & Company ought not to have large stock-holding interests in other financial institutions, and, while I think that the public is misled on this subject and that Mr. Untermyer's own ideas are colored by prejudice, nevertheless we all feel that it behooves us to pay more or less attention to public feeling of that kind, particularly as our relations to our friends do not depend on our stock-holding interests.²²⁵

Peter Knight notes that Exhibit 243 in the Pujo Report, a diagram (six feet long and more than three feet in width) showing the affiliations of J.P. Morgan & Co., National City Bank, First National Bank, Guaranty Trust Co. and Bankers Trust Co. of New York City with large American corporations,²²⁶ provides a 'startlingly original attempt' to provide a visual representation 'that pushes to the limit the representational technologies of the era'.²²⁷ The diagram was prepared by a statistician, Philip J. Scudder of the Investor's Agency, with the assistance of twelve clerks. Knight observes Scudder most probably received specifications for the diagram from Untermyer.²²⁸ The focus on J.P. Morgan & Co. and allied financial institutions suggests Knight is correct. He notes that it was Untermyer's 'training in the organizational efficiency of the railroads' in 'undertaking corporate reorganizations' that allowed him 'to visualize financial corruption as a *system*. Exhibit 243 thus reveals insider dealing not as an occasional and incidental corruption of proper business, but as a structural component of it, part of a complete ecosystem'.²²⁹ The Pujo Report's Exhibit 244 also provides a similar diagram comparing the affiliations of selected New York, Boston and Chicago banks with American corporations.²³⁰

The Pujo Report was well received by those who had taken an interest in the question of the 'Money Trust'. Brandeis, for example, asked Untermyer to send him a copy.²³¹ He was impressed by the report.

> It is admirable, and most of your recommendations I should heartily approve. In some respects it seems to me that the recommendations do not go far enough, and

I should not be surprised to find that in these instances your Committee failed to follow your advice.[232]

Untermyer was to meet with Brandeis to discuss the proposed legislation that resulted from the report.[233] Brandeis also wrote his series of articles in *Harper's Weekly* reviewing the Money Trust and the work of the Pujo Investigation. Untermyer spent over $1,800 to secure publicity for the articles.[234] The following year Brandeis used the articles to publish a best-selling book.[235] Untermyer later observed to Louis Marshall's son-in-law, Jacob Billikopf:[236]

> This is a funny world, in which it is a good thing to have a sustaining sense of humor. Justice Brandeis' articles, that were afterwards gathered together in the form of a book, called 'The Money Trust', first appeared in Harper's Weekly. They were a mere rehash of the Pujo Report. In fact, the book was 'cribbed' almost in its entirety from the Report and much of it was gone over with me by the then Mr. Brandeis at 'Greystone'. But what's the difference, after all.[237]

The Pujo Committee's proposed legislation caused great concern on the part of the stock exchange, which responded by making a personal attack on Untermyer's integrity. On 1 April William C. Van Antwerp of the New York Stock Exchange delivered an address before the Economic Club of Providence in which he recalled Vice-Chancellor Pitney's decision which condemned the conduct of Untermyer and his business associates in connection with the Columbia Straw Paper Company. A few days later the New York *Sun* published an editorial entitled 'Vice-Chancellor Pitney and Mr. Justice Brown on Samuel Untermyer'. The *Sun* questioned Untermyer's good character by casting doubt on his refutation of Pitney's opinion. It also reprinted the statement by Charles Peabody that had led Untermyer to sue the financier for libel in 1910. This editorial and Van Antwerp's address were clearly intended to undermine the proposed legislation resulting from the work of the Pujo Committee.[238]

The Pujo Committee's Report also recommended further state securities market regulation. Untermyer actively supported such legislation in his own state. Governor William C. Sulzer was a political ally of Louis Marshall. Sulzer had been the Progressive Democrat victor of the 1912 gubernatorial election.[239] He sent a special message to the New York State Assembly at the end of January 1913 supporting stock exchange regulation. He left the issue of stock exchange incorporation open.[240] However, Sulzer subsequently included a bill to incorporate the stock exchange among the stock exchange regulation bills introduced to the State Legislature.[241] In early April he invited Untermyer to meet him in Albany to discuss the question of making the New York Stock Exchange incorporate. Untermyer believed that the governor would sign the incorporation bill, if it was passed by the State Legislature.[242] While he was in Albany Untermyer appeared before the New York Senate Judiciary Committee, where he made a long argument in support of the incorporation bill.[243] The New York *Sun* published a cartoon which suggested that Untermyer was secretly pulling the strings behind the governor's chair to achieve stock exchange reform.[244] There may be some truth to this allegation. Untermyer was an ally of Tammany Hall

Illustration 8 Oscar Cesare's 'The People Demand Stock Exchange Legislation' Cartoon, 1913.

Boss Murphy. Sulzer had fallen out with Murphy, so Untermyer could not publicly support the governor.

Sulzer's efforts were to no avail. In early May, the Senate Judiciary Committee's adverse report on the incorporation bill was sustained by the full Senate. Van Antwerp later claimed credit for successfully lobbying against the bill. His allies, the elite investment bankers' organization, the Investment Bankers Association, also made a significant contribution to the bill's defeat. Sulzer also had to withdraw two of his reform bills. He did, however, succeed in enacting laws to tighten the law against bucket shops, a law introducing a penalty for the manipulation of quotations on securities, a law prohibiting brokers from trading against the orders of customers and a law requiring brokers to provide customers with a memorandum detailing the day and hour of transactions undertaken on their behalf on the Exchange.[245] Ott notes that the New York Stock Exchange supported the law against bucket shops, firms 'that accepted wagers on the movement of stock prices as recorded on ticker tape, with no physical trade of stock'.[246] Untermyer later observed that these laws were 'worse than worthless'.[247] Later that year in August Tammany Hall orchestrated a vote in the State Assembly to initiate impeachment proceedings against Sulzer. Sulzer assembled an impressive group of lawyers for his defence, including Untermyer's partner, Marshall.[248] Sulzer was the first of only two New York state governors to lose office as the result of impeachment.[249] Untermyer undoubtedly regarded the impeachment of Sulzer as a mistake. In a speech the following February he described Tammany Hall as an organization 'for which every self-respecting Democrat must apologize' and demanded the overthrow of Tammany Hall Boss Murphy.[250]

The work of the Pujo Committee made a major contribution to the Federal Reserve Act of 1913. Although Glass tried to prevent Untermyer from getting hold of copies of the proposed bill and other relevant information,[251] he was unsuccessful. Untermyer later recalled that his ally Senator Robert L. Owen had provided him with a copy of the bill. He was told it had been prepared by Willis for Glass and had been presented by the latter to the president. It provided for a central bank, for banking money and banking control. During May 1913 word was conveyed to Untermyer in New York that such a bill had been submitted to the president, and he was urged to come immediately to Washington to endeavour to dissuade the president from accepting or submitting it. On 18 May he took the midnight train to Washington and appeared early the following morning at the home of Secretary of State Bryan. Untermyer recounted to him what was happening, and he suggested that he see the President. Bryan was greatly excited, and they drove immediately to the White House, where they met with the president. Bryan told the president that he would use his personal influence to defeat any bill such as he understood had been submitted to him by Glass, providing for a central bank and banking control and that he hoped Wilson would not support any such legislation. After discussion of the merits of Untermyer and Bryan's plan for regional banks and government control, Wilson stated that he was in accord with their views, and they were led to believe that Glass's bill would never see the light of day.

When the bill reached the Senate, it was referred to the Banking and Currency Committee, of which Senator Owen was chairman. From that time on, he and Untermyer were in frequent conference. They had the same view. They both believed in the regional banking system governed by a Federal Reserve Board controlled by the government and with government money. Untermyer later recollected that 'A great hue and cry went up from the banking community all over the country, but principally from the great bankers of New York. They joined in the chorus that the proposed legislation would ruin the country.' Neither Owen nor Untermyer could see it that way. They accordingly initiated several Sunday morning conferences at Untermyer's home at Greystone, to which they invited one by one several of the leading bankers who were opposed to the bill, including Vanderlip, A. Barton Hepburn and Paul M. Warburg. As a result of these conferences, they concluded that there was no substance in the opposition and that its purpose was to bring about the defeat of Untermyer and Owen's plan and to substitute one that would give the bankers the control of the money system of the country.[252]

Untermyer also sought the assistance of House to get the recommendations of the Pujo Report enacted. In early May Untermyer met with House and Owen at Greystone.

Untermyer also held a luncheon at Greystone in mid-May for Bryan where financial legislation was discussed. Untermyer and Bryan both believed the federal government should exercise the function of issuing money. Among the fifty guests at the lunch were Governor James M. Cox of Ohio, Brandeis, George W. Perkins and George Foster Peabody, a wealthy banker and member of the New York Stock Exchange who had become a reformer. There was a pre-lunch reception attended by Bryan, House, Brandeis and Norman Hapgood, the editor of *Harper's Weekly*. The latter three were unable to stay for the lunch. House recorded in his diary that Untermyer did not seem to have an orthodox view of the currency question.[253]

On 17 May[254] Untermyer met Senator Owen and Paul M. Warburg at Greystone to discuss the banking bill. House observed the day before to Warburg 'that Untermyer did not like Carter Glass, and I thought he was doing all he could to make trouble between Owen and Glass, and to get a bill as different from Glass' as was possible.'[255] Warburg later recalled that after the meeting House shared with him the complete text of the draft bill that Owen and Untermyer had discussed with him at Greystone. Later while en route to Europe he wrote a memorandum in which he tried to disabuse Untermyer and Owen of the views that they had expressed to him in their meeting with him, adding at the end an argument against the draft bill. He sent the memorandum to Untermyer asking him to forward to Owen. Warburg also sent a copy to House[256] who shared it with Wilson.[257]

Untermyer had a further meeting with House on 19 May. House then advised President Wilson that a currency bill along the lines suggested by Untermyer could be drafted in a way acceptable to Bryan and Owen.

House observed in his diary that

> Untermyer has much influence with the House Committee on Currency, other than Glass, and it is exceedingly desirable that all elements get together and agree on such a bill as the President can approve.
>
> ... I suggested that he send for Untermyer and talk with him. He asked if McAdoo could not do it. I thought not, because the question of vanity entered so largely into these matters and the Jews were already more or less disgruntled because they had not been officially recognized.[258]

House also advised Wilson the following day that he believed Untermyer's

> plan is not different from the one we have in mind excepting that it is his purpose to have the Government issue all currency and to be responsible for its payment ... The difficulty is that Untermyer wants too large a share in the making of the measure but I think this can be overcome by bringing about a general agreement between Primus [William Jennings Bryan], Pythias [William Gibbs McAdoo], Owen and Glass, after first getting Untermyer committed to it.[259]

McAdoo did in fact arrange a meeting with Untermyer later that month. Before the meeting Untermyer wrote to McAdoo questioning whether 'such a visit may possibly embarrass you or furnish the pretext for raising a false issue as affecting pending

Currency Reform. The New York financial interests are not anxious that I shall have any connection with financial legislation'. He further observed

> Accompanying [the letter] you will find clippings from the Journal of Commerce of Tuesday, Wednesday and today which I may say in confidence I am reluctantly forced to suspect have been inspired by Mr. Glass or Mr. Willis. The latter, as you know, has long been a financial writer on the Journal of Commerce and is said to have prepared the tentative bill presented by Mr. Glass. I cannot understand how these articles could have emanated from any other source.
>
> The attitude of Mr. Glass for months past has been a continual surprise to me and is entirely at variance with his repeated professions to me. Mr. Glass, Senator Owen and I happen to have been born in the same town and I have for a long time refused to believe the stories that have come to me.
>
> My sole aim is to be helpful, provided those concerned and who have the responsibility of this great task believe that there is any direction in which I can be of aid in the performance of the most important public service of many years.
>
> I want no credit or notoriety in connection with it. Above all things I want to avoid being made the occasion of friction or disturbance, for that would complicate instead of help the result that I am anxious to see achieved. If friction is within the range of possibility I would like to be kept entirely out of any connection with the work.[260]

McAdoo's reply has not survived, but he must have advised Untermyer not to stand down.

Untermyer later met with McAdoo again on 19 June together with Senator Owen to discuss the pending Currency Legislation. As agreed at this meeting he subsequently wrote a synopsis of the conversation for McAdoo on 21 June. It was agreed that Untermyer

> gather information and make a report (1) as to the modus operandi of inaugurating a more effective system of dealing in commercial paper that will render such paper marketable through the introduction of the European methods of drafts, acceptances and rediscounts; and (2) as to the objections, if any, that may be legitimately urged from the point of view of the leading European students of finance to the pending proposal for the issue of currency by the Government, carrying the direct obligation of the latter redeemable in gold as against the existing system here and abroad, of bank-note currency.

Untermyer further observed it seemed 'grotesque' that the United States had no market for the discount of bills and acceptances unlike elsewhere in other parts of the world. He noted that the proposed bill was 'crude and indefinite in this respect'. He argued that it should authorize the national banks and proposed reserve banks to sell commercial paper bearing their endorsements in the international commercial markets. Untermyer suggested he could confer with the leading financial experts on this subject in and out of official life in London, Paris and Berlin during his annual

European tour and make a report to assist the Wilson administration in perfecting the Currency Bill and the National Banking Act in that respect.²⁶¹ McAdoo and Owen agreed to Untermyer's 'unofficial inquiry'.²⁶²

Untermyer also wrote to Glass expressing his disappointment at three features of the proposed bills, issues he had also raised with McAdoo.

1. The limitation of the issue of Government Currency to $500,000,000;
2. The elimination of the provisions for the retirement of the bond-secured bank-note currency; and
3. The fact that State institutions may in the discretion of the Federal Reserve Board become members of a Reserve Bank without being restricted as to their loans or investments to the limitations of a National Bank.

The limitation upon the issue of currency will invite rather than prevent disaster. It is likely to lead to a scramble for currency that is not needed when the limit is about to be reached, from fear that there will be none left.

The elimination of the provision for the retirement of the bond-secured bank-note currency converts the entire Bill into a mere emergency measure instead of its being the basis of a comprehensive system.

The third feature may disrupt the National Banking system as it would furnish every incentive for the conversion of National Banks into State Banks.²⁶³

Untermyer also felt that it would be impossible to mobilize the gold reserves with as many as twelve banks. He felt half that number would be far better because that would

> also to avoid having New York City dominate the other Reserve banks by reason of its abnormal power as compared with a number of smaller institutions. New York should be segregated and constituted a region of its own and only four or five other Reserve Banks almost – if not quite as – powerful should be constituted.²⁶⁴

However, Untermyer chose not to raise this issue with Glass in his letter. However, his concern was prescient. The Federal Reserve Bank of New York did dominate the other eleven banks after the establishment of the Federal Reserve System.

While he was in Europe Untermyer met with several British, French and German bankers, including Arthur Salomonsohn, a German banker affiliated with the Disconto-Gesellschaft Bank,²⁶⁵ and Karl Helfferich of the Deutsche Bank and a member of the central committee of the Reichsbank,²⁶⁶ to discuss the proposed American banking legislation.²⁶⁷ Helfferich, as he later reported to Warburg, pointed out to Untermyer the misgivings that he had with regard to certain important provisions of the bill. Although Untermyer had taken note of his concerns, Helfferich did not think that the revisions to the bill had gone far enough.

> Even the Federal Advisory Council, which has been inserted in the Bill during the course of the current discussions, does not dispel my misgivings. I assume that this Advisory Council is a result of Mr. Untermyer's European trip, and possibly

this proposal has reference to the conversations which Mr. Untermyer had with German bankers. In all these conversations, he was doubtless referred to the very sound arrangement of the Reichbank's Central Committee.[268]

In September Glass decided to enlist the support of Untermyer in support of the banking bill.[269] On 22, 23 and 29 September Untermyer testified at the hearing held by the Senate Committee on Banking and Currency on the bill. He suggested important modifications. Untermyer's principal suggestion was that security for the notes to be issued under the proposed system be limited to commercial paper in the strictest meaning of that term. Issues of currency based on the looser definition in the bill would lead to great inflation, as the term would include paper that would prove upon test to be anything but liquid.[270] Untermyer's testimony was followed with an article in *The North American Review* entitled 'Why the Pending Bill Should Pass'. Once again, he suggested some modifications to the bill.[271] The Federal Reserve Act was finally passed and signed into law on 23 December 1913.

Earlier, on 5 December, Benjamin Strong, Jr. of the Bankers' Trust Co. had written to Republican senator Theodore E. Burton that he was afraid there might be another Untermyer investigation following the enactment of the Federal Reserve legislation. He observed

> One reason why it seems wise to endeavor to clip the wings of Mr. Samuel Untermyer is because Senator Owen, in making his presentation [on the legislation], stated that Mr. Untermyer was one of the most patriotic gentlemen in this country, or words to that effect, which would seem to imply that it is the present intention of those in control of the Democratic program to again employ Mr. Untermyer to carry on some sort of investigation that may seriously disrupt business. There is undoubtedly a very strong undercurrent of fear existing in the minds of business men, not because of any truth that might be brought out concerning business methods, etc., but because that they anticipate further misrepresentation, and consequently do not know where they stand. Mr. Untermyer used his position as counsel for the Pujo committee entirely for the purpose of exploiting himself and his unusual ability as a cross-examining lawyer.[272]

Later that month Strong received better news in a memorandum from a partner on a conference between Wilson and some members of the House of Representatives Judiciary Committee on 9 December where an understanding had been reached as to the scope of the anti-trust legislation. 'The President's position was said, by one of those present at the conference, to be conservative ... This would indicate that Untermeyer [sic] has not been retained to write any of this legislation, as he confided to a newspaper man recently.'[273] The newspaper report was untrue.[274] However, Untermyer and Louis D. Brandeis had held an informal meeting in Washington four days earlier with Congressman Henry D. Clayton, chairman of the House Judiciary Committee, who was to have charge of the Wilson administration's anti-trust programme, Joseph E. Davies, Wilson's Commissioner of Corporations, and Congressman Robert Lee Henry to discuss their ideas for anti-trust legislation.[275]

Strong's fears about another Untermyer investigation were unjustified. In fact, a few days earlier in an address to the Economic Club of Springfield, Massachusetts, Untermyer had argued in favour of a halt in the investigation of past business misdeeds because of the damage it might do to the economy. He told the club

> I am in favor of a general amnesty. Let us wipe the slate and begin the work of so reframing and strengthening our laws that there can be no repetition of the past without the certainty of prompt detection and punishment.

Untermyer proposed a federal industrial commission to attend to the details of dissolving trusts and with power to authorize temporary agreements fixing prices and output. He also advocated 'living rates' for the railroads and declared the New York Stock Exchange had inaugurated 'sweeping reforms', but still needed incorporation to regain public confidence.[276] Untermyer was not pleased with the effect of this speech and felt the press had misrepresented it.[277]

Several members of the Wilson administration, including McCombs and Joseph P. Tumulty, proposed Untermyer as the next ambassador to France in late November 1913, apparently at the lawyer's behest. House did not offer his support.[278] However, according to House, Wilson was emphatic in his decision not to appoint Untermyer. House then observed to Wilson that in his opinion

> Untermyer was trying to do right and was accomplishing a great deal of good; that he had made all the money he desired and was now devoting himself to public and charitable purposes. I related a discussion I had heard concerning Untermyer, one man taking the stand that his success had a bad influence upon the youth of the country, the other contended that his failure to obtain public recognition was in itself a good lesson to the youth of the country. The President thought both gentlemen were correct. Personally I am not certain, for Untermyer has done many things of great public value.[279]

Untermyer also asked McAdoo to speak with Bryan and Wilson on his behalf.[280] It would appear McAdoo neglected to report back to Untermyer that Wilson was unwilling to appoint him ambassador to France.[281]

In January 1914, on his way to meet a court engagement in Kansas City Untermyer stopped over a few hours in Chicago to address the Illinois Manufacturers' Association.[282] In his address he again advocated an industrial commission to break up trusts and regulate corporations. Untermyer argued that

> The reactionary advocates of a 'let-alone' policy fail to realize that we [sic] cannot build an enduring structure upon rotten foundations and that the clearing of the debris is as important a part of the work of construction as is the rearing of the new structure.[283]

In this speech Untermyer focussed on violations of the spirit of the law by J.P. Morgan & Co. Untermyer referred to the existence of holding companies in the railroad industry and the inappropriateness of railroads being vertically integrated. He proposed various further financial and corporate reforms. Untermyer also attacked the recent Union Pacific-Southern Pacific dissolution as well as that in the Standard Oil case as ineffective.[284] On his return to New York Untermyer wrote to his friend Colonel House:

> I found the West – Republicans and Democrats alike – enthusiastic over the Administration, far beyond anything I had expected or have ever before seen. The transition was like coming from a charnel house into the fresh air.[285]

A few days later the Wilson administration published its tentative plans for anti-trust legislation. Five of the six proposals were similar to those made by Untermyer in his Chicago address.[286] He felt that the proposed trade board should have broader inquisitorial power.[287] On 6 February Untermyer testified before the House Judiciary Committee on their three tentative anti-trust bills. The *New York Times* reported that he disagreed with those who would absolutely prohibit all corporations from acquiring or holding the stocks of other companies. Such a prohibition would prevent the organization of purely security holding companies, which Untermyer thought were very desirable as a means of equalizing the risks of investment for small holders. He also felt it would prevent many useful cooperative enterprises from exploiting mines, patents and similar enterprises.[288] Untermyer was asked by the House Judiciary Committee to redraft the five new trust bills in accordance with his suggestions as a basis for future conferences with the committee.[289]

On 25 January Untermyer had written a confidential letter to House, which was seen by Wilson, regarding his fears regarding the anti-trust legislation being considered by Congress. Untermyer believed that the character of the legislation enacted would be the supreme test of the Wilson administration.

> The proposed Bills are in my judgment lamentably weak and ineffective. As to some of them one would imagine they were purposely so drawn but I know that is not the case. It reflects merely ignorance of the subject...
>
> The depressing feature of the situation is that there is apparently no capacity among the Chairman of the Committees to deal with this complex question. They are 'all in the air' and we are likely to get a body of meaningless legislation which when dissected and tested in years to come – as it is bound to be – will discredit the party.[290]

Untermyer also campaigned in support of the 'Pujo Investigation' subsidiary bill he drafted to regulate and incorporate the stock exchanges on behalf of his friend Senator Owen.[291] As already noted, in early January 1914 he had addressed the Illinois Manufacturers' Association in Chicago. As already noted, in his wide-ranging speech he also called for the incorporation of the nation's stock exchanges. He argued this lay at the foundation of all corporate reform. He observed:

> Until Government protection is furnished against wash sales, matched orders and manipulation of prices the Exchange cannot be helpful as the medium between the

corporations and the investing public which it can and should be made. So long as its members may with impunity rehypothecate the securities of their customers in excess of the debt owing them and pay one another in full out of the proceeds of the membership seat in case of insolvency to the exclusion of the defrauded customers, the Stock Exchange is no fit instrument for carrying out the great reforms in corporate management for which it might otherwise be used.[292]

During the same month Untermyer returned to the theme of stock exchange reform when he appeared before the Senate Committee on Banking and Currency to explain the Owen bill.[293] In further testimony in February, opponents of the Owen bill sought to undermine it by impugning Untermyer's integrity. He was accused of short selling and Nebraska Democratic senator Gilbert M. Hitchcock also questioned him at length about the Columbia Straw Paper affair.[294] Hitchcock also suggested Untermyer 'had experience with the stock exchange and stock-exchanges rules which had embittered him against it'. Untermyer vigorously defended himself.

> I am glad that you said that, Senator Hitchcock, because it is absolutely false. I have no feeling against the stock exchange or any of its members. I have never had any unpleasant experience with the stock exchange in my life.[295]

Meanwhile the New York Stock Exchange presented a lengthy brief and reply brief opposing the bill and refuting the case made for the incorporation and regulation of the exchange.[296] John G. Milburn, counsel for the exchange, argued that

> Mr. Untermyer devotes a great deal of space [in the Pujo Report] to what purports to be a discussion of the necessity of the incorporation of the exchange, but which is really a discussion of all sorts of matters that have no relation whatsoever to the subject. The one fundamental point for him to meet he avoids. That point is, that every requirement of this bill and every mode of regulation that has been suggested by him or anyone can be applied to an unincorporated exchange as well as to one that is incorporated, and therefore incorporation is not essential to any form of regulation... Mr. Untermyer does not answer it. Failing to do so, his whole case for incorporation falls to the ground.[297]

Jacob Lippman praises Untermyer's 'brilliant and hard-hitting defense' of the bill during the hearings.[298] But it was insufficient to get the bill enacted. By the time it was reported to the Senate Committee on Banking and Currency in late June 1914 it had failed to gain the necessary support.[299] One senator claimed he knew only one man in favour of the bill, Untermyer. Owen replied that there was one other, because he was also in favour. It was stricken from the Senate's calendar, at which time Owen was at sea on his way to Europe with Untermyer.[300] One of the reasons of the bill failed to gain sufficient support in the Senate was because stock exchange reform was not part of Wilson's 1912 platform. Wilson was ambivalent at best about the bill and declined to publicly support it.[301] Untermyer also argued that much of the opposition to the bill came from newspapers which feared the bill would infringe on the freedom of the press. Hitchcock, who was a newspaper proprietor, argued Untermyer was incorrect. The newspapers did not object to the exclusion of fraudulent and improper material from the mail; they opposed the establishment of the Postmaster General or any other federal official as public censor.[302]

Untermyer's campaign for the stock exchange regulation generated a lot of criticism from supporters of the status quo, including the *New York Times*. He wrote a long letter at the end of November 1914 to the *Times* reiterating his case for government regulation of the stock exchange.[303] Untermyer was also to make the stock exchange one of the main themes of his paper presented at the twenty-seventh annual meeting of the American Economic Association in Princeton, New Jersey, on 29 December.[304] The American Economic Association had been founded in 1885 to promote a 'New Political Economy' by, among others, Woodrow Wilson.[305] In his paper Untermyer noted that during the previous two years the New York Stock Exchange had established a press bureau called the 'Library Committee' to promote its reforms in response to the public disquiet resulting from the revelations of the Money Trust investigation. He argued 'its reforms are exaggerated and its abuses and defects are hidden as never before in its history.'[306] Untermyer also noted in a comprehensive expose of the New York Stock Exchange how it unilaterally imposed its rules on the New York Curb Market. The Curb was prohibited from dealing in any securities listed on the exchange or that the latter may choose at any time to place on its list.[307] One of the designated discussants of Untermyer's paper was William C. Van Antwerp, a governor of the exchange, who complained Untermyer had not provided him with an advance copy of his paper.[308] Untermyer subsequently replied that he had no knowledge of any association rule requiring him to submit an advance copy or of the fact Van Antwerp was to be a discussant.[309] Van Antwerp in his response to Untermyer's paper strongly opposed a break with the status quo.[310] He and his fellow members of the exchange were deeply offended that the press only gave brief coverage to the replies to Untermyer's argument for federal regulation of the stock exchange.[311] In response the *New York Times* published on 2 January most of Van Antwerp's refutation at Princeton of Untermyer's arguments and proposed remedies.[312] Untermyer replied to Van Antwerp the following day citing the evidence in the 1909 report of the commission appointed by Governor Hughes and the testimony before the Pujo Committee. He offered to debate the subject with a representative of the exchange before the Economic Club or in Carnegie Hall.[313]

At the end of March 1914, the *New York Times* reported that Untermyer had condemned the Trade Commission bill as 'an empty shell' in the forthcoming number of *The North American Review*.[314] Untermyer argued that

> The latest Bill . . . is most disappointing to the friends of corporate regulation and reform. It relegates the Commission to the position of a mere annex to the office of Attorney General. It cannot even enforce the attendance of witnesses or the production of books without his approval. It can inaugurate no inquiry on its own account to determine whether the law is being violated. . .
>
> This bill does not permit the Commission to go 'hunting for the rat' until some other body or official has 'smelled him' and directed the chase. There is no

provision for complaints by injured parties, and no power to act independently upon them. The bill has been carefully stripped of all vitality and is a mere empty shell...

...It should be the province of the Trade Commission, and of the Interstate Commerce Commission in the case of railroads, to perform for the courts the burden of framing Plans of Segregation and Readjustment of unlawful combinations, subject to the approval of the Court, and to retain jurisdiction, under the direction of the Court, of all corporations that have been thus regulated, *so as to see to the proper enforcement of the decree.* Until we have such a body, charged with that duty, there will be no such thing as an effective dissolution of unlawful combinations. This bill refrains from granting that much-needed power.[315]

Untermyer also privately shared his concerns with President Wilson's secretary, Joseph P. Tumulty.

I trust there is no truth in the persistent newspaper reports from Washington to the effect that all Anti-Trust legislation is to be abandoned for the present session except the passage of the Trade Commission Bill with limited powers of investigation. It seems to me that such a policy instead of quieting the so-called business apprehension would intensify and protract the present state of uncertainty that is alleged to be due to this impending legislation...

To my mind it would be a serious political blunder after all these months of agitation and investigation to enact a colorless Bill that would amount to an abandonment of the program – for that is what the postponement will amount to.[316]

Meanwhile Untermyer continued to give speeches on the trust legislation. In mid-April he addressed the Western Economic Society in Chicago on the relation of the farmer to the trust question. He observed that 'ruinous cutthroat competition' was an 'economic curse'. It disturbed 'the natural currents of trade, leads to spasmodic periods of over-production and under-production and consequent instability of prices, and is the highway to monopoly. It is quite as important to regulate competition as to suppress monopolies and trusts'.[317] He further observed that the incredible situation of extending general immunity to the farmers to violate the law while they are demanding and securing its enforcement against the industrial world would not long be tolerated. The real attitude of the farmer as a producer to the trust question, he declared, was unjust, inconsistent and unwise.[318] Later in a debate at the end of April at the Economic Club of New York Untermyer noted that he did not think the Federal Trade Commission bill went far enough in the direction of regulating competition, although he was very supportive of the proposed new commission. Regarding the omnibus bill, which was to be later enacted as the Clayton Anti-Trust Act, he noted that interlocking directorships were not the fundamental evil to be corrected. The bill needed to be aimed at the interlocking control of competing corporations.[319]

In early May Untermyer appeared before the Senate Committee on Interstate Commerce to propose several detailed amendments to the Trade Commission bill.

These were mostly based on his view that the bill's restrictions should apply not only to incorporated organizations in commerce but also to individual partnerships and other comparatively informal combinations tending to restrain trade.[320] Towards the end of June, the Senate Committee on Interstate Commerce received from Untermyer a series of amendments in the nature of a substitute for Chairman Francis G. Newlands's measure for the establishment of a Federal Trade Commission. The amendments were prepared at the request of the committee and added several features to the original measure. One of Untermyer's amendments was intended to replace the long, expensive and sometimes scandalous process of railroad reorganizations in the United States with court action similar to that of the Companies Act in Great Britain. Another amendment, to the holding company provisions, would require that in cases where such relations are permitted the controlled company must make provision for minority representation on its board, preferably through a plan of cumulative voting. He also suggested prohibiting interlocking stockholding on any large scale between companies that are actual or potential competitors, as well as interlocking directors. He proposed enlarging the scope of the bill so that it should apply to pools, gentlemen's agreements and other devices for fixing prices, as well as to more formal combinations. Another of his provisions was to make it a crime for an interstate corporation to destroy any of its books or to remove them from the jurisdiction of the United States. Untermyer also proposed many textual changes in his amendatory bill.[321]

At the end of June Untermyer left New York to take his annual summer vacation in Europe.[322] He spent a week of his vacation in the City of London engaged in professional business. During his stay in London, Untermyer condemned the Senate for failing to confirm Warburg as a member of the new Federal Reserve Board.[323] This was a particular disappointment because he had had to get Wilson to persuade a reluctant Warburg to accept the nomination. Untermyer had regarded Warburg as 'peculiarly essential' to the success of the Federal Reserve System in its initial stages. He believed there was 'unfortunately no one in our country to take his place'.[324] Wilson declined to withdraw the nomination and persisted with his effort to gain the Senate's approval, achieving success in early August.[325] Earlier in the year Untermyer had also tried to persuade Wilson to nominate him as member of the Federal Reserve Board too. The president had declined his offer:

> I have seen your letter of February second to Mr. Tumulty and want to tell you how much I admire the spirit in which it was written and the conception of public duty by which it was prompted. Certainly no one in the country would doubt your entire fitness and remarkable equipment for the Federal Reserve Board. On that question I differ with you, but I have particularly in mind your very high conception of public duty. That conception is never genuine unless it includes the impulse and principle of self-abnegation.[326]

Wilson's letter is indicative of his unwillingness to provide recognition to Untermyer, who had worked tirelessly on behalf of his administration. Furthermore, neither of the two bills resulting from the Pujo Investigation drafted by Untermyer was ever enacted as such. Had Wilson been more supportive the outcomes might have been different.

However, on the other hand Swaine notes many of his ideas to outlaw various corporate and financial abuses were to be embodied in subsequent federal legislation. For example, recommendations relating to the Clearing House and to bank collection rates were incorporated in the Federal Reserve Act of 1913; restrictions upon interlocking directorships, in the Clayton Act of 1914; and some of the proposals relating to the Stock Exchange, in the Securities Act of 1933 and the Securities Exchange Act of 1934.[327]

3

Untermyer's quest for national public recognition, 1914–40

When the First World War began Untermyer and his family were on vacation in the Bohemian spa town of Carlsbad in Austria-Hungary. They had a strenuous time getting from Carlsbad to London. After they arrived in London, Untermyer spent two weeks assisting thousands of stranded Americans. The Conservative Party Leader, Andrew Bonar Law, helped get the Untermyer party a passage back home to the United States. The Untermyer party arrived in New York on 22 August.[1] On the day of his return to New York he gave a lengthy interview to the *New York Times* in which he revealed his pro-German sympathies

> The impression studiously circulated by the English press, and that has to some extent found its echo in this country, that Germany provoked or encouraged or did nothing to avert the conflict is in flagrant contradiction of the facts as disclosed by the case made by Great Britain herself in the diplomatic correspondence that her government has had the enlightened good sense to publish to the world as the justification for her course.[2]

The First World War pushed Untermyer into a much closer relationship with the Jewish community. Before America's entry into the war, he assisted the efforts of the German government to covertly influence the community in its favour. After America entered the war Untermyer felt it necessary to prove his loyalty by campaigning in elections against left-wing Jewish pacifists who were seeking the support of the community. Then during the Red Scare immediately after the war, as already discussed, he defended some of the very same pacifists.

At the beginning of the war the Wilson administration adopted a policy of neutrality. Untermyer tried to secure the position of American ambassador to Germany to be better able to influence events. In late October he got Treasury Secretary McAdoo to advocate his appointment to replace James W. Gerard. However, George Harvey, editor of *The North American Review*, observed to House while Untermyer 'was well equipped mentally for the place, he doubted whether Germany would receive him'. House felt that McAdoo, who was thinking of leaving the Cabinet, had been influenced by the offer of a position at the Metropolitan Life Insurance Company which had been arranged by Untermyer. Joseph Palmer Knapp, Untermyer's long-standing client, controlled Metropolitan Life. In the event McAdoo stayed in the Cabinet and Gerard retained his post.³ Later that year House asked the German ambassador, Johann Heinrich Count von Bernstorff, if his government would accept Untermyer. He replied that they would during the continuation of the war, but if the war ended, he believed that they would not desire him. The reason for accepting Untermyer during the war was his well-known pro-German sympathies.⁴

Given their strong ties with Germany, both Untermyer and his wife Minnie strongly supported American neutrality in the period before America entered the war. Untermyer argued against an increase in expenditure on the army and navy. He advocated waiting until the militarily exhausted European combatants had ended the war. America might then be able to get a global reduction in arms. However, Untermyer did advocate the creation of a government-owned merchant marine.⁵ Since his advice was not heeded, in December 1916 he proposed a tax on munitions which would have meant that the European combatants would help pay for America's program of military preparedness.⁶

Untermyer's wife Minnie actively campaigned for neutrality in the interest of peace, a cause also supported by his friend Bryan.⁷ House recorded in his diary that she solicited his support in June 1915.

> Mrs. Samuel Untermyer asked over the telephone whether I saw any objection to the German-Americans raising a fund for the purpose of sending a commission to Europe for the purpose of investigating alleged German atrocities. I saw no objection to it. She said that they very much wanted me to be one of the committee, the idea being to have no one who was of German birth or descent, and only those well known throughout the country. She spoke of Jane Addams as having agreed to act. It is not necessary to say that I declined to act.⁸

On 9 June after Bryan had resigned as secretary of state because he feared Wilson's anti-German stance would drag the United States into the First World War, Minnie Untermyer wrote him a letter of support.

> Please forgive me if I say to you that I feel that you are the greatest man of the century, for you have given hope of lasting peace and benefit to all mankind and have given a vision of a glorious sunrise and a new day . . . And have uplifted the hearts of all those Americans who have been bowed with horror and anguish at the thought of war.⁹

Minnie Untermyer continued to support the cause of peace after America's entry into the war by, for example, contributing to the Emergency Peace Federation.¹⁰

After the outbreak of the First World War Untermyer became a counsellor to the German Embassy in Washington. For example, in August 1915 he advised Bernstorff on the wording of a note that he wished to send to the Department of State.¹¹ Francis P. Garvan¹² later described Untermyer as the ablest pro-German propagandist in the United States during the war. America's entry into the war was apparently postponed for months by Bernstorff's semi-official and half-hearted interview in September 1915 to the effect that a break in diplomatic relations would mean war. This was inspired by Untermyer and had a profound effect in Washington; the interview was so well arranged that Bernstorff could not be accused of breaching protocol and addressing the American people directly.[13] Untermyer also assisted German efforts to influence American public opinion. He worked closely with German commercial attaché, Privy Councillor Heinrich Friedrich Albert, who was the representative of the German Imperial Central Purchasing Company in the United States. Untermyer was unaware that Albert was also linked to a campaign of sabotage against American exports of munitions to the Entente Powers.[14]

Unbeknownst to Untermyer, on 14 May 1915 McAdoo was authorized by executive order to employ the Secret Service to conduct surveillance of German diplomats and German American 'suspects'. On Saturday 24 July 1915 Albert[15] lost his briefcase which was full of paperwork on his covert activities on behalf of his government's war effort on an 'El' train in New York City, where it fell into the hands of a Secret Service Agent, Frank Burke.[16] The chief of the Secret Service, William Flynn, informed McAdoo, who was at his summer home in Maine, of the briefcase incident. Flynn met with McAdoo the next day to review the contents of the briefcase, and the Treasury Secretary concluded they were of great significance. The matter was then referred to Wilson and House. They agreed with McAdoo that although much of the material related to perfectly legitimate activities, it should be used against the German government. It was decided that they should be selectively published in an embellished way in the New York *World*.[17] According to a later account by Untermyer's friend, German American writer George Sylvester Viereck, among the documents was an option on a large press association for $900,000 and a plan to purchase the *New York Evening Mail*.[18] These documents almost certainly included correspondence with Untermyer. Viereck later recalled that he, Albert and Dr Karl Alexander Fuehr, Albert's colleague, made a 'hectic automobile trip' to the home of an unnamed influential lawyer who was most likely Untermyer. This lawyer talked to Tumulty, Wilson's secretary, and to a member of the cabinet, on behalf of Viereck and the two Germans. Untermyer did indeed arrange a meeting with McAdoo.[19] It would appear that McAdoo agreed to speak to Wilson on Untermyer's behalf. There is a cryptic reference in a letter from Wilson to his future wife, Edith Boling Galt, to a meeting on 3 August:

> It turned out to be something ... personal to Mr. Sam'l Untermyer, the New York Lawyer, for whom Mac. has a very warm feeling of friendship – not a matter of general interest at all, but one in which he thought we might do Mr. Untermyer a good turn. That and a secret service matter took up all of our hour.[20]

It is likely McAdoo agreed with Wilson to keep Untermyer's name out of the copies of the documents to be published in the *World*.

Untermyer also tried unsuccessfully to persuade the editor of the *World*, Frank J. Cobb, not to publish the papers.[21] It was to no avail. The New York *World* published the papers leaked by Wilson, McAdoo and House. They showed that Germany had many friends in the United States, including Untermyer's friend Viereck. Delicate negotiations regarding the cessation of German submarine warfare and the controversy of Britain's enforcement of its blockade of Germany against neutral American ships were also revealed.²² Viereck later recalled, 'The publication of the Albert papers was a German catastrophe. It dramatized German propaganda. Henceforth the Allied propagandists could go as far as they liked.'²³

Bernstorff and other members of his embassy continued to be honoured guests at Untermyer's home during their frequent visits to New York in 1916, as they had been before this incident.²⁴ Madame Aino Malmberg,²⁵ a German government agent, also claimed Untermyer helped her organize a 'League of Oppressed Nations' to campaign on behalf of the nations oppressed by Russia.²⁶ Malmberg described Untermyer as a 'multi-millionaire and Wall Street banker as well as a close friend of President Wilson'. She also reported that Untermyer gave her a strong letter of recommendation to William Randolph Hearst, whose 2,000 newspapers she hoped to secure for the German cause.²⁷

The German government tried to acquire newspapers to influence public opinion. In 1916 it acquired the *New York Evening Mail*. This did not have much success in changing the public view of Germany. So the embassy in Washington tried to acquire further newspapers, including the New York *Sun*, *Washington Post*, *New York Tribune* and *Harper's Weekly*. Untermyer, and his friend Caleb M. Van Hamm, who was now editor of Hearst's *New York American*, conducted the negotiations on behalf of the embassy. But the German Foreign Ministry refused to approve the purchase and the *Sun* was acquired by another purchaser.²⁸ An investigation by the Military Intelligence Division (MID) later concluded that since Van Hamm was William Randolph Hearst's right-hand man in the procurement of properties, it was probable that had the *Sun* been purchased by Germany, it would have been sold to Hearst after the First World War.²⁹

Untermyer also acquired an interest on behalf of the German government in the *Warheit (Di Varhayt)*, an independent socialist Yiddish paper that had been founded in 1905 to compete with *Forverts* (the *Jewish Daily Forward*).³⁰ Under its editor, Louis E. Miller, the *Warheit* was against Bryan's position on the First World War and anti-German, which had put it at odds with all of the other Jewish daily newspapers. Miller was forced out because he would not turn the *Warheit* into a pro-German publication.³¹ Ehud Manor suggests Miller accepted Untermyer's money because the *Warheit*'s readers were unwilling to forgo their animosity against Russia and their rage at anyone who supported the tsar.³² Untermyer later claimed he had only loaned money to Judge Aaron Jefferson Levy, a Tammany Hall ally and close friend,³³ to purchase stock in the *Warheit*.³⁴ The *Warheit* proved to be a short-term investment because it was taken over and closed in 1919 by the newly founded independent liberal Yiddish newspaper *Der Tog (The Day)*.³⁵

Unbeknownst to Untermyer, he was placed under investigation by the MID before America's entry into the war because of his close contact with German diplomats. An extract from a letter from Captain Karl Boy-Ed, the naval attaché at the German Embassy in Washington, to the Chief of Admiralty Staff of the German Navy, referring to the press statements issued at the time of his expulsion from the United States, suggests where Untermyer's sympathies may have lain.³⁶ The letter was captured by the British at Nazareth.³⁷

> It was no 'boundless carelessness,' but rather a deliberate intention, to attack the American Press at that opportunity. Every statement was drawn up in its

original form by Counsel Samuel Untermyer. He was, at the time of my stay in New York, the unpaid juridical and legal-political adviser to the Imperial Embassy. He is one of the most important, if not the greatest, counsel of the United States, the presumptive successor of Mr. Gerard, if he should leave his Ambassadorial post.[38]

However, Untermyer was to claim that documents such as this one had been fabricated by the British Secret Service, which is not implausible.[39]

The sympathy of many East European Jewish immigrants for left revolutionaries, especially in tsarist Russia, led to questions being raised about their loyalty to the United States. In 1917, Untermyer, in common with some of his fellow elite Jewish peers, spent considerable time and money prior to the passage of the Conscription Law fighting Bolshevism among the Jews on the Lower East Side. As America's entry into the First World War began to become increasingly probable, editors and publishers of New York daily newspapers held a meeting in March 1917 at Greystone to discuss his proposal for the organization of a Jewish League of American Patriots. Untermyer was elected president and Joel Slonim of the *Warheit* was elected secretary. The organization was formally launched at another meeting at the office of Guggenheimer, Untermyer & Marshall. All the Yiddish newspapers excepting *Forverts* were represented on the board of directors. Herman Bernstein represented the Jewish weeklies printed in English. Headquarters were opened in the *Warheit* Building at 163 East Broadway. Several rabbis were persuaded to urge Jewish young men to enlist in the army and navy in their 1917 Passover sermons.[40] After several misleading press reports, Untermyer was keen to stress that the League did not propose the establishment of sectarian army or naval units.[41] He believed Jews should enlist in the American armed forces:

> To those among you who have known the curse and despair of the despotism and persecution that have pursued our race throughout the centuries and to those whose loved ones have suffered from this 'brand of Cain' fostered by religious hatred and bigotry, the opportunity that now comes to you to prove the gratitude and loyalty that are in you and to help shake from the breaking backs of your suffering brethren the yoke of tyranny under which they have so long been struggling, the appeal should be irresistible. America's bugle call for soldiers and sailors in the Army of Humanity must find us ready and responsive.[42]

Untermyer also sought to prove his own family's loyalty to their country through the purchase of Liberty Bonds. In May 1917 he topped the list of Liberty Loan subscribers through a rotogravure section in the *New York Times* with $2 million.[43] In October he undertook a speaking tour through New Jersey, Pennsylvania, Kentucky and Tennessee on behalf of the Treasury Department in support of the Liberty Loan. He reported to McAdoo's assistant, George R. Cooksey, that he found

> considerable apathy among the masses of the people with respect to the Loan. Strangely they do not yet seem to understand why we are at war and many of them hardly realise the grim fact that we are at war. I am confident that when the true

situation dawns upon them the country will respond with all the money that is needed to carry the country to a victorious conclusion.[44]

In October Untermyer purchased another $1 million of Liberty Bonds.[45] At the end of the month McAdoo announced that the Second Liberty Loan had been greatly oversubscribed and that in four weeks the American people had subscribed more than $5 billion.[46] Untermyer sent his friend a telegram to offer

> Hearty congratulations[!] It is a magnificent and a great personal triumph for you. It is the most effective blow yet struck in vindication of our self[-]respect since we declared war. All honor also to the bankers of the country whose patriotic [sic] and enthusiasm have known no bounds[.] The war has kindled a new spirit[.] It was almost worth[-]while for that alone[.][47]

In January 1918 Untermyer urged people to buy War Savings Stamps.[48] In September he purchased another $500,000 of Liberty Bonds as his contribution to the Fourth Liberty Loan Campaign.[49] His bountifulness encouraged Jacob H. Schiff to invite him to join the United War Work Campaign. The banker observed that he wanted to ensure that the Jewish Section did not amount to less than $3½ million.[50] Untermyer responded with a contribution of $10,000 which he noted was in addition to the sum he intended to subscribe to the Jewish end of the campaign at Yonkers.[51] Schiff acknowledged Untermyer's contribution and observed:

> May I assure you that I feel highly honoured that you have chosen the team of which I am Captain to make this very generous contribution, and also, that I do not under-estimate your kind recognition of the service Providence has permitted me to render to our people and mankind?[52]

However, Untermyer's generosity was the result of necessity not conviction.[53]

During the month before the mid-term elections of 1914 Untermyer was out West trying a case in Oklahoma City. On the way home to New York, he stopped off in Denver, Colorado, where he gave a campaign speech in support of Senator Charles S. Thomas. Then at the request of Thomas he gave a speech in Salt Lake City on behalf of the Democratic candidate for the US Senate who was hoping to unseat the Republican incumbent, Reed Smoot.[54] While the Democrats performed well across the country this was not the case in New York. Untermyer commissioned an analysis of the result of the Democratic campaign in his State by Thomas D. McCarthy, who had been Judge James W. Gerard's campaign manager in his unsuccessful campaign for election to the US Senate. McCarthy concluded that supporters of Sulzer had declined to vote for the Democratic ticket. McCarthy observed that Sulzer's impeachment in 1913 was 'one of the greatest political blunders of our political life. This surely deprived the gubernatorial candidate, Martin H. Glynn, and Gerard of at least 100,000 votes'.[55]

In mid-January, Untermyer testified before the Federal Commission on Industrial Relations. He argued that the captains of industry did not seem to recognize the rights of labour until they were forced to do so, and they had industrial organization so arranged that a small group of bankers in Wall Street could control a very large number of enterprises. He read out a list of railroads, which he said were controlled by J.P. Morgan & Co. and Kuhn, Loeb & Co., and denounced the proxy system. He also regretted that the federal act, which forbade interlocking directorates, had not gone further, and prohibited the ownership by the same group of men of corporations in competition with each other.[56]

Jacob H. Schiff of Kuhn, Loeb & Co. and J.P. Morgan, Jr. both denied Untermyer's claims. Schiff argued in his testimony to the commission that it was 'sheer nonsense' to claim that the railroads were controlled by two large firms of bankers. He stated:

> There is absolutely no control of the railroads, except such as is exercised indirectly by officers and Directors for the time being, who send out proxies, which the stockholders can return if they wish or let alone. When shareholders are neglectful and are not watchful, then things go wrong. Whenever there is railroad mismanagement, it is due to the neglect of the shareholders.

Schiff was then asked to comment on Untermyer's claim that after a reorganization, bankers, though they retained but a small number of shares, were able to keep control of the company. He replied that

> Mr. Untermyer may be correct in some cases, . . . but the attitude of bankers, to whom widely scattered shareholders look for protection, is that they would be gladly rid of the burden. The stockholders still look to the bankers to protect them.[57]

Untermyer responded to Morgan's denial by observing:

> The fact that Mr. Morgan has 'never noticed' that his firm and that of Kuhn, Loeb & Co. together dominate a majority of the great systems (I did not say of all the railroads of the country) is neither persuasive nor surprising if he knows as much or as little about such conditions as he professes to know about the corporations of which he is a Director.[58]

The following month Untermyer gave a speech in which he said government control of the railroads was preferable to that of the banks.[59]

In April Untermyer was retained by the US attorney general to assist Brandeis in the defence of the Comptroller of the Currency, John Skelton Williams, and McAdoo in the suit against them by the Riggs National Bank.[60] The two men were accused of conspiring to destroy the bank.[61] Senator Henry F. Hollis observed to Williams that

> This fight will keep the Democratic Party on the radical side and opposed to the money power. After President Wilson's election, I was afraid that the Wall Street interests would find a way to get the National Administration under their influence so that the Party might serve them rather than the whole people. This fight will settle that question for many years.[62]

Untermyer had previously acted as counsel on behalf of the Blair-Warfield interests in opposition to Williams in the reorganization of the Seaboard Air Line Railway.[63] The following month Judge Walter I. McCoy in the Equity Division of the Supreme Court of the District of Columbia ruled in favour of Williams and McAdoo and in Untermyer's opinion the suit was 'shown to be a grossly groundless and malicious suit'.[64] However, as McAdoo observed to Untermyer the court had failed to uphold the government on the $5,000 fine which Williams had imposed on the bank. This allowed the Riggs Bank, through 'the subservience of the news agencies', to convey the impression to the country that it had won a victory. McAdoo thought this was 'extremely disgusting'.[65] McAdoo consulted Untermyer on the comptroller's official response to the Riggs Bank's subsequent request to abrogate its national charter in favour of a state one.[66] The following year Attorney General Thomas W. Gregory refused to employ Untermyer in the subsequent Riggs Bank criminal prosecution case against the wishes of McAdoo. House recorded that Wilson supported Gregory's position.[67]

During the same month Untermyer was among the representatives of the United States who attended the six-day Pan American Financial Conference held from 24 to 29 May in Washington. It had been organized by McAdoo as part of an effort by the Wilson administration to increase trade between North and South America.[68] Untermyer was one of the American representatives appointed by the treasury secretary to a conference committee to consider 'Uniformity in the Laws Relating to Trade and Commerce and the Establishment of an International Commercial Court'. The twelve American representatives also included one of Untermyer's former clients, Benjamin Strong, Jr., now governor of the Federal Reserve Bank of New York. The committee held several sessions and, in its final report, recommended the establishment of an International High Commission composed of nine members resident in each country represented at the conference appointed by the respective ministers of finance.[69] McAdoo accepted the committee's recommendation and formed an International High Commission on Uniform Legislation. He appointed Untermyer to the commission the following month.[70] The conference may have inspired him to write to McAdoo on 19 June asking him whether the administration would be interested in him arranging a loan to organize and equip an army of at least 100,000 men to establish a constitutional government in Mexico, to restore and maintain order, and to assure the stability of the new government.[71] At the time of Untermyer's proposal Mexico had been a failed state for several years. McAdoo referred it to Wilson, who replied:

> I have read the ... letter with a great deal of attention and you may be sure [to] fully credit the motive Mr. Untermyer had in writing it. My great trouble is this: I do not see how it is going to be possible to allow the private interests most concerned in Mexico to finance her government without putting that government virtually under their control, and I fear that, whatever the understanding might be, the country would feel most uneasy about it. Do you see any way of working it out?[72]

Kendrick A. Clements notes a few weeks later Wilson was angered by a rumour that the National City Bank was offering financial support to Mexico's Constitutionalist leader Venustiano Carranza in exchange for mining and banking concessions. Clements notes the president raised the same concern as he had in his response to Untermyer's proposal.[73]

The following spring the International High Commission held a conference in Argentina. Untermyer and his wife Minnie were among the delegation headed by McAdoo and his wife Eleanor that travelled to the conference. They left Washington Navy Yard on 7 March aboard the president's yacht, the *Mayflower*. Wilson and House were there to say goodbye. At Hampton Roads the delegation transferred to the armoured cruiser *Tennessee*, on which they were to sail to South America.[74] They arrived in Buenos Aires on 1 April.[75]

Untermyer served as the American representative on the conference committee on negotiable instruments. He made a detailed proposal as to how further progress toward uniformity regarding bills of exchange might be achieved without interfering with the binding force of the Hague Convention of 1912.[76] Untermyer also served on the conference subcommittee on patents, trademarks and copyrights. He urged the importance of the early ratification of the trademarks convention of the Fourth International Conference of American States by governments which had not already done so. He also proposed some amendments to two articles of the 1910 Buenos Aires convention and an addition to one of them. Untermyer failed to persuade the subcommittee to make a decision on these proposals.[77] The conference reached several important decisions, including the establishment of a permanent organization with headquarters in Washington, DC. The McAdoo delegation left Buenos Aires on 14 April, travelling on a special train provided by the Argentine government across the pampas and over the Andes to Santiago in Chile.[78] The delegation received an enthusiastic reception in Chile.[79] After spending a few days as guests of the Chilean government the McAdoo delegation re-joined the *Tennessee*, where they learnt that further up the west coast of South America there had been a suspected outbreak of bubonic plague. Major General George W. Goethals, governor of the Panama Canal Zone, advised McAdoo that he was introducing strict quarantine regulations.[80] So the McAdoo delegation did not go ashore when they docked in Lima, Peru. Only Secretary McAdoo went ashore to meet the president of Peru.[81] The *Tennessee* arrived back at Hampton Roads on the evening of 3 May.[82] Although the Wilson administration worked to build on the progress made with the project in Buenos Aires, the Harding administration dropped the entire project.[83]

Untermyer was considered for the Democratic Party nomination as its candidate to succeed Senator O'Gorman in the 1916 general election.[84] The New York *Sun* observed:

> Mr. Untermyer is a close friend of Louis D. Brandeis, nominated by President Wilson for the United States Supreme Court, and Washington influences are seen in the suggestion that Mr. Untermyer be a delegate at large as forerunner to other party honors later. With Brandeis upon the Supreme Court bench and Untermyer in the United States Senate, friends of President Wilson pointed out that the progressives of the country in both parties readily could appreciate that President Wilson was certainly progressive, If not radical.[85]

In early August Untermyer withdrew his name from those being considered, announcing to the press that his poor health meant he would be unable to withstand the strain of a campaign. The following month he was operated on at Greystone for intestinal trouble.[86] However, in private he had informed McAdoo on 7 August

> I have today definitely declined. I did not care to take responsibility of possibly affecting National Ticket although party leaders here seemed to feel it would be strengthened. This leaves me free to assist.[87]

The New York *Sun* suggested that Untermyer had concluded that the Democratic Party would not win statewide in the upcoming general election. Referring to the nomination it observed:

> if Samuel Untermyer wouldn't take it, they say, it is pretty good evidence that Wilson will run so poorly in this State as to make a Senate nomination worthless. The disposition among Tammany leaders is to assume that Untermyer knew when to quit.[88]

Tammany chose William F. McCombs to reward him for Wilson's ungrateful disregard for his services in the 1912 campaign.[89] The *New York Tribune* concluded in September that McCombs's prospects for victory were nil unless he was able to win all of the votes of those who voted for the Progressive Party in 1914. The *Tribune* concluded that was unlikely because the Progressive Party had endorsed the Republican candidate, William M. Calder.[90] Calder defeated McCombs in the November election.[91]

In June, on the eve of the Democratic National Convention, Untermyer commented on the nomination of US Supreme Court justice Charles Evans Hughes by the Republican Party as its presidential candidate.

> The acceptance of this nomination by Mr. Hughes is a great disappointment to many of his best friends and warmest admirers in the legal profession. It was generally believed by them that he would refuse to set the precedent of encouraging the use of exulted post of Supreme Court Justice as a hatching nest for political ambition. Until now we have rested secure that this great court and every member of it were dedicated beyond recall to the sacred duty of construing and safeguarding our Constitution, and that here, at least, neither political ambition nor political expediency could enter. Henceforth our people will have to scan with a jealous eye every decision of that court affecting the rights and obligations of labor and of corporations and every construction of our Constitution involving principles of economic government and social justice.[92]

In early September Untermyer took his houseboat *Nirodha* on a trip up to Maine. While he was there, he gave two speeches in support of the Wilson administration.[93] Referring to the forthcoming presidential election Untermyer said that 'The one great issue ... is the struggle between invisible government and the people.' He explained what he meant by 'invisible government.'

It means rule under hidden influence, by a handful of the most ambitious money kings with which any country has ever been afflicted, bound together by a common malign purpose to exploit our great wealth and resources for their own selfish ends. It means that through their control over the lawmakers they mould our policies of tariffs, taxation, finance, railroads and business and that we must pay tribute to them in known and unknown ways in almost every phase of our industrial life.[94]

At McAdoo's behest Untermyer paid for the publication of his speeches to be distributed on behalf of the Democratic National Committee.[95]

Untermyer was in Maine to explain national issues to the voters for the Democratic Party in their September election campaign – the state held its election for the US Senate and House of Representatives in September rather than November. Untermyer observed to McAdoo he had concluded no prospect of the Democrats carrying the state in the election.[96] The *Chicago Tribune* suggested he might not have helped his party:

Untermyer appears to have encountered an antagonistic atmosphere, presumably due to temperamental reasons. At any rate his experience inspired him to respond to an impulse to express an opinion which was exploited by the Republicans 'as an insult to the intelligent voters of Maine'.

This opinion in effect was that the rural voters of the state did not know anything about the international situation, with which he concerned himself, and cared less. Democratic leaders, possessing an appreciation of the sensitiveness of the rural voter of Maine, deplore the indiscretion of Untermyer and wish he had refrained from expressing his purely personal view.[97]

Untermyer's prediction of the election result was correct. The Democrats lost the gubernatorial election, a seat in the US Senate and a seat in the House of Representatives.[98] Untermyer observed to McAdoo that the election result indicated the return of the Progressives to the Republican Party. It would give 'the Republicans new hope and courage and a tremendous impetus for the real work of the [general election] campaign'.[99]

While he was in Maine Untermyer became involved in the 'Mrs. Peck Affair'. A former mistress of President Wilson, Mary Allen Peck, was allegedly trying to blackmail him with some compromising personal correspondence. Rumours were apparently circulating and in early September Untermyer forwarded to McAdoo a copy of a letter he had received from a lawyer in Indiana informing him of an article in the September issue of *McClure's Magazine*, 'That Parkinson Affair', which referred to the scandal using pseudonyms.[100] McAdoo observed that 'this is one of the lowest and most wanton attempts at assassination of character I have yet encountered. I am, myself, puzzled to know how it ought to be dealt with.'[101] In response Untermyer noted that the 'story is a cleverly veiled libel'. Furthermore, 'The vile thing in varying forms has spread into every corner of this country. Every leading member of our party will, I think, agree that it is doing serious harm'. He suggested that the president sue the publication for libel to mitigate the damage.[102] By late September Untermyer's wife, Minnie, had been informed by a friend from Rhode Island that a story was circulating there that Wilson had retained Untermyer to contain the scandal. He had paid Peck $50,000 on behalf of Wilson. In return Brandeis was appointed to the US Supreme Court.[103] Later the State Department received a translation of another version of the story which appeared in the Berlin newspaper *Kreuz Zeitung* on 24 October 1917. The newspaper reported that Wilson had received a gift of $75,000 from Untermyer to prevent Mrs Peck from raising a breach-of-promise suit against him. Wilson had promised to marry Mrs Peck while his first wife was still alive. He persuaded Peck to secure a divorce from her husband. In the meantime, he had met Mrs Galt who was wealthier and beautiful than Peck and therefore he married her. Untermyer only gave Wilson the $75,000, upon condition that his friend Brandeis was appointed to the US Supreme Court.[104]

Peck, who later reverted to the surname Hulbert, by her own account (published 1924–5),[105] had in her possession some 200 personal letters from Wilson. She was offered $100,000 for them by a New York lawyer, claiming to represent the president, at a time when she was financially distressed. She later learned the lawyer really did represent Wilson. She was also offered $250,000 from someone claiming to represent the Republican Party. She declined both offers. Hulbert claimed in a series of articles in 1924 that the letters were always at the command of Wilson. She would have willingly returned them to him or alternatively destroyed them if he had asked her. Hulbert also in the same series said Wilson had advanced her $7,500 on the security of some mortgages sometime in 1916.[106] It seems plausible that Wilson, who had limited personal funds, might have been given the money by Untermyer. But it is unlikely that Untermyer asked for Brandeis's nomination in exchange.

Untermyer denied he was involved in Brandeis's selection as the nominee, although he wholeheartedly supported him and noted that it had 'put new heart into the Progressive element of our party'.[107] He cabled his friend to offer his 'heartfelt congratulations' and observed, 'We all feel greatly honored.'[108] He also later offered to testify before the Senate Judiciary Sub-Committee on Brandeis's behalf.[109] On the evening of the day Wilson sent the Brandeis nomination to the US Senate McAdoo hosted a dinner at his Washington home. The guests included Wilson and his wife, Brandeis and his wife, Untermyer and his wife, Chief Justice Hughes and his wife, and Justice Mahlon Pitney and his wife.[110] This suggests that Untermyer was at the very least consulted on the nomination. Clarence W. Barron claims that at a subsequent dinner at which McAdoo and Untermyer were guests Wilson remarked to the latter that he wondered if he had made mistake nominating Brandeis. Untermyer rose in response and delivered a passionate speech in defence of the nomination and its impact on American Jewry. Wilson was reputedly moved to tears.[111] There was also speculation in the *Wall Street Journal* that Untermyer had demanded it of the Wilson administration and that it was part of a move headed by the lawyer to win New York State for Wilson by securing the votes of New York City's East Side. It also observed that Untermyer might control millions of dollars, but it was not clear that he controlled millions of votes.[112] But Untermyer's private reflections on the nomination to McAdoo might suggest otherwise.

> the President has not, during his entire Administration, done a single act that has so strengthened him politically where he most needed strength or so endeared

him to millions of countrymen who misunderstood him. At the same time he has dispelled the suspicion that he has surrendered to or temporized with the financial interests and has put new hope into the hearts of the progressives of his party. It was a fine thing to do and incidentally a master-stroke politically.

[Samuel] Gompers came down with me on the train [to Florida]. He also was tremendously enthusiastic about it. I feel as grateful and jubilant as though it happened to me – I think more so for . . . [Brandeis] is temperamentally better fitted for the . . . [United States Supreme Court].[113]

The nomination was bitterly fought by the WASP legal establishment. In mid-March ex-president Taft and six former presidents of the American Bar Association protested to the Senate Judiciary Sub-Committee that Brandeis was not a fit person to be a member of the court.[114] Untermyer had earlier condemned the

bigots and smug, self-righteous 'blue-bloods' of the Boston bar, who do the bidding of corrupt corporations and whose conceptions of professional standing exclude every lawyer who champions corporate reform. If he happens also to be a Jew no punishment short of complete social and professional ostracism will fit his double crime. . .

I am looking forward with unusual satisfaction to seeing the Senate prick this bubble of New England bigotry and snobbery. It will be a great triumph for true democracy and the most severe blow yet dealt to instructed corporate corruption.[115]

The nomination was also opposed by Southern Democrats. They were aggrieved that Wilson had not consulted them. They also suspected it was an appeal to the Progressive wing of the party who were harassing them on the issue of child labour. Furthermore, parts of the South, in particular Georgia, had fallen under the influence of the anti-Catholic and anti-Semitic demagogue, Tom Watson. Eventually party unity was restored and only one Democrat voted against confirmation of the nomination in early June.[116] Josephus Daniels, Wilson's Secretary of the Navy, helped overcome the opposition of the Southern senators to Brandeis.[117] Nonetheless, in May a report had circulated through the Senate that Brandeis's name would be withdrawn and Untermyer's would be substituted.[118] Later just before the general election George Harvey noted that there was some speculation that as part of securing the Jewish vote Wilson might select Untermyer to succeed Edward Douglass White as Chief Justice.[119] White, whose health was failing, planned to retire in 1916, but in the end decided not to give the appointment to Wilson.[120]

After he returned from Maine in mid-September 1916, as already previously noted, Untermyer was operated on for an intestinal complaint. He had been suffering from the problem that led to the operation for nearly a year.[121] His recovery from the operation took over two weeks.[122] Wilson wrote to Untermyer expressing concern.

May I not send you a line of sincere sympathy in your illness? It has grieved me very much to learn that you overtaxed yourself, and I cannot help feeling that it was partly due to your great zeal in behalf of the present administration. I hope with all my heart that you are rapidly recovering.[123]

Untermyer wrote back to reassure Wilson that his work for the administration was not the cause of his illness.

> I am sure you will believe it is no mere figure of speech when I say that I deeply appreciate the generous impulse that prompted your gracious letter. I feel honored that in the turmoil of your incredibly busy life with the overwhelming cares of State that beset you, you should have found the time & thought to write me.[124]

Untermyer's public support for Wilson's re-election masked his disappointment regarding his refusal to publicly recognize him. House recorded a conversation late in October a few days before the general election.

> Samuel Untermyer called to relate his grievances against the administration. He considers that he has been badly treated. I sympathized with him in looks rather than in words, and he left with the promise that he would aid the campaign by a very liberal subscription, although I asked for nothing.[125]

Untermyer had also diplomatically observed to Wilson earlier in the month:

> Referring to your undeservedly flattering references to my connexion with Administration measures permit me to assure you, Sir, that I am your grateful debtor for whatever humble aid I may have had the opportunity to render in the support of those measures of the policies they embody. It has been to me a source of never-to-be forgotten gratification to have had the privilege of having had a part, however inconspicuous, in the partial realization of ideals of government that I have cherished & championed all my life.
>
> Whatever of personal disappointment may have come to me from not having been permitted to have a more conspicuous part in the working out of the vast problems, many of which are now well on the way to solution, has been entirely overshadowed by my gratitude & admiration for the superb statesmanship & the steadfast progressive aims that have characterized your management of the affairs of the nation.[126]

By the end of October Untermyer had recovered sufficiently to re-enter the election campaign with an address entitled 'A Historical Review of Mr. Hughes' Surrenders to Invisible Government' delivered in New York City on 30 October. He observed to McAdoo he could not understand in view of Hughes's record while governor of New York, how anyone could regard him as a progressive.[127] Untermyer accused the Republican presidential candidate of having surrendered the people's interest to 'invisible government' when he was governor of New York. He recalled that Hughes had failed to persuade his party to adopt his recommendations for a public legislative investigation into the New York Stock Exchange. So, before his renomination as

Republican gubernatorial candidate he had made an agreement with the New York Stock Exchange to drop this proposal. Instead, he appointed an ineffective commission which achieved nothing. Untermyer implied that he did this to secure his re-election. The speech signalled Untermyer's unhappiness that stock market regulation was absent from the party's platform.[128] He recalled that during the first decade of the twentieth century:

> The so-called 'washing' and manipulation of stocks and the fictitious transactions on the Stock Exchange and the practice of all manner of fraud and oppression upon the investing public through the machinery of the Exchange had reached the proportions of a National scandal.[129]

The first Wilson administration had proved a great personal disappointment to Untermyer. Prevented from becoming a US senator by the Morgan family and its associates, he had had high hopes of achieving national recognition through appointment to a high-profile government position by his friend Woodrow Wilson. His friends Henry Morgenthau Sr. and Abram I. Elkus[130] were in succession appointed ambassador to Turkey. Nonetheless, Untermyer and McAdoo celebrated Wilson's 'glorious victory'[131] in the November general election. Untermyer enthusiastically observed, 'it fairly revives one[s] confidence in popular government.'[132]

Untermyer's health deteriorated again in January 1917.[133] He went down to Palm Beach on his houseboat *Nirodha* for a few weeks to try and recover.[134] While he was moored off West Palm Beach there was a coup d'état by General Frederico Tinoco in Costa Rica. According to a diplomat representing the overthrown government, Tinoco was a long-standing friend of Minor C. Keith of the United Fruit Co. The company had objected to a new system of taxation introduced by the former government, which had also rejected Keith's project to gain control over all of the water power of Costa Rica.[135] Untermyer, who was counsel to the United Fruit Co., sent a telegram to Secretary of State Robert Lansing on behalf of his client.

> You will please note ... there have been no bloodshed or casualties and none are likely unless intervention is threatened. Country is absolutely tranquil and without disorder. [The United] Fruit Company, which is an American company owned by Americans, owns railways, steamships and other great interests there, and has the only important American interests in Costa Rica. It does not need protection and advises against landing or sending troops as best means of avoiding complication. We respectfully urge that before taking action you send a distinguished agent to investigate and report as best means of safeguarding our many millions of capital invested there and of doing justice.[136]

Wilson instructed Lansing on 7 February that he would never recognize any government established by Tinoco and no contracts made by any American citizen with such a government would be recognized by the American government. He observed, 'A word to Mr. Untermyer, who seems to speak as their attorney, might give them immediate pause.'[137] On 19 February McAdoo informed Untermyer that

The President has determined not to recognize any Government founded on revolution nor would any Government with which the principal revolutionist has to do receive the sanction of this Government. He feels, also, that any privileges or concessions obtained from such a Government should not receive the support of this Government.[138]

Untermyer continued to try to persuade the Wilson administration to recognize the Tinoco regime. In late June 1917 he met with Lansing to discuss the matter.[139] Later in July 1918 Bryan also lobbied the administration at Untermyer's behest to try and arrange a meeting for a confidential representative of the Tinoco regime to discuss necessary business with the State Department.[140] The intervention was unsuccessful.[141] Wilson regarded Tinoco as a 'scoundrel' and was disinclined to do anything to help his cause.[142] Instead, he instituted legal action against United Fruit. However, the government failed to find sufficient evidence to indict Keith for aiding Tinoco's coup d'état. Wilson also subsequently declined to recognize the governments that succeeded Tinoco after he resigned and fled to Jamaica in August 1919.[143]

Untermyer's patriotism and that of his political allies did not go unchallenged. The previous March, the Republican mayor of New York, John Purroy Mitchel, had accused Robert F. Wagner, the leader of the Democratic minority in the New York State Senate and a future US senator, of working in the interests of the German government. Mitchel was called before the Senate to answer to the charge that he made a 'false and malicious statement' against Wagner. Wagner retained Untermyer as counsel. On 4 April Untermyer subjected Mitchel to an especially severe cross-examination, which lasted a day. As a result, the State Senate endorsed Wagner and ended the inquiry.[144] In October, Mitchel retaliated against Untermyer by observing in a speech that

> New York is offered Hylan, the nominee of Murphy and of Hearst, the candidate of Untermyer and his kind, who, out of association with [Dr. Konstantin Theodor] Dumba[, the Austro-Hungarian Ambassador,] and Bernstorff and their like, raise their heads to spit venom at those who have taken a strong and active stand with America and against Germany.[145]

Much to Untermyer's disgust, many figures associated with the White House supported Mitchel in the 1917 New York mayoral election against Tammany Hall's candidate, John F. Hylan. Untermyer thought it was 'distressing and quite inexplicable' given how Tammany had exerted itself to the utmost in aid of the administration ticket in 1916 and completely exhausted its resources in the face of the strong antagonism of the German and Irish vote. He noted that Mitchel, who was standing as an independent, and his Republican appointees had posed the most important obstacle the previous year to Wilson's re-election campaign in the city. Untermyer observed to McAdoo, 'it seems to me that the gentlemen who pose as the reform end of the party are not the most reliable factors upon which to rely.'[146]

This was a particularly bitter contest in which a strong challenge was made by Untermyer's pacifist friend, Morris Hillquit. Untermyer, afraid, like many of the American Jewish leadership, that there would be an anti-Semitic backlash if Hillquit was elected, was one of the most active campaigners for Hylan, who went on to win the election. Untermyer's intervention was resented by many on the Jewish East Side. *Forverts* observed that the Jewish multimillionaire was asking them to revert to the same servile status they had held in medieval Poland. It felt Untermyer and the other leaders did not really believe in America or in democracy.[147]

As the November election approached Untermyer reported to McAdoo on 1 November:

> I have been making speeches opposing Mayor Mitchell [*sic*], largely on the ground of his treachery and ingratitude to the President in 1916. My main fear, however, is of Hillquit and his seditious appeal to the ignorance of the Russian Jews. I am making speeches every night this week.[148]

Untermyer included with his letter a copy of one of his speeches which he was to deliver that evening in the Bronx. Untermyer began by declaring that the Jews were the 'aristocrats of the world'. He then urged his audience to show loyalty to the country that given them 'the blessings of freedom and equal opportunity'. Untermyer then traced the history of the current war to date recognizing there had been an issue of the 'despotic bigot-ridden Russia' fighting on the side of the Allies. However, that was no longer an issue because autocracy had been overthrown in Russia. He urged his audience not to vote for Hillquit, who he counted as a friend. It would be supporting sedition to vote for him because he refused to support the Wilson administration while it was at war. The most charitable view of his platform was that it 'spelt national disaster and dishonor' for the Jewish community. He foresaw if they voted for Hillquit 'It will arouse a storm of hate, resentment and anti-Semitism such as our race has never before encountered in this country'. He asked them if they were 'willing to put this burden upon your people, yourselves, your children and your children's children?'[149] He also lambasted Germany as 'the enemy of freedom, the focus of anti-Semitism, the prompter of the Russian autocracy, the old persecutor and oppressor of the Jews'.[150] This was probably the only occasion he made comments in public of this kind before Hitler came to power.

The speech caught the attention of the Jewish community. Rabbi Samuel Shulman of New York City's Temple Beth-El referred to it in his Saturday sermon. Untermyer wrote him an open letter in which he objected to being described as a 'politician' and the rabbi's criticism of his appeal to Jewish voters to not vote for the Socialist candidate. He observed

> You are in error in referring to me as a 'politician', unless by that you mean to include every citizen who takes an active interest in public affairs and who believes that in a republic, government by party is essential to the expression of public will. Except in that sense I am no more of a politician than you are, for I have never held or sought public office.

Untermyer also defended his position on the election.

> The Jews are the bulwarks and constitute the main voting body of the Socialist party in this city. Their candidate also happens to be a Jew. You are well aware of

this as are the rest of us and of the community at large. The Jews will be held largely responsible in the public estimate for the seditious creed that is masquerading in the respectable habiliments of that party if they support that creed by their votes. It is idle to attempt to blink that fact.

If I can do anything toward averting such a catastrophe for my race, I believe that I am performing a far greater service than by keeping silence whilst they are blindly plunging into an abyss. Your counsel of blindness and timidity can result only in disaster where courage and honesty applied in time will save the situation.[151]

Shulman thought it was 'somewhat presumptuous' of Untermyer to teach him patriotism. He noted in his reply to Untermyer that he had 'violated an American Jewish tradition, which forbids any man to address himself as a Jew to Jews in a political campaign'.[152] Untermyer replied to Shulman. His friend Beck thought it 'was a fine reply . . . in your best vein . . . I judge from your reply that in your address on Hilquilt [sic] you were doing a public service'.[153]

After Hylan was elected mayor Untermyer sought to act as 'kingmaker' in the words of a political enemy, the mayor's adviser, Henry H. Klein. Hylan was later described as 'perhaps one of the most honest public officers ever to serve the city [of New York], [but] was far from one of the wisest'.[154] Untermyer succeeded in having his client, Frederick Bugher, appointed police commissioner.[155] However, Bugher would not take orders from Hylan. Bugher was dismissed after a mere twenty-three days in his post. As a result, Hylan and Untermyer subsequently became estranged.[156]

Part of the legislative agenda in the early part of Wilson's second term was the income tax bill. Ajay K. Mehrotra has observed that the Wilson administration created a new tax system based on a system of steeply graduated taxes. He notes that 'Among the Treasury officials who took part in creating the new tax system, a group of elite lawyers was central to the project of building the administrative capacity of the new fiscal state'.[157] Untermyer was part of this group. He was a strong supporter of the Wilson administration's new tax system apart from the tax on stock dividends.[158] At the beginning of November, he was unofficially appointed to the group of special legal advisers together with Arthur A. Ballantine, a Republican lawyer. Untermyer and Ballantine also worked on the preparation of a new regulation affecting the stamp taxes appertaining to the stock and produce exchanges. After a Washington journalist learnt of the committee's existence Untermyer suggested that McAdoo make the appointments a matter of public record and that another lawyer was required to complete the committee's work.[159] McAdoo acquiesced by both publicly announcing the committee and adding a third member, Judge John Barton Payne.[160] The committee's purview also included the excess profits tax. Its work was completed in late January, at which time Untermyer stood down. In the meantime, Ballantine had been appointed Internal Revenue Solicitor.[161]

Untermyer had already shared with House in late 1916 his unhappiness about the Wilson administration's unwillingness to give him appropriate public recognition. At the beginning of December, he wrote a lengthy complaint to McAdoo. He began by observing

> At the risk of seeming to be a nuisance I am going to ask you to pause in your important labors long enough to read this letter & when occasion permits to make certain inquiries so as to let me know frankly for my own satisfaction & peace of mind why it is that of all the men who for almost six years have loyally & with boundless confidence & admiration championed & followed the President & his Administration I have been singled out to be denied any sort of recognition. I do not of course include you in this complaint for you have uniformly considerate & I am now deeply appreciative of your genuine friendship & have lost no opportunity to give evidence of that fact.

Untermyer then reflected that he had been one of the early supporters of Governor Wilson before he had won the Democratic Party presidential nomination. He noted that before his annual tour of continental Europe he had expressly gone to see George Harvey, Wilson's adviser at that time, to offer financial assistance. He had subsequently supported his candidacy with press interviews and speeches. He was a delegate at the 1912 Democratic Convention, where he had been outspoken in his support for Wilson. He contributed $7,000 to Wilson's pre-nomination campaign through William F. McCombs. He further observed:

> During the campaign of 1912, besides contributing perhaps the largest sum that was expended by any single individual, barring none, as Col. House knows, I stumped various parts of the country. During the first Administration I spent fully one third of my time in writing, speaking & otherwise championing & assisting before Committees of Congress & in other ways, the Federal Reserve Act, the Clayton & Federal Trade Acts & other policies of the Administration. I was a Delegate at Large to the 1916 Convention, was a large contributor to the campaign fund & spoke in Maine at the request of the speakers bureau in the September elections but was prevented by illness from taking an active part thereafter until two weeks before the election.

Untermyer also reflected that his 'loyalty & services' were 'utterly ignored whilst the men who did their utmost to defeat [Wilson] are honored & strengthened for the next national struggle to wrest control of the Government from our party'. It was not as if there had only been 'limited opportunities' for his recognition. He then observed:

> The opportunities have been well-nigh without limit & the difficulty has been to find the men for important tasks until it has become almost impossible to resist the conviction that there is in the mind of the President a substantial reason for his attitude. Whilst Col. House has always indulged the most generous & unsolicited assurances of friendship & good will I have the feeling (possibly unjust) that he dislikes me although I have never put him to the test.

Untermyer ended his complaint with the following appeal to McAdoo:

I feel that I am at least entitled to know the situation & to have the opportunity to set myself right. When at almost the outset of the Administration McCombs, with whom I quarrelled on account of his attitudes, told me that I need never expect recognition, I set him down as a vicious liar, but he seems to have been right in his conclusion, although his assertion may have had no basis.

McAdoo's response to the complaint has not survived. But as Untermyer promised his friend, he would continue to assist the administration regardless of whether his suspicion regarding Wilson was correct or not.[162]

Perhaps it is not a coincidence that at the end of December Wilson proposed to Herbert Hoover the appointment of Untermyer as Chief Counsel to the Food Administration to replace Judge Curtis H. Lindsey, who had resigned.[163] However, Hoover rejected this suggestion in his letter to Wilson on 1 January 1918.

I have found that his German associations prior to our going into the War were most intimate. While he is a perfectly loyal citizen I am afraid it would bring a great deal of criticism on an Administration so much founded on voluntary devotion of the extreme, patriotic type. There is in the Food Administration an idealism amounting almost to a crusader's spirit and I am afraid that the appointing of Mr. Untermyer where he would be in such intimate relation with all of these men would not tend to maintain this spirit, which is so vital to successful work.[164]

Untermyer was probably unaware Hoover had blocked his appointment. In April 1920 after lunching with Hoover at the Bankers' Club in New York City he told a reporter, 'I am a Democrat. Herbert Hoover is a fine fellow, and I wish he was a Democrat.'[165]

At the end of 1917, the Wilson administration assumed operation of all railroads in the United States. McAdoo was appointed the new director general of Railroads, a position which he added to his existing one of treasury secretary.[166] McAdoo had met with Untermyer in Washington on the day of the announcement. After the meeting Untermyer wrote to him with a series of suggestions regarding his new role. These included the employment one of the three 'great' firms of English chartered accountants that had branches in the United States whose first duty would be to present a statement of the net revenues for the years 1915–17, the cash now in hand, liabilities and so on. This firm would also inaugurate a system of accounts based on the Interstate Commerce Commission's rules of railway accounting. Untermyer suggested McAdoo select Deloitte, Plender, Griffiths & Co. or Touche Niven & Co. or perhaps both in preference to Price Waterhouse & Co. because of the financial affiliations of the last named. He noted, 'Sir John Plender of the first named firm is Mr. Lloyd George's right hand man & has long been the intimate financial adviser to the English Gov't. Sir Geo. Touche of the second named firm is a prominent member of the House of Commons. I consider him one of the ablest men in the contemporary public life of Gt. Britain.'[167] Dale N. Shook suggests that this was the 'most useful advice McAdoo received on the program for implementing the government takeover of the railroads'.[168] McAdoo asked Untermyer to become his special counsel as director general. An issue arose regarding retainers from railroad companies for which Untermyer had long been acting as general counsel. He was willing to forgo the retainers, even though it would mean a loss of 'hundreds of thousands of dollars', if McAdoo determined this was a conflict of interest.[169] McAdoo decided it was. So Untermyer began arranging the surrender of his railroad retainers. He asked McAdoo if there would be any objection to Louis Marshall accepting railway retainers. He incorrectly noted that he had had no interest in his former law firm for the past four years. He further noted Marshall would decline the retainers if required. However, another issue arose. Untermyer was not prepared to be subordinate to the director general's proposed general counsel, Judge Payne.[170] This issue proved to be insurmountable. So Untermyer declined the position.[171]

Later in the year in May Untermyer became joint counsel to the National Association of Owners of Railroad Securities which had been organized by his client, Sol Davies Warfield, the previous May.[172] Untermyer represented the railroad owners in the compensation contract negotiations between the railroad industry and the federal government following the temporary wartime nationalization of the industry. Untermyer and Warfield objected to the final draft of the contract. However, the acceptance of the final draft in early September by the Railway Executives' Advisory Committee representing about ninety per cent of America's railroad mileage meant their objections did not carry a great deal of weight. McAdoo declined a proposal by Untermyer on behalf of the association later in the month for 'co-operation in securing an adjudication' upon the questions at issue between the government and the association as to the form of the contract which the director general had previously decided against them.[173]

In May 1918 McAdoo offered Untermyer a place on the board of the War Finance Corporation, but Untermyer declined it because he did not want to forgo his legal practice or spend his entire time in Washington.[174] McAdoo had long been finding the pressure of work unbearable. On 23 November 1918 he announced he was stepping down from his role as treasury secretary the following month and from his other role as director general of railroads in January 1919.[175] Untermyer agreed with his decision, even though it meant Glass succeeded him as treasury secretary. Untermyer cabled McAdoo:

> I congratulate you on having at last found the opportunity consistent with your high ideals of duty to your country to relieve yourself of the intolerable cares and responsibilities under which you have so long been staggering and at last look after your long neglected health and material welfare. Your unexampledly [sic] brilliant administration of the many great tasks allotted you have made your place in the people[']s admiration and esteem secure for the present and coming generations.[176]

Untermyer refused to be intimidated by his political enemies. In April 1918 he spoke out against the wave of hostility towards German Americans saying that it was wrong to embitter them by questioning their patriotism[177] and condemned attempts to outlaw the publication of German-language newspapers.[178] Untermyer also tried to prevent the expropriation of German American businesses by the American government.[179] In October 1917 the Wilson administration had established the

Office of Alien Property Custodian to assume control and dispose of enemy-owned property in the United States and its possessions. Untermyer frequently protested to the Alien Property Custodian, A. Mitchell Palmer, on behalf of clients and friends who had had their property expropriated. Palmer had been appointed custodian in October 1917 and was to be promoted to attorney general in March 1919. He was a member of the White House faction that was to gain ground after Wilson's stroke in October 1919. It may be no coincidence that Untermyer's friend Colonel House was not a member of this faction.[180] Palmer later recalled he was repeatedly compelled to deny Untermyer's requests. He also recalled that on one occasion in the office of the Alien Property Custodian in Washington, DC, Untermyer had concluded an interview with a threat. Palmer claimed Untermyer declared that 'he hoped for "for my sake" that I would act otherwise in the matter then pending, "for," he said, "you ought to be more careful about opposing the wishes of men with bitter tongues and vitriolic pens."'[181]

One of the cases involving the Alien Property Custodian involved Untermyer's relative Norvin R. Lindheim. The previous December the New York *Evening Mail* had sent a report to the Alien Property Custodian. In June 1918 the newspaper's lawyers S. Walter Kaufmann, Arthur Garfield Hays and Lindheim were asked to appear at the office of the attorney general of New York State. They testified that the German government had invested in the loss-making newspaper in 1916 with Albert acting as intermediary. Their inquisitors were not satisfied with the lawyers' account. Hays, who had not been involved in the preparation of the report, later recalled that they consulted Untermyer. Untermyer feared that this might be more than a mere investigation. He thought an 'indictment' might lie ahead which Hays thought was 'horrifying'. Untermyer proved to be prescient. The following month, Kaufmann and Edward Rumely, the publisher of the *Mail*, were charged with knowingly making a false report to the Alien Property Custodian. Rumely sought the assistance of Untermyer's friend Colonel House. House, who thought Rumely was probably guilty, chose not to become involved and disclaimed any influence with the custodian. Instead, he suggested Rumely should employ the services of Untermyer. Untermyer agreed to represent Rumely and Kaufmann. In April 1919 Lindheim's name was added as a defendant. The case appeared on the federal court calendar in June 1920. Untermyer used his ill health to get an adjournment to the autumn. When the trial began in November, he was still unwell. However, Untermyer sometimes used the ploy of ill health to sidestep unwinnable cases. The defendants were represented by Stephen C. Baldwin, Fred J. Powell, Max D. Steuer and William M. Wemple. Kaufmann and Lindheim were found guilty and disbarred.[182] It is ironic that the man who had initiated this prosecution, Palmer, had himself assisted Albert. In 1915 he had helped him ship foodstuffs and cotton to Germany.[183]

During the congressional election of 1918, Untermyer was again forced to prove his patriotism by campaigning against a Jewish socialist candidate. He joined with other Jewish leaders in appealing to the Jews of the lower East Side not to re-elect the Socialist Congressman, Meyer London. Melech Epstein says that their apparent hostility to London belied the cooperation between the socialist and mainstream Jews in the immense program of war relief and rehabilitation of East European Jewry. London was chairman of the People's Relief Committee, which was an indispensable part of the Joint Distribution Committee.¹⁸⁴ London was defeated but was to regain his seat in November 1920.¹⁸⁵

Untermyer's attempts to prove his patriotism failed to convince his enemies. In December, the war now over, A. Bruce Bielaski, Director of the Justice Department's Bureau of Investigation, the predecessor of the Federal Bureau of Investigation, alleged before a Senate subcommittee investigating German and Bolshevik propaganda, chaired by Senator Lee Slater Overman, that Untermyer was an agent of the German government. He said that Untermyer had tried to buy the New York *Sun* and, in a letter to Heinrich Albert, had said that a 'morning and evening' newspaper with 'valuable real estate on Park Row' could be bought for as little as $2 million. Untermyer's name was also brought up in connection with the acquisition of a controlling interest in the *Warheit*. However, it was conceded unless it could be proved the money came from the German government, the transaction was legitimate. It was reported that the British Secret Service claimed the purchase was made to influence Jewish public opinion.¹⁸⁶

Untermyer denied that he had ever acted in any capacity, either as counsel, agent, or otherwise for the German government.¹⁸⁷ In fact Bielaski did not have definitive proof for his allegations.¹⁸⁸ On 9 December Untermyer demanded the right to rebut Bielaski's testimony either in person or in writing. He also refuted another allegation by Bielaski that the Citizens' Committee for Food Shipments had been founded at his home to campaign against the British blockade.

> I did not know of the circumstances, but it now appears that in 1915 Mrs. Untermyer committed the heinous crime of not only permitting, but of actually abetting, a meeting at her home to devise ways and means of urging upon our State and Post Office Departments that they secure the consent of Great Britain to the lifting of its blockade in so far as to permit dried milk to be sent to the starving babies of Germany. Our Government was then insisting that the blockade was contrary to international law, and a personal appeal was made to President Wilson.

Untermyer also pointed out that at the time, America was at peace with Germany. After his wife Minnie found that the government was unable to help get the milk through the blockade, she reluctantly resigned from this organization.¹⁸⁹

Untermyer was granted his request to appear in person before the Senate committee. He gave seven hours of testimony on 17 December, including four hours of cross-examination by Major E. Lowry Humes, counsel for the MID.¹⁹⁰ He was very evasive, and it became clear that the MID had illegally tapped his telephone. Untermyer repeatedly asked Humes to show him the transcripts of these illegal intercepts. Humes refused. Once again Untermyer denied being counsel to the German Embassy. However, he could not deny that he had associated with the German ambassador and other diplomats based in Washington. He admitted that he was a friend of Dr Bernhard Dernburg (the financier in charge of German propaganda in the United States). When Untermyer was questioned about the publication of the papers that had been in Albert's mislaid briefcase, that the Secret Service had passed on to the New York *World*, he was not very forthcoming.¹⁹¹

After he had given his testimony Untermyer wrote a letter of complaint to the attorney general, Thomas W. Gregory, regarding the material supplied by the Department of Justice to the Overman Committee.[192] The Justice Department carried out a lengthy and thorough examination of Untermyer's complaint. Gregory's reply was not the one Untermyer desired. The attorney general said that Bielaski's testimony was in direct response to a formal request from the Overman Committee. He was satisfied that all of it was truthful and authentic. He concluded by observing

> If any embarrassment to you has resulted, it arose, not from the action of this Department, but from your participation with German agents in activities disseminating and attempting to disseminate German propaganda throughout the United States.[193]

Untermyer was incensed and replied on 1 March:

> My respect for the high office from which you are about to retire prevents me from appropriately characterizing the assertions and innuendoes in the last paragraph of your letter of February 22nd, which I deeply resent.

Untermyer also said he resented the Justice Department's agents providing the Senate Committee with fabricated evidence from the British and French Secret Services. He concluded by restating his original complaint, this time focusing on the placing in the public domain of his letter of January 1916 to Albert without first giving him the opportunity to explain its context. Untermyer argued it was Gregory's

> duty to have given me the protection to which any decent citizen was justly entitled and with which a sense of common fairness would have dictated. Instead of this you permitted and apparently encouraged your notoriety-seeking agents to make a sensation out of an innocent, casual, legitimate business offer that never materialized and that had about as much relation to 'propaganda' as chalk has to cheese.[194]

Later the same day Untermyer realized that in his rage he had gone too far in the letter because he was

> Smarting under a feeling of injustice at the unwarranted tone of your letter to me of February 22nd, which I regard as a poor return for the public services I have rendered both before and during the war.[195]

Later Gregory's successor as attorney general, Palmer, revived the allegations against Untermyer by quoting from the official report of the former naval attaché at the German Embassy in Washington, Captain Karl Boy-Ed, and an entry about a visit to Greystone from the handwritten diary of Albert.[196] This was retaliation for Untermyer's attacks on his record as attorney general. J. Edgar Hoover, Palmer's special assistant, ordered an investigation of the State Department's records to see if there was any other embarrassing information that could be used against Untermyer.[197] Palmer must have been very disappointed when Hoover's investigator reported back to him that

> In none of the files was there any information of any kind or character of MR. UNTERMYER'S dealings, or having any connection with any foreign German Agencies, or any connection with BOY-ED or VON PAPEN. Investigation closed.[198]

Hoover also contacted the Director of Military Intelligence at the War Department regarding Untermyer.[199] There is no record of the reply.

During the final year of the Wilson administration Untermyer made another attempt to achieve public recognition. In late 1919 his friend Folk had informed him that his name was under discussion at the State Department regarding his appointment as ambassador to Germany. Folk consulted Bryan, who wrote an enthusiastic unsolicited letter of endorsement.[200] Untermyer then asked McAdoo whether he would be willing to make a personal appeal to the president. He declared:

> I believe that in short time remaining of the present term I would be able, by reason of my acquaintance with men now in the German Gov't & who shared well in the confidence of the people, to perform useful service for my country in healing the wounds made by the war & towards restoring something of our historic friendship. The job will in the very nature of the case be an unpleasant one in many respects but I am satisfied that I could do much to overcome the feeling. It is only because I think that I see an opportunity for real service, which I have long sought, that I am making the request.

However, Untermyer observed that he had no idea how Secretary of State Bainbridge Colby would take the suggestion. He recalled that he and Colby had had quite an acrimonious dispute back in 1905 over the affairs of the Equitable Life when his then-law firm Alexander & Colby represented its president, James W. Alexander, and Untermyer had represented James Hazen Hyde. He reminded McAdoo that it was the row between Colby's firm and its rival, Alexander & Green, that had precipitated the life insurance scandals. Although their relationship had been friendly since that time, Untermyer noted he had been surprised when Colby had accepted the previous autumn the chairmanship of the re-election campaign committee for Justice Joseph E. Newburger, a Republican, in the judiciary election for the New York Supreme Court.[201] He did not mention to Folk that his son Irwin was the unsuccessful Democratic Party candidate and that Colby had alleged during the campaign that he had used his ownership of a farm at Brant Lake, in upstate New York, previously owned by Untermyer, to evade the draft.[202] Untermyer was to be disappointed because he failed to secure the ambassadorship.

Untermyer believed that the Versailles Treaty was 'hurried and confused as well as detestable'. The *Berliner Tageblatt und Handels-Zeitung*'s Washington correspondent, Dr Max Jordan, reported in 1925 that Untermyer regarded the treaty as 'as a betrayal equally towards America as well as Germany' and believed that 'the terms of the treaty need to be revised'.[203] Earlier in June 1920 Folk had shared with Colby a proposal from

Untermyer for a special mission to Europe.[204] In a later version Untermyer proposed an American mission based in Berlin headed by himself to investigate and formulate plans to revive American trade with Germany, Austria, Hungary and other former enemy countries. Untermyer suggested Russia should also be included. He observed to Colby:

> I take it that it is quite as necessary in order to effect an advantageous peace to be prepared for peace, as it is necessary in order to wage a successful war to be prepared for war, but our country alone of all the countries appears to have made no systematic arrangements in that direction.'[205]

Folk was strongly supportive of Untermyer's proposal:

> It seems to me that this is a matter of tremendous importance to the commerce of the United States, and know of no one who could fill such a mission with more credit to his country and honor to the Administration than Mr. Untermyer.[206]

Unbeknownst to Untermyer and Folk, Colby sought the advice of his Acting Chief of the Division of Western European Affairs, William R. Castle, Jr.,[207] an anti-Semite,[208] who stymied the proposal by disingenuously advising the secretary that the department's diplomats in Europe were already doing what Untermyer proposed.

> An ambassador at large, so to speak, would simply confuse the work of these various missions which keep in touch constantly with each other.
> It will not be necessary to say to [Folk] that to send a Jew to do this work would be utterly and absolutely disastrous.[209]

Colby was more diplomatic when he replied to Folk's letter observing that

> Mr. Untermyer possesses qualifications that would make him very serviceable in connection with many aspects of such a mission, but the underlying question has not been brought up for serious consideration as yet.[210]

However, Folk persisted in his advocacy of Untermyer's proposal. Folk discussed it with Colby on a train journey to San Francisco in July and persuaded Colby to meet with Untermyer to 'explain just what he had in mind'.[211] However, the meeting on 28 July[212] did not persuade Colby to override the advice he had received from Castle. Folk continued to lobby Colby on behalf of Untermyer[213] and sent his office in October a proposed outline of a letter from the State Department to Untermyer appointing him head of a three-man High Commission for the approval of Colby.[214] But Colby did not change his mind. Thus, an opportunity to potentially avert the next world war was missed.

The Democrats were defeated in the presidential election the following month. The Democrats did not win another presidential election until 1932. During the interregnum Untermyer continued to promote Progressive economic and financial reform, for example by assisting and testifying at congressional hearings. His most noteworthy contribution was to a Senate investigation into campaign finance in 1924. Untermyer had called for campaign finance law reform for candidates seeking federal office during the 1920 presidential campaign.[215] He believed J.P. Morgan & Co. had tried to buy control of the White House.[216] During the closing days of the 1924 general election campaign Untermyer agreed to assist Senator Robert La Follette's personal counsel, Frank P. Walsh, with an investigation chaired by Senator William E. Borah into an alleged huge Republican Party national campaign 'slush' fund being raised for use in swing states.[217] At hearings held in Chicago,[218] Untermyer sought to implicate Henry Ford in the scandal[219] and to reveal that J.P. Morgan & Co. was underwriting the Republican national campaign. Untermyer and Walsh considered the proposed Corrupt Practices bill was inadequate to tackle the abuses uncovered by the Borah investigation. They proposed a much tougher bill.[220] Untermyer thought contributions from all sources should be restricted in a presidential campaign to $1,000,000. Walsh thought the maximum should not exceed $300,000. Both advocated that no contribution be allowed within two weeks of the election, that the reallocation of large sums of money collected in other parts of the country into swing states be prohibited and that campaign committees be barred from incurring obligations in excess of their receipts. None of these proposals was included in the bill subsequently reported by the Borah committee.[221]

Untermyer understood the chances of any of his proposals being enacted during the period of Republican dominance in Washington were minimal. Therefore, he had agreed to be associate counsel to the New York State Joint Legislative Committee on Housing's investigation of the building material trust, commonly known as the Lockwood Committee after its chairman, Republican senator Charles C. Lockwood.[222] The investigation was the result of an initiative of a Democratic assemblyman, M. Maldwin Fertig.[223] Untermyer's exposure of corruption in the building industry resulted in several prosecutions. The New York District Attorney designated Untermyer Special Assistant District Attorney to facilitate the indictments.[224] Untermyer also used the inquiry as an opportunity to probe the New York Stock Exchange.[225] During the investigation the state enacted in 1921 its first Blue Sky Law, the Martin Act, which gave the state's attorney general the power to investigate stock market fraud. Untermyer considered it to be an ineffective law.[226] Meanwhile the committee completed its work in 1922 and chapter 6 of its final report was devoted to stock exchange practices.[227] The report noted that

> Another nine years have elapsed [since the Pujo Committee reported its findings] and the State of New York has still done nothing toward regulating these exchanges. Meantime numerous reforms have been effected in the practices of the New York Stock Exchange but the major abuses remain uncorrected and we find this Exchange today [1922] with its rapidly increasing powers still operating with its grip upon the public and its members more complete than at any time in its history.[228]

The Lockwood Committee recommended the enactment of a law regulating brokers and dealers in securities, stock exchanges and the transactions thereon.[229] Winsmore reported that

The new Untermeyer [sic] plan contains nothing novel. It is important, however, because of the steady growing radicalism that considers the stock market an integral part of the capitalistic system and that listens attentively to proposals to disorganize it and to contract its facilities. The Stock Exchange's policy of standing pat on its theoretical rights and refusing to bend to the tendencies of the times by correcting abuses which leave it open to criticism is what makes Untermeyerism [sic] appealing to the masses.[230]

Untermyer devised a program of legislation which included a bill to regulate the stock exchange, provided for the supervision of stock brokers and exchanges by the State Superintendent of Banks, the equivalent of a Blue Sky Law with teeth.[231] None of the legislation was enacted.[232] Untermyer subsequently observed that 'The influence of the big private bankers and of the Stock Exchanges dominated the Legislature, as I fear it always will in this State.'[233]

Untermyer also devoted a significant part of his final years to a resolution of New York City's transit problems.[234] He produced several plans for the unification and municipal control of the city's privately owned transit system between 1921 and 1931.[235] Untermyer also defended the 5 cent fare, even though as a stockholder in the IRT he would have benefitted from an increased fare.[236] Clifton Hood has also observed that 'the nickel fare led to disinvestment in underground rapid transit.'[237] In 1938 he used his position as delegate at large to the New York State Convention to prepare a proposed constitutional amendment which would permit New York City to buy the privately operated IRT and Brooklyn-Manhattan Transit Corporation systems for city bonds exempted from the debt limit. This formed the basis of the eventual amendment tabled by M. Maldwin Fertig of the State Transit Commission[238] with the support of Mayor Fiorello La Guardia.[239] The amendment was approved in mid-August subject which was subsequently approved by the voters in the November general election.[240] The unification and municipal ownership of New York's rapid transit system were finally achieved by La Guardia a few months after Untermyer's death in June 1940 at a cost of $326 million.[241]

Untermyer also anticipated banker Felix Rohatyn's financial rescue plan when New York City faced bankruptcy in 1976.[242] In 1933 during the depths of the Great Depression the city also faced bankruptcy. In July, the Tammany council appointed its sternest critic as its special financial adviser.[243] His first financial reorganization plan in the form of a bill raising taxes was approved by the State Senate but was blocked by the State Assembly in mid-August.[244] Undaunted Untermyer proceeded to appoint a committee of six, headed by Peter Grimm, the chairman of the Citizens Budget Commission, to assist him in another attempt to restore the city's finances.[245] Untermyer put together a second financial reorganization plan.[246] It included a proposed stock transfer tax of 4¢ per share. In response the New York Stock Exchange threatened to relocate the bulk of its business to a proposed branch in northern New Jersey.[247] The city was forced to abandon the proposed stock transfer tax.[248] A comprehensive plan to extricate the city from its financial plight was finally agreed at all-day conference at Governor Herbert H. Lehman's New York City apartment, attended by the governor, Untermyer, Mayor John P. O'Brien, Comptroller George McAneny and a committee representing the private banks and Clearing House institutions.[249] Untermyer then held secret negotiations on behalf of the city with its principal creditors, the New York City banks and J.P. Morgan & Co. A provisional agreement was reached in mid-October. Lehman called a special session of the New York State Legislature on 16 October to agree to its terms. The agreement to reorganize the city's debt was finally implemented on 30 October.[250] Untermyer considered that he deserved the credit for the agreement, later observing in 1934 'the richest city in the world, that was literally trembling on the verge of bankruptcy when I negotiated the contract with the Bankers that saved it from that catastrophe and disgrace ... is headed toward the financial rehabilitation and high credit to which it is entitled'.[251]

The failure of President Hoover to alleviate the Great Depression meant that by 1932 the prospects for a Democratic Party victory in the November election looked good. In April, the Senate Banking and Currency Committee began an investigation into the stock exchange. The committee's chairman, Progressive Republican Senator Peter Norbeck, asked Untermyer to be the inquiry's counsel. Untermyer declined.[252] Following the election of Franklin D. Roosevelt as president, Norbeck asked Untermyer in December to replace the investigation's first counsel who had resigned. Untermyer was unavailable because Roosevelt had asked him to draft a stock exchange and securities bill. Norbeck appointed Ferdinand Pecora instead.[253]

At the beginning of January, the president-elect asked Untermyer to meet with him to discuss the drafting of the bill while they were in Albany for the inauguration of Herbert H. Lehman as the new governor. The political commentators Drew Pearson and Robert S. Allen recalled the following year that Untermyer was delighted, indeed so delighted that he could not resist leaking to the *New York American* news of the meeting the evening before his departure. Pearson and Allen note there was nothing Roosevelt disliked 'so much as having his plans published'. So he cancelled the meeting.[254] In response Untermyer issued a statement to the press denying that he had a planned appointment with the president-elect.[255] Rebuffed, Untermyer left New York for his winter vacation in Palm Springs.[256] Roosevelt was also apparently irritated when Untermyer issued a press statement a couple of days after his arrival in which he said he had discussed with the president-elect on several occasions the activities of the New York Stock Exchange and the problem of government regulation.[257] However, unlike Wilson, Roosevelt understood the importance of rewarding those who had helped fund his campaign. Untermyer and his nephew, Laurence A. Steinhardt, had contributed $11,000 and $5,000 respectively to his presidential campaign fund. Steinhardt was an early supporter of Roosevelt's candidacy.[258] Roosevelt was impressed by Steinhardt. In March he suggested to Cordell Hull, his secretary of state, that he appoint him assistant secretary in charge of legal work.[259] Hull did not make the appointment. Meanwhile Untermyer told his nephew he could realistically expect to be made ambassador to Switzerland or Sweden. Steinhardt was appointed ambassador to Sweden in April.[260]

While he was in California Untermyer gave two speeches calling for stock exchange regulation.[261] He described the New York Stock Exchange as 'the most powerful and despotic institution on earth'.[262] Upon his return from California in March, he immediately travelled to Washington, DC, where Roosevelt had now been inaugurated as president. He discussed with members of the new administration details of the legislation to bring federal regulation of the stock exchange. While he was in

Washington, Senator Duncan U. Fletcher, who had replaced Norbeck as chairman of the Senate Banking and Currency Committee, asked Untermyer to assist Ferdinand Pecora. Untermyer declined again.[263] Raymond Moley believed that Untermyer would have done 'vastly better job' than Pecora.[264] He declined the position once more. Michael Perino notes, in his history of Pecora's investigation, Untermyer subsequently made repeated and unsuccessful attempts to secure the post of counsel to the committee, even after Pecora had begun work.[265]

Untermyer's draft bill did not please Roosevelt. The bill, like the Owen bill of 1914, provided for supervision through the Post Office Department. Untermyer had endeavoured to ensure that the bill conformed the US Constitution. Roosevelt wanted a less conformist bill. Unbeknownst to Moley, Roosevelt had also asked the ex-chairman of the Federal Trade Commission Huston Thompson to draft a bill as well. Moley and Untermyer were unimpressed by Thompson's legal draftsmanship. According to Louis D. Brandeis Thompson possessed 'every quality that makes a great lawyer except one: "Brains"'. Roosevelt held a meeting at the end of March, at which he tried to get Untermyer and Thompson to agree to merge their bills. It was not a success. Roosevelt decided two bills were required: a securities bill and a stock exchange regulation bill. Felix Frankfurter was tasked to organize a draft of the first bill, while Untermyer was asked to produce a draft of the second bill. By the time Untermyer had produced his draft bill Roosevelt had decided to put off stock exchange regulation until January 1934. Roosevelt subsequently decided not to use Untermyer's bill and instead commissioned another draft bill from two young associates of Frankfurter.[266]

Undaunted Untermyer continued to opine on stock exchange regulation outside the Washington arena. He gave a couple of speeches on the subject in southern California during his winter 1934 vacation.[267] In January Moley, in his role as editor of *Today*, published an article by Untermyer based on a speech on 'The Outlaw Stock Exchange', which he had given to the University Club of Los Angeles the previous February.[268] In early April, after his return from winter vacation, Untermyer testified before the Senate Committee on Banking and Currency on the Fletcher-Rayburn Securities Exchange bill. He started his testimony by reminding the senators of his long-standing interest in the regulation of the New York Stock Exchange.

> Perhaps I may be pardoned . . . for referring to the fact that I have been for at least a quarter of a century actively agitating for such legislation, both in the Congress of the United States and in the State of New York, and am the author of a number of bills looking to that end, beginning with the bill recommended in the Pujo Committee report, and followed in 1913 by a bill which was before the Senate Committee on Banking and Currency, of which Senator Owen, of Oklahoma, was then chairman, and known as the 'Owen bill', and ending with the submission of a bill last year that was prepared by me at the request of the President.[269]

Untermyer made many suggestions as to how the bill might be improved based on his long career as a corporate attorney.[270] Pecora said at the close of Untermyer's testimony:

Might I make again the statement that the communication addressed to us by Mr. Untermyer and which contained many suggestions, most of which he has referred to in detail today, was very, very carefully and favorably considered, and I think it should be stated to Mr. Untermyer that many of them have been adopted.

Untermyer replied, 'I am very intensely interested in this thing. The passage of this legislation I would regard as the culmination of one of my ambitions of a quarter of a century'.[271] The Fletcher-Rayburn bill became law on 6 June 1934. The *Brooklyn Daily Eagle* observed that it was 'The most bitterly fought legislation in many years, . . . crammed down the throats of moneyed interests by . . . Congress'.[272]

Untermyer's testimony at the hearings on the Fletcher-Rayburn bill was not his final intervention on securities reform. He returned to the fray in June 1937 at the hearings on Senator Alben W. Barkley's Regulation of Sale of Securities bill. Untermyer observed that while he was 'a great admirer of the work of the [Securities and Exchange] Commission' it was not infallible, it made mistakes as 'we all do'.[273] Untermyer was interested in a particular provision of the bill, the accessibility of bondholders' lists. He noted that as a representative of a committee of bondholders during the Krueger & Toll and International Match reorganization, he had been unable to gain access to the lists. Untermyer argued that the provision in the bill relating to bond holders lists required amendment to fully secure the objective of making the lists accessible to interested parties.[274] After the proposed additional powers of the Securities and Exchange Commission in the bill were radically restricted, it was enacted two years later as the Trust Indenture Act of 1939,[275] less than a year before Untermyer's death.

It is unlikely without the Great Crash of 1929 that Roosevelt would have supported federal regulation of America's stock markets. The political power of the New York Stock Exchange and its allies, the elite investment banks, was too great under normal circumstances. Untermyer must have undoubtedly felt a great sense of achievement at the successful conclusion to his

> thankless fight for the protection of innocent investors against the fraudulent promoters, the highly respected swindlers posing as 'stockbrokers', and the many other frauds that have been made possible by the absence of Federal laws regulating the public issue of securities through the machinery of the Stock Exchanges by which the public [was] being swindled out of hundreds of millions of dollars annually.

This had been achieved at the cost of 'persistent personal attacks and misrepresentations'.[276]

4

Untermyer as a Zionist leader in the 1920s

To be or not to be?[1]

Unlike some of his contemporaries Untermyer did not serve as a steward of the American Jewish community[2] until circumstances forced his hand during the First World War. Emanuel Neumann, an American Zionist, later claimed that before Untermyer accepted the presidency of the American branch of the Keren Hayesod (Palestine Foundation Fund) in 1921, he 'had been as far removed from Jewish affairs as his [law firm] partner, Louis Marshall, had been involved in them all his life.' Indeed, Neumann felt that 'except for the circumstances of his birth, there was nothing Jewish about him.'[3] More recently Susie J. Pak has observed Untermyer 'was . . . not of the German Jewish "Our Crowd," the Jewish social and economic elite in New York.'[4]

Neumann was wrong. In 1921 *The New Palestine*, the official organ of the Zionist Organization of America (ZOA), observed of Untermyer that 'The Jew who in his youth delved into the learning of the Talmud can never be very far from the heart-pulse of his people.'[5] Indeed, he had been actively involved with Jewish affairs since the 1880s when he was a supporter of the Society for Ethical Culture.[6] It was founded by Felix Adler who had split from the Reform Judaism of his father, Temple Emanu-El's Rabbi Samuel Adler. Later in 1895 Untermyer became a member of Temple Emanu-El, the synagogue favoured by 'Our Crowd'.[7] After his purchase of Greystone in 1900 he also became an active member and pewholder of Temple Emanu-El of Yonkers.[8] Furthermore, unlike his fellow German American Jew, Otto H. Kahn, Untermyer never disguised the fact that he was a Jew.[9] In fact he was proud of being Jewish.[10]

Pak's assertion that Untermyer was not a member of 'Our Crowd'[11] is also wrong. Indeed, as already noted in Chapter 1, he had been part of the German Jewish economic and social elite since his mother had moved the Untermyer family from Lynchburg to New York City. From the 1890s Untermyer was a financial benefactor of New York's elite Jewish charities such as the Purim Association,[12] the Hebrew Orphan Asylum of New York City[13] and the Montefiore Home for Chronic Invalids, the last of which he was also a director for several years. He also served as the home's lawyer.[14] The home was the charitable project of Kuhn, Loeb & Co. banker Jacob H. Schiff. Schiff oversaw its finances from its foundation in 1884 and served as its president from 1885 to 1920.[15] Later Untermyer was a founder member of a branch of the Young Men's Hebrew Association in Yonkers.[16] At a mass meeting in Yonkers to organize the branch in May 1912 he said that he owed his success in no small measure to the influence of the Young Men's Hebrew Association in New York City with which he was also associated.[17] He also subsequently helped organize and support a branch of the Young Women's Hebrew Association in Yonkers.[18] During the First World War he was one of the leaders of a campaign for Jewish Relief in Europe. He believed that

> The Jews who do not contribute to this fund to the full extent of their abilities are not taking a just view of their obligations to their race . . . They have no right to withhold their aid while their brethren are starving by the hundreds of thousands by the wayside in the far corners of the earth and cannot be rescued without their assistance.[19]

In the aftermath of the war Untermyer supported the international relief efforts of the American Jewish Joint Distribution Committee (JDC).[20]

In addition to his own contributions to Jewish community life, Untermyer also created the space for his law firm partner, Louis Marshall, to play the role that Neumann attributes to him. Marshall's contribution to the firm's work normally took precedence over everything else. Untermyer probably considered Marshall's community leadership to be a form of corporate social responsibility. Even before Marshall became a community leader, he was active in combatting anti-Semitism in American society. Untermyer privately shared Marshall's abhorrence of social anti-Semitism.[21] However, unlike him, he normally did not take a public stand against it. For example, in September 1920 Henry Clay Silver, managing partner of Melhuish & Company, a Wall Street brokerage firm, sent Untermyer a copy of an anti-Semitic tract entitled *Protocols of the Zionists* being circulated by Henry W. Marsh, of the New York insurance firm Marsh & McCain. In the tract Marsh referred to the Rand School case.[22] Untermyer dismissed it as 'nothing more than the usual bigoted anti-Semitic outputs'.[23] However, Untermyer made an exception during the 1920s when became involved in a high-profile case against the anti-Semitic automobile manufacturer Henry Ford.

Untermyer's enmity with Ford predated the case. He had been insulted by the manufacturer in 1920, when Ford had ignored a letter Untermyer had written on behalf of a Yonkers lawyer, David Gorfinkel. Gorfinkel had worked for Guggenheimer, Untermyer & Marshall as a boy. After graduating from there he had gone on to practice law in Yonkers. Gorfinkel and some friends had taken over the bankrupt Ford agency in Yonkers and made it profitable. However, the Ford Motor Co. had decided to take away their agency without good reason. Untermyer asked Ford to investigate the matter. Ford ignored his letter.[24]

However, Ford was not unaware of Untermyer. The following year, he published two articles in his anti-Semitic newspaper *The Dearborn Independent*, identifying Untermyer as one of the Jews allegedly directing 'Tammany's Gentile puppets'.[25] The second article also observed that

> Tammany is no longer denounced by the public press, but the Jewish leaders of Tammany live daily to a chorus of praise in the Jewish-controlled newspapers of New York. Samuel Untermeyer [sic], for example, receives more publicity in New York than does the President of the United States, but it is

not discriminating publicity; it does not penetrate to the inner purposes and consequences of his actions.[26]

Untermyer reciprocated in December by describing Ford as a 'mad hatter'.

> Having put his colossal egotism up against all civilization on war, having next gone into the Jew-baiting business, and then into politics, in all of which he has proven a dismal failure, he now tries to create social unrest by his latest bizarre excrescence on world finance.
>
> The man is so densely ignorant on every subject except automobiles and so blinded by a depth of bigotry that belongs to the dark ages from which he has not yet emerged, that he is fool enough to publicly exploit this madhouse bug of his about the international bankers of the world owning the gold of the world. He imagines that the great international bankers of the world are Jews, which is not true, and has not been true for fifty years or more. It so happens that there are no Jews in such great banking houses as J.P. Morgan & Co., Lee Higginson & Co., or in the great English houses.[27]

The articles defaming Untermyer were part of a series derived from the infamous *Protocols of the Elders of Zion*. Louis Marshall as president of the American Jewish Committee was involved in the efforts to put a stop to Ford's anti-Semitic project. Victoria Saker Woeste notes that Marshall's characteristic approach to such matters 'was working behind the scenes rather than "provoking great public controversies"'.[28] This episode was no exception. At the beginning of January 1922 Henry Ford libelled Herman Bernstein, the Jewish journalist, writer and editor of *The Jewish Tribune*, in a syndicated newspaper interview with Allan L. Benson. He claimed Bernstein was a source of information and inspiration for the anti-Semitic articles in *The Dearborn Independent*.[29] Bernstein issued a denial that he was the source[30] and decided to sue Ford for libel. He visited his friend Marshall for advice. Bernstein was of the view that there were none better to represent him than Marshall or Untermyer. Marshall declined on behalf of both himself and Untermyer. It is not clear whether Untermyer was consulted. Marshall doubted whether Bernstein could prove he was legally harmed by Ford and pointed to the jurisdictional challenge of suing Ford in New York. As to suing Ford in Detroit Marshall believed no jury in that city would return a verdict unfavourable to the manufacturer. He directed Bernstein to a fellow New York lawyer, Martin W. Littleton. However, Littleton proved to be an ineffective advocate for Bernstein.[31]

In frustration in July 1923 Bernstein appealed directly to Untermyer, who agreed to represent Bernstein in a $200,000 libel suit against Henry Ford. The basis of the action was an article in the 20 August 1921 issue of *The Dearborn Independent*.[32] The article, according to Bernstein, had charged him with being a 'spy' of 'the mythical combination of international Jewish bankers'. Bernstein declared:

> Regarding the article in question and those that preceded and have succeeded it as part of a consistent campaign of vilification and misrepresentation of the people of

my race on your part. I am determined to seek redress for the injury you have done me, and, incidentally, to expose the wanton falsehoods you have been spreading over the country concerning the Jews of the land, based largely upon documents that I heretofore exposed as forgeries, and the prejudice you have been trying to create based upon these figments of a diseased imagination.

It is high time for the American people to get a true picture of the manner of man you are, and I feel that in prosecuting this suit I am performing an important public service.[33]

Bernstein believed, as he wrote to Untermyer in September 1923, that there was no doubt that Ford was an anti-Semite.

As I said to you when I saw you last, The Dearborn Independent has attacked the Jews in various articles during the last six months, and every issue of the Dearborn Independent carries . . . advertisement of the four books Mr. Ford is selling now- 'The International Jew', 'Jewish Activities in the United States', 'Jewish Influences on American Life' and 'Aspects of Jewish Power in the United States'. This material, taken from The Dearborn Independent, is also reproduced now serially in various publications in Europe. To say that Ford is not conducting an anti-Jewish campaign is to close one's eyes to what he is doing. The books are now sold in large numbers throughout the country.[34]

Marshall opposed Untermyer representing Bernstein[35] and later told Julius Rosenwald he 'never had anything to do with' with the libel suit. He also claimed that Untermyer was acting independently of Guggenheimer, Untermyer & Marshall because he had not been his partner[36] since 1912. In fact Untermyer was still a member of the firm with the designation 'counsel'. All the paperwork for the case used the firm's stationery and Untermyer was assisted by one of the firm's partners, his nephew, Laurence A. Steinhardt. The firm also bore nearly all the costs during the four years of discovery.[37] Robert S. Rifkind is wrong to conclude Marshall was correct when he implied that Untermyer was no longer a member of his firm and that Victoria Saker Woeste is wrong to make the 'serious charge' that this was a 'rhetorical disguise' intended to conceal Marshall's violation of the canons of professional ethics. Rifkind's evidence is a letter from Marshall to his father from the beginning of January 1912 reporting Untermyer's retirement and legal directory entries for the firm that subsequently designated Untermyer as 'counsel' rather than as 'partner'. This overlooks the fact, as shown in Chapter 1, unlike his brother Isaac and former partner Moses Weinman, Untermyer subsequently rescinded his decision to retire. Untermyer continued to represent clients as a member of the firm for many more years. Nor is Rifkind correct to suggest that Marshall's uncharacteristic fit of pique 'was meant to indicate that relations between the two men, once close, had become distant'. In fact, Untermyer remained a close friend throughout the last years of Marshall's life.[38]

Henry Ford tried to avoid being sued personally by suggesting the suit be brought against the Dearborn Publishing Company. Bernstein insisted on serving Ford personally. Since the action was brought in the New York County Supreme Court, if Ford did not set foot in New York State, he could avoid being served. Untermyer responded by attaching whatever property or interest Ford had in New York State.³⁹ There then began a long, protracted campaign of obstruction by Ford in the courts to avoid the suit being heard. He got the case transferred to the United States District Court for the Southern District of New York. The manufacturer surrounded himself with armed guards to avoid being served. Steinhardt noted in a memorandum to his uncle that it was impossible to get near Ford to serve him with a subpoena.⁴⁰ Meanwhile another victim of *The Dearborn Independent*'s libels, Aaron Sapiro, brought suit in Detroit. The case ended in a mistrial in April 1927.⁴¹

Following the mistrial Ford conferred with various friends, including Arthur Brisbane. Ford concluded that the publicity generated by the libel suits was affecting sales of his cars. He decided to reach out to a suitable representative of American Jewry with a view to a resolution of the controversies and ill feeling. Negotiations were started with Marshall, who drafted a statement of apology and retraction on behalf of the manufacturer. Ford agreed to put his signature to Marshall's seventh draft. The statement was released by its official recipient, Marshall,⁴² in early July. Ford apologized for the anti-Semitic articles in *The Dearborn Independent*, claiming that the wide scope of his activities had made it impossible to devote his personal attention to the conduct and policies of his publications, and that he was obliged to delegate their management to others.⁴³

Before Ford's statement was released Marshall had informed Untermyer on 1 July and observed he had also already told Bernstein. Marshall claimed, probably disingenuously, that he had been unable to contact Untermyer for several days. Woeste observes that 'Instead of minimizing his own impact on his firm's client, he subtly pressured Untermyer to subordinate the lawsuit to the "moral effect" of Ford's apology.'⁴⁴ Untermyer understandably was aggrieved. He replied to Marshall that Bernstein wanted Ford to make retraction and settlement with him simultaneously with the statement or alternatively he and Bernstein wanted Ford to know that they intended to issue a statement challenging the sincerity of his excuse that he was deceived.⁴⁵ Untermyer concluded by observing:

> By insisting, as usual, on 'going it alone,' I think you have made a mistake. However, if you can arrange so that our statement commenting on this will not be understood and not regarded as a breach of faith by you or me I do not see that I have any right to object. Otherwise I do object – decidedly.⁴⁶

Marshall fired back:

> For once I insist that you do not interfere ... I tried to inform you of the proceedings but apparently you had no time for me, besides it was certain what your natural reaction would be and I did not regard your recent treatment conducive to confidences.⁴⁷

Untermyer replied:

> [I b]itterly resent your amazing intolerant attitude. [I]t is you who are wantonly inconsiderately interfering in my affairs and autocratically dictating what I shall

do without consulting me[,] taking unto yourself credit for [a] situation you did nothing to create and which could not have been created if you had your way.

Your absurd statements about having no time for you and about my treatment of you ... simply bewilder me.[48]

Untermyer was forced to submit to Marshall, to avoid humiliating him. However, he believed Marshall had a duty to withhold the statement until Bernstein and Sapiro had been satisfied. Although Marshall tried to get the publication of the statement delayed for a few days, he was too late.[49]

Marshall subsequently disingenuously observed to Julius Rosenwald that

In my opinion, except remotely, neither the Sapiro nor the Bernstein cases had anything to do with the retraction. There were other psychological forces at work. The retraction, on the other hand, ... will result in a settlement of the Bernstein case.[50]

Untermyer subsequently negotiated an out-of-court settlement of the Bernstein libel suit with Ford.[51] Steinhardt and Bernstein were willing to accept Ford's initial offer of $60,000. But Untermyer ignored them and persuaded Ford to raise his offer to $75,000.[52] At the end of July Ford wrote a letter of apology to Bernstein. In his letter, Ford wrote that

From the explanations made to me by my counsel through your counsel, Mr. Samuel Untermyer, I realize the damage that may have been caused you among the people of your race and in your profession as an author, editor and newspaper correspondent by the article of which you complain in your suit, and the expense, which you could ill afford, to which you have been put by the protracted litigation to vindicate the good name of the Jewish people and your own reputation against the charges contained in those articles.[53]

Bernstein accepted the apology and agreed to drop his libel suit against Ford. Ford also promised to contribute liberally toward defraying the expenses incurred by Bernstein in connection with the suit. Untermyer also insisted that Ford agree to make an energetic effort to counteract the effects of the libel in all parts of the world where it was published. The settlement was reached at a conference held at Greystone on 24 July between Untermyer and three representatives of Ford, Clifford B. Longley of Detroit, De Lancey Nicoll, Jr. and Martin C. Ansorge of New York.[54] Guggenheimer, Untermyer & Marshall received half of the $75,000. Bernstein told Untermyer that he hoped that Laurence A. Steinhardt would be 'substantially compensated' for the 'enormous amount of hard and conscientious work' he had put into the case.[55] Untermyer did indeed pay Steinhardt for his time. He also reimbursed his firm for its costs and as a peace offering sent a cheque for half the balance to Marshall as his share in connection with the settlement of the case.[56]

Unfortunately, Marshall's agreement with Ford did not prevent the publication of translations of *The International Jew* from being published in Europe. Contrary to the agreement Ford chose not to prevent these publications. *The International Jew* had never been copyrighted, and Ford was unwilling to financially compensate the European publishers for withdrawing the translations.[57] In November 1927 Untermyer learnt that Hammer Verlag of Leipzig had denied that Henry Ford had ordered them to stop the publication of the German translation of his book *The International Jew*. Untermyer wrote to Clifford B. Longley, the general counsel to the Ford Motor Company, asking him to ensure that Ford honoured the agreement with Bernstein by compelling Hammer Verlag to seize publication of his book and to surrender the books on hand to be destroyed as agreed.[58] Untermyer also sent a copy of the letter to the *New York Times*.[59] Longley responded by saying that he had received a telegram from Bernstein saying that Untermyer did not speak for him in this matter and that he was satisfied with the action Ford was taking with regard to the book in question.[60]

Untermyer's most important contribution to the Jewish community during the 1920s was his fundraising for Jewish settlement in Palestine. He was to serve as the first president of the Keren Hayesod's American branch, the fundraising arm of the World Zionist Organization (WZO) led by Dr Chaim Weizmann. American Jewry made substantial financial donations to support the Zionist Project after the establishment of the British Mandate in Palestine. The League of Nations Mandate was assigned to Britain at the San Remo Conference in 1920, and it was regarded at the time as the fulfilment of the Balfour Declaration of 1917, in which the British government had declared its support for 'the establishment in Palestine of a national home for the Jews'.[61] However, it was not until 1922 that the Council of the League of Nations formally approved the award of the mandate to Britain.[62] During the early years of the Mandate the Keren Hayesod was the principal conduit for American donations. It had been created by the annual conference of the WZO held in London in July 1920 and officially registered in England the following year.[63]

Untermyer had already had some contacts with the American Zionist movement dating back to the early 1910s before he accepted the presidency of the Keren Hayesod's American branch.[64] For example, he had previously given money to the emergency fund of the Provisional Executive Committee for General Zionist Affairs during the First World War. It would appear, according to Eugene Meyer,[65] he had had doubts about the merits of the Zionist Project. He apparently needed further persuasion by his nephew Laurence before he parted with his money.[66] Untermyer confessed to Louis D. Brandeis that he had an imperfect knowledge of the merits of the Zionist Project except that he was sure it was worthwhile because Brandeis and Rabbi Stephen S. Wise were so unselfishly devoting themselves to its promotion.[67] Brandeis had been an ardent Zionist since 1912.[68]

However, it was his niece's brother-in-law who convinced him to actively support the Zionist Project. In October 1920 Untermyer's niece, Therese Steinhardt[69] married William Rosenblatt.[70] William's brother, Magistrate Bernard A. Rosenblatt, was president of the American Zion Commonwealth. Rosenblatt was already acquainted with Untermyer and had sent him Zionist literature the previous year.[71] At the wedding, Rosenblatt asked Untermyer if they could meet to discuss the Jewish work in Palestine. Rosenblatt was very diplomatic in the way he approached Untermyer. He assured him that his object was not to collect money. Instead, he was very interested in the creation of a profitable financial institution. If such an institution was able to pay dividends it might become instrumental in creating a Jewish majority in Palestine. He appreciated the burden of work upon the lawyer, and if the matter could bear long delay, he would not have approached him. Rosenblatt said he was convinced that after a hearing Untermyer would conclude that he was able to become the most important factor in the future of Palestine. Indeed, Untermyer could become the American connection with Palestine, without any undue interference on the part of his present public and private duties. Untermyer's reputation and advice would, Rosenblatt was convinced, be sufficient for the Zionist Project.[72] Rosenblatt succeeded in capturing the wary lawyer's interest. Untermyer held at least two meetings with Rosenblatt in late 1920 to discuss the work of the American Zionists.[73] Rosenblatt followed up these meetings by sending Weizmann a letter of introduction to Untermyer.[74]

The following February Rosenblatt had a long talk with Untermyer at his home. As a result, it was agreed that Untermyer should not undertake American Zion Commonwealth work, but that he should wait the arrival of Chaim Weizmann in the United States in April and hold a conference with the British Zionist leader and Rosenblatt. This was to

Illustration 9 Photograph of Samuel Untermyer and Albert Einstein, Palm Springs, 7 February 1933.

be Untermyer's first meeting with Weizmann. Rosenblatt observed that Untermyer was firmly convinced that Palestine could only be rebuilt based on a single concentrated financial scheme. Rosenblatt felt that meant either the Keren Hayesod or a similar body with an explicit connection with the WZO executive could be launched in the United States under the best of auspices.[75] During Weizmann's visit Untermyer and his wife also entertained at lunch him and his wife at Greystone together with Albert Einstein and his wife in early April 1921. Einstein was also a member of the Keren Hayesod's first fundraising delegation to visit the United States. He was particularly interested in raising funds for the proposed establishment of a Hebrew university in Jerusalem.[76]

Untermyer became a member of the Keren Hayesod (Palestine Foundation Fund) Committee following the meeting[77] and decided to support the president of the WZO, Dr Chaim Weizmann, against the faction in the ZOA led by Louis D. Brandeis and Julian W. Mack.[78] Unlike some of the wealthy Jewish supporters of Zionism, Untermyer was familiar with the challenges European Jewish immigrants faced in a Middle Eastern setting having visited Egypt for a vacation before the First World War.[79] Untermyer also observed at a meeting in May, 'Somebody said that I am a convert to Zionism. That is not so. I have been a Zionist for years. Unfortunately I have had no practical part in the shaping of the policy.'[80] In May 1921 Untermyer was elected head of the board of trustees of the American branch of Keren Hayesod.[81] Rosenblatt then persuaded Untermyer to accept the post of president as well.[82] He accepted on the understanding that the Weizmann Faction would not promote a sectarian Jewish state in Palestine in the foreseeable future. As he told Weizmann:

I cannot conceive of any American or British citizen who above all things loves his country and its institutions assenting to be identified with any movement that involves a virtual separation or conflict in thought or feeling between his loyalty to his country and his racial aspirations.[83]

Untermyer succeeded Louis D. Brandeis as president of the American branch of the Keren Hayesod in June after the latter, Judge Julian W. Mack and their followers resigned from their official positions in the ZOA at its twenty-fourth annual convention in Cleveland.[84]

At the request of his friend Nathan Straus, he had tried to mediate an end to the split between Weizmann's WZO and the Brandeis–Mack Faction at a meeting held at the Hebrew Technical School for Girls a few weeks before the Cleveland convention. Untermyer was tasked with preparing a written agreement to end the schism. Both sides appear to have signified their approval of Untermyer's document. However, when the two factions arrived in Cleveland a last-minute misunderstanding meant the Brandeis–Mack Faction withdrew its approval.[85] Esther Panitz argues that the intractability of the positions held by each position 'doomed the Untermeyer [sic] project',[86] as the heated debates at the convention revealed.[87] Nonetheless, the chairman of the convention's sixth session, Judge Henry C. Dannenbaum, considered Untermyer's 'willingness to serve and to lend his name as a practical endorsement of the Keren Hayesod, as a most valuable acquisition; verily the hand of the God of Israel is at the steering wheel'.[88] However, the *American Hebrew* observed:

What a pity that a man like Samuel Untermyer permitted himself to be dragged into a factional squabble! He is one man who has in no wise been tainted by the mistakes and foolhardiness of either of the Zionist groups. Standing aside from both and appealing in [sic] behalf of Palestine, as a non-Zionist he could have marshalled them all for the rehabilitation of Palestine through American commercial methods.[89]

When Chaim Weizmann returned to England in June he received a tribute in the form of a letter from Untermyer which, he said, moved him to tears.[90] Untermyer also accompanied Weizmann on his return voyage to Europe.[91] Later in early September 1921 Untermyer attended the Twelfth World Zionist Congress in Carlsbad, Czechoslovakia, as the head of the ZOA's delegation.[92] After his return to New York he helped organize a national conference that was held in the city in mid-November to launch the Keren Hayesod's fundraising campaign.[93]

Rosenblatt and his colleagues knew that to successfully raise funds for the development of Jewish settlement in Palestine they needed a man with Untermyer's public profile to replace Brandeis and Mack. Untermyer's previous lack of affiliation was not a problem.[94] The fund was deliberately autonomous so that it could attract donations from non-Zionists. Untermyer's selection served this purpose well. Maier Bryan Fox also argues that it was inspired politics because it gave the Keren Hayesod legitimacy among non-Zionist Jews. Untermyer's high public profile

> contributed to widespread publicity in addition to that generated by Weizmann's national tour. In the sense that Untermyer's pronouncements often antagonized Zionists, they were a two-edged sword. But Zionists could be depended upon to overcome their pique, and his words were balm to the ears of the rest of the community.[95]

Albert Einstein, who was a member of the Weizmann Faction, wrote to Untermyer later in 1921,

> I hope and am convinced that your influence on the Zionist project will be beneficial, since you are particularly suited to bringing about mutual understanding between the various groups and to helping to turn the whole undertaking in a positive economic and political direction.[96]

Untermyer was to address fundraising events across the United States during his presidency. He also organized a Keren Hayesod Thousand Dollar Club which secured donations from multimillionaires such as his former partner Louis Marshall, client Adolph Lewisohn and others such as Jefferson Seligman.[97]

Emanuel Neumann, the Keren Hayesod's general secretary,[98] later claimed that Untermyer never once participated in the meetings of their committee and did not know many of the people he was working with. Neumann took on the role of intermediary. He would go and see Untermyer at either his city home or out at Greystone. The young Zionist found him a very difficult person to deal with.[99] Neumann undoubtedly exaggerated Untermyer's disengagement from the everyday affairs of the Keren Hayesod. In June 1923 Untermyer was sufficiently involved to uncover what he considered to be financial irregularities on the part of the local committees of the Keren Hayesod in the United States. He wrote to Weizmann asking him to assist him in enforcing proper methods of accounting.[100] Untermyer's rather abrasive approach to his inferiors was often misinterpreted. Later when Neumann left the Keren Hayesod to study law at New York University he found out that the elderly attorney had a high opinion of him. Neumann recalled:

> He even offered me a place in his law firm once I had passed the bar examination and had been admitted to practice. The offer was unexpected and most enticing, for the firm was a very prestigious one, and I already imagined myself seated comfortably at one of the impressive mahogany desks in that magnificent office, 'on top of the world' as a successful corporation lawyer with opulent clients. The subject crossed my mind at different times, but it never went any further: my Zionist interests inevitably overshadowed all thoughts of personal advancement.[101]

Untermyer's election as president created tensions with the Zionists who did the daily work under his nominal direction. They had to be constantly on guard to ensure he did not say something inappropriate. Fox observes, 'they had to monitor his statements carefully and remove the anti-nationalistic rhetoric which would undermine Zionist support for the infant fund.'[102] Untermyer's attendance at his son Alvin's church wedding in November 1923 caused great offence. The Orthodox community unsuccessfully tried to remove Untermyer from the Keren Hayesod presidency because this appeared to be an acceptance of apostasy.[103] However, many of the prominent Zionist activists in Palestine were, like Untermyer, not especially observant Jews. This no doubt helps explain why he retained his position.

The Keren Hayesod had great hopes of Untermyer as Neumann observed in a report to Chaim Weizmann at the end of May 1921. Neumann reported that Untermyer had helped them considerably, particularly in the American cities. However, they had not yet begun to exploit possibilities of his adherence. He argued they should try and secure a donation for the Keren Hayesod from Untermyer. Untermyer could afford to donate millions of dollars, but Neumann incorrectly claimed that he had hitherto given very little to Jewish causes, or charity in general. Rosenblatt had suggested Weizmann now had great influence over Untermyer, so he should raise the question of a donation with him. If Untermyer was not attracted to the idea of contributing to the Keren Hayesod, Weizmann could suggest the land mortgage bank project or the Rutenberg Scheme. Weizmann should try to get Untermyer to promise at least $1 million, at $200,000 a year. That was the minimum they should expect. Weizmann should make Untermyer feel that this was an opportunity to become an international figure in Jewish affairs; that what was proposed was not philanthropy, but Jewish statecraft, in which he was becoming interested.[104] Neumann obviously failed to realize that Untermyer's idea of a generous donation was $10,000.[105]

Untermyer's involvement with the Zionist movement may also have cost it the potential support of some other wealthy prominent Jews, as a confidential report received by Weizmann in July of the following year revealed. The case of Felix M. Warburg was cited. Untermyer had attacked Kuhn, Loeb & Co. during the Pujo Money Trust Investigation. This gave Warburg, who was a partner in the bank, another reason to oppose the Zionist Project.[106] However, Warburg overcame his ill-feeling towards Untermyer by the end of the year and became a supporter of the Keren Hayesod.[107]

In the summer of 1921 Untermyer wrote an article, published in the September number of *The Forum*, on behalf of the Keren Hayesod[108] in reply to an anti-Zionist article by Henry Morgenthau in the July number of *World's Work*.[109] Morgenthau had called Zionism 'the most stupendous fallacy in Jewish history'.[110] Untermyer retorted that Morgenthau claimed to be an expert on East European Jewry and yet failed to realize how Zionism had captured their imagination. He wrote that Morgenthau argued that Zionism was a 'betrayal'. This showed his ignorance of Jewish history and literature. Throughout the annals of the Jewish people there had been a persistent and irrepressible longing for the restoration of the Jewish homeland. Untermyer went on to observe that Morgenthau taunted the Zionists with having temporarily abandoned their plans for a sovereign Jewish state in Palestine and accepted instead a national home for the Jewish people. Untermyer claimed the Zionist leaders had no plans for a sovereign Jewish state.

Implicit to Morgenthau's article was a belief in the 'Melting Pot' ideal whereby Jews took full advantage of the opportunities in countries such as the United States where they had the same rights as citizens of other faiths. Untermyer, who also believed in the 'Melting Pot' ideal, had a less positive view of the opportunities available to Jews living outside the United States, Britain and France. He observed:

> Mr. Morgenthau emphasizes that the 'anti-Zionist Jews of America have found that the spiritual life in modern times can be most fully enjoyed by those people who accept the beneficent progress which the world at large has made in science, industry, and the art of government.' Does he suggest that Zionists, whether in America or elsewhere, are indifferent or opposed to the benefits of science, industry and the art of government? ... Or has he not heard that the greatest thinker of the day, the second Newton, Professor Einstein, is an ardent Zionist and is working for the successful promotion of the [Hebrew] University [in Jerusalem]? ...
>
> ...Mr. Morgenthau's article seems to have been written in a mood of personal egotism and a sort of moral vacuum, alive only to the financial success, the social position, and the material reward that the Jews in America can gain. He tells us that the Jews in France have found France to be their Zion, the Jews of England, England, and the Jews of America, America. But what of the millions of Jews in distracted Russia, in blood-stained Ukraine, in intolerant Poland and Rumania, in Anti-Semetic [sic] Austria, Hungary and Germany? Have they found their Zion yet? They are seeking it where their forefathers have always sought it, and where hundreds of thousands of their brethren in other countries are helping them to find it – in Palestine. But they will not reach it unless there is greater cooperation and more generous sacrifice on the part of all Jews who are enjoying the financial success, the social position, and the material reward which Mr. Morgenthau holds in such high esteem.[111]

Morgenthau, who was an old friend of Untermyer, never forgave him for this highly personalized attack.[112] Rabbi Wise tactfully observed to Untermyer that 'the article would have been still better if certain rather personal references had been omitted.'[113] Morgenthau responded by asserting that while Untermyer might pass muster as a radical Jew, he was rather an indifferent brand of Jew from the religious point of view. Untermyer refuted Morgenthau's assertion in a speech at the second annual dinner of the Jewish Telegraphic Agency in October.[114]

In private Untermyer did not disagree with all of Morgenthau's observations about the Zionist Project.[115] Indeed one Wall Street contemporary, Harry Bronner of Blair & Company, doubted whether Untermyer really believed in the Zionist Project at all.[116] After Untermyer's return to New York from his 1921 European summer vacation he revealed publicly for the first time that he was opposed to Jewish nationalism.[117] The non-Zionist *American Hebrew* took great interest in Untermyer's perspective on Zionism. They wholeheartedly approved of his opposition to Jewish nationalism and wondered how Untermyer was able to reconcile his views on Zionism with those of men like Weizmann. They also noted that Untermyer's views on Jewish nationalism were not shared by most Zionists throughout the world.[118] In their 28 October issue they published excerpts from Untermyer's recent Jewish Telegraphic Agency dinner speech in which he had observed:

> I am as fundamentally opposed as any man in the movement to any Nationalist movement outside of Palestine and would have nothing to do with it on that basis, as was made quite plain to Dr. Weizmann before I consented to head the Keren Hayesod in America and to which he readily assented...
>
> I was greatly surprised that in some of these [central and southeast European] countries there is a large body of opinion that goes to the extreme of regarding Zionism as a purely nationalistic movement even to the extent of championing and insisting upon the view that the Jews in the various countries should set themselves apart in their communities and constitute themselves a sort of pseudo-nation.[119]

Untermyer sought to include non-Zionists such as Rabbi Samuel Shulman in the cause of upbuilding Palestine as a homeland of the Jews.[120] Rabbi Morris S. Lazaron wrote to Untermyer suggesting that his statement in the *American Hebrew*

> has made me think that at last, we have a statement from an official in the Zionist Organization, which would make it possible for the Central Conference of American Rabbis to carry out their intention of co-operating in practical work in Palestine, provided certain expressions in your statement could find official formulation by an act of the Zionist Organization.[121]

Although there were rumours circulating in Palestine in early 1922 that the American government was obstructing the ratification of Britain's League of Nations' mandate because it was opposed to the realization of the Balfour Declaration,[122] the Keren Hayesod began a campaign in March by calling for 5,000 volunteers to help raise $3 million to support Jewish settlement. Untermyer sent a message to Dannenbaum, the chairman of the campaign, observing that eastern and central European Jews had no hope of improving their living conditions in 'the lands of persecution'. Palestine was the only promise on the horizon.[123] Untermyer chaired the opening of the New York campaign at a meeting of 5,000 Zionists at Carnegie Hall on 16 April. In the audience were 3,200 men and women who had volunteered to seek contributions in all the city's boroughs during the following ten days. In his speech to the meeting Untermyer argued that Zionists and non-Zionists should put aside their differences so that a homeland could be built for the downtrodden of the Jewish race.[124] The fundraising drive was opposed by certain sections of American Jewry. Untermyer alleged that 'a handful of notoriety-seeking pygmies among the men of our own race' were spreading 'insidious propaganda' against the Keren Hayesod.[125] He argued that

> The movement is not nationalistic... Neither is it charitable, and yet it is distinctly humanitarian. The purpose is one of helping to self-help the Jews who want but have not the means to escape from the hate and the pogroms and massacres of the crazed, bigoted and Jew-baiting peoples of eastern and southeastern Europe.
>
> Truly, it is most 'un-American' to hold out such opportunities to the persecuted and downtrodden people of our race, is it not?[126]

Untermyer wrote a feature article on Zionism which appeared on the front page of the 14 April issue of *The Jewish Tribune*. Although he later claimed that he had not personally become a Zionist at this stage, his opening statement seemed to suggest otherwise.

> The ideals of Zionism are among the most thrilling and inspiring of which the human mind and heart are capable. The hope and dream of centuries, now well-nigh realized, that our race is at last to re-inhabit its ancient home, surrounded by the religions and historic traditions and landmarks so dear to us, and is there to resume its industrial life and cultural development on a broader and more comprehensive scale than could have been forecast by our forefathers in their wildest dreams, is one that must inspire the imagination of every Jew.

Untermyer went on to identify what he felt would be one of the most important aspects of the work of the Zionist settlers in the British Mandate. Palestine would provide Jews freedom of expression and the ability to fully realize their potential. Untermyer spoke of the foundation of a new university in Jerusalem.[127] He hoped that it would become a seat of learning that would surpass in its idealism and the variety of its culture, anything that the world had ever known. He observed

> We know that the material is among us. This university is to be the medium for its outlet and opportunity. Our mission is to be one of peace, liberty and goodwill. Surely such a vision and to work towards its realization are sufficient to stir the hearts of all mankind and to still the ancient hatreds of which our race has been victim through all the centuries that have gone before. This is my conception of Zionism.[128]

Later following the opening of the Hebrew University of Jerusalem in 1925,[129] Rabbi Dr Judah Leon Magnes, who was married to Untermyer's second cousin, Beatrice Lowenstein, was appointed its chancellor.[130] Untermyer welcomed the new university 'as a symbol of the mission of the Jews on a platform where all Jews are able to meet, whether they are Zionists, non-Zionists or anti-Zionists'.[131]

In addition to Lowenstein another member of Untermyer's family made her home in Palestine during the 1920s, his niece Madeleine Steinhardt. New York-born Madeleine appears to have embraced the Zionist Project perhaps inspired by her sister's brother-in-law, Bernard A. Rosenblatt. She travelled[132] to 'Palestine the beautiful' in the early 1920s and adopted it as her 'homeland'.[133] In 1924 she married Major Frederic A. Partridge, deputy commandant of police in the Jerusalem-Jaffa District. Madeleine's husband had first come to Jerusalem in January 1918 to serve as staff captain of the Headquarters Staff of General Edmund Allenby.[134] He subsequently took control of policing in the city.[135] When the Palestine Police Force was established in 1920 Madeleine's husband was appointed as one of the senior aides to Lieutenant Colonel Percy B. Bramley, Palestine's first commandant of Police and Prisons.[136] Partridge was one of the 'very few Palestine Police officers . . . [to] enjoy the confidence of the Jewish inhabitants of Palestine'.[137] After his service in the Jerusalem-Jaffa District he was subsequently transferred to a senior position based in Gaza,[138] which he held until late 1929.[139]

In May 1922 Untermyer took the fundraising drive to Philadelphia, where he also promoted its work in Palestine. He announced the establishment of a mortgage bank for the relief of the acute housing shortage. This joined the previously established Workmen's Bank, which was assisting the working class of Palestine in their enterprises, most of which were cooperative. The Keren Hayesod was also maintaining and developing agricultural settlements and farms through the Department of Agricultural Colonization. Untermyer also said that all Christian and Moslem shrines and other holy places would be respected and protected. He further observed that the Keren Hayesod was not competing with the private initiative. It was facilitating the success of private initiative. Construction, agricultural settlement, immigration, sanitation, health care and education in Palestine would barely exist without private Jewish initiative.[140] However, Lawrence Davidson observes Untermyer did not elaborate on the fact that the leaders of the agricultural colonies in Palestine aspired to create a Jewish proletariat rather than another Jewish bourgeoisie.[141]

It is probable that Untermyer's new Zionist friends persuaded him to join the American Jewish Congress (AJCong). Untermyer had previously tried to become a member of the administrative committee of the nascent AJCong in 1918. He must have been infuriated to be rebuffed by Julian W. Mack, who was not impressed by his contribution of $13,000.[142] Untermyer attended the AJCong's two-day convention in Philadelphia in late May 1922. At this convention, the AJCong was transformed into a permanent organization. Nathan Straus of New York's R.H. Macy & Co. department store was elected president, with Untermyer and his friend Aaron Jefferson Levy as vice-presidents. Stephen S. Wise was chosen as executive secretary with the prominent Zionist journalist and writer Bernard G. Richards as treasurer.[143]

Rabbi Wise, who was the leading force in the AJCong, found it extremely difficult to impose his authority on the convention, and Untermyer was among several temporary chairmen at the convention. Untermyer used the opportunity to promote the Zionist Project in Palestine. He told the convention that

> To say that an American Jew is lacking in loyalty to his country because he wants to secure for his own people the home toward which they have been for centuries straining their eyes and where they will be safe from the bolts and shafts of hate, bigotry and persecution, and where they may enjoy the same liberties and opportunities with which we are blessed, is a form of psychology that it has been difficult for most of us to understand.
>
> In a few weeks' time the struggle will be over, the mandate will be an accomplished fact. Then our real responsibility will begin. The pride and reputation of Jewry the world over are at stake. We have had our differences while the problem was a debatable one; now it is settled, let us forget these difficulties and stand shoulder to shoulder for the redemption of our promises.[144]

Untermyer's role as a Democratic politician was also to bring him into conflict with the AJCong in 1924. The New York *World* published confidential correspondence between his nephew Laurence and Julius Peyser, a Washington, DC, banker, and lawyer, that revealed Untermyer had advised presidential primary candidate William Gibbs McAdoo not to disown the anti-Semitic Ku Klux Klan (KKK), albeit for political reasons. He apparently counselled him to accept the KKK's votes at the Democratic National Convention and dump it afterwards. Rabbi Wise appointed Untermyer to a committee to urge the Resolutions Committee of the convention to condemn the KKK by name in the Democratic platform. Untermyer refused the appointment.[145] Although he was opposed to the KKK and continued to campaign against it,[146] he was not prepared to embarrass the Democratic Party and his friend McAdoo.[147]

Many American Jews were opposed to Zionism. Among them was Untermyer's friend Adolph S. Ochs. In May 1922 Untermyer wrote to Ochs asking if it might be possible for the *New York Times* to report on the activities of the Keren Hayesod, although he appreciated the publisher's position. Untermyer also deconstructed an article on Zionism written by Ochs. He took issue with an observation Ochs had made regarding the proposed Hebrew University:

> I am greatly surprised at your statement that it is not intended that the proposed University at Jerusalem shall include a theological department. From all that Dr. Weizmann, Mr. [Nahum] Sokolow, Sir Alfred Monds [sic], Mr. Rothschild and other leaders have told me again and again, I gather that the theological department is intended to be the chief feature of the University in the same way as Hebrew is being taught in the schools and is intended to be the language of the Jews in Palestine.

Untermyer also took issue with Ochs's contention that, even assuming that Judaism was and should be preserved as a religion and discouraged as a race, this militated against the establishment of a homeland in Palestine. Untermyer argued to the contrary that Jews were both a race and a religious community. He believed there is no conflict between the two and why should not the fact that the Jews are a race and that they have a home and Government increase the respect for them and the ability to protect the people of their race in other lands? They could enforce their rights through diplomatic channels which they cannot now do.[148]

This was an important point, and Untermyer, who was a frequent visitor to Europe, was no doubt mindful of the growth of anti-Semitism there since the end of the First World War.

Untermyer continued to take issue with Morgenthau's position on Zionism. During December 1922 Untermyer wrote to Ochs noting that the *New York Times* had reported some anti-Zionist remarks made by Henry Morgenthau. Untermyer observed that he was sure it was not Ochs's intention to 'alienate or antagonize a large section of the Jewish community' with Morgenthau's remarks. He further observed to Ochs,

> Whatever may be said of the Zionist cause . . . the fact remains that during the last year or more the Keren Hayesod has collected $2,500,000 in money and has secured in addition $2,000,000 in subscriptions that are being gradually paid, and that the prospects for the coming year are still more encouraging. This constitutes about 65% of the contributions that have recently gone to Palestine, the balance having been raised in European countries. Even poor Poland, with its worthless currency, contributed more for the year 1922 than Great Britain. This money is being used exclusively in the upbuilding of Palestine – none of the funds are being diverted for political or extraneous purposes. They have all gone to help the oppressed Jews of Eastern and South Europe to self-help and I am assured on all sides that the Arabs in Palestine are awakening to the helpfulness of this movement and that they will soon be working hand in hand and in friendly intercourse with the Jews in that country.[149]

Untermyer's presidency of the Keren Hayesod introduced him to people who would later play a leading role in the formation of the State of Israel. They included the future Revisionist Zionist Vladimir (Zeev) Jabotinsky, who was part of the first Keren Hayesod delegation to the United States which arrived in November 1921 on a seven-month tour. Jabotinsky was a member of the executive of the WZO which had organized the Keren Hayesod.[150] The four-man delegation also included Nahum Sokolow, the chairman of the WZO executive. As well as helping to raise funds the delegation sought to counter the expected opposition to the Keren Hayesod concept from the Brandeis–Mack Faction. Untermyer was toastmaster at the banquet reception on 13 November in New York City which welcomed the delegation to the United States. He introduced Jabotinsky as a 'militant Zionist' known throughout the world as the 'Jewish Garibaldi'.[151] Untermyer actively supported the work of Jabotinsky and the other delegates during their tour, including accompanying him to the fourth American Jewish Congress in Philadelphia in May 1922.[152]

In January 1923 Untermyer published another article in *The Forum* entitled 'Zionism and the Crane Report'.[153] The King-Crane Report had been prepared by the American Section of the Interallied Commission that had been appointed by the Paris

Peace Conference to prepare a statement on conditions in former Turkish territory as a guide to the Allied and Associated Powers in their disposal of the conquered countries. Stuart E. Knee has described the commission 'as the articulation of political anti-Zionism'.[154] Its report was suppressed for some time before being published in the *Editor & Publisher*. The report condemned Zionism, which it considered to have an extreme program aimed at a 'Jewish State'. This would be at the expense of the civil and religious rights of the non-Jewish inhabitants of Palestine.[155] In response, in his article in *The Forum*, Untermyer observed that the Zionists were not going to dispossess the non-Jewish inhabitants of Palestine. Indeed, in fact it was the Jews of Palestine who were 'practically dispossessed'. While they formed a quarter of the population of Palestine, they owned less than one-twentieth of the land in the British Mandate. Furthermore,

> Of the arable land of Palestine only twenty-five per cent is under cultivation, and three-quarters is lying waste – as it always had done under the Arab and Turkish régime. Of the arable land only a fragment is owned by the Jews. There is ample room for Jewish expansion for generations to come, without infringing on anyone's rights.[156]

Untermyer refuted the report's assertion that the Zionists claimed they had a 'right' to Palestine based on an occupation of 2,000 years ago. He observed:

> True enough, if in two thousand years the Jews had found a permanent home, if they had not been, ever since their dispersion, a despised and persecuted people. But is a history of sixty generations of martyrdom not to be 'seriously considered'? ... If there ever were a people whose sad predicament invoked the true meaning and application of the twelfth of the 'Fourteen Points' it was that of the Jewish people in its relation to Palestine.[157]

This was something Untermyer felt very strongly about. Later that year the writer Israel Zangwill gave an address to the AJCong in which he proposed the expulsion and expropriation of the Arab population of Palestine. Untermyer wrote a letter of resignation from his post of vice-president observing that 'such an idea is abhorrent to anyone who is imbued with the just, humanitarian and constructive spirit of our [Zionist] movement.'[158] Untermyer was subsequently persuaded to rescind his resignation.[159]

In his *Forum* article Untermyer also pointed to the contribution that the Jews were making to the economic development of Palestine. He wrote of how the Jews were transforming a desert into wheat fields, orange orchards, almond groves and vineyards. Palestine owed most of its export trade to Jewish initiative. Furthermore, the mandate's future economic development mostly depended on the concrete plans of the Zionists. This was

> Not only in detail work, but in larger schemes for the whole country, the Zionists are ushering in a new age. In the four years from 1918 to 1922 the Jewish

investments in Palestine have exceeded £4,000,000. The Rutenberg scheme, which is collecting funds in this country, will harness the waters of the Jordan to supply Palestine, poor in coal and oil, with light and power. 'Never in a thousand years,' declared Mr. Winston Churchill in the British House of Commons, 'would the Arabs have brought forth a Rutenberg scheme.' True! And the Arabs will benefit by this scheme equally with the Jews. In uplifting ourselves we shall carry them along with us.[160]

When Weizmann visited New York in March he was distressed to find that Untermyer was on his annual winter vacation in Florida. He wrote to him impressing upon him how the success or failure of the Keren Hayesod's first important meeting would depend largely on his presence or absence.[161] In fact Weizmann's fears proved unfounded. Untermyer gave his promised address to the Keren Hayesod meeting on 18 March at the Hotel Pennsylvania to delegates from thirty cities.[162] He praised Weizmann, who addressed the meeting after him. As he wrote later in the year,

> If there is such a thing as a statesman in these times, Dr. Weizmann fills my conception of that rôle. Few will ever know of the skill and infinite pains and patience with which he has piloted us through the troubled waters of European and Asiatic politics, through the plots and counter-plots for the control of Palestine, that highway between the continent of Europe and the Far East, until we now have in Palestine our 'place in the sun,' and a secure one, from which Jewish industry, agriculture, science and art and all the pent-up and suppressed genius of the Jew of eastern and south-eastern Europe bids fair to radiate over the face of the earth and to convert the name of the Jew from one of reproach into the synonym for all that is most humane and progressive in our civilization of the future.[163]

In his speech Untermyer also argued that Zionism was 'the most potent force to stem the tide of anti-Semitism the world over'.[164]

During the same month Arthur Ruppin, who was the chief colonization expert in Palestine, unveiled a plan for the establishment of an American Palestine Investment Bank to finance sound commercial and industrial enterprises in the British Mandate. Writing to Weizmann he observed that at the head of the bank there must be a board made up of Jewish people of established, commercial or banking reputation. Ruppin gave several examples of such Jews, including Untermyer and Louis Marshall. Marshall had supported the Zionist Project since 1917 on the assumption that it would lead to the creation of a Jewish state.[165] Of these men Ruppin reported Untermyer had already offered his support for the first business which the investment company might do in Palestine, the financing of commercial centres in Jerusalem and Haifa.

> When I spoke to Mr. Samuel Untermyer about these commercial centers, he was very interested in it and told me that he would participate in such an enterprise. Afterwards, he told Judge Rosenblatt that my plans pleased him very much and that he would be ready to participate with 10% – that would mean in $60,000 in commercial centers in Jerusalem and Haifa which require about $600,000.[166]

Untermyer subsequently assisted Ruppin with work on the proposed bank.[167]

As well as helping to raise funds Untermyer also provided practical help to the Zionist Project. In September he was recognized by the new Jewish Palestinian city of Tel Aviv with the award of honorary citizenship for his assistance in placing a loan of $75,000 in the United States. He was the second honorary citizen, the first being Albert Einstein. Bernard A. Rosenblatt, acting on behalf of the mayor of Tel Aviv, Meyer Diezengoff, had brought the loan to the United States.[168] Diezengoff had embarked upon an ambitious program of development.[169] Untermyer had managed to clear up a 'terrible mess'. Rosenblatt had originally issued the bonds through Harvey Fisk & Sons, although Untermyer had strongly advised him against it. The outcome was that the banking house literally stole the money. Untermyer managed to recover the bulk of the money, but only after a 'desperate fight'.[170] He later retrieved all the money, at some personal cost as he observed to Weizmann.

> My chief trouble arose from the fact that at the same time they [Harvey Fisk & Sons] had stolen funds of the Bethlehem Steel Co., of which I am one of the largest shareholders and in which my son is a Director. The Bethlehem people are deeply aggrieved at the fact that the Tel-Aviv money was saved whilst theirs has been lost, and will not be consoled by the reflection that part of the money thus lost to them was mine.[171]

In early 1924 Untermyer had to deputize Judge Aaron Jefferson Levy, his old and intimate friend, to carry on the work on his behalf regarding the proposed investment bank because his wife, Minnie, was unwell.[172] In February Weizmann asked Untermyer if he would be prepared to increase his subscription to the proposed bank from $50,000 to $100,000.[173] He regretfully declined.[174] Untermyer was unable to attend the non-partisan Palestine conference held in February by Weizmann and Marshall to establish the bank and an extended Jewish Agency because his wife was still in a very poor state of health. Untermyer cabled Louis Marshall on 16 February a plan to be read at the conference,[175] outlining his position regarding the two proposed new bodies. His proposed plan was for an investment company with a capital $5 million in 50,000 shares of one class only, of which ten or twenty prominent men should take together one million at par. Untermyer indicated that he was willing to subscribe $50,000 if the balance could be secured on a satisfactory basis. He also told Marshall that he did not agree with Warburg's plan to invite Keren Hayesod contributors to subscribe to the investment company. Untermyer argued that 'We should do everything to maintain [a] broad line of demarcation between contributions and investments leaving Keren Hayesod subscribers alone.' He also told Marshall that he assumed that the proposed Jewish Agency would also take shape at the conference. Untermyer argued that leading Jews distinctly known as non-Zionists should in his judgement constitute at least half of the agency's directors and executive committee. He observed, 'There are numerous recognized non-Zionists like myself in Keren Hayesod who should have representation in [the] Agency.' It is interesting that in this private communication with a man whom Untermyer regarded as his closest friend, he described himself as a 'non-Zionist'.[176] However, the telegram did not reach Marshall in time for his plan to be presented at the conference.[177] Nonetheless Untermyer was subsequently chosen to serve on the committee of the Jewish Agency when it was established.[178]

Untermyer continued to work hard to raise money for the Keren Hayesod. In a speech at Carnegie Hall alongside Rabbi Abba Hillel Silver of Cleveland at the end of May, Untermyer reiterated the reasons why American Jewry should support Jewish settlement in Palestine. He also added an important new reason. He noted that before the First World War Jewish refugees could find a home in the United States. However, since the war 'the Nordic superstition' had captured the popular imagination and the US Congress. It had embodied this 'silly superstition' into brutal legislation that excluded most non-'Nordic' immigrants, including East European Jews. As a result, Palestine had become 'the one place of refuge for the eternal wanderer'.[179]

By December Untermyer was able to report to a conference of the National Council of the Keren Hayesod at the Hotel Astor that it had spent more than $6 million on the rebuilding of the Jewish homeland. About one-third of this sum had come from the Jews of New York City. Louis Marshall reported to the same meeting that the Palestine Economic Corporation (with a capital of $3 million) was almost ready to start functioning.[180] It was brought into being in February 1925 and merged with the Palestine Cooperative Company and the Palestine activities of the JDC. The new corporation, which was headed by Bernard Flexner, sought to help develop cooperatives as well as private businesses, and to prevent unemployment. Untermyer, Marshall, Felix M. Warburg and Herbert H. Lehman were among the prime movers. Ruppin wrote in his diary that its board of directors included men such as Untermyer, in his opinion 'the best names'.[181] As Untermyer had observed to Ruppin in late January, personal circumstances prevented him from playing a significant role in the creation of the new body. He was still recovering from the death of his beloved wife the previous August. This was regrettable because he was not at 'all satisfied with the progress that is being made by the Investment Corporation or by the World Agency in America'.[182]

The previous year the League of Nations' Mandate Commission had published a report on Palestine. Untermyer strongly objected to a statement in this report to the effect that the recent Jewish emigrants to Palestine were not prepared by training for the manual and agricultural work necessary in the present state of the country. He observed:

> The manner in which this commission has characterized the Jewish immigrants in Palestine cannot but arouse widespread astonishment and raise questions as to the reasons that led this body to make such utterly ungrounded assertions. Is it possible that this commission yielded to influences that are hostile to the Jewish reclamation of Palestine or were they really misled? Fortunately the clear and vigorous denial of Austen Chamberlain and, what is even more important, the indisputable facts themselves will furnish all fair-minded people the necessary reassurance and will give to the Jews of America the guarantees and encouragement to continue their labors for one of the greatest causes of civilization that the history of mankind records.[183]

Although Louis Marshall was Untermyer's closest friend, the two men possessed very different characters. Marshall was much more cautious than Untermyer. He had serious doubts regarding the direction the Zionist Project was taking, as Untermyer revealed in a meeting with Weizmann in London during his 1925 European summer vacation.[184] Untermyer was apparently very angry with Marshall 'for his procrastination' in connection with the completion of the establishment of the Jewish Agency.[185] Weizmann later wrote to Untermyer in November expressing the concern that Marshall might have decided to support an autonomous Jewish region created by the Soviet Union in the Crimea, which was sponsored by the JDC. Some Zionists perceived this project as an unwelcome alternative to their project in Palestine.[186] Weizmann's concern regarding Marshall was correct – he did support the Crimean colonization project.[187] Felix M. Warburg was chairman of the JDC. He was second to Louis Marshall among the non-Zionist supporters of the yet-to-be-established Jewish Agency. Herbert Parzen observes the project 'threatened to tear apart the [American] Jewish community'.[188]

After his return from Europe Untermyer announced in September that during the next year the Keren Hayesod would invest $5 million in an agricultural, industrial, public health and educational program for the development of the Jewish homeland in Palestine. The Keren Hayesod hoped to raise $3 million from American Jewry and the remainder from Jews in fifty-two other countries. He reported that the Keren Hayesod had spent $8 million in Palestine during the previous four years, of which two-thirds had come from the United States. The increase in expenditure was necessitated by the growth of Jewish immigration to Palestine.[189]

Although Untermyer had proved to be a highly effective fundraiser for the Keren Hayesod, his unwillingness to fully embrace the organization's interpretation of Zionism was not appreciated. Furthermore, Rabbi Wise, an influential American Zionist, had opposed the involvement of other Jewish millionaires in American Jewish life.[190] In November 1925 Weizmann's American associates decided to merge the fundraising activities of the Keren Hayesod with the Jewish National Fund, the Hebrew University Fund, the Special Palestine Fund of the Mizrachi and the Hadassah. The creation of the United Palestine Appeal (UPA) was also related to the failure of a joint fundraising campaign, the United Jewish Campaign (UJC), agreed at the 1924 conference, between the Keren Hayesod and the JDC. Marshall had attempted to focus the UJC on the Crimea project at the expense of Palestine. As a result of the creation of the UPA Marshall and Warburg refused to contribute to the 1926 Keren Hayesod campaign.[191]

Neumann decided not to inform Untermyer of the plans because he was afraid the lawyer would oppose them or insist on the active top position in the new organization. Untermyer learnt about the foundation of the UPA with Rabbi Wise as its chairman, after the press carried the news on 22 November. Neumann recalled:

> I immediately had a telephone call from Untermyer early in the morning at my home. He was enraged, and there was nothing I could say to appease his wrath. I went to see him, explained the situation and apologized for my failure to consult him. He did not resign from the presidency of Keren Hayesod, as I thought he might do, but he was still very angry. I decided to go ahead as planned.[192]

However, Untermyer did not hold Wise personally responsible and offered the rabbi his support in his new role.[193] Nonetheless, Marshall complained to Weizmann about the way his friend had been treated, observing:

Although Mr. Samuel Untermyer had been the President of Keren Hayesod and as such devoted loyal service to the cause, to say nothing of his contributions and influence, he was not even informed that there was any intention to organize the United Palestine Appeal, but was shoved to one side and practically stripped of his office, without the slightest consideration. This was an inexcusable mortal affront. It was, however, merely symptomatic of the fanaticism with which American Jews who have tried to help Palestine have been pursued.[194]

After Untermyer ceased to oversee fundraising there was a fall in donations during the late 1920s. In 1930 the Keren Hayesod ceased to conduct independent drives in the United States and its fundraising activities were subsumed by the UPA.[195]

Despite his humiliation, Untermyer continued to take an active interest in the Zionist Project. He became a member of the executive committee of the UPA[196] and supported its fundraising.[197] He also later served as joint chair of the Westchester County Division of the UPA.[198] In November of the following year he was one of several Jewish leaders who responded to an unfavourable report on Jewish settlement in Palestine by Dr Henry S. Pritchett of the Carnegie Endowment for International Peace. Pritchett was critical of the impact of Jewish settlement on the Arab population. He was also dismissive of the Rutenberg electrification project. Untermyer said that Pritchett seemed to be labouring 'under the delusion' that the Palestine project intended to establish a Jewish State by means of the expulsion of the Arabs. He further observed:

> If Dr. Pritchett has traveled through Palestine and has seen the superb specimens of young manhood and womanhood who are with their own hands tilling the soil, building the cities, feeding the poor – Arab and Jew alike – and cultivating the confidence and friendship of the Arab population, one wonders through what sources he received the misinformation upon which his conclusions are based.[199]

Rafael Medoff observes that the American supporters of the Zionist Project had not yet realized that Arab hostility to Jewish settlement in Palestine was rooted in religious and political beliefs that economic development could not alter.[200]

Although Untermyer continued to act as a spokesman for the Zionist Project, in September 1926 Bernard A. Rosenblatt reported to Weizmann that the lawyer was still resentful about the way the UPA had been launched in 1925. Rosenblatt felt that they might have been able to reconcile Untermyer to their position by now, because he had been strongly opposed to the Crimean colonization project. However, he reported Marshall had begun to succeed in influencing Untermyer against the policies of the Weizmann Faction, after much effort.[201] This probably explains why Untermyer's support for Jewish settlement in Palestine appeared to have cooled. Untermyer now apparently supported the Crimean colonization project.[202] However, he continued to support the Hebrew University, perhaps because he shared Magnes's interpretation of Zionism.[203] Like Untermyer, Magnes did not believe in Jewish nationalism and believed that Palestine's future was best based on cooperation between the Arabs and Jews.[204]

The problems regarding Marshall and the establishment of the Jewish Agency were subsequently successfully resolved.[205] In October 1926, the JDC had agreed at a conference in Chicago to deemphasize the Crimean project and upgrade other relief programmes. Morris Frommer suggests that the JDC had always been suspicious of the Soviet Union and its treatment of its Jewish minority. They may have wanted to blame the Zionists for the expected failure of the Crimean project. Over the next few months Marshall and Weizmann had also settled their differences and agreed on terms for an enlarged Jewish Agency. The Jewish Agency was launched at the Zurich World Zionist Congress in the summer of 1929 shortly before Marshall's death.[206]

During his 1926–7 world cruise Untermyer took the opportunity to visit Palestine when the cruise liner *Bergenland* berthed in Alexandria. On 2 April 1927 he chartered an Imperial Airways aeroplane to travel from Cairo to Jerusalem. The flight was very turbulent, and the aeroplane had to make a detour of thirty miles to avoid a sandstorm. Since he was the president of the Keren Hayesod's American branch and had donated funds in 1925 for the construction of an open-air amphitheatre at the Hebrew University in honour of his late wife, Untermyer received a great reception in Jerusalem.[207] One of the people he met was Magnes, the chancellor of the Hebrew University.[208] The next day he was driven to Tel Aviv, where at a reception in his honour at the City Hall he was made a first citizen. In his address he criticized the policies of the leaders of the ZOA, which he characterized as gravely injurious to the cause. He dismissed talk of a Jewish state in Palestine. That issue had become null and void with the acceptance of the British Mandate. He then returned to Jerusalem, where he accompanied the British high commissioner, Lord Herbert Plumer, and his wife to a Beethoven concert. They afterwards entertained him at tea followed by a discussion between Untermyer and Plumer on Palestinian affairs. While he was in Jerusalem Untermyer also subscribed $100,000 to the $5,000,000 endowment fund of the Hebrew University and arranged details for the financing of the open-air amphitheatre.[209]

The following year Untermyer agreed to act as legal counsel for the WZO in negotiations with the Wall Street investment banks Kelley, Converse & Co. and Hemphill, Noyes & Co. to secure a loan of $2.5 million to $3.25 million for a proposed Jewish National Loan Fund. However, after negotiating with the banks Untermyer advised against the loan without underwriting. It was postponed and later indefinitely.[210] He also publicly supported Chaim Weizmann's leadership that year after another Zionist split led to the resignation of Stephen S. Wise and two other members of the administrative committee of the ZOA.[211]

Unlike some of Weizmann's associates Untermyer had always believed in the need to ensure that the rights of the Arab inhabitants of Palestine were fully respected. The 1929 Arab uprising was a rude awakening for Untermyer. Untermyer's niece Madeleine's husband, Major Partridge, acted heroically during the uprising. When he learnt of a pogrom taking place in Hebron he travelled there from Gaza and re-established law and order in the city, thus saving many Jewish lives. Partridge then learnt of a column of 2,000 fully armed Bedouin on their way from the Sinai peninsula, who had been misinformed that the Jews were desecrating the Muslim holy places in Jerusalem. Partridge intercepted them on the outskirts of Gaza. He spoke with several of the Bedouin sheikhs, who had known him for ten years He assured them the desecration rumours were untrue and persuaded them to return to

Sinai, thus saving yet more Jewish lives.[212] The British administration in Palestine had failed to protect the Jewish community during the uprising. If Partridge had not acted on his own initiative, countless more Jews would have been slaughtered. Untermyer observed in a statement to the Jewish Telegraphic Agency on 25 August that world Jewry, and in particular American Jewry, had during the last few years been pouring tens of millions of dollars into Palestine to support its colonization and development. They relied upon the will and ability of the British government to carry out the spirit of the Balfour Declaration. However, they had 'been relying on a broken reed'. No amount of belated protection could now undo the shock to their confidence of the terrible events of the previous week. The least they had the right to expect from the British in return for what American Jews had been doing for Palestine and its Arab population was adequate protection, and they had 'miserably failed us'. Untermyer also observed that 'We have generously carried out our part of the bargain involved in the mandate, but the British Government has, I fear, fallen down in the performance of its obligations.' However, Untermyer was by no means a defeatist. He argued that there should be no thought of their surrender of the sacred task they had undertaken, and he was sure that would be the reaction of American Jewry to this staggering setback to their optimistic hopes and plans. Hundreds of thousands of Arabs had profited and were daily profiting from the Zionist Project. The disaster only served to confirm their worst fears that they were dealing with a race of fanatical barbarians who could be governed only by the sternest of repressive measures.[213] Untermyer chaired a protest meeting organized by New York's Jewish community at Madison Square Garden on 29 August against British rule in Palestine. Among the other speakers were US Senator William E. Borah and Untermyer's friends Governor Herbert H. Lehman and New York City mayor, James Walker.[214] The response from the audience was so spontaneous that Untermyer turned to Rosenblatt and said, 'It was the most impressive occasion that I ever witnessed.'[215]

At a subsequent mass meeting of the Palestine Emergency Fund at the Jewish Community Center in Yonkers on 9 September Untermyer went further in his condemnation of the British government. He demanded that the American government use its influence to obtain Jewish representation on whatever body investigated the Arab uprising in Palestine.[216] Samuel Halperin notes that Untermyer was one of those who contributed generously to the Palestine Emergency Fund, which raised over $2 million to assist the riot victims.[217]

In the aftermath of the 1929 Arab uprising Major Partridge transferred to another senior position based in Haifa, a long-sought-after move by him and his wife which had been approved before the disturbances.[218] However, it would appear that his heroism had not been appreciated by the British administration in Palestine. In November 1931, several senior positions in the Palestine Police Force were abolished as part of a reduction in government expenditure.[219] As a result, Partridge was dismissed.[220] This would not have improved Untermyer's opinion of the British administration. Partridge subsequently secured a position as manager of the Haifa office of Imperial Chemical Industries (ICI).[221] Untermyer was acquainted with Lord Melchett, a director of ICI, and may have helped Partridge secure the job. Partridge's wife Madeleine died in a hospital in Zurich, Switzerland, a couple of years later in January 1934.[222]

Meanwhile Weizmann had concluded that a Jewish state in Palestine was unacceptable to the Arab inhabitants. In September 1930 he proposed at a meeting in Berlin that the idea of a Jewish state should be given up, and that instead the Jews should establish a binational government in Palestine. Jacob Billikopf recalled what Untermyer told him at his Fifth Avenue home five or six years before. At that time Untermyer had urged Weizmann to tell the world that the Zionists did not have any nationalist aspirations and that if the Zionists gave up nationalism as a creed, they would have the support, not only of non-Zionists, but the world at large. Weizmann, according to Untermyer, shared his conviction, but he was afraid that his constituency would not back him in the proposition. Billikopf further observed:

> What a pity that Weizmann's announcement in Berlin came five or six years too late! The story in Palestine would have been altogether different had he followed your advice. Much more progress would have been achieved in that country and the relations between the Jews and the Arabs would be infinitely more amicable.
>
> I recall so clearly almost every conversation you [Untermyer] and I have ever had that I may shortly apply for the position of Sam Untermyer's Boswell![223]

Untermyer continued to take an interest in events in Palestine during the 1930s. When Weizmann visited the United States in the summer of 1933 Untermyer served as chairman of the reception committee. He also chaired the first public reception organized by the American Palestine Campaign, the ZOA and the Jewish Agency for Palestine, at which Weizmann outlined a proposal for the resettlement of 250,000 victims of anti-Semitism in Germany and elsewhere in Europe.[224] Later in July 1937 he met with Felix M. Warburg, George Backer[225] and others to discuss the problems presented by the report of the Palestine Royal Commission headed by Earl Peel. Peel recommended the division of Palestine into two sovereign states. Warburg and Backer asked Untermyer whether he would be available in case it was believed his presence might be useful at the fifth meeting of the Jewish Agency Council in Geneva. Untermyer declined because he was about to embark on a thirty-four-day cruise to the Baltic.[226]

During the same year Untermyer reflected on his evolving view of Zionism and on the implications of the report of the Peel Commission in a letter to Rabbi Wise.

> You know, of course, that I was not a Zionist, in the sense that I did not believe in a Jewish State, although I have always been a supporter of the idyllic dream of a Jewish Homeland until the intervention of the cruel, barbaric devil [Adolf Hitler] (who is probably no more of an 'Aryan' than you or I), of the ghastly Aryan myth, which was distorted to drive the Jews from the land of which they had been for centuries a part.
>
> When that catastrophe befell our people, and it became necessary for them and their brethren to find a refuge from Germany and other lands equally stricken with that poisonous plague, I became a Zionist.[227]

Untermyer also recalled, in the same letter, that when Weizmann had asked him to assume the leadership of the Keren Hayesod in the United States, he did so with the express understanding, publicly announced, that he did not believe in a Jewish state. At the same time, he was sympathetic, deeply so, to a Jewish Homeland in Palestine. He further observed:

> And now, at the end of it all, we are confronted with the proposed partitioning of Palestine, which I regard as a major disaster to World Jewry, especially at this critical time. It is a great shock and disillusionment to those of us who until now had supreme faith in British honor, which demands that it carry out its plighted word.
> ... What a pity that the wonderful transformation from a sterile neglected land under Arab domination into a country that has blossomed like a rose, under the magic touch of Zionist genius, should be rewarded with such treachery. We have the right to demand and should demand of our Government that, as a party to the Mandate, it shall effectively protest against the proposed rape of Palestine and shall insist upon the carrying out of the Mandate.
> It has been well said by Dr. Magnes ... that all that would be left to the Jews would be a 'toy' State, which would not enable us to realize any of the fond dreams that have stirred our imagination and urged us onward toward the road to victory on which we were embarked when this disaster overtook us.
> It seems to me that at the present time there is only one thing for us to do, and that is to stand and fight to the end. Perhaps out of this turmoil there may come some arrangement with the Arabs on which we can rely, although I doubt it. The responsibility that rests upon you and your associates is a grave one for World Jewry. My best wishes are with you.[228]

Untermyer's belief that it was unlikely the Zionists could reach an accommodation with the Arabs proved to be prescient.

Although Rabbi Wise opposed the influence of other Jewish millionaires in American Jewish life, there is no doubt that Untermyer had a wide following among the Jewish masses. Unlike most of the other Jewish leaders, he did not hide in the shadows, and thus he was seen as a 'hero'. During the 1920s Untermyer together with Marshall ensured that Ford was held accountable for his anti-Semitic publications. As president of the Keren Hayesod's American branch, his popularity helped raised far more money for the organization than if the campaign had been led by someone less well known. Barnard suggests that if Brandeis and Mack had stayed as leaders of the Zionist movement, unlike Untermyer, they might have been able to raise money for Jewish settlement in Palestine from a wider spectrum of American Jewry that also included wealthy non-Zionists.[229] It is hard to see how they would have succeeded with non-Zionists where Untermyer had failed. Furthermore, Mack was relatively unknown, and Brandeis would not have been able to address public fundraising meetings because this would have undermined his position as a US Supreme Court justice. But it is clear from the 1937 letter from Untermyer to Wise, quoted earlier, that he did not support all the Zionist Project. Indeed, throughout his time as president of the Keren Hayesod he was unable to make up his mind whether he was a Zionist or a non-Zionist. However, the funds he raised for the Keren Hayesod may have helped save Zionism from collapse. Tom Segev has observed regarding the Palestinian Jewish immigrant community during the mid-1920s, 'it looked like everything was going to crash' because of a lack of funds.[230]

5

Untermyer's finest hour

The boycott of Nazi Germany in the 1930s[1]

On 30 January 1933 Adolf Hitler was appointed chancellor of Germany. Several weeks later James G. McDonald, secretary of the New York City–based Foreign Policy Association, met with Hitler in Berlin on 8 April. McDonald subsequently confided in Rabbi Stephen S. Wise, the honorary president of the AJCong, that Hitler had told him, 'We will annihilate the Jews of Germany in every way. They do not belong to the White race. What is more, we will show the other nations, including America, how to get rid of its Jews.' Wise subsequently told Harry J. Stern, a Canadian rabbi, that McDonald had 'despite a thousand entreaties, . . . refused to make public his statements to individuals, including the President, statements which, if publicly made, might almost avail to save the Jews of Germany from their tragic fate'. However, Wise did not break his confidence with McDonald. He also told Stern that while 'no decent, self-respecting Jews' could do business with Germany anymore, 'in view of the Jewish hostages in Germany, a publicly organized and officially proclaimed boycott might prove a danger'.[2]

Untermyer disagreed with Wise's opposition to a publicly proclaimed boycott. While it is not known whether McDonald told him about his meeting in Berlin, Untermyer had no doubts as to Hitler's true intentions towards German Jewry. At a luncheon given in his honour by the American Friends of the Hebrew University on 13 April, he reflected that,

> Nothing could better illustrate the long-sustained suffering and ultimate despair and the blighting, brutalizing after-effects of a disastrous war upon a once prosperous, enlightened nation than the ascendancy to power of a bigoted brute of the Hitler type and the tame submission to his yoke of a proud, self-respecting people. Deep is our pity for the persecution, akin to that of the Dark Ages, of our unfortunate brethren, it should be still greater for the remaining ninety-nine per cent of the German people who are thereby relegated to semi-barbarism.
>
> It is now definitely established that there is deep-seated, continuing official propaganda to minimize and mislead the Jews and the rest of the civilized world as to the extent of the persecution with the deliberate purpose of withdrawing interest and support . . .

> But we are not without means of defense. The first step of world Jewry must be to find ways to care for our disfranchised men, women and children, and more particularly to so enlarge the scope of the Hebrew University to receive our youth to whom the doors of the German universities have now been closed by this brutal decree.
>
> Our next act should be to see to it that nowhere in the world and under no circumstances should a Jew, from this day forth, buy or use merchandise manufactured in Germany or support Germany industry in any form. The action taken in that respect by the Jewish shopkeepers in London should be followed the world over.[3]

Untermyer was aware that most of the leaders of the American Jewish community, in particular the American Jewish Committee (AJC), publicly opposed a trade boycott.[4] It was a difficult decision for him. As Untermyer later observed to Edward M. House,

> As one of German parentage, whose ancestors were for centuries imbedded in the soil of that land, and as one who has spent long periods of time in that country and has many dear friends there, I cannot resist the strongest feeling of sympathy toward the German people, nor a corresponding feeling of revulsion against the sadistic cruelties of the present regime.[5]

Nonetheless, from the early days of Hitler's regime there were Jews in America and elsewhere, who advocated a boycott of German goods and services. Among the groups declaring a boycott was the Jewish War Veterans (JWV) in the United States.[6] This was initially in response to the 1 April boycott of German Jewish businesses organized by the Nazi government.[7] While neither American nor world Jewry were united behind the boycott, the resulting campaign was to be the most ambitious boycott attempted in the United States since the boycotts of British merchandise in the period immediately before the American Revolution.[8]

A few days after Untermyer's address, the Russian-born Dr Abram Coralnik, associate editor of the Yiddish national daily newspaper *Der Tog*, announced the formation of the American League for the Defense of Jewish Rights (the League) and the creation of a provisional Boycott Committee.[9] It was unusual in that it had been specifically formed as a boycott organization. The League had first been mooted in May 1932.[10] This may have been in response to the adverse impact of the boycott of Jewish businesses in Germany organized by the Nazi Party during the late 1920s and early 1930s.[11] The actual organization of the League is thought to have been inspired by a speech given by Untermyer, in which he criticized the US Congress for its relative lack of response to Nazi Germany's human rights violations.[12] Meanwhile on 7 May Untermyer used a Keren Hayesod campaign speech in Boston[13] to extend his call for a boycott to the whole American nation, with its scope to include patronage of German ships and visits to Germany. He also observed,

> I am, however, aware that there is a very large and respectable element among our people, for whose opinion I have the highest regard, that advises against this

course but fails to suggest any other remedy. Their argument is based upon the fear that if the boycott proves effective Hitler and his fellow ruffians in office will carry out their implied threats and let loose their hatred by indulging and encouraging bloody pogroms against their unfortunate victims, which they otherwise would not dare.

That is what they started to do and what I fear they will do in any event unless restrained by some remaining shred of fear of the opinion of the civilized world.[14]

Untermyer believed that German economy could be brought to its knees by a successful boycott. Unlike many of his fellow American Jewish leaders he had a first-hand and in-depth knowledge of the German economy. It was his opinion that it was far weaker than was believed at the time – a view that has been supported by the research of Adam Tooze.[15] Rabbi Abba Hillel Silver, who was to become a key adviser to Untermyer behind the scenes, disagreed with his prediction that the boycott had the potential to cause starvation in Germany and the collapse of the Nazi government. He correctly foresaw that it would be 'a long battle'.[16]

Dr Alfred E. Cohn, a member of the Emergency Committee in Aid of Displaced German Scholars, suggested to Untermyer that if the boycott was successful one possible outcome might be the replacement of the Nazi government with a 'new Communist government'. Cohn asked him, 'What will be the attitude of the democratic peoples and governments now not too unsympathetic to the Jews?'[17] Untermyer replied:

Your concern as to what may happen if the present Government in Germany is defeated through this economic boycott is one that I am unable to set at rest but, so far as our people are concerned, nothing worse can happen to them than the cold-blooded, planned annihilation of their brethren in Germany. One would imagine, from your questions, that you would rather see the Jews in Germany annihilated than the possibility of a Communist government there. If that should come to pass I do not see on what theory the responsibility can be charged against the Jews.[18]

The founders of the League were radical left-wing Jews of East European heritage and recognized that their cause required a leader who was able to appeal to the Jewish community as a whole and operate within mainstream American society. It had become self-evident their boycott campaign needed more funds than their membership was able to raise in the depths of the Great Depression of the 1930s. Ezekiel Rabinowitz, the executive secretary of the League, decided to approach Untermyer to ask him to become a member of their organization. He agreed and made a plea for unity on the boycott in a speech on 12 May.[19]

Rabinowitz invited Untermyer to speak at a boycott conference held at the Hotel Astor on 14 May.[20] The first conference of the League attracted nearly 600 delegates representing 288 organizations in New York, New Jersey and Connecticut. It was also addressed by New York City mayoral candidate Fiorello H. La Guardia, Untermyer's friend James W. Gerard, Wilson's first Ambassador to Berlin and Jacob de Haas, a well-known British-born Zionist.[21] In his address, Untermyer condemned the 'timid'

American Jewish leaders who opposed the boycott but proposed no alternative means of defending their brethren in Germany. He also noted that

> It has been brought to my attention that since this boycott was announced the . . . brands and tickets, or what-not, that are required to be on all imported goods, are being removed, and that some of the greatest offenders are the proprietors of department stores. I do not believe that the heads of these stores, many of whom are Jews, know what their subordinates have been doing in this direction, and am sure that when their attention is called to these violations of law they will be immediately corrected. The Jewish people should, however, in their own defense, be careful to see to it that they are not imposed upon and should withdraw their patronage from any merchant who seeks to deceive them.
>
> Meantime, the attention of the authorities in Washington should be called to these violations of law, and they should be asked to enforce the penalties prescribed by the statutes.[22]

The conference resolved to mount a boycott of German goods and services, in cooperation with the committee of Jews in Britain represented by Lord Melchett.[23]

Untermyer formally accepted the League's invitation to serve as honorary president of the National Boycott Committee of America on 15 June.[24] In late June 1933, together with La Guardia, Gerard and others, Untermyer addressed the Women's Conference on the Boycott at the Hotel Astor. The conference launched a nationwide boycott of German goods and services. It supplemented a boycott by professional trades and industries previously begun by the League. In the early 1930s the United States imported several significant categories of merchandise from Germany, including luxury goods, such as fine porcelain china, and cheap variety goods, such as toys and Christmas decorations.[25]

The JWV were one of the first national Jewish organizations to support the League's boycott campaign.[26] They circulated half a million stamps to paste on the back of letters urging a boycott of German goods. Unfortunately, in June 1933 the postmaster general issued a ruling barring this action.[27] In July Untermyer addressed the annual convention of the JWV over a nationwide NBC radio hook-up. Responding to Hitler's libel that the Jews were cowards, Untermyer stressed the patriotism of American Jewry.

> We may well hold up our heads, for the record is one of which we are and should be intensely proud . . . It demonstrates that at all times patriotism has been the guiding star of the American Jew. In all the wars of the Republic his deeds have cast the fragrance of heroism and sacrifice over every page of the military and naval annals of the nation.[28]

Untermyer soon came under attack from other American Jewish leaders for meddling in a matter outside his area of expertise. Morris Waldman, executive secretary of the AJC, observed to him at the beginning of May,

> Above all, it is imperative that in this grave and highly delicate situation, no individual should speak or act for the Jewish people, but all should entrust the

responsibility to recognized organizations like the American Jewish Committee and B'nai B'rith who have been dealing with these problems for many years.

Untermyer replied:

> I have given considerable study to this subject and gathered a mass of information, all leading to the conclusion that the Hitler party is bent upon the extermination of the Jews in Germany, or upon driving them out of the country. The men in control are bigoted fanatics to whom neither reason, justice nor humanity makes the slightest appeal. Their hatred is deep-seated and nothing but the fear of consequences will affect them.

This reply provoked an even stronger rebuke from Waldman, who commented:

> Strong as your conviction, which we respect, may be, I keenly regret, frankly, that a man of your outstanding position in the community whose utterances exert a great influence upon public opinion, did not consult with the American Jewish Committee to ascertain the reasons for their attitude, and what methods they have been following, before giving public utterance to views which, you must have known, would be widely published and profoundly influence public sentiment.[29]

Notwithstanding Untermyer's irresolvable difference of opinion over the boycott, he did support the AJC's efforts to assist refugee Jews in flight from Nazi Germany. Ernst H. Feilchenfeld, an émigré German legal scholar, observed to him and Waldman that the League of Nations was the only international organization with clear jurisdiction regarding relief measures. At Untermyer's request, Feilchenfeld prepared a sixty-page memorandum proposing the re-establishment of the League's office of High Commissioner for Refugees. In early July Untermyer sent a copy of the memorandum to James N. Rosenberg, a lawyer who was a member of the executive boards of the JDC and AJC. Rosenberg set about realizing the goal which required securing private funding and countering the opposition of Germany. On 11 October, the League of Nations agreed to establish an office of the High Commissioner for Refugees (Jewish and Other) Coming from Germany headquartered in Lausanne, Switzerland, voluntarily funded from private and other sources. The position was subsequently offered to James G. McDonald.[30] Untermyer was a key stakeholder in the new office. McDonald met with Untermyer at his apartment on 1 November. He observed that Untermyer 'was most cordial personally and will, I think, refrain from any open attacks even if he later disagrees on policies adopted by the High Commission'. Untermyer subsequently agreed to help with fundraising to support McDonald's work. McDonald met with Untermyer in June 1934 to seek his support for the United Appeal. He was really impressed by what McDonald told him and promised his support.[31] Later in the month Untermyer supported McDonald at a fundraising event and made a personal contribution of $2,000.[32] After McDonald resigned as high commissioner at the end of 1935, he continued his friendship with Untermyer. They were both among the sponsors of a Youth Aliyah Fete held at movie tycoon Harry Warner's Westchester estate in July 1938 to raise money to support the emigration of young German Jews to Palestine.[33]

Meanwhile a committee of British Jews led by Lord Melchett and the British Trades Union Congress had announced an international boycott conference, the World Jewish Economic Conference, to be held at the end of June in London. The League requested that the conference be postponed for two weeks to allow Untermyer to attend.[34] In response Melchett's committee postponed the start of the conference until 15 July.[35] However, the conference was opposed by the Zionist movement because it was incompatible with the Transfer Agreement. It was also opposed by the British Jewish establishment represented by the Board of Deputies of British Jews. Furthermore it was opposed by Untermyer's nemesis from the 1920s, Rabbi Stephen S. Wise.[36] As Edwin Black observes, Wise feared Untermyer 'as the popular hero of the boycott movement ... would be catapulted into a dominant position in both the anti-Nazi movement and the world Jewish leadership' if the conference convened.[37] Thus in early July, while Untermyer was at sea en route to London, Lord Melchett postponed the conference until early October.[38] However, when Untermyer reached London he found that many other delegates to the conference had arrived before its postponement. He decided to take control and go ahead with the conference under his leadership in Amsterdam.[39] Untermyer did not mention Melchett's postponement of the conference when he was interviewed on 15 July by the London *Sunday Express*. The *Sunday Express* described him as one of Hitler's bitterest foes, whose righteous indignation had fired him with youthful vigour in his old age. Untermyer claimed that Hitler had tried to negotiate through one of his henchmen, but he had refused. Untermyer told the newspaper, 'I have no intention of going to see Hitler, although asked by his friends to do so. It is an essential part of the Hitler policy that the Jews shall be persecuted to the point of extermination.'[40]

Untermyer flew from London to Amsterdam on the afternoon of 19 July.[41] The American delegation to the postponed conference comprised the League and the JWV. Untermyer and J. George Fredman, the leader of the JWV delegation, reconvened the conference at the Hotel Carlton in Amsterdam to which all the international delegates to the postponed London conference were invited.[42] Two days of sessions were held on 20 and 21 July. Untermyer labelled the reconvened conference as 'preliminary' to spare Lord Melchett embarrassment. This allowed Melchett's committee to participate in the conference. There was not enough time at such short notice for all thirty-five of the national boycott committees to attend the reconvened conference.[43] In addition to Untermyer and Fredman, the League's Dr Abram Coralnik, Polish Sejm Deputy Waclav Wislicki[44] from Warsaw and Leon Castro, a lawyer and journalist from Egypt, were elected to the conference's presidium. There were some thirty delegates at the conference representing the United States, Poland, Britain, France, the Netherlands, Belgium, Switzerland, Czechoslovakia, Latvia, Lithuania, Finland, Rhodes, Egypt and South Africa. Amsterdam's *De Telegraaf* reported on 21 July that another delegation was on its way from Palestine.[45]

Rabbi Wise bitterly opposed the preliminary conference.[46] A Dutch ally, Prof. David Cohen, secretary of the Special Jewish Interests Committee, informed the London *Jewish Chronicle* on Wise's behalf that the conference had been 'arranged without the consent and indeed against the wishes of the accredited leaders of Netherlands Jewry.[47] He also informed Amsterdam's *De Telegraaf* that the conference been organized without the involvement of the AJC, the AJCong and the official Jewish committees and organizations in Britain, the Netherlands or elsewhere.[48] Cohen also published a letter authorized by Rabbi Wise on the day before the conference in a number of Dutch newspapers in which he condemned Untermyer's conference and claimed a majority of American Jews were against a boycott.[49] On the first day of the conference Untermyer issued a statement condemning Rabbi Wise as a 'trouble maker' and questioning whether he was for or against the boycott.[50] The German Embassy in the Hague reported that support for the boycott at the conference was particularly strong among the Polish delegates.[51] The conference adopted a resolution that called for a boycott by world Jewry of German goods and services and agreed to form a World Jewish Economic Federation with Untermyer as president.[52] Shortly after the conference Lord Melchett decided to resign as chairman of the federation's executive committee because of the opposition of the Board of Deputies.[53] The British Foreign Office also later noted that the multinational company, which Melchett played 'a leading role in the creation by amalgamation and development of',[54] ICI, had dealings with IG Farben of Germany.[55] He was replaced by his uncle, Sir Robert Mond. Mond pledged to keep in close contact with Untermyer.[56]

The federation was not a success because it had insufficient funds and poor intelligence. Untermyer and Harry Salomons, the federation's organizing secretary and former Dutch Consul in Zurich, also thought that Sir Robert Mond was not sufficiently committed to the cause.[57] The international conference postponed earlier in the year was eventually abandoned. Instead, a conference focussed on the boycott in Britain and the British Empire took place in early November under the auspices of a newly formed Jewish Representative Council, formed by Jews dissatisfied with the established British organizations such as the Board of Deputies. Untermyer sent a message of support from New York. Mond, who was a member of the new organization, was too ill to attend the conference.[58] He subsequently accepted the presidency of the council.[59] His uncle Lord Melchett also made a public declaration of support for the new boycott organization.[60]

Untermyer had informed his friend Adolph S. Ochs that he was participating in an international boycott conference before he departed from New York.[61] Although the publisher replied observing

> I have my doubts about the wisdom of a Jewish World Conference looking to united action by Jews throughout the world, but you and I do not always see things from the same angle ... I am greatly depressed by the German situation, and I have the gravest apprehension of a catastrophe that may precede the inevitable overthrow of the Hitler regime.[62]

Notwithstanding Ochs' misgivings about the conference, the *New York Times* chief European correspondent, Frederick T. Birchall, wrote some very positive reports.[63]

Untermyer returned to New York on 6 August. Chartered boats greeted him in Quarantine carrying placards welcoming him home. Fredman had organized a magnificent reception for Untermyer. Five thousand cheering supporters were waiting on the pier when his ship docked. Jewish War Veterans and members of other organizations such as the ZOA and Hadassah paid tribute to him at the pier. After the reception committee at the pier Untermyer was applauded by a further 10,000 supporters waiting on the street outside. He was then rushed flanked by police motorcycles uptown to the WABC radio studio,[64] where he made an appeal, which was also broadcast by the Columbia Broadcasting System network, in which he described the boycott as a 'holy war in the cause of humanity'. In his appeal, the transcript of which was published in the *New York Times*, Untermyer criticized some of his fellow Jews.

> As to the boycott, strange to say a mere handful in number, but powerful in influence, of our thoughtless but doubtless well intentioned Jews seem obsessed and frightened at the bare mention of the word 'boycott.' It signifies and conjures up to them images of force and illegality, such as have on occasions in the past characterized struggles between labor unions and their employers. As these timid souls are capitalists and employers, the word and all that it implies are hateful to their ears.
>
> In point of fact, it signifies nothing of the kind. These gentlemen do not know what they are talking or thinking about. Instead of surrendering to their vague fears and half-baked ideas, our first duty is to educate them as to what is meant by a purely defensive economic boycott, and what we are doing and proposing. Admittedly, the boycott is our only really effective weapon . . .
>
> What then have these amiable gentlemen accomplished and what do they hope or expect to accomplish in the way of stemming this conflagration of civilization by their 'feather-duster' methods? You cannot put out a fire, and especially that kind of fire, by just looking on until the mad flames, fanned by the wind of hate, have destroyed everything. What we are proposing and have already gone far toward doing, is to prosecute a purely defensive economic boycott that will undermine the Hitler regime and bring the German people to their senses by destroying their export trade on which their very existence depends.

In the same broadcast, he condemned the AJC and the leadership of the AJCong for failing to support the boycott.[65]

Later that month Untermyer conferred with Secretary of State Cordell Hull and Joseph Avenol, secretary-general of the League of Nations, on the possibility of an appeal by the AJCong to the League on behalf of German Jewry.[66] However, the AJCong decided not to follow through on Untermyer's initiative[67] which was based on a resolution from the Amsterdam conference.[68]

As noted earlier, Rabbi Wise had obstructed Untermyer. This was despite the fact many members of the AJCong, including some of its leaders such as Dr Joseph Tenenbaum, supported the boycott. Black argues Wise wanted to lead the boycott himself.[69] In August 1933, the National Executive Committee of the AJCong decided to join the boycott. Like Untermyer, the AJCong had become exasperated by the lack of response by Roosevelt and Hull to the persecution of Germany's Jews. Untermyer was a guest speaker at the AJCong meeting. He expressed the hope that the AJCong would

Illustration 10 Photograph: The Fearless Champion of Jewish Rights, New York Harbour, 6 August 1933.

coordinate its boycott campaign with that of the League.[70] This did not happen, although Wise and Bernard S. Deutsch visited Untermyer for this purpose in mid-September.[71] Rabbi Abba Hillel Silver, who had become a key adviser to Untermyer behind the scenes, strongly advised him against this move, because it would cause friction and eventually submerge the League. Silver believed that the League's fundraising campaign would suffer from being associated with the AJCong 'concerning whose program and activities there is a sharp division of sentiment in American Jewry. Many who favor boycott will not contribute when it becomes known that part of fund will go to [the American Jewish] Congress'.[72] Untermyer ultimately heeded Silver's advice.

The second World Jewish Conference held in Geneva in early September 1933 adopted a resolution endorsing the worldwide Jewish anti-Nazi boycott after it was strenuously advocated by Wise.[73] However, Black notes the resolution provided neither for the establishment of a committee to organize the boycott nor any enforcement apparatus. He further observes, 'It quickly became clear that the Geneva conference simply did not advance the boycott cause.'[74] He also observes that when Wise returned to New York on 15 September 'unlike the return of Samuel Untermyer, there were no welcoming committees, no fanfares, no radio broadcasts.'[75]

While Untermyer was trying to reach an understanding with the AJCong the world Zionist Organization signed the Haavara Agreement with Germany. Funds confiscated from emigrant Jews were to be used to buy German machinery for Palestine. Untermyer observed that 'the Zionist Organization has no business to enter upon any such negotiation . . . Why sell our birthright for a mess of pottage?'[76] The Zionists were aware that the agreement would be badly received in America as Morris Rothenberg observed in a letter to Chaim Weizmann:

> The agreement which the Anglo-Palestine Bank made with the German authorities has made a terrible impression everywhere, particularly in America, where Untermyer is playing havoc with the Zionists for it. The sentiment of the public is entirely with his point of view and I am inclined to believe that the instinct of the Jewish masses is correct. You cannot in one breath call upon Jews and the friends of Jews to help us boycott German goods and at the same time violate the boycott ourselves. They cannot and will not understand the argument in favor of the transaction.[77]

The Zionists tried unsuccessfully to placate their 'good friend Mr. Untermyer', who threatened 'all sorts of reprisals'.[78] Their efforts were doomed to failure despite a letter from Louis Lipsky to Weizmann in late September reporting some progress.

> The situation has improved with regard to the German contract, as far as Mr. Untermyer is concerned. He understands the matter a little better. At the same time, it is of the greatest importance that you communicate with him without delay, to explain the whole matter. He is under the impression, first, that the orange contract is involved under the second arrangement for the transfer of goods to Palestine on behalf of German Jews, and, second, he regards the contract with regard to German goods as being reprehensible in that, in effect, it makes a breach in the boycott, to which he has given a great deal of his time and quite a good deal of his money.[79]

Weizmann does not appear to have written to Untermyer. However, the advantage of having Zionists involved with the League was later shown in September 1935 when Rabbi Silver reported from Lucerne that he had succeeded in persuading the nineteenth biennial World Zionist Congress to sharply limit the scope of the Haavara Agreement of 1933 to the bare necessities of German Jews actually emigrating to Palestine. All other arrangements were outlawed. Silver regarded it as a 'victory for the boycott'.[80] Untermyer did not agree. He believed 'the Haavarah (sic.) agreement has been a great blow to the boycott, and that it will have to be repudiated in its entirety'.[81] However, Silver convinced Untermyer that he was mistaken in his view of the outcome of the congress.[82]

The Zionists also sought to persuade Albert Einstein to distance himself from his good friend Untermyer.[83] Einstein had met with Untermyer in England after the 1933 Amsterdam conference.[84] He subsequently wrote to him applauding his efforts regarding the boycott.

> I have thought a great deal about your efforts and sincerely admire your energy. I hope for nothing more than that you may create a strong and effective organisation, because the international trade boycott is a powerful weapon. I regret that innocent Jews and also non-Jews will have to suffer the consequences of this boycott. But

this must not prevent us from doing what will be really useful there in the long run. Make use of this message if you think it useful. I feel the need to tell the individuals who are being considered for carrying out this endeavour that I wish nothing more sincerely than that they may find enthusiastic support and approval from all sides. I myself do not want to be a member of this committee. That would have – as you undoubtedly realise without lengthy explanations – a number of serious disadvantages. Also, it will generally be felt that the possibility of such an official role would be completely outside my field of expertise. It is, however, my wish that those involved know that I consider it as the duty of all good Jews to stand by you.[85]

Later when Einstein returned to the United States that autumn to take up the position at Princeton University he had been appointed to the previous August, the Head of the Institute of Advanced Study, Abraham Flexner, arranged for his ship to be met by a tug which took the 'bewildered' scientist directly to Manhattan's Battery where two cars were waiting for the onward journey to Princeton.[86] He had been persuaded at the last moment by Flexner and Felix M. Warburg to avoid the 'publicity and notoriety' of the welcoming mayor's reception committee headed by Untermyer[87] at the Red Star Line pier. Untermyer was left waiting in vain.[88] After Einstein arrived in Princeton, he wrote to Untermyer to apologize saying, 'You can imagine how difficult it was for me to leave the ship before arrival even though I knew what a reception had been prepared by you and the authorities of New York.' He added:

> If I wish to devote myself here [Princeton] to my scientific work, I must refrain from involvement in public affairs . . . I am also convinced that in the present circumstances it is incumbent on the Jews to largely refrain from involvement in public political struggles. I firmly believe that much more can be achieved by working quietly and unobtrusively than by making a lot of noise in public.[89]

Given Einstein's previous letter to Untermyer it would appear his Princeton benefactor, Flexner, had persuaded him to distance himself from Untermyer.

The following April Untermyer received a letter from Einstein's wife Elsa asking him whether they were still friends. He replied that they were and that he did not hold her husband's position against him.

> Don't you know that I regard you and your distinguished husband as among my most treasured friends, and that I cherish my dear wife's admiration for both of you?
>
> Why should I be angry or think of criticizing his enforced silence? I realize why he felt that he could not raise his voice, although I may not agree with the wisdom of his attitude, as you may recall from our talk in England.[90]

Einstein, who had a guilty conscience, visited Untermyer at his Greystone country estate the following month to apologize and explain in person what had happened the previous October. Untermyer soon became engaged in a debate on the persecution of

Jews in German and the importance of intensifying the boycott of German goods in the United States. Einstein is reported to have expressed the opinion that Hitler could not be stopped.[91] Einstein's fatalism can be explained by his belief in determinism.[92] Later in 1937 Einstein declined a pro forma invitation from the League with Untermyer's signature to publicly support the boycott. He replied to Untermyer,

> Despite my greatest respect for the cause for which you are tirelessly fighting, I cannot nevertheless comply with your friendly request. I regard it as bad taste when an amateur pretends to be an artist. I can only make an effective contribution in the long run to the cause of freedom and the Jews by making permanent advances in my own field of work.[93]

The League was also approached by Vladimir Jabotinsky, with whom Untermyer had worked to raise funds for the Keren Hayesod during the 1920s. At a press conference in August 1933 Jabotinsky noted several fellow Revisionist Zionists, including Elias Ginsburg and Israel Posnansky, were members of Untermyer's League. He subsequently cabled Untermyer from Prague, 'Should like to coordinate Revisionist boycott activity with League'. Informing Ginsburg of the cable in early September 1933 Jabotinsky observed, 'I need not add what decisive importance we attach to Untermyer's personality and to the League headed by him. It is our fervent wish to coordinate all our activity with this powerful factor.' Jabotinsky agreed with Untermyer that the boycott would succeed only if it was supported by non-Jews as well as Jews. However, Untermyer decided not to work with Jabotinsky.[94]

On 10 September 1933 at a League conference Untermyer was elected president to replace Coralnik.[95] Max Ornstein, another early member of the League, argued that apart from inviting Untermyer to join, the League 'had been floating around without intelligent direction'. It reminded him of Don Quixote. He urged Untermyer in September to transform the League into a more effective organization.[96] One of the first things Untermyer did was to reform the League's board of directors. He drew upon his professional, political and social networks to recruit prominent non-Jewish men, such as Theodore Roosevelt, Jr.,[97] the Rev. John Haynes Holmes of Manhattan's Community Church,[98] his old friend Republican congressman James M. Beck,[99] James W. Gerard[100] and New York City politician Fiorello H. La Guardia.[101] They gave the boycott credibility outside the Jewish community where the founders of the League, such as Coralnik, were unknown. Silver, who was also a member of the board of directors, argued that speeches and articles by non-Jews rather than by Jews would have greater impact on the non-Jewish community.[102] Salmon O. Levinson, who had organized a boycott committee in Chicago mainly with non-Jews, suggested that the League should also be non-sectarian. Untermyer agreed.[103]

An added factor that reduced the impact of speeches of prominent Jewish leaders, such as Untermyer, was the anti-Semitism present in American society. For example, *Time* magazine in a report on a speech given by Untermyer in Cleveland in November 1933 referred to him as 'distinguished Jew Untermyer' with a photograph that was captioned 'Jew Untermyer'.[104] Untermyer wrote a letter of complaint to *Time* observing, 'It seems to me incredible in this 20th Century a publication of wide circulation such as yours should have anti-Semitic tendencies, which I believe is contrary to the spirit of Americanism and will offend the sense of propriety of non-Jews as well as Jews'. The social anti-Semite editor[105] Henry R. Luce replied:

> In decrying Nazi activities in the U.S. and agitating for a boycott of German goods and services, Lawyer Untermyer is acting not as lawyer, not as U.S. citizen, not as religionist, but as a Jew outraged by persecutions of fellow Jews . . . In labelling Lawyer Untermyer 'Jew' in contrast to 'German' for Ambassador Luther, TIME was strictly, significantly accurate. TIME did not thereby intend affront to Jewish sensibilities or express sympathy with the Nazi cause.[106]

After a great deal of discussion and deliberation Untermyer persuaded the League to change its full name in November to the 'Non-Sectarian Anti-Nazi League to Champion Human Rights'.[107] He may also have been influenced by the AJC. It opposed the boycott and had sought to persuade Untermyer to change his movement into a non-Jewish boycott. The AJC's Sol. M. Stroock, a fellow lawyer[108] who was an old friend of the Untermyer family, had discussed the matter with Untermyer personally in August.[109] Coralnik and Ezekiel Rabinowitz, the first executive secretary of the League, had opposed Untermyer's plan to convert the League into a non-sectarian organization. They 'were intensely bent upon continuing it as a Jewish affair'. However, they had finally given way.[110] On 23 December, Untermyer was elected president, Silver became first vice-president and Coralnik became second vice-president. Rabinowitz remained executive secretary.[111] Coralnik later argued that 'non-sectarian is synonymous with Jewish'. He argued that it was naive to believe that others would not know what the mask covers especially since the mask had been put on after the face had been seen.[112] The AJC subsequently modified its position. It still opposed the boycott but accepted that Jews as individuals could support the boycott.[113] Stroock continued to try to contain the boycott through his relationship with the Untermyer family, without much success.[114]

From the beginning of his involvement with the League Untermyer sought to micromanage it. Benjamin Dubovsky,[115] one of the League's founders, called Untermyer the 'Fuhrer'.[116] The League's work was to be marred by factionalism and personality clashes.[117] The surviving records suggest that only one member of the League, Rabbi Silver, had anything approaching the stature to keep Untermyer's dictatorial tendencies in check. However, after the first year and a half of the boycott campaign even the strong-willed Silver was forced to admit defeat. At the end of 1934 he wrote to inform Untermyer that he would cease to be actively involved in the management of the League.

> You have your own way of running an organisation and inasmuch as you largely finance this organization you are, I suppose, entitled to your way. But it is not my way. I joined the League at its very inception and accepted office in it believing that I was joining a National organization and not the private retinue of one individual (for whom, by the way, I have very high regard). Very soon thereafter it became apparent that the League was being run dictatorially by you and that no policies or

programs could be carried through without continual and frequent interference on you part. I wrote to you about it in the interest of the League and at the solicitation of the members of the Board but you chose to misunderstand the purpose and the spirit of my writing.[118]

Untermyer failed to recognize that an organization staffed mainly by volunteers required a more collegiate management style. This was despite his experience of presiding over the Keren Hayesod during the 1920s.

The League was administered by an executive secretary, who was directly employed by Untermyer. During the time Untermyer was president of the boycott organization there was a succession of executive secretaries because he was not prepared to give them agency. Untermyer did not always exercise good judgment in his appointments. Dr Boris E. Nelson, appointed in January 1937, claimed to have a doctorate in philology from the University of Heidelberg and be a survivor of Dachau concentration camp. Unbeknownst to Untermyer and the League he was an imposter.[119]

Untermyer's staunchest supporter in the League was Mary Harris, also known as Mrs Mark Harris. She was the New York–born wife of a Yiddish-speaking Polish immigrant vice-president of a family-owned raincoat manufacturing company.[120] Harris had been an active member of the Jewish Consumptive Relief Society of Denver (JCRS) for many years.[121] The JCRS was one of the New York City Jewish community's most important charities. It had been founded in 1903 by East European-American Jews to create a refuge near Denver, Colorado, for destitute Jewish consumptives from across the United States.[122] She had joined the League in May 1933[123] and was elected chairman of its Women's Division, a position she held throughout Untermyer's presidency of the League.[124] She was also the sole female member of the League's National Boycott Committee and its subsequent board of directors.[125] Untermyer regarded Harris as 'a splendid type of womanhood, and one of the most useful and intelligent women I have ever known, besides being a fine speaker'.[126] However, her critics in the League were to argue contrary to Untermyer that she lacked the dynamism of the women leading the boycott campaign at the American Jewish Congress.[127] Harris's most notable achievement was in February 1934 when she secured the endorsement of the boycott by the powerful Federation of Jewish Women's Organisations of Greater New York. This organization, which represented 100,000 women, had been opposed to the boycott. The reversal of their position had been achieved by the militancy of Harris and her colleagues in the League's Women's Division.[128]

Some satellite committees were also created. In September 1933 Philadelphia newspaper publisher J. David Stern visited New York City to find out how he could help Untermyer. Stern later recalled Untermyer set him three tasks. First, to get the large Philadelphia stores to boycott German goods. Second, to organize a public protest meeting with prominent non-Jewish speakers. Third, to raise money. Later that month the League's administrative committee named Stern chairman of a subcommittee to report on the best way of raising a fund of $500,000 to further the ant-Nazi boycott in the United States.[129] Stern organized a protest rally in June 1934 at the Metropolitan Opera House in Philadelphia with speeches by Untermyer; Oswald Garrison Villard, the liberal editor; Congressman James M. Beck; Francis Biddle, Chairman of the

Foreign Policy Association; and others.[130] The composition of the audience of 4,000 disheartened Stern. A third were Christians, of whom the majority were Quakers. Jews of East European heritage made up the remainder. Stern was concerned that, except for two others and himself, there were no Jews of German heritage in the audience. Stern soon discovered that Philadelphia's storekeepers followed the pattern of the audience at the rally, for stores owned by Christians were more willing to boycott German imports than those owned by fellow Jews of German origin.[131] The League subsequently founded a Pennsylvania Committee with Richard J. Beamish, a prominent Catholic layman,[132] as chairman, and Gifford Pinchot and Francis Biddle as honorary chairmen.[133] However, the boycott was probably not very active between 1934 and 1938 in Pennsylvania.[134] Stern made a much bigger contribution to the boycott through his acquisition, with Untermyer's financial support, of the New York *Evening Post* in December 1933. Stern's association with Untermyer did not endear him to some of the *Post's* most important advertisers, the New York department store owners, who, as will be shown, were initially opposed to the boycott. Stern later recalled his old friend Bernard F. Gimbel of the eponymous department store chain told him, 'That smart Sam Untermyer got you into this fix with Macy's. Let him figure a way out. We'll increase our advertising but Macy's is the leader and most of the merchants play follow-the-leader.'[135]

Meanwhile in Cleveland, Rabbi Abba Hillel Silver established the Cleveland Committee for the Defense of Human Rights Against Nazism. In Chicago, Dr Paul Hutchinson, editor of the *Catholic World*, and Salmon O. Levinson, an attorney and Nobel Prize winner, formed the Chicago Committee for the Defense of Human Rights against Nazism, of which the former was president.[136] In Newark, Dr S. William Kalb of the JWV formed an organization which became the League's division in New Jersey in 1936.[137] In Los Angeles the Hollywood Anti-Nazi League received extensive publicity after movie stars became involved from April 1936.[138] Elsewhere in North America, in 1934 the newly reorganized Canadian Jewish Congress began a boycott campaign modelled on the methods of Untermyer's League with which it was in frequent contact.[139] In 1935 a Canadian branch of the League was established with a head office in Montreal.[140] As was the case in Britain, the Canadian government opposed any acts 'that would injure the relations' between Canada and Germany.[141] There were periodic efforts to reinforce the boycott across Canada which were closely monitored by the German government.[142]

In early November 1934, the League launched a 140-page paperback book, *Nazis against the World*, containing speeches and articles by American and British anti-Nazis together with selected addresses and writings by Untermyer. The League printed 100,000 copies, some of which he distributed as complimentary copies to opinion formers.[143] It also announced that a world conference organized with Britain's Jewish Representative Council would begin on 25 November in London. Its aim was to intensify and coordinate the boycott of Germany.[144] Some 200 delegates attended the London conference from eighteen countries in Europe, North and South America, and Africa. There were representatives of nearly fifty organizations, including Socialists, trade unionists, Trotskyites, Zionists and Quakers.[145] Significantly there was no representative from the Soviet Union. The public session of the conference on 26 November established a World Non-Sectarian Anti-Nazi Council to Champion

Human Rights, which replaced the defunct World Jewish Economic Federation. The new organization, chaired by Sir Walter Citrine, the general secretary of the British Trades Union Congress, received the endorsement of the British labour movement.[146] It appears to have remained active until spring 1936,[147] although Citrine still listed it among his positions as late as September 1938.[148] Regardless of the length of its existence the council does not appear to have achieved anything substantive.

Untermyer was rather disappointed that although the four-day conference was attended by eminent delegates from many countries and culminated in a vast meeting attended by thousands, 'not a line appeared in any important daily newspaper'. He believed that the British government had instructed the newspapers to boycott the meeting on demand of the German government.[149] The Gestapo suggested otherwise:

> If the leader of the boycott had hoped to win over more of the English population to the cause of the boycott through this conference in London, he appears to have been unsuccessful. The British public scarcely took any notice of these events. This lack of interest was also seen at the mass meeting at the end of the conference that was attended by only approximately 4,000 people. There was no discussion of the conference in the English press. Only two dailies, the *Daily Herald* and the *Manchester Guardian*, mentioned the conference in an inconspicuous position in their newspapers.[150]

The conference also resulted in the establishment of a British Non-Sectarian Anti-Nazi Council to Champion Human Rights with Sir Walter Citrine, as president, which replaced the Jewish Representative Council.[151] The new organization does not appear to have survived more than three years.[152]

The boycott had four stages. The first involved discovering which businesses stocked German goods, either overtly or covertly. Intelligence was acquired from one of three sources: information from concerned citizens; questionnaires sent out to businesses by the League and interviews or fieldwork by members of the League. The second stage involved writing to businesses and asking them to comply with the boycott. When appropriate, the League provided information about American or other non-German substitutes. The third stage involved waiting for the responses of the businesses it had contacted. They varied from instant compliance to steadfast resistance. If the business refused to comply, the League moved on to the fourth stage and instituted a boycott of that concern. Karen J. Greenberg says blacklisting was the main type of boycott used. Sometimes circulars were distributed informing customers of the firm's links with Germany. After the establishment of the League's journal, the *Economic Bulletin*, it also published the names of offending firms.[153]

It could be argued that picketing would have been more effective which Untermyer and the League publicly opposed.[154] But as he told his son Irwin,

> Whilst our organization does not and cannot from motives of policy support picketing, and has taken every opportunity of so explaining, between you and me we are glad that it is being done, and hope that it will continue. It has had very effective results.[155]

Anna Cahane, a New York City lawyer,[156] headed the League's Vigilance Committee. She organized a group of 'Minutemen' who took a census in spring 1934 of groups and dealers in New York City to assess the extent of their adherence to the boycott. Efforts were made to assist these dealers in finding American substitutes for German products.[157] It is not clear whether these Minutemen were linked to the Anti-Nazi Minutemen of the JWV.[158] However, the League's Newark satellite formed an alliance with the Anti-Nazi Minutemen. The Minutemen picketed Newark businesses stocking German goods such as the largest department store, L. Bamberger, which was owned by Macy's of New York. In 1934 the national JWV organization disowned the Minutemen because it disapproved of the use of violence. The Young Men's Hebrew Club assumed sponsorship of the Minutemen from May 1934. They formed an alliance with the city's crime boss, Abner 'Longy' Zwillman, and his Third Ward Gang. Zwillman also helped fund the boycott in his city.[159]

Untermyer's high profile among New York Jewry meant that he got tips, many unsigned, from people working near the docks, in factories or stores, on where to find German goods. Mitchell Salem Fisher and his wife Esther later recalled a typical example. Fisher had been a well-known rabbi before he went to law school. He was the only lawyer at Guggenheimer & Untermyer apart from Untermyer active in the Boycott.[160] An anonymous note had been received from a clerk in Macy's that clocks with backs stamped on the outside 'Imported from Switzerland' and 'Imported from Czechoslovakia' had 'Made in Germany' inside on the works. The Fishers went to Macy's pretending to be shoppers. They asked the salesman in the clock department to call the buyer, and they demanded to know whether a 'Swiss' clock was actually German. When the buyer removed the back, he expressed much surprise at the German inscription underneath. The Fishers had no way of establishing whether the Swiss cover was added in the United States or in Germany or Switzerland. So they went up to the Eighth Floor and delivered with youthful militancy a sermon to the Macy executives on trade with Nazi Germany.[161]

Untermyer also received helpful suggestions from some of the Zionists he had worked with in the 1920s. For example, in December 1934 Morris Rothenberg, president of the ZOA, forwarded him a letter from Max Brod, the well-known Czech novelist and Franz Kafka's executor. Brod observed Czechoslovakian film importers depended exclusively on products from Germany. If American film companies were to make concessions to the Czechoslovakian importers this would render a great service to the Jewish cause and at the same time add great strength to the anti-Nazi boycott movement.[162]

Untermyer was well acquainted with the department store sector where many imported German goods were retailed. His extended family included the founders of the department stores Guggenheimer's in his birthplace, Lynchburg, and B. Lowenstein & Bros. in Memphis. Furthermore, his social network included the owners of many of the department stores in the New York metropolitan area such as the Straus family, who owned Macy's. Untermyer was particularly furious at Macy's for continuing to sell German goods, because the owners were descended from German Jews like himself. However, in summer 1933 the mass circulation New York newspapers refused to publish his attacks on their biggest advertiser, unlike the

Yiddish national daily *Der Tog*.¹⁶³ Therefore he persuaded J. David Stern, the owner of the *Philadelphia Record*, to publish his attacks on Macy's. Untermyer then circulated thousands of reprints in New York City.¹⁶⁴ On 2 October R.H. Macy & Co. published a full-page advertisement against the boycott in the New York daily newspapers. Furthermore, a statement was issued by the Retail Dry Goods Association on behalf of twenty leading New York department stores, many of which were owned by Jews, stating they had minimized their purchases of German merchandise, but that the boycott of their stores by the League would 'create a dangerous precedent'.¹⁶⁵

A half-page advertisement in response to that of Macy's, signed by Untermyer as president of the League, was refused for publication on 3 October by three New York morning newspapers: the *Times*, the *Herald-Tribune* and the *American*. Untermyer challenged the accuracy and sincerity of some of the statements in Macy's advertisement. The progressive magazine *The Nation* opposed this attempt at censorship and considered that the newspapers' 'refusal to publish even as paid advertising a statement from a man of the standing of Mr. Untermyer, who could be held liable for any libelous material therein contained, constitutes a unique and flagrant suppression'. *The Nation* offered to publish the advertisement without payment in its next issue.¹⁶⁶ On 25 October, it published an article on 'The Suppressed Advertisement Concerning R.H. Macy'¹⁶⁷ within which was the text of Untermyer's advertisement. It took the form of an open letter to Percy S. Straus, Macy's president, in which Untermyer observed,

> That the decision of the New York department stores to which you refer [in your advertisement of October 2], against refusing to further handle goods made in Germany, is said to have been influenced largely by your leadership as the most important store in the group, supported by another Jewish-managed store in New York City; that so long as you persisted in continuing to buy German goods you would have maintained an unfair advantage over them if they had failed to follow your lead; that they preferred not to subject themselves to such unequal competition.

He also wrote,

> That the 'dangerous precedent' of the boycott, to which you so feelingly refer, is in no respect dangerous nor is it a 'precedent' in that it is a purely defensive counter-boycott against a vastly more impressive and all-embracing boycott that is being enforced against all Jews in Germany. It follows the precedent that was set by Germany when it was brutally inaugurated and actively continued to prosecute the boycott of Jewish manufacturers and shopkeepers and professional men by the entire German nation for the avowed purpose of destroying their means of livelihood and of ruining and exterminating the German Jews.

Untermyer's open letter was followed by a summary of Macy's response. Straus denied asking any New York newspaper to suppress the advertisement. He went on further to observe that

Action on the part of a large business house which tends to accelerate racial cleavage in the United States is un-American. The policy of a mercantile establishment ought not to be directed to inculcating or to opposing the views of anyone on the ground of race, creed, or politics.[168]

Ironically, Lord & Taylor, a non-Jewish-owned New York department store, had 'recalled its buyers from Germany shortly after Hitler inaugurated his reign of terror, and regardless of price established the policy of not buying one pfennig's worth of Nazi goods'.[169] Joseph E. Pridday, president of the company, 'withstood many pressures against his courageous action'. The major New York newspapers, unwilling to alienate the other department store advertisers, chose not to publicize the store's action. However, Ernest Gruening, the editor of *The Nation*, did run the story in early October. Other news magazines and broadcasters then followed his example.[170] Ira Hirschmann, Lord & Taylor's publicity director, had visited Berlin in July and after his return to New York reported that Germany was in a state of terror.[171] He delivered a speech at the Annual Conference on Retail Distribution in Boston in September 1933 calling for a boycott of German goods.[172] Prof. Felix Frankfurter read about the speech in the *Boston Transcript* and invited Hirschmann to tea at his home in Cambridge to personally congratulate the store executive.[173]

In March 1934 John Wanamaker, one of the few large non-Jewish department stores, decided to stop dealing in German goods.[174] The German Consulate General in New York reported that similar commitments regarding German goods were made by R.H. Macy & Co., Saks, Gimbel's, Bloomingdale's, Hearn, Best's, Constable and Lord & Taylor.[175] However, not all of these stores completely adhered to the boycott. Nonetheless, by early 1935 the boycott had begun to have a severe effect on sales of German goods in the city's department stores.[176] Nonetheless later that year R.H. Macy appointed Francis X. Fay as its chief of detectives ostensibly to tackle the theft of merchandise by employees.[177] However, it is probably not a coincidence that in his previous job as head of the New York field office of the Federal Bureau of Investigation[178] Fay had undertaken an investigation into the activities of those engaged in boycotting German merchandise in the United States.[179]

In many other metropolitan centres, the boycott seems to have varied in its success. Some department store owners outside New York City supported the boycott. Albert M. Greenfield supported the complete elimination of German merchandise. Greenfield, a Philadelphia financier, controlled City Stores, a chain with stores in New Orleans; Memphis, Tennessee; Birmingham, Alabama; Louisville, Kentucky; Elizabeth and Newark, New Jersey; and Philadelphia. The Memphis store was B. Lowenstein & Bros. which had been acquired by City Stores in 1923.[180] However, the boycott was less effective in Los Angeles. Tom May of the May Company department store observed to Untermyer in January 1935 that his support for the boycott put him at a big competitive disadvantage because all the other stores in Los Angeles were handling German china and gloves.[181] One might have expected Sears, Roebuck & Co., the Jewish-owned mail order and department store retailer based in Chicago, to support the boycott. Indeed, Untermyer had claimed in a letter to Woolworth that Sears absolutely adhered to the boycott.[182] In fact, although Sears had suggested it would support the boycott, it continued to purchase German merchandise until the outbreak of the Second World War, although it claimed in its defence that these were kept to the minimum.[183]

Jews of East European heritage were probably more supportive of the boycott than the established middle-class and upper-class Jews of central European heritage. So there may have been a greater impact on the stores patronized by lower-income citizens of the New York metropolitan area such as the 5¢ to $1 chain stores, which included Woolworth, McCrory, Kresge, Kress, F. & W. Grand and W.T. Grant. By 1935 the League had persuaded these chains to minimize their inventories of German merchandise. However, the League suspected that some of the chains which had German contracts and were somewhat sympathetic to the Nazi German regime, rather than attempting to sell German merchandise in the New York market, were dumping it throughout the rest of the United States.[184] In 1937 Claude W. Kress, the German-American president of S.H. Kress & Co., a chain of 235 five- and ten-cent stores with headquarters in New York City,[185] was asked in an interview with the *Seattle Jewish Transcript*, why he, who prayed in church on Sunday to the Prince of Peace, sold German-made goods on the other days of the week, which put money in the hands of persecutors and war-makers in the Nazi regime. Kress replied, 'We handle merchandise the people want. We take the stand that if they don't like our merchandise policy, they can stay out of our store.' Reminded that his New York stores had recently been picketed for handling German goods, he declared, 'Mr. Untermyer knows our attitude. To hell with his boycott. I don't like the man. I've received insulting letters from him about the boycott. But as long as a Kress is at the head of our stores we will carry German goods.'[186]

Another of the chains targeted by the League was F.W. Woolworth Co. In October 1933 Untermyer had met with Woolworth's president, Byron D. Miller, who assured him that his company was buying no goods in Germany except in fulfilment of contracts heretofore made. Woolworth was in a precarious situation because they had eighty-two stores and an investment of $5 million in Germany. The subsidiary had been established only in 1927[187] although Woolworth had been purchasing merchandise in Germany since the 1890s.[188] Miller claimed Woolworth was nonetheless anxious to help.[189] Subsequent to this interview Untermyer acting on information received[190] sent many letters to Miller detailing the sale of German goods[191] and the illegal obscuring of country-of-origin marks on German goods.[192] Miller once again claimed that the company was not purchasing goods from Germany and was seeking to end the purchase of goods finished in America, which contained items of German manufactures.[193] Untermyer continued to receive complaints about the sale of German goods by the company,[194] although he was apparently satisfied that it was cooperating with the boycott.[195] Miller sent a telegram to the League in March 1934 saying, 'Replying your ... query as to policy of this company regarding importation of goods from Germany. Beg to advise that we have discontinued importation owing to extreme sales resistance.'[196] For example, Woolworth stopped purchasing 'Soft Luna' pencils from J.S. Staedtler, a Nuremberg pencil manufacturer.[197]

However, Woolworth was unable to honour its agreement. This may have partly been the result of retaliation against its German subsidiary in May 1934.[198] The German Foreign Ministry reported the following month that Woolworth had continued to purchase goods from Germany through its subsidiaries in Canada and Great Britain.

The German Consulate General in New York also reported that Woolworth was still purchasing goods from Germany for resale in the majority of its stores in the United States.[199] This is substantiated by reports received by the League regarding German goods on sale at American and British branches of Woolworth in August 1934.[200] The League resumed its boycott of Woolworth. Woolworth, together with Sears, was regarded as the largest and most conspicuous violator of the boycott. In November 1935 Rabbi Silver reported that Woolworth was flooding its stores with German-made Christmas toys.[201] The League highlighted this in its *Economic Bulletin*.[202] However, Gabriel Lowenstein, a manufacturer who supported the League, argued in December 1938 that the League was being unfair to Woolworth. The chain could only repatriate their German subsidiary's profits in offset purchases. Nonetheless Woolworth had tried to minimize its German purchases by helping American manufacturers develop substitutes for many German products.[203]

Although the League induced hundreds of wholesalers to cease handling German merchandise,[204] as in the case of the retail trade there were importers willing to break the boycott.[205] In October 1934 Bernard Lubow of the Manhattan Import Co. Inc. reported to Untermyer that several Jewish importers were breaking the boycott by importing German goods and that it had become the most profitable business. Lubow observed that 'We fight such a gang – Jewish importers – who stoop low enough in their greed to profiteer from the misery of their brethren.' Lubow claimed that importers could go to Germany, purchase one of a half-a-dozen phoney currencies and acquire merchandise as low as 40 cents on the dollar. While German merchandise was not generally available in New York City, when Lubow travelled further west he encountered almost everywhere large quantities of German goods. He claimed that these were generally purchased from Jewish importers in New York City.[206] In response Untermyer initiated a drive against Jewish importers.[207]

The German government closely monitored the reaction abroad to its depredations on its Jewish Community. A 2010 German Foreign Ministry official report on its conduct during the Nazi era and its aftermath notes that German diplomats showed no qualms about trivializing and justifying the terror campaign. The German ambassador to the United States at the time Hitler came to power, Dr Friedrich Wilhelm von Prittwitz und Gaffron, in a remarkable telegram sent on 21 March, warned the German Foreign Office that it must ensure that Germany's reputation as a nation of law and order was upheld because the foreign agitators would not miss any opportunity to pick up, distort and exaggerate real events. According to the 2010 report Prittwitz also advised 'Hitler must put a stop to the anti-Semitic agitation and convince other countries that law and justice are still supreme in the German Reich.' When the reports of anti-Semitic outrages from Germany did not abate Prittwitz renewed his call for moderation. He noted that one cause for concern above all was the 'boycott movement against German goods and German ships' which was already having an impact. The official report notes that Prittwitz's dispatches caused the opposite of what he intended. By explicitly referring to American Jews as the instigators of the protests and suggesting that in the United States the impression prevailed that the government in Berlin was no longer in control of the situation, he provided Hitler with the decisive pretext for a 'counter-boycott' of German Jewish businesses on 1 April.[208] Prittwitz had tendered his resignation on 14 March because he was unsympathetic to the Nazi regime.[209] In 1930 in reply to a question on the anti-Semitic policy of Hitler, he had said his 'is not the voice of Germany'. He further observed, 'the Jews have nothing to fear in Germany'.[210] Prittwitz's resignation was accepted as of 15 April. He retired[211] at the age of forty-nine. The German Foreign Office report notes, contrary to Prittwitz's expectation, none of his fellow ambassadors followed his example.[212]

Prittwitz was succeeded by Dr Hans Luther, who had had to give up his position as Reichsbank president and had been compensated with the post of ambassador to the United States. Although he was non-party,[213] he was to defend his government with an enthusiasm not shown by his predecessor.[214] He arrived in Washington in mid-April and after barely two months he returned to Berlin on family leave.[215] However, the Washington *Evening Star* subsequently reported that Luther's fellow diplomats in Washington believed that the real purpose of his visit was to report to Hitler the American reaction to recent events in Germany, which had caused wide repercussions in the United States, especially the Nazis' persecution of the Jews.[216] During Luther's absence the German chargé d'affaires, Dr Rudolf Leitner, responded to Untermyer's advocacy of the trade boycott in an article on 7 August in the *New York Times* by calling on Hull on 11 August to protest. Hull suggested in response 'that the best remedy would be for the German people or the German Government or both to conclude as quickly as possible whatever may be their activities relating to assaults upon or mistreatment of Jews in Germany; that this would enable [the American government] to make suitable appeals to discontinue the boycott'.[217] From this point onwards the German government repeatedly complained to Hull about the boycott.

Luther returned to Washington in mid-August observing that during his six weeks in Germany he had made a close examination of conditions there and witnessed a complete transformation. He undoubtedly witnessed the persecution of German Jewry. Luther told the Associated Press he intended 'to deepen and increase the mutual understanding between [Germany and the United States] which are so resolutely striving to master their own destiny'.[218] On 14 September Leitner at Luther's behest called on Hull again to complain about the boycott. Hull responded by citing evidence of the persecution of Germany's Jews and suggested again that the only chance for the Roosevelt administration to make an appeal against the boycott would be if the mistreatment of the Jews was 'absolutely discontinued and abandoned'.[219] On 21 September, Luther also met with Hull to complain about the boycott of German goods. According to Luther,

> [Hull] talked about the difficulties that were arising for the American Government from the continuous propaganda undertaken by the Jews. Pressure was continuing to increase in an attempt to get the American Government of its own accord to take a definitive stand against Germany on account of the treatment of Jews in Germany. Hull said he did not know, for example, whether news used for propaganda purposes or reports on speeches from Germany were in fact correct. However, they certainly had an effect in America. He was worried that the situation could get considerably more difficult by the beginning of January [1934] when

Congress met, and also more difficult in general through the fact that some of the Senators would then be involved in election campaigns.[220]

Hull's account suggests that he had become less sympathetic to the plight of Germany's Jews. He reported:

> I stated, unofficially, that officials of our Government had been subjected to personal criticisms, which were really offensive in their denunciatory and condemnatory nature, about the alleged treatment of Jews by the German population and government while I and other officials had been endeavoring to avoid complications with the German government by refusing to attack it on account of the alleged mistreatment of Jewish nationals.

Once again, he suggested that, if Germany ceased mistreating its Jews, then it would be possible to curtail the boycott and similar activities in the United States.[221] This is not mentioned in Luther's report.

In November 1933, Untermyer decided to respond to the attempts by the German government to undermine the boycott by attacking Luther, in a speech to a League meeting held in Cleveland on 1 November[222] chaired by Silver. In his speech Untermyer referred to the congressional hearings on Nazi propaganda in the United States, and denounced the German ambassador, saying, 'One of the most destructive of propagandists is Dr. Luther who, I say, is masquerading as the German ambassador and is really a propagandist.'[223]

Luther quickly complained to the State Department about Untermyer's speech. Hull told Luther he regretted the situation.[224] He also issued a press release expressing 'his concern that an Ambassador accredited to the Government of the United States should be subjected to a public attack'.[225] Untermyer in turn thought Hull was 'most precipitous and unjudicial' in expressing his regrets to Luther. He argued that Hull had no right, without inquiry into his allegation that Germany was funding propaganda in the United States, to give credence to Luther's 'monstrous falsehood' by denying the allegation.[226] Untermyer told Silver that 'The lying statement of Dr. Luther that he knew of no propaganda in this country is about the most brazen piece of impertinence I have encountered in a long time.'[227] Among the correspondence received by Hull concerning this incident was a telegram from Cyrus Adler, president of the AJC, saying that his committee wished to be entirely disassociated from Untermyer's attack on the Department of State.[228]

On 6 December 1933 Luther gave a speech at a German Day celebration held at Madison Square Garden in New York City.[229] In it he sought to counter the bad publicity Germany had been receiving by suggesting America was receiving 'incomplete reports' from Germany.[230] A few days later on 12 December he gave a speech at Columbia University in a similar vein.[231] Untermyer responded to the speeches in a feature article in the January issue of the *Southern Israelite* of Augusta, Georgia, in which he once again sought to expose Luther as a 'Propagandist in Disguise'.[232]

In March 1934, a furious Luther called on Hull again to complain at length about anti-German activities in the United States. Hull reported that he specifically mentioned

Untermyer's advocacy of the boycott of German goods and efforts to counteract Nazi propaganda in the United States; the proposed House of Representatives' investigation of this propaganda by Untermyer's ally, Congressman Samuel Dickstein; and boycotts by R. H. Macy & Co., Gimbel Brothers and F. W. Woolworth Co. He went on to proclaim that the boycotts of German businesses should not be tolerated and strenuously called upon the American government to find ways to suppress them. Hull reported that the 'Ambassador's language was critical of our government and at times became almost violent.' Hull suggested more than once that the way to resolve this matter was the cessation of the persecution of Germany's Jews. Luther declined to give a definitive reply. Hull then 'inquired if he thought the Jews should resume buying goods from Germany? He said, 'Yes, it would help to restore good relations.' Hull 'said, "Do you think we here could persuade them to do so?" He hesitated, and then smiled.' The unpleasant interview continued going round in circles until Hull was required to forcefully terminate it.[233]

Untermyer tried negotiating with the German government. At the end of November 1933, the German Consulate General in New York had reported to the Embassy in Washington that Untermyer was understood to be prepared under certain conditions to revoke the boycott. His conditions were the repeal of the laws against the Jews and that an acceptable minimum number were reinstated as state officials. He also suggested that Hitler include the Jews in a published message of peace for the forthcoming Christmas holiday. Untermyer made a solemn pledge of secrecy, which the Consulate General observed was out of character. It argued that his desire to reach an understanding had to be seen in the context of the growing anti-Semitic mood in the United States. The report also observed,

> It is certainly possible that he hopes to gain in stature through his role as a peace mediator. I consider it beyond doubt that he is in a position, despite hostility in his own camp, to influence the boycott decisively in one direction or another; it is precisely the radical wing that listens to him. I agree therefore with my informant who considers Untermyer's statement very important.[234]

Untermyer's initiative resulted in a confidential approach by House in June 1934 to the American ambassador in Berlin, William E. Dodd. He asked him to try to negotiate a change in Germany's policy towards its Jews.[235] House had been invited to Germany to discuss the Jewish situation but had refused.[236] Unbeknownst to Untermyer, House not only wanted to ease off the boycott, he also sought, according to Dodd, a reduction in the number of Jews in high positions in the United States.[237] Untermyer seems to have agreed with his friend McDonald's assessment of the likely success of this approach. McDonald told Untermyer that he 'had no faith in such an effort'. Untermyer 'agreed it would be difficult for the Jews to accept favors if the other persecuted groups were not included'. McDonald 'agreed, but more important seemed to be the unlikelihood that the regime could make real terms or that these would be kept if made'.[238]

On 4 June, Ambassador Dodd visited the German foreign minister, Konstantin Baron von Neurath, alone in his home. He read a letter from House and suggested that he see Hitler and sound him out. Von Neurath said he would do so as soon as

Hitler was home again, and that Hjalmar Schacht, president of the Reichsbank, and Kurt Schmitt, Reich economics minister, would join him. He suggested that restraining propagandists Julius Streicher and Dr Josef Goebbels was the first move, and that some Nazi leader deliver a speech calling for moderation.[239] Von Neurath recorded in a memorandum that Dodd had met with House on a recent trip to the United States. House had said a precondition for the suspension of the boycott was that further measures against the Jews must cease. In particular, Streicher's hate campaign must end and his publication, Der Stürmer, be banned. The letter that Dodd read to him was in reference to the ambassador's conversation with House.[240] Dodd was probably not an ideal emissary because he observed to von Neurath in the meeting that 'we have had difficulty now and then in the United States with Jews who had gotten too much of a hold on certain departments of intellectual and business life.'[241] Afterwards in late June, House informed Untermyer that Dodd had been told that 'official assurances [were] not possible but unofficial moderation emphasized.'[242] By mid-July, however, it was clear that the secret negotiations had been unsuccessful because the German government intensified, rather than moderated, its anti-Semitic policies.[243]

In late July 1934, Untermyer was visited by a German secret agent posing as a journalist. The agent reported that

> It is very difficult to arrange an appointment. Even with the most reputable letters of introduction you are thoroughly questioned as to what you want and mostly you are turned away. I was lucky; apparently, I did not give the impression I was carrying a revolver.
>
> You have to force yourself to remain calm when you hear this ruthless little man speak so openly and freely about all the things he has brought upon our country.

The agent reported that Untermyer told him that

> Boycotts in general are a weapon that I personally do not like and whose use does not therefore appeal. This weapon was and is, however, the only one with which I can damage and influence Germany. I would give up the boycott today rather than tomorrow if the Jews in Germany were given the rights again that they had. I am very German; my wife was Aryan. I have done much for Germany; I spoke and wrote extensively against the Treaty of Versailles. After the [outbreak] of the war I was appointed Counsellor of the German Embassy in Washington. My and our boycott does not only extend to the Jews but above all to the Catholics and the American workers. A boycott of this kind does not succeed with the Jews alone. I have never relied upon newspapers. I have always had my own investigations carried out and then led the boycott not only in America but also in various countries in Europe, especially Holland.[244]

The following year another German secret agent succeeded in infiltrating Untermyer's inner circle to gain intelligence on the progress of the boycott from the lawyer himself.[245]

Dodd had acted unofficially on behalf of Untermyer. The Roosevelt administration remained opposed to the boycott throughout the 1930s. The League had requested a message of support from Roosevelt for a testimonial dinner in autumn 1933 honouring Untermyer for his work in defence of German Jewry. Hull advised the president's secretary that 'it would be hard to frame a message that would not be interpreted as at least an implied endorsement of such a boycott, which is contrary to this Government's beliefs.'[246] However, it would be wrong to infer from this that Roosevelt was indifferent to the plight of Germany's Jews. According to McDonald at a meeting earlier in 1933 Roosevelt had seemed 'very much disturbed about the Jewish situation' in Germany and suggested 'that he had a plan in mind to appeal over the head of Hitler to the German people'.[247] However, as Conrad Black has argued, domestic political considerations led him to decide against this course of action.[248] The following year In late April, the German Embassy reported to Berlin that it had been informed that Untermyer had a meeting with Roosevelt, which was also attended by Hull and Henry Morgenthau, Jr. Referring to similar cases in the past, namely Russia, Untermyer urged the president to make representations to Germany regarding its anti-Semitic policies. He was confronted by a very reserved attitude on the part of the president. Roosevelt told Untermyer that he did not intend to take such action under any circumstances, partly because the American Jewish community was itself divided, and partly because fundamental considerations led him to the conviction that such a step was not appropriate. The Embassy reported Untermyer was said to attribute Roosevelt's position to the influence of Hull. It also cautioned Berlin against concluding from Roosevelt's position that he approved of Germany's Jewish policy.[249] Untermyer himself later observed:

> Mr. Hull has been always, at heart, a 'free trader' . . . All I know is that although I give Mr. Hull credit for being a friend to Jews and liberalism generally, his way of expressing himself is so inconclusive that in the end he does us more harm than good.[250]

In fact, Hull may have been less of a friend than Untermyer thought. In 1937 Hull observed to Ambassador Luther that 'the more intelligent and thinking people of . . . [the United States] look upon these racial and religious occurrences [in Germany] more as a matter of temporary abnormality or the outcroppings of highly wrought-up emotions.'[251]

Some members of the Roosevelt administration were more sympathetic to the boycott than Hull. In November 1935 Untermyer discovered that German steel piling had been purchased for use in the construction of the Triborough Bridge in New York City. In response to a telegram from Untermyer, Harold L. Ickes, Federal Emergency Administrator of Public Works, responded by assuring Untermyer

> that this Administration has not and will not compel the Triborough Bridge Authority to approve or require the purchase of German steel for use in the construction of the Triborough Bridge. Furthermore, I am changing the [Public Works Administration] order so as to provide that no foreign materials may be approved on any PWA non-Federal project without my express approval. That approval will be given only if the American bids are collusive or the prices are

so unreasonably high as to justify the belief that advantage is being taken of the Government in administering its relief funds.[252]

By the autumn of 1933, it had become apparent that agents of the German government were seeking to seize control of German American community organizations. Untermyer observed that American immigration policy had allowed

> swarms of German propagandists to infest our shores and to sow their vile creed against Jews while scientists, college professors and many other distinguished victims of the bigotry and fanaticism of these savages are denied admittance to this country.[253]

In October New York City mayor, John P. O'Brien, upheld a ban on a pro-Nazi rally in celebration of German Day. In a radio address Untermyer supported the mayor's decision. He also spoke of how a Nazi agent, Heinz Sparknoebel, had tried unsuccessfully to gain control of the *New Yorker Staats-Zeitung und Herold* by intimidating the proprietor, Bernard Ridder.[254] In an interview with the *New York Times*, Untermyer also urged the Immigration Bureau to deport immediately several people associated with the organizers of the rally, the United German Societies.[255] His cover exposed, Sparknoebel was suddenly recalled to Berlin.[256] McDonald observed that, according to Untermyer, he also caused 'dissensions in the ranks of the German societies'. He regarded this as 'proof' of 'the pertinacity and the intelligence of the old man. He would, indeed, be a dangerous enemy'.[257]

In May 1934, the United German Societies established an organization called the German-American Protective Alliance (DAWA) to boycott the boycotters. The DAWA argued that the League was directed against everything German, including German Americans and their businesses.[258] It began to post German blue eagles on the windows of stores that refused to boycott German goods.[259] The Friends of New Germany also participated in the counter-boycott.[260] In response, Untermyer prepared an advertisement entitled 'To Our Patriotic German Citizens'. In a lengthy text over his signature, he said that he had no quarrel with American citizens of German birth or ancestry. The boycott was aimed only at German goods, ships and shipping. Unlike the case of the advertisement about Macy's, the New York newspapers published it on 15 May.[261] Two days later, on 17 May, a mass meeting against the boycott was held at Madison Square Garden by the Friends of New Germany. Against a backdrop of Nazi swastikas, various speakers condemned Untermyer and the boycott. His name was booed and met with chants of 'Hang him!'[262]

Untermyer's concern over the activities of German secret agents in the United States also led to his support for initiatives to monitor and counter them. He supported Los Angeles' attorney Leon Lewis's private espionage organization which monitored German government agents and their local collaborators during the 1930s. During his winter 1933–4 vacation in California, he flew by aeroplane from Palm Springs to Los Angeles to attend an afternoon session of a trial involving a disputed Friends of New Germany election which Lewis used to expose their plans which included the recruitment of veterans for a potential armed insurrection. Untermyer signalled his support for Lewis's cause by sitting alongside the plaintiff's attorneys.[263] The *Los Angeles Times* reported that he said, 'I have come . . . because of the international importance this case may assume if the issues involved will permit of proof of the startling facts I understand to be probable.' He further observed:

> For some time past I have been insisting and expect to be able at the proper time to prove to the American people that there exists and is being conducted an insidious, traitorous country-wide propaganda and conspiracy aimed at the peace and security of our country.[264]

A couple of days before Untermyer's appearance in the Los Angeles court, he had delivered a speech to a mass meeting of 12,000 people in San Francisco on 13 February at the Civic Auditorium advocating a boycott of Nazi Germany as a response to its 'unbelievable crimes against humanity'.[265] There were frequent disturbances by Nazi sympathizers. For example, at the beginning of his speech a blond youth on the main floor leaped to his feet, raised his hand dramatically in the Nazi salute and shouted 'Heil Hitler'. The youth and a dozen of his neighbours were quickly ejected by irate spectators and the police.[266] The civic authorities were obviously expecting trouble because Untermyer had been assigned a twenty-four-hour police guard.[267] The *San Francisco Examiner* reported that he made a dire prediction about the fate of German Jewry.

> From the little that can be gleaned of the tragic circumstances, they could not possibly be worse for these unfortunates. We know from the laws passed by the Hitler government it is its openly avowed official, widely heralded policy and boasted purpose eventually to exterminate them – whether by murder, suicide or starvation is immaterial.[268]

As already noted earlier, Untermyer had made the same prescient prediction in private to Waldman the previous May.

Untermyer subsequently formed a secret alliance with Congressman Samuel Dickstein. In March 1934, Dickstein persuaded the House of Representatives to establish a Special Committee on Un-American Activities Authorized to Investigate Nazi Propaganda and Certain Other Propaganda Activities.[269] Jewish organizations such as the Anti-Defamation League refused to assign any of their investigators to the investigation.[270] The committee submitted its report in February 1935. It wrongly concluded that the committee's work had caused the activities of German government agents in the United States to cease and the American Nazi movement to disintegrate. Dickstein felt that the 74th Congress had buried the committee.[271] Untermyer considered that the hearings 'had been harmful to the general cause'.[272] Concerned about his and Dickstein's failure to halt Nazi subversion in the United States, Untermyer called a secret meeting at Greystone during the first week of May 1935. The group of middle-aged men present included three film studio and radio executives, a priest, a rabbi, a clergyman, a group of Wall Street industrialists, a labour leader and two former government officials. The meeting agreed to form a secret organization known as the Board to help Dickstein and Untermyer expose German subversion. One of Dickstein's staff, Richard Rollins (a pseudonym for Isadore Rothberg), was appointed as the Board's chief investigator. Untermyer paid Rollins a small salary and operating expenses from at least as early as May 1934.[273] Rollins carried out investigations of German subversion for Dickstein as requested by Untermyer.[274] Investigations on behalf of the Board were still being carried out by Rollins in October 1938.[275] He also investigated far-right groups for the League and various other Jewish organizations during the 1930s and 1940s.[276]

While the League's work was publicized by the Jewish press in New York and elsewhere Untermyer believed that coverage by the daily non-Jewish press, in particular the press supplied by the Associated Press nationwide, was much more important. He belittled the League's Publicity Bureau and claimed if it were not for the efforts of the office staff at his law firm the League would get virtually no news in the daily press.[277] This was unfair. Many of the leading daily newspapers were unsympathetic to the boycott. The retail trade was a major source of advertising revenue.[278] America's newspaper of record, the *New York Times*, opposed the boycott. Arthur Hays Sulzberger, who was to succeed his father-in-law, Adolph S. Ochs, as the newspaper's publisher in 1935, resented both the boycott activities of Untermyer and those of the AJCong.[279]

There were some exceptions. Fox Movietone broadcast Untermyer's announcement of a world boycott after the Amsterdam conference as part of one of its cinema newsreels.[280] The following year Fox Movietone interviewed Untermyer about the result of the Saar Referendum and the boycott.[281] Scripps-Howard's *New York World-Telegram* published a series of eight interviews on the boycott in early 1934. Joseph M. Proskauer of the AJC gave an interview opposing the boycott arguing it was 'emotional product of a noisy minority'. Reflecting the views of State Department officials, he warned that the boycott would threaten German financial assets in America and obstruct trade relations between the two countries.[282] Untermyer and a League director, George Gordon Battle, presented the case for the boycott. With Proskauer's interview in mind, Untermyer observed:

> The grotesque and tragic feature of it all is that, unlike the non-Jews, a small section of well-intentioned, noisy, self-important Jews, who are barely a factor in the movement and whose duty to their people should have dictated their being in the front ranks of the boycott, are its only carping critics, although they have no other remedy to suggest. Have they done anything to alleviate the plight of the German Jews? If so, what?[283]

The press baron William Randolph Hearst, Untermyer's client and friend, also initially provided Untermyer with a platform for the boycott, although this did not include his newspapers. Like Fox Movietone, Hearst Metrotone News broadcast his announcement of a world boycott after the Amsterdam conference.[284] Hearst subsequently became sympathetic to Nazi Germany after meeting with Hitler.[285] On 1 May 1935 the American Communist Party's *Daily Worker* condemned Untermyer for his uncritical support for the anti-Communist publisher. Quoting from a preliminary copy of Untermyer's speech at the League's all-star variety benefit show at the Hippodrome the previous night, the *Daily Worker* reported that he praised Hearst as one 'whose courage, ability, and editorial policies I have, in the main, admired'. Untermyer also chided those who, he said, had 'detected an absence of sympathy in Hearst's press with the long continued inhuman persecution of the German Jews ... I gravely doubt the justice of that charge'.[286] Nasaw suggests that even in 1935 Hearst 'continued to believe that Hitler would, in due course, change his policies toward the Jews'.[287] Nonetheless Untermyer remained a friend of Hearst. As late as January 1938 he sent the publisher a telegram supporting his opposition to Hull's free trade policy.[288]

Untermyer shared the Communist's Party's critique of the AFL's position on the Boycott. In October 1933 the AFL had voted in favour of a trade boycott of Germany at its convention in Washington.[289] The *Daily Worker* said a subsequent statement on the boycott by William Green, president of the AFL, 'was one of his crudest swindles'[290] because of his unwillingness to support a transportation boycott advocated by Béla Kun of the Communist International.[291] Untermyer told McDonald that he planned 'to work on the A. F. of L. with a view to making their contribution something more than mere resolutions'.[292] He appears to have been unsuccessful. Nonetheless the League organized a testimonial dinner in Green's honour at New York's Aldine Club in February 1934, at which he gave an address on the Nazi assault on organized labour. Mayor La Guardia also addressed the dinner, observing the boycott was the only effective way to deal with the Nazi menace and a speech by Untermyer was read on his behalf.[293]

Untermyer tried to form an alliance with the Roman Catholic Church. However, he only succeeded in winning the support of a handful of liberal Catholics such as Richard J. Beamish, a Pennsylvanian Roman Catholic lawyer and senior state official. Beamish became a member of the League's executive committee in January 1935.[294] The official position of the Roman Catholic Church was hostile to the boycott as Untermyer discovered when he took up a suggestion by Beamish and travelled to Rome in the summer of 1935 with the intention of securing an audience with Pope Pius XI – which he regarded as 'worth a long chance'. He was unsuccessful. Although he did get to meet with some Vatican officials, they were unsympathetic to his cause.[295] This is not surprising given David I. Kertzer's research shows Pius XI had unenlightened perspectives on world Jewry at that time.[296] This was despite the hostility of the Nazi regime to the Roman Catholic Church.

Although the position of the Roman Catholic Church towards the Nazi government was, to say the least, ambivalent, a senior American Roman Catholic, Cardinal Mundelein of Chicago, unequivocally condemned it on 19 May 1937. Untermyer sent Mundelein a telegram praising him. The League redoubled its efforts to win the support of America's twenty million Roman Catholics.[297] The following day, the *Berliner Illustrierte Nachtausgabe* published a front-page article on Untermyer's praise for the cardinal with a headline that included 'Samuel Untermeyer [sic] senses new business opportunities'. It reported,

> The Anti-Nazi League wants to use the favorable opportunity to have new meetings to oppose National Socialist Germany in order to extend the boycott of German goods from Jewish groups to Catholic groups.

Samuel Untermeyer [sic] has shown in his well-known and crude way in this telegram what the Jewish elements in New York really want: the extension of a front created purely for business purposes against a competitor who is inconvenient because it supplies quality goods instead of the poor goods commonly found in Jewish trade.[298]

In February 1935 Dr Julius Lippert, the Nazi Commissioner for Berlin, reported in an address before the city's American Chamber of Commerce, that the boycott of German goods in the United States had seriously affected trade between the two countries. He appealed to 'America's sober business sense' to end the boycott.[299] Untermyer responded to Lippert in a speech before a mass meeting at the Philharmonic Auditorium in Los Angeles. He said the 'only answer to such a plea' was 'not only to continue but to intensify the boycott'.[300] In September 1935 he called for an American boycott of the 1936 Olympic Games.[301] Untermyer had urged Jewish athletes the previous September to boycott the games, followed by a call in December supported by former governor Alfred E. Smith that the American Athletic Union (AAU) refuse to certify entries from the United States to the 1936 Olympiad which would have meant American teams could not compete in the leading sports of the Olympic Games.[302] The AAU, which was at its fortieth national convention, chose to ignore the Berlin Olympics issue. However, Untermyer hoped with the replacement of Avery Brundage by Jeremiah Mahoney as president of the AAU[303] there might be a possibility of transferring the Olympic Games from Berlin.[304] While this did not happen Mahoney proved to be sympathetic to the position taken by the League which brought him into conflict with Brundage who in his new role as president of the American Olympic Committee was not. Untermyer and Ferdinand Pecora organized a tribute dinner in November 1935 at New York City's Commodore Hotel in recognition of 'Judge Mahoney's splendid and courageous stand against American participation in the 1936 Olympiad in Berlin'.[305] The following month at the AAU's forty-first national convention Mahoney proposed America's withdrawal from the Berlin Olympics. But he was outmanoeuvred by Bundage. Recognizing he had lost Mahoney withdrew his candidacy for the presidency of the AAU. He was replaced by Bundage.[306]

At the end of December 1936 the League turned its attention to boxing when J. George Fredman,[307] as a short-lived executive secretary, committed the League to a boycott of the Schmeling–Braddock boxing match the following June and the preceding goodwill tour of exhibition fights in twenty-two cities, seventeen in the South, by the German boxer Max Schmeling.[308] Dr S. William Kalb, chairman of the League's research department, told the press in early January that they did not want American money from the match to go back to Germany.[309] The official German news agency responded by observing, 'It signifies the hatred, rage and envy of the New York Jewish mob which realized that the boycott of German commodities was unsuccessful. The mob now sees the failure of its own political prediction and vents its anger on the German boxer.'[310] Untermyer, who was at his winter vacation home in Palm Springs, had not approved the boycott of Schmeling and made it known that he preferred the fight to go on, but with the stipulation that the German boxer keep his end of the purse in the United States.[311] He feared that the League's action against Schmeling would alienate its most important directors. Indeed, James W. Gerard felt that it would be unpopular and counterproductive, a position supported by Untermyer's two sons.[312] Nonetheless, as soon as James J. Braddock's manager had confirmed the League had indeed voted for a boycott he decided to break the boxer's contract to fight Schmeling.[313] Neither the June prize fight nor the tour took place which vindicated Fredman.[314] Untermyer supported a subsequent boycott of Schmeling's mid-December fight with Harry Thomas in New York, stressing that the League had nothing against the boxer as an individual but was against any of the money he earnt going to Germany. It failed to stop it from taking place, and, although it was not a sell-out, Schmeling's promoter, Mike Jacobs, made a profit.[315] Nonetheless Julius Streicher was so incensed by the latest boycott actions of the 'Jew Untermyer' that he organized a retaliatory boycott of all Jewish shops in his home district of Franconia.[316] Undaunted the League then threatened a boycott of Schmeling's June 1938 heavyweight championship fight with African American boxer Joe Louis in New York unless Jacobs donated his share of the gate to a fund for the relief of refugees from Germany.[317] Jacobs responded with a letter to President Roosevelt with an offer to donate 10 per cent of his profits to his new Advisory Committee on Political Refugees if the League lifted its boycott.[318] After the fight in which Louis defeated Schmeling Jacobs reneged on his offer to donate the funds which were reported to be close to $14,000. Apparently, James G. McDonald, the chairman of Roosevelt's committee, had refused the offer because it was in no position to accept a private donation. Jacobs's lawyer said that the funds would not be given to other refugee aid organizations because he felt they had not cooperated with his client before the fight.[319]

In December 1937 Untermyer gave his last major public address on the boycott in Baltimore. The address was broadcast by Radio Station WCBM of the Mutual Broadcasting Network. In his address, he reflected:

> I cannot understand why Catholics, Protestants, Organized Labor, Rotarians, Masons and Americans generally have been so indolent, callous and shortsighted as to have failed long since to effect a mutual protective organization to safeguard civilization, or why they permit this perilous situation aimlessly to drift, when they have within easy reach the means of self-protection for themselves and their brethren in Germany – by the simple expedient of the boycott of German goods and services.

Untermyer also reflected on the lack of unity in the American Jewish community.

> The wave of world-wide anti-Semitism, led and encouraged by Germany, that is inundating our country should serve only to make us more race conscious, tie us closer together and confirm us in our determination to combat and overcome by every means in our power the vast propaganda of this world-bully and braggart and the forces of evil that inspire it. There are still too many turn-coats, hyphenated Jews and apostates in our ranks. The sooner we expose them and root them out, the better it will be for our welfare and self-respect. They are an undiluted liability.[320]

On 24 April 1938, Untermyer resigned as chairman and president of the League.[321] His health had deteriorated to the point that his work on behalf of the boycott had become too great a burden. He could not sleep because he was worrying so much about the League.[322] After Untermyer's resignation the League continued to promote the boycott and sought to extend its organization. There was a battle to succeed him as president. The candidates included Dr S. William Kalb, the leader of the League's Newark Division. In 1935 he had succeeded in persuading Kraft Foods to switch from using German ships to Holland-America Line to transport Swiss cheese to the United States, and the following year to cease importing cheese from Germany, apart from a small amount of Gruyere.[323] However, the League's fractious convention in May was unable to agree on a successor.[324] Eventually the post of president was replaced by chairman of the board of directors. Kalb was the first chairman.[325] Surprisingly, given the League's financial dependence on Untermyer during his presidency, it survived the loss of his support.

Although Untermyer is often blamed for the failure to achieve a unified anti-Nazi boycott movement in the United States,[326] the AJCong bears a far greater share of the blame for this than the elderly lawyer. As shown above, Frommer has argued that most of leaders of the AJCong believed that the boycott was a hopeless cause.[327] The slogan of the Non-Sectarian Anti-Nazi League to Champion Human Rights was 'the boycott is the moral substitute for war.' However, Untermyer was prescient when he predicted in February 1934 that if Hitler was unable to rid Germany of its Jews by any other means he would exterminate them.[328] It was his desire to prevent this from happening that explains why Meyer F. Steinglass observed, 'something Jehovah-like in [Untermyer's] fanatical devotion to the boycott movement.'[329] It is unfortunate that the boycott did not prove to be a substitute for war.

Conclusion

A British politician, Enoch Powell, has suggested that 'All political lives, unless they are cut off in midstream at a happy juncture, end in failure, because that is the nature of politics and human affairs.'¹ During his bouts of acute illness during his final three years which were accompanied by severe depression, Untermyer might well have been inclined to agree. His last major project, the economic boycott of Nazi Germany, failed to achieve its objective, the downfall of Hitler's government and the salvation of German Jewry. As he observed in reaction to the Anschluss, the German annexation of Austria in March 1938,

> It does not seem possible that a callous world that is apparently so paralyzed that nothing can any longer arouse it to action intends to stand idly and helplessly by and witness the continuous march of the reign of terror by a government that was once a member of the human family in a carnage of slaughter, tramping civilization under foot in cold blood by the hundreds of thousands without rhyme, reason or pretext.²

Untermyer did not live to see his worst fears realized because he died on 16 March 1940. However, he correctly foresaw Hitler's annihilation of German Jewry. He was also one of the first American Jewish leaders to recognize that Polish Jewry was facing an existential threat. He became a benefactor of the American Committee Appeal for the Jews in Poland in 1937.³ In June, he was one of the speakers at the opening session of the twenty-ninth annual convention of the Federation of Polish Jews in America. Untermyer proposed extending the trade boycott to Poland to encourage its government to improve its treatment of its Jewish minority. He also recalled that the 1919 Paris Peace Treaty, to which Poland was a signatory, guaranteed minority protection there. Hence the Roosevelt administration 'should demand either its enforcement or sever all diplomatic and trade relations with Poland'.⁴ The boycott call went unheeded, and the American government did not act. So at the beginning of December, he organized a conference for the Federation of Polish Jews to form an emergency campaign committee. He reported to the conference that of the 3,150,000 Jews in Poland at least 2,000,000 were starving. Untermyer read a cablegram from the American Committee Appeal for the Jews in Poland pleading for more help. He presciently observed that 'The situation of the Jews in Poland is extremely grave. An entire nation of more than three million souls is threatened with annihilation.' Untermyer accepted the honorary chairmanship of the campaign.⁵ After the outbreak of the Second World War he received permission from the State Department for the emergency campaign committee to raise funds for his stricken fellow Jews.⁶ Untermyer was proved correct about the annihilation of Polish Jewry. But the genocide was committed by Nazi Germany rather than Poland's authoritarian government.

Monroe Friedman, in his assessment of the anti-Nazi boycott in the United States, concludes that it may have succeeded more in its value-expressive goals than in its instrumental goals. Instrumentally it failed to stop the Holocaust.[7] Although in 1937 the League pointed to trade statistics that showed that during the previous four and half years Germany had lost more than 50 per cent of her importance as an exporting nation to the United States which they attributed to the boycott. Even if the boycott was responsible it had not brought about the collapse of the German economy.[8] Sharon Gewirtz is undoubtedly correct in arguing that Untermyer's optimism was exaggerated to boost the boycott campaign when he predicted in November 1933 that Germany would economically crack within one year if the boycott was properly prosecuted.[9] Nonetheless, Joseph Tenenbaum, who was chairman of the AJCong's Boycott Committee and subsequently from February 1936 of the Joint Boycott Council in which the AJCong was an equal partner with the Jewish Labor Committee,[10] later recalled that Untermyer's 'zeal, courage and devotion as well as his personal prestige were of inestimable value to the boycott movement. His name became a challenge and a symbol of the boycott'.[11] The German government did not appreciate Untermyer publicizing its suppression of the human rights of its Jewish community and his prediction their ultimate goal was extermination. He was demonized in their propaganda which was disseminated in the United States by collaborators such as 'the influential and rabidly anti-Semitic' Father Charles Coughlin, the spiritual leader and spokesman of the Christian Front.[12] A supporter of Nazi Germany, he preached to millions of Americans on his weekly national radio show.[13] After Untermyer's death, Coughlin republished in the 16 March 1942 issue of *Social Justice* the lawyer's 6 August 1933 speech with a commentary saying it proved the Jews, not Germany, started the Second World War.[14] This contributed to the newspaper being barred from the US mail and it ceasing publication at the beginning of May.[15]

Despite Untermyer's optimism in 1933 that he could make a difference, he faced serious obstacles. The Jewish leadership in the United States, Britain and many other countries in the diaspora were afraid a boycott would encourage anti-Semitism. Indeed, by 1939 Untermyer's nephew Laurence A. Steinhardt believed that what had happened in various parts of Europe during the 1930s could also happen in the United States.[16] The scenario in Philip Roth's *The Plot against America* (2004)[17] is far from implausible. Another obstacle to the boycott's success was that governments in countries such as the United States and Britain prioritized economic recovery over human rights during the Great Depression of the 1930s. Neil Forbes observes the 'revival of lagging exports was a fundamental objective' of the British government and 'remained so throughout the 1930s'.[18] US secretary of state, Cordell Hull, opposed the boycott and promoted trade liberalization for the same reason.[19] However, following an objection by Untermyer in October 1934 he did subsequently intervene to prevent a barter deal to sell cotton to Nazi Germany proposed by Roosevelt's foreign trade adviser.[20]

The rest of Untermyer's political career does not conform to Powell's dictum. As a fundraiser for Jewish settlement in Palestine he helped save the Zionist Project from financial collapse. Perhaps if Untermyer's concerns about Palestine's Arab population had been heeded the subsequent history of Palestine would have been less violent. Although it is unlikely the influx of European Jewish refugees during the 1930s would have been friction free even if the Zionist leadership had been more accommodative to the Palestinian Arabs.

Untermyer also achieved successful outcomes in his quest for economic and financial reform. He made a major contribution to the creation of the Federal Reserve System notwithstanding Carter Glass's insistence that he did not.[21] While Untermyer failed to achieve regulation of securities and America's stock exchanges during the Wilson administration, he was able to contribute to the successful enactment of legislation during Roosevelt's first and second New Deals. He also had successes in New York, most notably saving the city from bankruptcy in 1933, and he also made a major contribution to the unification of the city's mass transit system under municipal ownership. Finally, and not least, he had phenomenal success in his profession as a corporate lawyer. He used the wealth he accumulated to fund his political activities.

During his long career Untermyer made a lot of enemies. He observed in 1908 to Eppa Hunton, a Virginian lawyer and former Congressman,

> I suppose that every aggressive lawyer who has led a busy professional life for thirty years has accumulated a host of unknown enemies. Mine is further an aggravated case in that respect because of the circumstance that, although representing corporate interests, I have spent some considerable part of my life in attacking corporate evils and have incurred powerful enmities, which I do not, however, in the least regret.[22]

Virginian politician Carter Glass was probably Untermyer's worst enemy. As noted earlier he had tried to prevent Untermyer from becoming counsel to the Pujo Investigation in 1912. Glass remained a bitter enemy of Untermyer, whom he considered to be 'a common swindler & defrauder of his business associates',[23] for the rest of his life.[24] It is thus rather odd that in October 1936 he delivered the dedicatory speech in Lynchburg's Agudath Sholom Synagogue at the unveiling of the only known monument dedicated to Untermyer. However, Glass was up for re-election the following month and probably did not want to alienate Lynchburg's Jewish community. The ceremony was attended by, among others, Untermyer's cousin, Nathaniel S. Guggenheimer, a retired former president of Lynchburg's Guggenheimer's Department Store. Glass would also not have wanted to offend the Guggenheimer family whose department store and promotion of manufacturing had revived the Lynchburg economy from the post-Civil War economic depression.[25] The dedication ceremony was part of the week-long celebrations of Lynchburg's sesquicentennial.[26] The bronze tablet honouring Untermyer was attached to a boulder from a local quarry donated by the city. It was funded by popular subscription in which many of the city's residents participated.[27] Untermyer had been expected to attend the sesquicentennial celebrations.[28] In the event, illness prevented him from travelling to Lynchburg. The *Lynchburg News* reported that Glass observed in his dedication on 13 October, 'I am one of them who thinks it is better to praise a person while he is still living than to strew flowers on his grave after he is dead. Few men have ever lived who have possessed a more brilliant intellect than

Mr. Untermyer.' He went on to observe that the distinguished New York attorney had applied his intellect effectively and that he had provided 'invaluable service to those legislative bodies of which I happened to be a member'. As counsel to the Pujo Money Trust Investigation Glass observed Untermyer 'through keen insight and great energy enabled the [C]ongress to bring about drastic reforms that had been of great benefit to the nation'. He had also provided Glass from time to time great assistance in his own legislative activities.[29] There is no doubt that Glass did not believe anything he said about Untermyer in his speech.

Untermyer died three and a half years later at his Palm Springs villa, the Willows, aged eighty-one.[30] Among those who paid tribute to him were Governor Lehman, who said

> Samuel Untermyer, . . . was my friend ever since I was a boy. He was one of the leading lawyers of our time and a man of unusual forcefulness and of indomitable courage. Always concerned with what he considered the best interests of his State and nation, he was for more than half a century a leader in the business and civic life of New York.

New York City mayor Fiorello La Guardia observed of Untermyer: 'On many occasions he had the courage to differ with his associates when it was unpopular to do so. To me his death is a personal loss.' Senator Robert F. Wagner also paid tribute.

> The life of Samuel Untermyer was marked by brilliant achievement in every phase of a varied and remarkable career. As a leader of the bar, patron of the arts and of innumerable charitable endeavors, champion of public causes, and defender of the rights of man in every land, he won the admiration of his countrymen in every phase and walk of life. I join in mourning the loss of a dear friend and great American.[31]

At the funeral service held at his Yonkers estate on 23 March Rabbi Abba Hillel Silver observed in his eulogy that Untermyer

> believed in the American way of life and valiantly championed and defended it when subversive elements attempted to undermine it. In the spread of dictatorships and forms of intolerance abroad in recent years he saw a distinct threat to those political values of life which he knew were at the heart of the classic American tradition and which he believed were indispensable also to civilization as a whole.[32]

Jerold S. Auerbach has observed of one of the Jewish stewards who opposed the economic boycott of Nazi Germany that it was 'his uneasiness as a Jew that required silence, deference – and, ultimately, capitulation'.[33] Unlike Joseph M. Proskauer, Untermyer refused to be silent, deferential or capitulate to the greatest existential threat in the history of world Jewry. Although he was unsuccessful, at least he tried to avert the apocalypse unlike so many of his peers.

Epilogue

As in many family businesses dominated by a founder, Untermyer failed to nurture a successor at Guggenheimer & Untermyer. Although both his sons graduated from Columbia Law School – Alvin in 1906 and Irwin in 1910 – neither of them[1] nor any of his nephews, came close to matching his legal prowess with the possible exception of his nephew Laurence A. Steinhardt. This is probably why Irwin was encouraged by his father to seek election to the New York Supreme Court. He failed to secure sufficient votes in 1919.[2] However, his second attempt in 1929 was successful.[3] He retired in 1945 following the suicide of his wife the previous year.[4] Although Guggenheimer & Untermyer established a branch in Washington, DC in 1935, subsequently a subsidiary partnership[5] and further expanded after the Second World War, none of the partners were able to match Untermyer's achievements. In 1985 it was decided to dissolve the firm.[6] Untermyer would have been displeased that the rival white shoe Cravath firm has survived and is still a leading Wall Street firm.[7]

Untermyer also had a granddaughter and two grandsons, children of his youngest son Irwin. None of them pursued a legal career. Joan became a philanthropist with a particular interest in the rehabilitation of juvenile delinquents.[8] Frank became an academic specializing in political science and African studies. In 1933 his grandfather, who had great respect for academics, had observed he was 'developing on the right lines'.[9] After Frank graduated at Cornell University with an AB in 1938, he pursued graduate studies, became a part-time teaching assistant in government and started a doctorate. After serving in the US Army during the Second World War in Alaska's Aleutian Islands he joined the newly established progressive Roosevelt College (subsequently University) in Chicago, where he was to become a professor. His University of Chicago PhD dissertation on 'The Problem of Federation in the British Central African Colonies' was never completed. He was an early adherent of what has since become the 'Black Lives Matter' movement. His students included Harold Washington, the first African American mayor of Chicago.[10]

Frank's brother, Samuel II, graduated from MIT with an SB in mechanical engineering in 1934. His grandfather thought his father should have given him more direction in his choice of career. After several years as a mechanical engineer at Mack Manufacturing Co., a motor truck producer, he served as an engineering officer in the United States Navy during the Second World War. In 1946, after the war, he joined the Atomic Energy Commission at Oak Ridge, Tennessee, where the uranium enrichment plants had been constructed for the Manhattan Project. He moved to the University of Chicago's Argonne National Laboratory at Lemont, Illinois, in 1948. It was the first national laboratory in the United States contracted by the commission to develop nuclear power for peaceful purposes. While carrying out experiments, he had the groundbreaking insight that it would be safe to allow bulk boiling within the reactor. He prepared a successful proposal for the construction of the first boiling water experimental reactor. He next served as chief engineer on the design of a 5,000-kW experimental boiling water reactor that provided electric power within the Argonne complex and prepared the path for the commercialization of the concept. He convinced General Electric (GE) to adopt his boiling water design. GE recruited him in 1954 and formed an atomic power equipment department in Schenectady, New York, from where he directed the design and construction of what became the Vallecitos Boiling Water Reactor, which went into operation in 1957. He and his department moved to expanded operations at GE's new Vallecitos Atomic Laboratory at Pleasanton, California. He retired from GE in 1964 and founded the National Nuclear Corporation in 1968 to design and produce machinery for the nuclear industry. It produced a device that measured the purity of nuclear fuel and how much further residual nuclear fuel was available. This was sold all over the United States to the big utility companies. In 1985 the company was purchased by Thermo Instrument Systems.[11]

Notes

Preface

1 Richard A. Hawkins, 'Samuel Untermyer', in *American National Biography: 22: Tunnicliff-Welk*, ed. John Arthur Garraty and Mark Christopher Carnes (New York: Oxford University Press, 1999), 105–7.
2 Geoffrey T. Hellman to Alvin Untermyer, 16 May 1940; Alvin Untermyer to Geoffrey T. Hellman, 20 May 1940, MS 251, SUC, AJA, Cincinnati, OH.
    Hellman was a writer at the *New Yorker* magazine whose article on Untermyer's Greystone estate was published shortly after the lawyer's death.
    Geoffrey T. Hellman, 'The Boutonnières of Mr. Untermyer', *New Yorker*, 18 May 1940, 54–65.
3 Charlotte Himber, *Famous in Their Twenties* (New York: Association Press, 1942), 51–67.
4 'Nanette Dembitz Trying to "Crash" Male Stronghold', *Ocean Times Herald*, 26 October 1972, 12.
5 Nanette Dembitz to Frank Untermyer, 7 September 1973, FUPP, Evanston, IL.
6 'Judge Nanette Dembitz, 76, Dies', *NYT*, 5 April 1989, B10; Jacob De Haas, *Louis D. Brandeis: A Biographical Sketch* (New York: Bloch Publishing Company, 1929), 36.
7 Nanette Dembitz to Frank Untermyer, 7 September 1973, FUPP, Evanston, IL.
8 Coleman T. Mobley, 'Venerable Firm Torn Apart by Modern Pressures', *Legal Times*, 26 May 1986, 6, 16–17.
9 https://www.immigrantentrepreneurship.org/entries/samuel-untermyer/, accessed 23 August 2020.

Introduction

1 Kenneth D. Wald, *The Foundations of American Jewish Liberalism* (Cambridge: Cambridge University Press, 2019), 5, 6.
2 Morton Keller, *In Defense of Yesterday: James M. Beck and the Politics of Conservatism, 1861–1936* (New York: Coward-McCann, Inc., 1958), 70.
    Untermyer and Beck's friendship dates to 1900, and possibly even earlier. Untermyer was one of the honorary pall bearers at his friend's funeral in 1936.
    'About New Haven People', *New Haven Morning Journal and Courier*, 30 July 1900, 8; 'Why He Is a Convert', *NYDT*, 3 August 1900, 4; FMD, 1902, 11 May, RPHSFA, New York, NY; 'Happy Hunting Grounds', *Maine Woods*, 17 October 1902, 6; 'Becks The Hosts', *PI*, 14 February 1903, 4; JMB to SU, 7 November 1917, Folder 1, Box 1,

MS 251, SUC, AJA, Cincinnati, OH; SU to JMB, 13 March 1935, Folder 18, Box 10, JMBP, SGMML, PU, Princeton, NJ; 'James M. Beck is Dead at 75', *PI*, 16 April 1936, 6; 'Notables Attend Funeral of Beck', *PI*, 13 April 1936, 1.
3 'Louis Marshall Dies Abroad in 73rd Year after a Brave Fight', *NYT*, 12 September 1929, 24. 'Joins a New York Firm: Louis Marshall, One of Onondaga's Ablest Attorney's Goes to the Metropolis', *Syracuse Daily Standard*, 19 January 1894, 4.
4 'Changes in a Law Firm', *NYH*, 14 February 1894, 4.
5 SU to WGM, 24 May 1916, Box 159, WGMP, LCMD, Washington, DC.
6 Max Eastman, *Is Woman Suffrage Important?* (New York: Men's League for Woman Suffrage, 1912), 23.
7 Brooke Kroeger, *The Suffragents: How Women Used Men to Get the Vote* (Albany: State University Press of New York, 2017), 55–6, 157–8, 219, 222, 227–8.
8 'Untermyer to Plead for Suffrage Bill', *NYT*, 26 February 1910, 7.
9 'Sees Woman Suffrage Coming', *NYT*, 12 June 1910, II:8.
10 General Federation of Women's Clubs, *Eleventh Biennial Convention, June 25 to July 5, 1912, San Francisco, CA: Official Report* (Newark, NJ: The Federation, 1912), 338.
11 'Took Tea in Suffrage Cause', *NYS*, 18 October 1909, 2.
12 'War on Suffragists', *NYDT*, 31 October 1908, 4; 'A Suffragist Recruit: Mrs. Samuel Untermyer Cheers Dobbs Ferry Meeting', *NYDT*, 18 October 1909, 3; 'Suffrage Gains Pair of Noted Women Converts', *New York World*, 18 October 1909, 2; 'For Suffrage Benefit', *NYH*, 15 March 1910, 6; 'Suffragists in Court Fight for Show Booth', *NYS*, 16 March 1912, 1.
13 'Suffragists to Dine', *New York Press*, 26 July 1915, 7; 'Bryan Sees Real Peace Here Only by Women's Vote', *Thrice-A-Week World*, 20 October 1915, 6.
14 'Big Suffrage Party for Mrs. Whitman', *NYT*, 10 October 1915, II:14.
15 'Untermyer Speaks at Pioneer's 100th Anniversary', *NYDT*, 31 October 1915, 8.
16 Margaret Sanger, *Pioneering Advocate for Birth Control: An Autobiography* (New York: First Copper Square Press, 1999), 183–90; SU to Margaret Sanger, 6 December 1915, Margaret Sanger Papers, LCMD, Washington, DC.
17 'City and State Reject Suffrage Amendment by Decisive Majority', *NYS*, 3 November 1915, 1.
18 'Col. House Boosts Woman Suffrage', *NYS*, 25 April 1917, 7; SU to WJB, 24 July 1917, Box 31, WJBP, LCMD, Washington, DC; SU to WGM, 24 July 1917; WGM to SU, 26 July 1917, Box 184; SU to WGM, 14 August 1917; Vira Boarman Whitehouse to WGM, 17 August; WGM to Vira Boarman Whitehouse, 20 August 1917, Box 185, WGMP, LCMD, Washington, DC.
19 'The Woman's Parade', *The Woman Citizen*, 29 September 1917, 337; 'No Real Democracy without Suffrage', *New York Call*, 4 October 1917, 4.
20 'Seen in the Great Suffrage Parade', *NYDT*, 28 October 1917, 8.
21 WGM to Violet Morawetz, 7 November 1917, Box 191, WGMP, LCMD, Washington, DC.
22 SU to WGM, 2 December 1917, Box 192, WGMP, LCMD, Washington, DC.
23 'Democratic Fight on Short Ballot Due at Spa Today', *Knickerbocker Press*, 26 August 1914, 5.
24 *The Suffragist*, 22 July 1916, 2; 26 July 1919, 2.
25 SU to WGM, 24 May 1916, Box 159, WGMP, LCMD, Washington, DC.
26 'Wilson Hears Suff's Plea', *Washington Herald*, 19 July 1917, 1; 'Big Pardon Splits Suffrage Factions', *NYS*, 20 July 1917, 5.

27 Samuel Gompers, *Seventy Years of Life and Labour: An Autobiography: 1* (New York: E.P. Dutton & Company), 346.
28 Joseph Barondess to SU, 30 October 1919, Folder 4, Box 1, MS 251, SUC, AJA, Cincinnati, OH.
29 Benjamin Schlesinger to SU, 18 January 1922, Folder 20, Box 4, Collection 5780/009, ILGWU: Benjamin Schlesinger, President, Records, 1914–1923, Kheel Center for Labor-Management Documentation & Archives, Cornell University Library, Ithaca, NY; 'Cloak Union Gives Untermyer a Cup', *NYT*, 27 March 1922, 27.
30 U.S. Congress, Senate, *Industrial Relations: Final Report and Testimony Submitted to Congress by the Commission on Industrial Relations Created by the Act of August 23, 1912: 8*, 64th Cong., 1st sess. (Washington, DC: G.P.O., 1916), 7429–55.
31 Senate, *Industrial Relations*, 7429.
32 Senate, *Industrial Relations*, 7440.
33 'Mr. Untermyer on the Minimum Wage Decision', *American Federationist*, May 1923, 408.
34 U.S. Congress, Senate, Committee on Education and Labor, *West Virginia Coalfields: Hearings on S. Res. 80: 2*, 67th Cong., 1st sess. (Washington, DC: G.P.O., 1921), 700.
35 Senate, *West Virginia Coalfields*, 700.
36 Senate, *West Virginia Coalfields*, 704.
37 'Untermyer for A.E.A', *Variety Daily Bulletin*, 16 August 1919, 26.
38 This was an anti-Communist, anti-Semitic and anti–New Deal organization that had been founded in 1927.
    Peter H. Amann, 'A "Dog in the Nighttime" Problem: American Fascism in the 1930s', *The History Teacher* 19, no. 4 (1986): 567.
39 Memorandum Report on Samuel Untermyer, R408, Box 3, RG46, Records of the United States Senate Internal Security Subcommittee, NA, Washington, DC.
    Deman's copy of this memorandum does not say who compiled it. However, another copy sent to the anti-Communist businessman Myers G. Lowman does acknowledge the organization that compiled it.
    Memorandum Report on Samuel Untermyer, Box 81, Collection 67019, Myers G. Lowman Papers, Hoover Institution Archives, Palo Alto, CA.
40 'Brands Company Union Biggest Fake in Nation', *Daily Worker* [New York], 6 December 1926, 5.
41 'Porters Are Hosts at A Labor Dinner', *Philadelphia Tribune*, 11 December 1926, 9.
42 'Untermyer to Aid Porters', *NYT*, 1 December 1926, 47.
43 'Brotherhood of Sleeping Car Porters', *Topeka Plaindealer*, 17 December 1926, 4.
44 Jervis Anderson, *A. Philip Randolph: A Biographical Portrait* (New York: Harcourt Brace Jovanovich, 1972), 188–9.
45 'Investigate Porters' Pay', *NYT*, 7 May 1927, 8.
46 'Samuel Untermyer', *Pittsburgh Courier*, 2 July 1927, A8.
47 Anderson, *A. Philip Randolph*, 192.
48 Walter Dyson, *Howard University: The Capstone of Negro Education: A History: 1867–1940* (Washington, DC: The University, 1941), 228; Jacob Billikopf to Charles E. Hughes, Jr., 22 November 1948, RPHSFA, New York, NY.
49 Jason Schulman, 'The Limits of Liberalism: A Constitutional Reconsideration of American Jewish Politics' (PhD diss., Emory University, Atlanta, GA, 2014), 379.
50 W.A. Swanberg, *Pulitzer* (New York: Charles Scribner's Sons, 1967), 359–65.
51 'Indict Five Editors for Panama Libel', *NYT*, 18 February 1909, 2.

52 'Will Fight Extradition', *NYT*, 18 February 1909, 2.
53 Swanberg, *Pulitzer*, 371–2.
54 'More Indictments for Panama Libel', *NYT*, 5 March 1909, 18; Swanberg, *Pulitzer*, 373.

   Untermyer had previously clashed with Roosevelt when he was the governor of New York. In late 1899 Roosevelt began a campaign to remove the New York County District Attorney, Colonel Asa Bird Gardiner, from office. Roosevelt appointed his friend, the lawyer Ansley Wilcox, to investigate allegations of corruption against Gardiner. Untermyer defended Gardiner on a pro bono basis at the hearings held the following year. Wilcox found insufficient evidence to sustain the charges against Gardiner. However, Roosevelt subsequently presented new charges against Gardiner. After a hearing at the end of the year he dismissed the district attorney.

   'Gov. Roosevelt: Declares Criticisms of His Conduct Are Unfair', *NYT*, 2 December 1899, 10; 'Mr. Gardiner Now Faces His Accusers', *NYT*, 20 February 1900, 4; 'Charges Gardiner Nothing', *NYT*, 1 September 1900, 1; 'Governor Dismisses Gardiner Charges', *NYT*, 14 September 1900, 14; 'Gardiner Likely to Go', *NYDT*, 18 December 1900, 1; 'Governor Ousts Gardiner', *NYDT*, 23 December 1900, 1.
55 'Panama Libel Case Pleas', *NYT*, 16 March 1909, 4.
56 'Publishers Rejoice over Libel Decision', *Los Angeles Herald*, 31 January 1910, 12.
57 Walter Lippmann and Charles Merz, 'A Test of the News', *New Republic*, 4 August 1920, S1–S42.
58 SU to Upton Sinclair, 27 October 1919, Upton Sinclair Papers, Lilly Library, Indiana University, Bloomington, IN.
59 Senate, *Industrial Relations*, 7429.
60 'Calls Committee Lawless', *NYT*, 9 July 1919, 17.
61 Samuel Untermyer to Clayton R. Lusk, 9 July 1919, in Rand School of Social Science, *The Case of The Rand School* (New York: The School, 1919), 5–9.
62 'Attorneys Clash Over Rand School', *NYT*, 11 July 1919, 24.
63 Thomas Wirth, 'A Beautiful Public Life: George D. Herron, American Socialism, and Radical Political Culture at the Rand School of Social Science, 1890–1956' (PhD diss., Binghamton University, State University of New York, Binghamton, NY, 2014), 384.
64 'Untermyer Assails Attorney General', *NYT*, 28 July 1919, 4.
65 'Court Dismisses Rand School Case', *NYT*, 31 July 1919, 15.
66 Max Eastman to Florence Deshon, 31 July 1919, Deshon mss., Lilly Library, Indiana University, Bloomington, IN.
67 'Untermyer Charges Persecution in Rand School Case', *NYH*, 7 October 1919, 2:6.
68 Todd J. Pfannestiel, 'Rethinking the Red Scare: The Lusk Committee and New York State's Fight against Radicalism, 1919–1923' (PhD diss., College of William and Mary, Williamsburg, VA, 2001), 224.
69 Zechariah Chafee, Jr., *Free Speech in the United States* (Cambridge, MA: Harvard University Press, 1946), 308, 311, 316–7.
70 Chafee, Jr., *Free Speech*, 317.
71 'Sweet Wins Fight to Expel 5 Socialist Assemblymen', *NYDT*, 1 April 1920, 1, 2; 'Socialists Outline War against Ouster', *NYT*, 4 April 1920, 5.
72 'Untermyer Aids Ousted 5', *NYT*, 1 September 1920, 3.
73 'Five Expelled Socialists Win Again at Polls', *NYDT*, 17 September 1920, 20.
74 '5 Socialists Seated', *NYDT*, 21 September 1920, 1, 6.
75 'Assembly Ousts Three Socialists; Two Resign', *NYDT*, 22 September 1920, 1, 2.

76 'Ouster Means More Socialists in Legislature, Leaders Say', *NYDT*, 22 September 1920, 2.
77 'Edgar Speyer Dies on Visit to Berlin', *NYT*, 18 February 1932, 21; 'Sir Edgar Speyer', *The Times* [London], 18 February 1932, 17; Jean Starr Untermeyer, *Private Collection* (New York: A.A. Knopf, 1965), 118.
   For an in-depth study of the Speyer case see the following:
   Antony Lentin, *Banker, Traitor, Scapegoat, Spy? The Troublesome Case of Sir Edgar Speyer* (London: Haus Publishing, Ltd., 2013).
78 'Privy Councilor Quits after Attack', *Washington Herald*, 18 May 1915, 1.
79 Nationality and Naturalisation: Sir Edgar Speyer, HO144/12981, TNA, Kew, UK; 'Sir E. Speyer's Reply', *The Times* [London], 9 January 1922, 12.
80 'Sir Edgar Speyer Denaturalized', *The Times* [London], 14 December 1921, 10; 'Speyer Silently Becomes Man of No Country', *NYDT*, 15 December 1921, 6.
81 'Sees Liberty Going Amid Indifference', *NYT*, 16 May 1925, 10.
82 'Mine Owner Defies Untermyer To Sue', *NYT*, 1 June 1922, 4; 'Gov. Sproul Promises Mine Field Justice', *NYT*, 12 June 1922, 28.
83 'Untermyer to Aid Baldwin', *NYT*, 1 November 1925, II:3.
84 'Baldwin Sentence Upheld in New Jersey', *NYT*, 2 November 1927, 29.
85 'Assails Saklatvala Ban', *NYT*, 20 September 1925, 29.
86 Jacob A. Zumoff provides a definitive account of the strike in his forthcoming monograph. I would like to thank him for providing me with an advance copy.
   Jacob A. Zumoff, *Red Thread: The Passaic Textile Strike* (New Brunswick, Camden, and Newark, NJ and London: Rutgers University Press, 2021).
87 Mary Heaton Vorse, *The Passaic Textile Strike, 1926-1927* (Passaic, NJ: General Relief Committee of Textile Strikers, 1927), 11–59; 'Armed Guards Ring Jersey Mill Pickets', *NYEP*, 19 April 1920, 1, 6; Zumoff, *Red Thread*, 51.
88 'Textile Mills Open', *NYT*, 20 April 1926, 29.
89 'Untermyer Pleads for Senate Probe of Passaic Strike', *BDE*, 20 April 1926, 2.
90 Vorse, *Textile Strike*, 59–60.
91 'Strikers Accept Parley to End Textile Tieup', *BDE*, 22 April 1926, 2.
92 'Strikers Ready for Mediation', *NYS*, 21 April 1926, 3.
93 Zumoff, *Red Thread*, 72.
94 Zumoff, *Red Thread*, 72–3.
95 Vorse, *Textile Strike*, 125.
96 Jacob A. Zumoff, *The Communist International and US Communism, 1919-1929* (Leiden: Brill, 2014), 196.
97 'Hillquit Funeral to be Wednesday', *NYEP*, 9 October 1933, 36.
98 Samuel Untermyer and Morris Hillquit, *Shall Trade Unions be Regulated by Law?: Affirmative, Mr. Samuel Untermyer; Negative, Mr. Morris Hillquit* (New York: Hanford Press, 1923), 15.
99 Harold Seidman, *Labor Czars: A History of Labor Racketeering* (New York: Liveright Publishing Corporation. 1938), 92–3.
100 O. F. Lewis, 'County Jails as Farm Labor Center', *The American City*, March 1918, 215–6.
101 SU to Nathan Snyder, 20 October 1927, Folder 8, Box 2, MS 251, SUC, AJA, Cincinnati, OH.
102 'Lewis E. Lawes Dies', *PI*, 24 April 1947, 14.
103 'To Fight Capital Punishment', *NYT*, 4 January 1926, 40.
104 'Debate Abolition of Death Penalty', *NYT*, 15 January 1928, 27.

105 Samuel Untermyer, *Resolved, That Capital Punishment be Abolished: Opening Argument of Mr. Samuel Untermyer: Debate before the Roebling Unit, Steuben Society, University Club, Brooklyn, January 14, 1928* (New York: The League to Abolish Capital Punishment, 1928), 11.
106 Untermyer, *Capital Punishment*, 18–19.
107 Untermyer, *Capital Punishment*, 23.
108 Himber, *Famous*, 56.
109 Henry H. Klein, *My Last Fifty Years: An Autobiographical History of "Inside" New York* (New York: The Author, 1935), 275.
110 Klein also estimated in 1921 the Untermyer family's combined wealth was an estimated $50 million.
　　Henry H. Klein, *Dynastic America and Those Who Own It* (New York: The Author, 1921), 155–7.
111 SU to his Children, 7 June 1926, FUPP, Evanston, IL.
112 *Trow's New York City Directory for the Year Ending July 1, 1893* (New York: Trow Directory, Printing and Bookbinding Company, 1892), 1446; 'The Social World', *NYT*, 27 March 1892, 2.
113 'At Old Greystone', *Kansas City American Citizen*, 4 February 1900, 3; 'Greystone As Restored', *NYT*, 17 June 1900, 15.
114 'Seventy-Four Pictures Bring Total of $63,635', *NYT*, 22 March 1906, 9.
115 'The Verestchagin Sale', *NYT*, 19 November 1891, 5.
116 Sidney Starr to James McNeill Whistler, 2 September 1892; James McNeill Whistler to SU, 3 September 1892; SU to James McNeill Whistler, 11 October 1892; James McNeill Whistler to SU, 30 October 1892; SU to James McNeill Whistler, 7 November 1892, *The Correspondence of James McNeill Whistler, 1855–1903*, ed. Margaret F. MacDonald, Patricia de Montfort and Nigel Thorp, online edition, University of Glasgow, http://www.whistler.arts.gla.ac.uk/correspondence, accessed 2 July 2020.
117 'Whistler v. Ruskin', *The Times* [London], 26 November 1878, 9; 'Whistler v. Ruskin', *The Times* [London], 27 November 1878, 9, 11; Daniel E. Sutherland, *Whistler: A Life for Art's Sake* (New Haven: Yale University Press, 2014), 262–3.
118 'Greystone on the Hudson', *Town and Country*, 2 January 1904, 10–14.
119 Beatrice L. Magnes, *Episodes: A Memoir* (Berkeley: Judah L. Magnes Memorial Museum, 1977), 25.
120 James Creelman, 'The Mastery of a Billion Dollars', *Pearson's Magazine*, April 1907, 359–60.
121 Jerome Myers and Guy Pène DuBois, 'Greystone', *Arts & Decoration* 6, no. 11 (1916): 508.
122 Gove Hambidge, 'Samuel Untermyer in His Enchanted Gardens', *Better Homes and Gardens*, February 1928, 18, 128.
123 Caroline Seebohm, *Paradise on the Hudson: The Creation, Loss, and Revival of a Great Garden* (Portland, OR: Timber Press, 2020) 11–13, 17–18.
124 I thank Caroline Seebohm for the following reference.
　　Philadelphia Public Ledger, 17 April 1918, Scrapbooks: March 1918–September 1919, 2, page 43, Box 52, MS 251, SUC, AJA, Cincinnati, OH.
125 Untermeyer, *Collection*, 118.
126 'Live Topics About Town', *NYS*, 4 February 1905, 4.
127 'New York Scoops in a Fee in Cooper Merger that Makes Eyes Bulge', *Omaha Sunday Bee*, 6 February 1910, 2.

128 *NYT*, 22 March 1903, 14.
129 'Gen Ives Owns the World's Fastest Steam Yacht', *NYT*, 18 June 1905, 3–6.
130 'Rival Hudson River Flyers', *NYH*, 20 May 1903, 12.
131 'Crucial Equitable Meeting Is Called', *New York Press*, 22 May 1905, 3; Dexter Marshall, 'Who Is Samuel Untermyer?', *Duluth Evening Herald*, 27 May 1906, 2.
132 United States Department of Commerce, Bureau of Navigation, *Forty-Fifth Annual List of Merchant Vessels of the United States for the Year Ended June 30, 1913* (Washington, DC: G.P.O., 1913), 74; *Lloyd's Register of American Yachts* (New York: Lloyd's Register of Shipping, 1914) 58.
133 'Canopy of Lilies for Her Wedding', *NYT*, 6 February 1914, 9; 'Packers Run It', *Topeka Daily State Journal*, 22 December 1917, 5; 'Mrs. Juliana H.A. Ferguson', *NYT*, 28 November 1921, 11.
134 'Houseboat for Lorillard', *NYT*, 13 January 1901, 8; 'Pierre Lorillard Dead', *NYT*, 8 July 1901, 1; 'Col. Phelps' Houseboat Launched', *NYT*, 15 June 1902, 6; 'Sheffield Phelps Dead', *New Haven Morning Journal and Courier*, 10 December 1902, 2; 'Furnish Bond For Untermyer's Boat', *Wilmington Morning Star*, 6 January 1921, 12; Works Progress Administration, *Ship Registers and Enrollments of Providence, Rhode Island, 1773–1939* (Providence, RI: The National Archives Project, 1941), 801.
135 'Cape Sable', *Tropic Magazine*, February-March 1917, 81–2, 130; 'Cape Sable', *Tropic Magazine*, April 1917, 5–9.
136 In the late 1920s Untermyer sold the *Nirodha* to the South Florida Yacht Club.
       United States Department of Commerce, Bureau of Navigation, *Merchant Vessels of the United States: Year Ended June 30, 1928* (Washington, DC: G.P.O., 1928), 802–3; United States Department of Commerce, Bureau of Navigation, *Merchant Vessels of the United States: Year Ended June 30, 1929* (Washington, DC: G.P.O., 1929), 102–3.
137 It is not known when they first became acquainted. However, by 1905 Rice was living near Greystone with her brother, Henry, and eleven-year-old niece, Molly Tackaberry.
       Third Ward, Yonkers, Westchester County, New York State Census, 1905, https://www.familysearch.org/, accessed 24 July 2019.
138 SR District/Reg Area – Tralee: 1870, https://civilrecords.irishgenealogy.ie/, accessed 26 July 2019; *Calendar of Grants of Administration and Letters of Probate of Her Majesty's Court of Probate, Ireland: 1872* (Dublin: H.M.S.O., 1873), 561.
139 *Who's Who in New York: 1914* (New York: Who's Who in New York City and State, Inc., 1914), 404–5; *The India List and India Office List for 1902* (London: Harrisons & Sons, 1902), 541.
140 Interview with Frank Untermyer, 25–28 April 2000.
141 Imre Jösicka-Herczeg was a staunch Hungarian patriot. Jösicka-Herczeg's nationalism became an issue after the war. In 1928 Untermyer was attacked by the Anti-Horthy League for his involvement with Jösicka-Herczeg in a Louis Kossuth statute unveiling ceremony because a large delegation from Hungary was in attendance. He replied by arguing his involvement did not involve 'condonation of or sympathy with Hungarian or other Jew-baiters'. Jösicka-Herczeg died at the relatively young age of sixty in 1935. His wife outlived him by eleven years.
       'New York to Honour Kossuth Pilgrims', *NYT*, 10 March 1928, 17; 'De Josika-Herczeg Patriot, Dies At 60', *NYT*, 1 April 1935, 19; 'Mrs. I. De Josika-Herczeg', *NYT*, 13 March 1947, 28.
142 *Who's Who in New York: Fourth Biennial Edition* (New York: L. R. Hamersly & Company, 1909), 755; *Who's Who in New York: 1914*, 404–5.

143 Ward 15, New York City, NY, 19 April 1910, United States Census, https://www.familysearch.org, accessed 24 July 2019.
144 'William G. McAdoo, Jr., Is Married to Divorcee', *Yonkers Statesman and News*, 23 May 1922, 7.
   Billy was an alcoholic and ne'er-do-well. She separated from him in 1934 and two years later was granted a divorce.
   'Wins Divorce', *New York Post*, 13 May 1936, 2.
145 'Untermeyer Appeals $48,122 Tax Charge', *BDE*, 9 July 1939, 1.
146 'Dinner to Count Apponyi', *NYS*, 3 March 1911, 2.
147 SU to Hon. Ira Morris, United States Embassy, Stockholm, Sweden, 7 June 1919, Box 222, Papers of WGM, LCMD, DC.
148 The apartment had fourteen rooms and five baths.
   'Samuel Untermyer Leases Large Fifth Ave. Suite at 74th St. Corner', *NYS*, 18 September 1930, 51.
149 'Untermyer's Home Leased', *NYEP*, 24 June 1926, 23.
150 Tracy Conrad to Richard Hawkins, 24 December 2001; 9 January 2002; Jim Welsh to Tracy Conrad, 27 January 2011.
151 SU to JMB, 4 January 1933, Folder 21, Box 7, JMBP, SGMML, PU, Princeton, NJ.
152 Cleveland Amory, *The Last Resorts* (Westport: Greenwood Press, 1973), 481.
153 WGM to SU, 14 January 1931, Box 355, Papers of WGM, LCMD, Washington, DC.
154 SU to WGM, 16 January 1931, Box 355, Papers of WGM, LCMD, Washington, DC.
155 'Socialites at 'The Willows', *Palm Springs News*, 9 April 1936; 'Prominent Villagers', *Palm Springs News*, 23 April 1936.
156 Passenger Manifest, SS Kronprinzessin Cecilie, 18 November 1913; 'Passenger Manifest, SS Olympic, 9 September 1925', https://familysearch.org, accessed 22 August 2019.
157 'Alien Rejected for Drinking Finally Granted Citizenship', *Yonkers Statesman*, 20 July 1928, 7.
158 'Untermyer in Hopeful View of Economy', *San Bernardino Sun*, 9 January 1934, 2:1.
159 Interview with Frank Untermyer, 25–28 April 2000.
160 LAS to SU, 12 May 1933, Letterbook 1933, Box 75, LASP, LCMD, Washington, DC.
161 Interview with Frank Untermyer, 25–28 April 2000.
   Blair died just over a decade later in Lancaster, Pennsylvania, of acute alcohol poisoning.
   Certificate of Death, 1 January 1952, Bureau of Vital Statistics, Department of Health, PA.

Chapter 1

1 These were rural ghettos to which the Jews of Augsburg had been expelled in the early fifteenth century.
2 Acta des konigl. Landesgerichts Krumbach Betreff: Guggenheimer Salomon Kaufmann von Lynchburgh in Nordamerica, dessen Verehelichung mit Landauer Therese von Hürben 1847, 2, Bezirksamt Krumbach 2829, Staatsarchiv Augsburg, Augsburg, Germany.

3 Hürben-Krumbach Community Registers, https://www.jgbs.org, accessed 22 February 2019; Doris Pfister, *Dokumentation zur Geschichte und Kultur der Juden in Schwaben: 2: Hausbesitz um 1835/40* (Augsburg: Bezirk Schwaben, 1993), 85.
4 Rolf Hofmann, Wallerstein Jewish Cemetery Grave List, Version 1 (2003–2005), http://www.alemannia-judaica.de, accessed 15 February 2019; Isidor Singer, ed., *The Jewish Encyclopedia: IX: Morawczyk-Phillipson* (New York and London: Funk and Wagnalls Company, 1912), 447–8.
5 Selma Stern, *The Court Jew: A Contribution to the History of the Period of Absolutism in Central Europe* (Philadelphia: The Jewish Publication Society of America, 1950), 57–8, 182.
6 Singer, *Jewish Encyclopedia: IX*, 447–8.
7 Advertisement, *LV*, 4 August 1844, 3.
8 Rötgerber (red or bark) tanneries employed the oldest method of tanning.
    Hippolyte Dussauce, *A New and Complete Treatise on Tanning, Currying and Leather Dressing*, 2nd edn. (Philadelphia: Henry Carey Baird, 1867), 24.
9 Hürben-Krumbach Community Registers, https://www.jgbs.org, accessed 22 February 2019; Pfister, *Hausbesitz um 1835/40*, 92, 96; *Lynchburg News*, 5 February 1962, 9.
10 *Betreff: Guggenheimer Salomon*, Staatsarchiv Augsburg, Augsburg, Germany.
11 Advertisement, *LV*, 30 October 1848, 2.
12 Henry Hall, ed., *America's Successful Men of Affairs: I* (New York: New York Tribune, 1895), 282–3.
13 Lynchburg (VA) Hustings Court, Law Order Book No.5, November 1848–September 1852, 39, Clerk's Office, LCC, Lynchburg, VA.
14 Virginia, Vol.9, Campbell County, p.11, R.G. Dun & Co. Credit Report Volumes, Baker Library, Harvard Business School, Cambridge, MA.
15 Entry No. 20: Marriage Register, Congregation Beth Ahabah Museum and Archives, Richmond, VA.
16 Iva was born in 1849 and died in 1855.
    Town of Lynchburg, Campbell County, VA, 23 September 1850, United States Census, https://www.familysearch.org, accessed 7 December 2020; Account Books, Diuguid Funeral Home, Lynchburg, Virginia, 4 March 1855, JML, Lynchburg, VA.
17 Helen Untermyer Siesfeld was born on 20 May 1852 and died on 9 September 1932.
    Grave marker, Salem Fields, New York City, transcribed by Frank Untermyer.
18 Isaac was born on 22 June 1853 and died on 31 August 1926.
    'Isaac Untermyer, Lawyer, Dies At 73', *NYT*, 1 September 1926, 23.
19 Maurice was born on 19 February 1860 and died on 29 December 1908.
    'Maurice Untermyer', *NYDT*, 30 December 1908, 7.
20 Account Books, Diuguid Funeral Home, Lynchburg, Virginia, 7 November 1861, JML, Lynchburg, VA.
21 Addie was born on 2 May 1866 and died on 24 November 1921.
    'Mrs. Addie Steinhardt', *NYT*, 3 December 1921, 23.
22 Lynchburg (VA) Hustings Court, Chancery Court and Law Order Book: Justices: February 1846–August 1849, 469, Clerk's Office, LCC, Lynchburg, VA.
23 Lynchburg (VA) Hustings Court, Chancery Court and Law Order Book: Justices: February 1846–August 1849, 4 May 1847, 184, Clerk's Office, LCC, Lynchburg, VA.
24 The Hürben death register says Isaak Untermayer was born *c.* 1761 and died on 24 January 1838 and Jette Untermayer was born *c.* 1771 and died on 6 April 1839. Shenef records Isaak's death as 7 January 1838.

Acta konigl. Landgerichts. Krumbach, Verlassenschaft des Handelsmannes Josef Guggenheimer zu Hürben 1852, 23, LgäO Krumbach, NA, Hürben Nr.156, Staatsarchiv Augsburg, Augsburg, Germany; Yehuda Shenef, *Das Haus der Drei Sterne: Die Geschichte des jüdischen Friedhofs von Pfersee, Kriegshaber und Steppach bei Augsburg, in Österreich, Bayern und Deutschland* (Norderstedt: Books on Demand, 2016), 152, 172.

25 Dr. Reinhard H. Seitz, Ltd. Archivdirektor Staatsarhiv Augsburg, to Dr. Arthur S. Obermayer, 13 October 1997.

26 Shenef, *Haus der Drei Sterne*, 92–3, 123; Arthur Obermayer, 'Tracing German-Jewish Ancestry to the 17th Century – And Much Earlier', *Avotaynu* 27, no. 2 (2011): 35–7.

27 *Augsburgische Ordinari Postzeitung*, 17 May 1821, 8; Pfister, *Hausbesitz um 1835/40*, 142; Heinz Wember, Umschlüsselung Hausnummer alt zu Straße und Hausnummer 1918, sortiert nach vorhandener Hausnummer von 1840, http://www.heinz-wember.de, accessed 12 February 2019.

28 Isidor Singer, ed., *The Jewish Encyclopedia: II: Apocrypha-Benash* (New York and London: Funk and Wagnalls Company, 1912), 604.

29 Acta konigl. Landgerichts. Krumbach, Verlassenschaft des Handelsmannes Josef Guggenheimer zu Hürben 1852, 23, LgäO Krumbach, NA, Hürben Nr.156, Staatsarchiv Augsburg, Augsburg, Germany.

30 Phillip W. Rhodes, JML, Lynchburg, to Frank Untermyer, 21 September 1990, FUPP, Evanston, IL; Advertisement, *LV*, 4 April 1850, 3.

31 'Fire', *LV*, 12 January 1853, 2; Untermyer v. Shelton Case File, 9, 13, Clerk's Office, LCC, Lynchburg, VA.

32 Virginia, Vol. 9, Campbell County, 83, R.G. Dun & Co. Credit Report Volumes, Baker Library, Harvard Business School, Cambridge, MA.

33 Advertisement, *LV*, 15 September 1859, 2.

34 Advertisement, *LV*, 26 December 1859, 2.

35 'Legislature of Virginia', *Richmond Enquirer*, 28 February 1860, 4; Advertisement, *LV*, 12 April 1860, 2.

The bank was short-lived. John Jay Knox notes that all of Virginia's banks 'practically went out of existence with the surrender of Lee's Army at Appomattox'. The Lynchburg Savings Bank was no exception.

John Jay Knox, *A History of Banking in the United States* (New York: Bradford Rhodes & Company, 1903), 534.

36 *The Occident*, 31 March 1859, 5–6.

37 Robert D. Gardner, M.D., Lynchburg Jewish community historian, to Richard Hawkins, 23 April 1998.

38 'Death of an Old Merchant', *LV*, 27 March 1866, 3.

39 Isidor had been a member of congregation since at least 1848.

Account Book c.1848–1855; List of Members as of 1851, Congregation Beth Ahabah Museum and Archives, Richmond, VA.

40 'Guggenheimer Advises Newsboys', *NYDT*, 19 January 1901, 5; Theodor Lemke, *Geschichte des Deutschthums von New York: Von 1848 auf die Gegenwart* (New York: Verlag von Theodor Lemke, 1891), 105.

41 Cornelius J. Heatwole, *A History of Education in Virginia* (New York: The Macmillan Company, 1916), 269.

42 Advertisement, *LV*, 9 December 1862, 4.

43 Untermyer v. Shelton Case File, 168–71.
44 Lynchburg Corporation Court, Deed Book W: December 1859 to January 1863, 479–80, Clerk's Office, LCC, Lynchburg, VA.
45 Washington County Deed Book Vol. 38, 572–3, Sherrod Library, East Tennessee State University, Johnston City, TN.
46 Entry No.69, Marriage Register, Congregation Beth Ahabah Museum and Archives, Richmond, VA.
47 'Death of an Old Merchant', *LV*, 27 March 1866, 3.
48 Phillip W. Rhodes, JML, to Frank Untermyer, 21 September 1990.
49 Untermyer v. Shelton Case File, 1–2, 63.
50 Untermyer v. Shelton Case File, 209; 'An Act staying the Collection of Debts for a Limited Period Passed December 19, 1865'; 'An Act to stay the Collection of Debts for a limited period Passed March 2, 1866' in State of Virginia, *Acts of the General Assembly, Passed in 1865–1866, in the Eighty-Ninth Year of the Commonwealth* (Richmond: Allegre & Goode, Printers, 1866), 179–84.
51 Richard A. Hawkins, 'Lynchburg's Swabian Jewish Entrepreneurs in War and Peace', *Southern Jewish History* 3 (2000): 64–6.
52 Advertisement, *LV*, 21 September 1867, 2; Advertisement, *LV*, 1 January 1868, 3.
53 Virginia, Vol. 9, Campbell County, p.150, R.G. Dun & Co. Credit Report Volumes, Baker Library, Harvard Business School, Cambridge, MA.
54 Virginia, Vol. 9, Campbell County, p.174, R.G. Dun & Co. Credit Report Volumes, Baker Library, Harvard Business School, Cambridge, MA.
55 Words Spoken at the Bier of Therese Untermyer by Rabbi Gustav Gottheil, 14 January 1895, FUPP, Evanston, IL.
56 Julius Katzenberg, 'Theresa Untermeyer [sic]', *AH*, 18 January 1895, 336.
57 'Deaths', *Jewish Messenger*, 19 August 1864, 53.
58 Isaac Untermyer's obituary incorrectly says that he moved with his family to New York City in 1868.
  NYT, 1 September 1926, 23; College of the City of New York, *Eighteenth Report of the Faculty to the Board of Trustees* (New York: The College, 1869), 22.
59 Cornelius Grinnell, 24 February 1854, Passenger Lists of Vessels Arriving in New York, New York, 1820–1897, Roll 136, M237, RG36, Records of the U.S. Customs Service, NA, Washington, DC.
60 *Trow's New York City Directory for the Year Ending May 1, 1856* (New York: John F. Trow, 1855), 494; 'Curious Case', *NYT*, 4 February 1856, 6.
61 'Admissions to Bar', *NYDT*, 10 May 1859, 7.
62 *History of Bench and Bar of New York City: 2* (New York: New York History Company, 1897), 379.
63 Lynchburg Corporation Court Deed Book Aug. 1866 to Jan. 1870, 561–3, LCC, Lynchburg, VA.
64 Washington County, Tennessee, Deed Book Vol.42, 370–2; Vol.43, 518–20, Sherrod Library, East Tennessee State University, Johnston City, TN.
65 Himber, *Famous*, 59; '*Trow's New York City Directory for the Year Ending May 1, 1870* (New York: John F. Trow, 1869), 1117; Advertisement', *NYH*, 26 March 1871, 3; 'Advertisement', *Jewish Messenger*, 18 May 1877, 6.
66 Beatrice L. Magnes to Louise Frankel, 14 December 1965, FUPP, Evanston, IL.
67 *Trow's New York City Directory for the Year Ending May 1, 1879* (New York: Trow City Directory Company, 1878), 1481; *Trow's New York City Directory for the Year Ending*

May 1, 1881 (New York: Trow City Directory Company, 1880), 1570; *Trow's New York City Directory for the Year Ending May 1, 1882* (New York: Trow City Directory Company, 1881), 1642.

68 Edwin G. Burrows and Mike Wallace, *Gotham: A History of New York City to 1898* (New York: Oxford University Press, 1999), 1078.

69 'He Was A Leader in Social Reform', *NYT*, 6 December 1963, 28; Memorandum by Governor Lehman Regarding Death of Samuel Untermyer, 17 March 1940, FUPP, Evanston, IL; Allan Nevins, *Herbert H. Lehman and His Era* (New York: Charles Scribner's Sons, 1963), 45, 143, 192; Michael R. Cohen, *Cotton Capitalists: American Jewish Entrepreneurship in the Reconstruction Era* (New York: New York University Press, 2017), 126–8; 183; Hebert H. Lehman Oral History Volume 1, 69–70, RBML, CUL, New York, NY; Herbert H. Lehman to SU, 20 August 1917; SU to Herbert H. Lehman, 21 August 1917; SU to Herbert H. Lehman, 24 August 1917; Herbert H. Lehman to SU, 27 August 1917; SU to Herbert H. Lehman, 28 August 1917, Folder 1, Box 2, MS 251, SUC, AJA, Cincinnati, OH.

70 'Disclosures Promised', *Rochester Democrat and Chronicle*, 24 March 1904, 2; Anthony Lehman to SU, 6 May 1918, Folder 1, Box 2, MS 251, SUC, AJA, Cincinnati, OH.

71 'Guggenheimer', *Rome Daily Sentinel*, 15 August 1898, 4.

72 *Real Estate Record*, 27 September 1873, 446; 21 February 1874, 85; 21 March 1874, 137.

73 *Real Estate Record*, 15 April 1882, 364.

74 *Real Estate Record*, 23 February 1884, 187; 21 June 1884, 674; 18 October 1884, 1068; Alva Johnston, 'Profiles: Little Giant – I', *New Yorker*, 17 May 1930, 30; Himber, *Famous*, 56.

75 'Hugo Kafka', *Journal of the American Institute of Architects* 3, no. 7 (1915): 305; 'Hugo Kafka', *New Rochelle Pioneer*, 1 May 1915, 8.

76 'Off for Europe', *Jewish Messenger*, 1 June 1883, 6; New York Passenger Lists, 1820–1891, https://www.familysearch.org, accessed 21 July 2020; 'Obituary Notes', *NYS*, 13 January 1895, 2.

77 Dexter Marshall, 'Samuel Untermyer', *New York Press*, 27 May 1906, 3:3; 'Reunion for No.35 Boys', *NYH*, 24 October 1910, 4; 'Alumni Notes', *Columbia Alumni News*, 1 December 1910, 192; Anna M. Hunter and Jenny Hunter, eds, *The Autobiography of Thomas Hunter* (New York: The Knickerbocker Press, 1931), 3, 61–7, 368–9, 374–5.

78 Samuel Untermyer, *The Ideals of Zionism: An Address Delivered before the Jewish Telegraphic Agency at Hotel Brevoort, October 1, 1921* (New York: The Author, 1921), 1.

79 College of the City of New York, *Twenty-Fourth Annual Register: 1872–1873* (New York: The College, 1872), 66.

80 College of the City of New York, *Nineteenth Report of the Faculty to the Board of Trustees* (New York: The College, 1870, 7–8.

81 *Merit Roll of the College of the City of New York: First and Second Collegiate Terms: September 1872 to June 1873* (New York: The College, 1873), 17.

82 *Merit Roll of the College of the City of New York: First Academic Term: July 1889 to February 1870* (New York: The College, 1870), 19.

83 'Samuel Untermyer', in *National Cyclopædia of American Biography* 17 (New York: James T. White & Company, 1920), 396; 'Samuel Untermyer', in *Who's Who in Banking and Finance: 1920–1922* (New York: Who's Who in Finance, Incorporated, 1922), 695.

84 Richard A. Hawkins, 'The Marketing of Legal Services in the United States, 1855–1912: A Case Study of Guggenheimer, Untermyer & Marshall of New York and the Predecessor Partnerships', *American Journal of Legal History* 53, no. 2 (2013): 239–64; 'Legal Notices', *Real Estate Record*, 22 January 1876, 70; 'The Alleged Flight of Levinger', *NYEP*, 28 February 1876, 3; 'Fate of a Fugitive Lawyer', *NYH*, 30 May 1878, 9; 'Old Byrnes Man Dead', *NYT*, 7 March 1906, 9.

85 'Levinger & Co. Fail', *NYH*, 25 September 1875, 5; 'City and Suburban News', *NYT*, 26 September 1875, 12; 'Long Island', *NYDT*, 17 December 1875, 8; 'Seizure of the College Point Brewery', *NYDT*, 18 December 1875, 2.

86 *Resolutions Passed by the Trustees of Columbia College from 1874 to 1879* (New York: The College, 1879), 52.

87 Allan Nevins and Milton Halsey Thomas, eds, *The Diary of George Templeton Strong: 4: Post-War Years, 1865–1875* (New York: Macmillan Company, 1952), 544; 'George Templeton Strong', *NYDT*, 22 July 1875, 5.

88 *A History of Columbia University, 1754–1904* (New York: Columbia University Press, 1904), 216, 224–5.

89 'Tributes to Louis Marshall', *Jewish Tribune*, 10 December 1926, 2.

90 Samuel Untermyer, 'What Every Present-Day Lawyer Should Know', *The Annals of the American Academy of Political and Social Science* 167 (1933): 173.

91 *Jewish Tribune*, 10 December 1926, 2; Entry for 16 February 1877: Minutes of Columbia Law Club, 20 December 1873 – 6 February 1880, 172, Law Library, CUL, New York, NY.

92 Johnston, 'Little Giant – I', 29–30.

93 'New Lawyers', *American Israelite*, 24 May 1876, 6.

94 'Lawyer, 19, Must Wait for the Bar', *NYT*, 20 August 1988, 1:31.

95 Hastings vs. Andrews, December 1881, FUPP.

96 'Important Trustees' Sale of Eastern Boulevard Lots', *New York Evening Telegram*, 17 May 1873, 3; 'Small Bequest to an Erring Son', *NYH*, 5 January 1894, 5.

97 Matthew P. Breen, *Thirty Years of New York Politics Up-To-Date* (New York: The Author, 1899), 361–2.

98 New York, Vol. 382, 307, R.G. Dun & Co. Credit Report Volumes, Baker Library, Harvard Business School, Cambridge, MA; 'New York Building Items', *Manufacturer and Builder*, 15 September 1884, 200; Sophie Guggenheimer Untermeyer and Alix Williamson, *Mother is Minnie* (Garden City, NY, Doubleday, 1960), 59.

99 John Franklin Sprague, *New York, The Metropolis: Its Noted Business and Professional Men: 1* (New York: The New York Recorder, 1893), 89–90; *Trow City Directory Co.'s Formerly Wilson's Business Directory of New York City: 1885* (New York: Trow City Directory Company, 1885), 449.

100 John Oller, *White Shoe: How a New Breed of Wall Street Lawyers Changed Big Business and the American Century* (New York: Dutton, 2019), 4.

101 'R. Guggenheimer Dies of Apoplexy', *Richmond Times-Dispatch*, 13 September 1907, 1.

102 *The Trow Copartnership and Corporation Directory of the Boroughs of Manhattan and the Bronx, City of New York, March 1908* (New York: Trow Directory, Printing & Bookbinding Co., 1908), 337.

103 *Trow's General Directory of the Boroughs of Manhattan and Bronx, City of New York for the Year Ending July 1, 1906* (New York: Trow Directory, Printing & Bookbinding Co., 1905), 1455.

104 *The Trow Copartnership and Corporation Directory of the Boroughs of Manhattan and Bronx, City of New York, March 1909* (New York: Trow Directory, Printing & Bookbinding Co., 1909), 319, 802.
105 'Arthur M. Wickwire', *NYS*, 12 April 1937, 23.
106 New York City Births, 1846–1909, https://familysearch.org; NYC Municipal Archives, https://italiangen.org, accessed 20 March 2019.
107 Marriage Certificate, FUPP, Evanston, IL; Frank Untermyer to Richard Hawkins, 14 June 1999; Annie Polland and Daniel Soyer, *Emerging Metropolis: New York Jews in the Age of Immigration* (New York: New York University Press, 2012), 73–6, 85–6.
108 United States Passport Applications, 1795–1925, https://familysearch.org, accessed 20 March 2019.
109 'Irwin Untermyer, 87, Retired Judge, Dies', *NYT*, 19 October 1973, 44.
110 Friedrich Lorenz Schmidt, *Darstellende Geschichte der Stadt Zeulenroda, 1325–1867, 2: Zeulenroda in der Zeit von 1651–1867*: 2 (Weimar: Hermann Böhlaus Nachfolger, 1953), 709, 772; 'Aus Thüringen, Osterland & Vogtland', *Zeulenroda Kreisblatt*, 2 November 1878, 1, 4; ' Zeulenroda', *Zeulenroda Tageblatt*, 23 September 1887, 3.
111 Alfred Spitzner, *1813–1913: Das Völkerschachtdenkmal Weiheschrift* (Leipzig: Breitkopf & Härtel, 1913), 77, 80, 82–3.
112 *Official Army Register of the Volunteer Force of the United States Army: 7* (Washington, DC: G.P.O., 1867), 79; Manilius Carl, Compiled Service Records of Volunteer Union Soldiers Who Served in Organizations from the State of Missouri, M405, RG94, NA, Washington, DC.
113 'Mrs. S. Untermyer Dies at Greystone', *NYT*, 17 August 1924, 24.
114 New Orleans Passenger Lists, 1820–1945, https://familysearch.org, accessed 15 March 2019.
115 'The German Drama Represented in the Police Court', *Cincinnati Enquirer*, 29 September 1857, 3; 'The Late Erring Wife and Her Husband Reconciled', *Cincinnati Enquirer*, 30 September 1857, 3; 'Nicknacks', *Sacramento Union-Supplement*, 9 April 1859, 1; Depositions of William E. Schubert, 1 June 1893; John A. Adolph, 2 June 1893; Arnold Beck, 3 June 1893; Christoph Geissler, 7 June 1893; Transcript of General Court Martial, 8 August 1863; Copy of Burial Certificate: Francis Ehrler, 7 August 1886, WO225-079, Louisa Ehrler, Civil War Widows' Pension Files, Records of the Veterans Administration, RG15, NA, Washington, DC; *Trow's New York City Directory for the Year Ending May 1 1871* (New York: Trow City Directory Company, 1870), 187; *Trow's New York City Directory for the Year Ending May 1 1877* (New York: Trow City Directory Company, 1876), 205; *Trow's New York City Directory for the Year Ending May 1 1878* (New York: Trow City Directory Company, 1877), 400.
116 *Edwards' Annual Directory* (St. Louis, MO: Southern Publishing, 1868), 216; *Edwards' Annual Directory* (St. Louis, MO: Southern Publishing, 1870), 206; E.D. 360, New York, New York County, NY, 1 June 1880, United States Census, https://www.familysearch.org, accessed 15 March 2019; Pauline Carl Mesker to Frank Untermyer, 1988, FUPP, Evanston, IL; Last Will and Testament of Manilius Carl, New York, Wills and Probate Records, 1659–1999, www.Ancestry.com, accessed 15 March 2019.
117 'Guggenheim Hearing Ends', *NYT*, 1 January 1913, 17.
118 Harvey O'Connor, *The Guggenheims: The Making of an American Dynasty* (New York: Covici, Friede, 1937), 146–51; Grace B. Guggenheim, *The Power and Influence of Money: A True Story of the Guggenheim Divorce Case*, c.1922, 58, File SNY 226407,

RG60, Records of the Dept. of Justice, NA, College Park, MD; 'Guggenheim Tells His Marriage Story', *NYT*, 2 January 1913, 6.
119 'Would Disbar Untermyer', *NYT*, 28 February 1913, 3.
120 'Prosecutor Drops Guggenheim Case', *Brooklyn Standard Union*, 24 July 1913, 3.
121 Gregory J. Kupsky, '"The True Spirit of the German People": German-Americans and National Socialism, 1919–1955' (PhD diss., The Ohio State University, Columbus, OH, 2010), 23.
122 'A Charge of Conspiracy', *NYT*, 4 February 1883, 5; 'A Partner Alleging Fraud', *NYT*, 17 April 1883, 3; New York Court of Appeals, Records and Briefs of Baur v. Betz (1885), Respondent's Brief, J2002, New York State Archives, Albany, NY.
123 Newcombe was a partner of Albert Cardozo, the father of future US Supreme Court justice Benjamin Cardozo.
  'Death of Richard S. Newcombe', *NYT*, 27 July 1891, 5; 'Death of R.S. Newcombe', *NYDT*, 27 July 1891, 1.
124 'Richard Wightman Fox, *Trials of Intimacy: Love and Loss in the Beecher-Tilton Scandal*' (Chicago: University of Chicago Press, 1999); 'Mr. Baur's Money "Up the Spout"', *NYT*, 2 May 1884, 3; 'Mr. Betz Wins His Suit', *NYT*, 9 May 1884, 8.
125 New York Court of Appeals, Case on Appeal from Order, of 31 October 1884, William C. Baur, Plaintiff vs. John F. Betz, Henry Daily, Jr., Appellant and Attorney in Person, Randolph Guggenheimer, Respondent's Attorney, New York, 1885, 281–5, New York State Archives, Albany, NY; 'Court of Appeals', *NYDT*, 27 June 1885, 8.
126 'Real Estate', *NYEP*, 29 March 1898, 11; 'Marionville, Horicon', *Warrensburgh News*, 12 May 1898, 7; 'Horicon', *Warrensburgh News*, 21 July 1898, 7; 'Horicon', *Warrensburgh News*, 17 November 1898, 7; 'Supreme Court – County of Warren', *Glens Falls Daily Times*, 10 June 1909, 3.
127 'Untermyer Paid No Warren County Tax', *NYS*, 1 November 1919, 10.
128 'British Gold in America', *NYH*, 21 July 1889, 22.
129 In the September 1888 issue of the *Brewers' Journal* Samuel Untermyer is described as 'the brilliant' young lawyer responsible for the genesis of the company promotions.
  'The Capitalisation of Breweries', *Brewers' Journal*, 1 September 1888, 428; Johnston, 'Little Giant – I', 30; Himber, *Famous*, 56.
130 Richard A. Hawkins, 'American Boomers and the Flotation of Shares in the City of London in the late Nineteenth Century', *Business History* 49, no. 6 (2007): 802–22.
131 'Advertisement', *The Times* [London], 30 October 1889, 14.
132 Untermyer later secured a position on behalf of the English bondholders for his brother-in-law, Alvin Carl, as one of two receivers for this company in May 1895. Carl helped reorganize the company.
  'Bought By English Money', *NYT*, 14 July 1889, 1; U.S. Congress, Senate, Subcommittee on the Committee on the Judiciary, *Prohibiting Intoxicating Beverages: Hearings on The Bills to Prohibit the Liquor Traffic and to Provide for the Enforcement of Such Prohibition and the War Prohibition Act*, 3, 66th Cong., 1st sess. (Washington, DC: G.P.O., 1919), 250; 'Receivers for the Otis Steel Company', *NYT*, 10 May 1895, 1; 'Otis Steel Company Fails', *Indianapolis Journal*, 10 May 1895, 5; *The Iron Age*, 16 May 1895, 1029; 'Will Stay at Cleveland', *Evening Bulletin* [Maysville, Kentucky], 21 November 1895, 1.
133 Alvin Carl served as the British company's resident manager in Cincinnati. He was also associated with the Jung Brewing Company from 1890, subsequently serving as vice-president and general manager.

One Hundred Years of Brewing (Chicago and New York: Western Brewer, 1903), 229; 'A Trust Mortgage for $775,000', *Pittsburg Dispatch*, 20 January 1891, 2; *History of Cincinnati and Hamilton County, Ohio* (Cincinnati: S.B. Nelson & Co., 1894), 329; 'Manufacturing', *The Iron Age*, 16 May 1895, 1029; George Mortimer Roe, ed., *Cincinnati: The Queen City of the West* (Cincinnati: Cincinnati Times-Star Co., 1895), 171.

134 Hawkins, 'American Boomers', 812.
135 'Levy Mayer', in *National Cyclopædia of American Biography* 6 (New York: James T. White & Company, 1929), 531.
136 *National Cyclopædia of American Biography* 1, 241.
137 'New York Lawyers', *The Advance*, 30 January 1908, 139–40.
138 Richard A. Hawkins, 'Leopold Salomons, 1841–1915, Financier and Landowner', in *Oxford Dictionary of National Biography* (Oxford: Oxford University Press, 2012), https://doi.org/10.1093/ref:odnb/101300, accessed 3 March 2019.
139 Isaac Untermyer to SU, 18 December 1889, FUPP, Evanston, IL; 'Sir Henry Isaacs: A Retrospect of the Nineties', *City Press*, 7 August 1909, 5.
140 'Sir F. Crisp', *The Times* [London], 1 May 1919, 10.
141 'Friar Park', *Henley Advertiser*, 6 April 1889, 4.
142 'Friar Park, Henley', *The Gardener's Chronicle*, 28 October 1899, 321–4.
143 Jack Londoner, 'Man About Town', *Essex Newsman*, 19 August 1933, 1.
144 'Calls Peabody Figurehead', *NYS*, 9 April 1906, 1; 'Mr. Choate and Son Plead First Case', *NYH*, 24 November 1911, 7.
145 Sir Thomas H.D. Berridge to SU, 21 December 1917, Folder 1, Box 1, MS 251, SUC, AJA, Cincinnati, OH.
146 SU to LM, 25 September 1908, Folder 4, Box 22, MS 359, LMC, AJA, Cincinnati, OH.
147 From 1896 Alvin Carl also served as general manager of the Roessle brewery, one of the British company's four American breweries, and as general manager of the New England Brewing Company from the late 1890s until his death in 1907. He was succeeded as manager of the Roessle brewery by his son, Walter Alvin Carl.

Zachary Nowak, 'Something Brewing in Boston: A Study of Forward Integration in American Breweries at the Turn of the Twentieth Century', *Enterprise & Society* 18, no. 2 (2017): 337–8, 341, 346–7; 'The Death Roll: Alvin Carl', *American Brewers' Review*, 1 November 1907, 530; *Harvard College Class of 1904: Secretary's Second Report* (Cambridge, MA: Crimson Printing Co., 1910), 55, 254.
148 'Industrial & General Trust, Limited v. Tod', in *New York Supplement* 64 (1900): 1093–101; 'The Industrial and General Trust, Limited, Respondent, v. J. Kennedy Tod et al., Appellants, Impleaded with Another', in *Reports of Cases Decided in the Court of Appeals of the State of New York* 170 (1902): 233–70.
149 Clarence Winthrop Bowen, ed., *The History of the Centennial Celebration of the Inauguration of George Washington as First President of the United States* (New York: D. Appleton and Company, 1892), 244.
150 'Samuel Untermyer', in *National Cyclopædia of American Biography* 1 (New York: James T. White & Company, 1893), 241–2.
151 Samuel Untermyer', in *Who's Who in America: 4* (Chicago: A.N. Marquis and Company, 1906), 1824.
152 George Cohen, *The Jews in the Making of America* (Boston, MA: The Stratford Co., 1924), 218.
153 *National Cyclopædia of American Biography* 1, 241.
154 Emmanuel Pilpel to James T. White & Co., 17 June 1898, FUPP, Evanston, IL.

155 New York City Municipal Deaths, 1795–1949, https://familysearch.org, accessed 9 September 2020.
156 *New York Press*, 27 May 1906, 3:3.
157 Johnston, 'Little Giant – I', 29.
158 Slave Schedule, Lynchburg, Campbell County, VA, 18 June 1860, United States Census, https://www.familysearch.org, accessed 25 September 2020.
159 'Carter Glass', in *National Cyclopædia of American Biography* A (New York: James T. White & Company, 1961), 36–8; Writers' Program of the Works Projects Administration, *The Negro in Virginia* (New York: Hastings House, 1940), 239.
160 The duty was to take effect on 1 July 1893. If the output of American tin mines had not exceeded 5,000 tons in any one year prior to 1 July 1895 then all imported tin after that date would be admitted free of duty.
  National Cyclopædia of American Biography 1, 241–2; U.S. Congress, House, Committee on Ways and Means, *Revision of the Tariff: Hearings 1889–1890*, 51st Cong., 1st sess. (Washington, DC: GPO, 1890), 1187–96; U.S. Dept. of State, *The Statutes at Large of the United States, December 1889 to March 1891* (Washington, DC: G.P.O., 1891), 582.
161 'Englishmen Charge Fraud', *NYT*, 30 June 1894, 9.
162 'Where is American Tin?', *NYDT*, 8 December 1887, 10.
163 SU to LM, 29 June 1894, Folder 22, Box 79, MS 359, LMC, AJA, Cincinnati, OH.
164 'The Tin-Mine Fiasco', *NYEP*, 25 August 1894, 3.
165 SU to LM, 27 June 1908, Folder 4, Box 22, MS 359, LMC, AJA, Cincinnati, OH.
166 SU to Charles Fairchild, 5 February 1892, FUPP, Evanston, IL.
167 'Louis Marshall Dies Abroad in 73rd Year After a Brave Fight', *NYT*, 12 September 1929, 24.
168 Weinman had joined the firm in 1883 after his graduation from Columbia Law School.
  'Moses Weinman "81"', *City College Quarterly*, June 1912, 179; *Hubbell's Legal Directory* 21 (1890): 1008.
169 'Joins a New York Firm: Louis Marshall, One of Onondaga's Ablest Attorney's Goes to the Metropolis', *Syracuse Daily Standard*, 19 January 1894, 4.
170 'Harry Hoffman', in *Who Was Who in America: 9: 1985–1989* (Wilmette, IL: Marquis Who's Who, 1989), 169.
171 Harry Hoffman to Nanette Dembitz, n.d., FUPP, Evanston, IL.
172 James Marshall to CW, 1 January 1931, WA, Rehovot, Israel.
173 'James Marshall, Lawyer, Is Dead', *NYT*, 12 August 1986, D20.
174 'Samuel Untermyer', *Harper's Weekly*, 29 July 1911, 32.
175 Creelman, 'Billionaire', 364.
176 'Umbrella Trust Incorporated', *NYT*, 5 June 1892, 15; 'The Wall-Paper Trust: Its Capital Increased and Its Growth Keeping Pack', *NYT*, 31 December 1892, 8; 'Steam Pump Makers Combine', *NYT*, 9 March 1899, 14; 'Enamel Ware Trust Organized', *NYDT*, 22 January 1899, 7; *Moody's Manual of Industrial and Miscellaneous Securities 1900* (New York: O.C. Lewis Company, 1900), 900.
177 Hebert H. Lehman Oral History Volume 1, 82–3, RBML, CUL, New York, NY.
178 'Enamel Ware Trust Organized', *NYDT*, 22 January 1899, 7.
179 New York City Marriage Records, 1829–1940, https://www.familysearch.org, accessed 6 July 2020.
180 SU to LM, 24 September 1903, Folder 21, Box 10, MS 359, LMC, AJA, Cincinnati, OH; 'Saved By His Dog', *NYS*, 11 February 1908, 9.

181 William L. Chenery, *So It Seemed* (New York: Harcourt, Brace and Company, 1952), 166.
182 Agreement: Joseph P. Knapp with F. Heppenheimer's Sons, 2 January 1892, FUPP, Evanston, IL.
183 Maxwell Bloomfield, 'Joseph Palmer Knapp', in *Dictionary of American Biography, Supplement 5* (New York: Charles Scribner's Sons, 1977), 394–5; *Moody's Manual 1900*, 900.
184 Joseph Palmer Knapp to ASO, 28 October 1903; ASO to Joseph Palmer Knapp, 30 October 1903; Joseph Palmer Knapp to SU, 2 November 1903, FUPP, Evanston, IL.
185 Thomas Peterson, *Magazines in the Twentieth Century* (Urbana: University of Illinois Press, 1984), 133; *Poor's Manual of Industrials: 1911* (New York: Poor's Railroad Manual, 1911), 860.
186 Chenery, *So It Seemed*, 166–7; 'Thomas William Lamont', in *National Cyclopædia of American Biography 41* (New York: James T. White & Company, 1956), 6–8.
187 'Statement of Ownership', *Collier's*, 1 November 1924, 48.
188 'Crowell Co. Gets Control of 'Collier's', *NYDT*, 26 July 1919, 16.
189 SU to Eppa Hunton, 10 February 1908, Folder 4, Box 1, MS 251, SUC, AJA, Cincinnati, OH.
190 Dupee and Willard of the Chicago law firm, Dupee, Judah & Willard, had helped initiate the trust in 1892.
    'Harry W. Dickerman, Trustee, et al., Petitioners v. Northern Trust Company et al. (176 U.S. 181) [Argued 5–6 April 1899, Decided 22 January 1900]' in *The Supreme Court Reporter* 20 (1900), 311–20; *Transcript of Record in the United States Circuit Court of Appeals for the Seventh Circuit, October Term, 1895, No.344, Henry W. Dickerman, Trustee, Et Al. Appellants vs. The Northern Trust Company and Ovid B. Jameson, Trustees, Etc., Appellants*, File 16724, Box 2847, RG267, United States Supreme Court Appellate Cases, NA, Washington, DC.
191 *The Supreme Court Reporter* 20 (1900), 313–20; 'Fraud in Making a Trust', *NYT*, 23 January 1900, 10; 'Paper Trust's Victory', *New York World*, 23 January 1900, 6; 'Paper Mills To Be Sold', *Chicago Daily Tribune*, 23 January 1900, 12.
192 'A Straw Paper Trust', *NYT*, 24 March 1897, 3.
193 'Strawboard Suits End', *NYDT*, 29 June 1905, 9.
194 'William G.E. See, receiver of the Columbia Straw Paper Company, v. William C. Heppenheimer, Samuel Untermyer et al. [Decided 3 April 1905]', in *Reports of Cases Decided in the Court of Chancery of the State of New Jersey: 69* (Newark: Soney & Sage, 1907), 36–88.
195 'With A Capital of $20,000,000', *NYDT*, 31 March 1899, 11.
196 'The New United Fruit Company', *NYDT*, 1 September 1899, 9.
197 *United Fruit Company* (Boston: Edgerly & Crocker, 1901), 4, 7.
198 'Controls the Fruit Market', *NYDT*, 29 August 1902, 9.
199 Mike Wallace, *Greater Gotham: A History of New York City from 1898 to 1919* (New York: Oxford University Press, 2017), 809.
200 SU to LM, 21 September 1903, Folder 21, Box 10, MS 359, LMC, AJA, Cincinnati, OH; 'Banana Trust Beaten', *Fruit Trade Journal and Produce Record*, 8 June 1912, 1; Eugene W. Ong, Vice-President United Fruit Company to SU, c. November 1920; SU to Eugene W. Ong, Vice-President United Fruit Company, 17 November 1920, Box 58, MS 359, LMC, AJA, Cincinnati, OH; Eugene W. Ong to SU, 3 December 1917; SU to Eugene W. Ong, 4 December 1917, Folder 8, Box 2, MS 251, SUC, AJA,

Cincinnati, OH; LAS to United Fruit Company, 20 May 1938, Family, Box 95, LASP, LCMD, DC.
201 *Second Annual Report to the Stockholders of the United Fruit Company for the Fiscal Year Ended August 31, 1901* (Boston: The Company, 1901), 3; *Eighth Annual Report to the Stockholders of the United Fruit Company for the Fiscal Year Ended September 30, 1907* (Boston: The Company, 1907), 2; 'United Fruit Co.', *Commercial & Financial Chronicle*, 12 October 1901, 794; 'United Fruit Co.', *Commercial & Financial Chronicle*, 25 July 1907, 164.
202 Susan E. Tifft and Alex S. Jones, *The Trust: The Private and Powerful Family Behind The New York Times* (New York: Little, Brown and Company, 1999), 31–40; *NYT*, 3 July 1928, 5; SU to ASO, 6 June 1933, b42, f.13-15, NYTCR: ASOP, NYPL, New York, NY.
203 SU to ASO, 8 June 1899, b42, f.13-15, NYTCR: ASOP, NYPL, New York, NY.
204 SU to ASO, 23 March 1901, b42, f.13-15, NYTCR: ASOP, NYPL, New York, NY.
205 'Statement of Ownership', *Brewer's Journal*, 1 November 1915, 45.
206 SU to ASO, 13 November 1907; ASO to SU, 15 December 1907, b42, f.13-15, NYTCR: ASOP, NYPL, New York, NY.
207 ASO to SU, 1 February 1910, b42, f.13-15, NYTCR: ASOP, NYPL, New York, NY.
208 SU to Louis Wiley, 13 June 1933, Louis Wiley Papers, Collection A.W67, Department of Rare Books and Special Collections, University of Rochester, NY; 'Louis Wiley', *BDE*, 20 March 1935, 17; Isaac M. Brickner, *The Jews of Rochester* (Rochester, NY: Historical Review Society, 1912), 93–5; 'Lawyers and Legal Events', *Bench and Bar*, May 1917, 47; 'Abraham Benedict', *NYT*, 5 March 1943, 7.
209 *A Souvenir of New York's Liquor Interests* (New York: American Publishing and Engraving Co., 1893), 50; 'Isaac Danenberg', *NYDT*, 4 March 1899, 7.
210 'A New York Firm Retained by the Brewers Association to Fight the Raines Law', *Poughkeepsie News-Press*, 24 March 1896, 1; 'To Fight to the End', *East-Hampton Star*, 27 March 1896, 1.
211 'Mr. Choate's Great Fee', *NYDT*, 4 May 1896, 1; William E. Schenk, ed., *Decisions Relating to the Liquor Tax Law of the State of New York: 1* (Albany: State of New York, 1905), 1–31.
212 SU to LM, 15 May 1896, Folder 11, Box 6, MS 359, LMC, AJA, Cincinnati, OH.
213 SU to Charles Fairchild, 5 February 1892, FUPP, Evanston, IL.
214 Alvin Untermyer to SU, 26 July 1907, FUPP, Evanston, IL.
215 '$20,000,000 Company', *NYDT*, 29 July 1910, 12; 'Big Cotton Mills Fight Dissolution', *NYS*, 27 May 1914, 16; Walter C. Noyes, ed., *Making of the Modern Law: Trials 1600–1926: Francis A. Lazenby, Etc., Plaintiff against International Cotton Mills Corporation, and Others, Defendants [1915]* (Belmont, CA: Gale, 2012).
216 G. Samuel Bradshaw, 'Moses Herman Cone' and 'Ceasar Cone', in *Biographical History of North Carolina From Colonial Times to the Present: 8* (Greensboro, NC: Charles L. Van Toppen, 1917), 109–21; Carl J. Balliett, *World Leadership in Denims Through Thirty Years of Progress* (Greensboro, NC: Proximity Mfg. Co., 1925), 9.
217 'Breach of Contract Suit', *Daily Charlotte Observer*, 23 February 1896, 3.
218 'Bernard Milton Cone', in *National Cyclopædia of American Biography* 43 (New York: James T. White & Company, 1961), 86; 'Dunham v. Hastings Pavement Co.', in *New York Supplement* 68 (1901): 221–4.
219 Hynda Rudd, 'Samuel Newhouse: Utah Mining Magnate and Land Developer', *Western States Jewish Historical Quarterly* 11, no. 4 (1979): 291, 307.

220 Company Registration File No: 46526: Utah Consolidated Gold Mines Ltd., BT31/6612/46526, TNA, Kew, UK; Leonard J. Arrington and Gary B. Hansen, *"The Richest Hole on Earth": A History of the Bingham Copper Mine* (Logan: Utah State University Press, 1963), 17–18.
221 Arrington and Hansen, *Richest Hole*, 19–20; 'New Investments', *Financial Times* [London], 9 June 1898, 8.
222 'Utah Copper Deal', *NYT*, 14 May 1903, 16; '$85,000,000 Ore Find', *NYT*, 25 October 1904, Frank C. Robertson and Beth Kay Harris, *Boom Towns of the Great Basin* (Denver: Sage Books, 1962), 133.
223 'Reorganization of Newhouse Company'; 'Newhouse Mines & Smelters Advertisement', *Salt Lake Herald*, 14 June 1909, 7; 'More Activity in South Utah Mines', *Salt Lake Herald-Republican*, 30 September 1910, 10.
224 Walter Harvey Weed, *The Mines Handbook: 15* (New York: Stevens Copper Handbook Co., 1922), 1582.
225 Untermyer's firm had probably represented the Lewisohn Brothers since at least 1897. FMD, 1897, 22 February, RPHSFA, New York, NY; GU&M to Leonard Lewisohn, 10 May 1899; Leonard Lewisohn to GU&M, 11 May 1899; GU&M to Leonard Lewisohn, 13 May 1899, Folder 5, Box 7, MS 251, SUC, AJA, Cincinnati, OH.
226 Richard E. Lingenfelter, *Bonanzas & Borrascas: Copper Kings & Stock Frenzies, 1885–1918* (Norman, OK: Arthur H. Clark Company, 2012), 194; 'Lewisohns Absorbed by Concern That Will Handle 70 Per Cent of Output', *Butte Daily Inter Mountain*, 2 February 1900, 5.
227 'Leonard Lewisohn, Financier Dead', *NYH*, 6 March 1902, 5.
228 Walter Harvey Weed, *The Mines Handbook: 12* (New York: Stevens Copper Handbook Co., 1916), 509.
229 'The Butte Companies Are Busy', *Duluth Evening Herald*, 24 February 1906, 13; 'Lewisohns Back In Globe', *Duluth Evening Herald*, 23 March 1907, 17, 28; 'Will Offer Mining Stock', *NYH*, 29 March 1908, 5–8; *Moody's Manual of Railroads and Corporation Securities: Eleventh Annual Number: 1910* (New York: Moody Manual Company, 1910), 3282; *Moody's Manual of Railroads and Corporation Securities: Twelfth Annual Number: 1911* (New York: Moody Manual Company, 1911), 3661.
230 'Death of Leonard Lewisohn', *Arizona Silver Belt*, 13 March 1902, 4; *Duluth Evening Herald*, 23 March 1907, 17, 28; 'Deal for the Copper Butte', *Duluth Evening Herald*, 13 April 1907, 17; 'Lewisohns Mine in Globe', *Duluth Evening Herald*, 29 December 1907, 13.
231 *Moody's Manual of Railroads and Corporation Securities: Twenty-Fourth Annual Number: Industrial Section: II – K-Z: 1923* (New York: Poor's Publishing Company, 1923), 418–9.
232 *Duluth Evening Herald*, 23 March 1907, 17.
233 'Sixty Per Cent Dividend', *Duluth Evening Herald*, 3 July 1909, 12; Weed, *Mines Handbook: 15*, 105.
   Moody's Manual of Railroads and Corporation Securities: Twenty-First Annual Number: Industrial Section: 1920 (New York: Poor's Publishing Company, 1920), 2582.
234 'More Copper Talk', *NYT*, 26 April 1899, 1.
235 'Refuse to Talk', *Butte Weekly Miner*, 27 April 1899, 3.
236 Thomas W. Lawson, 'Frenzied Finance: The Story of Amalgamated: II', *Everybody's Magazine*, April 1905, 485–97, A65.
237 'Lawson's Pen Digs Up the Utah Copper Boom', *NYT*, 21 March 1905, 7.

238 'Samuel Untermyer Sounds a Warning', *NYT*, 11 June 1905, 3:1; Edward W. Russell to C.E. Lovejoy, 1 February 1938, Untermyer File, RBML, CUL, New York, NY.
239 O'Connor, *Guggenheims*, 109.
240 SU to WGM, 27 June 1915, Box 140, WGMP, LCMD, Washington, DC.
241 O'Connor, *Guggenheims*, 111; 'Brief Bits of News', *Kansas City Journal*, 6 June 1899, 2.
242 'Guggenheims Own Only 15 Per Cent of Guggenheim Exploration Co. Stock', *United States Investor*, 23 September 1911, 1590–2.
243 J.H.M. Shaw to GU&M, 5 July 1899, Folder 4, Box 25, MS 251, SUC, AJA, Cincinnati, OH.
244 O'Connor, *Guggeheims*, 120–3.
245 Bernard M. Baruch, *Baruch: My Own Story* (New York: Henry Holt and Company, 1957), 196–9.
246 Gatenby Williams and Charles Monroe Heath, *William Guggenheim* (New York: Lone Voice Publishing Company, 1934), 224; Marvin D. Bernstein, *The Mexican Mining Industry, 1890–1950: A Study of the Interaction of Politics, Economics and Technology* (New York: State University of New York Press, 1964), 36–9, 50–6, 67–9, 72–3.
247 LM to SU, 5, 7 and 26 August 1903, Folder 22, Box 1572, MS 359, LMC, AJA, Cincinnati, OH; Bernstein, *Mexican Mining*, 56; Company Registration File No. 62457: Esperanza Gold Mining Co. Ltd. BT31/16216/62457, TNA, Kew, UK; Bernstein, *Mexican Mining*, 56.
248 'Advertisement', *NYEP*, 21 July 1909, 11; *Moody's Manual of Railroads and Corporation Securities: Twelfth Annual Number: 1911* (New York: Moody Publishing Co., 1911), 3598.
249 'Great Copper Mine', *Ogden Evening Standard*, 25 November 1912, 3; 'Guggenheim's New Chile Deal', *Bisbee Daily Review*, 27 April 1913, 2:2; 'Chile Copper Co. Financing', *NYS*, 15 May 1913, 4; *Moody's Manual of Railroads and Corporation Securities: Fourteenth Annual Number: II: 1913* (New York: Moody Manual Co., 1913), 4863; Wallace, *Greater Gotham*, 47.
250 SU to WGM, 27 June 1915, Box 140, WGMP, LCMD, Washington, DC.
251 *Listings Statements of the New York Stock Exchange* 13 (New York: Francis Emory Fitch, Inc., 1916), A-2524.
252 'Antofagasta (Chili) and Bolivia Railway Co.', *The Times* [London], 11 December 1908, 4; 'Samuel Untermyer', in *Who's Who in Finance* (New York: Joseph & Sefton, 1911), 707.
253 'Guggenheim Gets Utah Copper', *NYDT*, 23 November 1905, 12.
254 SU to his Children, 7 June 1926, FUPP, Evanston, IL.
255 'Washington Is Sounded Out as To Copper Merger', *New York Press*, 12 December 1909, 6; 'Denies Big Copper Merger', *NYT*, 13 December 1909, 16.
256 'Copper Merger Ratified', *NYT*, 6 January 1910, 12.
257 'Untermyer $775,000 The Biggest Fee Yet', *NYT*, 27 January 1910, p.1; Arrington and Hansen, *Richest Hole*, 65–6.
258 Guthrie was paid directly. So there is no record of the amount of the fee, although one partner recalled he had been told by Guthrie it was $1 million.
  'What Great Lawyers Receive for Their Work', *NYT*, 19 January 1908, B9; Robert T. Swaine, *The Cravath Firm and Its Predecessors, 1819–1947: 1: The Predecessor Firms, 1819–1906* (New York: Cravath, Swaine & Moore, 1946), 686.
259 'The Erie Negotiations – Copper Financing', *The Economist*, 18 April 1908, 840–1.
260 '400 "Alaska Railroad Men Incorporate"', *San Francisco Call*, 4 June 1905, 29; Mile Road for Alaska', *Newport News Daily Press*, 4 February 1906, 1.

261 Elizabeth A. Tower, *Icebound Empire: Industry and Politics on the Last Frontier, 1898–1938* (Anchorage: The Author, 1996), 109–13.
262 'Bonanza Mine, World's Greatest Copper Deposit', *Valdez Prospector: Mining Edition*, 15 January 1909, 3; U.S. Congress, Senate, Committee on Territories, *Government of Alaska: Statements on the Bill S.5436, To Create a Legislative Council in the District of Alaska, to Confer Legislative Powers Theron and for Other Purposes*, 61st Cong., 2nd sess. (Washington, DC: G.P.O, 1910), 142.
263 SU to WGM, 27 June 1915, Box 140, WGMP, LCMD, Washington, DC.
264 'Part of the "Flatiron" Sold', *NYDT*, 5 May 1899, 8; 'Great Wave of Real Estate Investment Sweeps Salt Lake City', *Salt Lake Herald*, 4 December 1906, 1; 'Career Like Epic Recalled by Death', *Washington Sunday Star*, 28 September 1930, A-7.
265 SU to Samuel Newhouse, 11 November 1907; Samuel Newhouse to SU, 13 November 1907; 13 November 1907; 1 April 1908, FUPP, Evanston, IL; Rudd, 'Samuel Newhouse', 297–306.
266 Rudd, 'Samuel Newhouse', 306; 'Untermyers Sued for $825,000 in Utah Case', *NYDT*, 12 January 1918, 11; 'Untermyer Alleges Plot', *NYT*, 4 February 1918, 9.
267 'Sam Newhouse Is a Believer in Nevada', *Goldfield News and Weekly Tribune*, 22 June 1918, 6.
268 'Control Gained of Newhouse Holding', *Salt Lake Telegram*, 10 October 1919, 11; 'J.H. Waters Buys Newhouse Hotel', *Salt Lake Tribune*, 10 October 1919, 24.
269 Hermann Hagedorn, *The Magnate: William Boyce Thompson and His Time, 1869–1930* (New York: Reynal & Hitchcock, 1935), 132, 163.
270 Edwin P. Hoyt, Jr., *The Guggenheims and the American Dream* (New York: Funk & Wagnells, 1967), 153–5; Hagedorn, *The Magnate*, 114–27.
271 O'Connor, *Guggenheims*, 185; 'The Guggenheims Lose $1,700,000 in Nipissing', *NYT*, 2 December 1906, 1; 'Another Curb Panic in Nipissing Stock', *NYT*, 4 December 1906, 4.
272 *Moody's Manual of Railroad and Corporation Securities: Eighth Annual Number* (New York: Moody Publishing Co., 1907), 2461–2.
273 Swaine, *Cravath Firm 1819–1906*, 640; SU to LM, 12 January 1899, Folder 41, Box 8, MS 359, LMC, AJA, Cincinnati, OH.
274 'Samuel Untermyer's Mission', *NYDT*, 20 March 1903, 3; 'S. Untermyer Forms New Company', *NYDT*, 7 April 1903, 3; *Poor's Manual of Industrials: 1st Annual No., 1910* (New York: Poor's Railroad Manual Co., 1910), 1610–11; 'International Steam Pump Co.', *Commercial & Financial Chronicle*, 23 May 1903, 1611.
275 Hebert H. Lehman Oral History Volume 1, 82–3, RBML, CUL, New York, NY.
276 Hoyt, *The Guggenheims*, 217–9, 272–3.
277 'Untermyer Out of International Steam Pump', *NYT*, 6 July 1914, 10.
278 O'Connor, *The Guggenheims*, 352–3.
279 'Merger of Copper Companies Under Way', *NYEP*, 17 November 1915, 13.
   Moody's Analyses of Investments: II: Public Utilities and Industrials: Seventh Year, 1916 (New York: Moody's Investor's Service, 1916), 1292.
280 'Kennecott Copper Holders', *NYEP*, 17 May 1916, 2.
281 'Andrew Freedman Dies of Apoplexy', *NYT*, 5 December 1915, II-19.
282 Jacques Coe, 'Andrew Freedman Capitalist', *Commercial & Financial Chronicle*, 10 May 1973, 10.
283 Freedman left the company in 1903 to form the Casualty Company of America.
   Clarke J. Fitzpatrick and Elliott Buse, *Fifty Years of Suretyship and Insurance: The Story of the United States Fidelity and Guaranty Company* (Baltimore, MD:

The Authors, 1946), 35, 37, 40; 'Obituary', *Electric Railway Journal*, 11 December 1915, 1193.

284 'Croker & Co., Bondsmen', *New York World*, 9 December 1897, 3; 'Croker-Maryland Company', *NYEP*, 8 December 1897, 8.
285 'Pretty Penny for Freedman', *NYS*, 1 March 1907, 12.
286 Andrew Freedman Home, *Celebrating the 50th Anniversary of the Dedication of the Andrew Freedman Home Founders' Day May 16, 1974* (New York: The Home, 1974), 8.
287 'Troubles of Businessmen', *NYT*, 12 February 1884, 8; 'Joseph P. Freedman Dead', *NYH*, 23 June 1903, 6.
288 'In the Hands of a Receiver', *NYS*, 29 January 1893, 8; 'A New Baseball Magnate', *Rome Daily Sentinel*, 1 March 1895.
289 'No Baseball Trust', *NYT*, 26 September 1901, 10; 'Freedman's Record in National Game', *Brooklyn Eagle's Sporting Section*, 5 December 1915, 1; James D. Hardy, Jr., *The New York Giants Baseball Club: The Growth of a Team and a Sport, 1870–1900* (Jefferson, NC: McFarland & Co, 1996), 156–91; Wallace, *Greater Gotham*, 622.
290 Fitzpatrick and Buse, *Fifty Years*, 40–1.
291 Ray Stannard Baker, 'The Subway "Deal": How New York Built Its New Underground Railroad', *McClure's Magazine*, March 1905, 451–62; 'M'Donald Gets the Contract', *NYDT*, 17 January 1900, 1.
292 'August Belmont's Tribute', *NYT*, 5 December 1915, II:19.
293 'Vanderbilt Is Dead At 68', *NYS*, 2 March 1942, 2; 'Gen. C. Vanderbilt Dies on Yacht', *NYT*, 2 March 1942, 21.
294 'Belmont Plan Accepted', *NYS*, 8 February 1900, 1; Interborough Rapid Transit, *The New York Subway: Its Construction and Equipment* (New York: The Company, 1904), 10–11; *Moody's Manual of Corporation Securities: Fifth Annual Number: 1904* (New York: Moody Publishing Co., 1904), 970–1; 'John B. M'Donald Is Dead', *NYS*, 17 March 1911, 2; Fitzpatrick and Buse, *Fifty Years*, 71.
295 State of New York, *Minutes and Testimony of the Joint Legislative Committee Appointed to Investigate the Public Service Commissions: 4* (Albany: State Legislature, 1916), 938.
296 'Untermyer Passes the Lie to Hylan', *NYT*, 2 November 1921, 3.
297 State of New York, *Minutes and Testimony of the Joint Legislative Committee Appointed to Investigate the Public Service Commissions: 3* (Albany: State Legislature, 1916), 134–5, 296–9, 306–20, 373–7; 874–905; State of New York, *Public Service Commissions: 4*, 935–43; 954–61.
298 *Moody's Manual of Railroads and Corporation Securities: Ninth Annual Number: 1908* (New York: Moody Publishing Co., 1908), 1363–86.
299 'Mr. Untermyer Quits', *NYEP*, 4 October 1907, 2; 'Fight to Keep Off A State Receiver', *NYT*, 15 October 1907, 2; 'Seabury Names Receivers', 30 November 1907, 1; Swaine, *Cravath Firm Since 1906*, 45–8.
300 'Receivership Is Upheld', *NYH*, 14 January 1908, 17.
301 In January 1904 Freeedman, Untermyer and Shubert served on a committee who tried to persuade the Democratic National Committee to bring that year's convention to New York City.

   'Committee Ready to Bid for Convention', *New York Evening World*, 5 January 1904, 6.
302 Lee Shubert was apparently a client of the notorious Tammany Hall–protected male brothel, Paresis Hall, according to a later recollection by William Klein of their first

meeting in March 1900. Fortunately for him Untermyer did not care whether his clients were gay and nor presumably did Klein.

Maryann Chach, ed., 'William Klein's Early Years With The Shuberts', *The Passing Show* 13/14, Nos. 2/1 (1991): 3; 'Dive Bosses Pay the Local Tammany Boss's Tax and Cops Leave Them Alone', *NYS*, 27 October 1898, 4.

303 'Two Theatres Change Hands', *NYT*, 28 March 1900, 2; 'Herald Square Management', *NYT*, 29 March 1900, 7.
304 Chach, 'William Klein's Early Years', 5; 'William Klein, 90, Shubert Lawyer', *New York World-Telegram and Sun*, 18 January 1966, 23.
305 Jerry Stagg, *The Brothers Shubert* (New York: Ballantine Books, 1969), 76.
306 'Sires Get Control of Casino Theatre', *New York Evening World*, 21 May 1902, 2; Stagg, *Brothers Shubert*, 37, 44–5; Brooks McNamara, *The Shuberts of Broadway: A History Drawn from the Collections of the Shubert Archive* (New York: Oxford University Press, 1990), 5; Rudolph Aronson, *Theatrical and Musical Memoirs* (New York: McBride, McNast and Company, 1913), 159–60; Chach, 'William Klein's Early Years', 3–4.
307 Stagg, *Brothers Shubert*, 58–9.
308 William Winter, *The Life of David Belasco*, 2 (New York: Moffat, Yard and Company, 1918), 156.
309 Alfred L. Bernheim, *The Business of the Theatre* (New York: Actors' Equity Association, 1932), 31–56.
310 'David Belasco and Mrs. Carter', *New York Sunday Telegraph*, 31 August 1902, 2–5; 'Belasco Drops Agencies', *NYT*, 24 September 1903, 5; 'Belasco Declares War', *NYT*, 28 November 1903, 6; 'David Belasco Tells Theatrical Secrets', *NYT*, 7 April 1905, 9; 'Theatre Trust Action', *NYDT*, 6 July 1905, 2; Winter, *Belasco*, 2, 178–9. 'David Belasco; Dean of Theatre, 76, Had Long Been Ill', *NYT*, 15 May 1931, 1, 16.
311 *NYT*, 7 April 1905, 9.
312 'Erlanger Threatened to Crush Me – Belasco', *NYT*, 8 April 1905, 9.
313 Thomas Powers, 'A Hit! – "Crushed to Earth" Pleases All', *New York Evening World*, 14 April 1905, 3.
314 '$20,000 Is Small Part of Erlanger's Income', *NYT*, 14 April 1905, 5.
315 'Mrs. Carter Describes War Against Belasco', *NYT*, 18 April 1905, 11.
316 '$227,673 One Season's Profits for Syndicate', *NYT*, 27 April 1905, 6.
317 Chach, 'William Klein's Early Years', 5; 'Buy A Washington Theatre', *NYT*, 13 September 1905, 9.
318 'Samuel S. Shubert Is Dead', *New York Morning Telegraph*, 13 May 1905, 1, 10; '"Theatre Trust Foes Unite', *NYT*, 9 July 1905, 12; Shubert Roasts Syndicate', *NYS*, 15 July 1905, 2; 'Anti-Trust Actors In New Combine', *PI*, 15 July 1905, 2; 'A Shubert Corporation', *NYDT*, 2 September 1905, 7; Wallace, *Greater Gotham*, 397–403; Bernheim, *Business of the Theatre*, 64–5.
319 'To Free the Theatre', *New York Dramatic Mirror*, 21 October 1905, 15; 'Shuberts Surely Coming Here', *Minneapolis Journal*, 15 October 1905, 1; 'Theatre Deal Against Trust', *Buffalo Courier*, 16 October 1905, 1; 'Cox Becomes Good Angel', *Syracuse Journal*, 21 December 1905, 2.
320 Jerome had been elected in 1901 on the Fusion ticket headed by Seth Low.
'Mr. Belasco Loses Suit', *NYDT*, 20 December 1905, 12; 'Klaw Defies Jerome In Theatre Syndicate Row', *New York Press*, 20 December 1905, 5.
321 'Theatre Quiz Stopped by Writ of Injunction', *NYT*, 22 December 1905, 9.
322 Chach, 'William Klein's Early Years', 7; 'The Trust Inquiry', *New York Dramatic Mirror*, 2 February 1907, 13; 'Klaw & Erlanger Win: Jerome Is Badly Beaten', *New*

York Press, 20 June 1907, 10; Ivan Joe Fillipo, 'Landmark Litigation in the American Theatre' (PhD diss., University of Florida, Gainesville, FL, 1972), 301–4; Court of General Sessions, New York Co., June 1907, The People v. Marc Klaw and Erlanger (55 Misc. 72), in *New York Criminal Reports* 21 (1908), 353–75.
323 Hirsch, *Boys from Syracuse*, 65.
324 John Tenney, 'In the Trenches: The Syndicate-Shubert Theatrical War', *The Passing Show* 21, No. 2 (1998): 8.
325 'New Shubert Investors Hand the Boys $300,000', *Variety*, 2 December 1911, 1.
326 'Buying Out Klaw And Erlanger Hope of Shubert Backers', *Variety*, 6 September 1912, 1; 'Will They Make Up', *New York Dramatic Mirror*, 15 January 1913, 26; 'K & E And Shubert "Talk" Running Rampant Once More', *Variety*, 7 February 1913, 1; 'Cox Buys For $600,000', *Variety*, 5 December 1913, 11; 'Buys More Shubert Stock', *NYT*, 6 December 1913, 22.
327 '"Military Girl" in New York?', *Variety*, 11 October 1912, 12; 'Erect Theatre in Memory of Brother', *NYS*, 28 September 1913, 7–11; 'New Theatre To Open In New York', *Brooklyn Daily Star*, 9 October 1913, 7; 'Name Of Theatre Changed', *NYS*, 17 December 1913, 7; 'Andrew Freedman Dies', *Variety*, 10 December 1915, 11.
328 Maryann Chach, 'The Heart of Broadway Still Beats Strong at 100', *The Passing Show* 30 (2013–2014): 47–8.
329 Hirsch, *Shuberts*, 73.
330 'Untermeyer for A.E.A.', *Variety*, 16 August 1919, 4.
331 'Andrew Freedman Buried', *NYT*, 8 December 1915, 15.
332 'Freedman Gifts May Be Changed by Another Will', *New York Evening World*, 8 December 1915, 12; 'Freedman Millions to Found a Charity', *NYT*, 9 December 1915, 8.
333 *NYT*, 9 December 1915, 8.
334 *NYT*, 9 December 1915, 8.
335 JHS to SU, 19 January 1916; 22 May 1916; 11 July 1916; 24 July 1916; 11 December 1916; 15 May 1917; 18 May 1917; 18 July 1917; 23 October 1917, Minutes of the Finance Committee of the Andrew Freedman Home, 20 December 1916; 18 May 1917; SU to JHS, 18 January 1916; 20 January 1916; 10 July 1916; 11 July 1916; 21 July 1916; 8 December 1916; 17 May 1917; 17 July 1917; 24 October 1917, Folder 15, Box 452, MS 456, JHSC, AJA, Cincinnati, OH.
336 Pat Edith Ayres, *The Andrew Freedman Story* (New York: The Home, 1976), 15.
337 Andrew Freedman Home, *50th Anniversary*, 6.
338 'Dedicate a Refuge for Cultured Poor', *NYT*, 26 May 1924, 17.
339 In 1897 Untermyer's brother Isaac successfully bid at an auction on behalf of two New York clients for three bankrupt railroads in Utah.
   'The Utah Central Sale', *Salt Lake Herald*, 9 May 1897, 2.
340 Henry H. Swain, 'Economic Aspects of Railroad Receiverships', *Economic Studies* 3, no. 2 (1898): 66–7.
341 Peter Tufano, 'Business Failure, Judicial Intervention, and Financial Innovation: Restructuring U.S. Railroads in the Nineteenth Century', *Business History Review* 71, no. 1 (1997): 11, 24.
342 Leslie Hannah, 'J.P. Morgan in London and New York before 1914', *Business History Review* 85, no. 1 (2011): 121–2.
343 Johnston, 'Little Giant – I', 30.
344 'Coates Ask a Chance to Bid', *NYH*, 29 October 1897, 11.
345 'English Offer for the Roads was Declined', *San Francisco Call*, 30 October 1897, 1.

346 'Asked for More Money', *NYH*, 1 November 1897, 9; Naomi W. Cohen, *Jacob H. Schiff: A Study in American Jewish Leadership* (Hanover: University of New England Press, 1999), 12–15.
347 'Field of Politics One Vast Bedlam', *NYH*, 10 October 1897, 1:5.
348 'The Union Pacific Deal Smashed by the World', *New York World*, 26 October 1897, 1; 'The Ohio Election', *Richmond Dispatch*, 27 October 1897, 6.
349 'Suit to Recover $700,000', *NYT*, 11 July 1899, 2.
350 'Receiver Appointed', *Richmond Daily Palladium*, 6 July 1904, 5.
351 'Advertisement', *NYT*, 27 July 1904, 8; 'Advertisement', *NYS*, 15 February 1905, 11.
352 'Thomas F. Ryan Dies as One of World's Richest Men', *NYEP*, 23 November 1928, 1, 8.
353 'Old Rail Fight Takes New Turn', *Chicago Daily Tribune*, 2 January 1908, 1, 3.
354 Advertisement, *Richmond Times-Dispatch*, 14 January 1905, 7; Advertisement, *NYDT*, 28 June 1905, 15.
355 'James A. Blair, Retired Banker', *BDE*, 28 November 1939, 9.
356 'Davies Warfield Dies in Baltimore', *WES*, 25 October 1927, 3.
357 'Seek Receiver for Seaboard', *NYS*, 2 January 1908, 1; 'Sharp Criticism of Mr. Williams', *Richmond-Times Dispatch*, 4 January 1908, 1, 5; 'Plea for Seaboard', *Richmond Times-Dispatch*, 22 January 1908, 7; 'Dissolve Voting Trust', *Richmond Times-Dispatch*, 12 March 1908, 10; U.S. Congress, Senate, Committee on Banking and Currency, *Nomination of John Skelton Williams: Hearings on the Nomination of John Skelton Williams to be Comptroller of the Currency*, 66th Cong., 1st sess. (Washington, DC: G.P.O., 1919), 641.
358 Edwina H. Wilson, *Her Name Was Wallis Warfield: The Life Story of Mrs. Ernest Simpson* (New York: E.P. Dutton, 1936), 28–31, 77.
359 Kansas City Southern Railway Legal Correspondence, 1905–6, Folder 11, Box 10, MS 251, SUC, AJA, Cincinnati, OH; 'After Another Voting Trust', *NYS*, 11 February 1905, 10.
360 'New Harriman Syndicate', *NYDT*, 28 October 1899, 1.
361 'Sielcken Proxies on Kansas City', *NYDT*, 16 May 1905, 12; 'Harriman Out of K.C.S.', *NYDT*, 18 May 1905, 8.
362 Kansas City Southern Railway Legal Correspondence, 1910, Folder 10, Box 10, MS 251, SUC, AJA, Cincinnati, OH; The Wheeling and Lake Erie Railway Company to SU, 19 November 1920, Folder 21, Box 58, MS 359, LMC, AJA, Cincinnati, OH.
363 'Kansas City Southern Railway Company, Appt. v. United States of America and Interstate Commerce Commission (231 U.S. 423) [Argued 29 and 30 October 1913, Decided 1 December 1913]', in *The Supreme Court Reporter* 34 (1913): 125–36.
364 U.S. Congress, House, Committee on the Judiciary: Subcommittee III, *Appeals from Circuit Court of Appeals: Hearings on H.R. 10736: January 23, 1914*, 63rd Cong., 2nd sess. (Washington, DC: G.P.O., 1914), 1–16; *The Statutes At Large of the United States of America from March, 1913, to March, 1915*, Vol. XXXVIII, Part I (Washington, DC: G.P.O., 1915), 803–5.
365 'Kansas City Southern Railway Company, Appt. v. Guardian Trust Company, Central Improvement Company, Cambria Steel Company, and Kansas City Suburban Belt Railroad Company (240 U.S. 166) [Argued 13, 14 and 15 December 1915, Decided 21 February 1916]', in *The Supreme Court Reporter* 36 (1915), 334–7.
366 'John D. to Boss Wabash Terminal', *New York Press*, 2 June 1908, 8; 'Bondholders Dissatisfied', *NYDT*, 23 June 1910, 13; 'Gould Shuts Out Public and Testifies in Secret', *New York Evening World*, 31 March 1911, 12; 'Sue Gould and Others for $90,000 in

R.R. Deal', *Thrice A Week New York World*, 30 April 1913, 2; '$1,000,000 is Needed for Wabash-Pittsburg', *NYS*, 19 December 1913, 19; 'George Jay Gould', *WES*, 16 May 1923, 1, 2.

367 U.S. Congress, Senate, Committee on Interstate Commerce, *Hearing Pursuant to S.R. 98, A Resolution Directing the Committee to Investigate and Report Desirable Changes in the Laws Regulating and Controlling Corporations, Persons, and Firms Engaged in Interstate Commerce: 3*, 62nd Cong., 2nd sess. (Washington, DC: G.P.O, 1912), 2567-8, 2574-5.

368 'Delavan to Lead Fight', *NYDT*, 4 November 1910, 13; 'Calls it Mellen Trick', *NYDT*, 23 May 1912, 13.

369 'C.S. Mellen Dies Suddenly at Concord Home', *NYS*, 17 November 1927, 1-2.

370 David W. Sargent, Jr., 'The Rutland Railroad', *The Railway and Locomotive Historical Society Bulletin* 58a (1942): 81.

371 'St. Jo and Grand Island', *NYS*, 7 November 1911, 15; 'Minority Holders of St. J. & G.I. Must Be Given the Control', *Omaha Bee*, 28 May 1914, 1.

372 'Rites for N.L. Amster Tomorrow', *BDE*, 23 September 1939, 9.

373 Barnard Powers, 'That Rock Island Fiasco: 1: The Fall of Rock Island', *The Magazine of Wall Street*, 31 March 1917, 873-6; Advertisement, *NYEP*, 31 July 1914, 9; Advertisement, *NYT*, 26 September 1914, 12.

374 Barnard Powers, 'That Rock Island Fiasco: 2: The New Rock Island', *The Magazine of Wall Street*, 14 April 1917, 10.

375 'To Sift Road Sale Plan', *NYDT*, 28 September 1914, 10; 'Fight Rock Island Foreclosure Suit', *NYT*, 3 October 1914, 14.

376 Swaine, *Cravath Firm Since 1906*, 177; 'Sol M. Stroock, 67, Noted Lawyer, Dies', *NYT*, 12 September 1941, 21; Interview with Frank Untermyer, 25-28 April 2000.

377 Swaine, *Cravath Firm Since 1906*, 175; Powers, 'Rock Island Fiasco: 2', 10.

378 Swaine, *Cravath Firm Since 1906*, 176-7; 'Stops Rock Island Sale', *NYT*, 20 November 1914, 12.

379 'The Folklore of Rock Island', *Railway Age Gazette*, 23 October 1914, 727.

380 'Attorney is Quizzed on Rock Island Deal', *WES*, 4 June 1915, 21; 'Defends His Course in Rock Island Case', *WES*, 5 June 1915, 2.

381 'No.6834: In Re Financial Transactions, History, and Operation of the Chicago, Rock Island & Pacific Railway Company', in *Interstate Commerce Commission Reports, 34, Decisions July 1915 to December 1915* (Washington, DC: G.P.O, 1916), 43-61.

382 'Rock Island Receivership Stirs Protest', *NYS*, 21 April 1915, 14.

383 Swaine, *Cravath Firm Since 1906*, 178-80.

384 'New Rock Island Plan', *NYT*, 23 June 1916, 17.

385 Swaine, *Cravath Firm Since 1906*, 177-8; 'Offer of Settlement in Amster Suit', *NYDT*, 10 January 1917, 16.

386 'Court Approves Settlement of Rock Island Refund Suit', *Omaha Bee*, 30 January 1917, 9.

387 Samuel Untermyer, *Hobson's Choice Between Government Ownership and Bankruptcy of the Railroads: Address of Samuel Untermyer of New York Before the University Club of Los Angeles, Monday, February 27, 1933* (New York: The Author, 1933), 39-45.

388 'Answer to Standard Oil', *NYT*, 9 April 1912, 14.

389 'Seek to Reopen Oil Dissolution', *NYT*, 29 September 1912, 2-4.

390 'May Examine Oil Men Here', *NYT*, 15 September 1912, 2-7.

391 Wellman included Untermyer's cross-examination of Henry L. Doherty in *Boran v. Pierce Oil Corporation* in the revised edition of his textbook as a classic case study of the art.
   Francis L. Wellman, *The Art of Cross-Examination* (New York: Macmillan, 1923), 347–63.
392 'J.D. Rockefeller A Wary Witness', *NYT*, 29 May 1912, 1, 14.
393 'Stanadard Oil Sells Waters-Pierce Holdings to Henry Clay Pierce', *Washington Herald*, 3 November 1912, 8.
394 'City of New York v. Hearst', in *New York Supplement* 126 (1911), 917–23.
395 Advertisement, *Motor Boating*, November 1912, 105; 'Statement of the Ownership', *Motor Boating*, May 1914, 68; 'Statement of the Ownership', *Cosmopolitan*, June 1922, 110.
396 SU to WRH, 5 July 1918, Folder 6, Box 1, MS 251, SUC, AJA, Cincinnati, OH; Palm Beach Benefit for Tobacco Fund the Climax of a Season of Unusual Activity', *NYS*, 3 March 1918, 9.
397 SU to Upton Sinclair, 27 October 1919, Upton Sinclair Papers, Lilly Library, Indiana University, Bloomington, IN.
398 'Testifies on Value of A.P. Membership', *NYT*, 26 March 1915, 14.
399 'Decision Reserved in A.P.-Hearst Suit', *NYT*, 28 March 1915, E4; 'Hearst Wins Against Associated Press', *NYS*, 14 October 1915, 5.
400 Neil MacNeil, *Without Fear or Favor* (New York: Harcourt, Brace and Company, 1940), 242.
401 'Defer News Service Case', *NYT*, 11 January 1917, 11; 'Judge Hand Hears News Service Case', *NYT*, 18 January 1917, 10.
402 'Court Bars News Piracy', *NYS*, 17 July 1917, 2.
403 'International News Service v. Associated Press (248 U.S. 215) [Argued 2 and 3 May 1918, Decided 23 December 1918]', in *The Supreme Court Reporter* 39 (1918), 68–82.
404 'News Pirating Case in Supreme Court', *NYT*, 3 May 1918, 14.
405 *The Supreme Court Reporter* 39 (1918), 68–82.
406 SU to Upton Sinclair, 27 October 1919, Upton Sinclair Papers, Lilly Library, Indiana University, Bloomington, IN.
407 Untermyer, *Hobson's Choice*, 44; SU to WRH, 4 January 1933; WRH to SU, 5 January 1933, Folder 17, Box 10, Subseries 1.2, BANC MSS 71/121c, WRHP, Bancroft Library, University of California, Berkeley, CA.
408 'Untermyer To Washington', *NYT*, 13 January 1912, 14.
409 Victor Rosewater to President Taft, 24 November 1909, Folder 6, Box 6 of 21, MS 359, LMC, AJA, Cincinnati, OH.
410 Isador Sobel to LM, 14 December 1909, Folder 7, Box 6 of 21, MS 359, LMC, AJA, Cincinnati, OH.
411 Lloyd P. Gartner, 'The Correspondence of Mayer Sulzberger and William Howard Taft', *Proceedings of the American Academy for Jewish Research* 46–47, no. 1 (1979–1980): 130–2.
412 Mayer Sulzberger to LM, 10 April 1910, Folder 7, Box 6 of 21, MS 359, LMC, AJA, Cincinnati, OH.
413 Stephen Wise, *Challenging Years: The Autobiography of Stephen Wise* (New York: Putnam's Sons, 1949), 144–5.
414 Charles Reznikoff, ed., *Louis Marshall, Champion of Liberty: Selected Papers and Addresses: 2* (Philadelphia: Jewish Publication Society of America, 1957), 1160;

M.M. Silver, *Louis Marshall and the Rise of Jewish Ethnicity in America: A Biography* (Syracuse: Syracuse University Press, 2013), 161–4.
415 Silver, *Louis Marshall*, 164–70.
416 Silver, *Louis Marshall*, 169.
417 Silver, *Louis Marshall*, 170.
418 'Samuel Untermyer "Retires" to Increased Activity', *Bench and Bar*, January 1912, 37.
419 Nanette Dembitz, *The Trials of Mr. and Mrs. Stokes*, unpublished manuscript, c.1964, FUPP, Evanston, IL
420 Nanette Dembitz, *The Battle for Mrs. Stokes' Dower Rights*, unpublished manuscript, c.1964, FUPP, Evanston, IL.
421 'Untermyer Wants Perjury Punished', *NYT*, 12 November 1923, 19.
422 SU to ASO, 10 January 1925, b42, f.13-15, NYTCR: ASOP, NYPL, New York, NY; 'S.D. Warfield Dies', *NYT*, 25 October 1927, 31; U.S. Congress, Senate, Subcommittee of the Committee on Interstate Commerce, *Hearings Pursuant to S. Res. 71 Authorizing an Investigation of Interstate Railroads: Part 26: Sea Board Air Line Railway*, 75th Cong., 2nd sess. (Washington, DC: G.P.O, 1942), 11720–1; 11544; 11572–3; 11576–9; 11583, 11727–8; 11731–5; 11756–9; 11876–7; 11881–3.
423 U.S. Congress, Senate, Subcommittee on Monopoly of the Select Committee on Small Business, *The International Petroleum Cartel (Reprint)*, 94th Cong., 1st sess. (Washington, DC: GPO, 1975), 47.
424 Hagedorn, *The Magnate*, 299.
425 'To Fight for Billion and Rich Oil Lands for Sultan's Heirs', *NYT*, 2 December 1922, 1, 6.
426 SU to Charles Evans Hughes, 14 December 1922, File 867.602 at 8/12, RG59, Records of the Department of State, NA, College Park, MD.
427 Allen W. Dulles to SU, 20 December 1922, File 867.602 at 8/12; SU to Allen W. Dulles, 26 December 1922; SU to Charles Evans Hughes, 26 December 1922, File 867.602 at 8/13; Charles Evans Hughes to SU, 2 January 1923, File 867.602 at 8/14, RG59, Records of the Department of State, NA, College Park, MD; U.S. Department of State, *Papers Relating to the Foreign Relations of the United States: 1923: 2* (Washington, DC: G.P.O., 1938), 1198–9.
428 'Outcome at Lausanne Satisfies Washington', *NYT*, 19 July 1923, 3.
429 'Abdul Hamid's Heirs: Two Adverse Decisions', *The Times* [London], 17 December 1930, 11.
430 Glyn Roberts, *The Most Powerful Man in the World: The Life of Sir Henri Deterding* (New York: Covici Friede, 1938), 343; U.S. Congress, *International Petroleum Cartel*, 54, 64–5.
431 Interview with Frank Untermyer, 25–8 April 2000; 'Untermyer's Home for "Zaza"', *New York Morning Telegraph*, 29 July 1923, 15; 'Zaza', *Pictures*, 20 September 1923, 23; 'Getting Atmosphere No Easy Thing', *PI*, 14 October 1923, 34; 'Famous Estate Used in Pictures', *PI*, 3 February 1924, 35.
432 'Sue Electric Firms over Sound Films', *NYT*, 10 September 1929, 48; Edward W. Russell to C.E. Lovejoy, 1 February 1938, Untermyer File, RBML, CUL, New York, NY.
433 'Film War May Go On', *NYT*, 4 May 1912, 15; 'Says There's A Film Trust', *NYT*, 16 July 1912, 2; Dembitz, *The Fox and 'The Reptile'*, unpublished manuscript, c.1964, 18–19, FUPP, Evanston, IL; U.S. Congress, Senate, Committee on Interstate Commerce, *Hearing Pursuant to S.R. 98, A Resolution Directing the Committee to*

Investigate and Report Desirable Changes in the Laws Regulating and Controlling Corporations, Persons, and Firms Engaged in Interstate Commerce: 1, 62nd Cong., 2nd sess. (Washington, DC: G.P.O, 1912), 1338–41.
434 Swaine, *Cravath Firm Since 1906*, 534–6; Sinclair, *William Fox*, 75–183.
435 'Fox Relates His Version of Film Control Battle', *Chicago Tribune*, 13 April 1933, I:16.
436 Dembitz, *The Fox And 'The Reptile'*, 18–19; Upton Sinclair, *Upton Sinclair Presents William Fox* (Los Angeles: (West Branch): The Author, 1933), 221–2.
437 Sinclair, *William Fox*, 222; Alva Johnston, 'Profiles: Little Giant II', *New Yorker*, 24 May 1930, 27.
438 Dembitz, *The Fox And 'The Reptile'*, 20–4.
439 Dembitz, *The Fox And 'The Reptile'*, 26; Sinclair, *William Fox*, 222–31; '$45,000,000 Funding Halts Fox Receiver', *NYT*, 29 January 1930, 25.
440 Swaine, *Cravath Firm Since 1906*, 535–6.
441 Sinclair, *William Fox*, 294–6.
442 Sinclair, *William Fox*, 296–302; Dembitz, *The Fox And 'The Reptile'*, 55–61.
443 Dembitz, *The Fox And 'The Reptile'*, 61–3; 'Praises Fox Financing', *NYT*, 19 April 1930, 14; 'Gets Million Fee', *Chicago Tribune*, 13 April 1930, I:21.
444 'Untermyer Retained By Kreuger Shareholders', *WES*, 15 April 1932, B14; 'Untermyer Scores Rules of Brokers', *NYT*, 16 May 1932, 28; 'Kreuger and Toll', *Financial Times* [London], 24 May 1932, 5; 'Untermyer Hits Kreuger Plans', *Yonkers Herald Statesman*, 8 August 1932, 4; '"Preference" Hit in Kreuger Deal', *WES*, 21 December 1932, B7.
445 SU to ASO, 3 July 1933, b42, f.13-15, NYTCR: ASOP, NYPL, New York, NY.
446 'Untermyer Hails Roosevelt's Plan', *NYT*, 6 July 1933, 11.
447 Norman H. Davies to LAS, 24 May 1934, Box 68, LASP, LCMD, Washington, DC.
448 Wallenberg's cousin Raoul later saved hundreds of Hungarian Jews in German-occupied Budapest from deportation to Auschwitz.
    Gert Nylander and Anders Perlinge, 'Raoul Wallenberg in Documents, 1927–1947', *Banking & Enterprise* 3 (2000): 11.
449 'Kreuger Reorganizers Here from Abroad', *NYT*, 11 November 1934, N11; Ernst Söderlund, *Skandinaviska Banken I Det Svenska Bankväsendets Historia, 1914–1939* (Uppsala: Almqvist & Wiksell, 1978), 527.
450 Söderlund, *Skandinaviska Banken*, 522–30; Hans Sjögren, 'The Financial Contracts of Large Firms: A Longitudinal Study of Swedish Firms and Commercial Banks, 1919–1947', *Scandinavian Economic History Review* 39, no. 3 (1991): 78.
451 'God start på Kreuger-förhandlingar', *Svenska Dagbladet*, 28 November 1934, 4.
452 'Kreuger and Toll Talks', *Financial Times* [London], 23 February 1935, 7; 'Kreuger and Toll Talks', 28 March 1935, *Financial Times* [London], 9; 'Kreuger and Toll Debentures', *Financial Times* [London], 13 June 1935, 9.
453 'Kreuger and Toll 5% Debentures', *Financial Times* [London], 22 February 1936, 5; 'Kreuger & Toll Secured Dollar Debentures, *Financial Times* [London], 6 May 1936, 5; 'Kreuger and Toll Assets Sale', *Financial Times* [London], 8 June 1936, 1.
454 Correspondence with G&U, 1936-8, Kreuger & Toll File, Box 38, BCP, LCMD, Washington, DC; 'Kreuger & Toll Payments Bared', *Washington Sunday Star*, 28 February 1937, A13.
455 'Une réunion des commerçants juifs parisiens', *Le Matin*, 26 April 1933, 3; 'La conférence juive mondiale', *Le Temps*, 23 July 1933, 2; 'Le comité de défense des juifs persécutes', *Le Temps*, 21 April 1934, 2.
456 Rudy Behlmer, *Inside Warner Bros. (1935–1951)* (New York: Viking, 1985), 35–6.

Chapter 2

1 'Randolph Guggenheimer', *NYDT*, 10 October 1897, 7.
2 Louis Marshall had married Untermyer's second cousin Florence Lowenstein in 1895. FMD, 1895, 6 May; 1897, 2 November, RPHSFA, New York, NY.
3 *Richmond Times-Dispatch*, 13 September 1907, 1.
4 'Here's Col. Ruppert', *New York World*, 5 October 1897, 2; 'Ruppert Kicked Off by Croker', *New York Press*, 8 October 1897, 1; 'Col. Ruppert, 71, Dies of Lingering Malady', *BDE*, 13 January 1939, 1, 18.
5 'Tammany Names a M'Kinley Man', *NYH*, 10 October 1897, 1–6.
6 'Brewers for Van Wyck', *BDE*, 22 October 1897, 2.
7 Lauren Beth Aker, 'Savannah's New South: The Politics of Reform, 1885–1910' (PhD diss., University of California, Los Angeles, CA, 2012), 2.
8 Aker, 'Savannah's New South', 9, 76–118, 160–252.
9 'Cleveland For President', *NYT*, 29 May 1892, 9; 'At The New York Hotels', *NYT*, 10 January 1896, 4; 'Two Mayors in the City Hall', *New York Press*, 3 March 1899, 5; 'Savannah's Mayor Here', *NYDT*, 17 August 1900, 8.
10 *Memoirs of Georgia: 2* (Atlanta, GA: Southern Historical Association, 1895), 403–4.
11 'Backer in A New Light', *NYT*, 8 August 1891, 8; 'Abram Backer's Affairs', *NYT*, 11 August 1891, 8; 'The Affairs of H. Myers & Brothers', *NYT*, 27 August 1891, 2.
12 'To Feed the Poor', *NYH*, 13 October 1898, 4:3; Randolph Guggenheimer, 'Guggenheimer's Charity Plan', *NYH*, 11 December 1898, 4:11.
13 'While Van Wyck Is Away the Public Library Has the Support of The Mayor', *New York World*, 2 August 1898, 6.
14 'A Municipal Problem', *NYDT*, 16 December 1900, II-6.
15 'Homeless City Boys and Girls', *BDE*, 17 December 1900, 4.
16 *Brooklyn Daily Standard Union*, 11 August 1900, 6.
17 'Enough of Mayor's Cares', *NYDT*, 1 September 1900, 1.
18 'Bryan To Be Here To-Day', *NYDT*, 22 January 1900, 1; 'Guggenheimer Goes West', *NYDT*, 23 January 1900, 2.
19 'Mr. Untermyer For Bryan', *NYT*, 12 September 1900, 3.
20 'Glorious Larceny New Bryan Term', *NYT*, 5 February 1908, 3; 'Democratic Dinners Feel Bryan's Spell', *NYT*, 14 April 1912, 1, 4; WJB to Sue Kerr Hicks, 10 June 1925, Box 57, WJBP, LCMD, Washington, DC.
21 *NYT*, 12 September 1900, 3.
22 'Well Known Corporation Lawyer, Interviewed in London, Praises Nebraskan', *NYH*, 6 September 1908, 2:5.
23 'Bryan Campaign Fund $261,123; Only $22,604 Left', *Thrice-A-Week World*, 16 October 1908, 2; 'Untermyer Gives Bryan $1,500', *New York Press*, 28 October 1908, 2.
24 Gregory Weinstein, *Reminiscences of an Interesting Decade: The Ardent Eighties* (New York: The International Press, 1928), 101; 'SU to Gregory Weinstein, 5 December 1929, Folder 2, Box 4, MS 251, SUC, AJA, Cincinnati, OH; 'Tenement-House Cigar Factories', *NYT*, 27 March 1888, 2.
25 State of New York, Board of Mediation and Arbitration, *Second Annual Report* (Albany: Troy Press Company, 1889), 14–309; 'Boycotters Hard At It', *NYS*, 4 June 1888, 1; Hermann Schlüter, *The Brewing Industry and the Brewery Workers' Movement in America* (New York: Burt Franklin, 1970), 148–66.

26 Gompers, *Seventy Years: 1*, 346.
27 Keller, *In Defense of Yesterday*, 70, 73.
28 'Samuel Untermyer', in *Who Was Who in America: 1: 1897–1942* (Chicago: Marquis – Who's Who Incorporated, 1968), 1264.
29 SU to ASO, 17 August 1902, b42, f.13-15, NYTCR: ASOP, NYPL, New York, NY.
30 W. J. Lampton, 'Coincidental Coincidences', *Collier's*, 24 October 1908, 21.
31 'Works to be Included', *NYDT*, 11 June 1902, 6; 'Buys Bethlehem Steel Co', *NYDT*, 15 June 1902, 1:1; 'To be Reorganized', *NYDT*, 9 May 1903, 9; 'Must Defend Shipyard Trust', *New York Evening World*, 12 June 1903, 9.
32 'Intended No Attack on J.P. Morgan & Co', *NYT*, 11 October 1903, 12; 'Doesn't Blame Morgan', *Baltimore Sun*, 14 October 1903, 10.
33 '"It's Survival of the Fittest Now" Says Morgan', *St. Louis Post-Dispatch*, 7 November 1903, 7.
34 'Schwab Yields All in Shipyard Fight', *NYT*, 5 February 1904, 1–2.
35 Swaine, *Cravath Firm Since 1906*, 72–3; SU to His Children, 7 June 1926, FUPP, Evanston, IL.
36 '$4,500,000 for One Case', *Toronto Star*, 6 August 1915, 3.
37 Susie J. Pak, *Gentlemen Bankers: The World J.P. Morgan* (Cambridge, MA and London: Harvard University Press, 2013), 28.
38 'Trusts the Real Issue, Samuel Untermyer Says', *NYT*, 4 November 1904, 7.
39 '"Good" and "Bad" Trusts', *NYT*, 4 November 1904, 8.
40 Cyrus Adler, 'Louis Marshall: A Biographical Sketch', *American Jewish Yearbook* 32 (1930): 22.
41 Untermyer as a member of the Democratic National Committee had been on the platform at Madison Square Garden when Parker had addressed thousands of New Yorkers at a campaign rally on 31 October. He had also been a delegate at the Democratic Party's National Convention in St. Louis which had nominated Parker earlier in the year.
    'What They Think of Parker', *NYT*, 11 July 1904, 7; 'Parker, Wildly Cheered by Thousands, Accuses Roosevelt of Duplicity', *New York Press*, 1 November 1904, 1, 3.
42 'How They Fear the Trusts! Why Many Big Corporation Lawyers Work for Parker', *NYDT*, 6 November 1904, 7.
43 'Favors Federal Control of the Trusts', *NYH*, 22 December 1904, 5.
44 'Federal Licence not the Remedy in Samuel Untermyer's Opinion', *NYH*, 22 December 1904, 5.
45 'Untermyers' and Morgan's Rivalry', *WSJ*, 10 September 1906, 3.
46 *American Kennel Club Stud Book* 21 (1904): 457, 621–2.
47 Milo G. Denlinger, *The Complete Collie*, 2nd edn (Washington, DC: Denlinger's, 1947), 58–61.
48 'Photo of Untermyer', *NYT*, 24 June 1906, I:7; '$3,000 For Collie Puppy', *NYT*, 23 March 1905, 7; 'Mr. Samuel Untermyer's Record Collie Purchase', *Field and Fancy*, 25 March 1905, 12.
49 'Pure Blood Collies', *NYDT*, 2 April 1905, II:3.
50 After the death of Morgan at the end of March 1913 Untermyer lost interest in competing at dog shows. In November 1913 he disposed of his kennels, scattered his fine and costly collection of dogs to different buyers, dismissed his kennel master and kept for himself only six collies of no great prize-winning history to serve as sentinels at Greystone.

'Untermyer and Morgan in Show Ring', *NYT*, 14 January 1907, 9; Henry F. Pringle, 'Front Page Stuff', *American Mercury*, January 1927, 160–1; 'Untermyer Sells His Dogs', *NYT*, 23 November 1913, II:1; Interview with Samuel Untermyer II, 12 March 2000.

51 William Griffith, 'Samuel Untermyer Sounds a Warning', *NYT*, 11 June 1905, 3:1.
52 Swaine, *Cravath Firm 1819–1906*, 750–5; R. Carlyne Buley, *The Equitable Life Assurance Society of the United States, 1859–1964: 1* (New York: Appleton-Century-Crofts, 1967), 539–699; 'Surplus is Policyholders'', *NYS*, 8 May 1905, 3.
53 When Hughes was later appointed chief justice of the US Supreme Court in 1930 Untermyer observed, 'Not since Chief Justice Marshall has a man of such outstanding ability, experience and judicial temperament been called to that exalted office.' However, according to Upton Sinclair, Hughes told his client, William Fox, just before his appointment that Untermyer 'was the lowest type of human that ever lived' and called him a 'reptile'. Untermyer was not happy about 'the scandalous, insulting and lying observation'.

'Untermyer Backs Hughes', *NYEP*, 13 February 1930, 2; Sinclair, *William Fox*, 222; SU to Upton Sinclair, 30 March 1933, Sinclair mss., Lilly Library, Indiana University, Bloomington, IN.
54 'Warns New York Life Not to Seek Proxies', *NYT*, 19 March 1906, 1–2; 'Untermyer on Trustees', *NYT*, 22 March 1906, 2.
55 'Choate Accepts', *Topeka State Journal*, 8 March 1906, 10; Lawrence F. Abbott, *The Story of NYLIC: A History of the Origin and Development of the New York Life Insurance Company from 1845 to 1929* (New York: The Company, 1930), 180–1.

An earlier committee had been formed by Thomas W. Lawson but in February 1906 Untermyer persuaded him to sever himself entirely from the movement.

'T.W. Lawson is Busy', *WES*, 8 October 1905, 2; 'Lawson Quits Committee', *Los Angeles Herald*, 15 February 1906, 1.
56 Creelman, 'Billionaire', 375.
57 'Untermyer to Lawmakers', *NYS*, 22 March 1906, 3.
58 'Discussed by Untermyer', *NYT*, 2 June 1906, 4.
59 'Untermyer Declines Any Insurance Office', *NYT*, 7 August 1906, 6.
60 'Untermyer Wants Kelsey Disciplined', *NYT*, 23 October 1906, 5; 'Untermyer Protests Against Pony Ballots', *NYT*, 16 November 1906, 18; 'Forgery Charged in Insurance Campaign', *NYT*, 11 December 1906, 16.
61 'New York Life's Case in the Supreme Court', *NYT*, 9 November 1906, 7; 'A Lively Court Day in the Insurance Fight', *NYT*, 10 November 1906, 7; Abbott, *NYLIC*, 184–7.
62 Udo J. Keppler, 'Watcher Got?', *Puck*, 3 October 1906, 1.
63 'Both Sides Claim Insurance Victory', *NYT*, 19 December 1906, 1–2.
64 Abbott, *NYLIC*, 183.
65 Roscoe Carlyle Buley, *The American Life Convention, 1906–1952: A Study in the History of Life Insurance: 1* (New York: Appleton-Century-Crofts, Inc., 1953), 298.
66 'Untermyer Sees Hughes', *NYT*, 25 January 1907, 12.
67 'Policy Holders Quit Insurance Fight', *NYT*, 1 October 1907, 5.
68 'Untermyer Attacks Life Insurance Men', *NYT*, 19 April 1910, 2; 'Report of the New York Insurance Department on an Examination of the Mutual Life Insurance Company', *The Weekly Underwriter*, 23 April 1910, 331–2.
69 'Untermyer Sues Peabody For Libel', *NYT*, 22 April 1910, 1.
70 'Untermyer Sues Peabody For Libel', *NYT*, 22 April 1910, 1.

71 SU to ASO, 27 June 1910, b42, f.13-15, NYTCR: ASOP, NYPL, New York, NY.
72 SU to Harry Hoffman, 17 July 1919, Folder 6, Box 1, MS 251, SUC, AJA, Cincinnati, OH.
73 'Monroe Affairs in Court's Hands', *NYH*, 13 December 1904, 16.
74 'Drag City Bank in Monroe Deals', *NYH*, 5 January 1905, 7; '"All Right," Said Loomis', *NYDT*, 13 January 1905, 14.
75 'Loomis Gets Out', *NYS*, 14 January 1905, 1.
76 'Montreal and Boston Sold', *NYS*, 20 June 1905, 11.
77 'Disclosures Promised', *Rochester Democrat and Chronicle*, 24 March 1904, 2; Advertisement, *NYDT*, 18 June 1910, 14; Advertisement, *NYDT*, 13 June 1912, 12; Anthony Lehman to SU, 6 May 1918, Folder 1, Box 2, MS 251, SUC, AJA, Cincinnati, OH; Advertisement, *NYDT*, 17 October 1919, 18; Advertisement, *WES*, 25 January 1923, 27.
78 Lazard Fréres to GU&M, 1 July 1903; Lazard Fréres to GU&M, 14 December 1905, FUPP, Evanston, IL; SU to LM, 12 September 1904, Folder 8, Box 13, MS 359, LMC, AJA, Cincinnati, OH; Lazard Fréres to GU&M, 13 January 1903; Tillinghast & Tillinghast to GU&M, 21 July 1906, Folder 15, Box 7, MS 251, SUP, Box 13, AJA, Cincinnati, OH.
79 'Bankers Named to Plan Merger', *Birmingham Age-Herald*, 7 April 1911, 5; 'Southern Iron & Steel Co.', *Algemeen Handelsblad*, 11 April 1911, 10; 'Merger Committee', *The Iron Trade Review*, 13 April 1911, 744; 'Southern Iron & Steel Co., N.Y.', *Commercial & Financial Chronicle*, 13 October 1913, 1119–20.
80 'Prominent Young Lawyer', *Birmingham Age-Herald*, 5 September 1912, 4; 'Standard Steel Co. Will Be New Name When Reorganized', *Birmingham Age-Herald*, 1 February 1913, 5.
81 Advertisement, *NYS*, 10 March 1908, 9.
82 Jean Strouse, *Morgan: American Financier* (London: The Harvill Press, 1999), 575–89.
83 'Control by Depositors', *NYDT*, 30 October 1907, 2.
84 'Receivers Report Soon', *NYDT*, 14 November 1907, 3.
85 'To Issue More Stock', *NYDT*, 21 November 1907, 2.
86 'Plan of Depositors', *NYDT*, 30 November 1907, 9.
87 'Untermyer's Reply to Compromise Plan', *NYT*, 19 December 1907, 6.
88 'Unwarranted Delay in Knickerbocker Trust Company Re-Organization Plans', *Trust Companies*, December 1907, 831.
89 'Doelger's Knickerbocker Assent', *NYDT*, 25 January 1908, 9.
90 Pak, *Gentlemen Bankers*, 25.
91 Pak, *Gentlemen Bankers*, 28.
92 'Sugar Men Left Trail for Earle', *NYT*, 13 June 1909, 10.
93 'Trusts Enthroned, Untermyer Says', *NYT*, 16 June 1909, 1.
94 'Untermyer Would Fix Trust Prices', *NYT*, 21 September 1910, 3.
95 Samuel Untermyer, *Extermination vs. Regulation of the Trusts. Which Shall It Be?: An Address Delivered at the Annual Meeting of the National Civic Federation, at New York City on January 12th, 1911* (New York: The Author, 1911), 1–30.
96 'Untermyer Wants Corporate Reforms', *NYT*, 6 January 1911, 10; Samuel Untermyer, *Some Needed Legislative Reforms in Corporate Management: An Address Delivered Before the New York County Lawyers' Association, at Hotel Astor, N.Y., January 5, 1911* (New York: The Author, 1911), 1–26.
97 Samuel Untermyer, 'The Supreme Court Decisions: The Remedy', *The North American Review*, July 1911, 70–95.

98 Untermyer, 'The Remedy', 73.
99 Untermyer, 'The Remedy', 88–93.
100 'Federal Charters for Big Business', *NYT*, 13 November 1911, 15.
101 'Untermyer Attacks Steel and Tobacco', *NYT*, 19 November 1911, 9; U.S. Congress, Senate, Committee on Interstate Commerce, *Hearing Pursuant to S.R. 98, A Resolution Directing the Committee to Investigate and Report Desirable Changes in the Laws Regulating and Controlling Corporations, Persons, and Firms Engaged in Interstate Commerce: 1*, 62nd Cong., 2nd sess. (Washington, DC: G.P.O., 1912), 181–240, 487–97, 1338–41.
102 Samuel Untermyer, 'The Tobacco Trust Farce: Corporation Attorney Advocates a Government Commission to Regulate Trusts', *The World To-Day*, December 1911, 1429–38.
103 Robert Erskine Ely, ed., *Yearbook of the Economic Club of New York: II: Containing the Addresses of the Season 1911–1912* (New York: The Knickerbocker Press, 1912); Samuel Untermyer, *Government Regulation of the Trusts with Special Reference to the Sherman Act: Address Delivered at the Dinner of the Economic Club of New York at the Hotel Astor, November 22nd, 1911* (New York: The Author, 1911), 1–27; 'Untermyer Tells Where States Fail', *NYT*, 29 November 1911, 16.
104 Intercollegiate Socialist Society to Edwin Markham, 23 March 1912, Edwin Markham Correspondence, Horrmann Library, Wagner College, New York, NY; 'Fifth Ave. and East Side Attend Debate', *New York Press*, 28 April 1912, 5.
105 SU to William J. Gaynor, 19 February 1911, Folder 751, Box 64, Series IV, RG 001.WJG: Office of the Mayor, William J. Gaynor, New York City Municipal Archives, NY.
106 Samuel Untermyer, *Is There a Money Trust?: An Address Delivered Before the Finance Forum in the City of New York, December 27th, 1911* (New York: The Author, 1911), 16–17.
107 SU to Bernard M. Baruch, 23 October; 28 October; 30 October 1912; Bernard M. Baruch to SU, 30 October 1912, Folder 1, Box 1, MS 251, SUC, AJA, Cincinnati, OH.
108 Henry W. Sites, *Investment Bankers and Brokers* (New York: The Author, 1918).
109 Sites, *Investment Bankers*, 167, 173.
110 'Stocks React After Early Advance', *PI*, 16 December 1922, 22.
111 'Untermyer Says Money Trust Is Big Menace', *Washington Times*, 7 September 1911, 5.
112 Untermyer, *Money Trust*, 1.
113 Untermyer, *Money Trust*, 1–2.
114 Untermyer, *Money Trust*, 2, 15.
115 Untermyer, *Money Trust*, 2.
116 Untermyer, *Money Trust*, 17–19.
117 'Charge That Morgan Defeated Sheehan', *NYT*, 31 May 1911, 6; 'Denial from F.L. Stetson', *NYEP*, 31 May 1911, 3.
118 'Untermyer Wrong, Stetson Asserts', *NYT*, 1 June 1911, 5; 'Letter About Boss Stetson', *NYS*, 31 May 1911, 1–2.
119 'James A. O'Gorman', *BDE*, 18 May 1943, 11; 'Passing of James A. O'Gorman', *The Advocate*, 29 May 1943, 4.
120 Bruce L. Larson, *Lindbergh of Minnesota: A Political Biography* (New York: Harcourt, Brace Jovanovich, Inc., 1973).
121 Frank A. Vanderlip to James Stillman, 15 December 1911; 29 December 1911, Vanderlip Collection, RBML, CUL, NY.

122 Charles A. Lindbergh, *Banking and Currency and the Money Trust* (Washington, DC: National Capital Press, 1913), 75.
123 U.S. Congress, House, Committee on Rules, *Hearings on House Resolution No. 314, Authorising the Appointment of a Committee to Investigate as to Whether There are Not Combinations of Financial and Other Concerns Who Control Money and Credits, and Operate in Restraint of Trade Through That Control*, 62nd Cong., 2nd sess. (Washington, DC: G.P.O., 1911).
124 'Plan Inquiry into the Money Trust', *NYT*, 22 December 1911, 5.
125 'Untermyer To Lead Money Trust Inquiry', *NYT*, 5 January 1912, 1, 3.
126 'Samuel Untermyer on Money Trust', *The Commoner*, 5 January 1912, 5.
127 Untermyer later told Brandeis that Henry was

> the man who more than every other one man is responsible for having secured the passage of the Resolution under which the Investigation was made and who thereafter gave to me loyal and consistent support at a time when the financial interests, through their powerful inspired press bureau and through their friends on the floor of the House, were exhausting every effort to discredit and defeat the Inquiry...
>
> It was on his insistence and in the face of great opposition that the Resolution was forced upon the floor of the House and was afterwards passed through caucus action. That was only the beginning of his fight. He wanted the Resolution referred to a Special Committee but it was sent to the Banking and Currency Committee; and he had to struggle against a hostile element in that Committee at every stage of the proceedings. He defended the action of the Sub-Committee and its Counsel against the persistent attacks of its enemies.
>
> At the outset the Chairman was openly opposed to the Inquiry, although he was subsequently converted and became its most loyal supporter; but from the beginning nothing could have been accomplished without the aid and encouragement of Mr. Henry.

SU to LDB, 1 December 1913, Reel 32, LDBC, UA, UL, Louisville, KY.
128 'Untermyer To Washington', *NYT*, 13 January 1912, 14.
129 'Money Inquiry Assured', *NYT*, 23 January 1912, 1; 'To Hear Untermyer To-Day', *NYT*, 26 January 1912, 12.
130 'Untermyer Scores Money Oligarchy', *NYT*, 27 January 1912, 12.
131 U.S. Congress, House, Committee on Rules. *Investigation of the Money Trust: No. 1: Hearings on Rules of the House of Representatives on House Resolutions 314 and 356, Friday, January 26, 1912*, 62nd Cong., 2nd sess. (Washington, DC: GPO, 1912), 15.
132 'Nation Menaced By Money Trust, Witness Avers', *Washington Times*, 26 January 1912, 1, 3.
133 William A. Glasgow to CG, 26 March 1912, Box 64, MSS 2913, CGP, SSC, UVL, Charlottesville, VA.
134 CG to A.W. Page, 24 June 1927, Box 64, MSS 2913, CGP, SSC, UVL, Charlottesville, VA.
135 CG to SU, 13 February 1912, Box 64, MSS 2913, CGP, SSC, UVL, Charlottesville, VA.
136 SU to CG, 17 February 1912, Box 7, MSS 2913, CGP, SSC, UVL, Charlottesville, VA.
137 CG to SU, 22 February 1912, Box 24, MSS 2913, CGP, SSC, UVL, Charlottesville, VA.
138 SU to Charles M. Guggenheimer, 12 February 1912, Folder 2, Box 2, MS 251, SUC, AJA, Cincinnati, OH.
139 Charles M. Guggenheimer to SU, 15 February 1912, Folder 2, Box 2, MS 251, SUC, AJA, Cincinnati, OH.
140 'Bryanites Beaten in Latest Money Trust Row', *NYDT*, 15 February 1912, 1.

141 'Radical Probe of Money Trust Wins', *Washington Times*, 24 February 1912, 1; 'House Passes "Money Trust" Investigation Resolution and Has Two Others before It', *NYDT*, 25 February 1912, 1.
142 'Delay Money Trust Inquiry', *NYS*, 29 February 1912, 13.
143 'Untermyer Won't Serve', *NYT*, 1 March 1912, 6.
144 Charles Edward Shields, *Samuel Untermyer, The Pujo Committee, and the Federal Reserve Act (A Preliminary Study)* (Mechanicsburg: The Author, 1979), 22.
145 SU to Robert L. Henry, 8 April 1912, 10 April 1912, 11 April, 15 April, 20 April 1912; Robert L. Henry to SU, 5 April 1912, 8 April 1912, 9 April 1912, 16 April, 17 April 1912, Folder 6; SU to James F. Byrnes, 17 April 1912, Folder 3, Box 2; SU to Arsene Pujo, 20 April 1912, Folder 1, Box 3, MS 251, SUC, AJA, Cincinnati, OH.
146 Shields, *Samuel Untermyer*, 35.
147 'Money Trust Inquiry to Have Wider Scope', *NYT*, 23 April 1912, 7.
148 'Act in Money Inquiry', *Washington Post*, 24 April 1912, 4; 'Ready to Open Inquiry', *WES*, 26 April 1912, 11.
149 J.P. Morgan, Jr. to J.P. Morgan, 25 April 1912, Box 32, Papers of J.P. Morgan, Jr., Archives of The Pierpont Morgan Library, New York, NY.
150 'Untermyer Fears for Money Inquiry', *NYT*, 3 June 1912, 3.
151 'Five Men the Power in Clearing House', *NYT*, 7 June 1912, 3.
152 'Vanderlip Attacks the Money Inquiry', *NYT*, 11 June 1912, 1, 8.
153 'Untermyer Invites Critics to Testify', *NYT*, 10 June 1912, 8.
154 Swaine, *Cravath Firm Since 1906*, 100
155 SU to WJB, 18 July 1912, Folder 3, Box 2, MS 251, SUC, AJA, Cincinnati, OH.
156 SU to WJB, 21 November 1912, Folder 3, Box 2, MS 251, SUC, AJA, Cincinnati, OH.
157 WJB to SU, 26 November [1912], Folder 3, Box 2, MS 251, SUC, AJA, Cincinnati, OH.
158 'Samuel Untermyer Stresses Friendly Sentiment Existing', *Japan Times & Mail*, 23 January 1927, 1.
159 'Sam Untermyer Says Al Smith Can Be Elected', *Panama American*, 23 December 1926, 1.
160 In August 1915 Wilson wrote to Untermyer thanking him for a telegram of sympathy. He said, 'It is very delightful to feel the warm touch of a friend's hand at such a time and your telegram has served to give me strength and courage.'
    WW to SU, 15 August 1914, WWP, LCMD, Washington, DC.
161 A mutual acquaintance of Untermyer and Wilson, Johann Heinrich Count von Bernstorff, observed in 1920 that Wilson 'has not the reputation of being a loyal friend, and is accused of ingratitude by many of his former colleagues and enthusiastic adherents'.
    Johann Heinrich Bernstorff, *My Three Years in America* (London: Skeffington & Son, Ltd., 1920), 53.
162 House observed in 1913 that 'Notwithstanding his reputation, Untermyer gives one the impression of being a cultured gentleman with very progressive tendencies'.
    Entry for 30 March 1913, Volume 1, 162–3, EMHD, MA, YUL, New Haven, CT.
163 Untermyer had been an ally of Folk since at least 1906. Folk was one of several Progressive Democratic state governors such as William C. Sulzer of New York and John A. Johnson of Minnesota who Untermyer supported and advised during this period.
    'Folk Urges The Need Of Active Patriotism', *NYT*, 1 September 1906, 5; Richard Young, 'Joseph Wingate Folk: Graft Killer', *Hearst's*, August 1914, 238–41; 'Joseph W.

Folk', *Rome Daily Sentinel*, 29 May 1923, 4; Winifred G. Helmes, *John A. Johnson: The People's Governor: A Political History* (Minneapolis: University of Minnesota Press, 1949), 182–3, 232, 253, 255, 272, 283–4; 'Our New York Letter', *The Reform Advocate*, 9 November 1912, 404.

164 Arthur S. Link, *Wilson: Volume I: The Road to the White House* (Princeton, NJ: Princeton University Press, 1947), 402–4, 485; Arthur S. Link, *Wilson: Volume II: The New Freedom* (Princeton, NJ: Princeton University Press, 1956), 26, 31, 219, 202, 207, 426.
165 'James Stillman', *NYT*, 16 March 1918, 1, 11.
166 Frank A. Vanderlip to James Stillman, 20 September 1912, Vanderlip Collection, RBML, CUL, NY.
167 SU to WW, 3 July 1912, WWP, LCMD, Washington, DC.
168 SU to WW, 3 July 1912, WWP, LCMD, Washington, DC.
169 SU to WW, 3 July 1912, WWP, LCMD, Washington, DC.
170 SU to WW, 31 July 1912, WWP, LCMD, Washington, DC.
171 William Gibbs McAdoo, *Crowded Years: The Reminiscences of William G. McAdoo* (London: Jonathan Cape, 1932), 157; William F. McCombs, *Making Woodrow Wilson President* (New York: Fairview Publishing Company, 1921), 104, 167.
172 Link, *Wilson: The Road*, 402–4, 485.
173 'Untermyer Sees Dawn of New Era', *NYT*, 1 September 1912, II:6.
174 WJB to EMH, 28 December 1911, Box 28, WJBP, LCMD, Washington, DC.
175 *NYT*, 1 September 1912, II:6.
176 Frank A. Vanderlip to James Stillman, 20 September 1912, Vanderlip Collection, RBML, CUL, NY.
177 SU to WGM, 6 November 1912, Box 94, WGMP, LCMD, Washington, DC.
178 SU to WGM, 5 March 1913, Box 96, WGMP, LCMD, Washington, DC.
179 LDB to WGM, 5 March 1913, Box 96, WGMP, LCMD, Washington, DC.
180 'Our Cabinet', *Twentieth Century Magazine*, June 1912, ii.
181 'Talk of Probable Cabinet of Wilson', *Mexican Herald*, 13 November 1912, 8.
182 H. Parker Willis to CG, 7 November 1912, Boxes 25 & 26, MSS 2913, CGP, SSC, UVL, Charlottesville, VA.
183 CG to James F. Byrnes, 8 November 1912, Boxes 25 & 26, MSS 2913, CGP, SSC, UVL, Charlottesville, VA.
184 CG to Robert J. Bulkley, 8 November 1912, Boxes 25 & 26, MSS 2913, CGP, SSC, UVL, Charlottesville, VA.
185 Arsène Paulin Pujo (1861–1939) Biographical Information, http://bioguide.congress.gov, accessed 8 July 2019.
186 CG to Arsène P. Pujo, 8 November 1912, Box 64, 1912–1927, MSS 2913, CGP, SSC, UVL, Charlottesville, VA.
187 Arsène P. Pujo to CG, 11 November 1912, Box 64, MSS 2913, CGP, SSC, UVL, Charlottesville, VA.
188 'Split Is Expected On Currency Reform', *NYT*, 19 November 1912, 5; 'Untermyer May Quit Money Trust Hunt', *NYT*, 20 November 1912, 19; 'Peace In Money Inquiry', *NYT*, 21 November 1912, 4; 'E.H. Farrar Quits Money Trust Quiz', *New Orleans Daily Picayune*, 20 November 1912, 3.
189 SU to CG, 22 November 1912, Box 64, MSS 2913, CGP, SSC, UVL, Charlottesville, VA.
190 CG to SU, 2 December 1912, Box 64, MSS 2913, CGP, SSC, UVL, Charlottesville, VA.
191 'Attacks Pujo Committee', *NYT*, 3 December 1912, 3.

192 'Pujo Now Questions Big Wall St. Banks', *NYT*, 8 December 1912, 3-4; SU to Harvey, Fiske & Sons, 26 December 1912, Folder 2, Box 2, MS 251, SUC, AJA, Cincinnati, OH; Swaine, *Cravath Firm Since 1906*, 100.
193 Swaine, *Cravath Firm Since 1906*, 100.
194 'Bankers Meet Untermyer', *NYT*, 31 October 1912, 10.
195 'Five Men Control $368,000,000 Here', *NYT*, 11 December 1912, 1-2.
196 'Stock Exchange Ways Discussed', *NYT*, 13 December 1912, 1-2.
197 'Robert S. Winsmore', *NYS*, 9 November 1937, 25.
198 'Widespread Break in Stock Market', *PI*, 6 December 1912, 15.
199 'Stocks Dull and Generally Heavy', *PI*, 15 December 1912, 19.
200 Mary O'Sullivan, *Dividends of Development: Securities Markets in the History of U.S. Capitalism, 1866-1922* (Oxford: Oxford University Press, 2016), 261.
201 O'Sullivan, *Dividends*, 262.
202 As quoted in Strouse, *Morgan*, 666.
203 Henry F. Pringle, 'Front Page Stuff', *American Mercury*, January 1927, 158; U.S. Congress, House, Subcommittee of the Committee on Banking and Currency. *Money Trust Investigation, Investigation of Financial and Monetary Conditions in the United States under House Resolutions Nos. 429 and 504*, 62nd Cong., 3rd sess. (Washington, DC: GPO, 1913), 1003-91.
204 House, *Money Trust Investigation*, 1084.
205 House, *Money Trust Investigation*, 1050-1.
206 Boardman Robinson, 'Gulliver before the Lili-*Pujoans*', *NYDT*, 20 December 1912, 1.
207 Oscar Cesare, 'Who Said Panic?', *NYS*, 20 December 1912, 9; 'Wilson Throws Down Gauntlet to Wall Street', *Washington Herald*, 18 December 1912, 1.
   The proprietor of the *Sun*, William C. Reick, believed that Untermyer had done him in by confidentially advising a friend concerning him. After Frank A. Munsey purchased the *Sun* in 1916 Untermyer appealed successfully to him to put an end to its unfavourable coverage of his activities in its editorial and news columns.
   Frank Michael O'Brien, *The Story of the Sun: New York, 1833-1928*, New edn. (New York: D. Appleton & Co., 1928), 198-9, 204; SU to Frank A. Munsey, 20 May 1920, Folder 7, Box 1, MS 251, SUC, AJA, Cincinnati, OH.
208 'Character First in His Philosophy', *NYT*, 1 April 1913, 6.
209 Entry for 30 March 1913, Volume 1, 162-3, EMHD, MA, YUL, New Haven, CT.
210 John Douglas Forbes, *J.P. Morgan, Jr., 1867-1943* (Charlottesville: University Press of Virginia, 1981), 73-4.
211 J.P. Morgan, Jr. to Herbert L. Satterlee, 18 March 1913, Box 9, Papers of J.P. Morgan, Jr., Archives of The Pierpont Morgan Library, New York, NY.
212 Forbes, *J.P. Morgan, Jr.*, 73-4.
213 House, *Money Trust Investigation*, 1419-568.
214 J.P. Morgan, Jr. to J.P. Morgan, 11 January 1913, Box 32, Papers of J.P. Morgan, Jr., Archives of The Pierpont Morgan Library, New York, NY.
   Milton Friedman and Anna Schwartz note an entry from 1917 in Charles S. Hamlin's diary says that J.P. Morgan, Jr. reportedly believed that the Jews (presumably Untermyer) had killed his father and that some time he would get even with them. They suggest that Morgan, Jr. did indeed get even with them by allowing the Bank of United States to fail in 1930.
   Milton Friedman and Anna J. Schwartz, 'The Failure of the Bank of United States: A Reappraisal: A Reply', *Explorations in Economic History* 23, no. 2 (1986): 201-2;

Entry for 20 January 1917, November 1916-27 March 1919, 68–9, Reel 1, Box 4, Volume 4, Charles S. Hamlin Diaries, LCMD, Washington, DC.
215 'Would Have Nation Control Exchange', *NYT*, 16 January 1913, 2.
216 'Schiff Believes in Individual Concentration', *NYT*, 17 January 1913, 1–2.
217 House, *Money Trust Investigation*, 2049.
218 House, *Money Trust Investigation*, 2141–2, 2144–5.
219 'Probers Place William Rockefeller on Grill Today', *Newark Evening Star*, 7 February 1913, 1.
220 House, *Money Trust Investigation*, 2143, 2226.
221 'Morgan Defense In as Pujo Finishes', *NYT*, 28 February 1913, 7.
222 U.S. Congress, House, Subcommittee of the Committee on Banking and Currency, *Report of the Committee Appointed Pursuant to House Resolutions 429 and 504 to Investigate the Concentration of Control of Money and Credit*, 62nd Cong., 3rd sess. (Washington, DC: GPO, 1913).
223 'The Pujo Report', *NYT*, 1 March 1913, 14.
224 'Pujo Guns Spiked', *NYH*, 22 December 1912, 2–3.
225 J.P. Morgan, Jr. to James Stillman, 12 March 1913, Box 9, Papers of J.P. Morgan, Jr., Archives of The Pierpont Morgan Library, New York, NY.
226 House, *Concentration of Control of Money and Credit*, Appendix F.
227 Peter Knight, 'Representations of Capitalism in the Gilded Age and Progressive Era', in *American Capitalism: New Histories*, ed. Sven Beckert and Christine Desan (New York: Columbia University Press, 2018), 248.
228 Peter Knight, *Reading the Market: Genres of Financial Capitalism in Gilded Age America* (Baltimore: Johns Hopkins University Press, 2016), 242.
229 Knight, *Reading the Market*, 243.
230 House, *Concentration of Control of Money and Credit*, Appendix G.
231 SU to LDB, 17 March 1913, Reel 32, LDBC, UA, UL, Louisville, KY.
232 LDB to SU, 18 March 1913, Reel 32, LDBC, UA, UL, Louisville, KY.
233 SU to LDB, 3 October 1913; 8 October 1913; LDB to SU, 2 October 1913, Reel 32, LDBC, UA, UL, Louisville, KY.
234 SU to WGM, 27 December 1915, Box 151, Papers of WGM, LCMD, Washington, DC.
235 Louis Dembitz Brandeis, *Other People's Money, and How the Bankers Use It* (New York: F.A. Stokes Co., 1914).
236 Untermyer had a lot of respect for Billikopf.
    Interview with Frank Untermyer, 25–28 April 2000.
237 SU to Jacob Billikopf, 10 November 1932, Folder 16, Box 30, MS 13, Jacob Billikopf Collection, AJA, Cincinnati, OH.
238 'Vice-Chancellor Pitney and Mr. Justice Brown on Samuel Untermyer', *NYS*, 5 April 1913, 6.
239 Silver, *Louis Marshall*, 231–4.
240 'Sulzer for Curbs on the Exchanges', *NYT*, 28 January 1913, 1.
241 'Incorporation Bill for All Exchanges', *NYT*, 13 February 1913, 7.
242 'For Federal Board to Pass on Stocks', *NYT*, 22 February 1913, 2.
243 'Untermyer Goes to Albany', *NYT*, 2 April 1913, 2.
244 Oscar Cesare, 'The People Demand Stock Exchange Legislation', *NYS*, 5 April 1913, 7.
245 'Untermyer Again Attacks Exchange', *NYT*, 4 April 1913, 8; Macey and Miller, *Blue Sky*, 370, 379; 'New Giants of Wall Street: William Clarkson Van Antwerp', *BDE*, 25 June 1916, B1.

246 Julia C. Ott, '"The Free and Open People's Market": Political Ideology and Retail Brokerage at the New York Stock Exchange, 1913-1933', *Journal of American History* 96, no. 1 (2009): 54.
247 Samuel Untermyer, *A Legislative Program to Restore Business Freedom and Confidence: An Address Delivered Before the Illinois Manufacturing Association at the Hotel La Salle, Chicago, January 5, 1914* (New York: The Author, 1914), 28.
248 Jay W. Forrest and James Malcolm, *Tammany's Treason: Impeachment of Governor William Sulzer* (Albany: The Fort Orange Press, 1913), 153.
249 Silver, *Louis Marshall*, 237-40.
250 'Tammany A Target at Tilden Dinner', *NYT*, 10 February 1914, 2.
251 CG to H. Parker Willis, 23 March 1913, Box 283, MSS 2913, CGP, SSC, UVL, Charlottesville, VA.
252 SU to WGM, 12 February 1931, Box 356, WGMP, LCMD, Washington, DC.
253 'Bryan Visits Untermyer', *NYDT*, 16 May 1913, 2; 'Bryan Is Untermyer's Guest', *NYS*, 16 May 1913, 16; 'G.F. Peabody Dead', *NYT*, 5 March 1938, 17; Entry for 15 May 1913, Volume 1, 223-4, EMHD, MA, YUL, New Haven, CT; EMH to WW, 15 May 1913, WWP, LCMD, Washington, DC.
254 Warburg later recalled, probably incorrectly, that the meeting took place on 18 May.
Paul M. Warburg, *The Federal Reserve System: Its Origin and Growth: Reflections and Recollections, 1* (New York: Macmillan Company, 1930), 97.
255 Entry for 16 May 1913, Volume 1, 225-6, EMHD, MA, YUL, New Haven, CT.
256 The letter and the accompanying memorandum are reproduced in full in Warburg's 1930 memoir.
Warburg, *Federal Reserve System*, 97-8, 636-52.
257 EMH to WW, 26 May 1913, WWP, LCMD, Washington, DC.
258 Entry for 19 May 1913, Volume 1, 227-9, EMHD, MA, YUL, New Haven, CT.
259 EMH to WW, 20 May 1913, WWP, LCMD, Washington, DC.
260 SU to WGM, 24 May 1913, Box 100, WGMP, LCMD, Washington, DC.
261 SU to WGM, 21 June 1913, Box 102, WGMP, LCMD, Washington, DC.
262 SU to WGM, 25 June 1913, Box 102, WGMP, LCMD, Washington, DC.
263 SU to CG, 21 June 1913, Box 23, MSS 2913, CGP, SSC, UVL, Charlottesville, VA.
264 SU to WGM, 21 June 1913, Box 102, WGMP, LCMD, Washington, DC.
265 *Neue Deutsche Biographie* 22 (Berlin: Duncker & Humblot, 2004), 395-6.
266 *Neue Deutsche Biographie* 8 (Berlin: Duncker & Humblot, 1968), 470-2.
267 SU to Arthur Salomonson, 31 July, 3 August 1913; Arthur Salomonson to SU, 1 August 1913, Box 7, Folder 83 - 84, MS 535, Paul Moritz Warburg Papers, MA, YUL, New Haven, CT.
268 Karl Helfferich to Paul M. Warburg, 28 October 1913, Box 17, MSS 2913, CGP, SSC, UVL, Charlottesville, VA.
269 'House Speeds Up on Currency Bill', *WES*, 16 September 1913, 2.
270 'Untermyer Urges Money Bill Changes', *NYT*, 23 September 1913, 9; 'Wilson To Clear Way for Currency', *NYT*, 30 September 1913, 3; U.S. Congress, Senate, Committee on Banking and Currency. *Banking and Currency: Hearings on H.R.7837 (S.2639) - A Bill to Provide for the Establishment of Federal Reserve Banks, for Furnishing an Elastic Currency, Affording Means of Rediscounting Commercial Paper, and to Establish a More Effective Supervision of Banking in the United States and for Other Purposes, I & II*, 63rd Cong., 1st sess. (Washington, DC: GPO, 1913), 808-942, 1288-369.

271 Samuel Untermyer, 'Why the Currency Bill Should Pass', *The North American Review*, October 1913, 498–526.
272 Benjamin Strong to Theodore E. Burton, 5 December 1913, 0021.2, Papers of Benjamin Strong, Jr., Federal Reserve Bank of New York Archives, New York, NY.
273 William C. Heinkel to Benjamin Strong, 22 December 1913, 0610.2, Papers of Benjamin Strong, Jr., Federal Reserve Bank of New York Archives, New York, NY.
274 'New Legislation on Trusts Topic of Conference', *NYH*, 6 December 1913, 6.
275 'Clayton Gets Views on Anti-Trust Bill', *NYS*, 6 December 1913, 5; '"Trust Busters Plan for Battle: Samuel Untermyer and Others Confer on Coming Democratic Bill', *NYDT*, 6 December 1913, 4.
276 'Urges End of War on Corporations', *NYT*, 29 November 1913, 19.
277 Melvin I. Urofsky and David W. Levy, ed., *Letters of Louis D. Brandeis: III: 1913–1915: Progressive and Zionist* (Albany: State University of New York Press, 1973), 222.
278 Entry for 28 November 1913, Volume 1, 372–3, EMHD, MA, YUL, New Haven, CT.
279 Entry for 29 November 1913, Volume 1, 375–7, EMHD, MA, YUL, New Haven, CT.
280 SU to WGM, 18 December 1913, Box 112, WGMP, LCMD, Washington, DC.
281 SU to WGM, 14 January 1914, Box 110, WGMP, LCMD, Washington, DC.
282 SU to EMH, 12 January 1914, Folder 3882, Box 122, MS 466, EMHP, MA, YUL, New Haven, CT.
283 Untermyer, *A Legislative Program*, 2.
284 Untermyer, *Business Freedom*, 1–40; 'Untermyer Favors Industrial Board', *NYT*, 6 January 1914, 15.
285 SU to EMH, 12 January 1914, Folder 3882, Box 122, MS466, EMHP, MA, YUL, New Haven, CT.
286 'Adopt Untermyer Curbs', *NYT*, 16 January 1914, 2.
287 'Untermyer's Trust Plan', *NYT*, 24 January 1914, 11.
288 'Wouldn't Bar All Holding Concerns', *NYT*, 7 February 1914, 2; U.S. Congress, House, Committee on the Judiciary. *Trust Legislation: Hearings on Trust Legislation in Two Volumes, Serial 7 – Parts 1 to 24 Inclusive, 1*, 63rd Cong., 2nd sess. (Washington, DC: GPO, 1915), 815–59.
289 'Untermyer Busy On 5 New Trust Bills', *NYT*, 9 February 1914, 9.
290 SU to EMH, 25 January 1914, WWP, LCMD, Washington, DC.
291 SU to WJB, 21 November 1912, Folder 3, Box 2, MS 251, SUC, AJA, Cincinnati, OH.
292 Untermyer, *A Legislative Program*, 28.
293 U.S. Congress, Senate, Committee on Banking and Currency, *Regulation of the Stock Exchange: Hearings on S.3895: A Bill to Prevent the Use of the Mails and of the Telegraph and Telephone in Furtherance of Fraudulent and Harmful Transactions on Stock Exchanges*, 63rd Cong., 2nd sess (Washington, DC: GPO, 1914), 5–108.
294 Senate, *Regulation of the Stock Exchange*, 383–427.
295 Senate, *Regulation of the Stock Exchange*, 385.
296 John G. Milburn and Walter F. Taylor, *Brief and Reply Brief Submitted on Behalf of the New York Stock Exchange to the Senate Committee on Banking and Currency, March 5, 1914, and March 30, 1914, Respectively* (New York: New York Stock Exchange, 1914).
297 Senate, *Regulation of the Stock Exchange*, 682–3.
298 Jacob Lippman, 'The Securities Exchange Act of 1934 and the Commerce Clause', *United States Law Review* 69, no. 1(1935): 20–1.
299 'Sees State Control of Stock Markets', *NYT*, 13 February 1914, 15.
300 'Owen Reports Bill on Stock Exchange', *NYT*, 26 June 1914, 11.

301 Cedric B. Cowing, *Populists, Plungers, and Progressives: A Social History of Stock and Commodity Speculation* (Princeton, NJ: Princeton University Press, 1965), 62.
302 'Says Press Opposes 'Change Regulation', *NYT*, 5 February 1914, 18.
303 'The Stock Exchange', *NYT*, 24 November 1914, 12.
304 'Program of Twenty-Seventh Annual Meeting', *American Economic Review* 5, no. 1 (Supplement: Papers and Proceedings of the Twenty-Seventh Annual Meeting of the American Economic Association) (1915): 1–2.
305 William J. Novak, 'Institutional Economics and the Progressive Movement for the Social Control of American Business', *Business History Review* 93, no. 4 (2019): 680–1.
306 Samuel Untermyer, 'Speculation on the Stock Exchanges and Public Regulation of the Exchanges', *American Economic Review* 5, no. 1 (Supplement: Papers and Proceedings of the Twenty-Seventh Annual Meeting of the American Economic Association) (1915): 27.
   This was not the first time Untermyer had presented a paper at an academic conference. He had previously done so in April 1910 at the annual meeting of the American Academy of Political and Social Science in Philadelphia.
   'Notes on Recent and Current Events', *Journal of the American Institute of Criminal Law and Criminology* 1, no. 1 (1910): 132.
307 Untermyer, 'Speculation', 33.
308 'Speculation on the Stock Exchanges—Discussion', *American Economic Review* 5, no. 1 (Supplement: Papers and Proceedings of the Twenty-Seventh Annual Meeting of the American Economic Association) (1915): 100.
309 'Untermyer Speech Tactics Criticised', *NYS*, 31 December 1914, 9.
310 'Discussion', 100–11.
311 'Untermyer Under Fire', *NYT*, 31 December 1914, 12.
312 'Asks Untermyer For His Evidence', *NYT*, 2 January 1915, 10.
313 'Offers to Debate on Stock Exchange', *NYT*, 3 January 1915, III:3.
314 'Untermyer Views Latest Trust Bills', *NYT*, 29 March 1914, 14.
315 Samuel Untermyer, 'Completing the Anti-Trust Programme', *The North American Review*, April 1914, 535–8.
   Untermyer had sent a copy of this article to the White House.
   SU to Joseph P. Tumulty, 30 March 1914, WWP, LCMD, Washington, DC.
316 SU to Joseph P. Tumulty, 13 April 1914, WWP, LCMD, Washington, DC.
317 Samuel Untermyer, *The Relation of the Farmer to the Trust Question: An Address Delivered Before the Western Economic Society and the Second National Conference on Marketing and Farm Credits at Chicago, April 15th, 1914* (New York: The Author, 1914), 3.
318 'Farmers and the Trust Law', *Yonkers Statesman*, 16 April 1914, 5.
319 Robert Erskine Ely, ed., *Yearbook of the Economic Club of New York: IV: Containing the Addresses of the Season 1913–1914* (New York: The Knickerbocker Press, 1914), 209, 212, 216.
320 'Hear Untermyer On Trusts', *NYT*, 7 May 1914, 13; U.S. Congress, Senate, Committee on Interstate Commerce. *Interstate Trade: Hearings on Interstate Commerce: Bills Relating to Trust Legislation, 1 & 2*, 63rd Cong., 2nd sess. (Washington, DC: GPO, 1914), 127–58.
321 'To Put All Pools Under Trade Board', *NYT*, 22 June 1914, 12.
322 'Untermyer Optimistic', *NYT*, 28 June 1914, II:10.
323 'A Blow to Our Credit', *NYT*, 12 July 1914, III:1.

324 SU to WW, 9 July 1914, WWP, LCMD, Washington, DC.
325 'Hamlin Chosen to Head Reserve Board', *New York Evening World* [War Extra], 8 August 1914, 5.
326 WW to SU, 4 February 1914, WWP, LCMD, Washington, DC.
327 Swaine, *Cravath Firm Since 1906*, 99-103.

Chapter 3

1 'American's Relief Work', *Toronto Globe*, 7 August 1914, 11; 'Untermyer Cables Bryan For Tourists', *NYT*, 7 August 1914, 3; 'Baltic In With 2,072', *NYT*, 23 August 1914, II:9; SU to Ira Morris, 7 June 1919, File 364.64/390, RG59, Records of the Department of State, NA, College Park, MD; U.S. Congress, Senate, Subcommittee of the Committee on the Judiciary. *Brewing and Liquor Interests and German and Bolshevik Propaganda: Report and Hearings Submitted Pursuant to S. Res. 307 and 439 65th Congress Relating to Charges Made Against the United States Brewers' Association and Allied Interests: 2*, 66th Cong., 1st sess. (Washington, DC: G.P.O., 1919), 1836-7.
2 'Untermyer Points the War's Lessons', *NYT*, 23 August 1914, I:9.
3 Entries for 27, 29 and 30 October 1914, Volume 2, 203-6, EMHD, MA, YUL, New Haven, CT.

Although Harvey had supported Untermyer's campaign for economic and financial reform, he was also an anti-Semite. He later claimed Untermyer's 'racial activities' helped contribute to the failure of Elihu Root's 1917 mission to Russia. He undoubtedly exaggerated Untermyer's contribution.

George Harvey, '"Thank God for Wilson": The President at His Best', *The North American Review*, January 1918, 9; George Harvey, 'Mr. Root as Envoy to Russia', *The North American Review*, June 1917, 832-4; C. Howard Hopkins and John W. Long, 'American Jews and the Root Mission to Russia in 1917: Some New Evidence', *American Jewish History* 69, no. 3 (1980): 343.
4 Entry for 11 November 1915, Volume 3, 284-5, EMHD, MA, YUL, New Haven, CT.
5 'Untermyer Decries Preparedness Now', *NYT*, 29 November 1915, 4.
6 'Urges Tax on Munitions', *NYT*, 6 December 1915, 3.
7 Minnie Untermyer to Judah Leon Magnes, 19 June 1916, File P3/1214, Central Archives for the History of the Jewish People, Jerusalem, Israel.
8 Entry for 24 June 1915, Volume 3, pa173-80, EMHD, MA, YUL, New Haven, CT.
9 Minnie Untermyer to WJB, 9 June 1915, Box 30, WJBP, LCMD, Washington, DC.
10 List of Contributors to the Emergency Peace Federation, 25 July 1918, File 10110-1694, RG165, Records of the Military Intelligence Division, NA, College Park, MD.
11 SU to Johann Heinrich Bernstorff, 20 August 1915, File 60765, M1085, Investigative Reports of the Bureau of Investigation: Old German Files, 1909-21, NA, College Park, MD.
12 As a student at New York Law School Garvan had been a clerk in the law offices of Untermyer's friend Abram I. Elkus. During the First World War he served as Director of the Bureau of Investigations at the Office of the Alien Property Custodian from November 1917. He succeeded A. Mitchell Palmer as Alien Property Custodian in March 1919.

'Garvan Succeeds Palmer', *NYT*, 4 March 1919, 21.

13 'German Envoy's War Threat Is Denounced as An Amazing Affront', *New York Evening Telegram*, 12 September 1915, 3; Alva Johnston, 'Profiles: Little Giant – II', *New Yorker*, 24 May 1930, 25.
14 Henry Landau, *The Enemy Within: The Inside Story of German Sabotage in America* (New York: G.P. Putnam's Sons, 1937).
15 Bernstorff, *My Three Years*, 31.

    Heinrich Albert (1874–1960) was a lawyer by training. From the mid-1920s he was general counsel to Ford's German subsidiary, Ford Werke A.G. He was elected to the Ford Werke board of directors in 1930. Albert became the first German chairman of the board in 1937, a position he held until 1947. He was arrested in September 1944 in connection with the Stauffenberg Plot and held by the Gestapo for six months. Albert later claimed he was also accused of violating the racial decrees against Jews because so many of his friends were Jewish. However, although he does not appear to have been a member of the Nazi party, his position at Ford Werke meant he was complicit in the human rights crimes of the Nazi government.

    Simon Reich, *Ford's Research Efforts in Assessing the Activities of Its Subsidiary in Germany* (Dearborn, IN: Ford Motor Company, 2001), 6–7, 123; 'Die neuen Männer', *Deutsche Allgemeine Zeitung*, 24 November 1922, 1; 'In Memoriam', *Der Spiegel*, 16 November 1960, 95.
16 'Man Who First Revealed German Plan in First World War Leaves Secret Service', *Milwaukee Journal*, 20 July 1942, Green Sheet: 1–2.
17 Stewart Halsey Ross, *Propaganda for War: How the United States Was Conditioned to Fight the Great War of 1914–1918* (Jefferson, NC, and London: McFarland & Company, Inc. Publishers, 1996), 128–31.
18 George Sylvester Viereck, *Spreading Germs of Hate* (London: Duckworth, 1931), 74.
19 SU to George R. Cooksey, 26 July 1914; George R. Cooksey to SU, Box 140, WGMP, LCMD, Washington, DC.
20 Arthur S. Link, ed., *The Papers of Woodrow Wilson: 34: July 21 – September 30, 1915* (Princeton, NJ: Princeton University Press, 1980), 74.
21 'Untermyer Tells of His Call on Editor', *NYT*, 30 December 1918, 18.
22 Bernstorff, *My Three Years*, 31; Kaiserlich Deutsches Generalkonsulat New York, 25 August 1915, Bd. 145 f. Bd. 146, R20010, Akten Krieg 1914, PAAA, Berlin, Germany.

    'How Germany Has Worked in U.S.', *New York World*, 15 August 1915, 1; McAdoo, *Crowded Years*, 324–30.
23 Viereck, *Germs of Hate*, 75.
24 Senate, *German and Bolshevik Propaganda*, 1842–3.
25 Aino Malmberg (1866–1933) was an anti-Russian Finnish nationalist and suffragette who had been exiled from the Russian Empire in 1910. She was a frequent visitor to the United States between 1912 and 1918 where she gave lectures. Malmberg assailed the massacres of Russian Jews as the result of incitement by the secret police, who told lies about the Jews to inflame their neighbours.

    'Mme. Malmberg Dies in Finland', *NYT*, 26 February 1933, 27.
26 'Oppressed Nations Form New League', *BDE*, 26 November 1916, 5.
27 Brief von Frau Malmberg datiert New York 20. Dezember 1916, Bd. 5 f. Bd. 6, R21824, Akten Krieg 1914, PAAA, Berlin, Germany.
28 Reinhard R. Doerries, *Imperial Challenge: Ambassador Count Bernstorff and G erman-American Relations, 1908–1917* (Chapel Hill: University of North Carolina

Press, 1989), 54–5, 268; 'Caleb Van Hamm Dies At Miami, Fla', *NYT*, 28 December 1919, 23.
29 Memorandum: Samuel Untermyer, the Administration and Pro-Germanism, 4 February 1920, File 10110-1694, RG165, Records of the Military Intelligence Division, NA, College Park, MD.
30 Melech Epstein, *Profiles of Eleven* (Lanham, MD: University Press of America, 1987), 41, 153.
31 Louis E. Miller to WGM, 10 June 1915, Box 137, WGMP, LCMD, Washington, DC.
32 Ehud Manor, 'Louis Miller, the *Warheit*, and the *Kehillah* of New York, 1908–1909', *Australian Journal of Jewish Studies* 25 (2011): 179.
33 Untermyer later parted ways with Levy. In 1937 he declared Levy to be unworthy of re-election to the New York Supreme Court and unsuccessfully campaigned for his Republican opponent, Nathan D. Perlman.

  Irving Howe and Kenneth Libo, *World of Our Fathers* (New York: Galahad Books, 1994), 369–72, 374; 'Justice Levy Called Unfit By Untermyer', *New York Post*, 21 October 1937, 1, 16; 'Levy and Noonan Win Re-Election', *New York Post*, 3 November 1937, 14; 'Aaron J. Levy', *NYT*, 22 November 1955, 35.
34 'Untermyer Replies Again', *NYT*, 7 October 1917, I:8.
35 'Jewish Papers Unite', *NYT*, 28 February 1919, 6.
36 Memorandum: Subject: Samuel Untermyer, 17 January 1919, File 9146-3085, RG165, Records of the Military Intelligence Division, NA, College Park, MD.
37 John Lord O'Brian to T.W. Gregory, 6 May 1919, File 9-5-1487-2, RG60, Records of the Department of Justice, NA, College Park, MD.
38 Memorandum: Subject: Samuel Untermyer, 17 January 1919. File 9146-3085, RG165, Records of the Military Intelligence Division, NA, College Park, MD.
39 SU to Thomas W. Gregory: Letter 1, 1 March 1919. File 198437-11, RG60, Records of the Department of Justice, NA, College Park, MD.
40 SU to Rev. Dr. Charles H. Parkhurst, 20 January 1919, Folder 8, Box 2, MS 251, SUP, AJA, Cincinnati, OH; 'Jews To Aid Recruiting', *NYT*, 6 April 1917, 8; 'Jews in Patriot League', *NYT*, 27 March 1917, 2; 'Rabbis to Plead for Recruits', *NYT*, 7 April 1917, 3.
41 'The Jewish Patriotic League', *NYT*, 8 April 1917, II:2.
42 'Untermyer Joins Protest on Root', *NYT*, 4 May 1917, 7.
43 'Untermyer Tops List of Loan Subscribers Through Rotogravure Section', *NYT*, 30 May 1917, 1.
44 SU to George R. Cooksey, 19 October 1917, Box 189, WGMP, LCMD, Washington, DC.
45 'Total Loan Grows to 250 Million in Its Poorest Day', *NYT*, 9 October 1917, 1.
46 'McAdoo Announces Overwhelming Success of Second Bond Issue', *NYDT*, 28 October 1917, 7:1.
47 SU to WGM, 29 October 1917, Box 190, WGMP, LCMD, Washington, DC.
48 'Samuel Untermyer Points to Patriotic Advantages of Thrift', *NYT*, 21 January 1918, 15.
49 'New York Takes $200,000,000 Bonds First Day of Drive', *NYT*, 29 September 1918, 1.
50 JHS to SU, 21 October 1918, Folder 15, Box 460, MS 456, JHSC, AJA, Cincinnati, OH.
51 SU to JHS, 8 November 1918, Folder 15, Box 460, MS 546, JHSC, AJA, Cincinnati, OH.

52 JHS to SU, 8 November 1918, Folder 15, Box 460, MS 456, JHSC, AJA, Cincinnati, OH.
53 Bernard A. Rosenblatt, *Two Generations of Zionism: Historical Recollections of an American Zionist* (New York: Shengold Publishers, 1967), 65.
54 SU to WGM, 28 October 1914, Box 125, WGMP, LCMD, Washington, DC.
55 SU to WGM, 16 November 1914, Box 126, WGMP, LCMD, Washington, DC.
56 'Urges Federal Rein on Big Foundations', *NYT*, 19 January 1915, 7.
57 'Schiff Denies Bankers Control', *NYT*, 21 January 1915, 1, 4.
58 'Research Bureau Assailed, Upheld', *NYT*, 7 February 1915, I:8.
59 *NYT*, 19 January 1915, 7; 'Lays Railroad Ills to Banking Control', *NYT*, 1 February 1915, 16.
60 'Hear Williams Will Retain Untermyer', *NYT*, 17 April 1915, 5; SU to WGM, 20 April 1915, Box 519, WGMP, LCMD, Washington, DC.
61 *NYT*, 17 April 1915, 5; Senate, *John Skelton Williams*, 641.
62 Henry F. Hollis to John Skelton Williams, 17 April 1915, Box 519, WGMP, LCMD, Washington, DC.
63 Senate, *John Skelton Williams*, 641.
64 'Court Questions Riggs Bank Fine', *NYT*, 20 May 1915, 16; Senate, *John Skelton Williams*, 648, 654.
65 WGM to SU, 1 June 1916, Box 160, WGMP, LCMD, Washington, DC.
66 SU to WGM, 3 June 1916; SU to WGM, 13 June 1916; SU to WGM, 14 June 1916, Box 160; WGM to SU, 21 June 1916; SU to WGM, 23 June 1916, Box 161, WGMP, LCMD, Washington, DC.
67 Entry for 3 May 1916, Volume 4, 171–9, EMHD, MA, YUL, New Haven, CT.
68 U.S. Department of the Treasury, *Proceeding of the First Pan American Financial Conference, Washington May 24 to 29, 1915* (Washington, DC: G.P.O., 1915), 50; 'Pan-American Meeting Epoch-Making Event in World's History', *WES*, 24 May 1915, 1.
69 Treasury, *Pan American Financial Conference*, 30–1, 70, 142–3, 301–3, 527.

Later in July 1918 Strong tried to expand the Federal Reserve Bank of New York's quarters in the Equitable Building at 120 Broadway to include the 23rd Floor where Guggenheimer, Untermyer & Marshall's office was located. The bank, like Untermyer's firm, had moved into the building relatively recently in 1916. It had outgrown its initial quarters on the first, fourth and fifth floors and had recently acquired the 24th and 25th floors from the Public Service Commission. Untermyer was extremely displeased at the prospect of the further disruption that acceding to Strong's request would cause and made him forcefully aware of this. The firm remained put and did not move again until 1931.

LM to SU, 17 February 1916, Folder 3, Box 1585; Benjamin Strong to SU, 15 July 1918; SU to Benjamin Strong, 16 July 1918, Folder 10, Box 115, MS 359, LMC, AJA, Cincinnati, OH; James F. Curtis to Benjamin Strong, 8 August 1918, 0320.152, Papers of Benjamin Strong, Jr., Federal Reserve Bank of New York Archives, New York, NY; 'New Home for Reserve Bank', *NYDT*, 19 December 1915, III & IV:8; 'Equitable Building Corporation', *Real Estate Record and Guide*, 25 March 1916, 483; 'Service Board to Move', *NYT*, 9 January 1916, 13; 'Lawyers Lease in Pine Street', *NYS*, 14 January 1931, 47.
70 WGM to RL, 4 July 1915, File 810.51/266, RG59, Records of the Department of State, NA, College Park, MD.
71 SU to WGM, 19 June 1915, Box 510, WGMP, LCMD, Washington, DC.

72 WW to WGM, 22 June 1915, Box 510, WGMP, LCMD, Washington, DC.
73 Kendrick A. Clements, 'Woodrow Wilson's Mexican Policy, 1913–15', *Diplomatic History* 4, no. 2 (1980): 127–8.
74 'Start for South America', *NYT*, 8 March 1916, 18.
75 'McAdoo Arrives at Rio', *NYT*, 26 March 1916, 18; 'McAdoo In Buenos Aires', *NYT*, 2 April 1916, I:8.
76 International High Commission, *First Edition of the Committee Reports and Resolutions Adopted at the First General Meeting, Held in Buenos Aires, in April 1916* (Washington, DC: G.P.O., 1916), 15–21.
77 International High Commission, *First Edition*, 31–5.
78 'McAdoo Heads Commission', *NYT*, 14 April 1916, 8; American Bar Association, *Annual Report* 41 (1916): 893–6.
79 'Chile Welcomes McAdoo Party', *NYT*, 18 April 1916, 6.
80 'May Quarantine McAdoo', *NYT*, 23 April 1916, I:12.
81 'McAdoo Angers Peru', *NYT*, 24 April 1916, 6; 'McAdoo Thanks Peru', *NYT*, 26 April 1916, 12.
82 'M'Adoo Returns, Reporting Success', *NYT*, 5 May 1916, 5.
83 McAdoo, *Crowded Years*, 349–63.
84 'Mr. Untermyer for Senate Now Democratic Talk', *NYH*, 6 February 1916, 1:10.
85 'Reelection of Wilson Keynote at Syracuse', *NYS*, 1 March 1916, 7.
86 'Untermyer Won't Run', *NYT*, 9 August 1916, 7; 'Untermyer out of Race', *NYDT*, 9 August 1916, 9; 'Operation on Untermyer', *NYEP*, 14 September 1916, 1; 'Samuel Untermyer Undergoes Operation', *NYDT*, 15 September 1916, 2.
87 SU to WGM, 7 August 1916, Box 164, WGMP, LCMD, Washington, DC.
88 'Murphy Hears T.R. Wars on Whitman', *NYS*, 11 August 1916, 1.
89 *NYS*, 11 August 1916, 1.
90 'Watchful Rainbowing', *NYDT*, 22 September 1916, 8.
91 'Ex-U.S. Senator Dies on His 76th Birthday', *BDE*, 4 March 1945, 1, 28.
92 'Leaders Confident of Wilson Victory', *NYT*, 12 June 1916, 1.
93 Samuel Untermyer, *An Answer to Mr. Roosevelt – "The Only True American of Us All", Delivered at Newfield Maine, September 4th, 1916: Shall Invisible Government Be Restored? – The Only Real Issue, Delivered at Portland, Maine, September 7th, 1916* (New York: The Author, 1916), 1–38.
94 Untermyer, *Answer to Mr. Roosevelt*, 36.
95 SU to WGM, 13 September 1916; WGM to Robert W. Woolley, 14 September 1916, Box 166, WGMP, LCMD, DC.
96 SU to WGM, 8 September 1916, Box 166, WGMP, LCMD, DC; 'Rival Parties Claim Victory In Maine Today', *Chicago Daily Tribune*, 11 September 1916, 1–2.
97 *Chicago Daily Tribune*, 11 September 1916, 1–2.
98 'Republicans Win Sweeping Victory in Maine Election', *WES*, 12 September 1916, 1.
99 SU to WGM, 13 September 1916, Box 166, WGMP, LCMD, DC.
100 SU to WGM, 8 September 1916, Box 166; SU to WGM, 20 September 1916, Box 167, WGMP, LCMD, DC; Sophie Kerr, 'That Parkinson Affair', *McClure's Magazine*, September 1916, 15–17, 46–8.
101 WGM to SU, 12 September 1916, Box 166, WGMP, LCMD, DC.
102 SU to WGM, 13 September 1916, Box 166, WGMP, LCMD, DC.
103 Harrison S. Morris to Minnie Untermyer, 17 September 1916, Box 167, WGMP, LCMD, DC.

104 John W. Garrett to RL, 26 November 1917, File 763.72/8167, RG59, Records of the Department of State, NA, College Park, MD.
105 Wilson's Attorney General and Director of the Bureau of Investigation, Thomas W. Gregory, and A. Bruce Bielaski, respectively, found inaccuracies in Hulbert's account which raises questions about its reliability as an historical source.
   Thomas W. Gregory to A. Bruce Bielaski, 27 January 1925; A. Bruce Bielaski to Thomas W. Gregory, 3 February 1925, Box 2, Papers of Thomas Watt Gregory, LCMD, DC.
106 Mary Ann Hulbert, 'The Woodrow Wilson I Knew: 2', *Liberty Magazine*, 27 December 1924, 14–5; Mary Ann Hulbert, 'The Woodrow Wilson I Knew: 5', *Liberty Magazine*, 17 January 1925, 21–2.
107 'Senate Softens Toward Brandeis', *NYT*, 30 January 1916, 1:1.
108 SU to LDB, 28 January 1916, Reel 44, LDBC, UA, UL, Louisville, KY.
109 SU to LDB, February 17, 1916, Reel 41, LDBC, UA, UL, Louisville, KY.
110 'Newspaper Specials', *WSJ*, 31 January 1916, 2.
111 Arthur Pound and Samuel Taylor Moore, eds, *They Told Barron: Conversations and Revelations of An American Pepys in Wall Street: The Notes of Clarence W. Barron* (New York: Harper & Brothers, 1930), 234–5.
112 'The Wall Street Straws', *WSJ*, 8 March 1916, 2.
113 SU to WGM, 30 January 1916, Box 154, WGMP, LCMD, DC.
114 'Taft Opposes Brandeis', *NYT*, 15 March 1916, 4.
115 'Brilliant Diplomacy of President in Grave National Crisis Insures His Reelection, Untermyer Holds', *Washington Post*, 6 March 1916, 3.
116 'Look on Brandeis As A Great Jurist', *NYT*, 3 June 1916, 7; Richard M. Abrams, 'Woodrow Wilson and the Southern Congressmen', *Journal of Southern History* 22, no. 4 (1956), 430–1.
117 Joseph L. Morrison, 'A Southern Philo-Semite: Josephus Daniels of North Carolina', *Judaism* 12, no. 1 (1963): 83–4.
118 'Untermyer May Get Brandeis Nomination', *Washington Herald*, 10 May 1916, 4.
119 'The Paramount Issue: Character', *The North American Review*, November 1916, 648.
120 Walter F. Pratt, *The Supreme Court Under Edward Douglass White, 1910–1921* (Columbia: University of South Carolina Press, 1999), 156; Artemus Ward, *Deciding to Leave: The Politics of Retirement from the United States Supreme Court* (Albany: State University of New York Press, 2003), 112–13.
121 'Untermyer Operated Upon', *NYT*, 15 September 1916, 22.
122 'Untermyer Recovering Rapidly', *NYT*, 2 October 1916, 22.
123 WW to SU, 10 October 1916, WWP, LCMD, Washington, DC.
124 SU to WW, 14 October 1916, WWP, LCMD, Washington, DC.
125 Entry for 23 October 1916, Volume 4, 263–4, EMHD, MA, YUL, New Haven, CT.
126 SU to WW, 14 October 1916, WWP, LCMD, Washington, DC.
127 SU to WGM, 28 October 1916, Box 230, WGMP, LCMD, DC.
128 Samuel Untermyer, *A Historical Review of Mr. Hughes' Surrenders to Invisible Government: An Address Delivered at the New Star Casino, New York City, October 30, 1916* (New York: The Author, 1916).
129 Untermyer, *Hughes' Surrenders*, 6–7.
130 Untermyer had known Elkus since 1887 and he was one of his oldest friends. Elkus was a fellow Jewish lawyer with progressive beliefs.

SU to Martin H. Glynn, 23 December 1912, WWP, LCMD, Washington, DC; 'Abram Elkus Dies; Diplomat, Lawyer', *NYT*, 16 October 1947, 27.
131 WGM and Mrs W.G. McAdoo to SU and Mrs Samuel Untermyer, 10 November 1916, Box 169, WGMP, LCMD, Washington, DC.
132 SU and Mrs Samuel Untermyer to WGM and Mrs W.G. McAdoo, 9 November 1916, Box 169, WGMP, LCMD, Washington, DC.
133 'Samuel Untermyer Is Ill', *NYT*, 19 January 1917, 4.
134 'Untermyer Assails Peace Leak Inquiry', *NYT*, 20 January 1917, 1.
135 U.S. Department of State, *Papers Relating to the Foreign Relations of the United States with the Address of the President to Congress, December 4, 1917* (Washington, DC: G.P.O., 1926), 312.
136 SU to RL, 31 January 1917, File 818.00764, RG59, Records of the Department of State, NA, College Park, MD.
137 U.S. Department of State, *Papers Relating to the Foreign Relations of the United States: The Lansing Papers, 1914–1920: II* (Washington, DC: G.P.O., 1940), 518.
138 WGM to SU, 19 February 1917, File 818.00/108-1/2, RG59, Records of the Department of State, NA, College Park, MD.
139 SU to RL, 26 June 1917; Richard Crane to SU, 26 June 1915; SU to Richard Crane, 26 June 1917, Vol. 36, RLP, LCMD, Washington, DC.
140 WJB to RL, 30 July 1918, Vol. 37, RLP, LCMD, Washington, DC.
141 RL to WJB, 14 August 1918, Vol. 38, RLP, LCMD, Washington, DC.
142 WW to RL, 27 June 1919, Vol. 44, RLP, LCMD, Washington, DC.
143 George W. Baker, Jr., 'Wilson's Use of the Non-Recognition Policy in Costa Rica', *The Americas* 22, no. 1 (1965): 16–21.
144 'Senate Will Put Mitchel At Mercy of Tammany Foes', *NYT*, 29 March 1917, 1, 3; 'Senate Indorses Wagner, Ending Mitchel Inquiry', *NYT*, 5 April 1917, 1, 11.
145 'Mayor Will Fight, He Tells Citizens at Great Meeting', *NYT*, 2 October 1917, 1.
146 SU to WGM, 18 June 1917, Box 182, WGMP, LCMD, Washington, DC.
147 SU to WGM, 14 August 1917, Folder 7, Box 1, MS 251, SUP, AJA, Cincinnati, OH; Zosa Szajkowski, 'The Jews and New York City's Mayoralty Election of 1917', *Jewish Social Studies* 32, no. 4 (1970): 295–6; Howe, *Our Fathers*, 320.
148 SU to WGM, 1 November 1917, Box 190, WGMP, LCMD, Washington, DC.
149 Summary of Address of Mr. Samuel Untermyer Delivered at Hunt's Point Casino, Bronx, Thursday Evening, 1 November 1917, Box 190, WGMP, LCMD, Washington, DC.
150 'A Warning', *NYT*, 3 November 1917, 14.
151 SU to Samuel Shulman, 5 November 1917, Folder 17, Box 4, MS 90, Samuel Shulman Collection, AJA, Cincinnati, OH.
152 Samuel Shulman to SU, 7 November 1917, Folder 17, Box 4, MS 90, Samuel Shulman Collection, AJA, Cincinnati, OH.
153 JMB to SU, 7 November 1917, Folder 1, Box 1, MS 251, SUC, AJA, Cincinnati, OH.
154 Grover A. Whalen, *Mr. New York: The Autobiography of Grover A. Whalen* (New York: G.P. Putnam's Sons, 1955), 52.
155 SU to WRH, 5 July 1918, Folder 6, Box 1, MS 251, SUC, AJA, Cincinnati, OH.
156 Klein, *My Last Fifty Years*, 172; Whalen, *Mr. New York*, 35–8.
157 Alay K. Mehrotra, 'Lawyers, Guns, and Public Moneys: The U.S. Treasury, World War I, and the Administration of the Modern Fiscal State', *Law and History Review* 28, no. 1 (2010): 174–5.
158 SU to WGM, 26 April 1917, Box 178, WGMP, LCMD, Washington, DC.

159 SU to George R. Cooksey, 25 November 1917, Box 192, WGMP, LCMD, Washington, DC.
160 George R. Cooksey to SU, 28 November 1917, Box 192, WGMP, LCMD, Washington, DC.
161 SU to WGM, 12 January 1918, Box 194, WGMP, LCMD, Washington, DC; 'New Internal Revenue Solicitor Appointed', *Washington Herald*, 6 January 1918, 12.
162 SU to WGM, 2 December 1917, Box 192, WGMP, LCMD, Washington, DC.
163 Francis William O'Brien, ed., *The Hoover-Wilson Wartime Correspondence, September 24, 1914, to November 11, 1918* (Ames, IA: Iowa State University Press, 1974), 125–6.
164 O'Brien, *Hoover-Wilson*, 127–8.
165 'Lunch Puzzles Politicians', *NYDT*, 21 April 1920, 2.
166 'Government Operation of All Railroads in U.S. Will Begin at Noon Tomorrow', *WES*, 27 December 1917, 1.
167 SU to WGM, 27 December 1917, Box 193, WGMP, LCMD, Washington, DC; WGM to SU, 28 December 1917, Box 193, WGMP, LCMD, Washington, DC.
168 Dale N. Shook, 'William G. McAdoo and the Development of National Economic Policy, 1913–1918' (PhD diss., University of Cincinnati, Cincinnati, OH, 1975), 317.
169 SU to WGM, 12 January 1918, Box 194, WGMP, LCMD, Washington, DC.
170 SU to WGM, 23 January 1918, Box 195, WGMP, LCMD, Washington, DC.
171 WGM to SU, 28 January 1918, Box 195, WGMP, LCMD, Washington, DC.
172 'Railroad Owners Organize', *Syracuse Journal*, 24 May 1917, 9; 'Gossip of the Street', *Philadelphia Evening Public Ledger*, 9 May 1918, 15.
173 SU to WGM, 17 May 1918, Box 204; SU to M.B. Claggett, 8 June 1918, Box 206, SU to WGM, 9 August 1918; WGM to SU, 10 August 1918; SU to WGM, 17 August 1918; WGM to SU, 19 August 1918, Box 208; WGMP, LCMD, Washington, DC; Samuel Untermyer, *Brief on Behalf of National Association of Owners of Railroad Securities* (Washington, DC: The Author, 1918); 'M'Adoo Gives Out Text of Rail Contract', *NYDT*, 6 September 1918, 1, 12; 'The Compensation Contract', *Railway Age*, 13 September 1918, 469-70; 'Director General Declines Proposal for Test Suit on Compensation Contract', *Railway Age*, 27 September 1918, 577; Samuel Untermyer, *The Operating Contract and the Future of Railroad Securities Thereunder: An Address Delivered Before the American Bankers Association at Chicago, September 24, 1918* (New York: The Author, 1918).
174 SU to WGM, 17 May 1918, Box 204, WGMP, LCMD, Washington, DC.
175 'McAdoo Quits as Treasury Head and Rail Chief', *NYDT*, 23 November 1918, 1–2.
176 SU to WGM, 23 November 1918, Box 214, WGMP, LCMD, DC.
177 *NYT*, 9 April 1918, 20.
178 'Untermyer Assails $5,000,000,000 Gift', *NYT*, 27 April 1918, 6.
179 'Search for German Stock Was Blocked', *NYT*, 16 May 1918, 10.
180 Entry for 14 February 1919, Volume 7: 1 January 1919–29 June 1919, 49; Entries for 20 November 1919, 31 January 1920, 16 March 1920, 16 August 1920; Volume 8: 14 July 1919–1921, I:64, II:8, II:31, II:83, EMHD, MA, YUL, New Haven, CT.
181 'Palmer Answers Untermyer Attack', *NYT*, 20 January 1921, 3.
182 Entry for 7 July 1918, Volume 6, I:178, EMHD, MA, YUL, New Haven, CT; 'Lindheim Held in $5,000 Bail', *NYT*, 19 April 1919, 12; 'Dr. Rumely's Trial Opens', *NYT*, 4 November 1920, 22, Arthur Garfield Hays, *City Lawyer: The Autobiography of a Law Practice* (New York: Simon and Schuster, 1942), 78–94.
183 Stanley Cohen, *A. Mitchell Palmer: Politician* (New York: Columbia University Press, 1963), 119–21.

184 Epstein, *Profiles*, 182.
185 'Meyer London Wins in 12th District', *NYH*, 4 November 1920, 8.
186 Senate, *German and Bolshevik Propaganda*, 1444–8, 1456, 1537.
187 'Untermyer Again Defends Loyalty', *NYT*, 8 December 1918, I:3–4.
188 Senate, *German and Bolshevik Propaganda*, 1446–7.
189 Senate, *German and Bolshevik Propaganda*, 1547.
190 'Untermyer Denies Aiding Propaganda', *NYT*, 18 December 1918, 1, 3.
191 Senate, *German and Bolshevik Propaganda*, 1835–1910; Bernstorff, *My Three Years*, 36–7.
192 SU to Thomas W. Gregory, 26 December 1918, File 198437-11, RG60, Records of the Department of Justice, NA, College Park, MD.
193 Thomas W. Gregory to SU, 22 February 1919, File 198437-11, RG60, Records of the Department of Justice, NA, College Park, MD.
194 SU to Thomas W. Gregory: Letter 1, 1 March 1919, File 198437-11, RG60, Records of the Department of Justice, NA, College Park, MD.
195 SU to Thomas W. Gregory: Letter 2, 1 March 1919, File 198437-11, RG60, Records of the Department of Justice, NA, College Park, MD.
196 'Palmer Retorts to Untermyer', *NYT*, 26 January 1921, 3.
197 W.L. Hurley, State Department, to J. Edgar Hoover, 16 February 1921, File 9-5-1487-8, RG60, Records of the Department of Justice, NA, College Park, MD.
198 SAMUEL UNTERMYER – Activities – Information from files of State Department, 24 February 1921, File 9-5-1487-10, RG60, Records of the Department of Justice, NA, College Park, MD.
199 J. Edgar Hoover to Brigadier-General C. E. Nolan, 22 February 1921, File 9-5-1487-4, RG60, Records of the Department of Justice, NA, College Park, MD.
200 SU to WJB, 22 December 1919, Box 32, WJBP, LCMD, Washington, DC.
201 SU to WGM, 29 February 1920, Box 230, WGMP, LCMD, DC.
202 'Evasive Irwin Untermyer', *NYDT*, 2 November 1919, 3:1.
203 Max Jordan, 'Amerika und das neue Deutschland', *Berliner Tageblatt und Handels-Zeitung: Morgen Ausgabe*, 1 January 1925, 1–2. [Translated by Doris Jaeger.]
204 Joseph W. Folk to BC, 12 June 1920, Box 3, BCP, LCMD, Washington, DC.
205 SU to BC, 29 July 1920, File 763.72119/11145, File 364.64/390, RG59, Records of the Department of State, NA, College Park, MD.
206 Joseph W. Folk to BC, 12 June 1920, Box 3, BCP, LCMD, Washington, DC.
207 *Register of the Department of State: 1 May 1922* (Washington, DC: Government Printing Office, 1922), 101.
208 Richard Breitman and Allan J. Lichtman, *FDR and the Jews* (Cambridge, MA: Harvard University Press, 2013), 144.
209 William R. Castle, Jr., to George Howland Shaw, 18 June 1920, Box 3, BCP, LCMD, Washington, DC.
210 BC to Joseph W. Folk, 21 June 1920, Box 3, BCP, LCMD, Washington, DC.
211 Joseph W. Folk to BC, 12 July 1920, Box 3, BCP, LCMD, Washington, DC.
212 SU to BC, 29 July 1920, File 763.72119/11145, RG59, Records of the Department of State, NA, College Park, Md.
213 Joseph W. Folk to BC, 12 August 1920, File 763.72119/11146, RG59, Records of the Department of State, NA, College Park, MD.
214 Joseph W. Folk to James H. Beck, 4 October 1920, File 763.72119/11147, RG59, Records of the Department of State, NA, College Park, MD.
215 Samuel Untermyer, 'Domestic Issues of the Campaign', *NYT*, 18 July 1920, II:6.
216 SU to Eugene Untermyer, 7 February 1920, FUPP, Evanston, IL.

217 'Borah Will Widen Party Fund Inquiry', *NYT*, 20 October 1924, 1–2; 'Dry Law Scandal Seen By Untermyer', *NYT*, 23 October 1924, 1, 6; 'Republicans Raise $487,027 In 5 Days; Total Is $2,187,027', *NYT*, 24 October 1924, 1.
218 U.S. Senate, Special Committee to Investigate Contributions and Expenditures of Any and All Candidates for President, Vice President, Presidential Electors, and Senators of the United States, Transcript of Hearings Held in Chicago, 29–31 October 1924, 1–3, Senate Library, Washington, DC.
219 'Borah Goes West to Question Butler', *NYT*, 28 October 1924, 1, 6.
220 'Demand New Curb on Campaign Funds', *NYT*, 6 November 1924, 1, 3.
221 Richard Boeckel, *Presidential Campaign Funds* (Washington, DC: Editorial Research Reports, 1928), http://library.cqpress.com/cqresearcher/cqresrre1928040600, accessed 13 August 2020.
222 'Lockwood Retires from Public Life', *NYT*, 1 July 1922, 1.
223 'M. Maldwin Fertig', in *National Cyclopædia of American Biography: Current Volume F: 1939–1942* (New York: James T. White & Company, 1942), 191.
224 'Jury to Be Asked to Indict Four in Building Graft', *NYT*, 30 October 1920, 1, 12.
225 'Untermyer to Aid Inquiry into Building Costs', *NYDT*, 15 October 1920, 21.
226 'The Farcical Martin Act', *NYT*, 20 July 1923, 12.
227 State of New York, *Legislative Document No. 48: Final Report of the Joint Legislative Committee on Housing* (Albany: J.B. Lyon Company, Printers, 1923), 89–102.
228 *Legislative Document No. 48*, 98.
229 *Legislative Document No. 48*, 105.
230 'Stocks React After Early Advance', *PI*, 16 December 1922, 22.
231 'Plans State Law for Labor Unions', *NYT*, 15 December 1922, 7.
232 'Assembly Buries 3 Untermyer Bills, And Blue Sky Curbs', *NYT*, 23 March 1923, 1.
233 Samuel Untermyer, *Stop Thief! A Constructive Attack on Bucket Shops, "Blue Sky" Stocks, and Market Manipulation* (Washington, DC: People's Legislative Service, 1923), 6.
234 Arthur J. Waterman, Jr., 'New York Solves Transit Problems', *National Municipal Review* 29, no. 11 (1940): 728–35, 766.
235 Samuel Untermyer, *A Constructive Criticism of the Transit Plan: Address by Samuel Untermyer Before the City Club, Thursday, October 13th, 1921* (New York: The Author, 1921); 'Untermyer Pleads for Municipal Domination of Operating Companies', *NYT*, 31 December 1921, 24; 'State Board Starts On A Transit Plan; Untermyer To Aid', *NYT*, 14 December 1926, 1, 14; Samuel Untermyer, *Report and Recommendations of Special Counsel to the Transit Commission on Proposed Plan of Readjustment Directed by Legislature* (New York: The Author, 1927); Samuel Untermyer, *Report of Special Counsel to the Transit Commission Accompanying Proposed Tentative Plan of Readjustment* (New York: The Author, 1928); Samuel Untermyer, *Second Supplemental Report of Special Counsel to the Transit Commission on the Unification of the Rapid Transit Lines Accompanying Proposed Legislation And Proposed Plan of Unification* (New York: The Author, 1930); Samuel Untermyer, *Proposed Alternative Plan for the Unification by Recapture or Purchase of All or Part of the Rapid Transit Railroads in the City of New York* (New York: The Author, 1931); Samuel Untermyer, *Report and Recommendations of Mr. Samuel Untermyer on Transit and His Letter of Resignation As Special Counsel* (New York: The Author, 1931); Samuel Untermyer, *The Solution of the Transit Problem: An Address by Samuel Untermyer, Broadcast by Station WOR, Thursday Evening, June 16, 1932* (New York: The Author, 1932).

236 Samuel Untermyer, *The Social and Economic Justice and Wisdom of Maintaining a Five-Cent Fare: Address Before the Summer Class in Government and Sociology at the College of the City of New York Thursday, August 8, 1929* (New York: The Author, 1929).

237 Clifton Hood, *722 Miles: The Building of The Subways and How They Transformed New York* (New York: Simon & Schuster, 1993), 221–2.

238 Fertig had been appointed to the commission by Governor Lehman earlier in 1938. He was a friend of Untermyer and had been a member of the board of directors of the Non-Sectarian Anti-Nazi League since 1934.
Ezekiel Rabinowitz to Bertha V. Corets, 30 June 1934, Folder 1, Box 1, MS 307, Bertha Corets Papers, AJA, Cincinnati, OH; 'Maldwin Fertig, Legislator, Dies', *NYT*, 24 July 1972, 30.

239 'City Bonds to Buy Subways Proposed', *NYT*, 1 May 1938, 2:1; 'Transit Unity Debt is Put Up in Albany', *NYT*, 11 May 1938, 1, 6.

240 'Parley Passes Transit Plan', *BDE*, 18 August 1938, 1–2; 'Boro Leaders Hail Victory on Amendments', *BDE*, 10 November 1938, 7.

241 George J. Lankevich, *American Metropolis: A History of New York City* (New York: New York University Press, 1998), 177.

242 'Felix Rohatyn, 91, Who Kept City Finances Afloat, Dies', *NYT*, 16 December 2019, A26.

243 'Untermyer's Aid on City Financing and Transit Asked', *NYT*, 7 July 1933, 1, 10.

244 'New City Tax Bill Is Voted in Senate but Faces Defeat', *NYT*, 18 August 1933, 1, 4; 'City Taxes Blocked by Assembly Snarl', *NYT*, 19 August 1933, 12.

245 'Six Aid Untermyer In Finance Reform', *NYT*, 21 August 1933, 1, 6.

246 City of New York, Board of Estimate and Apportionment, Report and Recommendations of Samuel Untermyer (New York: The Board, 1933); 'Drastic City Tax Program Submitted by Untermyer', *NYT*, 8 September 1933, 1, 12.

247 'Brokers Push Plan to Move Exchange in City Tax Fight', *NYT*, 14 September 1933, 1, 16.

248 'City to Drop Stock Tax If Exchange Will Remain', *NYT*, 26 September 1933, 1–2.

249 'Banks Agree to City Finance Plan', *NYT*, 28 September 1933, 1.

250 Hebert H. Lehman Oral History: 1, 178–9, Herbert H. Lehman Papers, CUL, New York, NY; SU to John B. O'Brien, 1 November 1933, Box 22, Series IV, RG 001.JPO: Office of the Mayor, John P. O'Brien, Municipal Archives, New York, NY.

251 SU to Fiorella H. La Guardia, 10 May 1934, Frame 2467, Roll 185, Subject Files – Personal Correspondence 'U', RG 001.FHL: Office of the Mayor, Fiorello H. La Guardia, Municipal Archives, New York, NY.

252 'Favor Untermyer For Stock Inquiry', *NYT*, 14 April 1932, 33; James Burk, 'The Origins of Federal Securities Regulation: A Case Study in the Social Control of Finance', *Social Forces* 63, no. 4 (1985): 1023.

253 Raymond Moley, *After Seven Years* (New York: Harper & Brothers Publishers, 1939), 84, 176.

254 Drew Pearson and Robert S. Allen, 'How Untermyer's Whim Led to the Great Stock Market Fight', *The Daily Washington Merry-Go-Round*, 8 May 1934, 1, https://dra.american.edu/islandora/object/pearson:33735#page/1/mode/1up, accessed 6 April 2021.

255 'Stock Regulation May be Albany Topic', *NYT*, 2 January 1933, 37.

256 'Untermyer Urges Unification Delay', *NYT*, 4 January 1933, 3; 'Roosevelt's Policies to Ultimately Aid Recovery, Samuel Untermyer Says', *San Bernardino Sun*, 7 January 1933, 11.

257 'Untermyer Urges Stock Regulation', *NYT*, 9 January 1933, 21.
258 Untermyer had contributed $25,000 to Al Smith's presidential campaign in 1928 which suggests he was more confident he would receive recognition from him than Roosevelt.
U.S. Congress, Senate, Report No. 2024, *Presidential Campaign Expenditures* (Washington, DC: G.P.O., 1929), 31; 'How the Small Fry Got Paid Off', *In Fact*, 17 March 1941, 3; Ralph Robert Stackman, 'Laurence A. Steinhardt: New Deal Diplomat, 1933–1945' (PhD diss., Michigan State University, Ann Arbor, IN, 1967), 1.
259 Frank Freidel, *Franklin D. Roosevelt: Launching the New Deal* (Boston: Little, Brown and Company, 1973), 362.
260 After four years as ambassador to Sweden, Roosevelt appointed him ambassador to Peru in 1937. Two years later he was promoted to ambassador to the Soviet Union. In 1942 he was appointed ambassador to Turkey, followed by Czechoslovakia in 1945, and Canada in 1948. His career as one of America's most senior diplomats was cut short by his untimely death in an air crash in 1950.
LAS to SU, 23 February 1933, Letterbook 1933, Box 75, LASP, LCMD, Washington, DC; 'Steinhardt, 4 Others Killed When Plane Falls in Canada', *NYT*, 29 March 1950, 1, 14; 'Laurence A. Steinhardt', in *National Cyclopædia of American Biography* 40 (New York: James T. White & Company, 1955), 70; Barry Rubin, 'Ambassador Laurence A. Steinhardt: The Perils of a Jewish Diplomat, 1940–1945', *American Jewish History* 70, no. 3 (1981): 331–46; Dennis J. Dunn, *Caught Between Roosevelt & Stalin: America's Ambassadors to Moscow* (Lexington, KY: The University Press of Kentucky, 1998), 95–144; Igor Lukes, 'Ambassador Laurence Steinhardt: From New York to Prague', *Diplomacy & Statecraft* 17, no. 3 (2006): 523–45; David Mayers, 'The Great Patriotic War, FDR's Embassy Moscow, and Soviet—US Relations', *International History Review* 33, no. 2 (2011): 299–333; Norman Eisen, *The Last Palace: Europe's Extraordinary Century Through Five Lives and One House in Prague* (London: Headline, 2018), 177–240.
261 'Financial Troubles Blamed on Morgan', *Los Angeles Examiner*, 28 February 1933, Folder 11, Box 1782, Collection 7000.1c, Hearst Corporation Los Angeles Examiner photographs, negatives and clippings--portrait files (N-Z), Regional History Collection, University of Southern California, Los Angeles, CA; Samuel Untermyer, *Federal Regulation of the Stock Exchange; Address by Samuel Untermyer Before the Law Alumni of the University of Southern California, March 8, 1933* (New York: The Author, 1933).
262 Untermyer, *Federal Regulation of the Stock Exchange*, 1.
263 'Untermyer Considered', *NYT*, 30 March 1933, 24.
264 Moley, *Seven Years*, 177.
265 Michael Perino, *The Hellhound of Wall Street: How Ferdinand Pecora's Investigation of the Great Crash Forever Changed American Finance* (New York: Penguin Books, 2010), 107–8, 217–8, 282–3.
266 Freidel, *Roosevelt*, 341–6; Moley, 177–83, 284; Anthony J. Badger, *FDR: The First Hundred Days* (New York: Hill and Wang, 2008), 124.
267 Samuel Untermyer, *A Friendly Criticism of the Stock Exchange Bill: An Address By Samuel Untermyer Before the Los Angeles Breakfast Club, February 21st, 1934* (New York: The Author, 1934); Samuel Untermyer, *Is the Reign of the Money Trust Over Government Ended or Only Suspended?: An Address at the Community Playhouse Pasadena, February 26th, 1934* (New York: The Author, 1934).

268 SU to Raymond Moley, 27 January 1934; 'The Outlaw Stock Exchange' by Samuel Untermyer, 27 February 1933, File No.6, Box No.56, Raymond Moley Papers, Hoover Institution Archives, Palo Alto, CA; Samuel Untermyer, 'A Plan for Regulating the Stock Exchange', *Today*, 27 January 1934, 3–4, 22.
269 U.S. Congress, Senate, Committee on Banking and Currency, *Stock Exchange Practices: Hearings Before the Senate Committee on Banking and Currency: 16, National Securities Act (Continued) March 23 to April 5, 1934*, 73rd Cong., 2nd sess. (Washington, DC: G.P.O., 1934), 7704.
270 Senate, *Stock Exchange Practices*, 7701–47.
271 Senate, *Stock Exchange Practices*, 7747.
272 'Will New Stock Exchange Law Check Gambling?', *BDE*, 7 June 1934, 19.
273 U.S. Congress, Senate, Subcommittee of the Committee on Banking and Currency, *Regulation of Sale of Securities: Hearing on S. 2344, A Bill to Provide for the Regulation of the Sale of Certain Securities in Interstate and Foreign Commerce, and the Trust Indentures under Which the Same Are Issued, and for Other Purposes*, 75th Cong., 1st sess. (Washington, DC: G.P.O., 1937), 99.
274 Senate, *Sale of Securities*, 94–103.
275 'Trust Indenture Bill Is Signed by President', *PI*, 5 August 1939, 20.
276 Untermyer, *Stop Thief*, 3.

Chapter 4

1 This chapter is derived, in part, from an article published in *Australian Journal of Jewish Studies* 21 (2007).
2 A term used by Cohen to describe the German American leaders of the American Jewish community.
   Cohen, *Jacob H. Schiff*, 44.
3 Emanuel Neumann, *In the Arena: An Autobiographical Memoir* (New York: Herzl Press, 1976), 60.
4 Pak, *Gentlemen Bankers*, 29.
5 'Editorial Notes', *The New Palestine*, 14 October 1921, 1.
6 Weinstein, *Ardent Eighties*, 101.
7 Board of Trustees Minute Book, 1893–1897, Folder 2, Box 3a, MS 547, Temple Emanu-El (New York, NY) Records, AJA, Cincinnati, OH. [Transcribed by Frank Untermyer.]
8 'Mr Untermyer Lays Cornerstone', *Jewish Exponent*, 29 March 1912, 7; Morris Freudenheim to SU, 13 September 1920, Folder 21, Box 58, MS 359, LMC, AJA, Cincinnati, OH; Untermyer, *Ideals of Zionism*, 1.
9 Theresa M. Collins, *Otto Kahn: Art, Money, & Modern Time* (Durham, NC: University of North Carolina Press, 2002), 120–1, 259–62.
10 SU to ASO, 23 March 1901, b42, f.13–15, NYTCR: ASOP, NYPL, New York, NY.
11 This is a reference to Stephen Birmingham's book *Our Crowd*. He mistakenly omits Untermyer from New York's Jewish elite. However, he does include his law firm partner, Louis Marshall.
   Stephen Birmingham, *'Our Crowd': The Great Jewish Families of New York* (London: Futura, 1985), 374.

12 'The Charity Ball and Banquet', *Jewish Messenger*, 14 January 1898, 2.
13 *Proceedings of the Seventieth Annual Meeting of the Hebrew Benevolent and Orphan Society of the City of New York Held at The Asylum, Sunday, April 30th, 1893* (New York: Stettiner, Lambert & Co., 1893), 82.
14 'The Montefiore Home', AH, 10 January 1896, 290; 'The Montefiore League Ball', *Jewish Messenger*, 12 February 1897, 2; 'Montefiore Home for Chronic Invalids', AH, 19 November 1897, 79; 'No Damages For His Death', NYH, 12 February 1898, 12; 'Montefiore Home', *Jewish Messenger*, 18 November 1898, 7; 'Montefiore Home', *Jewish Messenger*, 9 November 1900, 7-8.
15 Cohen, *Jacob H. Schiff*, 64-9.
16 Young Men's Hebrew Association to SU, 11 November 1920, Folder 21, Box 58, MS 359, LMC, AJA, Cincinnati, OH.
17 'To Establish a Yonkers Y.M.H.A.', NYT, 20 May 1912, 2; 'New York Happenings', *American Israelite* 18 January 1912, 2.
18 'Mme. Pevsner at Y.W.H.A. Meeting', *Yonkers Stateman*, 23 November 1916, 3.
19 'Urge Harder Work for Jewish Relief', NYT, 12 December 1917, 15.
20 George Kupsky, 'Germanness and Jewishness: Samuel Untermyer, Felix Warburg, and National Socialism, 1914-1938' *AJAJ* 63, no. 2 (2011): 27.
21 Untermyer told Marshall after he joined his firm that this was the reason for his alliance with the Irish American–dominated New York City Democratic Party, popularly known as 'Tammany Hall', because 'between the Irish leaders of Tammany & the high-toned Jew-hating Presbyterians on the other side I consider Tammany the lesser evil for men of our race.'
SU to LM, 17 November 1894, Folder 3, Box 3, MS 359, LMC, AJA, Cincinnati, OH.
22 Henry Clay Silver to SU, 18 September 1920, Folder 21, Box 58, MS 359, LMC, AJA, Cincinnati, OH.
23 SU to Henry Clay Silver, 20 September 1920, Folder 21, Box 58, MS 359, LMC, AJA, Cincinnati, OH.
24 SU to Henry Ford, 13 August 1920, Folder 21, Box 58, MS 359, LMC, AJA, Cincinnati, OH.
25 'How the Jews Rule and Ruin Tammany Hall', *Dearborn Independent*, 24 September 1921, 8-9; 'Jew Wires Direct Tammany's Gentile Puppets', *Dearborn Independent*, 1 October 1921, 8-9.
26 *Dearborn Independent*, 1 October 1921, 8-9.
27 'Ford A 'Mad Hatter' Untermyer Says', NYT, 5 December 1921, 33.
28 Victoria Saker Woeste, *Henry Ford's War on Jews and the Legal Battle Against Hate Speech* (Stanford, CA: Stanford University Press, 2012), 87.
29 Allan L. Benson, 'Henry Ford Has Nothing Against the Jew', *Bridgeport Times*, 6 January 1922, 5.
30 'Gave No Facts on Jews, Claim of Bernstein', *Chicago Evening American*, 9 January 1922, 5.
31 Woeste, *Henry Ford's War*, 113-16.
32 'A Glimpse of International Jewish Politics: Herman Bernstein Brings Home A Whopper', *Dearborn Independent*, 20 August 1921, 8-9; 'Editor to Sue Ford', NYT, 9 July 1923, 17.
33 NYT, 9 July 1923, 17.
34 Herman Bernstein to SU, 17 September 1923, Folder 352 'U', R.G.713 (Bernstein), Yivo Institute for Jewish Research, New York, NY.

35 Woeste, *Henry Ford's War*, 116-17.
36 Charles Reznikoff, ed., *Louis Marshall, Champion of Liberty: Selected Papers and Addresses: 1* (Philadelphia: Jewish Publication Society of America, 1957), 381.
37 Woeste, *Henry Ford's War*, 117, 289.
38 Robert S. Rifkind, 'Confronting Antisemitism in America: Louis Marshall and Henry Ford', *American Jewish History* 94, no. 1/2 (2008): 82; Victoria Saker Woeste, 'Insecure Equality: Louis Marshall, Henry Ford, and the Problem of Defamatory Antisemitism, 1920-1929', *Journal of American History* 91, no. 3 (2004): 902-3; Interview with Frank Untermyer, 25-28 April 2000.
39 Supreme Court of the State of New York, County of New York, Herman Bernstein, Plaintiff, against Henry Ford and the Dearborn Publishing Company, Defendants, 1923 Folder 1, Box 122, Accession 1; E.G. Liebold to Charles S. Whitman, 24 July 1923, Folder 572, Box 203, Accession 285; Charles S. Whitman to Henry Ford, 18 July 1923; GU&M to Whitman, Ottinger & Ransom, 12 July 1923; Henry A. Patten to E.G. Liebold, 22 August 1923; E.G. Liebold to Corn Exchange Bank, 20 August 1923, Folder 32, Box 156, Accession 285, Henry Ford Museum, Dearborn, MI.

Unfortunately, no correspondence from Henry Ford himself regarding the Bernstein case has survived. The relevant file in the Henry Ford Office Papers is empty.

Cathleen Latendresse, Henry Ford Museum Research Services, to Richard Hawkins, 15 October 2001.
40 LAS to SU: Memorandum Re: Bernstein v. Ford, 23 May 1927; Brief: United States District Court, Southern District of New York, Herman Bernstein v. Henry Ford and the Dearborn Publishing Company, Plaintiff's Memorandum in Opposition to Defendant's Request for Leave to File an Additional Affidavit of Henry Ford to Vacate the Attachment and Dismiss the Complaint, Laurence A. Steinhardt, *c*. June 1925, FUPP, Evanston, IL; 'Henry Ford Is Rebuked For Delaying Trial Of $200,000 Libel Action', *NYEP*, 7 July 1925, 1.
41 Woeste, *Henry Ford's War*, 119-260.
42 Woeste, *Henry Ford's War*, 261-86.
43 'Assert Ford Acted Alone on Apology', *NYT*, 10 July 1927, 1, 18; Statement by Henry Ford to LM, 30 June 1927, FUPP, Evanston, IL.
44 Woeste, *Henry Ford's War*, 286-7.
45 Woeste, *Henry Ford's War*, 287.
46 Quoted in Woeste, *Henry Ford's War*, 287.
47 Reznikoff, *Louis Marshall: 1*, 376.
48 Quoted in Woeste, *Henry Ford's War*, 287-8.
49 Woeste, *Henry Ford's War*, 288.
50 Reznikoff, *Louis Marshall: 1*, 381.
51 'Sum Paid to Sapiro Is Put At $140,000', *NYT*, 19 July 1927, 13.
52 Woeste, *Henry Ford's War*, 289.
53 Henry Ford to Herman Bernstein, 23 July 1927, FUPP, Evanston, IL.
54 'Ford Again Recants; Bernstein Ends Suit', *NYT*, 25 July 1927, 1-2.
55 Herman Bernstein to SU, 4 August 1927, Folder 526 'U', R.G.713 (Bernstein), Yivo Institute for Jewish Research, New York, NY.
56 Woeste, *Henry Ford's War*, 289-90.
57 Woeste, *Henry Ford's War*, 300-10.
58 SU to Clifford B. Longley, 25 November 1927, Folder 3, Box 122, Accession 1, Henry Ford Museum, Dearborn, MI.

59 'Asks Ford to Press Ban on Sale of Book', *NYT*, 26 November 1927, 17.
60 Clifford B. Longley to SU, 16 December 1927, Folder 3, Box 122, Accession 1, Henry Ford Museum, Dearborn, MI.
61 'Greatest Day in Jewish History', *American Jewish World*, 16 November 1917, 3; 'Palestine Declared Jewish Homeland', *American Jewish World*, 30 April 1920, 2.
62 'Jews Rejoice Over Palestine Mandate', *American Jewish World*, 28 July 1922, 1.
63 'An Appeal to Jewry', *The Times* [London], 24 December 1920, 9; Joseph B. Schechtman, *Rebel and Statesman: The Vladimir Jabotinsky Story: The Early Years* (New York: Thomas Yoseloff, Inc., 1956), 370; The Erez Israel (Palestine) Foundation Fund Keren Hayesod Limited, Company No. 00173860, Registration Documents, 23 March 1921, https://find-and-update.company-information.service.gov.uk, accessed 30 October 2020.
64 Untermyer, *Ideals of Zionism*, 2.
65 Meyer had dated Untermyer's daughter Irene for several years. However, the future publisher of the *Washington Post* felt unable to marry her on a mere Lazard Frères clerk's salary.
   Merlo J. Pusey, *Eugene Meyer* (New York: Alfred A. Knopf, 1974), 28.
66 Melvin I. Urofsky, *American Zionism From Herzl To The Holocaust* (Garden City: Anchor Press, 1975), 120, 152–3; Urofsky and Levy, *Letters of Louis D. Brandeis: III*, 665–6; LDB to SU, 21 June 1915, Reel 72, LDBC, University Archives, University of Louisville, Louisville, KY; Melvin I. Urofsky and David W. Levy, ed., *Letters of Louis D. Brandeis: IV: 1916–1921: Mr. Justice Brandeis* (Albany: State University of New York Press, 1975), 246.
67 LDB to SU, 22 June 1915, Reel 72, LDBC, University Archives, University of Louisville, Louisville, KY.
68 Charles Israel Goldblatt, 'The Impact of the Balfour Declaration in America', *American Jewish Historical Quarterly* 57, no. 4 (1968): 458.
69 'Mrs. W. Rosenblatt, Wife of Financier', *NYT*, 3 April 1948, 15.
70 Bernard A. Rosenblatt, *Two Generations of Zionism: Historical Recollections of an American Zionist* (New York: Shengold Publishers, 1967), 200.
   William Rosenblatt was a classmate of Therese's brother Laurence at Columbia Law School.
   Felix H. Levy to SU, 7 September 1920; Therese Steinhardt to SU, 29 September 1920, Folder 21, Box 58, MS 359, LMC, AJA, Cincinnati, OH.
71 Bernard A. Rosenblatt to SU, 12 July 1919; Bernard A. Rosenblatt, 9 December 1919; SU to Bernard A. Rosenblatt, 18 December 1919; Bernard A. Rosenblatt to SU, 22 December 1919; SU to Bernard A. Rosenblatt, 24 December 1919, Folder 4, Box 3, MS 251, SUC, AJA, Cincinnati, OH.
72 Bernard A. Rosenblatt to SU, 29 October 1920, Folder 21, Box 58, MS 359, LMC, AJA, Cincinnati, OH.
73 Bernard A. Rosenblatt to SU, 1 November 1920; 7 November 1920, Folder 21, Box 58, MS 359, LMC, AJA, Cincinnati, OH.
74 Rosenblatt, *Two Generations*, 100.
75 'Samuel Untermyer's Zionism', *AH*, 28 October 1921, 631; Bernard A. Rosenblatt to CW, 8 February 1921, WA, Rehovot, Israel.
76 'Zionist Mission to America', *The Times* [London], 29 March 1921, 4; '"Don't Worry" Einstein Advises Public', *NYDT*, 4 April 1921, 9; 'Social Events', *AH*, 8 April 1921, 580.
   Einstein became a client and good friend of Untermyer. Untermyer also acted as his American banker and, for example, invested on his behalf some of the money

earned on his 1921 visit to the United States in American securities. Later in 1931 Untermyer handled Einstein's legal action against the unauthorized publication of a collection of his writings and speeches by the New York publisher Donald Friede. Einstein's visits to Untermyer's Palm Springs villa, *The Willows*, during the early 1930s were reported by newspapers throughout the United States. After Einstein's death in 1955 his estate entrusted Guggenheimer & Untermyer with carrying out his final wishes regarding his personal library, manuscripts and papers.

AE to SU, 15 September 1921, 45–158; AE to SU, 8 September 1924, 45–160; Elsa Einstein to SU, 25 February 1931, 42–59, AEP, JNUL, Jerusalem, Israel; 'Untermyer Host to Prof. Einstein', *Brooklyn Standard Union*, 26 January 1931, 4; '"Mystery" Woman is Einstein', *Los Angeles Times*, 27 February 1933, II-8; Coleman T. Mobley, 'Firm's Archives Reveal Rich History', *Legal Times*, 26 May 1986, 16.

77 'Seeks to Heal Zion Breach', *NYT*, 20 April 1921, 11.
78 Harry Barnard, *The Forging of An American Jew: The Life and Times of Judge Julian W. Mack* (New York: Herzl Press, 1974), 261–83; '$1,100,000 Is Added to Palestine Fund', *NYT*, 16 May 1920, 17.
79 SU to LM, 20 December 1894, Folder 3, Box 3, MS 359, LMC, AJA, Cincinnati, OH; 'Cook's Nile Service', *Egyptian Gazette*, 11 December 1894, 3.
80 Keren Hayesod Press Release, 16 May 1921, WA, Rehovot, Israel.
81 'The Merry Zionist War', *AH*, 20 May 1921, 1–2; 'Untermyer Upholds Weizmann in Zionist Controversy', *AH*, 20 May 1921, 17; 'From the Four Corners', *AH*, 8 June 1923, 80.
82 Rosenblatt, *Two Generations*, 97–101.
83 SU to CW, 2 August 1921, WA, Rehovot, Israel.
84 'Zionists Split on Palestine Fund', *NYH*, 8 June 1921, 2.
85 Rosenblatt, *Two Generations*, 97; Untermyer, *Ideals of Zionism*, 6–7.
86 Esther Panitz, 'Louis Dembitz Brandeis and the Cleveland Conference', *American Jewish Historical Quarterly* 65, no. 2 (1975): 161.
87 Maurice Samuel, *Report of the Proceedings of the 24th Annual Convention of the Zionist Organization of America* (New York: Zionist Organization of America, 1921), 22–4, 32–3, 35–7, 43, 61.
88 Samuel, *Zionist Organization of America*, 150.
89 *AH*, 20 May 1921, 1–2.
90 'Zionist Minority Organize to Fight', *NYT*, 8 June 1921, 17.
91 'Dr. Weizmann Leaves America', *American Jewish World*, 24 June 1921, 3.
92 'Twelfth Zionist Congress Opens on Sept. 4', *AH*, 26 August 1921, 358.
93 'To Hold Keren Hayesod Conference', *AH*, 11 November 1921, 706.
94 Maier Bryan Fox, 'American Zionism in the 1920s' (PhD diss., George Washington University, Washington, DC, 1979), 113.
95 Fox, 'American Zionism', 127.
96 AE to SU, 15 September 1921, 45 159, AEP, JNUL, Jerusalem, Israel. [Translated by Dr Peter Brown.]
97 'Keren Hayesod Thousand Dollar Club has 97 Members', *American Jewish World*, 7 April 1922, 2.
98 *AH*, 8 June 1923, 80.
99 Neumann, *In the Arena*, 61.
100 SU to CW, 28 June 1923, WA, Rehovot, Israel.
101 Neumann, *In the Arena*, 69.
102 Fox, 'American Zionism', 114–15.

103 Fox, 'American Zionism', 160; 'Untermyer-Schall', *NYT*, 23 November 1923, 17.
Shapiro incorrectly claims Untermyer resigned as president of the Keren Hayesod after the marriage.
Yonathan Shapiro, *Leadership of the American Zionist Organization, 1897–1930* (Urbana: University of Illinois Press, 1971), 228.
104 Emmanuel Neumann to CW, 27 May 1921, WA, Rehovot, Israel.
105 SU to CW, 28 September 1921, WA, Rehovot, Israel; 'The Carnegie Hall Meeting: $180,000 for Keren Hayesod', *The New Palestine*, 2 December 1921, 6.
106 Nahum Sokolow to CW, 23 June 1922, WA, Rehovot, Israel.
107 CW to Col. Frederick Hermann Kisch, 6 November 1923; CW to Sir John Shuckburgh, 26 December 1923, WA, Rehovot, Israel.
108 Draft of 'A Reply to Attacks Upon Zionism By Samuel Untermyer', 25 July 1921, WA, Rehovot, Israel.
109 Dennis Cohen to CW, 6 July 1921, WA, Rehovot, Israel.
110 Goldblatt, 'Balfour Declaration', 467.
111 Samuel Untermyer, 'Zionism a Just Cause', *The Forum*, September 1921, 224–6.
112 However, Morgenthau remained a good friend of Untermyer's former law firm partner, Louis Marshall, and nephew, Laurence A. Steinhardt.
LM to Henry Morgenthau, Sr., 30 April 1926, Henry Morgenthau, Sr., 1926 (Jan-Apr) Non-Family, Box 484; LAS to Henry Morgenthau, Sr., 28 April 1933, Henry Morgenthau, Sr., 1933 (Jan-July) Non-Family, Box 489, Morgenthau Papers, Franklin D. Roosevelt Library, Hyde Park, NY; Henry Morgenthau III, *Mostly Morgenthaus: A Family History* (New York: Ticknor & Fields, 1991), 208.
113 SSW to SU, 14 November 1921, Box 121-6, SSWC, RDFUASC, BU, Waltham, MA.
114 Untermyer, *Ideals of Zionism*, 1–2.
115 SU to LM, 16 February 1924, WA, Rehovot, Israel.
116 Pound and Moore, *They Told Barron*, 183.
117 Memorandum, 14 October 1921, WA, Rehovot, Israel.
118 'Mr. Untermyer's Zionism', *AH*, 28 October 1921, 629.
119 'Samuel Untermyer's Zioinism', *AH*, 28 October 1921, 631, 646.
120 SU to Samuel Shulman, 10 November 1921, Folder 17, Box 4, MS 90, Samuel Shulman Collection, AJA, Cincinnati, OH.
121 Morris S. Lazaron to SU, 1 November 1921, Folder 24, Box 8, MS 71, Morris S. Lazaron Collection, AJA, Cincinnati, OH.
122 The rumours were untrue. Hughes asked Untermyer not to make public a telegram to him regarding the rumours because it might compromise negotiations with the British government.
SU to Charles E. Hughes, 25 March 1922, File 867N.01/189, RG59, Records of the Department of State, NA, College Park, MD.
123 'Jews War Relief Drive Ends Tonight', *NYT*, 13 March 1922, 15.
124 '5,000 Begin Drive for Zionist Fund', *NYT*, 17 April 1922, 36.
125 'Untermyer Hits Back at Critics of Zionism', *NYT*, 3 May 1922, 24.
126 'Anti-Zionist Jews Scourged by Untermyer', *NYDT*, 3 May 1922, 13.
127 Samuel Untermyer, 'Building the Jewish Homeland', *Jewish Tribune*, 14 April 1922, 1.
128 *Jewish Tribune*, 14 April 1922, 1.
129 'Lord Balfour Opens Hebrew University in Jerusalem', *The Reform Advocate*, 18 April 1925, 28.
130 'Jewish News From Everywhere', *American Jewish World*, 9 October 1925, 4.
131 'Hails Palestine College', *NYT*, 6 April 1925, 19.

132 Steinhardt states she plans to travel to Palestine on her 1922 passport application. United States Passport Applications, 1795–1925, https://familysearch.org, accessed 6 April 2021.
133 Madeleine Steinhardt to CW, 18 December 1929, WA, Rehovot, Israel.
134 'Miss Steinhardt is Bride in Jerusalem of Major Partridge', *NYS*, 20 March 1924, 25.
135 'Captain Partridge', *Batavia Times*, 12 February 1927, 4.
136 Tyler Krahe, 'A History of Violence: British Colonial Policing in Ireland and the Palestine Mandate' (PhD diss., Eberly College at West Virginia University, Morgantown, WV, 2016), 43–6.
137 Memorandum: Major F. Partridge, Deputy Superintendent, Haifa, 10 December 1931, WA, Rehovot, Israel.
138 'Entertains King of Iraq: Mrs. Fred Partridge Gives Luncheon in Gaza', *NYT*, 28 August 1927, 33.
139 LAS to CW, 24 October 1929, WA, Rehovot, Israel.
140 'Untermyer Praises Work in Palestine', *NYT*, 15 May 1922, 6.
141 Lawrence Davidson, 'Zionism, Socialism and United States Support for the Colonization of Palestine in the 1920s', *Arab Studies Quarterly* 18, no. 3 (1996): 6.
142 Julian W. Mack to SU, 26 December 1918, Folder 8, Box 3, MS 251, SUC, AJA, Cincinnati, OH; Bernard G. Richards, 'The American Jewish Congress', in *The Jewish Communal Register of New York City, 1917–1918: Second Edition* (New York: Kehillah (Jewish Community) of New York City, 1918), 1429–44.
143 'Congress of Jews Pass Constitution', *PI*, 23 May 1922, 2; 'Bernard G. Richards, 94, Dies', *NYT*, 26 July 1971, 32.

Untermyer was re-elected at the fourth convention held in New York City in October 1923 and the fifth convention held in Philadelphia in October 1925. He did not stand for re-election as a vice-president of the AJCong at the sixth convention held in February 1927, and instead was elected as an honorary vice-president, a position he held until the seventh convention held in May 1929.

American Jewish Yearbook 26 (1924), 473; *American Jewish Yearbook* 28 (1926), 290; 'American Jewish Congress Appeals to World Public Opinion Against Mistreatment of Jews in Roumania', *JDB*, 24 February 1927, 7; 'American Jewish Congress Endorses Extension of Jewish Agency', *JDB*, 22 May 1929, 1.
144 'The American Jewish Congress', *AH*, 26 May 1922, 60.
145 'Samuel Untermyer's Advice to William G. McAdoo', *Jewish Criterion*, 18 July 1924, 3; 'Back Dr. Wise On Klan', *NYT*, 27 October 1924, 19; *Archives of Biography: Living Progressive Americans Prominent in the Social, Industrial and Financial World* (Chicago: American Blue Book Publishers, 1924), 333; James C. Prude, 'William Gibbs McAdoo and the Democratic National Convention of 1924', *Journal of Southern History* 38, no. 4 (1972): 621–8.
146 'Untermyer Hits Klan In Church Drive Talk', *NYT*, 25 November 1924, 16.
147 The Reminiscences of Bernard G. Richards (1960), 170–3, RBML, CUL, New York, NY.
148 SU to ASO, 9 May 1922, b42, f.13-15, NYTCR: ASOP, NYPL, New York, NY.
149 SU to ASO, 11 December 1922, b42, f.13-15, NYTCR: ASOP, NYPL, New York, NY.
150 'Zionist Delegation Given Memorable Welcome', *American Jewish World*, 18 November 1921, 1, 9.
151 Schechtman, *Rebel and Statesman*, 388–94; '1,200 at Astor Reception for Zionist Delegation', *Jewish Criterion*, 18 November 1921, 14; 'End Hatred as Well as Wars Jewry Pleads', *NYDT*, 14 November 1921, 5.

152 Vladimir Jabotinsky to the Zionist Organization, Executive, 27 March 1922, KH1/8//B/3, Central Zionist Archive, Jerusalem, Israel; 'Untermyer Gives Dinner for Zion Fund Campaign', *NYDT*, 3 April 1922, 9; 'Jews Want $3,000,000 for Palestine Fund', *NYH*, 10 April 1922, 20; 'American Jews Rallied to Fight Race Prejudice', *NYDT*, 22 May 1922, 7.
153 Samuel Untermyer, 'Zionism and the Crane Report', *The Forum*, January 1923, 1123.
154 Stuart E. Knee, 'The King-Crane Commission of 1919: The Articulation of Political Anti-Zionism', *American Jewish Archives* 29, no. 1 (1977): 22–52.
    Charles R. Crane, one of the leaders of the commission, considered Jews to be an 'anathema'.
    William E. Dodd and Martha Dodd (eds), *Ambassador Dodd's Diary, 1933–1938* (London: Victor Gollancz, 1941), 24–5.
155 'Report of American Section of Inter-Allied Commission on Mandates in Turkey', *Editor & Publisher*, 2 December 1922, iv–xxvi.
156 Untermyer, 'Crane Report', 1123.
157 Untermyer, 'Crane Report', 1128.
158 'Untermyer on Zangwill', *NYT*, 29 October 1923, 10.
159 SU to Bernard G. Richards, 26 June 1924, FUPP, Evanston, IL.
160 Untermyer, 'Crane Report', 1134.
161 CW to SU, 6 March 1923, WA, Rehovot, Israel.
162 'Palestine Fund Grows', *NYT*, 19 March 1923, 19.
163 Chaim Weizmann, *American Addresses* (New York: Palestine Foundation Fund, 1923), 5–6.
164 'Palestine Fund Grows', *NYT*, 19 March 1923, 19.
165 Goldblatt, Balfour Declaration, 478–9.
166 Arthur Ruppin to CW, 15 March 1923, WA, Rehovot, Israel.
167 Arthur Ruppin to SU, 6 January 1924, WA, Rehovot, Israel.
168 'Untermyer Honored', *NYT*, 12 September 1923, 18; 'New York Notes', *AH*, 21 September 1923, 482.
169 Barbara J. Smith, *The Roots of Separatism in Palestine: British Economic Policy, 1920–1929* (New York: I.B. Tauris, 1993), 154.
170 SU to CW, 17 August 1923, WA, Rehovot, Israel.
171 SU to CW, 12 November 1923, WA, Rehovot, Israel.
172 Extract from SU's letter to Emmanuel Neumann, 24 January 1924, WA, Rehovot, Israel.
173 CW to SU, 6 February 1924, WA, Rehovot, Israel.
174 SU to CW, Cable 2, 16 February 1924, WA, Rehovot, Israel.
175 SU to CW, Cable 1, 16 February 1924, WA, Rehovot, Israel.
176 SU to LM, 16 February 1924, WA, Rehovot, Israel.
177 SU to CW, 27 February 1924, WA, Rehovot, Israel.
178 CW to LM, 21 February 1924; LM to CW, 18 March 1924; Minutes of the meeting on the Jewish Agency held at the home of Louis Marshall, 4 May 1924, WA, Rehovot, Israel.
179 '$638,684 Raised Here for Palestine', *NYT*, 28 May 1924, 26.
180 '$6,000,000 Is Given to Aid Holy Land', *NYT*, 8 December 1924, 14; Herbert Parzen, 'The Enlargement of the Jewish Agency for Palestine: 1923–1929: A Hope – Hamstrung', *Jewish Social Studies* 39, no. 1–2 (1977): 138.

181 'Palestine Co. To Merge', *NYT*, January 31, 1925, 16; 'To Aid Power Plant On Jordan River', *NYT*, 1 June 1926, 16; Stephen J. Whitfield, 'Strange Fruit: The Strange Career of Samuel Zemurray', *American Jewish History* 73, no. 3 (1984): 319; Alex Bein, ed., *Arthur Ruppin: Memoirs, Diaries, Letters* (London: Weidenfeld & Nicolson, 1971), 212, 215.
182 SU to Arthur Ruppin, 28 January 1925, CZA/A107/557, Central Zionist Archive, Jerusalem, Israel.
183 'Untermyer Hits Palestine Report', *NYT*, 14 December 1924, II:2.
184 Weizmann's Secretary to SU, 23 June 1925, WA, Rehovot, Israel.
185 CW to Morris Rothenburg, 7 July 1925, WA, Rehovot, Israel.
186 CW to SU, 9 November 1925, WA, Rehovot, Israel; Fox, 'American Zionism', 144.
187 Oscar Handlin, *A Continuing Task: The American Joint Distribution Committee, 1914–1964* (New York: Random House, 1964), 56–9; Morris Frommer, 'The American Jewish Congress: A History, 1914–1950' (PhD diss., Ohio State University, Columbus, OH, 1978), 266–8; Neumann, *In the Arena*, 83–5.

Later in 1928 the JDC leaders established the American Society for Jewish Farm Settlements in Russia. Marshall was one of the directors. Weizmann's opposition to the Crimean settlement project proved to be prescient. Stalin proved to be untrustworthy. In 1938 Stalin closed the JDC-sponsored agricultural settlements in the Crimea and Ukraine.

Handlin, *Continuing Task*, 59, 71–2.
188 Parzen, 'A Hope – Hamstrung', 141–2.
189 'To Put $5,000,000 Into Palestine', *NYT*, 27 September 1925, II:16.
190 'Jewish Congress for United Relief', *NYT*, 27 October 1925, 8.
191 Urofsky, *American Zionism*, 323–7; Frommer, 'American Jewish Congress', 273–5.
192 Neumann, *In the Arena*, 86; 'Will Seek $5,000,000 to Help Palestine', *NYT*, 22 November 1925, 14.
193 SU to SSW, 26 December 1925, Box 51-9, SSWC, RDFUASC, BU, Waltham, MA.
194 Reznikoff, *Louis Marshall: 2*, 757.
195 Abraham Ulitzur, *Two Decades of Keren Hayesod: A Survey in Facts and Figures, 1920–1940* (Jerusalem: The Erez Israel (Palestine) Foundation Fund, Keren Hayesod, 1940), 9, 12–15.
196 'Jew and Christian Come to Wise's Aid', *NYT*, 28 December 1925, 3; 'Jewish Leaders Vote to Reject Wise Resignation', *BDE*, 4 January 1926, 5.
197 'Jacobs Leads Drive', *NYS*, 11 February 1938, 29; 'Big Show in Garden for Jewish Relief', *NYS*, 15 November 1938, 12.
198 'Peekskill Zionists Plan Benefit Dance', *Yonkers Herald Stateman*, 2 June 1936, 14.
199 'Zionist Heads Deny Pritchett Charges', *NYT*, 30 November 1926, 11.
200 Rafael Medoff, *Zionism and the Arabs: An American Jewish Dilemma, 1898–1948* (Westport: Praeger, 1997), 42–3.
201 Urofsky, *American Zionism*, 323–8; Bernard A. Rosenblatt to CW, 3 September 1926, WA, Rehovot, Israel.
202 CW to Sir Alfred Mond, 19 September 1926, WA, Rehovot, Israel.
203 Ferdinand M. Isserman, 'Dr. Magnes and Zionism', *The Nation*, 8 January 1930, 56; CW to Sir Alfred Mond, 19 September 1926, WA, Rehovot, Israel.
204 Tom Segev, *One Palestine, Complete: Jews and Arabs under the British Mandate* (London: Little, Brown & Company, 2000), 408–11.
205 SU to CW, 19 July 1928, WA, Rehovot, Israel.
206 Parzen, 'A Hope – Hamstrung', 149; Rosenblatt, *Two Generations*, 109, 143; Frommer, 'American Jewish Congress', 276; Urofsky, *American Zionism*, 328.

207 'Untermyer Flies from Cairo to Jerusalem', *NYT*, 3 April 1927, 1; 'Hebrew University Dedicates Stage', *NYT*, 14 April 1933, 15.

The $25,000 Minnie Untermyer Memorial Open-Air Amphitheatre was completed in spring 1933. It was designed by Benjamin Chaikin, F.R.I.R.A., and its construction was supervised by Louis Green, M.I.C.E. The theatre was modelled on the principles of the ancient open-air theatres of Rome and Greece. It had a seating capacity of 2,200. From it could be seen the Dead Sea, the Wilderness of Benjamin and, in the distance, across the Jordan, the mountains of Ammon and Moab. Beneath the stage was a light and spacious hall with seating for 250 people. The dedication of the theatre was made by the chancellor of the university, Judah Leon Magnes. The amphitheatre was subsequently renamed the Rothberg Amphitheatre. Untermyer's gift is now only acknowledged by the Minnie Untermyer Memorial Stage, which is in the amphitheatre.

'Hebrew University Open-Air Theatre', *Palestine Post*, 5 April 1933, 2; Judah L. Magnes, *Addresses by the Chancellor of the Hebrew University* (Jerusalem: Hebrew University, 1936), 199–202; 'Theatre To Be Ready Soon', *NYT*, 24 July 1932, 24; 'Untermyer Memorial Theater For Jerusalem', *NYS*, 11 April 1933, 31; *NYT*, 14 April 1933, 15; Norman Bentwich, *For Zion's Sake: A Biography of Judah L. Magnes* (Philadelphia: Jewish Publication Society of America, 1954), 170; 'Hebrew University Ampitheatre', *Palestine Post*, 14 April 1933, 5; Jerry Barach, Media Relations, The Hebrew University Jerusalem, to Richard Hawkins, 4 November 2002.

208 Bentwich, *For Zion's Sake*, 136.
209 'Untermyer Gives University $100,000', *NYT*, 4 April 1927, 3.
210 CW to Mark Schwartz, 31 March 1928; CW to SU, 1 April 1928; CW to Louis Lipsky, 23 May 1928; Abram Simon to CW, 15 June 1928; Abram Simon to CW, 19 June 1928; SU to CW, 20 June 1928, WA, Rehovot, Israel; 'Wall Street Bankers Negotiating Zionist $3,000,000 Loan', *The Sentinel*, 27 April 1928, 2; 'American Loan for Palestine Postponed', *Palestine Bulletin*, 12 November 1928, 3.
211 'Head of Hadassah Joins Zionist Split', *NYT*, 31 March 1928, 7; 'Untermyer for Weizmann', *NYT*, 1 April 1928, B37.
212 LAS to Jacob Landau, 24 October 1929, WA, Rehovot, Israel; 'The Hebron Incident', *The Times* [London], 30 August 1929, 12.
213 'Parade of Protest Is Planned Here', *NYT*, 26 August 1929, 6.
214 Rosenblatt, *Two Generations*, 145–8; 'Natives Behind Holy Land War, Says Untermyer', *Yonkers Statesman*, 30 August 1929, 2.
215 Rosenblatt, *Two Generations*, 148.
216 'Demands Jews Share in Palestine Inquiry', *NYT*, 10 September 1929, 6.
217 Samuel Halperin, *The Political World of American Zionism* (Detroit: Wayne State University Press, 1961), 17.
218 LAS to CW, 24 October 1929, WA, Rehovot, Israel.
219 '8 British Police Officers to Go, "Old Stagers" of the Force', *Palestine Bulletin*, 20 November 1931, 4.
220 *Annual Administrative Report 1932* (Jerusalem: Palestine Police and Prisons, 1932), 3.
221 'Social and Personal', *Palestine Bulletin*, 3 April 1933, 5.
222 'Bestattungen Stadt Zürich', *Neue Zürcher Nachrichten*, 1 February 1934, 4; 'Mrs. F.A. Partridge', *Palestine Post*, 9 February 1934, 5; 'Obituary: Lord Melchett', *The Times* [London], 24 January 1949, 7.

223 Jacob Billikopf to SU, 16 September 1930, Folder 16, Box 30, MS 13, Jacob Billikopf Collection, AJA, Cincinnati, OH.

Untermyer is on record as having said in May 1925 at a Keren Hayesod dinner that 'We seek no Jewish State, or dictatorship or political power or advantage over our Arab neighbors . . . All we ask is equal rights of citizenship and protection under British rule.' This observation probably had not been approved by the Keren Hayesod.
'$733,000 Raised Here for Palestine Fund', *NYT*, 12 May 1925, 2.
224 'Weizmann Outlines Plan for Colonization of 250,000 Jews in Palestine Within Five Years', *JDB*, 30 June 1933, 3.
225 Like Untermyer Backer was a UPA fundraiser. He was married to Dorothy Schiff, the granddaughter of Jacob H. Schiff.
'George Backer, Published Post', *NYT*, 2 May 1974, 50.
226 Urofsky, *American Zionism*, 403–5; SU to SSW, 20 July 1937, Box 124-4, SSWC, RDFUASC, BU, Waltham, MA.
227 SU to SSW, 20 July 1937, Box 124-4, SSWC, RDFUASC, BU, Waltham, MA.
228 SU to SSW, 20 July 1937, Box 124-4, SSWC, RDFUASC, BU, Waltham, MA.
229 Barnard, *Julian W. Mack*, 284.
230 Tom Segev, *A State at Any Cost: The Life of Ben Gurion* (London: Head of Zeus, 2019), 204.

Chapter 5

1 This chapter is derived, in part, from an article published in *Management and Organizational History* 5, no. 2 (2010): available online: https://www.tandfonline.com/doi/10.1177/1744935910361642 and an article published in *American Jewish History* 93, no. 1 (2007).
2 SSW to Harry J. Stern, 5 May 1933, Folder 15, Vol.1, MG31 F12, Harry Joshua Stern Collection, LAC, Ottawa, Canada.
3 Samuel Untermyer, *The Boycott Is Our Only Weapon Against Nazi Germany: Addresses By Samuel Untermyer* (New York: The Author, 1933), 1–4.
4 Moshe Gottlieb, 'The Anti-Nazi Boycott Movement in the American Jewish Community, 1933–1941' (PhD diss., Brandeis University, Waltham, MA, 1967), 53–60.
5 SU to EMH, 9 July 1934, Folder 3884, Box 122, MS 466, EMHP, MA, YUL, New Haven, CT.
6 For more on the JWV see Berkowitz's book chapter.
Michael Berkowitz, 'Kristallnacht in Context: Jewish War Veterans in America and Britain and the Crisis of German Jewry', in *American Religious Responses to Kristallnacht*, ed. Maria Mazzenga (Basingstoke: Palgrave Macmillan, 2009), 57–84.
7 Moshe Gottlieb, 'The First of April Boycott and the Reaction of the American Jewish Community', *American Jewish Historical Quarterly* 57, no. 4 (1968): 516-6.
8 Monroe Friedman, *Consumer Boycotts: Effecting Change through the Marketplace and the Media* (New York: Routledge, 1999), 3–4.
9 Gottlieb, 'Boycott Movement', 60; 460; 'Abram Coralnik, Editor, Dies At 54', *NYT*, 17 July 1937, 15; Benjamin Dubovsky to Samuel Margoshes, 11 February 1937, Box 16, NSANLCHRR, RBML, CUL, New York, NY.
10 Max Ornstein to the League, 20 September 1933, Box 59, NSANLCHRR, RBML, CUL, New York, NY.

11 Hannah Ahlheim, 'Establishing Antisemitic Stereotypes: Social and Economic Segregation of Jews by Means of Political Boycott in Germany', *The Leo Baeck Institute Year Book* 55, no. 1 (2010): 149, 173.
12 'Untermyer Scores Congress on Nazis', *NYT*, 17 April 1933, 6.
13 The speech was considered sufficiently important for the German Embassy in Washington to send a report to Berlin and from this time onwards Untermyer's anti-Nazi activities were closely monitored by the German government.
    An die Deutsche Botschaft in Washington, 9 May 1933, S. 100–2, Handel 37: USA, Bd. 1, R301/44483, Bundesarchiv, Berlin, Germany.
14 'Untermyer Urges German Boycott', *NYT*, 8 May 1933, 6; Untermyer, *Addresses*, 5–15.
15 'Smith Denounces Nazis as "Stupid"', *NYT*, 11 September 1933, 1, 8; Adam Tooze, *The Wages of Destruction: The Making and Breaking of the Nazi Economy* (London: Allen Lane, 2006).
16 '$500,000 Sought for Nazi Boycott', *NYT*, 11 September 1933, 8; Gottlieb, 'Boycott Movement', 128–37.
17 Alfred E. Cohn to SU, 10 August 1933, Folder 29, Box 1, Alfred E. Cohn Papers, Rockefeller University Faculty (FA802), Rockefeller Archive Center, Sleepy Hollow, NY.
    Lamberti observes Cohn believed that American Jews would lose the goodwill of people who were friendly or at least not unsympathetic to them if their community leaders organized boycotts of German goods and other protests.
    Marjorie Lambertie, 'The Reception of Refugee Scholars from Nazi Germany in America: Philanthropy and Social Change in Higher Education', *Jewish Social Studies* 12, no. 3 (2006): 167.
18 SU to Alfred E. Cohn, 12 August 1933, Folder 29, Box 1, Alfred E. Cohn Papers, Rockefeller University Faculty (FA802), Rockefeller Archive Center, Sleepy Hollow, NY.
19 'Untermyer Renews Plea for Boycott', *NYT*, 12 May 1933, 7; Gottlieb, 'Boycott Movement', 69.
20 Nanette Dembitz, The Anti-Nazi Boycott Campaign, unpublished manuscript, c. 1964, 7ff, FUPP, Evanston, IL.
21 Gottlieb, 'Boycott Movement', 69–72; 'Jews Here Decree Boycott on Reich', *NYT*, 15 May 1933, 1, 8; 'Jacob de Haas, Secretary and Biographer of Herzl Dead', *Jewish Criterion*, 2 April 1937, 7.
22 American League for the Defense of Jewish Rights Press Release, Address of Mr Samuel Untermyer, Hotel Astor, New York City, 14 May 1933, S. 77–82, Handel 37: USA, Bd. 1, R301/44483, Bundesarchiv, Berlin, Germany.
23 *NYT*, 15 May 1933, 1, 8.
24 'Untermyer Aids Boycott', *NYT*, 16 June 1933, 7.
25 'Boycott Is Begun by Jewish Women', *NYT*, 28 June 1933, 4; *The Economic Boycott of Germany: Address By Samuel Untermyer Before the Women's Conference on the Boycott, Hotel Astor, New York City, June 27, 1933*, Box 29, NSANLCHRR, RBML, CUL, New York, NY.
26 'Untermyer Picked for Fight on Nazis', *NYT*, 22 May 1933, 9.
27 'Protests Ban on Stamps', *NYT*, 30 June 1933, 3.
28 'Untermyer Hails Jewish Patriots', *NYT*, 5 July 1933, 8; SU to ASO, 3 July 1933, b42, f.13-15, NYTCR: ASOP, NYPL, New York, NY.
29 As quoted in Gottlieb, 'Boycott Movement', 80–1, 456.

30 Monty Noam Penkower, 'Honorable Failures against Nazi Germany: McDonald's Letter of Resignation and the Petition in its Support', *Modern Judaism* 20, no. 3 (2010): 247–53.
31 Diary Entries for 26 October and 2 November 1933, 5 June 1934, Richard Breitman, Barbara McDonald Stewart and Severin Hochberg, eds, *Advocate for the Doomed: The Diaries and Papers of James G. McDonald, 1932-1935* (Bloomington and Indianapolis: Indiana University Press, 2007), 134, 139, 403.
32 Entry for 13 June 1934, Breitman, McDonald Stewart and Hochberg, *Advocate for the Doomed*, 407–8.
33 'Aliyah Fete Set for Next Week', *Yonkers Herald Statesman*, 8 July 1938, 7.
34 Edwin Black, *The Transfer Agreement: The Untold Story of the Secret Agreement Between the Third Reich and Jewish Palestine* (New York: Macmillan Publishing Company, 1984), 188; 'Untermyer Celebrates 75th Birthday, Plans to Attend Boycott Parley', *JDB*, 7 June 1933, 3.
35 'Postpone World Boycott Conference', *JDB*, 9 June 1933, 3.
36 Black, *Transfer Agreement*, 189–202.
37 Black, *Transfer Agreement*, 202.
38 Black, *Transfer Agreement*, 203.
39 'U.S. Envoys to World Boycott Conference in Preliminary Parley', *JDB*, 16 June 1933, 11; 'Joodsche leiders te Amsterdam: Een conferentie tegen Hitler', *Het Volk*, 17 July 1933, 1.
40 'A Jew Who Comes to Lead All Jews against Hitler', *Sunday Express* [London], 16 July 1933, 5.
   There is no record of this approach in the German government papers. However, Untermyer repeated this claim in an address to the Assembly of Orthodox Rabbis in September.
   'Rabbi Group Vote to Boycott on Nazis', *NYT*, 7 September 1933, 6.
41 'Wider Boycott against Reich Goods Sought', *Buffalo Courier-Express*, 17 July 1933, 3.
42 *JDB*, 16 June 1933, 11; 'U.S. Envoys to World Boycott Conference in Preliminary Parley', *JDB*, 17 June 1933, 1, 4.
43 'Black, *Transfer Agreement*', 204–5.
44 'Deputy Wislicki Dead', *Jewish Telegraphic Agency: Latest Cable Dispatches*, 4 October 1935, 1.
45 'World Jews Push Boycott of Reich for "Inhuman" Acts', *NYT*, 21 July 1933, 1, 5; 'Joodsche Boycot-Conferentie in Amsterdam', *De Telegraaf*, 21 July 1933, 10; 'Mobilisatie der Joden', *Het Volk*, 21 July 1933, 1; 'De Joodsche bijeenkomst is gesloten', *Het Volk*, 22 July 1933, 1.
46 Black, *Transfer Agreement*, 204–5.
47 'World Jewish Economic Conference', *Jewish Chronicle* [London], 21 July 1933, 30.
48 'Joodsche boycot-actie tegen Duitschland', *De Telegraaf*, 20 July 1933, 1.
49 '"Een Conferentie" van den Heer Untermayer', *Algemeen Handelsblad*, 19 July 1933, 17; 'Likewise-Contrariwise!', *Jewish Chronicle* [London], 28 July 1933, 27.
   David Cohen, a professor of ancient history at the University of Amsterdam, later served as a member of the German-appointed Jewish Council from 1941 to 1943 after Germany occupied the Netherlands. He subsequently survived incarceration in Theresienstadt concentration camp. After the Second World War he was accused of being a collaborator.
   P.H. Schrijvers, '"Rome, Athens, Jerusalem": Aspects of the Life and Work of Dr. David Cohen', in *Dutch Jewry: Its History and Secular Culture (1500-2000)*, ed. Jonathan Israel and Reinier Salverda (Leiden: Brill, 2002), 240–51.

50 'Untermyer Assails Wise as Preliminary Boycott Meeting is Opened in Amsterdam', *JDB*, 21 July 1933, 1, 3; 'Aan het adres van prof. Cohen', *Het Volk*, 21 July 1933, 3.
51 Deutsche Botschaft, Den Haag, 25 July 1933, GFM33/4735, TNA, Kew, UK.
52 *NYT*, 21 July 1933, 1, 5; Gottlieb, 'Boycott Movement', 96–7.
53 'Lord Melchett And Anti-Nazi Boycott', *Daily Herald* [London], 14 November 1933, 15.
54 Frank Greenaway, 'Mond family', in Oxford Dictionary of National Biography (Oxford: Oxford University Press, 2011), https://doi.org/10.1093/ref:odnb/51124, accessed 15 April 2021.
55 Geoffrey Knox to Lord Balfour, 29 November 1939, FO371/25169/981, TNA, Kew, UK.
  Bill Reader in his history of Imperial Chemical Industries shows that it indeed has such dealings.
  W. J. Reader, *Imperial Chemical Industries: A History: Volume II: The First Quarter Century, 1926–1952* (London: Oxford University Press, 1975), 150–5.
56 'Sir Robert Mond Takes Helm of World Boycott Move against Germany', *JDB*, 30 July 1933, 11; 'Sir Robert Mond', *The Times* [London], 24 October 1938, 21.
57 Black, *Transfer Agreement*, 273; SU to Harry Salomons, 15 November 1933; Harry Salomons to SU, 6 December 1933, Folder 2, Box 1, MS 251, SUC, AJA, Cincinnati, OH; 'Het Ontdekken van Metalen', *Algemeen Handelsblad*, 18 November 1927, 10.
58 'Jews' Drastic Boycott Plan', *Daily Mirror*, 16 September 1933, 8; 'Jews Urged to Buy British', *Daily Mirror*, 6 November 1933, 4; 'Council of 50 to Direct Boycott Named by British Jews at Conference', *JDB*, 8 November 1933, 1, 4.
59 'Jewish Boycott', *Yorkshire Post*, 18 November 1933, 7.
60 *Daily Herald* [London], 14 November 1933, 15.
61 SU to ASO, 3 July 1933, b42, f.13-15, NYTCR: ASOP, NYPL, New York, NY.
62 ASO to SU, 5 July 1933, b42, f.13-15, NYTCR: ASOP, NYPL, New York, NY.
63 *NYT*, 21 July 1933, 1, 5; 'Sees Boycott Success', *NYT*, 28 July 1933, 7; 'Boycott Exceeds Untermyer's Hope', *NYT*, 1 August 1933, 5.
64 'Fredman Plans Reception to Saml. Untermyer Sun.', *Jersey City Jewish Standard*, 4 August 1933, 1, 4; 'Untermyer Back, Greeted in Harbor', *NYT*, 7 August 1933, 4; 'Enthusiastic Crowds Greet Untermyer Who Urges Boycott Spread in Broadcast', *JDB*, 8 August 1933, 2.
65 'Text of Untermyer's Address', *NYT*, 7 August 1933, 4; Samuel Untermyer Criticizes Hitler's Rule, 6 August 1933, Box 29, NSANLCHRR, RBML, CUL, New York, NY.
66 'Jewish Appeal to League', *Irish Times*, 21 August 1933, 8.
67 Moshe Gottlieb, *American Anti-Nazi Resistance, 1933–1941: An Historical Analysis* (Ktav Pub. House, 1982), 82.
68 *Daily News Bulletin* [Jewish Telegraphic Agency, London], 24 July 1933, 1–3.
69 Black, *Transfer Agreement*, 278–362.
70 Gottlieb, 'Boycott Movement', 102–7; 'Jews Here to Push Boycott on Hitler', *NYT*, 21 August 1933, 2.
71 Gottlieb, 'Boycott Movement', 161–3.
72 AHS to SU, 27 September 1933, Folder 1217, MS 4787, AHSP, WRHS, Cleveland, OH.
73 Black, *Transfer Agreement*, 278–362; 'Boycott of Reich Demanded by Wise', *NYT*, 6 September 1933, 12;
  'Geneva Conference Votes Anti-German Resolution', *JDB*, 10 September 1933, 1, 11.
74 Black, *Transfer Agreement*, 362.

75 Black, *Transfer Agreement*, 363.
76 'Untermyer See Hitler's End Soon', *NYT*, 28 August 1933, 5.
77 Morris Rothenberg to CW, 10 September 1933, WA, Rehovot, Israel.
78 Louis Lipsky to CW, 12 September 1933, WA, Rehovot, Israel.
79 Louis Lipsky to CW, 24 September 1933, WA, Rehovot, Israel.
80 AHS to NSANL, 3 September 1935, Box 3, NSANLCHRR, RBML, CUL, New York, NY; 'Zionist's 19th', *Time*, 2 September 1935, 54.
81 SU to George E. Harriman, 5 February 1936, Box 4, NSANLCHRR, RBML, CUL, New York, NY.
82 SU to AHS, 12 February 1935, Folder 1220, MS 4787, AHSP, WRHS, Cleveland, OH.
83 Felix M. Warburg to CW, 17 October 1933, WA, Rehovot, Israel.
84 'Jews' Next Step', *Daily Mail* [London], 22 July 1933, 11; 'Einstein in England', *Daily Telegraph* [London], 22 July 1933, 11.
85 AE to SU, 25 July 1933, 121 793.1, AEP, JNUL, Jerusalem, Israel.
    I thank Andrew Robinson, Visiting Fellow at Wolfson College, Cambridge, for sharing this letter.
86 'Einstein Elusive as Theory, Dodges Welcome Party Here', *NYEP*, 17 October 1933, 3.
87 Felix M. Warburg to CW, 17 October 1933, WA, Rehovot, Israel.
88 *New York Evening Post*, 17 October 1933, 3.
89 AE to SU, 19 October 1933, 52 115-1&2, AEP, JNUL, Jerusalem, Israel. [Translated by Dr Peter Brown.]
90 SU to Elsa Einstein, 19 April 1934, 52 117, AEP, JNUL, Jerusalem, Israel. [Translated by Dr Peter Brown.]
91 Leon L. Watters: Comments on the letters of Professor and Mrs Albert Einstein to Dr Leon L. Watters, *c.* 1959, 17–18, Folder 2, Box 1, MS 495, Leon Laizer Watters Collection, AJA, Cincinnati, OH.
92 George Sylvester Viereck, 'What Life Means to Einstein', *Saturday Evening Post*, 26 October 1929, 114.
93 AE to SU, 31 March 1937, FUPP, Evanston, IL. [Translated by Dr Peter Brown.]
94 Joseph B. Schechtman, *Fighter and Prophet: The Vladimir Jabotinsky Story: The Last Years* (New York: Thomas Yoseloff, 1961), 218–20.
95 '$500,000 Sought for Nazi Boycott', *NYT*, 11 September 1933, 8; Gottlieb, 'Boycott Movement', 128–37.
96 Max Ornstein to the League, 20 September 1933, Box 59, NSANLCHRR, RBML, CUL, New York, NY.
97 Roosevelt resigned in December 1934.
    Theodore Roosevelt to Henry H. Rosenfelt, 28 October 1933, Box 2; SU to George E. Harriman, 24 December 1934, Box 29, NSANLCHRR, RBML, CUL, New York, NY.
98 Holmes had been a friend of Untermyer's wife Minnie and conducted the services at her funeral. He was a left-wing cleric, albeit anti-Communist, and counted among his friends the anarchist Emma Goldman.
    'Simple Funeral Service for Mrs. Untermyer', *Brooklyn Standard Union*, 19 August 1924, 11; Emma Goldman to John Haynes Holmes, 11 July 1935; 15 October 1935, Folder 19, Vol.1, MG31 F12, Harry Joshua Stern Collection, LAC, Ottawa, Canada.
99 SU to JMB, 21 November 1933, Folder 21, Box 7, JMBP, SGMML, PU, Princeton, NJ.
100 Why the Boycott Against Germany Is Succeeding: Address of Samuel Untermyer at the Metropolitan Opera House, Philadelphia, 27 June 1934, Box 29, NSANLCHRR, RBML, CUL, New York, NY.

101 'Boycott Is Begun by Jewish Women', *NYT*, 28 June 1933, 4.
102 AHS to SU, 9 November 1933, Folder 1217, MS 4787, AHSP, WRHS, Cleveland, OH.
103 SU to AHS, 20 November 1933; AHS to SU, 20 November 1933, Folder 1217, MS 4787, AHSP, WRHS, Cleveland, OH.
104 'Masquerader!', *Time*, 13 November 1933, 9-10.
105 Robert E. Herzstein, *Henry R. Luce, Time, and the American Crusade in Asia* (New York: Cambridge University Press, 2005), 29.
106 'Letters', *Time*, 27 November 1933, 4.
107 SU to AHS, 22 November 1933, Folder 1217, AHSP, MS 4787, WRHS, Cleveland, OH.
108 James N. Rosenberg, 'Sol. M. Stroock', *American Jewish Yearbook* 44 (1942): 52-60.
109 Minutes of Committee on Policy, 1 September 1933, American Jewish Committee Archive, New York, NY.
110 SU to George E. Harriman, 22 January 1936, Box 4, NSANLCHRR, RBML, CUL, New York, NY.
111 Gottlieb, 'Boycott Movement', 157.
112 Abram Coralnik, 'The Sterilized Boycott', n.d., Box 412, NSANLCHRR, RBML, CUL, New York, NY.
113 Naomi W. Cohen, 'The Transatlantic Connection: The American Jewish Committee and the Joint Foreign Committee in Defense of German Jews, 1933-1937', *American Jewish History* 90, no. 4 (2002): 363.
114 Alvin Untermyer to SU, 1 February 1936; SU to Sol M. Stroock, 4 February 1936; SU to Alvin Untermyer, 4 February 1936, Box 4, NSANLCHRR, RBML, CUL, New York, NY.
115 Dr Benjamin Dubovsky (1888-1963) was a Ukrainian immigrant physician with an office on West 87th Street and an instructor on the teaching staff of the New York University School of Medicine. He was also a Yiddish journalist specializing in medical issues.
   Benjamin Dubovsky to SU, 21 April 1938, Box 16, NSANLCHRR, RBML, CUL, New York, NY; Benjamin Dubovsky to AHS, 26 August 1934, Folder 1217, MS 4787, AHSP, WRHS, Cleveland, OH; 'Physician-Writer B. Dubovsky Dies', *Detroit Jewish News*, 20 September 1963, 31; *American Jewish Yearbook* 65 (1964): 432.
116 Benjamin Dubovsky to AHS, 16 August 1934; 17 August 1934, Folder 1217, MS 4787, AHSP, WRHS, Cleveland, OH.
117 Ezekiel Rabinowitz to AHS, 17 August 1934, Folder 1218, MS 4787, AHSP, WRHS, Cleveland, OH.
118 AHS to SU, 31 December 1934, Folder 1219, MS 4787, AHSP, WRHS, Cleveland, OH.
119 In fact, Nelson had immigrated to the United States from Mannheim in 1926 with his parents, Rosa and David Leib Nitkewitsch. The Nitkewitschs subsequently changed their name to Nelson. I thank Nelson's ex-wife Mary Cheyney Nelson Gould for this information. It is probable that most, if not all, of Nelson's biography was invented apart from his place of birth, Heidelberg. The University of Heidelberg archivist Dr Werner Moritz says that he was not among the 125 Jewish students who had their doctorates revoked between 1937 and 1945.
   S.S. *Stuttgart*: Passengers Sailing from Bremen, 13 January 1926, Passenger and Crew Lists of Vessels Arriving at New York; E.D. 3, Brooklyn, Kings County, NY, 11 April 1930, United States Census, https://www.familysearch.org, accessed 11 October 2020; Boris E. Nelson to SU, 8 March 1937, Box 5, NSANLCHRR, RBML, CUL, New York, NY; 'You Should Know', *Jewish Criterion*, 26 February 1937, 29; 'Dr. Boris Nelson dies', *Toledo Blade*, 20 February 1995, 1:1, 1:5, 2:10; Dr. Werner Moritz

to Richard Hawkins, 28 August 2007; Mary Cheyney Nelson Gould to Richard Hawkins, 5 October 2009.
120 Manhattan, New York County, NY, U.S. Census, 26–8 April 1930; Manhattan, New York County, NY, U.S. Census, 26 April 1940, https://www.familysearch.org, accessed 20 August 2019.
121 'Jewish Relief Group Will Assemble Here', *NYT*, 13 March 1935, 26; *American Jewish Yearbook* 39 (1937): 616; *American Jewish Yearbook* 51 (1950): 454–5.
122 Jeanne Abrams, *Blazing the Tuberculosis Trail* (Denver: Colorado Historical Society, 1991), 30–43.
123 'Boycott Group Organizing Printing Trade, Plans Christian Division', *JDB*, 19 May 1933, 2.
124 'Untermyer to Address Women's Boycott Meeting', *JDB*, 21 June 1933, 3.
125 American League for the Defense of Jewish Rights, 18 September 1933 [Abschrift], S. 9, Handel 37: Bd. 2, R301/44484, Bundesarchiv, Berlin, Germany; Ezekiel Rabinowitz to BVC, 30 June 1934, Folder 1, Box 1, MS 307, BVCC, AJA, Cincinnati, OH; 'Women of Sinai to Meet Monday', *Mount Vernon Daily Argus*, 10 March 1938, 14.
126 SU to JMB, 13 March 1935, Folder 18, Box 10, JMBP, SGMML, PU, Princeton, NJ.
127 SU to George E. Harriman, 11 February 1935, Box 4; George E. Harriman to SU, 16 February 1935, Box 9; 28 February 1935, Box 4, NSANLCHRR, RBML, CUL, New York, NY.
128 'A Notable Boycott Victory', *Jewish Criterion*, 9 February 1934, 10.
129 Stern's recollections are not entirely reliable. For example, he recalled that the meeting with Untermyer took place in February 1933.
   J. David Stern, *Memoirs of a Maverick Publisher* (New York: Simon and Schuster, 1962), 214; *Jewish Criterion*, 29 September 1933, 5.
130 'Anti-Nazis to Rally', *PI*, 26 June 1934, 10; 'Untermyer Due at Anti-Nazi Rally', *PI*, 27 June 1934, 2; 'Nazi Horrors Assailed Here at Big Meeting', *PI*, 28 June 1934, 1.
131 Stern, *Memoirs*, 214.
132 'Richard Beamish Dies', *PI*, 2 October 1945, 12.
133 Deutsche Botschaft, Washington, DC, 12 August 1935, S. 35–6, Handel 37: USA, Bd.7, R301/44489, Bundesarchiv, Berlin, Germany; 'Pennsylvania Governor Protests Nazi Persecutions', *Jewish Telegraphic Agency Latest Cable Dispatches*, 6 August 1935, 3.
134 Murray Friedman, ed., *Philadelphia Jewish Life, 1940–2000* (Philadelphia: Temple University Press, 2003), 3.
135 Stern relaunched the conservative Republican tabloid *Evening Post* at the end of March 1934 as the liberal Democratic *New York Post*. In June 1939 he sold the loss-making paper to George Backer.
   Stern, *Memoirs*, 220–2; 'New Publisher Confers with Untermyer and Others Here', *NYT*, 9 December 1933, 12; 'Geo. Backer Acquires Control of the Post', *New York Post*, 22 June 1939, 1, 8.
136 *Address Read Before Anti-Nazi Non-Sectarian Meeting at Chicago Auditorium*, 28 November 1933, Box 29, NSANLCHRR, RBML, CUL, New York, NY; '15,000 Assail Hitlerism At Stadium Rally', *Chicago Tribune*, 4 December 1933, 5; Deutsches Generalkonsulat Chicago, 7 November 1934; 3 January 1935; 11 January 1935; 5 February 1935, R99531, PAAA, Berlin, Germany.
137 'Anti-Nazi Committee to Hold Conference Today', *Jewish Post*, 25 March 1937, 1; Warren Grover, *Nazis in Newark* (New Brunswick, NJ: Transaction Publishers, 2003), 111–37.

138 Steven J. Ross, *Hitler in Los Angeles: How Jews Foiled Nazi Plots Against Hollywood and America* (New York and London: Bloomsbury, 2017), 187, 192–7, 199–200, 204, 206–8, 212, 218–19, 237, 239, 243.
139 'Canadian Jews Push Boycott of German Goods', *JDB*, 9 July 1934, 5; 'Important Achievements Follow Canadian Jewish Congress Efforts', *The Jewish Standard* [Toronto], 31 May 1935, Folder 519, Vol. 1748, RG25, Records of the Department of External Affairs, LAC, Ottawa, Canada.
140 Deutsche Generalkonsulat für Kanada, 2 January 1935, S. 21, Handel 37: USA, Bd. 6, R301/44488, Bundesarchiv, Berlin, Germany; 'Montreal, Que.', *JDB*, 2 April 1935, 3; Leith A. Baldwin, Chairman, Non-Sectarian Anti-Nazi League to the Weaver F.P. Coal Company, Montreal, 27 August 1935, Folder 519, Vol. 1748, RG25, Records of the Department of External Affairs, LAC, Ottawa, Canada.
141 William Lyon MacKenzie King to John Bracken, 9 December 1938, Folder 519, Vol. 1748, RG25, Records of the Department of External Affairs, LAC, Ottawa, Canada.
142 'Anti-Nazi Boycott Launched in Toronto', *Globe and Mail*, 29 July 1938, 4.
143 'Book Sums Up Fight of World Against Nazis', *JDB*, 11 November 1934, 12; Anti-Nazi League, *Nazis Against the World*.
144 'Boycott Meeting Called in London', *NYT*, 9 November 1934, 5; 'German Trade', *Yorkshire Post*, 19 November 1934, 8.
145 Deutsche Gesandschaft Brüssel: Tagung der an Boykott Deutschlands interessierten Kreise in London, 1 December 1934, R99532, PAAA, Berlin, Germany; 'International Boycott Conference', *Jewish Chronicle* [London], 30 November 1934, 8, 25–6, 35.
146 'Boycott Body Acts To End Hitlerism', *NYT*, 27 November 1934, 9; Geheimes Staatspolizeiamt Berlin: Bericht über internationale Boykottkonferenz in London vom 26.-28-11.1934, 28 December 1934, R99532, PAAA, Berlin, Germany; 'Laborites Back German Boycott', *NYT*, 28 November 1934, 11.
147 'Hitler Regime's Sincerity', *Yorkshire Post*, 20 April 1936, 7.
148 Alfred Johns, 'From £2 a week Electrician to Ruler of 5,000,000 Workers', *Belfast Telegraph*, 7 September 1938, 8.
149 'Untermyer Home, Scores Saar Pact', *NYT*, 5 December 1934, 8.
150 Geheimes Staatspolizeiamt Berlin, 28 December 1934, R99532, PAAA, Berlin, Germany. [Translated by Dr Peter Brown.]
151 Karen J. Greenberg (ed.) *Archives of the Holocaust, VI, Columbia University Library, New York: The Non-Sectarian Anti-Nazi League to Champion Human Rights Papers: The Non-Sectarian Anti-Nazi League Pamphlet Collection* (New York: Garland Publishing, Inc., 1990), 58, 83.
152 'Proposed Boycott of German Goods', *South Wales Gazette and Newport News*, 11 June 1937, 1.
153 Greenberg, *Archives*, ix–x.
154 SU to David A. Brown, 14 July 1934, Box 3, Folder 14, MS 18, David A. Brown Collection, AJA, Cincinnati, OH.
155 SU to Irwin Untermyer, 9 February 1935, FUPP, Evanston, IL.
156 'Women's League Picks Mrs. Cahane', *Jewish Floridian*, 16 June 1961, B5.
157 'Vigilance Group Seeks to Ascertain the Extent of Drop in German Trade', *JDB*, 4 April 1934, 2.
158 Moshe Gottlieb, 'The Anti-Nazi Boycott Movement in the United States: An Ideological and Sociological Appreciation', *Jewish Social Studies* 35, no. 3/4 (1973): 203.

159 Grover, *Nazis in Newark*, 1–2, 7–8, 47, 54–5, 121–4.
160 'Mitchell Fisher, 86', *NYT*, 22 March 1990, B16.
161 Dembitz, Anti-Nazi Boycott, 20f, 33f.
162 Morris Rothenberg to SU, 26 December 1934, Box 4, NSANLCHRR, RBML, CUL, New York, NY.
163 Samuel Margoshes to AHS, 9 August 1933, Folder 344, MS 4787, AHSP, WRHS, Cleveland, OH.
164 Stern, *Memoirs*, 214.
165 'Three Personal Letters concerning the sale of German Goods by Department Stores in the United States', *NYT*, 2 October 1933, 7.
166 *The Nation*, 18 October 1933, 423.
167 The German Consulate General in New York City considered this to be an important turn of events. Deutsches Generalkonsulat New York, 25 October 1933, S. 42, Handel 37: Bd. 2, R301/44484, Bundesarchiv, Berlin, Germany.
168 'The Suppressed Advertisement Concerning R.H. Macy', *The Nation*, 25 October 1933, 478–80.
169 Richard Neuberger, 'The New Germany', *The Nation*, 4 October 1933, 379; 'Licensing of Retail Dealers Proposed', *Buffalo Evening News*, 19 September 1933, 9.
170 Ira Hirschmann, *Caution to the Winds* (New York: Davis McKay Company, Inc.), 46–50.
171 'I.A. Hirschmann Back, Tells of Nazi Myth', *NYT*, 28 July 1933, 7.
172 *Buffalo Evening News*, 19 September 1933, 9.
173 Hirschmann, *Caution to the Winds*, 48–9.
174 Gottlieb, 'Boycott Movement', 173.
175 Telegram, New York, 20 March 1934, S. 104, Handel 37: USA, Bd. 3, R301/44485, Bundesarchiv, Berlin, Germany.
176 Deutsches Generalkonsulat, New York, 8 February 1935, S. 130–5, Handel 37: USA, Bd. 6, R301/44488, Bundesarchiv, Berlin, Germany.
177 'Macy's Hires Notorious Detective in Effort To Stem Organization', *Daily Worker* [New York], 27 May 1935, 4.
178 'Whitley Named To New York Post', *WES*, 11 April 1935, B16.
179 Division of Investigation, U.S. Department of Justice, 14 January 1935, S. 175, Handel 37: USA, Bd. 6, R301/44488, Bundesarchiv, Berlin, Germany.
180 'Maison Blanche Co.', *The Cumulative Daily Digest of Corporation News: Fourth Quarterly Number: 1923* (New York: Poor's Publishing Co., 1924), 295; Andrew Robert Harrison, 'Mr. Philadelphia: Albert Greenfield (1887–1967)' (PhD diss., Temple University, Philadelphia, PA, 1997), 109, 172.
181 Tom May to SU, 26 January 1935, Box 9, NSANLCHRR, RBML, CUL, New York, NY.
    Untermyer's firm had represented Lehman Brothers in 1910 in the flotation of the May Department Stores Company.
    Advertisement, *NYDT*, 18 June 1910, 14.
182 SU to Byron D. Miller, 24 October 1934, Folder 2, Box 1, MS 251, SUC, AJA, Cincinnati, OH.
183 Greenberg, *Archives of the Holocaust*, 31–40.
184 Greenberg, *Archives of the Holocaust*, 50.
185 'Claude Washington Kress', in *National Cyclopædia of National Biography* 31 (New York: James T. White & Company, 1944), 142–3.
186 'Kress Flays Anti-Nazi Boycott', *Southern Israelite*, 19 February 1937, 1.

187 John K. Winkler, *Five and Ten, the Fabulous Life of F.W. Woolworth* (New York: R.M. McBride & Company, 1940), 242.
188 Winkler, *Five and Ten*, 84–5; James Brough, *The Woolworths* (New York: McGraw-Hill, 1982), 89–95; 'A Skyscraper Built by the Nickels of Millions', *NYT*, 1 January 1911, SM6.
189 SU to Ezekiel Rabinowitz, 3 November 1933, Box 3, NSANLCHRR, RBML, CUL, New York, NY.
190 Samuel Linsenberg to SU, 9 November 1933, Folder 2, Box 1, MS 251, SUC, AJA, Cincinnati, OH.
191 SU to Byron D. Miller, 24 October 1933, Folder 2, Box 1, MS 251, SUC, AJA, Cincinnati, OH.
192 SU to Vice-President, F.W. Woolworth Company, 20 September 1933, Folder 2, Box 1, MS 251, SUC, AJA, Cincinnati, OH.
193 Byron D. Miller to SU, 18 November 1933, Folder 2, Box 1, MS 251, SUC, AJA, Cincinnati, OH.
194 SU to Byron D. Miller, 20 December 1933, Folder 2, Box 1, MS 251, SUC, AJA, Cincinnati, OH.
195 SU to Sol Davison, 26 December 1933, Folder 2, Box 1, MS 251, SUC, AJA, Cincinnati, OH.
196 'Woolworth Bans All German Goods', *NYT*, 21 March 1934, 11; Greenberg, *Archives of the Holocaust*, 7.
197 J.S. Staedtler, Inc., New York to J.S. Staedtler, Nuremburg, 20 March 1934, S. 245, Handel 37: USA, Bd. 3, R301/44485, Bundesarchiv, Berlin, Germany.
198 J.S. Staedtler Mars-Beleistiftfabrik, Nürnberg, an die Aussenhandelstelle für Nordbayern und Südthüringen, Nürnberg, 4 July 1934, S. 249–51, Handel 37: USA, Bd. 4, R301/44486, Bundesarchiv, Berlin, Germany.
199 Auswärtiges Amt, 6 June 1934, R99530, PAAA, Berlin, Germany.
200 Cyril Quixano Henriques to SU, 14 August 1934; Nanette Silbert to SU, 30 August 1934, Folder 2, Box 1, MS 251, SUC, AJA, Cincinnati, OH.
201 Gottlieb, 'Boycott Movement', 289; AHS to George E. Harriman, 20 November 1935, Box 9, NSANLCHRR, RBML, CUL, New York, NY.
202 SU to Byron D. Miller, 24 October 1934, Folder 2, Box 1, MS 251, SUC, AJA, Cincinnati, OH.
203 Gabriel Lowenstein to Johan J. Smertenko, 22 December 1938; 29 December 1938, Box 399, NSANLCHRR, RBML, CUL, New York, NY.
204 Samuel Feller to SU, 30 August 1934, Box 3, NSANLCHRR, RBML, CUL, New York, NY.
205 SU to George E. Harriman, 27 June 1935, Box 29, NSANLCHRR, RBML, CUL, New York, NY.
206 Bernard Lubow to SU, 22 October 1934, Box 29, NSANLCHRR, RBML, CUL, New York, NY.
207 Entry for 1 January 1935, Breitman, McDonald Stewart and Hochberg, *Advocate for the Doomed*, 592.
208 Eckart Conze, Norbert Frei, Peter Hayes and Moshe Zimmermann, eds, *Das Amt und die Vergangenheit: Deutschen Diplomaten im Dritten Reich und in der Bundesrepublik* (Munich: Pantheon Verlag, 2012), 25–30.
209 'German Envoy to U.S. Yields His Portfolio', *Buffalo Courier-Express*, 15 March 1933, 2.
210 'German Envoy Says Jews Have Nothing to Fear', *Jewish Exponent*, 31 October 1930, 6.

211 'German Ambassador Bids Farewell to Diplomacy', *Buffalo Evening News*, 15 April 1933, 2.
212 Conze et al., *Das Amt*, 37.
213 Conze et al., *Das Amt*, 57.
214 'Luther Arrives, Sees Germany Resurrected', *BDE*, 14 April 1933, 3.
215 'Dr. Luther Sails', *WES*, 26 June 1933, B3.
216 Frederic William Wile, 'Washington Observations', *WES*, 30 June 1933, A8.
217 U.S. Department of State, *Foreign Relations of the United States: Diplomatic Papers: 1933: 2: The British Commonwealth, Europe, Near East and Africa* (Washington, DC: Government Printing Office, 1949), 357.
218 'Luther Says Hitler Is Fighting Despair', *WES*, 18 August 1933, A1.
219 *Diplomatic Papers: 1933: 2*: 357–8.
220 Telegram, 21 September 1933, GFM33/4734, German Foreign Ministry Archives, TNA, Kew, UK. [Translated by Dr Peter Brown.]
221 *Diplomatic Papers: 1933: 2*, 359.
222 'Untermyer Scores Luther', *NYT*, 2 November 1933, 11.
223 Address of Hon. Samuel Untermyer Given at Luncheon Meeting of American League for Defense of Jewish Rights at Cleveland Chamber of Commerce, 1 November 1933, Box 29, NSANLCHRR, RBML, CUL, New York, NY.
224 Memorandum of Conversation Between Secretary Hull and the German Ambassador, Herr Hans Luther, 2 November 1933, File 811.00 NAZI/31, RG59, Records of the Department of State, NA, College Park, MD.
225 'Hull Deprecates Attack on Luther', *NYT*, 3 November 1933, 10.
   This was unusual enough for the British Ambassador to include in a report to the Foreign Office.
   Nazi Activities in United States of America, 10 November 1933, FO371/1671, Foreign Office, TNA, Kew, UK.
226 'Untermyer Turns Attack Upon Hull', *NYT*, 4 November 1933, 8.
227 SU to AHS, 9 November 1933, Folder 1217, MS 4787, AHSP, WRHS, Cleveland, OH.
228 Cyrus Adler to Cordell Hull, 3 November 1933, File 811.00 NAZI/18, RG59, Records of the Department of State, NA, College Park, MD.
229 'Hitler Ignored in Speeches at Madison Square Garden', *BDE*, 7 December 1933, 9.
230 Samuel Untermyer, 'A Challenge to Luther', *Southern Israelite*, January 1934, 9, 21.
231 'Luther Urges Disarmament', *NYS*, 13 December 1933, 16.
232 *Southern Israelite*, January 1934, 9, 21.
233 U.S. Department of State, *Foreign Relations of the United States: Diplomatic Papers: 1934: 2: Europe, Near East and Africa* (Washington, DC: G.P.O., 1951), 516–20.
234 Deutsches Generalkonsulat New York, 28 November 1933, R99530, PAAA, Berlin, Germany. [Translated by Dr Peter Brown.]
235 EMH to SU, 20 June 1934; SU to EMH, 21 June 1934, Folder 3884, Box 122, MS466, EMHP, MA, YUL, New Haven, CT.
236 EMH to William E. Dodd, 25 May 1934, Folder 1210, Box 39, MS466, EMHP, MA, YUL, New Haven, CT.
237 Dodd and Dodd, *Diary*, 117–18, 156.
238 Entry for 5 June 1934: Breitman, McDonald Stewart and Hochberg, *Advocate for the Doomed*, 404.
239 William E. Dodd to EMH, 4 June 1934, Folder 1210, Box 39, MS466, EMHP, MA, YUL, New Haven, CT.

240 Freiherr von Neurath, S. 71-2, 4 June 1934, Handel 37: USA, Bd. 4, R301/44486, Bundesarchiv, Berlin, Germany.
241 Quoted in Erik Larson, *In the Garden of Beasts: Love and Terror in Hitler's Berlin* (London: Doubleday, 2011), 130.
242 EMH to SU, 26 June 1934, Folder 3884, Box 122, MS466, EMHP, MA, YUL, New Haven, CT.
243 EMH to SU, 12 July 1934, Folder 3884, Box 122, MS466, EMHP, MA, YUL, New Haven, CT.
244 Interview S.U., 24 July 1934, S. 380-1, Handel 37: USA, Bd. 4, R301/44486, Bundesarchiv, Berlin, Germany. [Translated by Dr Peter Brown.]
245 U.Nr.45: Bericht über eine Unterredung mit Samuel Untermyer, S. 332-5, Handel 37: USA, Bd. 6, R301/44488, Bundesarchiv, Berlin, Germany.
246 Cordell Hull to Louis McH. Howe, 6 September 1933, Official File 198A, Germany 1933, Roosevelt Papers, Franklin D. Roosevelt Library, Hyde Park, NY.
247 Entry for 1 May 1933, Breitman, McDonald Stewart and Hochberg, *Advocate for the Doomed*, 59-64.
248 Conrad Black, *Franklin Delano Roosevelt: Champion of Freedom* (London: Weidenfeld & Nicolson, 2003), 450.
249 Deutsche Botschaft, Washington, DC, S. 348-9, 26 April 1934, Handel 37: USA, Bd. 3, R301/44485, Bundesarchiv, Berlin, Germany.
250 SU to Jacob Billikopf, 28 October 1937, Folder 16, Box 30, MS 13, Jacob Billikopf Collection, AJA, Cincinnati, OH.
251 U.S. Department of State, *Foreign Relations of the United States: Diplomatic Papers: 1937: 2: The British Commonwealth, Europe, Near East and Africa* (Washington, DC: G.P.O., 1954), 376.
   Irving Abella and Harold Troper argue that Hull was unsympathetic to the plight of Germany's Jews and as late as 1938 deliberately sought to thwart their efforts to find refuge outside Germany at the international conference he organized in Evian, France.
   Irving Abella and Harold Troper, *None Is Too Many: Canada and the Jews of Europe, 1933-1948*, 3rd edn (Toronto: Lester Publishing Limited, 1991), 16.
252 Harold L. Ickes to SU, 27 November 1935, Box 25, NSANLCHRR, RBML, CUL, New York, NY.
253 'Untermyer Asks Deportation of Nazi Propagandists', *Jewish Criterion*, 29 September 1933, 5.
254 Address of Mr Samuel Untermyer over Station 'WOR', New York: 'Was the Mayor Right in Preventing the Nazi Meeting?', 23 October 1933, Box 29, NSANLCHRR, RBML, CUL, New York, NY.
255 'Ban on Nazi Rally Upheld by O'Brien', *NYT*, 26 October 1933, 1, 8.
256 'Nazi Agent Called Home to Explain', *NYT*, 27 October 1933, 10.
257 Entry for 1 January 1935, Breitman, McDonald Stewart and Hochberg, *Advocate for the Doomed*, 592.
258 'Chides Nazis On Protest', *NYT*, 7 May 1934, 10.
259 'German Societies Defend the DAWA', *NYT*, 10 May 1934, 22.
260 'Germans in College Point Score Jews', *North Shore Daily Journal*, 11 May 1934, 1-2.
261 'To Our Patriotic German-American Fellow Citizens', *NYT*, 15 May 1934, 15.
262 '20,000 Nazi Friends at A Rally Here Denounce Boycott', *NYT*, 18 May 1934, 1, 3; 'Nazi Rally Open Threat to Jews', *AH*, 25 May 1934, 33, 36.
263 Ross, *Hitler in Los Angeles*, 53-7
264 'Untermyer Sounds Alarm', *Los Angeles Times*, 16 January 1934, II-18.

265 'Untermyer Urges Use of Boycott against Hitlerism', *Schenectady Gazette*, 14 February 1934, 1.
266 'Untermyer Proposes Trade Boycott of Nazis for Persecution of Jews', *San Francisco Examiner*, 14 February 1934, 3.
267 'Police Guard Untermyer', *NYT*, 14 February 1934, 21.
268 *San Francisco Examiner*, 14 February 1934, 3.
269 Dorothy Waring, *American Defender* (New York: Robert Speller, 1935), 181–5.
270 SD to SU, 10 February 1934; SU to SD, 3 May 1934, Folder 6, Box 5, MS 8, SDC, AJA, Cincinnati, OH.
271 U.S. Cong., House, Report No. 153: Investigation of Nazi and Other Propaganda, 74th Cong., 1st sess. (Washington, DC: G.P.O., 1935), 9; Waring, *American Defender*, 202, 206.
272 SU to SD, 20 December 1934, Folder 6, Box 5, MS 8, SDC, AJA, Cincinnati, OH.

   McDonald recorded in his diary that at the beginning of 1935 Untermyer had 'not lost any of his contempt for Dickstein, whom he looks upon as a dangerous fool. He still regrets that he did not go into Dickstein's constituency [sic] at the last election, and defeat him'.

   Entry for 1 January 1935, Breitman, McDonald Stewart and Hochberg, *Advocate for the Doomed*, 592.
273 Newspaper clipping: Paul A. Peters, 'On the Q.T.', *San Francisco Emanu-El*, 23 April 1937, Box 77; SU to SD, 31 May 1934, Box 4, NSANLCHRR, RBML, CUL, New York, NY; Richard Rollins, *I Find Treason: The Story of an American Anti-Nazi Agent* (New York: William Morrow and Company, 1941), 62–5; Westbrook Pegler, 'Anti-Nazi Head Proficient In Whispering Campaigns', *Buffalo Evening News*, 9 January 1948, 22.

   No direct evidence of the Board exists except for Rollins's account. However, a telegram from Dickstein to Rollins in 1937 suggests that Rollins was employed by Untermyer and Dickstein.

   SD to Richard Rollins, 30 March 1937, Folder 7, Box 4, MS 8, SDC, AJA, Cincinnati, OH.
274 Investigation at request of Samuel Untermyer: Re: 'U.S. Malt Co., Inc.', 6 June 1934, Folder 7, Box 4, MS 8, SDC, AJA, Cincinnati, OH.
275 Hotel bill from Richard Rollins, 18 October 1938, Folder 7, Box 4, MS 8, SDC, AJA, Cincinnati, OH.
276 Richard Rollins to Boris E. Nelson, 28 April 1937, Box 77; NSANL: Summary of Facts Presented at Meeting of Survey Committee Held 20 June 1939, Box 59, NSANLCHRR, RBML, CUL, New York, NY; Percy E. Foxworth to Richard Rollins, 20 March 1942, File 100-9552, Non-Sectarian Anti-Nazi League, Federal Bureau of Investigation, Washington, DC.
277 SU to Bernard G. Richards, 27 September 1934, Box 4, NSANLCHRR, RBML, CUL, New York, NY.
278 Stern, *Memoirs*, 220.
279 Entry for 2 November 1933: Breitman, McDonald, and Hochberg, *Advocate for the Doomed*, 139; ASO to SU, 5 July 1933, b42, f.13-15, NYTCR: ASOP, NYPL, New York, NY; Arthur Hays Sulzberger to Ezekiel Rabinowitz, 22 August 1933, Box 7, NSANLCHRR, RBML, CUL, New York, NY; SU to ASO, 5 March 1935, Folder 8, Box 2, MS 251, SUC, AJA, Cincinnati, OH; 'Arthur Hays Sulzberger', *NYT*, 15 December 1968, E13.

280 Untermeyer [sic] Interview 1933, Story Number: 6482B, British Movietone Digital Archive, London, United Kingdom.
281 Samuel Untermyer and Countess De Covagodonga, 4 December 1934, MVTN 23-970, Cassette No. RC 2427, Moving Image Research Collection, University of South Carolina, Columbia, SC.
282 George Britt, 'The Boycott', *New York World-Telegram*, 5 February 1935, II-1; Jerold S. Auerbach, 'Review Essay: Proskauer: His Life and Times', *American Jewish History* 69, no. 1 (1979): 109–10.
283 George Britt, 'The Boycott', *New York World-Telegram*, 12 February 1935, 15.
284 Samuel Untermeyer [sic], noted New York lawyer, interviewed in London, announces world boycott plan, 5 July 1933, Vol. 4, no. 290, Hearst Metrotone News, ZVB2315 M, Hearst Newsreels Collection, UCLA Film and Television Archive, Los Angeles, CA.
285 David Nasaw, *The Chief: The Life of William Randolph Hearst* (New York: Houghton Mifflin Company, 2000), 488–99.
286 'Untermyer Joins Hands with Hearst', *Daily Worker* [New York], 1 May 1935, 1.
287 Nasaw, *The Chief*, 499.
288 'Untermyer Raps Hull's Policies', *Los Angeles Examiner*, 25 January 1938, Folder 11, Box 1782, Collection 7000.1c, Hearst Corporation Los Angeles Examiner photographs, negatives and clippings--portrait files (N-Z), Regional History Collection, University of Southern California, Los Angeles, CA.
289 'U.S. Labor Votes Boycott of Germany', *Buffalo Courier Express*, 14 October 1933, 1.
290 'Green's Boycott Swindle', *Daily Worker* [New York], 30 December 1933, 8.
291 The Hungarian Jew had been the leader of the short-lived Hungarian Soviet Republic in 1919. Kun was executed in 1938. He was a victim of Stalin's mass repression.
  Béla Kun, 'The Communist Position on the Boycott', *Daily Worker* [New York], 11 December 1933, 6; William J. Chase, 'Microhistory and Mass Repression: Politics, Personalities, and Revenge in the Fall of Béla Kun', *The Russian Review* 67, no. 3 (2008): 458.
292 Entry for 1 January 1935, Breitman, McDonald Stewart and Hochberg, *Advocate for the Doomed*, 592.
293 'Boycott on German Goods Again Urged', BDE, 15 February 1934, 6; William Green, 'Nazi Assault on Organized Labor', in Non-Sectarian Anti-Nazi League to Champion Human Rights, *Nazis Against the World: The Counter-Boycott is the Only Defensive Weapon against Hitlerism's World-Threat to Civilization* (New York: The League, 1934), 32–40; Samuel Untermyer, *Civilization's Only Weapon Against Hitlerism: Address Read at the Testimonial Dinner to Mr. William Green, at the Aldine Club, New York City, February 14, 1934* (New York: Non-Sectarian Anti-Nazi League to Champion Human Rights, 1934).
294 George E. Harriman to SU, 7 January 1935, Box 4, NSANLCHRR, RBML, CUL, New York, NY.
295 SU to George E. Harriman, 18 July 1935; Richard J. Beamish to George E. Harriman, c. 22 July 1935; George E. Harriman to Richard J. Beamish, 22 August 1935; George E. Harriman to Editor, The Forward, 6 August 1935, Box 24, NSANLCHRR, RBML, CUL, New York, NY.
  The Archivum Secretum Vaticanum have no record of this meeting. Marco Grilli to Richard Hawkins, 22 October 2018.

296 David I. Kertzer, *Unholy War: The Vatican's Role in the Rise of Modern Anti-Semitism* (London: Macmillan. 2002), 239–91.
297 'Untermyer Felicitates Cardinal', *NYT*, 20 May 1937, 4.
298 'Samuel Untermeyer wittert neue Geschäftsmöglichkeiten' *Berliner Illustrierte Nachtausgabe*, 20 May 1937, 1–2. [Translated by Doris Jaeger.]
299 'Trade Agreements', *Commercial & Financial Chronicle*, 2 March 1935, 1353.
300 Samuel Untermyer, *The World's Answer to the Mendacious Nazi Plea to End the Boycott: An Address at a Mass Meeting of the Los Angeles Americanization League Held at the Philharmonic Auditorium, Los Angeles, California, March 17th, 1935* (New York: The Author, 1935), 26.
301 'Public Men Urge Olympic Boycott', *NYT*, 12 September 1935, 28.
302 'Untermyer Sends A Letter', *NYT*, 27 September 1934, 28; 'Power Rests with A.A.U.', *NYT*, 8 December 1934, 20.
303 Moshe Gottlieb, 'The American Controversy Over the Olympic Games', *American Jewish Historical Quarterly* 61, no. 3 (1972): 196.
304 Entry for 1 January 1935, Breitman, McDonald Stewart and Hochberg, *Advocate for the Doomed*, 407.
305 SU to EMH, 18 October 1935, Folder 3884, Box 122, MS466, EMHP, MA, YUL, New Haven, CT; 'Mahoney Praised for Olympic Stand', *NYT*, 8 November 1935, 7.
306 Gottlieb, 'Olympic Games', 197–210.
307 The lawyer was a former commander-in-chief of the JWV who had led its anti-Nazi boycott campaign and was 'apparently its most active, if not avid' boycott advocate.
  Gottlieb, 'Ideological and Sociological', 202; 'George Fredman, Jersey Lawyer', *NYT*, 3 July 1958, 25.
308 'Schmeling Boycott Gains Supporters', *Daily Worker* [New York], 17 February 1937, 8.
  Although Schmeling was effectively an ambassador for the Nazi regime, he was not an anti-Semite. He hid the two sons of a Jewish friend in his Berlin apartment during the Kristallnacht pogrom of 9 November 1938 and allowed them to remain there for several days until another hiding place could be found for them. Mike Jacobs, his American promoter, was Jewish. In April 1940 when it was mistakenly reported Jacobs had died, Schmeling said he was 'deeply shocked and sorry'.
  Robert Weisbord and Norbert Hedderich, 'Max Schmeling Righteous Ring Warrior', *History Today* 43, no. 1 (1995): 40; 'Max Deeply Shocked by Death of Jacobs', *Buffalo Evening News*, 25 April 1940, 35.
309 'Teuton Target for Anti-Nazi League Blast', *PI*, 9 January 1937, 19, 21.
310 'Fight Boycott Irks Schmeling, Germans', *Syracuse Sunday American*, 10 January 1937, 15.
311 'Untermyer Against Fight Ban If Max Keeps Earnings Here', *Yonkers Herald Statesman*, 14 January 1937, 14.
312 SU to J. George Fredman, 12 January 1937; SU to J. George Fredman, 13 January 1937; SU to Mary Harris, 19 January 1937, Box 5, NSANLCHRR, RBML, CUL, New York, NY; Mary Harris to AHS, 21 January 1937, Folder 1221, MS 4787, AHSP, WRHS, Cleveland, OH.
313 'Braddock's Manager Agrees to Boycott Plan', *New York Post*, 9 January 1937, 24; 'Braddock Will Oppose Garden', *PI*, 14 April 1937, 21; 'Nazis Fume', *BDE*, 4 June 1937, 19.
314 'Anti-Nazi Boycott KO's Schmeling; He Leaves U.S.', *Daily Worker* [New York], 24 March 1937, 1, 8.

315 'Mike Jacobs Accepts Schmeling Ban as New Woe', *New York Post*, 16 November 1937, 22; 'Thomas Outclassed by Uhlan', *NYS*, 14 December 1937, 39.
316 'Streicher Askes Nazis Boycott Jewish Stores', *Buffalo Courier-Express*, 18 December 1937, 8.
317 'Plan Fight Boycott', *PI*, 27 April 1938, 19.
318 U.S. Department of State, *Press Releases* 18, no. 451 (1938): 586; 'Mike to Give 10 Per Cent of Receipts', *Buffalo Evening News*, 13 May 1938, 36.
319 'Jacobs' Attorney Defends Failure to Aid Refugee Fund', *Daily Worker* [New York], 2 September 1938, 8.
320 Samuel Untermyer, *"No Pasaran" (They Shall Not Pass): Religion Answers the Nazi Challenge: Address of Samuel Untermyer Before the Temple and Synagogue Brotherhoods at Baltimore, Md., Sunday, December 19, 1937* (New York: The Author, 1938), 1–32.
321 SU to the League, 24 April 1938, Folder 2, Box 1, MS 251, SUC, AJA, Cincinnati, OH.
322 SU to Alvin Untermyer, 27 April 1938, Folder 2, Box 1, MS 251, SUC, AJA, Cincinnati, OH.
323 Minutes of the Bronx Division of the League, 4 December 1935, Box 1, Folder 12, MS 307, BVCC, AJA, Cincinnati, OH; Grover, *Nazis in Newark*, 129–30, 221, 267–8.
324 Grover, *Nazis in Newark*, 267–8; 'Link, Not Shrink the Effort', *Jewish Criterion*, 13 May 1938, 6; 'We Pat Our Back', *Jewish Criterion*, 3 June 1938, 18
325 Benjamin Dubovsky to SU, 13 May 1939, Folder 3, Box 1, MS 251, SUC, AJA, Cincinnati, OH; Report on Non-Sectarian Anti-Nazi League, 20 January 1941, File 100-9552, Non-Sectarian Anti-Nazi League, Federal Bureau of Investigation, Washington, DC.
326 Grover, *Nazis in Newark*, 184.
327 Frommer, 'American Jewish Congress', 366–9.
328 'Untermyer Brands Nazi Rule by Extermination', *San Francisco Chronicle*, 14 February 1934, 3.
329 Meyer F. Steinglass, 'American Jewry's Fall of Fame', *Jewish Criterion*, 14 September 1934, 3.

Conclusion

1 Enoch Powell, *Joseph Chamberlain* (London: Thames & Hudson, 1977), 151.
2 'Untermyer Says Jews to Boycott Austria', *Desert Sun*, 25 March 1938, 11.
3 'Untermyer Aids Polish Jews', *NYT*, 5 May 1937, 16.
4 'Interfaith Boycott of Germany Urged', *NYT*, 13 June 1937, 31.
5 'Untermyer Asks Aid for Jews In Poland', *NYT*, 6 December 1937, 18; Samuel Untermyer, *Address of Mr. Samuel Untermyer at the Emergency Conference Appeal for the Relief of Jews in Poland, Waldorf-Astoria Hotel, New York, December 5, 1937* (New York: The Author, 1937).
6 'Permit Campaign for Polish Jews', *Detroit Jewish Chronicle*, 22 September 1939, 1, 4.
7 Friedman, *Consumer Boycotts*, 138.
8 'Nazi Exports to U.S. Hit New Low', *Detroit Jewish Chronicle*, 16 July 1937, 1.
9 Sharon Gewirtz, 'Anglo-Jewish Responses to Nazi Germany 1933–1939: The Anti-Nazi Boycott and the Board of Deputies of British Jews', *Journal of Contemporary History* 26, no. 2 (1991): 261.

10 Frommer, American Jewish Congress, 368–9; Joseph Tenenbaum, *Three Years Anti-Nazi Boycott* (New York: Joint Boycott Council of the American Jewish Congress and Jewish Labor Committee, 1936).
11 Joseph Tenenbaum, 'The Anti-Nazi Boycott Movement in the United States', in *Yad Vashem Studies on the European Jewish Catastrophe and Resistance, III*, ed. Saul Esh (Jerusalem: Yad Vashem, 1959), 148.
12 Sarah Churchwell, *Behold, America: A History of America First and the American Dream* (London: Bloomsbury Publishing, 2018), 227.
13 Jeffrey S. Gurock, *Jews in Gotham: New York Jews in a Changing City, 1920–2010* (New York: New York University Press, 2012), 32–4.
14 Charles Coughlin, *Is it OK to be Anti-Christian but a Crime in the United States to be Anti-Semitic?: Text of Samuel Untermeyer's 'Sacred War' Speech, August 7, 1933, Upon his Return from the World-Wide International Jewish Boycott Conference at Amsterdam, Holland, and Father Coughlin's Comments, March 16, 1942* (Hollywood, CA: Sons of Liberty, 1942).
15 '"Social Justice" Barred from U.S. Mails', *New York PM Daily*, 15 April 1942, 2; 'Fr. Coughlin Paper Stopped By Bishop', *PI*, 5 May 1942, 1, 7.
16 LAS to Charlie S. Guggenheimer, 4 January 1939, Box 27, LASP, LCMD, Washington, DC.
17 Philip Roth, *The Plot against America* (London: Vintage, 2018).
18 Neil Forbes, *Doing Business with the Nazis: Britain's Economic and Financial Relations with Germany, 1931–1939* (London: Frank Cass, 2000), 200.
19 'Boycott Opposed by Hull as Unwise', *NYT*, 19 September 1934, 4.
20 'Untermyer Fights Nazi Trade Treaty', 1 October 1934, 8; SU to Cordell Hull, 14 November 1934; 15 November 1934, File 662.1115/88, RG59, Records of the Department of State, NA, College Park, MD; Cordell Hull, *The Memoirs of Cordell Hull: 1* (New York: The Macmillan Company, 1948), 370–4.
21 In 1927 Glass published a book in which he took the credit for the Federal Reserve Act while minimizing Untermyer's contribution. Untermyer published a pamphlet refuting Glass's account. Reginald McKenna of Britain's Midland Bank observed to Senator Robert L. Owen that it was 'extraordinary that the need for this pamphlet should ever have been allowed to arise'. Owen disputed Glass's account and noted in 1935 that he had declined to reply to Untermyer's refutation. In his book on the Federal Reserve Act published in 1919 Owen had acknowledged that he 'particularly appreciated the valuable assistance of Hon. Samuel Untermyer of New York, who gave me many useful suggestions'. Owen's annotated copy of Glass's book also shows he considered the references to Untermyer to be inaccurate. Paul M. Warburg also agreed that Glass's account included false statements.

Carter Glass, *An Adventure in Constructive Finance* (Garden City, NY: Doubleday, Page & Company, 1927);

Samuel Untermyer, *Who is Entitled to the Credit for the Federal Reserve Act? An Answer to Senator Carter Glass, by Samuel Untermyer* (New York, The Author, 1927); Robert L. Owen, *The Federal Reserve Act* (Washington, DC: The Author, 1919), 102–3; Annotated copy of 'An Adventure in Constructive Finance'; Reginald McKenna to Robert L. Owen, 3 August 1927; Robert L. Owen to Duncan U. Fletcher, 27 March 1935; Robert L. Owen to CG, 26 March 1935, Box 1, Robert L. Owen Papers, LCMD, Washington, DC; Paul M. Warburg to SU, 28 June 1929, Folder 7, Box 3, MS 251, SUC, AJA, Cincinnati, OH.

22 SU to Eppa Hunton, 10 February 1908, Folder 4, Box 1, MS 251, SUC, AJA, Cincinnati, OH.
23 Newspaper Clipping, c. 30 January 1936, Box 64, MSS 2913, CGP, SSC, UVL, Charlottesville, VA.
24 As late as December 1938 Glass was still defaming Untermyer.
    CG to Chester Morrill, 22 December 1938, Box 332, MSS 2913, CGP, SSC, UVL, Charlottesville, VA.
25 Ernest C. Hastings, 'How Guggenheimers' Succeeded by Building Town to Support Store', *Dry Goods Economist*, 13 August 1921, 28, 237.
26 E. L. Jordan, 'Fete at Lynchburg', *NYT*, 11 October 1936, 11:1.
27 'Lynchburg Jews Plan Tablet to Untermyer', *Richmond Times-Dispatch*, 4 October 1936, 9.
28 'Lynchburg's Sesquicentennial', *Norfolk & Western Magazine*, September 1936, 318.
29 'Untermyer Dedication', *Lynchburg News*, 14 October 1936, 2; 'Two Native Sons Are Honoured at Lynchburg Celebration', *Richmond Times-Dispatch*, 14 October 1936, 1, 6.
30 'Untermyer Dead in His 82nd Year', *NYT*, 17 March 1940, 1, 48.
31 'Nation Mourns Samuel Untermyer', *Jewish Telegraphic Agency News*, 18 March 1940, 2–4.
32 'Governor Attends Untermyer Funeral Rites', *NYT*, 23 March 1940, 26.
33 Auerbach, 'Review Essay', 110.

Epilogue

1 'Alvin Untermyer Dead at 80', *NYT*, 21 September 1963, 21; 'Irwin Untermyer, 87, Retired Judge, Dies', *NYT*, 19 October 1973, 44.
2 'Untermyer Runs Last', *NYDT*, 5 November 1919, 1.
3 'Vote for Judges', *NYEP*, 6 November 1929, 3.
4 'Justice Untermyer's Wife Dies', *Yonkers Herald Statesman*, 28 March 1944, 2; 'Untermyer Retires from Post as Appellate Judge', *Yonkers Herald Statesman*, 1 August 1945, 3.
5 'Goodrich Resigns Tax Appeals Post', *WES*, 20 February 1935, B11; 'Harry Hoffman' in *Who Was Who in America: 9: 1985–1989* (Wilmette, IL: Marquis Who's Who, 1989), 169.
6 *Legal Times*, 26 May 1986, 6, 16–17.
7 James Fontanella-Khan, Sujeet Indap and Barney Thompson, 'Lockstep in the Dock', *Financial Times* [London], 10 April 2018, 9.
8 Joan Untermyer Erdmann, 'Youth House', *Legal Aid Review*, 62 (1964): 24–7; 'Youth House Acts to Drop Jail Aura', *NYT*, 2 October 1964, 39; *Warrentown – Lake George News*, 13 February 1969, 12.
9 SU to Irwin Untermyer, 15 February 1933, FUPP, Evanston, IL.
10 Cornell University, *Announcement of the College of Arts and Science for 1940–1941* (Ithaca, NY: The University, 1939), 11; 'Appointments Ratified', *Cornell Daily Sun*, 26 March 1940, 12; 'Liberalism Talks Begin Today', *Cornell Daily Sun*, 13 April 1940, 1; Frank Untermyer, *Recollections of the Untermyer Family* (Evanston, IL: The Author, 1995), 44, 71; *Yonkers Herald Statesman*, 28 March 1944, 2; 'Frank Untermyer, 88',

Chicago Tribune, 20 October 2004, 2:10; Laura Janota, 'Roosevelt University's First Decade', *Roosevelt Review*, Spring 2008, 31.
11 SU to Irwin Untermyer, 15 February 1933, FUPP, Evanston, IL; Hanover, Lehigh County, PA, 15 April 1940, United States Census, https://www.familysearch.org, accessed 10 September 2020; 'Samuel Untermyer II', *NYT*, 31 January 2001, A19; Frank Wicks, '50 Years of Nuclear Power', *Mechanical Engineering*, November 2007, 37–9; Untermyer, *Recollections*, 67.

Bibliography

Archival sources

American Jewish Archives, Cincinnati, OH.
American Jewish Committee Archive, New York, NY.
American University Digital Research Archive, Washington, DC.
Archives of The Pierpont Morgan Library, New York, NY.
Baker Library, Harvard Business School, Cambridge, MA
British Movietone Digital Archive, London, United Kingdom.
Bundesarchiv, Berlin, Germany.
Central Archives for the History of the Jewish People, Jerusalem, Israel.
Central Zionist Archive, Jerusalem, Israel.
Clerk's Office, Lynchburg Circuit Court, Lynchburg, VA.
Congregation Beth Ahabah Museum and Archives, Richmond, VA.
Federal Bureau of Investigation, Washington, DC.
Federal Reserve Bank of New York Archives, New York, NY.
Franklin D. Roosevelt Library, Hyde Park, NY.
Henry Ford Museum, Dearborn, MI.
Hoover Institution Archives, Palo Alto, CA.
Horrmann Library, Wagner College, New York, NY.
Jones Memorial Library, Lynchburg, VA.
Kheel Center for Labor-Management Documentation & Archives, Cornell University Library, Ithaca, NY
Law Library, Columbia University Library, New York, NY.
Library and Archives Canada, Ottawa, Canada.
Lilly Library, Indiana University, Bloomington, IN.
Manuscripts and Archives, Yale University, New Haven, CT.
Moving Image Research Collection, University of South Carolina, Columbia, SC.
National Archives, Kew, United Kingdom.
National Archives, Washington, DC and College Park, MD.
New York Municipal Archive, New York, NY.
New York Public Library, New York, NY.
Politisches Archiv des Auswärtigen Amts, Berlin, Germany.
Private Papers of the Late Frank Untermyer, Evanston, IL.
Rabbi Peter H. Schweitzer's Family Archive, New York, NY.
Rare Book and Manuscript Library, Columbia University Library, New York, NY.
Regional History Collection, University of Southern California, Los Angeles, CA.
Rockefeller Archive Center, Sleepy Hollow, NY.
Robert D. Farber University Archives & Special Collections, BUL, Waltham, MA.
Seeley G. Mudd Manuscript Library, Princeton University, Princeton, NJ.
Senate Library, Washington, DC.
Sherrod Library, East Tennessee State University, Johnston City, TN.

Staatsarchiv Augsburg, Augsburg, Germany.
Stadt Augsburg Stadtarchiv, Augsburg, Germany.
The Jewish National and University Library, Jerusalem, Israel.
The Weizmann Archive, Rehovot, Israel.
UCLA (University of California at Los Angeles) Film and Television Archive, Los Angeles, CA.
University Archives, University of Louisville, Louisville, KY.
Western Reserve Historical Society, Cleveland, OH.
Yivo Institute for Jewish Research, New York, NY.

Books

Abbott, Lawrence F. *The Story of NYLIC: A History of the Origin and Development of the New York Life Insurance Company from 1845 to 1929*. New York: The Company, 1930.
Abella, Irving, and Harold Troper. *None Is Too Many: Canada and the Jews of Europe, 1933–1948*. 3rd edn. Toronto: Lester Publishing Limited, 1991.
Abrams, Jeanne. *Blazing the Tuberculosis Trail*. Denver: Colorado Historical Society, 1991.
Anderson, Jervis. *A. Philip Randolph: A Biographical Portrait*. New York: Harcourt Brace Jovanovich, 1972.
Anon. *Proceedings of the Seventieth Annual Meeting of the Hebrew Benevolent and Orphan Society of the City of New York Held at The Asylum, Sunday, April 30th, 1893*. New York: Stettiner, Lambert & Co., 1893.
Anon. *A Souvenir of New York's Liquor Interests*. New York: American Publishing and Engraving Co., 1893.
Anon. *History of Cincinnati and Hamilton County, Ohio*. Cincinnati: S.B. Nelson & Co., 1894.
Anon. *Memoirs of Georgia: 2*. Atlanta, GA: Southern Historical Association, 1895.
Anon. *One Hundred Years of Brewing*. Chicago and New York: Western Brewer, 1903.
Anon. *A History of Columbia University, 1754–1904*. New York: Columbia University Press, 1904.
Anon. *Celebrating the 50th Anniversary of the Dedication of the Andrew Freedman Home: Founders' Day May 16, 1974*. New York: The Home, 1974.
Aronson, Rudolph. *Theatrical and Musical Memoirs*. New York: McBride, McNast and Company, 1913.
Arrington, Leonard J., and Gary B. Hansen. *'The Richest Hole on Earth': A History of the Bingham Copper Mine*. Logan: Utah State University Press, 1963.
Ayres, Pat Edith. *The Andrew Freedman Story*. New York: The Home, 1976.
Badger, Anthony J. *FDR: The First Hundred Days*. New York: Hill and Wang, 2008.
Balliett, Carl J. *World Leadership in Denims Through Thirty Years of Progress*. Greensboro, NC: Proximity Mfg. Co., 1925.
Barnard, Harry. *The Forging of An American Jew: The Life and Times of Judge Julian W. Mack*. New York: Herzl Press, 1974.
Baruch, Bernard M. *Baruch: My Own Story*. New York: Henry Holt and Company, 1957.
Behlmer, Rudy. *Inside Warner Bros. (1935–1951)*. New York: Viking, 1985.
Bein, Alex, ed. *Arthur Ruppin: Memoirs, Diaries, Letters*. London: Weidenfeld & Nicolson, 1971.

Bentwich, Norman. *For Zion's Sake: A Biography of Judah L. Magnes*. Philadelphia: Jewish Publication Society of America, 1954.
Berman, Myron. *Richmond's Jewry, 1769–1976: Shabbat in Shockoe*. Charlottesville: University of Virginia Press, 1979.
Berman, Myron. *The Last of the Jews?* Lanham: University Press of America, 1998.
Bernstein, Marvin D. *The Mexican Mining Industry, 1890–1950: A Study of the Interaction of Politics, Economics and Technology*. New York: State University of New York Press, 1964.
Bernstorff, Johann Heinrich. *My Three Years in America*. London: Skeffington & Son, Ltd., 1920.
Birmingham, Stephen. *'Our Crowd': The Great Jewish Families of New York*. London: Futura, 1985.
Black, Conrad. *Franklin Delano Roosevelt: Champion of Freedom*. London: Weidenfeld & Nicolson, 2003.
Black, Edwin. *The Transfer Agreement: The Untold Story of the Secret Agreement Between the Third Reich and Jewish Palestine*. New York: Macmillan Publishing Company, 1984.
Boeckel, Richard. *Presidential Campaign Funds*. Washington, DC: Editorial Research Reports, 1928. http://library.cqpress.com/cqresearcher/cqresrre1928040600, accessed 13 August 2020.
Bowen, Clarence Winthrop, ed. *The History of the Centennial Celebration of the Inauguration of George Washington as First President of the United States*. New York: D. Appleton and Company, 1892.
Brandeis, Louis Dembitz. *Other People's Money, and How the Bankers Use It*. New York: F.A. Stokes Co., 1914.
Breen, Matthew P. *Thirty Years of New York Politics Up-To-Date*. New York: The Author, 1899.
Breitman, Richard, and Allan J. Lichtman, *FDR and the Jews*. Cambridge, MA: Harvard University Press, 2013.
Breitman, Richard, Barbara McDonald Stewart, and Severin Hochberg, eds. *Advocate for the Doomed: The Diaries and Papers of James G. McDonald, 1932–1935*. Bloomington and Indianapolis: Indiana University Press, 2007.
Brough, James. *The Woolworths*. New York: McGraw-Hill, 1982.
Buley, Roscoe Carlyle. *The American Life Convention, 1906–1952: A Study in the History of Life Insurance: 1*. New York: Appleton-Century-Crofts, Inc., 1953.
Buley, Roscoe Carlyle. *The Equitable Life Assurance Society of the United States, 1859–1964: 1*. New York: Appleton-Century-Crofts, 1967.
Burrows, Edwin G., and Mike Wallace. *Gotham: A History of New York City to 1898*. New York: Oxford University Press, 1999.
Chafee Jr., Zechariah. *Free Speech in the United States*. Cambridge, MA: Harvard University Press, 1946.
Chenery, William L. *So It Seemed*. New York: Harcourt, Brace and Company, 1952.
Churchwell, Sarah. *Behold, America: A History of America First and the American Dream*. London: Bloomsbury Publishing, 2018.
Cohen, George. *The Jews in the Making of America*. Boston, MA: The Stratford Co., 1924.
Cohen, Michael R. *Cotton Capitalists: American Jewish Entrepreneurship in the Reconstruction Era*. New York: New York University Press, 2017.
Cohen, Naomi W. *Jacob H. Schiff: A Study in American Jewish Leadership*. Hanover: Brandeis University Press: Published by University Press of New England, 1999.
Cohen, Stanley. *A. Mitchell Palmer: Politician*. New York: Columbia University Press, 1963.

Collins, Theresa M. *Otto Kahn: Art, Money, & Modern Time*. Durham, NC: University of North Carolina Press, 2002.

Conze, Eckart, Norbert Frei, Peter Hayes, and Moshe Zimmermann, eds. *Das Amt und die Vergangenheit: Deutschen Diplomaten im Dritten Reich und in der Bundesrepublik*. Munich: Pantheon Verlag, 2012.

Coughlin, Charles. *Is it OK to be Anti-Christian but a Crime in the United States to be Anti-Semitic?: Text of Samuel Untermeyer's 'Sacred War' Speech, August 7, 1933, Upon his Return from the World-Wide International Jewish Boycott Conference at Amsterdam, Holland, and Father Coughlin's Comments, March 16, 1942*. Hollywood, CA: Sons of Liberty, 1942.

Cowing, Cedric B. *Populists, Plungers, and Progressives: A Social History of Stock and Commodity Speculation*. Princeton, NJ: Princeton University Press, 1965.

De Haas, Jacob. *Louis D. Brandeis: A Biographical Sketch*. New York: Bloch Publishing Company, 1929.

Denlinger, Milo G. *The Complete Collie*. 2nd edn. Washington, DC: Denlinger's, 1947.

Dodd, William E., and Martha Dodd, eds. *Ambassador Dodd's Diary, 1933-1938*. London: Victor Gollancz, 1941.

Doerries, Reinhard R. *Imperial Challenge: Ambassador Count Bernstorff and German-American Relations, 1908-1917*. Chapel Hill: University of North Carolina Press, 1989.

Dunn, Dennis J. *Caught Between Roosevelt & Stalin: America's Ambassadors to Moscow*. Lexington, KY: The University Press of Kentucky, 1998.

Dyson, Walter. *Howard University: The Capstone of Negro Education: A History: 1867-1940*. Washington, DC: Howard University, 1941.

Eastman, Max. *Is Woman Suffrage Important?* New York: Men's League for Woman Suffrage, 1912.

Eisen, Norman. *The Last Palace: Europe's Extraordinary Century Through Five Lives and One House in Prague*. London: Headline, 2018.

Ely, Robert Erskine, ed. *Yearbook of the Economic Club of New York: II: Containing the Addresses of the Season 1911-1912*. New York: The Knickerbocker Press, 1912.

Ely, Robert Erskine, ed. *Yearbook of the Economic Club of New York: IV: Containing the Addresses of the Season 1913-1914*. New York: The Knickerbocker Press, 1914.

Epstein, Melech. *Profiles of Eleven*. Lanham, MD: University Press of America, 1987.

Ezekiel, Herbert T., and Gaston Lichtenstein. *The History of the Jews of Richmond from 1769 to 1917*. Richmond: Herbert T. Ezekiel, 1917.

Fogelson, Robert M. *The Great Rent Wars: New York, 1917-1929*. New Haven and London: Yale University Press, 2013.

Forbes, John Douglas. *J.P. Morgan, Jr., 1867-1943*. Charlottesville: University Press of Virginia, 1981.

Forbes, Neil. *Doing Business with the Nazis: Britain's Economic and Financial Relations with Germany, 1931-1939*. London: Frank Cass, 2000.

Forrest, Jay W. and James Malcolm. *Tammany's Treason: Impeachment of Governor William Sulzer*. Albany: The Fort Orange Press, 1913.

Fox, Richard Wightman. *Trials of Intimacy: Love and Loss in the Beecher-Tilton Scandal*. Chicago, IL: University of Chicago Press, 1999.

Freidel, Frank. *Franklin D. Roosevelt: Launching the New Deal*. Boston: Little, Brown and Company, 1973.

Friedman, Monroe. *Consumer Boycotts: Effecting Change Through the Marketplace and the Media*. New York: Routledge, 1999.

Friedman, Murray, ed. *Philadelphia Jewish Life, 1940–2000*. Philadelphia: Temple University Press, 2003.
General Federation of Women's Clubs. *Eleventh Biennial Convention, June 25 to July 5, 1912, San Francisco, Cal.: Official Report*. Newark, NJ: The Federation, 1912.
Glass, Carter. *An Adventure in Constructive Finance*. Garden City, NY: Doubleday, Page & Company, 1927.
Gompers, Samuel. *Seventy Years of Life and Labor: An Autobiography: 1*. New York: E.P. Dutton & Company, 1925.
Gottlieb, Moshe. *American Anti-Nazi Resistance, 1933–1941: An Historical Analysis*. New York: Ktav Pub. House, 1982.
Greenberg, Karen J., ed. *Archives of the Holocaust, VI, Columbia University Library, New York: The Non-Sectarian Anti-Nazi League to Champion Human Rights Papers: The Non-Sectarian Anti-Nazi League Pamphlet Collection*. New York: Garland Publishing, Inc., 1990.
Grover, Warren. *Nazis in Newark*. New Brunswick, NJ: Transaction Publishers, 2003.
Gurock, Jeffrey S. *City of Promises: A History of the Jews of New York: 3: Jews in Gotham: New York Jews in a Changing City, 1920–2010*. New York and London: New York University Press, 2012.
Hagedorn, Hermann. *The Magnate: William Boyce Thompson and His Time, 1869–1930*. New York: Reynal & Hitchcock, 1935.
Halperin, Samuel. *The Political World of American Zionism*. Detroit: Wayne State University Press, 1961.
Handlin, Oscar. *A Continuing Task: The American Joint Distribution Committee, 1914–1964*. New York: Random House, 1964.
Hardy, James D. Jr. *The New York Giants Baseball Club: The Growth of a Team and a Sport, 1870–1900*. Jefferson, NC: McFarland & Co, 1996.
Hays, Arthur Garfield. *City Lawyer: The Autobiography of a Law Practice*. New York: Simon and Schuster, 1942.
Heatwole, Cornelius J. *A History of Education in Virginia*. New York: The Macmillan Company, 1916.
Helmes, Winifred G. *John A. Johnson: The People's Governor: A Political History*. Minneapolis, MN: University of Minnesota Press, 1949.
Herzstein, Robert E. *Henry R. Luce, Time, and the American Crusade in Asia*. New York: Cambridge University Press, 2005.
Himber, Charlotte. *Famous in Their Twenties*. New York: Association Press, 1942
Hirschmann, Ira. *Caution to the Winds*. New York: Davis McKay Company, Inc., 1962.
Hood, Clifton. *722 Miles: The Building of The Subways and How They Transformed New York*. New York: Simon & Schuster, 1993.
Hoyt, Edwin P. *The Guggenheims and the American Dream*. New York: Funk & Wagnalls, 1967.
Hull, Cordell. *The Memoirs of Cordell Hull: 1*. New York: The Macmillan Company, 1948.
Hunter, Anna M., and Jenny Hunter, eds. *The Autobiography of Thomas Hunter*. New York: The Knickerbocker Press, 1931.
Keller, Morton. *In Defense of Yesterday: James M. Beck and the Politics of Conservatism, 1861–1936*. New York: Coward-McCann, Inc., 1958.
Kertzer, David I. *Unholy War: The Vatican's Role in the Rise of Modern Anti-Semitism*. London: Macmillan. 2002.
Klein, Henry H. *Dynastic America and Those Who Own It*. New York: The Author, 1921.

Klein, Henry H. *My Last Fifty Years: An Autobiographical History of 'Inside' New York*. New York: The Author, 1935.
Knight, Peter. *Reading the Market: Genres of Financial Capitalism in Gilded Age America*. Baltimore: Johns Hopkins University Press, 2016.
Knox, John Jay. *A History of Banking in the United States*. New York: Bradford Rhodes & Company, 1903.
Kroeger, Brooke. *The Suffragents: How Women Used Men to Get the Vote*. Albany: State University Press of New York, 2017.
Landau, Henry. *The Enemy Within: The Inside Story of German Sabotage in America*. New York: G.P. Putnam's Sons, 1937.
Lankevich, George J. *American Metropolis: A History of New York City*. New York and London: New York University Press, 1998.
Larson, Bruce L. *Lindbergh of Minnesota: A Political Biography*. New York: Harcourt, Brace Jovanovich, Inc., 1973.
Larson, Erik. *In the Garden of Beasts: Love and Terror in Hitler's Berlin*. London: Doubleday, 2011.
Lentin, Antony. *Banker, Traitor, Scapegoat, Spy? The Troublesome Case of Sir Edgar Speyer: An Episode of the Great War*. London: Haus Publishing, 2013.
Lindbergh, Charles A. *Banking and Currency and the Money Trust*. Washington, DC: National Capital Press, 1913.
Lingenfelter, Richard E. *Bonanzas & Borrascas: Copper Kings & Stock Frenzies, 1885-1918*. Norman, OK: The Arthur H. Clark Company, 2012.
Link, Arthur S. *Wilson: Volume I: The Road to the White House*. Princeton, NJ: Princeton University Press, 1947.
Link, Arthur S. *Woodrow Wilson and the Progressive Era: 1910-1917*. New York: Harper & Brothers Publishers, 1954.
Link, Arthur S. *Wilson: Volume II: The New Freedom*. Princeton, NJ: Princeton University Press, 1956.
Link, Arthur S., ed. *The Papers of Woodrow Wilson: 34: July 21 – September 30, 1915*. Princeton, NJ: Princeton University Press, 1980.
MacNeil, Neil. *Without Fear or Favor*. New York: Harcourt, Brace and Company, 1940.
Magnes, Beatrice L. *Episodes: A Memoir*. Berkeley: Judah L. Magnes Memorial Museum, 1977.
Magnes, Judah L. *Addresses by the Chancellor of the Hebrew University*. Jerusalem: Hebrew University, 1936.
McAdoo, William Gibbs. *Crowded Years: The Reminiscences of William G. McAdoo*. London: Jonathan Cape, 1932.
McCombs, William F. *Making Woodrow Wilson President*. New York: Fairview Publishing Company, 1921.
McNamara, Brooks. *The Shuberts of Broadway: A History Drawn from the Collections of the Shubert Archive*. New York: Oxford University Press, 1990.
Medoff, Rafael. *Zionism and the Arabs: An American Jewish Dilemma, 1898-1948*. Westport: Praeger, 1997.
Milburn, John G., and Walter F. Taylor. *Brief and Reply Brief Submitted on Behalf of the New York Stock Exchange to the Senate Committee on Banking and Currency, March 5, 1914, and March 30, 1914, Respectively*. New York: New York Stock Exchange, 1914.
Moley, Raymond. *After Seven Years*. New York: Harper & Brothers Publishers, 1939.
Morgenthau III, Henry. *Mostly Morgenthaus: A Family History*. New York: Ticknor & Fields, 1991.

Nasaw, David. *The Chief: The Life of William Randolph Hearst*. New York: Houghton Mifflin Company, 2000.
Neumann, Emanuel. *In The Arena: An Autobiographical Memoir*. New York: Herzl Press, 1976.
Nevins, Allan. *Herbert H. Lehman and His Era*. New York: Charles Scribner's Sons, 1963.
Nevins, Allan and Milton Halsey Thomas, eds. *The Diary of George Templeton Strong: 4: Post-War Years, 1865-1875*. New York: Macmillan Company, 1952.
Non-Sectarian Anti-Nazi League to Champion Human Rights. *Nazis Against the World: The Counter-Boycott is the Only Defensive Weapon against Hitlerism's World-Threat to Civilization: Selected Speeches from World Leaders of Public Opinion*. New York: The League, 1934.
Noyes, Walter C. ed. *Making of the Modern Law: Trials 1600-1926: Francis A. Lazenby, Etc., Plaintiff against International Cotton Mills Corporation, and Others, Defendants [1915]*. Belmont, CA: Gale, 2012.
O'Brien, Francis William, ed. *The Hoover-Wilson Wartime Correspondence, September 24, 1914, to November 11, 1918*. Ames, IA: Iowa State University Press, 1974.
O'Brien, Frank Michael. *The Story of the Sun: New York, 1833-1928*: New edn. New York: D. Appleton & Co., 1928.
O'Connor, Harvey. *The Guggenheims: The Making of an American Dynasty*. New York: Covici Friede, 1937.
Oller, John. *White Shoe: How a New Breed of Wall Street Lawyers Changed Big Business and the American Century*. New York: Dutton, 2019.
O'Sullivan, Mary A. *Dividends of Development: Securities Markets in the History of US Capitalism, 1866-1922*. Oxford: Oxford University Press, 2016.
Owen, Robert L. *The Federal Reserve Act*. Washington, DC: The Author, 1919.
Pak, Susie J. *Gentlemen Bankers: The World J.P. Morgan*. Cambridge, MA and London: Harvard University Press, 2013.
Perino, Michael. *The Hellhound of Wall Street: How Ferdinand Pecora's Investigation of the Great Crash Forever Changed American Finance*. New York and London: Penguin Books, 2011.
Peterson, Thomas. *Magazines in the Twentieth Century*. Urbana: University of Illinois Press, 1984.
Pfister, Doris. *Dokumentation zur Geschichte und Kultur der Juden in Schwaben: 2: Hausbesitz um 1835/40*. Augsburg: Bezirk Schwaben, 1993.
Piott, Steven L. *Holy Joe: Joseph W. Folk and the Missouri Idea*. Columbia, MO and London: University of Missouri Press, 1997.
Polland, Annie, and Daniel Soyer. *City of Promises: A History of the Jews of New York: 2: Emerging Metropolis: New York Jews in the Age of Immigration, 1840-1920*. New York and London: New York University Press, 2012.
Pound, Arthur, and Samuel Taylor Moore, eds. *They Told Barron: Conversations and Revelations of An American Pepys in Wall Street: The Notes of Clarence W. Barron*. New York: Harper & Brothers, 1930.
Powell, Enoch. *Joseph Chamberlain*. London: Thames & Hudson, 1977.
Pusey, Merlo J.. *Eugene Meyer*. New York: Alfred A. Knopf, 1974.
Rand School of Social Science. *The Case of The Rand School*. New York: The School, 1919.
Reader, W.J. *Imperial Chemical Industries: A History: Volume II: The First Quarter Century, 1926-1952*. London: Oxford University Press, 1975.
Reich, Simon. *Ford's Research Efforts in Assessing the Activities of Its Subsidiary in Germany*. Dearborn, IN: Ford Motor Company, 2001.

Reznikoff, Charles, ed. *Louis Marshall, Champion of Liberty: Selected Papers and Addresses: 1 & 2*. Philadelphia: Jewish Publication Society of America, 1957.
Roberts, Glyn. *The Most Powerful Man in the World: The Life of Sir Henri Deterding*. New York: Covici Friede, 1938.
Robertson, Frank C., and Beth Kay Harris. *Boom Towns of the Great Basin*. Denver: Sage Books, 1962.
Rock, Howard B. *City of Promises: A History of the Jews of New York: 1: Haven of Liberty: New York Jews in the New World, 1654–1865*. New York and London: New York University Press, 2012.
Roe, George Mortimer, ed. *Cincinnati: The Queen City of the West*. Cincinnati: Cincinnati Times-Star Co., 1895.
Rollins, Richard. *I Find Treason: The Story of an American Anti-Nazi Agent*. New York: William Morrow and Company, 1941.
Rosenblatt, Bernard A. *Two Generations of Zionism: Historical Recollections of an American Zionist*. New York: Shengold Publishers, 1967.
Ross, Steven J. *Hitler in Los Angeles: How Jews Foiled Nazi Plots Against Hollywood and America*. New York and London: Bloomsbury, 2017.
Ross, Stewart Halsey. *Propaganda for War: How the United States Was Conditioned to Fight the Great War of 1914–1918*. Jefferson, NC, and London: McFarland & Company, Inc. Publishers, 1996.
Roth, Philip. *The Plot Against America*. London: Vintage, 2018.
Samuel, Maurice. *Report of the Proceedings of the 24th Annual Convention of the Zionist Organization of America*. New York: Zionist Organization of America, 1921.
Sanger, Margaret. *Margaret Sanger: Pioneering Advocate for Birth Control: An Autobiography*. New York: Cooper Square Press, 1999.
Schechtman, Joseph B. *Rebel and Statesman: The Vladimir Jabotinsky Story: The Early Years*. New York: Thomas Yoseloff, Inc., 1956.
Schechtman, Joseph B. *Fighter and Prophet: The Vladimir Jabotinsky Story: The Last Years*. New York: Thomas Yoseloff, 1961.
Schenk, William E. ed. *Decisions Relating to the Liquor Tax Law of the State of New York: 1*. Albany: State of New York, 1905.
Schlüter, Hermann. *The Brewing Industry and the Brewery Workers' Movement in America*. New York: Burt Franklin, 1970.
Schmidt, Friedrich Lorenz. *Darstellende Geschichte der Stadt Zeulenroda, 1325–1867, 2: Zeulenroda in der Zeit von 1651–1867: 2*. Weimar: Hermann Böhlaus Nachfolger, 1953.
Seebohm, Caroline. *Paradise on the Hudson: The Creation, Loss, and Revival of a Great Garden*. Portland, OR: Timber Press, 2020.
Segev, Tom. *One Palestine, Complete: Jews and Arabs Under the British Mandate*. London: Little, Brown & Company, 2000.
Segev, Tom. *A State at Any Cost: The Life of Ben Gurion*. London: Head of Zeus, 2019.
Seidman, Harold. *Labor Czars: A History of Labor Racketeering*. New York: Liveright Publishing Corporation. 1938.
Shapiro, Yonathan. *Leadership of the American Zionist Organization, 1897–1930*. Urbana: University of Illinois Press, 1971.
Shenef, Yehuda. *Das Haus der Drei Sterne: Die Geschichte des Jüdischen Friedhofs von Pfersee, Kriegshaber und Steppach bei Augsburg, in Österreich, Bayern und Deutschland*. Augsburg: Books on Demand, 2016.
Shields, Charles Edward. *Samuel Untermyer, The Pujo Committee, and the Federal Reserve Act (A Preliminary Study)*. Mechanicsburg: The Author, 1979.

Silver, M. M. *Louis Marshall and the Rise of Jewish Ethnicity in America.* Syracuse, NY: Syracuse University Press, 2013.
Sinclair, Upton. *Upton Sinclair Presents William Fox.* Los Angeles (West Branch): The Author, 1933.
Sites, Henry W. *Investment Bankers and Brokers.* New York: The Author, 1918.
Smith, Barbara J. *The Roots of Separatism in Palestine: British Economic Policy, 1920-1929.* New York: I.B. Tauris, 1993.
Söderlund, Ernst. *Skandinaviska Banken I Det Svenska Bankväsendets Historia, 1914-1939.* Uppsala: Almqvist & Wiksell, 1978.
Spitzner, Alfred. *1813-1913: Das Völkerschachtdenkmal Weiheschrift.* Leipzig, Breitkopf & Härtel, 1913.
Stagg, Jerry. *The Brothers Shubert.* New York: Ballantine Books, 1969.
Stern, J. David. *Memoirs of a Maverick Publisher.* New York: Simon and Schuster, 1962.
Stern, Selma. *The Court Jew: A Contribution to the History of the Period of Absolutism in Central Europe.* Philadelphia: The Jewish Publication Society of America, 1950.
Strouse, Jean. *Morgan: American Financier.* London: The Harvill Press, 1999.
Sutherland, Daniel E. *Whistler: A Life for Art's Sake.* New Haven: Yale University Press, 2014.
Swaine, Robert T. *The Cravath Firm and its Predecessors: I: The Predecessor Firms, 1819-1906.* New York: The Firm, 1946.
Swaine, Robert T. *The Cravath Firm and its Predecessors: II: The Cravath Firm Since 1906.* New York: The Firm, 1948.
Swanberg, W.A. *Pulitzer.* New York: Charles Scribner's Sons, 1967.
Tenenbaum, Joseph. *Three Years Anti-Nazi Boycott.* New York: Joint Boycott Council of the American Jewish Congress and Jewish Labor Committee, 1936.
Tifft, Susan E., and Alex S. Jones. *The Trust: The Private and Powerful Family Behind The New York Times.* Boston, New York and London, 1999.
Tooze, Adam. *The Wages of Destruction: The Making and Breaking of the Nazi Economy.* London: Allen Lane, 2006.
Tower, Elizabeth A. *Icebound Empire: Industry and Politics on the Last Frontier, 1898-1938.* Anchorage: The Author, 1996.
Ulitzur, Abraham. *Two Decades of Keren Hayesod: A Survey in Facts and Figures, 1920-1940.* Jerusalem: The Erez Israel (Palestine) Foundation Fund, Keren Hayesod, 1940.
Untermeyer, Jean Starr. *Private Collection.* New York: A.A. Knopf, 1965.
Untermeyer, Sophie Guggenheimer, and Alix Williamson. *Mother is Minnie.* Garden City, NY: Doubleday, 1960.
Untermyer, Frank. *Recollections of the Untermyer Family.* Evanston, IL: The Author, 1995.
Untermyer, Samuel. *Extermination vs. Regulation of the Trusts. Which Shall it Be?: An Address Delivered at the Annual Meeting of the National Civic Federation, at New York City on January 12th, 1911.* New York: The Author, 1911.
Untermyer, Samuel. *Government Regulation of the Trusts with Special Reference to the Sherman Act: Address Delivered at the Dinner of the Economic Club of New York at the Hotel Astor, November 22nd, 1911.* New York: The Author, 1911.
Untermyer, Samuel. *Is There a Money Trust?: An Address Delivered Before the Finance Forum in the City of New York, December 27th, 1911.* New York: The Author, 1911.
Untermyer, Samuel. *Some Needed Legislative Reforms in Corporate Management: An Address Delivered Before the New York County Lawyers' Association, at Hotel Astor, N.Y., January 5, 1911.* New York: The Author, 1911.

Untermyer, Samuel. *A Legislative Program to Restore Business Freedom and Confidence: An Address Delivered Before the Illinois Manufacturing Association at the Hotel La Salle, Chicago, January 5, 1914*. New York: The Author, 1914.

Untermyer, Samuel. *The Relation of the Farmer to the Trust Question: An Address Delivered Before the Western Economic Society and the Second National Conference on Marketing and Farm Credits at Chicago, April 15th, 1914*. New York: The Author, 1914.

Untermyer, Samuel. *Speculation on the Stock Exchanges and Public Regulation of the Exchanges: An Address Delivered Before the American Economic Association at Princeton, N.J., December 29th, 1914*. New York: The Author, c.1915.

Untermyer, Samuel. *An Answer to Mr. Roosevelt – "The Only True American of Us All", Delivered at Newfield Maine, September 4th, 1916: Shall Invisible Government Be Restored? – The Only Real Issue, Delivered at Portland, Maine, September 7th, 1916*. New York: The Author, 1916.

Untermyer, Samuel. *A Historical Review of Mr. Hughes' Surrenders to Invisible Government: An Address Delivered at the New Star Casino, New York City, October 30, 1916*. New York: The Author, 1916.

Untermyer, Samuel. *Brief on Behalf of National Association of Owners of Railroad Securities*. Washington, DC: The Author, 1918.

Untermyer, Samuel. *The Operating Contract and the Future of Railroad Securities Thereunder: An Address Delivered Before the American Bankers Association at Chicago, September 24, 1918*. New York: The Author, 1918.

Untermyer, Samuel. *What the War Will Do for America: Address Before Meeting of Speakers for the Fourth Liberty Loan at Chicago Wednesday, September 25, 1918*. New York: The Author, 1918.

Untermyer, Samuel. *A Constructive Criticism of the Transit Plan: Address by Samuel Untermyer Before the City Club, Thursday, October 13th, 1921*. New York: The Author, 1921.

Untermyer, Samuel. *The Ideals of Zionism: An Address Delivered Before the Jewish Telegraphic Agency at Hotel Brevoort, October 1, 1921*. New York: The Author, 1921.

Untermyer, Samuel. *Honest and Dishonest Trade Associations: An Address Delivered at Temple Beth-El, Sunday Evening, April 23rd, 1922*. New York: The Author, 1922.

Untermyer, Samuel. *How to Strengthen Labor Unionism: An Address Delivered at Paul Revere Lodge, Monday Evening, May 1, 1922*. New York: The Author, 1922.

Untermyer, Samuel. *Stop Thief! A Constructive Attack on Bucket Shops, "Blue Sky" Stocks, and Market Manipulation*. Washington, DC: People's Legislative Service, 1923.

Untermyer, Samuel. *How We Americans Muddle and Blunder Along; An Address Before the Rotary Club at West Palm Beach, Fla., Tuesday, March 11, 1924, by Mr. Samuel Untermyer*. New York: The Author, 1924.

Untermyer, Samuel. *Reflections on Armistice Day: Address of Mr. Samuel Untermyer at Temple Rodelph Sholom, 63rd Street and Lexington Avenue New York, Armistice Day, November 11, 1924*. New York, The Author, 1924.

Untermyer, Samuel. *The Most Urgent Economic and Political Issue of the Day; Shall the Water Power of the State be Developed by Private Enterprise under State Supervision or by the State Through a Water Power Authority?: Argument in Favor of State Development Before the Annual Convention of the Erie County League of Women Voters at Buffalo, N.Y., October 28, 1927, by Samuel Untermyer*. New York, The Author, 1927.

Untermyer, Samuel. *Report and Recommendations of Special Counsel to the Transit Commission on Proposed Plan of Readjustment Directed by Legislature*. New York: The Author, 1927.

Untermyer, Samuel. *Who Is Entitled to the Credit for the Federal Reserve Act? An Answer to Senator Carter Glass, by Samuel Untermyer*. New York, The Author, 1927.

Untermyer, Samuel. *'Looking Backward and Forward at Finance and Industry': Address of Samuel Untermyer Before the Constitutional Law Class of the College of the City of New York, Monday Evening, July 30, 1928*. New York: The Author, 1928.

Untermyer, Samuel. *Report of Special Counsel to the Transit Commission Accompanying Proposed Tentative Plan of Readjustment*. New York: The Author, 1928.

Untermyer, Samuel. *Resolved, That Capital Punishment be Abolished: Opening Argument of Mr. Samuel Untermyer: Debate Before the Roebling Unit, Steuben Society, University Club, Brooklyn, January 14, 1928: For the Affirmative: Mr. Untermyer: For the Negative: Senator Love*. New York: The League to Abolish Capital Punishment, 1928.

Untermyer, Samuel. *The Social and Economic Justice and Wisdom of Maintaining a Five-Cent Fare: Address Before the Summer Class in Government and Sociology at the College of the City of New York Thursday, August 8, 1929*. New York: The Author, 1929.

Untermyer, Samuel. *Second Supplemental Report of Special Counsel to the Transit Commission on the Unification of the Rapid Transit Lines Accompanying Proposed Legislation and Proposed Plan of Unification*. New York: The Author, 1930.

Untermyer, Samuel. *In the Matter of the Investigation Under Commission Issued by the Governor of the State of New York of Charges Made Against Thomas C. T. Crain, District Attorney of New York County, Respondent. Revised Summary of Argument of Mr. Samuel Untermyer with Extracts from brief of Messrs. Untermyer and Hartman*. New York, Hecla Press, 1931.

Untermyer, Samuel. *Proposed Alternative Plan for the Unification by Recapture or Purchase of all or Part of the Rapid Transit Railroads in the City of New York*. New York: The Author, 1931.

Untermyer, Samuel. *Report and Recommendations of Mr. Samuel Untermyer on Transit and His Letter of Resignation As Special Counsel*. New York: The Author, 1931.

Untermyer, Samuel. *Some of America's Social and Economic Follies: Address before the University Club of Los Angeles, February 17, 1931*. New York: The Author, 1931.

Untermyer, Samuel. *The Solution of the Transit Problem: An Address by Samuel Untermyer, Broadcast by Station WOR, Thursday Evening, June 16, 1932*. New York: The Author, 1932.

Untermyer, Samuel. *The Boycott Is Our Only Weapon Against Nazi Germany: Addresses By Samuel Untermyer*. New York: The Author, 1933.

Untermyer, Samuel. *Federal Regulation of the Stock Exchange; Address by Samuel Untermyer Before the Law Alumni of the University of Southern California, March 8, 1933*. New York: The Author, 1933.

Untermyer, Samuel. *Hobson's Choice Between Government Ownership and Bankruptcy of the Railroads: Address of Samuel Untermyer of New York Before the University Club of Los Angeles, Monday, February 27, 1933*. New York: The Author, 1933.

Untermyer, Samuel. *A Friendly Criticism of the Stock Exchange Bill: An Address By Samuel Untermyer Before the Los Angeles Breakfast Club, February 21st, 1934*. New York: The Author, 1934.

Untermyer, Samuel. *Civilization's Only Weapon Against Hitlerism: Address Read at the Testimonial Dinner to Mr. William Green, at the Aldine Club, New York City, February 14, 1934*. New York: Non-Sectarian Anti-Nazi League to Champion Human Rights, 1934.

Untermyer, Samuel. *Civilization's Only Weapon Against Hitlerism: Address of Mr. Samuel Untermyer, President of the Non-Sectarian Anti-Nazi League to Champion Human*

Rights, Read at the Testimonial Dinner to Mr. William Green, President of the American Federation of Labor, at the Aldine Club, New York City, February 14, 1934. New York: Non-Sectarian Anti-Nazi League to Champion Human Rights, 1934.

Untermyer, Samuel. *Is the Reign of the Money Trust Over Government Ended or Only Suspended?: An Address at the Community Playhouse Pasadena, February 26th, 1934*. New York, The Author, 1934.

Untermyer, Samuel. *'Why the Boycott Against Germany is Succeeding': At the Metropolitan Opera House, Philadelphia, Pa., Wednesday Evening, June 27, 1934 Under the Auspices of the Pennsylvania State Federation of Labor, Central Labor Union, American Legion, World War Veterans, and Other Civic Bodies*. New York: Columbia Broadcasting System, 1934.

Untermyer, Samuel. *A 'Call to Arms' Against Hitler's Destruction of Christianity*. New York: Non-Sectarian Anti-Nazi League, 1935.

Untermyer, Samuel. *The World's Answer to the Mendacious Nazi Plea to End the Boycott: An Address at a Mass Meeting of the Los Angeles Americanization League Held at the Philharmonic Auditorium, Los Angeles, California, March 17th, 1935*. New York: The Author, 1935.

Untermyer, Samuel. *Address of Mr. Samuel Untermyer at the Emergency Conference Appeal for the Relief of Jews in Poland, Waldorf-Astoria Hotel, New York, December 5, 1937*. New York: The Author, 1937.

Untermyer, Samuel. *'No Pasaran' (They Shall Not Pass): Religion Answers the Nazi Challenge: Address of Samuel Untermyer Before the Temple and Synagogue Brotherhoods at Baltimore, Md., Sunday, December 19, 1937*. New York: The Author, 1938.

Untermyer, Samuel, and Morris Hillquit. *Shall Trade Unions be Regulated by Law?: Affirmative, Mr. Samuel Untermyer; Negative, Mr. Morris Hillquit*. New York: Hanford Press, 1923.

Urofsky, Melvin I. *American Zionism From Herzl To The Holocaust*. Garden City: Anchor Press, 1975.

Urofsky, Melvin I. and David W. Levy, ed. *Letters of Louis D. Brandeis: III: 1913–1915: Progressive and Zionist*. Albany: State University of New York Press, 1973.

Urofsky, Melvin I. and David W. Levy, ed. *Letters of Louis D. Brandeis: IV: 1916–1921: Mr. Justice Brandeis*. Albany, NY: State University of New York Press, 1975.

Vaught, Steve, and Tracy Conrad. *Einstein Dreamt Here: The Willows Historic Palm Springs Inn*. Palm Springs: The Willows Historic Palm Springs Inn, 2015.

Viereck, George Sylvester. *Spreading Germs of Hate*. London: Duckworth, 1931.

Viereck, George Sylvester. *The Strangest Friendship In History: Woodrow Wilson and Colonel House*. London: Duckworth, 1933.

Vorse, Mary Heaton. *The Passaic Textile Strike, 1926–1927*. Passaic, NJ: General Relief Committee of Textile Strikers, 1927.

Wald, Kenneth D. *The Foundations of American Jewish Liberalism*. Cambridge: Cambridge University Press, 2019.

Wallace, Mike. *Greater Gotham: A History of New York City from 1898 to 1919*. New York: Oxford University Press, 2017.

Warburg, Paul M. *The Federal Reserve System: Its Origin and Growth: Reflections and Recollections, 1*. New York: Macmillan Company, 1930.

Waring, Dorothy. *American Defender*. New York: Robert Speller, 1935.

Weinstein, Gregory. *The Ardent Eighties*. New York: International Press, 1928.

Weizmann, Chaim. *American Addresses*. New York: Palestine Foundation Fund, 1923.

Wellman, Francis L. *The Art of Cross-Examination*. New York: Macmillan, 1923.
Whalen, Grover A. *Mr. New York: The Autobiography of Grover A. Whalen*. New York: G.P. Putnam's Sons, 1955.
Williams, Gatenby, and Charles Monroe Heath, *William Guggenheim*. New York: Lone Voice Publishing Company, 1934.
Wilson, Edwina H. *Her Name Was Wallis Warfield: The Life Story of Mrs. Ernest Simpson*. New York: E.P. Dutton, 1936.
Winter, William. *The Life of David Belasco, 2*. New York: Moffat, Yard and Company, 1918.
Wise, Stephen. *Challenging Years: The Autobiography of Stephen Wise*. New York: Putnam's Sons, 1949.
Winkler, John K. *Five and Ten, the Fabulous Life of F.W. Woolworth*. New York: R.M. McBride & Company, 1940.
Woeste, Victoria Saker. *Henry Ford's War on Jews and the Legal Battle Against Hate Speech*. Stanford, CA: Stanford University Press, 2012.
Writers' Program of the Works Projects Administration. *The Negro in Virginia*. New York: Hastings House, 1940.
Zumoff, Jacob A. *The Communist International and US Communism, 1919–1929*. Leiden: Brill, 2014.
Zumoff, Jacob A. *Red Thread: The Passaic Textile Strike*. New Brunswick, Camden, and Newark, NJ and London: Rutgers University Press, 2021.

Chapter in an edited collection

Ahlheim, Hannah. 'Establishing Antisemitic Stereotypes: Social and Economic Segregation of Jews by Means of Political Boycott in Germany'. In *The Leo Baeck Institute Year Book* 55, no. 1 (2010): 149–73.
Berkowitz, Michael. 'Kristallnacht in Context: Jewish War Veterans in America and Britain and the Crisis of German Jewry'. In *American Religious Responses to Kristallnacht*, edited by Maria Mazzenga, 57–84. Basingstoke: Palgrave Macmillan, 2009.
Green, William. 'Nazi Assault on Organized Labor'. In *Nazis Against the World: The Counter-Boycott is the Only Defensive Weapon against Hitlerism's World-Threat to Civilization*, 32–40. New York: Non-Sectarian Anti-Nazi League to Champion Human Rights, 1934.
Knight, Peter. 'Representations of Capitalism in the Gilded Age and Progressive Era'. In *American Capitalism: New Histories*, edited by Sven Beckert and Christine Desan, 236–56. New York: Columbia University Press, 2018.
Richards, Bernard G. 'The American Jewish Congress'. In *The Jewish Communal Register of New York City, 1917–1918*, 2nd edn, edited by the Kehillah (Jewish Community) of New York City, 1429–44. New York: The Kehillah, 1918.
Schrijvers, P.H. '"Rome, Athens, Jerusalem": Aspects of the Life and Work of Dr. David Cohen'. In *Dutch Jewry: Its History and Secular Culture (1500–2000)*, edited by Jonathan Israel and Reinier Salverda, 240–51. Leiden: Brill, 2002.
Tenenbaum, Joseph. 'The Anti-Nazi Boycott Movement in the United States'. In *Yad Vashem Studies on the European Jewish Catastrophe and Resistance, III*, edited by Shaul Esh, 141–59. Jerusalem: Yad Vashem, 1959.

Journal Articles

'Speculation on the Stock Exchanges—Discussion'. *American Economic Review* 5, no. 1 (Supplement: Papers and Proceedings of the Twenty-Seventh Annual Meeting of the American Economic Association) (1915): 86–111.

Abrams, Richard M. 'Woodrow Wilson and the Southern Congressmen'. *Journal of Southern History* 22, no. 4 (1956): 417–37.

Adler, Cyrus. 'Louis Marshall: A Biographical Sketch'. *American Jewish Yearbook* 32 (1930): 21–55.

Amann, Peter H. 'A "Dog in the Nighttime" Problem: American Fascism in the 1930s'. *The History Teacher* 19, no. 4 (1986): 559–84.

Auerbach, Jerold S. 'Review Essay: Proskauer: His Life and Times'. *American Jewish History* 69, no. 1 (1979): 103–16.

Baker, George W. Jr. 'Wilson's Use of the Non-Recognition Policy in Costa Rica'. *The Americas* 22, no. 1 (1965): 3–21.

Burk, James. 'The Origins of Federal Securities Regulation: A Case Study in the Social Control of Finance', *Social Forces* 63, no. 4 (1985): 1010–29.

Chach, Maryann, ed. 'William Klein's Early Years with the Shuberts'. *The Passing Show* 13/14, Nos. 2/1 (1991): 2–8.

Chach, Maryann. 'The Heart of Broadway Still Beats Strong at 100', *The Passing Show* 30 (2013–2014), 46–53.

Chase, William J. 'Microhistory and Mass Repression: Politics, Personalities, and Revenge in the Fall of Béla Kun'. *The Russian Review* 67, no. 3 (2008): 454–83.

Clements, Kendrick A. 'Woodrow Wilson's Mexican Policy, 1913–1915'. *Diplomatic History* 4, no. 2 (1980): 113–36.

Cohen, Naomi W. 'The Transatlantic Connection: The American Jewish Committee and the Joint Foreign Committee in Defense of German Jews, 1933–1937'. *American Jewish History* 90, no. 4 (2002): 353–84.

Davidson, Lawrence. 'Zionism, Socialism and United States Support for the Colonization of Palestine in the 1920s', *Arab Studies Quarterly* 18, no. 3 (1996): 1–16.

Evans, Arthur S. 'The Jim Braddock-Max Schmeling Affair: An Assessment of a Jewish Boycott of a Professional Prizefight'. *Journal of Sport and Social Issues* 6, no. 2 (1982): 1–12.

Friedman, Milton, and Anna J. Schwartz. 'The Failure of the Bank of United States: A Reappraisal: A Reply'. *Explorations in Economic History* 23, no. 2 (1986): 199–204.

Gartner, Lloyd P. 'The Correspondence of Mayer Sulzberger and William Howard Taft'. *Proceedings of the American Academy for Jewish Research* 46–47, no. 1 (1979–1980): 121–39.

Gewirtz, Sharon. 'Anglo-Jewish Responses to Nazi Germany 1933–1939: The Anti-Nazi Boycott and the Board of Deputies of British Jews'. *Journal of Contemporary History* 26, no. 2 (1991): 255–76.

Goldblatt, Charles Israel. 'The Impact of the Balfour Declaration in America'. *American Jewish Historical Quarterly* 57, no. 4 (1968): 455–515.

Gottlieb, Moshe, 'The First of April Boycott and the Reaction of the American Jewish Community'. *American Jewish Historical Quarterly* 57, no. 4 (1968): 516–56.

Gottlieb, Moshe. 'The American Controversy Over the Olympic Games'. *American Jewish Historical Quarterly* 61, no. 3 (1972): 181–213.

Gottlieb, Moshe. 'The Anti-Nazi Boycott Movement in the United States: An Ideological and Sociological Appreciation'. *Jewish Social Studies* 35, no. 3–4 (1973): 198–227.

Hannah, Leslie. 'J.P. Morgan in London and New York before 1914'. *Business History Review* 85, no. 1 (2011), 113–50.
Hawkins, Richard A. 'Lynchburg's Swabian Jewish Entrepreneurs in War and Peace'. *Southern Jewish History* 3 (2000): 45–82.
Hawkins, Richard A. 'American Boomers and the Flotation of Shares in the City of London in the Late Nineteenth Century'. *Business History* 49, no. 6 (2007): 802–22.
Hawkins, Richard A. '"Hitler's Bitterest Foe": Samuel Untermyer and the Boycott of Nazi Germany, 1933–1938'. *American Jewish History* 93, no. 1 (2007): 21–50.
Hawkins, Richard A. 'Samuel Untermyer and the Zionist Project: An Attempt to Reconcile the American "Melting Pot" with Zionism'. *Australian Journal of Jewish Studies* 21 (2007): 114–54.
Hawkins, Richard A. 'Boycotts, Buycotts and Consumer Activism in a Global Context: An Overview'. *Management & Organizational History* 5, no. 2 (2010): 123–43.
Hawkins, Richard A. 'The Internal Politics of the Non-Sectarian Anti-Nazi League to Champion Human Rights, 1933–1939'. *Management & Organizational History* 5, no. 2 (2010): 251–78.
Hawkins, Richard A. 'The "Jewish Threat" and the Origins of the American Surveillance State: A Case Study of the Untermyer Family'. *Australian Journal of Jewish Studies* 24 (2010): 74–115.
Hawkins, Richard A. 'The Marketing of Legal Services in the United States, 1855–1912: A Case Study of Guggenheimer, Untermyer & Marshall of New York and the Predecessor Partnerships'. *American Journal of Legal History* 53, no. 2 (2013): 239–64.
Hopkins, Howard, and John W. Long. 'American Jews and the Root Mission to Russia in 1917: Some New Evidence'. *American Jewish History* 69, no. 3 (1980): 342–54.
Jackson, William Turrentine. 'Dakota Tin: British Investment at Harney Peak, 1880–1900'. *North Dakota History* 33, no. 1 (1966): 22–63.
Knee, Stuart E. 'The King-Crane Commission of 1919: The Articulation of Political Anti-Zionism'. *American Jewish Archives* 29, no. 1 (1977): 22–52.
Kupsky, George. 'Germanness and Jewishness: Samuel Untermyer, Felix Warburg, and National Socialism, 1914–1938'. *American Jewish Archives Journal* 63, no. 2 (2011): 24–42.
Lambertie, Marjorie. 'The Reception of Refugee Scholars from Nazi Germany in America: Philanthropy and Social Change in Higher Education'. *Jewish Social Studies* 12, no. 3 (2006): 157–92.
Lippman, Jacob. 'The Securities Exchange Act of 1934 and the Commerce Clause'. *United States Law Review* 69, no. 1 (1935): 18–33.
Lukes, Igor. 'Ambassador Laurence Steinhardt: From New York to Prague'. *Diplomacy & Statecraft* 17, no. 3 (2006): 523–45.
Manor, Ehud. 'Louis Miller, the *Warheit*, and the *Kehillah* of New York, 1908–1909'. *Australian Journal of Jewish Studies* 25 (2011): 175–200.
Mayers, David. 'The Great Patriotic War, FDR's Embassy Moscow, and Soviet–US Relations'. *International History Review* 33, no. 2 (2011): 299–333.
Mehrotra, Alay K. 'Lawyers, Guns, and Public Moneys: The U.S. Treasury, World War I, and the Administration of the Modern Fiscal State'. *Law and History Review* 28, no. 1 (2010): 173–225.
Morrison, Joseph L. 'A Southern Philo-Semite: Josephus Daniels of North Carolina'. *Judaism* 12, no. 1 (1963): 78–91.
Myers, Jerome, and Guy Pène DuBois. 'Greystone', *Arts & Decoration* 6, no. 11 (1916): 508–11, 524.

Novak, William J. 'Institutional Economics and the Progressive Movement for the Social Control of American Business'. *Business History Review* 93, no. 4 (2019): 665–96.

Nowak, Zachary. 'Something Brewing in Boston: A Study of Forward Integration in American Breweries at the Turn of the Twentieth Century'. *Enterprise & Society* 18, no. 2 (2017): 324–59.

Nylander, Gert, and Anders Perlinge.'Raoul Wallenberg in Documents, 1927–1947'. *Banking & Enterprise* 3 (2000): 1–84.

Obermayer, Arthur. 'Tracing German-Jewish Ancestry to the 17th Century – And Much Earlier'. *Avotaynu* 27, no. 2 (2011), 35–7.

O'Sullivan, Mary. 'Yankee Doodle Went to London: Anglo-American Breweries and the London Securities Market, 1888–1892'. *Economic History Review*, 68, no. 4 (2015): 1365–87.

Ott, Julia C. '"The Free and Open People's Market": Political Ideology and Retail Brokerage at the New York Stock Exchange, 1913–1933'. *Journal of American History* 96, no. 1, 44–71.

Pak, Susie J. 'Reputation and Social Ties: J. P. Morgan & Co. and Private Investment Banking'. *Business History Review* 87, no. 4 (2013): 703–28.

Panitz, Esther. 'Louis Dembitz Brandeis and the Cleveland Conference'. *American Jewish Historical Quarterly* 65, no. 2 (1975): 140–62.

Parzen, Herbert. 'The Enlargement of the Jewish Agency for Palestine: 1923–1929: A Hope – Hamstrung'. *Jewish Social Studies* 39, no. 1–2 (1977): 129–58.

Penkower, Monty Noam. 'Honorable Failures Against Nazi Germany: McDonald's Letter of Resignation and the Petition in its Support'. *Modern Judaism* 20, no. 3 (2010): 247–98.

Prude, James C. 'William Gibbs McAdoo and the Democratic National Convention of 1924'. *Journal of Southern History* 38, no. 4 (1972): 621–8.

Rifkind, Robert S. 'Confronting Antisemitism in America: Louis Marshall and Henry Ford'. *American Jewish History* 94, no. 1/2 (2008): 71–90.

Rosenstock, Morton. 'The Role of Biography in American Jewish History'. *American Jewish Historical Quarterly* 54, no. 2 (1964): 182–97.

Rubin, Barry. 'Ambassador Laurence A. Steinhardt: The Perils of a Jewish Diplomat, 1940–1945'. *American Jewish History* 70, no. 3 (1981): 331–46.

Rudd, Hynda. 'Samuel Newhouse: Utah Mining Magnate and Land Developer'. *Western States Jewish Historical Quarterly* 11, no. 4 (1979): 291–307.

Sargent, Jr., David W. 'The Rutland Railroad'. *The Railway and Locomotive Historical Society Bulletin* 58a (1942): 73–90.

Sjögren, Hans. 'The Financial Contracts of Large Firms: A Longitudinal Study of Swedish Firms and Commercial Banks, 1919–1947'. *Scandinavian Economic History Review* 39, no. 3 (1991): 72–94.

Swain, Henry H. 'Economic Aspects of Railroad Receiverships'. *Economic Studies* 3, no. 2 (1898): 45–161.

Szajkowski, Zosa. 'The Jews and New York City's Mayoralty Election of 1917'. *Jewish Social Studies* 32, no. 4 (1970): 286–306.

Tenney, John. 'In the Trenches: The Syndicate-Shubert Theatrical War', *The Passing Show* 21, no. 2 (1998): 2–18.

Tufano, Peter. 'Business Failure, Judicial Intervention, and Financial Innovation: Restructuring U.S. Railroads in the Nineteenth Century', *Business History Review* 71, no. 1 (1997): 1–40.

Untermyer, Samuel. 'Evils and Remedies in the Administration of the Criminal Law'. *The Annals of the American Academy of Political and Social Science* 36, no. 1 (1910): 145–60.

Untermyer, Samuel. 'The Supreme Court Decisions: The Remedy'. *The North American Review*, July 1911, 70–95.
Untermyer, Samuel. 'Why the Currency Bill Should Pass'. *The North American Review*, October 1913, 498–526.
Untermyer, Samuel. 'Speculation on the Stock Exchanges and Public Regulation of the Exchanges'. *American Economic Review* 5, no. 1 (Supplement: Papers and Proceedings of the Twenty-Seventh Annual Meeting of the American Economic Association) (1915): 24–68.
Untermyer, Samuel. 'Zionism a Just Cause'. *The Forum*, September 1921, 210–27.
Untermyer, Samuel. 'Zionism and the Crane Report'. *The Forum*, January 1923, 1120–36.
Untermyer, Samuel. 'What Every Present-Day Lawyer Should Know'. *The Annals of the American Academy of Political and Social Science* 167 (1933): 173–6.
Untermyer, Samuel. 'A Plan for Regulating the Stock Exchange'. *Today*, 27 January 1934, 3–4, 22.
Waterman, Jr., Arthur J. 'New York Solves Transit Problems'. *National Municipal Review* 29, no. 11 (1940): 728–35, 766.
Weisbord, Robert, and Norbert Hedderich. 'Max Schmeling Righteous Ring Warrior'. *History Today* 43, no. 1 (1995): 36–41.
Whitfield, Stephen J. 'Strange Fruit: The Strange Career of Samuel Zemurray'. *American Jewish History* 73, no. 3 (1984), 307–23.
Woeste, Victoria Saker. 'Insecure Equality: Louis Marshall, Henry Ford, and the Problem of Defamatory Antisemitism, 1920–1929'. *Journal of American History* 91, no. 3 (2004): 877–905.
Woolf, David A. 'No Matter How You Do It, Fraud is Fraud: Another Look at Black Hills Mining Scandals'. *South Dakota History* 33, no. 2 (2003): 91–119.

Government publications

City of New York. Board of Estimate and Apportionment. *Report and Recommendations of Samuel Untermyer*. New York: The Board, 1933.
International High Commission. *First Edition of the Committee Reports and Resolutions Adopted at the First General Meeting, Held in Buenos Aires, in April 1916*. Washington, DC: G.P.O., 1916.
Interstate Commerce Commission. 'No.6834: In Re Financial Transactions, History, and Operation of the Chicago, Rock Island & Pacific Railway Company'. In *Interstate Commerce Commission Reports, 34, Decisions July 1915 to December 1915*. Washington, DC: G.P.O., 1916, 43–61.
State of New York. *Documents of the Assembly of State of New York. 95th sess. 6, no.71, Pt 2: Charges Against Justice G. Barnard, and Testimony Thereunder, Before the Judiciary Committee of the Assembly*. Albany: Weed, Parsons and Company, Printers, 1872.
State of New York. *Board of Mediation and Arbitration*. Second Annual Report. Albany: Troy Press Company, 1889.
State of New York. *Minutes and Testimony of the Joint Legislative Committee Appointed to Investigate the Public Service Commissions: 3*. Albany: State Legislature, 1916.
State of New York. *Minutes and Testimony of the Joint Legislative Committee Appointed to Investigate the Public Service Commissions: 4*. Albany: State Legislature, 1916.

State of New York. *Legislative Document No. 48: Final Report of the Joint Legislative Committee on Housing*. Albany: J.B. Lyon Company, Printers, 1923.

State of Virginia. *Acts of the General Assembly of the State of Virginia, Passed in 1865–1866, in the Eighty-Ninth Year of the Commonwealth*. Richmond: Allegre & Goode, Printers, 1866.

U.S. Congress. House. Committee on the Judiciary. *Trust Legislation: Hearings on Trust Legislation in Two Volumes, Serial 7 - Parts 1 to 24 Inclusive, 1*. 63rd Cong., 2nd sess. Washington, DC: G.P.O., 1915.

U.S. Congress. House. Committee on the Judiciary: Subcommittee III. *Appeals from Circuit Court of Appeals: Hearings on H.R. 10736: January 23, 1914*. 63rd Cong., 2nd sess. Washington, DC: G.P.O., 1914.

U.S. Congress. House. Committee on Rules. *Hearings on House Resolution No. 314, Authorising the Appointment of a Committee to Investigate as to Whether There are Not Combinations of Financial and Other Concerns Who Control Money and Credits, and Operate in Restraint of Trade Through That Control*. 62nd Cong., 2nd sess. Washington, DC: G.P.O., 1911.

U.S. Congress. House. Committee on Rules. *Investigation of the Money Trust: No.1: Hearings on Rules of the House of Representatives on House Resolutions 314 and 356, Friday, January 26, 1912*. 62nd Cong., 2nd sess. Washington, DC: G.P.O., 1912.

U.S. Congress. House. Committee on Ways and Means. *Revision of the Tariff: Hearings 1889–1890*. 51st Cong., 1st sess. Washington, DC: G.P.O., 1890.

U.S. Congress. House. *Report No. 153: Investigation of Nazi and Other Propaganda*. 74th Cong., 1st sess. Washington, DC: G.P.O., 1935.

U.S. Congress. House. Subcommittee of the Committee on Banking and Currency. *Money Trust Investigation, Investigation of Financial and Monetary Conditions in the United States Under House Resolutions Nos. 429 and 504*. 62nd Cong., 3rd sess. Washington, DC: G.P.O., 1913.

U.S. Congress. House. Subcommittee of the Committee on Banking and Currency. *Report of the Committee Appointed Pursuant to House Resolutions 429 and 504 to Investigate the Concentration of Control of Money and Credit*. 62nd Cong., 3rd sess. Washington, DC: G.P.O., 1913.

U.S. Congress. Senate. *Industrial Relations: Final Report and Testimony Submitted to Congress by the Commission on Industrial Relations Created by the Act of August 23, 1912: 8*. 64th Cong., 1st sess. Washington, DC: G.P.O., 1916.

U.S. Congress. Senate. Committee on Banking and Currency. *Banking and Currency: Hearings on H.R.7837 (S.2639) - A Bill to Provide for the Establishment of Federal Reserve Banks, for Furnishing an Elastic Currency, Affording Means of Rediscounting Commercial Paper, and to Establish a More Effective Supervision of Banking in the United States and for Other Purposes, I & II*. 63rd Cong., 1st sess. Washington, DC: G.P.O., 1913.

U.S. Congress. Senate. Committee on Banking and Currency. *Regulation of the Stock Exchange: Hearings on S.3895: A Bill to Prevent the Use of the Mails and of the Telegraph and Telephone in Furtherance of Fraudulent and Harmful Transactions on Stock Exchanges*. 63rd Cong., 2nd sess. Washington, DC: G.P.O., 1914.

U.S. Congress. Senate. Committee on Banking and Currency. *Nomination of John Skelton Williams: Hearings on the Nomination of John Skelton Williams to be Comptroller of the Currency*. 66th Cong., 1st sess. Washington, DC: G.P.O., 1919.

U.S. Congress. Senate. Committee on Banking and Currency. *Stock Exchange Practices: Hearings Before the Senate Committee on Banking and Currency: 16, National Securities*

Act (Continued) March 23 to April 5, 1934. 73rd Cong., 2nd sess. Washington, DC: G.P.O., 1934.

U.S. Congress. Senate. Committee on Education and Labor. *West Virginia Coalfields: Hearings on S. Res. 80: 2.* 67th Cong., 1st sess. Washington, DC: G.P.O., 1921.

U.S. Congress. Senate. Committee on Immigration. *Purchase of American Industries by Foreign Capital: Testimony Taken by the Committee on Immigration of United States Senate and the Select Committee on Immigration and Naturalization of the House of Representatives in Relation to the Purchase of American Industries by Foreign Capital.* 51st Cong., 2nd sess. Washington, DC: G.P.O., 1891.

U.S. Congress. Senate. Committee on Interstate Commerce. *Hearing Pursuant to S.R. 98, A Resolution Directing the Committee to Investigate and Report Desirable Changes in the Laws Regulating and Controlling Corporations, Persons, and Firms Engaged in Interstate Commerce: 1–3.* 62nd Cong., 2nd sess. Washington, DC: G.P.O., 1912.

U.S. Congress. Senate. Committee on Interstate Commerce. *Interstate Trade: Hearings on Interstate Commerce: Bills Relating to Trust Legislation, 1 & 2.* 63rd Cong., 2nd sess. Washington, DC: G.P.O., 1914.

U.S. Congress. Senate. Committee on Territories. *Government of Alaska: Statements on the Bill S.5436, To Create a Legislative Council in the District of Alaska, to Confer Legislative Powers Theron and for Other Purposes.* 61st Cong., 2nd sess. Washington, DC: G.P.O., 1910.

U.S. Congress. Senate. Report No. 2024. *Presidential Campaign Expenditures.* Washington, DC: G.P.O., 1929.

U.S. Congress. Senate. Subcommittee of the Committee on the Judiciary. *Brewing and Liquor Interests and German and Bolshevik Propaganda: Report and Hearings Submitted Pursuant to S. Res. 307 and 439 65th Congress Relating to Charges Made Against the United States Brewers' Association and Allied Interests: 2.* 66th Cong., 1st sess. Washington, DC: G.P.O., 1919.

U.S. Congress. Senate. Subcommittee of the Committee on Banking and Currency. *Regulation of Sale of Securities: Hearing on S. 2344, A Bill to Provide for the Regulation of the Sale of Certain Securities in Interstate and Foreign Commerce, and the Trust Indentures under Which the Same are Issued, and for Other Purposes.* 75th Cong., 1st sess. Washington, DC: G.P.O., 1937.

U.S. Congress. Senate. Subcommittee of the Committee on Interstate Commerce. *Hearings Pursuant to S. Res. 71 Authorizing an Investigation of Interstate Railroads: Part 26: Sea Board Air Line Railway.* 75th Cong., 2nd sess. Washington, DC: G.P.O., 1942.

U.S. Congress. Senate. Subcommittee of the Committee on the Judiciary. *Prohibiting Intoxicating Beverages: Hearings on the Bills to Prohibit the Liquor Traffic and to Provide for the Enforcement of Such Prohibition and the War Prohibition Act: 3.* 66th Cong., 1st sess. Washington, DC: G.P.O., 1919.

U.S. Congress. Senate. Subcommittee on Monopoly of the Select Committee on Small Business. *The International Petroleum Cartel (Reprint).* 94th Cong., 1st sess. Washington, DC: G.P.O., 1975.

U.S. Department of State. *Papers Relating to the Foreign Relations of the United States with the Address of the President to Congress, December 4, 1917.* Washington, DC: G.P.O., 1926.

U.S. Department of State. *Papers Relating to the Foreign Relations of the United States: 1923: 2.* Washington, DC: G.P.O., 1938.

U.S. Department of State. Press Releases 18, No. 451 (1938): 585–606.

U.S. Department of State. *Papers Relating to the Foreign Relations of the United States: The Lansing Papers, 1914–1920: II.* Washington, DC: G.P.O., 1940.

U.S. Department of State. *Foreign Relations of the United States: Diplomatic Papers: 1933: 2: The British Commonwealth, Europe, Near East and Africa.* Washington, DC: G.P.O., 1949.

U.S. Department of State. *Foreign Relations of the United States: Diplomatic Papers: 1934: 2: Europe, Near East and Africa.* Washington, DC: G.P.O., 1951.

U.S. Department of State. *Foreign Relations of the United States: Diplomatic Papers: 1937: 2: The British Commonwealth, Europe, Near East and Africa.* Washington, DC: G.P.O., 1954.

U.S. Department of the Treasury. *Proceeding of the First Pan American Financial Conference, Washington May 24 to 29, 1915.* Washington, DC: G.P.O., 1915.

Newspapers and journals

Algemeen Handelsblad [Amsterdam]
American Brewers' Review
American Federationist
American Hebrew
American Israelite
American Jewish World
American Mercury
Augsburgische Ordinari Postzeitung
Ballston Spa Daily Journal
Baltimore Sun
Belfast Telegraph
Bench and Bar
Berliner Tageblatt und Handels-Zeitung
Berliner Illustrierte Nachtausgabe
Better Homes and Gardens
Birmingham Age-Herald
Bisbee Daily Review
Brewers' Journal
Bridgeport Times
Brooklyn Daily Eagle
Brooklyn Daily Star
Brooklyn Eagle's Sporting Section
Brooklyn Standard Union
Buffalo Courier
Buffalo Courier-Express
Buffalo Evening News
Butte Daily Inter Mountain
Butte Weekly Miner
Chicago Daily Tribune
Chicago Evening American
Cincinnati Enquirer
City Press (London)
Collier's
Commercial & Financial Chronicle
Cosmopolitan

Daily Charlotte Observer
Daily Herald [London]
Daily Mirror [London]
Daily News Bulletin [Jewish Telegraphic Agency, London]
Daily Telegraph [London]
Daily Worker [New York]
Dearborn Independent
Der Spiegel
Desert Sun [Palm Springs]
De Telegraaf [Amsterdam]
Detroit Jewish News
Detroit Jewish Chronicle
Deutsche Allgemeine Zeitung
Deutscher Beobachter of New York
Dry Goods Economist
Duluth Evening Herald
East-Hampton Star
Egyptian Gazette
Electric Railway Journal
Essex Newsman
Evening Bulletin [Maysville, Kentucky]
Everybody's Magazine
Field and Fancy
Financial Times [London]
Fruit Trade Journal and Produce Record
Glens Falls Daily Times
Goldfield News and Weekly Tribune
Harper's Monthly Magazine
Harper's Weekly
Hearst's
Henley Advertiser
Het Volk [Amsterdam]
In Fact
Indianapolis Journal
Irish Times
Jamestown Evening Journal
Japan Times & Mail
Jersey City Jewish Standard
Jewish Chronicle [London]
Jewish Criterion
Jewish Daily Bulletin
Jewish Exponent
Jewish Floridian
Jewish Messenger
Jewish Post [Paterson, NJ]
Jewish Telegraphic Agency: Latest Cable Dispatches
Jewish Telegraphic Agency News
Jewish Tribune
Kansas City American Citizen

Kansas City Journal
Knickerbocker Press
Le Temps [Paris]
Legal Times
Liberty Magazine
Lynchburg News
Lynchburg Virginian
Los Angeles Examiner
Los Angeles Herald
Los Angeles Times
Maine Woods
McClure's Magazine
Memphis News Scimitar
Mexican Herald
Milwaukee Journal
Motor Boating
Mount Vernon Daily Argus
Neue Zürcher Nachrichten
New Haven Morning Journal and Courier
New Orleans Daily Picayune
New Republic
New Rochelle Pioneer
New York Call
New York Daily Tribune
New York Dramatic Mirror
New York Evening Post/New York Post
New York Evening Telegram
New York Evening World
New York Herald
New York Morning Telegraph
New York PM Daily
New York Press
New York Sun
New York Times
New York World
New York World-Telegram
New York World-Telegram and Sun
New Yorker
Newark Evening Star
Newport News Daily Press
Norfolk & Western Magazine
North Shore Daily Journal
Ocean Times Herald
Ogden Evening Standard
Omaha Bee
Omaha Sunday Bee
Palestine Bulletin
Palestine Post
Palm Springs News

Panama American
Pearson's Magazine
Philadelphia Public Ledger
Philadelphia Evening Public Ledger
Philadelphia Inquirer
Philadelphia Tribune
Pittsburg Dispatch
Pittsburgh Courier
Poughkeepsie News-Press
Puck
Railway Age Gazette/Railway Age
Real Estate Record
Richmond Daily Palladium
Richmond Dispatch
Richmond Enquirer
Richmond Times-Dispatch
Richmond Virginian
Rochester Democrat and Chronicle
Rome Daily Sentinel
Sacramento Union-Supplement
St. Louis Post-Dispatch
Salt Lake Herald
Salt Lake Herald-Republican
Salt Lake Telegram
Salt Lake Tribune
San Bernardino Sun
San Francisco Call
San Francisco Chronicle
San Francisco Emanu-El
San Francisco Examiner
Saturday Evening Post
Southern Israelite
Sunday Express [London]
Svenska Dagbladet
Syracuse Daily Standard
Syracuse Journal
Syracuse Sunday American
The Advance
The Advocate [New York]
The American City
The Commoner
The Economist [London]
The Forum
The Gardener's Chronicle
The Guardian [London]
The Iron Age
The Iron Trade Review
The Jewish Standard [Toronto]
The Magazine of Wall Street

The Nation
The New Palestine
The New Yorker
The North American Review
The Occident
The Reform Advocate
The Suffragist
The Tobacco World
The Weekly Underwriter
The World To-Day
Thrice A Week New York World
Time
Toledo Blade
Today
Topeka Daily State Journal
Topeka Plaindealer
Toronto Globe
Toronto Globe and Mail
Toronto Star
Town and Country
Tropic Magazine
Trust Companies
Twentieth Century Magazine
United States Investor
Valdez Prospector
Variety
Variety Daily Bulletin
Warrensburgh News
Warrentown - Lake George News
Washington Evening Star
Washington Herald
Washington Post
Washington Sunday Star
Washington Times
Wilmington Morning Star
The Woman Citizen
Yonkers Herald Statesman
Yonkers Stateman
Yonkers Statesman and News
Yorkshire Post
Zeulenroda Kreisblatt
Zeulenroda Tageblatt

Interviews

Prof. Frank Untermyer. 12 March 2000.
Prof. Frank Untermyer. 25–28 April 2000.
Prof. Frank Untermyer. 30 September 1999.
Samuel Untermyer II, 12 March 2000.

Dissertations

Aker, Lauren Beth. 'Savannah's New South: The Politics of Reform, 1885–1910'. PhD diss., University of California, Los Angeles, CA, 2012.

Filipo, Ivan Joe. 'Landmark Litigation in the American Theatre'. PhD diss., University of Florida, Gainesville, FL, 1972.

Fox, Maier Bryan. 'American Zionism in the 1920s'. PhD diss., George Washington University, Washington, DC, 1979.

Frommer, Morris. 'The American Jewish Congress: A History, 1914–1950'. PhD diss., Ohio State University, Columbus, OH, 1978.

Gottlieb, Moshe. 'The Anti-Nazi Boycott Movement in the American Jewish Community, 1933–1941'. PhD diss., Brandeis University, Waltham, MA, 1967.

Harrison, Andrew Robert. 'Mr. Philadelphia: Albert Greenfield (1887–1967)'. PhD diss., Temple University, Philadelphia, PA, 1997.

Kupsky, Gregory J. '"The True Spirit of the German People": German-Americans and National Socialism, 1919–1955'. PhD diss., The Ohio State University, Columbus, OH, 2010.

Pfannestiel, Todd J. 'Rethinking the Red Scare: The Lusk Committee and New York State's Fight Against Radicalism, 1919–1923'. PhD diss., College of William and Mary, Williamsburg, VA, 2001.

Schulman, Jason. 'The Limits of Liberalism: A Constitutional Reconsideration of American Jewish Politics'. PhD diss., Emory University, Atlanta, GA, 2014.

Shook, Dale N. 'William G. McAdoo and the Development of National Economic Policy, 1913–1918'. PhD Diss., University of Cincinnati, Cincinnati, OH, 1975.

Stackman, Ralph Robert. 'Laurence A. Steinhardt: New Deal Diplomat, 1933–1945'. PhD diss., Michigan State University, Ann Arbor, IN, 1967.

Wirth, Thomas. 'A Beautiful Public Life: George D. Herron, American Socialism, and Radical Political Culture at the Rand School of Social Science, 1890–1956'. PhD diss., Binghamton University, State University of New York, Binghamton, NY, 2014.

Index

Abdul Hamid II, Sultan 43
Abella, Irving 263 n.251
Actors' Equity Association 3
Adler, Cyrus 169
Adler, Felix 119
Adler, Samuel 119
Advisory Committee on Political Refugees 178
Agudath Sholom Synagogue, Lynchburg 183
Alaska Steamship Co. 32
Alaska Syndicate 31–2
Albert, Heinrich Friedrich 89–90, 108–10, 231 n.15
Aldine Club (New York City) 176
Aldrich, Nelson 58
Allen, Robert S. 115
Amalgamated Copper Co. 29–30
American Academy of Political and Social Science 229 n.306
American Athletic Union (AAU) 177
American Civil Liberties Union (ACLU) 8–9
American Civil War 15, 17–19, 21–2, 183
American Committee Appeal for the Jews in Poland 181
American Economic Association 82
American Federation of Labor (AFL) 176
American Hebrew 127–8, 131
American Jewish Committee (AJC) 121, 148, 150–1, 153–4, 159, 169, 175
American Jewish Congress (AJCong) 133–4, 136, 147, 153–5, 160, 175, 179, 182, 248 n.143
American Jewish Joint Distribution Committee (JDC) 120, 139–42, 151, 250 n.187
American Jewish Relief Committee for Sufferers from the War 120

American League for the Defense of Jewish Rights (the League) vii, 148–67, 169–79, 182, 240 n.238
American Lithographic Company 27
American Palestine Campaign 144
American Palestine Investment Bank 137
American Smelting and Refining Company 30
American Socialist Society 5–6
American Sugar Refining Co. 55
American Telephone and Telegraph Company (AT&T) 44–5
American Vigilant Intelligence Federation of Chicago 3–4
American Zion Commonwealth 125–6
Amster, Nathan L. 39–40
Andrew Freedman Home 37–8
Anglo-Palestine Bank 156
the Anschluss (German annexation of Austria) 181
Ansorge, Martin C. 124
Anti-Defamation League 174
Anti-Nazi Minutemen of the JWV 163
Antofagasta (Chili) and Bolivia Railway Co. 31
Arab Uprising, Palestine 1929 142–3
Archbold, John D. 40
Armstrong Committee 52
Arnold Constable and Company (New York City department store) 165
Assembly of Orthodox Rabbis 254 n.40
Associated First National Pictures, Inc. 44
Associated Press 41–2, 168, 173
Auerbach, Jerold S. 184
Avenol, Joseph 154

Backer, George 144, 252 n.225, 258 n.135
Bailey, Joseph W. 61
Baker, Abby Scott 2–3

Baker, George F.   70
Baldwin, Roger N.   8
Balfour Declaration   125, 131, 143
Ballantine, Arthur A.   104
Bancamerica-Blair Corporation   45
Bankers' Club, New York City   106
Bankers Trust Co.   27, 54, 66, 71, 78
Bank of America   28
Barkley, Alben W.   117
Barron, Clarence W.   43, 98
Barthelmess, Richard   44
Baruch, Bernard M.   30, 32, 56
Battle, George Gordon   175
B.B. & R. Knight Co.   28
Beach, William A.   23
Beamish, Richard J.   161, 176
Beck, James M.   1, 48, 104, 158, 160, 187 n.2
Belasco, David   35–6, 44
Belmont, August   33–4, 37
Bench and Bar   43
Benedict, Abraham   28
Berkowitz, Michael   252 n.6
Berlin 1936 Olympic Games   177
Berliner Illustrierte Nachtausgabe   176
Berliner Tageblatt und Handels-Zeitung   111
Bernstein, Herman   91, 121–5
Berridge, Thomas H. D.   24
Best & Co. (New York department store chain)   165
Bethlehem Steel Co.   3, 49, 138
Betz, John F.   23
Betz v. Baur   23
Biddle, Francis   160–1
Bielaski, A. Bruce   109–10, 235 n.105
Billikopf, Jacob   4, 72, 144
Birchall, Frederick T.   153
Birmingham, Sheffield and Tennessee River Railway Co.   38
Black, Conrad   172
Black, Edwin   152, 154–5
Blair, James A.   38, 94
Blair, Louis (a.k.a. Karel Bleha)   13, 194 n.161
Blake & Knowles Steam Pump Works Co.   23
Bloomingdale Brothers (department store)   165

B. Lowenstein & Bros. (Memphis department store)   163, 165
The Board (Secret Counter-Nazi German Subversion Organization)   174–5
Bolivia Railway Co.   31
Bonar Law, Andrew   87
Borah, William E.   113, 143
Boston and Montana Consolidated Copper & Silver Mining Co.   29
Boston Consolidated Copper and Gold Mining Company, Ltd.   29, 31
Boy-Ed, Karl   90, 110–11
Boy's Public School No. 35 (New York City)   19–20
Braddock, James J.   177–8
Braden Copper Mines Co.   30, 32
Brandeis, Louis D.   vi, 42, 64, 71–2, 75, 78, 93, 95, 98–9, 116, 125, 127–8, 135, 145, 222 n.127
Brant Lake (Adirondack Mountains estate)   vi, 23, 111
Brewers' Journal   28, 201 n.129
The Brewers' Journal, Inc.   28
Brewers Exchange of New York   28
Brisbane, Arthur   42
British Ambassador, Washington   262 n.225
British Foreign Office   153
British Gaumont Company   44
British Non-Sectarian Anti-Nazi Council to Champion Human Rights   162
British Secret Service   91, 109–10
British Trades Union Congress   152, 162
Brod, Max   163
Bronner, Harry   131
Brooklyn Daily Eagle   48, 117
Brooklyn–Manhattan Transit Corporation   114
Brotherhood of Sleeping Car Porters   4
Broward, Napoleon B.   52
Brundage, Avery   177
Bryan, William Jennings   2, 12, 48, 58, 61–3, 67, 74–5, 79, 88, 90, 102, 111
Bugher, Frederick   104
Bulkley, Robert J.   64
Burn & Berridge (law firm)   24
Burton, Theodore E.   78

Cahane, Anna   163
Calder, William M.   96
Canadian Jewish Congress   161
Carl, Alvin   21, 24, 201 n.132, 201–2 n.133, 202 n.147
Carl, Johann Erdmann Traugott   21
Carl, Manilius   21–2
Carl, Pauline   21–2
Carl, Walter Alvin   202 n.147
Carnegie Endowment for International Peace   141
Carter, Leslie   35, 44
Castle, William R. Jr.   112
Castro, Leon   152
Catholic World   161
Catt, Carrie Chapman   2
Central Trust Company   39
Chamberlain, Austen   139
Chicago, Rock Island & Pacific Railroad   39–40
Chicago and North-West Granaries Co.   23
Chicago Tribune   97
Chile Copper Co.   30–1
Chile Exploration Co.   30–1
Choate, Joseph H.   28
Chuquicamata copper mine   30–1
Churchill, Winston   137
Cincinnati Breweries Company   23
Citizens' Committee for Food Shipments   109
Citizens Budget Commission   114
Citrine, Walter   162
The City of Baltimore United Breweries   23
City of London   24–6, 84
City Stores   165
Clarke, Harley L.   45
Clausen, Henry Jr.   21
Clayton, Henry D.   78
Clayton Anti-Trust Act of 1914   83, 85, 105
Cleveland Committee for the Defense of Human Rights Against Nazism   161
cloak makers' strike (1921–2)   3
Coates, Son & Co.   38
Cobb, Frank J.   89

Cohen, David   152–3, 254 n.49
Cohn, Alfred E.   149, 253 n.17
Colby, Bainbridge   111–12
College of the City of New York   19–20
Columbia Broadcasting System   154
Columbia College of Law (subsequently Columbia Law School)   20, 185, 203 n.168, 245 n.70
Columbia Law Club   20
Columbia Straw Paper Co.   27, 59, 72, 81
Columbia University   vii, 20, 169, 185, 203 n.168, 245 n.70
Comité de Défense des Juifs Persécutes   46
Commercial Travelers League   49–51
The Commoner   58
Communist International   176
Cone, Bernard Milton   29
Cone, Ceasar   28–9
Cone, Herman   18, 28
Cone, Moses H.   28–9
Cone Export & Commission Company   28
Congregation Ahawath Chesed, New York City   21
Congregation Beth Ahabah, Richmond   15, 17
Congressional Union for National Suffrage and National Women's Party   2–3
Consolidated Stock Exchange of New York   56
Cooksey, George R.   91–2
Copper River and Northwestern Railway Co.   31–2
Coralnik, Abram   148, 152, 158–9
Corn Exchange Bank of New York   66
Coughlin, Charles   182
Cox, George B.   35–7
Cox, James M.   75
Crane, Charles R.   249 n.154
Cravath, Paul D.   31, 34, 65
Cravath firm   31, 34, 65, 185, 207 n.258
Creelman, James   11, 26
Crimean colonization project   140–2, 250 n.187
Crisp, Frank   24
Croker, Richard (Boss)   33, 47
Croker, Richard Jr.   37
Crowell Publishing Co.   27

Daily, Henry Jr. 23
Daily Herald (London) 162
Daily Worker (New York City) 175–6
Daniels, Josephus 99
Dannenbaum, Henry C. 127, 132
Davies, Joseph E. 78
The Dearborn Independent 120–3
Dearborn Publishing Company 122–4
De Ford, William A. 41
de Haas, Jacob 149
Deloitte, Plender, Griffiths & Co. 106
Dembitz, Louis vi
Dembitz, Nanette vi, 43
Dernburg, Bernhard 109
Der Stürmer 171
Der Tog (*The Day*) 90, 148, 164
De Telegraaf (Amsterdam) 152–3
Deutsch, Bernard S. 155
Deutsche Bank 77
Dickstein, Samuel 170, 174–5, 264 nn.272–3
Diezengoff, Meyer 138
Dillon, Read & Co. 45
Disconto-Gesellschaft Bank 77
Disraeli, Benjamin 11, 44
Dix, John Alden 57
Dodd, William E. 170–1
Doherty, Henry L. 214 n.391
Dominion Copper Co. of Toronto 54
Dreyfus, Alfred 46
Dreyfus, Pierre 46
DuBois, Guy Pène 11
Dubovsky, Benjamin 159, 257 n.115
Duluth Evening Herald 29
Dupee, Charles A. 27, 204 n.190
Dwight, Theodore W. 20

Eastman, Max 1, 6–7
Economic Bulletin 162, 167
Economic Club of New York 56, 82–3
Economic Club of Springfield, Massachusetts 79
Ehrler, Francis 22
Ehrler, Louisa 22
1848 German Revolution 21
Einstein, Albert 126–8, 130, 138, 156–8, 245–6 n.76
Einstein, Elsa 157

Elkus, Abram I. 101, 230 n.12, 235–6 n.130
Equality League of Self-Supporting Women 2
Equitable Building 233 n.69
Equitable Life Assurance Society 52, 111
Erdmann, Joan Untermyer 185
Erlanger, Abraham 34–7
Exploration Company (subsidiary of N.M. Rothschild & Sons of London) 30

F. & W. Grand 5–10–25 Cent Stores 166
Farrar, Edward Howard 60, 65
Fay, Francis X. 165
Federal Bureau of Investigation 165
Federal Commission on Industrial Relations 92–3
Federal Reserve Act of 1913 74–8, 85, 105, 268 n.21
Federal Reserve Bank of New York 77, 94, 233 n.69
Federal Reserve Board 74, 77, 84
Federal Reserve System 77, 84, 183
Federal Trade Commission 82–4, 116
Federal Trade Commission Act of 1914 82–3
Federation of Jewish Women's Organisations of Greater New York 109, 160
Federation of Polish Jews in America 181–2
Feilchenfeld, Ernst H. 151
Ferguson, Julianna Farquhar 12
Fertig, M. Maldwin 113–14, 240 n.238
F. Heppenheimer's Sons of New Jersey 26–7
First National Bank of New York 70
Fisher, Esther 163
Fisher, Mitchell Salem 163
Flagler, Henry M. 40
Fletcher, Duncan U. 116–17
Flexner, Abraham 157
Flexner, Bernard 139
Florida land boom of the 1920s 43
Flynn, William 89
Folk, Joseph W. 39–40, 61, 111–12, 223–4 n.163
Ford, Henry 13, 113, 120–5, 145, 244 n.39

Ford Werke A.G.   231 n.15
Foreign Policy Association   147, 160–1
The Forum   130, 135–6
Forverts (Jewish Daily Forward)   90–1, 103
Fox, William   44–5, 219 n.53
Fox Film Corporation   44
Fox Movietone   175
Fox Theatres Corporation   44
Frank, Leo   11
Frankfurter, Felix   116, 165
Frank Jones Brewing Company   23
Fredman, J. George   152–3, 177–8, 266 n.307
Freedlander, Joseph Henry   11
Freedman, Andrew   33–4, 37–8, 54, 208–9 n.283
Freedman, Daniel B.   37
French Secret Service   110
Frew, Walter E.   66
Friar Park   24
Friede, Donald   245–6 n.76
Friedman, Milton   225–6 n.214
Friedman, Monroe   182
Friends of New Germany   173
Fuehr, Karl Alexander   89
Fullerton, William   23
F.W. Woolworth Co.   165–7, 170

Gardiner, Asa Bird   190 n.54
Garfield, James R.   51
Garvan, Francis P.   88, 230 n.12
Gaynor, William J.   56–7
General Development Company   29
Gerard, James W.   87–8, 91–2, 149–50, 158, 178
German-American Protective Alliance (DAWA)   173
German Consulate General in New York City   165, 167, 170, 260 n.167
German Embassy in the Hague   153
German Embassy in Washington   88, 90, 109–10, 171–2, 253 n.13
German Foreign Ministry   90, 166–7
German Imperial Central Purchasing Company   89
Gestapo (Geheime Staatspolizei)   162, 231 n.15

Gewirtz, Sharon   182
Gimbel, Bernard F.   161
Gimbel Brothers (department store chain)   161, 165, 170
Ginsburg, Elias   158
Glasgow, William Jr.   59
Glass, Carter   25, 59, 64–5, 74–8, 107, 183–4, 268 n.21, 269 n.24
Glynn, Martin H.   92
Goebbels, Josef   171
Gompers, Samuel   3, 48, 99
Gorfinkel, David   120
Gould, George J.   39
Green, William   176
Greene, Belle da Costa   66–7
Greenfield, Albert M.   45, 165
Gregory, Thomas W.   94, 110, 235 n.105
Greystone (Yonkers estate)   1, 11–12, 44–5, 51, 56, 60, 72, 74–5, 91, 96, 110, 119, 124, 127–8, 157, 174, 187 n.2, 193 n.137, 218–19 n.50
Greystone Kennels   51, 218–19 n.50
Grimm, Peter   114
Gruber, Abraham   35–6
Guaranty Trust Company   66, 71
Guggenheim, Benjamin   32
Guggenheim, Daniel   22, 30–1
Guggenheim, William   22–3
Guggenheim Brothers   23, 30–2
Guggenheimer & Untermyer (Lynchburg retail business)   17
Guggenheimer & Untermyer/ Guggenheimer, Untermyer & Marshall (law firm)   vi, 20–1, 26, 28–9, 30, 33, 42, 91, 120, 122, 124, 163, 185, 233 n.69, 245–6 n.76
Guggenheimer, Abraham   15
Guggenheimer, Charley   59
Guggenheimer, Nathaniel   15, 17
Guggenheimer, Nathaniel S.   183
Guggenheimer, Randolph   15, 17–21, 24, 32, 38, 47–8
Guggenheimer, Salomon   15–16
Guggenheimer's (Lynchburg department store)   163, 183
Guggenheim Exploration Company   30, 32
Gulbenkian, Carlouste Sarkis   43
Guthrie, William   31, 207 n.258

Haavara Agreement   155–6
Hadassah   140, 154
Hamlin, Charles S.   225–6 n.214
Hammer Verlag, Leipzig   125
Hammond, John Hays   32
Hampton Court Palace gardens   24
Hand, Augustus Noble   41
Hanly, Frank   52
Hannah, Leslie   38
Hapgood, Norman   75
Harney Peak tin mine   23, 25, 59
Harper, Ida Husted   1
Harper's Weekly   72, 75, 90
Harriman, Edward H.   39
Harris, Mary   160
Harrison, Benjamin   24
Harvey, George   87, 99, 105, 230 n.3
Harvey Fisk & Sons   138
Hayden, Charles   32
Hays, Arthur Garfield   108
Hearn (New York city department store)   165
Hearst, William Randolph   41–2, 90, 102, 175–6
Hearst Metrotone News   175
Hebrew Orphan Asylum of New York City   119
Hebrew University, Jerusalem   127, 130, 133–4, 140–2, 147–8, 251 n.207
Hebrew University Fund   140
Heidelberg, Charles   20
Helfferich, Karl   77
Hellman, Geoffrey T.   187 n.2
Hemphill, Noyes & Co   142
Henry, Robert Lee   58–60, 78, 222 n.127
Hepburn, A. Barton   74
Herbert, Grace Brown   22
High Commission for Refugees (Jewish and Other) Coming from Germany   151
Highland Boy Gold Mining Company   29
Hillquit, Morris   9–10, 56, 102–3
Hirschmann, Ira   165
Hitchcock, Gilbert M.   81–2
Hitler, Adolf   103, 144, 147–54, 158, 165, 167–8, 170–2, 174–6, 179, 181, 254 n.40
Hoffman, Harry   26, 31
Hollis, Henry F.   93

Hollywood Anti-Nazi League   161
Holmes, John Haynes   4, 158, 256 n.98
Holmes, Oliver Wendell   42
Hoover, Herbert   106, 115
Hoover, J. Edgar   110–11
Howard University Law School   4
Huebsch, Adolph   21
Hughes, Charles Evans   42–4, 52–3, 82, 96, 98, 100, 219 n.53, 247 n.122
Hull, Cordell   115, 154, 168–70, 172, 176, 182, 263 n.251
Humes, E. Lowry   109
Hunter, Thomas   19
Hutchinson, Paul   161
Hyde, James Hazen   52, 111
Hylan, John F.   102–4

Ickes, Harold L.   172–3
IG Farben   153
Illinois Manufacturers' Association   79–80
Immigration Acts of 1921 and 1924   139
Imperial Chemical Industries (ICI)   143–4, 153, 255 n.55
Industrial & General Trust   24
Interborough Rapid Transit Company (IRT)   34, 37, 114
Intercollegiate Socialist Society   56
International Committee of Policy Holders of the New York and Mutual Life Insurance Companies   52–3
International Cotton Mills Corporation   28
International High Commission on Uniform Legislation   94–5
The International Jew   122, 124–5
International Ladies' Garment Workers' Union   3
International Magazine Co.   41
International Match Company   45
International News Service   41
International Steam Pump Company, New York   32
Interstate Commerce Commission   39–40, 56, 83, 106
Isaacs, Henry   24

Jabotinsky, Vladimir (Zeev)   135, 158
Jacobs, Mike   178, 266 n.308

Jerome, William Travers 36
Jewish Agency for Palestine 138–42, 144
Jewish Chronicle (London) 152–3
Jewish Consumptive Relief Society of
    Denver (JCRS) 160
Jewish League of American Patriots 91
Jewish National Fund 140
Jewish Representative Council
    (Britain) 153, 161–2
Jewish Telegraphic Agency 131, 143
The Jewish Tribune 121, 132
Jewish War Veterans (JWV) 148, 150,
    152, 154, 161, 163, 252 n.6,
    266 n.307
John F. Betz and Son's Brewery 23
Johnson, Hiram W. 41
Johnson, John A. 52, 223–4 n.163
John Wanamaker (department store) 165
Jonas, Abraham (a.k.a. Abraham ben Jona
    Schwab) 15
Jordan, Max 111
Jösicka-Herczeg, Imre 12, 193 n.141
Jösicka-Herczeg, Marguerite (Margaret)
    Roche Rice 12
Journal of Commerce 76
J.P. Morgan & Co. 31, 38, 45, 49, 51, 57,
    65–6, 69–71, 79, 93, 113, 115, 121
J.S. Staedtler 166
Jung Brewing Company 23, 201–2 n.133

Kafka, Hugo 19
Kahn, Otto H. 119
Kalb, S. William 161, 177, 179
Kansas City Southern Railway
    Company 39
Kaufmann, S. Walter 108
Keith, Minor C. 101–2
Kelley, Converse & Co. 142
Kennecott Copper Corporation 32
Kennecott Mines Co. 31–2
Keppler, Udo J. 52–3
Keren Hayesod (Palestine Foundation
    Fund) 119, 125, 127–35, 137–42,
    145–6, 148, 158, 160, 247 n.103,
    252 n.223
Keren Hayesod Thousand Dollar
    Club 128
King-Crane Report 135–6
Klaw & Erlanger 35, 37

Klein, Henry H. 104, 192 n.110
Klein, William 34, 209–10 n.302
Knapp, Joseph Palmer 26–7, 87
Knickerbocker Trust 54–5
Knight, Peter 71
Kraft Foods 179
Kraus, Mayer & Stein of Chicago 24
Kress, Claude W. 166
Kreuger & Toll Company 45–6
Kreuger, Ivar 45
Kreuz Zeitung (a.k.a. *Neue Preußische
    Zeitung*) 98
Kriegshaber 15–16
Kroeger, Brooke 1
Kuhn, Loeb & Co. 38, 65, 93, 119, 130
Ku Klux Klan (KKK) 134
Kun, Béla 176, 265 n.291
Kupsky, Gregory J. 23

La Follette, Robert 113
La Guardia, Fiorello H. 114, 149–50,
    158, 178, 184
Lakewood Preventorium 42–3
Lamont, Thomas W. 27
Landauer, Raphael Israel 15
Lansing, Robert 101–2
Lawes, Lewis Edward 10
Lawson, Thomas W. 30, 219 n.55
Lazard Frères 54, 245 n.65
Lazaron, Morris S. 131
L. Bamberger (Newark department
    store) 163
League for the Abolition of Capital
    Punishment 10
League for the Civic Education of
    Women 2
League of Nations' Mandate
    Commission 139
League of Nations 125, 131, 139, 151, 154
Lee Higginson & Co. 121
Lehman, Babette 19
Lehman, Herbert H. 26, 32, 114–15, 139,
    143, 184, 240 n.238
Lehman, Mayer 19
Lehman Brothers 19, 32, 45, 54,
    260 n.181
Leitner, Rudolf 168
Levinger, Adolph (Abraham) 18–21
Levinger, Mathias 18, 20

Levinson, Salmon O.   158, 161
Levy, Aaron Jefferson   90, 133, 138, 232 n.33
Lewis, Leon   173-4
Lewisohn, Adolph   29, 128
Lewisohn, Leonard   29
Lewisohn Brothers   29, 206 n.225
Liberty Bonds   91-2
Lindbergh, Charles A. Sr.   58, 60, 65
Lindheim, Norvin R.   108
Link, Arthur S.   62
Lippert, Julius   177
Lippmann, Walter   5
Lipsky, Louis   156
Littleton, Martin W.   121
Lloyd George, George   106
Lockwood, Charles C.   113
Lockwood Committee   9-10, 113
London, Meyer   108-9
London Stock Exchange   23, 29, 56
Longley, Clifford B.   124-5
Lord & Taylor (department store)   165
Los Angeles Times   174
'Lost Cause' mythology   25
Lotos Club   66
Louis, Joe   178
Lowenstein, Benedict   19
Lowenstein, Gabriel   167
Lowenstein, Sophia Mendelson   19
Lubow, Bernard   167
Luce, Henry R.   159
Lusk, Clayton R.   6-7
Lusk Committee   5-7
Luther, Hans   159, 168-70, 172
Lynchburg's Sesquicentennial, 1936   183
Lynchburg News   183
Lynchburg Savings Bank   17, 196 n.35

McAdoo, Molly (Mary) Tackaberry Ferguson   12-13, 193 n.137
McAdoo, William 'Billy' Gibbs Jr.   12, 194 n.144
McAdoo, William Gibbs   1-3, 12-13, 30-1, 61-2, 64, 75-7, 79, 87, 89, 91-8, 100-7, 111, 134
McAneny, George   114
McCarthy, Thomas D.   92
McClure's Magazine   97
McCombs, William F.   62, 79, 96, 105-6

McCrory Stores Corporation (chain store)   166
McDonald, James G.   147, 151-2, 170, 172-3, 176, 178, 264 n.272
McDonald, John B.   33-4
Mack, Julian W.   127-8, 133, 135, 145
McKenna, Joseph   42
McKenna, Reginald   268 n.21
McKinley, William   38, 47
Magnes, Beatrice Lowenstein   11, 113
Magnes, Judah Leon   141-2, 145, 251 n.207
Mahoney, Jeremiah   177
Malmberg, Aino   90, 231 n.25
Manchester Guardian   162
Manhattan Athletic Club   33
Manhattan Import Co. Inc.   167
Marsh, Henry W.   120
Marshall, Florence Lowenstein   47, 217 n.2
Marshall, James   26
Marshall, Louis   1, 4, 20, 25-8, 42-3, 47, 50, 72, 74, 107, 119-24, 128, 137-42, 145, 172, 217 n.2, 242 n.11, 243 n.21, 247 n.112, 250 n.187
May, Tom   164
May Department Stores Company   165, 260 n.181
Mayer, Levy   24, 36
Melchett, 2nd. Lord (a.k.a. Henry Mond)   143-4, 150, 152-3
Mellen, Charles S.   39
Men's League for Woman Suffrage   1
Mendelson, Adelheid Untermayer   vi, 15, 18-19
Merz, Charles   5
Metropolitan Life Insurance Company   87
Mexican Herald   64
Meyer, Eugene   125, 245 n.65
Miami Cooper Company   29
Michelbacher, Maximillian Josef   15
Milburn, John G.   81
Military Intelligence Division (MID)   3-4, 90, 109
Miller, Byron D.   166
Miller, Louis E.   90
Miller, Nathan L.   7

Minnie Untermyer Open-Air Amphitheatre   142, 251 n.207
Minutemen   163
Mitchel, John Purroy   102–3
Moley, Raymond   116
Mond, Robert   153
Montefiore Home for Chronic Invalids   119
Montreal and Boston Copper Co.   54
Moore, A. Harry   9
Morgan, J.P. (John Pierpont) Jr.   60, 69–71, 93, 101, 225 n.214
Morgan, J.P. (John Pierpont) Sr.   39, 49, 51, 54–5, 57, 61–3, 66–8, 70, 101, 218–19 n.50
Morgenthau, Henry   62, 101, 130–1, 135, 247 n.112
Morgenthau, Henry Jr.   63–4, 172
Morrow, Dwight   32
Morrow, Edwin P.   4
Motion Picture Patents Company   44
Mundelein, Cardinal George William   176
Munroe & Munroe   54
Munsey, Frank A.   225 n.207
Murphy, Charles F. (Boss)   57, 62, 72–4, 102
Mutual Broadcasting Network   178
Mutual Life Insurance Company   52, 57
Myers, Fred S.   47
Myers, Herman   47
Myers, Sigo   47

Nagel, Charles   58
Nathan, Max   42
The Nation   164–5
National Association of Owners of Railroad Securities   107
National Boycott Committee of America   150, 160
National City Bank of New York   54, 58, 62, 71, 94
National Civic Federation   55–6
National Cyclopædia of American Biography   24
National Socialist German Workers (Nazi) Party   148, 231 n.15
Nazis against the World   161
NBC radio   150

Nelson, Boris E. (a.k.a. Boris Nitkewitsch)   160, 257 n.119
Neumann, Emanuel   119–20, 128–9, 140
Newcombe, Richard S.   23, 201 n.123
New England Breweries Co.   23–4
Newhouse, Mott   31
Newhouse, Samuel   29, 31–2, 54
Newhouse Mines & Smelters Co.   29
Newhouse Realty Co.   31
New Jersey State Court of Chancery   27
Newlands, Francis G.   84
The New Palestine   119
New Republic   5
Newton, Charles D.   6
New York, New Haven & Hartford Railroad   33, 39
New York American   90, 115, 164
New York Breweries Co.   23
New York City Financial Reorganization, 1933   114–15
New York City Transit Unification   114
New York Clearing House   61, 64, 66, 70, 85, 114
New York Court of Appeals   21, 28
New York Curb Market   56, 82
New Yorker Staats-Zeitung und Herold   173
New York Evening Journal   42
New York Evening Mail   89–90, 108
New York Evening Post   161, 258 n.135
New York Evening Sun   60
New York Evening World   35–6
New York Female Suffrage Amendment (1915)   2
New York Giants   33
New York Herald-Tribune   164
New York Post, see New York Evening Post
New York Press   47, 56
New York State Assembly   7, 72, 74, 114
New York State Brewers' and Maltsters' Association   28
New York State Joint Legislative Committee Appointed to Investigate the Public Service Commissions   34
New York State Joint Legislative Committee on Housing, *see* Lockwood Committee
New York State Suffrage Association   2

New York Stock Exchange   56–7, 59, 66, 70, 72–3, 75, 79, 81–2, 85, 99, 100–1, 113–17
New York *Sun*   67, 69, 72–3, 90, 95–6, 109, 225 n.207
New York Supreme Court   6, 21, 28, 35–6, 41, 52, 111, 185, 232 n.33
New York Times   5–6, 27–8, 37, 40, 50–2, 54–5, 58, 62, 65, 71, 80, 82, 87, 91, 125, 134–5, 153–4, 164, 168, 173, 175
New York Tribune   51, 67–8, 90, 96
New York Woman Suffrage Amendment (1917)   2
New York Workingmen's School   48
New York *World*   5, 58, 89–90, 109, 134, 175
New York World-Telegram   175
Nicoll, De Lancey   5, 37
Nicoll, De Lancey Jr.   124
Nineteenth Amendment to the US Constitution (woman suffrage)   2–3
Nipissing Mines Company   31–2
Nirodha (houseboat)   12, 96, 101, 193 n.136
Non-Sectarian Anti-Nazi League to Champion Human Rights, *see* American League for the Defense of Jewish Rights
Non-Sectarian Anti-Nazi League to Champion Human Rights Pennsylvania Committee   161
Norbeck, Peter   115–16
The North American Review   55, 78, 82, 87

O'Brien, John P.   114, 173
Ochs, Adolph S.   27–8, 41, 49, 54, 134–5, 153, 175
O'Gorman, James A.   57, 95
Oller, John   21
Ornstein, Max   158
Orr, Alexander E.   52–3
Osiris (houseboat)   12
O'Sullivan, Mary   66
Otis Steel Company   23, 201 n.132
Otterson, John E.   44–5
Overman, Lee Slater   109

Overman Committee   109–10
Owen, Robert Latham   74–8, 80–1, 116, 268 n.21

Pak, Susie J.   49, 55, 119
Palestine (British Mandate)   125, 131–2, 134, 136–7, 139, 142–3, 145
Palestine Cooperative Company   139
Palestine Economic Corporation   139
Palestine Emergency Fund   143
Palestine Royal Commission Report, 1937   144–5
Palmer, A. Mitchell   108, 110–11, 230 n.12
Panama Libel Case   5
Pan American Financial Conference (1915)   94
Panic of 1907   28, 54–5
Paramount Pictures Corporation   44
Paresis Hall   209–10 n.302
Paris Peace Treaty, 1919   181
Parker, Alton B.   51, 218 n.41
Partridge, Frederic A.   133, 142–4
Partridge, Madeleine Steinhardt   133, 143–4
Passaic Strike   9, 191 n.86
Paterson Seven   8
Paul, Alice   2
Payne, John Barton   104, 107
Peabody, Charles A.   52–4, 72
Peabody, George Foster   75
Pearson, Drew   115
Peck, Mary Allen Hulbert   97–8, 235 n.105
Pecora, Ferdinand   116–17, 177
Peel, William Robert Wellesley (Earl Peel)   144
Penrose, Boise   61
Perkins, George W.   70, 75
Perlman, Nathan D.   232 n.33
Peyser, Julius   134
P.F. Collier and Son   27
Philadelphia Inquirer   66
Philadelphia Record   164
Pierce, Henry Clay   40
Pillsbury-Washburn Flour Mills Co.   23–4
Pinchot, Gifford   161
Pitney, Henry C.   27, 72

Pitney, Mahlon 98
Pittsburgh Courier 4
Pius XI, Pope 176
Plender, John 106
The Plot against America (2004) 182
Plumer, Herbert 142
Posnansky, Israel 158
Powell, Enoch 181–2
Press Publishing Company 5
Price Waterhouse & Co. 106
Pridday, Joseph E. 165
Prison Association of New York 10
Pritchett, Henry S. 141
Prohibition 23
Proskauer, Joseph M. 175, 184
Provisional Executive Committee for General Zionist Affairs 125
Puck 52–3
Pujo, Arsene 60–1, 65–6, 70
Pujo Money Trust Investigation 13, 37, 57–72, 74–5, 78, 80, 82, 84–5, 113, 116, 130, 183–4, 222 n.127
Pulitzer, Joseph 5
Pullman Company 4
Purim Association 119

Rabinowitz, Ezekiel 149, 159
Raines Liquor Tax Law, 1896 28
Rand School of Social Science 5–7, 120
Reichsbank 77, 168, 171
Reick, William C. 225 n.207
Reid-Moore syndicate 39–40
Retail Dry Goods Association (New York City) 164
R.G. Dun & Co. 15, 18
Rhinock, Joseph 35–7
R.H. Macy & Co. 133, 161, 163–5, 170
Richards, Bernard G. 133
Richmond Virginian 59
Richter, Irene Untermyer Myers 11, 21–2, 245 n.65
Ridder, Bernard 173
Rifkind, Robert S. 122
Riggs National Bank 93–4
Robinson, Boardman 67–8
Rockefeller, John D. 40
Rockefeller, William A. Jr. 29–30, 70
Rogers, Henry H. 29–30, 50–1
Rohatyn, Felix 114

Rollins, Richard (a.k.a. Isadore Rothberg) 175, 264 n.273
Roosevelt, Franklin Delano 45, 57, 115–17, 154, 168, 171–2, 178, 181–3, 241 n.258, 241 n.260
Roosevelt, Theodore 5, 50–1, 55, 61, 190 n.54
Roosevelt, Theodore Jr. 158, 256 n.97
Root, Elihu 230 n.3
Rosenblatt, Bernard A. 125–9, 133, 137–8, 141, 143
Rosenblatt, Therese Steinhardt 125
Rosenblatt, William 125, 245 n.70
Roth, Philip 182
Rothenberg, Morris 156, 163
Rumely, Edward 108
Ruppert, Jacob Jr. 47
Ruppin, Arthur 137–9
Rutenberg Scheme 129, 137, 141
Rutland Railroad 39
Ryan, Thomas Fortune 38, 52

St. Joseph & Grand Island Railway Co. 39
Saklatvala, Shapurji 8
Saks Fifth Avenue (department store) 165
Salomons, Harry 153
Salomons, Leopold 24
Salomonsohn, Arthur 77
San Francisco Examiner 174
Sapiro, Aaron 123–4
Satterlee, Herbert L. 54–5
Schacht, Hjalmar 171
Schiff, Jacob H. 37–8, 42, 70, 92–3, 119, 252 n.225
Schmeling, Max 177–8, 266 n.308
Schmeling–Braddock boxing match 177–8
Schmitt, Kurt 171
Schwartz, Anna 225 n.214
Scud (steam yacht) 12
Scudder, Philip J. 71
Seaboard Air Line 38, 43, 94
Sears, Roebuck & Co. 165–7
Seattle Jewish Transcript 166
Second World Jewish Conference 155
Securities Act of 1933 85
Securities Exchange Act of 1934 85, 116

Segal, Adolph   55
Seligman, Jefferson   128
Shelton, Samuel W.   18
Sherer, William   61
S.H. Kress & Co. (chain store)   166
Shubert, Jacob J.   34, 36–7
Shubert, Lee   34, 36–7, 209–10 n.302
Shubert, Samuel S.   34–5, 209 n.301
Shulman, Jason   5
Shulman, Samuel   103–4, 131
Sielcken, Herman   39
Siesfeld, Helen Untermyer   15, 195 n.17
Siesfeld, Max   18
Silver, Abba Hillel   139, 149, 155–6, 158–9, 161, 167, 169, 184
Silver, Henry Clay   120
Silver, Matt   42–3
Sinclair, Upton   5, 41, 219 n.53
Slonim, Joel   91
Smith, Alfred E.   7, 177, 241 n.258
Smith, William Alden   52
Smoot, Reed   92
Social Justice   182
Society for Ethical Culture   119
Sokolow, Nahum   134–5
South American Gold and Platinum Company   29
Southern Iron & Steel Co.   54
Southern Israelite   169
Southern Pacific Railroad Co.   80
South Utah Mines & Smelters Co.   29
Sparknoebel, Heinz   173
Special Palestine Fund of the Mizrachi and the Hadassah   140
Speyer & Co.   7, 65
Speyer, Edgar   7–8, 12, 191 n.77
S.S. Kresge Co. (chain store)   166
Standard Oil   30, 40, 49–50, 80
Standard Oil of New Jersey   44
Standard Oil of New York   44
Stanton, Elizabeth Cady   2
Steinglass, Meyer F.   179
Steinhardt, Addie Untermyer   vi, 15, 26, 195 n.21
Steinhardt, Adolph   26
Steinhardt, Laurence A.   13, 43, 45, 115, 122, 124–5, 134, 182, 185, 241 n.260, 245 n.70, 247 n.112
Stern, Harry J.   147

Stern, J. David   160–1, 164, 258 n.129, 258 n.135
Stetson, Francis Lynde   51, 55, 57
Stillman, James   61–2, 71
Stilwell, Arthur Edward   39
Stockholms Enskilda Bank   45
Stokes, Helen Elwood   43
Straus, Nathan   37, 42, 127, 133
Straus, Percy S.   164–5
Straus Family   163
Streicher, Julius   171, 178
Strong, Benjamin Jr.   54, 78–9, 94, 233 n.69
Strong, George Templeton   20
Stroock, Sol M.   39, 159
Stuart, Harry L.   44–5
Sturgis, Frank K.   66
Sulzberger, Arthur Hays   175
Sulzberger, Mayer   42
Sulzer, William C.   72–4, 92, 223–4 n.163
Sunday Express (London)   152
Svenska Dagbladet   46
Swanson, Gloria   44
Swedish Match Co.   46
Sweet, Thaddeus C.   7

Tackaberry, John   12, 193 n.137
Taft, William Howard   42, 61–2, 65, 99
Tammany Hall   21, 33–4, 47–8, 57, 62, 72–4, 90, 102, 209–10 n.302, 243 n.21
Tel Aviv Loan   138
Tel Aviv-Untermyer honoured by   138, 142
Temple Emanu-El, New York City   119
Temple Emanu-El, Yonkers   119
Tenenbaum, Joseph   154, 182
Theatrical Syndicate   34–6
Third Ward Gang, Newark   163
Thomas, Charles S.   92
Thomas Hunter Association   19
Thompson, Huston   116
Thompson, William Boyce   31–2, 43
Tilden, Samuel J.   11
Time   158–9
Tinoco, Frederico   101–2
Today   116
Topeka Plaindealer   4
Touche, George   106

Touche Niven & Co. 106
Triborough Bridge 172–3
Troper, Harold 263 n.251
Tumulty, Joseph P. 79, 83–4, 89
Tweed, William M. (Boss) 21
Twentieth Century Magazine 64

Ulmo, Meir ben Sanwil 16
Union Pacific Railroad Co. 38–9, 80
United Fruit Company 27, 101–2
United German Societies 173
United Jewish Campaign (UJC) 140
United Metals Selling Company 30
United Mine Workers of America 8
United Palestine Appeal (UPA) 140–1, 252 n.225
United States Brewers Association 48
United States Brewing Company 23
United States Fidelity and Guaranty Company 32–4
United States Shipbuilding Co. 49–50, 57, 60
United States Steel Corporation 49, 51, 62
United War Work Campaign 92
University Club of Los Angeles 116
Untermayer, Isaak 15–16, 195–6 n.24
Untermayer, Jette Guggenheimer 15–16
Untermayer, Zacharias 16
Untermyer, Alvin 13, 21–2, 37, 54, 129, 185
Untermyer, Eugene 46
Untermyer, Frank vi–vii, 185
Untermyer, Irwin 7, 13, 21–3, 31, 111, 162, 185
Untermyer, Isaac 15, 18–21, 23, 30, 42, 122, 195 n.18, 197 n.58, 211 n.339
Untermyer, Maurice 15, 23–4, 48, 195 n.19
Untermyer, Minnie Carl 2, 12, 21–2, 88, 95, 97–8, 109, 138, 251 n.207, 256 n.98
Untermyer, Samuel II vi, 185–6
Untermyer, Samuel xi
  anti-Nazi boycott leader 147–79, 181–2
  childhood 11–12, 15–20
  children 21
  conspicuous consumption 11–13, 142
  death 184
  education 17–20
  grandchildren vi, 185–6
  Jewish community leader 119–79
  legal career 21–46
  liberalism 1–11
  marriage 21
  mistress 12
  Polish Jewish relief (1937–9) 181–2
  political career 47–117, 183–4
  university education 20–1
  Zionist activist 125–46
Untermyer, Stein & Stiefel (law firm) 21
Untermyer, Therese Landauer Guggenheimer 11–12, 15–21, 119
Untermyer Bronze Memorial Tablet, Lynchburg 183
Untermyer/Untermayer, Isidor 15–18, 24–5, 196 n.39
US Department of Commerce and Labor 51
US Department of Justice 110
US Department of State 8, 43, 88, 98, 102, 111–12, 169, 175, 181
US Department of the Treasury 91
US Food Administration 106
US House Committee on Banking and Currency 58, 60, 64–5, 222 n.127
US House Committee on Rules 58
US House Committee on the Judiciary 78, 80
US House Committee on Ways and Means 25
US House Special Committee on Un-American Activities 174
US Office of Alien Property Custodian 107–8, 230 n.12
US Railway Mediation Board 4
US Secret Service 89, 109
US Senate Committee on Banking and Currency 74, 78, 81, 115–16
US Senate Committee on Interstate Commerce 84
US Senate Committee on Manufactures 9
US Senate Committee on the Judiciary 73
US Senate Subcommittee of the Committee on the Judiciary 98–9

US Supreme Court   vi, 8, 27, 39, 41–2, 55, 95–6, 98–9, 145, 201 n.123, 219 n.53
Utah Consolidated Gold Mines Ltd.   29
Utah Copper Company   31

Van Antwerp, William C.   72–3, 82
Van Deman, Ralph H.   3
Vanderbilt, Cornelius III   33, 37
Vanderlip, Frank A.   61–3, 74
Van Hamm, Caleb M.   5, 90
Van Wyck, Robert A.   33, 48
Vatican   176, 265 n.295
Viereck, George Sylvester   89–90
Villard, Oswald Garrison   9–10, 160
Vinton Colliery Company   8
von Bernstorff, Johann Heinrich Count   88–90, 102, 223 n.161
von Neurath, Konstantin Baron   170–1
von Prittwitz und Gaffron, Friedrich Wilhelm   167–8

Wabash Pittsburgh Terminal Railway Company   39
WABC radio   154
Wagner, Robert F.   102, 184
Wald, Kenneth D.   1
Waldman, Morris   150–1, 174
Walker, James   143
Wallenberg, Jacob   45–6
Wallenberg, Raoul   216 n.448
Wall Street Journal   98
Walsh, Frank P.   113
Warburg, Felix M.   130, 138–40, 144, 157
Warburg, Paul M.   74–5, 77, 84, 227 n.254, 268 n.21
Warfield, Solomon (Sol) Davies   28, 38, 43, 94, 107
Warfield, Wallis (Duchess of Windsor)   38
War Finance Corporation   107
Warheit (Di Varhayt)   90–1, 109
Warner, Harry   44, 152
Warner, Jack   152
Warner Bros.   13, 45–6
Washington *Evening Star*   168
Washington Post   90, 245 n.65
Waters-Pierce Oil Company   40
Watson, Tom   99

Weinman, Moses   25, 30, 42, 122, 203 n.168
Weinstein, Gregory   48
Weir, Thomas   29
Weizmann, Chaim   125–31, 134, 137–8, 140–2, 144–5, 156, 250 n.187
Westchester County Division of the UPA   141
Western Economic Society   83
Western Maryland R.R. Co.   54
West Side YMCA, New York City   57
Whistler, James McNeill   11
White, Edward Douglass   99
Whitman, Olive   2
Who's Who in America   24
Wickersham, George W.   58
Wickwire, Arthur Manley   21, 54
Wilcox, Ansley   190 n.54
Wiley, Louis   28, 37
Wilhelm II, Kaiser   21
Willard, Monroe L.   27, 204 n.190
Williams, John Skelton   38, 93–4
Willis, H. Parker   64, 74, 76
The Willows (Palm Springs winter estate)   vii, 12–13, 184, 245–6 n.76
Wilson, Edith Boling Galt   89
Wilson, Woodrow   2, 13, 55, 61–4, 67, 69, 74–5, 77–84, 87–90, 93–109, 111, 115, 149, 183, 223 nn.160–1, 235 n.105
Wilson Tariff Act of 1890   25, 203 n.160
Winsmore, Robert S.   66, 113–14
Wise, Henry A.   41
Wise, Stephen S.   42, 125, 131, 133–4, 140, 142, 144–5, 147, 152–5
Wislicki, Waclaw   152
Woeste, Victoria Saker   121–3
Wollman, Henry   50–1
Woman Suffrage Party   2
World Jewish Economic Conference   152
World Jewish Economic Federation   153, 162
World Non-Sectarian Anti-Nazi Council to Champion Human Rights   161–2
World To-Day   56
World Zionist Congress   128, 142, 156
World Zionist Organization (WZO)   125, 127, 135, 142, 155

Worthington Pump Company 32
W.T. Grant (chain store) 166

Young Men's Hebrew Association,
	New York City 120
Young Men's Hebrew Association,
	Yonkers 119–20
Young Men's Hebrew Club, Newark 163
Young Men's Union of the Ethical
	Society 48

Young Women's Hebrew Association,
	Yonkers 120
Yuengling, David G. Jr. 23

Zangwill, Israel 136
Zionist Organization of America
	(ZOA) 119, 127, 142, 144, 154, 163
Zumoff, Jacob A. 9, 191 n.86
Zwillman, Abner 'Longy' 163

www.ingramcontent.com/pod-product-compliance
Lightning Source LLC
Chambersburg PA
CBHW052149300426
44115CB00011B/1580